Oct, '07

Esther x

ORACLES, CURSES, AND RISK AMONG
THE ANCIENT GREEKS

Oracles, Curses, and Risk among the Ancient Greeks

ESTHER EIDINOW

OXFORD
UNIVERSITY PRESS

OXFORD
UNIVERSITY PRESS

Great Clarendon Street, Oxford OX2 6DP

Oxford University Press is a department of the University of Oxford.
It furthers the University's objective of excellence in research, scholarship,
and education by publishing worldwide in

Oxford New York

Auckland Cape Town Dar es Salaam Hong Kong Karachi
Kuala Lumpur Madrid Melbourne Mexico City Nairobi
New Delhi Shanghai Taipei Toronto

With offices in

Argentina Austria Brazil Chile Czech Republic France Greece
Guatemala Hungary Italy Japan Poland Portugal Singapore
South Korea Switzerland Thailand Turkey Ukraine Vietnam

Oxford is a registered trade mark of Oxford University Press
in the UK and in certain other countries

Published in the United States
by Oxford University Press Inc., New York

© Esther Eidinow 2007

The moral rights of the author have been asserted
Database right Oxford University Press (maker)

First published 2007

All rights reserved. No part of this publication may be reproduced,
stored in a retrieval system, or transmitted, in any form or by any means,
without the prior permission in writing of Oxford University Press,
or as expressly permitted by law, or under terms agreed with the appropriate
reprographics rights organization. Enquiries concerning reproduction
outside the scope of the above should be sent to the Rights Department,
Oxford University Press, at the address above

You must not circulate this book in any other binding or cover
and you must impose this same condition on any acquirer

British Library Cataloguing in Publication Data

Data available

Library of Congress Cataloging in Publication Data

Data available

Typeset by RefineCatch Limited, Bungay, Suffolk
Printed in Great Britain
on acid-free paper by
Biddles Ltd, King's Lynn

ISBN 978–0–19–927778–0

1 3 5 7 9 10 8 6 4 2

PLAYER. Uncertainty is the normal state. You're nobody special.

(He makes to leave again. GUILDENSTERN *loses his cool.)*

GUILDENSTERN. But for God's sake what are we supposed to *do*?!

PLAYER. Relax. Respond. That's what people do. You can't go through life questioning your situation at every turn.

Tom Stoppard, Rosencrantz and Guildenstern Are Dead

The relevance of historical fact for sociological analysis does not rest on the proposition that there is nothing in the present but the past, which is not true, or on easy analogies between extinct institutions and the way we live now. It rests on the perception that though both the structure and the expressions of social life change, the inner necessities that animate it do not.

Clifford Geertz, 'Centers, Kings, and Charisma:
Symbolics of Power', Local Knowledge

Acknowledgements

This book is based on my doctoral thesis, which I wrote at Oxford (1999–2003). There are many people from that time whom I must thank, in particular Robert Parker, my supervisor, for his kindly, thorough, and challenging guidance; Oswyn Murray, Simon Price, and Robin Lane Fox who examined, guided, and advised; and Helen King and Oswyn Murray who finally examined me, and whose idea it was to turn the thesis into a book. Magdalen College, where I had also been an undergraduate, and more particularly, Oliver Taplin, welcomed me back with great warmth and generosity. Finally, thanks to all the wonderful friends I made during that time.

There are many others who have generously given their support. David Jordan was, and continues to be, an essential guide to the meaning of curse texts. Mary Douglas has generously shared both her anthropological insights and her hospitality. I remember with tremendous gratitude the kindness of the late Anastasios-Ph. Christidis who told me about the unpublished oracle tablets from Dodona and that of the late Mike Jameson, who provided invaluable early encouragement. I owe a special debt of gratitude to Robin Osborne for all his help, advice, and encouragement over many years.

Robin Osborne and my father John Eidinow read and discussed drafts of both the doctorate and the book; Simon Hornblower read drafts of the book. They have all suggested immeasurable improvements and any errors that remain are mine. The team at OUP could not have been more helpful: thanks must go to Hilary O'Shea, Kathleen McLaughlin, Mary Morton and Heather Watson. A warm thank you goes to Douglas Matthews for all his help. I must also thank the Deutsche Archäologische Institut, Athens, for patiently tracking down the images of the curse tablets; the Archaeological Receipts Fund, Athens, for permission to print the images of the gold coin from Dodona and the map of the site of the sanctuary; and the Art and Archaeology Collection for the images of the oracle tablets.

Finally, my heartfelt gratitude to my family and all my friends for their love, patience, and support. This book is dedicated to my parents, and to Simon.

Contents

List of Figures   x
Abbreviations   xi
Note on Spellings and Inscription Conventions   xiii

Introduction	1
1. Exploring Uncertainty	10
2. A Lapse into Unreason	26
3. Individuals and Oracles	42
4. The Dwelling of the Spirit	56
5. A Catalogue and Summary of Published Questions by Individuals and Responses from the Dodona Oracle	72
6. Oracles and Daily Life	125
7. Curses!	139
8. Urban Drama	156
9. The Best Defence	165
10. Business as Usual?	191
11. Love and Curses	206
12. Curses and Risk	225
Conclusion	233

Notes   238
Appendices:
  1. Questions Presented by Communities at the Oracle of Dodona   345
  2. Texts Excluded from the Relationship Category   349
Catalogue of Binding Curses   352
Glossary   455
Bibliography   456
Index Locorum   481
General Index   501

List of Figures and Maps

List of Figures

1. Oracle question tablet from Dodona (the Kerkyraians and Orikians)	64
2. Bronze coin from Dodona with oak tree and three doves	66
3. Oracle question tablet from Dodona (Hermon and Kretaia)	90
4. Oracle question tablet from Dodona (Pistos and the fleeces)	118
5. Lead doll and coffin set: SGD 9	142–3
6. Curse tablet (SGD 14) from the Kerameikos	169

List of Maps

1. Synchronic map showing all the major sites mentioned in the text	xiv–xv
2. The sanctuary of Dodona today	xvi

Abbreviations

For ancient authors and for periodicals, the abbreviations in the *Oxford Classical Dictionary* (third edition) ed. S. Hornblower and A. Spawforth (1996) have been followed where available.

AAA	Ἀρχαιολογικά Ἀνάλεκτα ἐξ Ἀθηνῶν, Athens Annals of Archaeology, 1– (Athens, 1968–)
AE	Ἀρχαιολογική Ἐφημερίς
AGIBM	Ancient Greek Inscriptions in the British Museum
APF	J. K. Davies, *Athenian Propertied Families* (Oxford, 1971)
ARV²	J. D. Beazley, *Athenian Red-Figure Vases*, 2nd edn. (Oxford, 1963)
BE	J. Robert and L. Robert, 'Dodone', *Bulletin épigraphique* (1852–84)
CGFP	C. Austin, *Comicorum Graecorum Fragmenta in Papyris Reperta* (Berlin, 1973)
Christidis	Oracles presented in a lecture given by Professor Christidis in Oxford, July 2002, which he kindly gave me permission to include.
Didyma II	A. Rehm and R. Harder (eds.), *Didyma II: Die Inschriften* (Berlin, 1958)
D–K	H. Diels and W. Kranz *Fragmente der Vorsokratiker* (Berlin, 1952)
DT	A. Audollent, *Defixionum Tabellae* (Paris, 1904)
DTA	R. Wünsch, *Defixionum Tabellae Atticae Inscr. Gr.*, vol. 3, pt. 3 (Berlin, 1897)
Ep. Chron.	Ηπειρωτικά Χρονικά (Ioannina)
Fontenrose Didyma	Oracles listed in 'Catalogue of Responses of Didyma' in J. Fontenrose *The Delphic Oracle: Its Responses and Operations with a Catalogue of Responses* (University of California), pp. 417–29
ICos	W. R. Paton and E. L. Hicks *Inscriptions of Cos* (Oxford, 1891)
IC	M. Guarducci (ed.), *Inscriptiones Creticae*, 4 vols. (Rome, 1935–50)
K–A	R. Kassel and C. Austin (eds.) *Poetae Comici Graeci* (Berlin and New York, 1983)
Kovs.	W. K. Kovacsovics (ed.), 'Die Eckterrasse an der Gräberstrasse des Kerameikos', *Kerameikos*, xiv (1990), 145–7
Milet.	*Milet: Ergebnisse der Ausgrabungen und Untersuchungen dem Jahre 1899* (1966–)

ML	R. Meiggs and D. Lewis *A Selection of Greek Historical Inscriptions to the End of the Fifth Century* (Oxford, 1989)
NGCT	D. Jordan, 'New Greek Curse Tablets (1985–2000)', *GRBS* 41 (2000), 5–46
PAE	Πρακτικά τῆς ἐν Ἀθήναις Ἀρχαιολογικῆς Ἐταιρείας
Parke + cat. no.	Private oracle consultations listed in H. W. Parke *The Oracles of Zeus* (Oxford, 1967), 263–73
Parke State + cat. no.	State oracle consultations listed in H. W. Parke *The Oracles of Zeus* (Oxford, 1967) 259–62
PGM	*The Greek Magical Papyri in Translation*, ed. Hans Dieter Betz (Chicago, 1992)
Poikila Epigraphika	A. Ph. Christidis, S. Dakaris, J. Vokotopoulou, 'Oracular Tablets from Dodona', in C. Brixhe, *Poikila Epigraphika* (Paris, 1997), 105–10
Pomtow	H. R. Pomtow 'Die Orakelinschriften von Dodona', *Jahrbuch für klassische Philologie*, 29: 305 ff.
P/W	Oracles in H. W. Parke and D. E. W. Wormell, *The Delphic Oracle, vol. 2: The Oracular Responses* (Oxford, 1956)
SEG	*Supplementum Epigraphicum Graecum*
SGD	D. Jordan, 'A Survey of Greek Defixiones Not Included in the Special Corpora', *GRBS* 26 (1985), 151–97
SGDI	O. Hoffman, 'Die Orakelinschriften aus Dodona', in H. Collitz and F. Bechtel (eds.), *Sammlung der Griechischen Dialekt-Inschriften* (Göttingen, 1899), 1557–98
Syll.³	W. Dittenberger, *Sylloge Inscriptionum Graecarum*, 3rd edn. (1915–24)
TGF	A. Nauck, *Tragicorum Graecorum Fragmenta*, 2nd edn. (Leipzig, 1889)
TrGF	B. Snell *et al.* (eds.) *Tragicorum Graecorum Fragmenta* (Göttingen, 1971–)

Note on Spellings and Inscription Conventions

ALTHOUGH I have, in general, preferred to use Greek spelling, where this seems awkward, I have retained the more familiar Latin spelling of some names or terms.

The inscriptions in the text and catalogue reproduce the conventions of the relevant editions.

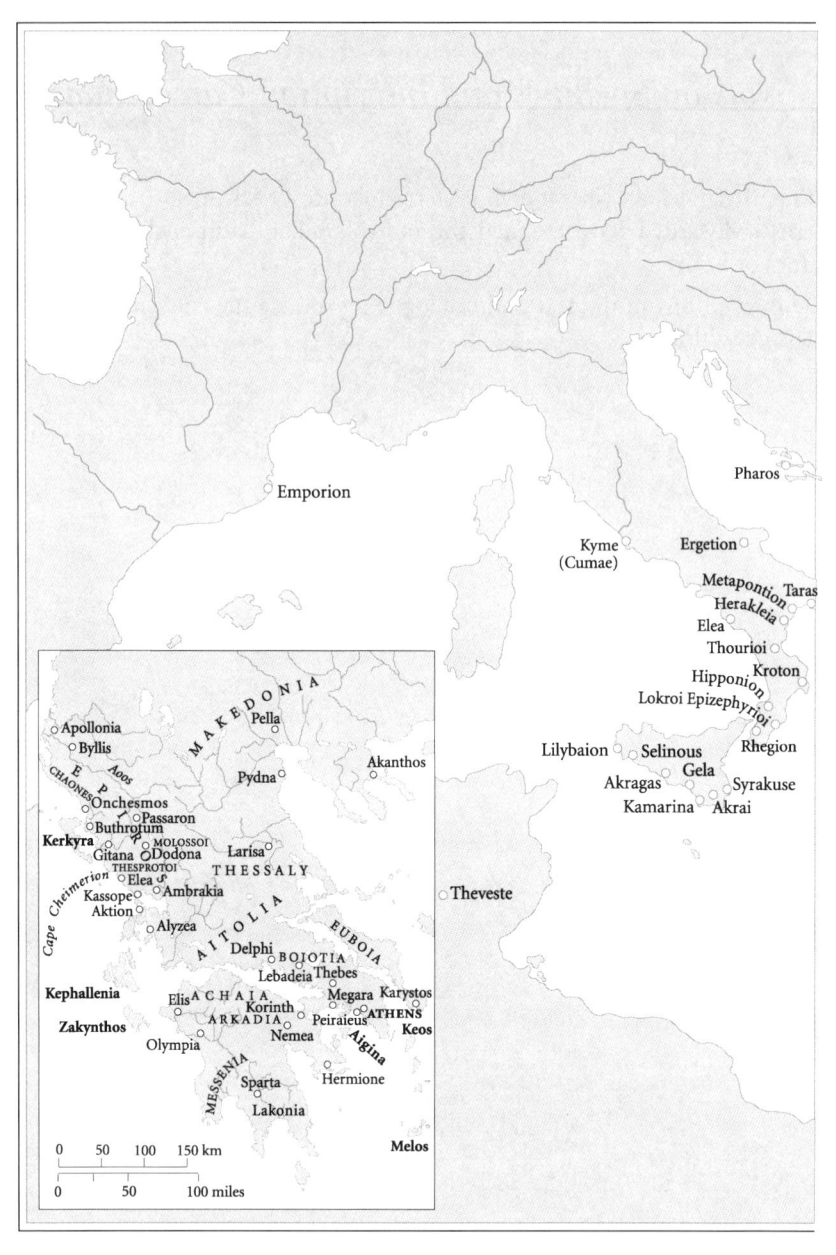

MAP 1. Synchronic map showing all the major sites mentioned in the text (it shows the fourth-century locations of the tribes in Epiros, according to Hammond 1967)

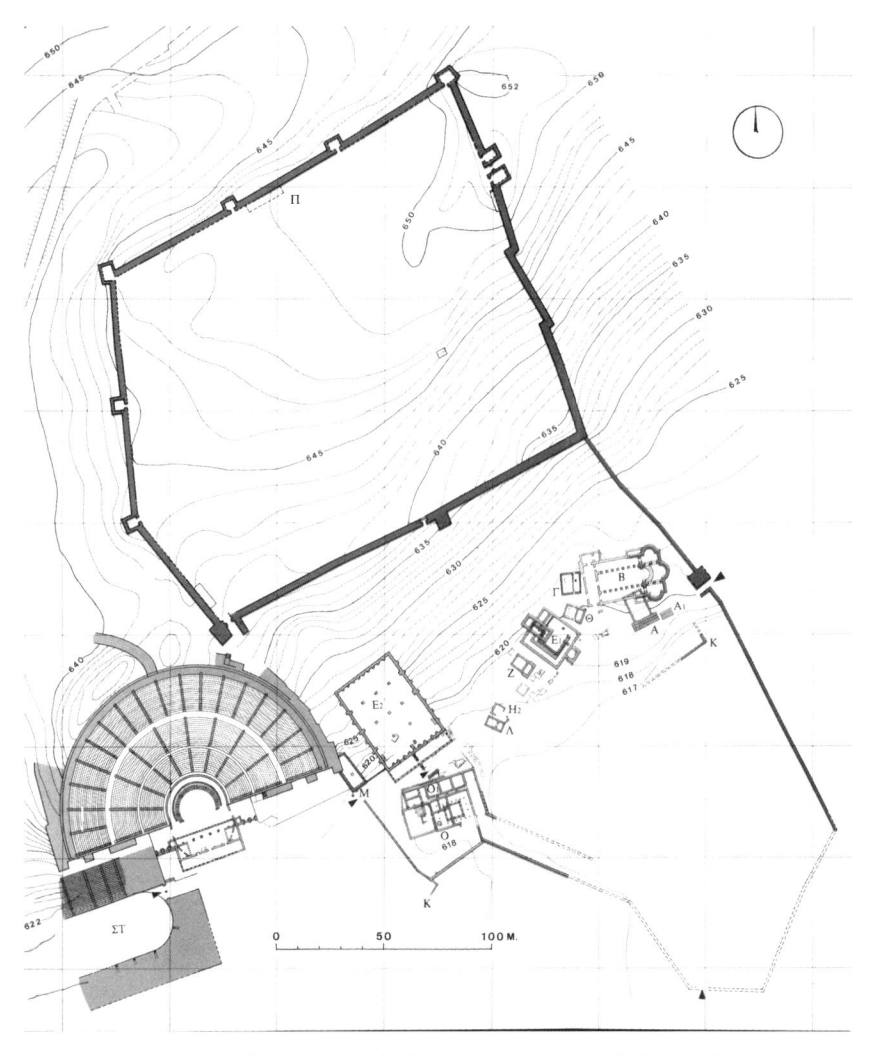

KEY A–A1. Temple of Herakles and the altar: Beginning of the third century BCE
B. Christian Basilica: Fifth to sixth centuries CE Γ. Ancient Temple of Dione: Second half of the fourth century BCE E1. Hiera Oikia: Earliest remains dating to the second half of fourth century BCE, with later additions dating to the beginning and end of the third century BCE E2. Bouleterion: Beginning of third century BCE ΣΤ. Stadium: End of third century BCE Z. Temple of Themis and the altar: Beginning of third century BCE H2. Roman building: Early Roman period Θ. New Temple of Dione: End of third century BCE K. Stepped retaining wall: End of third century BCE Λ. Temple of Aphrodite: Beginning of third century BCE M. House of the Priests (?): Second half of the fourth century BCE O–O1. Prytaneion and the extension to the north side: earliest remains dating to the second half of the fourth century, but most date to the third century BCE: some later additions. Π. Precinct wall: Second half of the fourth century

MAP 2. The sanctuary of Dodona today (adapted from S. Dakaris 1996: 24 and 25) © The Archaeological Receipts Fund, Athens

Introduction

> 'The king died and then the queen died' is a story. 'The king died and then the queen died of grief' is a plot.
>
> Forster 1927: 116–17

You are in a tavern in a small town somewhere in Epiros in north-west Greece, in the second century BCE. *A travelling* mantis—*a seer*—*comes round the tables offering oracles, healing, initiation into secret mysteries that will bring good fortune. He's standing close to you, whispering intensely about his awesome powers, when the tavern's owner overhears his pitch and tosses him out. The man standing next to you raises a cheer and then, in the way of tavern conversation, introduces himself, calls for more drinks and launches into a story.*

The man's name is Lysanias. A few years ago he and his woman, Annyla, were blessed with the birth of a child, a boy. Everything seemed to be going well, until he was visited by a disturbing dream. Not being one of these superstitious types, he could usually forget about such things, but this dream repeated itself a few nights later. Now, some people might go to the local wise woman, but he was afraid it might create gossip. So when a mantis *came knocking on his door, he invited him in for a consultation . . .*

The mantis *told him that his dream almost certainly meant that the child was not his—and, for a very reasonable additional fee, he could concoct a curse against the man who'd done the wicked deed; perhaps throw in an amulet to keep his woman out of trouble; maybe brew up a potion, so that she'd have eyes for no one but him . . . Now, some people might have bought everything the* mantis *had to offer, but Lysanias had never had much use for that sort of thing. He bid the protesting* mantis *goodbye, and tried to forget what had happened. But a seed of doubt had been planted that kept growing. What if it was true that the child wasn't his? Each day, his anxieties multiplied. He began to think that people were talking about him, laughing at him, behind his back. Maybe the* mantis *himself had spread the story, resentful that Lysanias had refused his wares. Finally, he felt he couldn't bear it any longer. He told his household he was going to make a pilgrimage—he must attend the* Naia *festival—and set off for Dodona. And when he reached the sancturary, this is the question he put to the oracle:*[1]

Ἐρωτῇ Λυσα-
νίας Δία Νάον
καὶ Δηώνα(ν) · ἦ οὐ-
κ ἐστὶ ἐξ αὐτοῦ
ΘΙ τὸ παιδάριον
ὃ Ἀννύλα κυεῖ

Lysanias asks Zeus Naos and Dione whether the child Annyla bears is from him.

Now, obviously, the context is my creation, but it is a fact that, some time in the second century BCE, a man called Lysanias did present a lead tablet inscribed with this question to the oracle at Dodona.[2] We do not know what procedure Lysanias or other consultants used to present their questions, nor is it clear how they received their answers. Nevertheless, since excavations started in 1875–6, approximately 1,400 lead tablets have been found at the site of the oracular sanctuary of Dodona. These tablets, dating from the sixth century to around the end of the second century BCE, contain questions from men and women, slave and free, addressed to the gods, for the most part to Zeus 'Naios' or 'Naos', and sometimes also to his companion at the site, the mysterious goddess Dione.[3] Occasionally they also seem to record replies.

Unfortunately, we do not know what answer Lysanias was given, but in such a situation, concern about Annyla's behaviour—or that of her possible lover—might well have prompted him to follow the advice of the *mantis* and commission a curse tablet against his rival, or, indeed, to control his wife. A similar scenario may have been behind the creation of the following vivid curse:[4]

Παρατίθομαι Ζο-
ίδα τὴν Ἐρετρικὴν
τὴν Καβείρα γυναῖκα
- [τ]ῇ Γῇ καὶ τῷ Ἑρμῇ, τὰ βρώ-
ματα αὐτῆς, τὸν ποτᾶ, τὸν ὕ-
πνον αὐτῆς, τὸν γέλωτα,
τὴν συνουσίην, τὸ κιθ{φε}άρισ[μα]
αὐτῆς κὴ τὴν πάροδον αὐ-
[τῆς], τὴν ἡδον<ὴν>, τὸ πυγίον,
[τὸ] (φρό)νημα, {ν} ὀφθα[λμοὺς]
- - ααπηρη(?) τῇ Γῇ.

I assign Zois, the Eretrian, wife of Kabeira, to Earth and to Hermes. I bind her food and her drink, her sleep and her laughter, her meetings and her cithara playing, her entrance, her pleasure, her little buttocks, her thoughts, her eyes . . . the earth.

The curse describes the binding of a woman, bringing her image more sharply into focus with each aspect of her that it binds. Taken out of context, the text might describe the crucial moments of a seduction, rather than a curse.[5] A description of her surroundings grows in detail, suggesting, first, how she behaves, then evoking how she moves, before focusing on parts of her body, until finally we look into her eyes. It is almost as if the reader has caught sight of Zois from across a room, perhaps at a party, and watches her for a while, until suddenly she feels the gaze and looks back.

It is something of a surprise to realize that this description, so evocative of this woman's charms, is a curse or *katadesmos*, designed to exert some form of control over its target. The writer 'dedicates' Zois to certain underworld gods, giving her over to their authority, 'binding' her (in the idiom used in these texts), along with certain parts of her body and particular aspects of her behaviour. Zois was probably a *hetaira*, a woman hired to entertain at *symposia*, or drinking parties. These words, scratched onto a lead tablet some time before the end of the Hellenistic period, survive as testimony to somebody's desire to stifle her attractions, and, perhaps, frustrate her commercial success.

Such vicious petitions to the gods are not what we expect from the Greeks, renowned for laying the foundations of Western civilization—scientific hypotheses, architectural concepts, political models, and other intellectual achievements. Nor, thinking back to Lysanias, do we expect the fathers of rational thought to try to resolve their problems by using a system as apparently arbitrary as an oracle. So, how should we regard these two activities: as simply early forays into what we could describe as 'black magic'—recasting their practitioners as masters of the Dark Arts—or would it be better to think of them as examples of the irrational, aberrant, and furtive behaviour of a silly few?[6]

In fact, although the term 'magic' still appears unselfconsciously in studies of certain ancient practices, most historians now take the approach that simply applying such culturally dependent labels as 'irrational' or 'magical' tends to be of little help in understanding particular activities or the society in which they are practised.[7] Instead, more recent approaches have sought to rehabilitate these practices. In the case of oracles, commentators have helped modern minds to grapple with this bewildering phenomenon either by elucidating their operation, for example, by explaining the mechanisms of kleromancy or inspired prophecy, or by finding functionalist explanations for their widespread use, for example, recognizing the potential of oracles as disseminators of international information to travellers and politicians.

Attention has largely focused on the oracle at Delphi and the notion of an oracle as an instrument for group decision-making. Scholars have noted the interaction of socio-political function and geographical location, in particular exploring the role of marginal interstate sanctuaries as political entities.[8] Although a great aid to understanding, such analyses tend to overlook the different contexts of consultations—this is particularly noticeable in their use of comparative material.[9] In particular, little consideration has been given to the place of divination in the lives of individuals and the kinds of concerns about which they chose to consult an oracle.

In the case of curse tablets, Faraone has argued that their essential feature is their use within agonistic relationships, 'that is, relationships between rival tradesmen, lovers, litigants, or athletes concerned with the outcome of some future event';[10] and he suggests that, in fact, a number of these relationships, across the curse categories, may relate to larger political conflicts.[11] In particular, he argues, curse tablets act as 'pre-emptive' strikes in competitive contexts where the curser (the weaker party) fears imminent defeat. This insightful explanation helps modern readers to see beyond the initial 'magical' aspect of these curses, and, crucially, locates the role of cursing within ancient Greek society, drawing attention to its adversarial context. However, although there may be what Faraone has called a 'defensive stance' in some of the texts, detailed examination suggests that it is not at all obvious that the person who would most often employ a binding curse is 'the perennial "underdog"' that he describes, resigned to losing the competition in question.[12] In fact, close inspection of the curse corpus raises questions about the extent to which an explanation that turns on competition is adequate for many of the curse texts.[13]

In current studies, we rarely find divination and curse-writing explored side-by-side. This seems to be a legacy of the discipline of ancient history, in which oracle consultation has been partially redeemed by scholars as a legitimate, if still bewildering activity of the ancients, while, in contrast, curse-writing for a long time has not featured on intellectual maps at all. Its shameful resemblance to 'black magical' activities seems to have pushed it *ne plus ultra*, beyond the bounds of what was considered worthy of study.[14] Nowadays, even though curses are stirring scholarly interest, the division seems to remain entrenched in our approach.

In contrast, this study is intended to further understanding of the nature and significance of these two practices for ordinary men and women of the ancient world. It considers these two activities together, in the belief that they share particular characteristics and a particular cultural role: that is, that oracle consultation and writing curses were both strategies by which ordinary ancient Greek men and women, individually and collectively, expressed and managed aspects of the uncertainty and risk of everyday life.

In using the term 'risk' I am fully aware that, like 'magic', this multivalent modern term is difficult to apply to contemporary activities with any precision, let alone to the activities and attitudes of a people in another time and place. After all, even relatively recently it was still being used to describe a statistically quantifiable, neutral entity. Nowadays, as any swift trawl of newspaper headlines quickly reveals, it has a far from technical meaning. We use it to describe the ghouls that have grabbed our imagination and resonate with our current fears, rather than those that may be, objectively, considered dangerous. Risk has entered the arena of corporate jargon, where it is energetically assessed using a variety of weapons: forecasting, expert advice, scenario-planning. But as it has gained in popularity, it has lost the sharp edges of definition.

This study will draw on the theory that risks are socially constructed, that is, that different societies, and different groups within a society, perceive, explain, and tackle uncertainty about the future—specifically, future dangers or risks—quite differently.[15] Facing the uncharted future, with all its horrible possibilities, means contemplating the impermanence of stability and prosperity, the inexplicable nature of misfortune—and different cultures map this unseen territory differently. Their choice of landmarks turns on their particular world-view. The dangers they select as important depend, at least in part, on a culturally specific network of beliefs, for example, about the origins of misfortune, their relationships with unseen powers, mortal and supernatural, their understanding of their own capacity to act. The theory of the social construction of risk draws attention to the ways in which society makes and remakes the meaning of this term; I explain this approach to risk in more detail in Chapter 1.

One way to explore risk or danger in ancient Greek culture would have been to trace use of the Greek word *kindunos* ('risk', 'threat', or 'danger') through the literary sources. Its meaning seems, at first glance, close to our own colloquial use.[16] However, this study set out to understand more fully the day-to-day experiences of risk and uncertainty among Greek men and women that were not captured in the literary sources. To this end, it concentrates on two bodies of texts: the published question tablets composed by individuals for use at the oracle at Dodona and the corpus of *katadesmoi* or curse tablets, dating from the sixth to first centuries BCE. The first part of this book will concentrate on oracles; the second on curses. Together, these texts provide comparative, as well as collective, indices of aspects of risk and uncertainty in ancient Greek culture. These can be summarized, very briefly, as follows: those who used oracles were uncertain and wanted to be sure they were making the right choice; those who turned to curses were usually already in a situation of danger and wanted to limit the damage their enemies might inflict.

Before turning to the texts themselves, I shall try to set them and the practices that they represented in their cultural context. In the ancient Greek world, engagements with the supernatural were mundane, many, and varied: a spectrum of interactions at different social levels, involving different mortal and supernatural personnel and conducted with a variety of intentions. Alongside state-organized events, we stumble on a vast market in supernatural services, made available to ancient Greek men and women by both institutions and individuals. Chapter 2 of this book examines the nature of this market: from the men and women who roam through our sources selling divination, curse-writing, healing, and initiations into mysteries, to the many different kinds of oracular sanctuaries scattered across the Greek landscape.

In such a world, in which the gods were constantly providing signs to those who could read them, why, when, and how did an individual engage with the supernatural? In Chapter 3 I use material from and about the oracles of Didyma, Delphi, and Dodona to investigate both how the Greeks represented oracular consultation to themselves, in terms of both explicit instructions and the stories they told about it, and the evidence for actual consultations. Chapter 4 provides more specific information about the oracle at Dodona— its geographical and socio-political context, as well as the possible methods of consultation that were used at the site.

Chapter 5 comprises a catalogue of questions (and, very occasionally, answers) that men and women posed to Zeus at his oracle at Dodona. The catalogue, organized by theme, includes the published texts, as well as a few as yet unpublished, presented by the late Professor Christidis of Thessaloniki University, at a seminar at the Centre for the Study of Ancient Documents in Oxford University, which he kindly gave me permission to use. He was kind enough to say that he thought that the management of risk and uncertainty provided a useful explanation of the use of the oracle at Dodona, and described to me a number of other oracle texts from Dodona, which he considered might be relevant to this study. His generosity and insights were invaluable. In Chapter 6, I have provided an overview of the catalogue, including consideration of the subject matter and timing of questions; the identities of the consultants; the language and behaviour of their inquiry; and, finally, how these tablets can help us to understand better the use of oracles by individuals between the sixth and first centuries BCE.

The texts in the corpus of ancient Greek curse tablets show individuals confronting risks of a different sort. Their authors seem usually to have been contemplating an imminent danger—often a person or people—that they wanted to control. Returning to the figure of the itinerant curse-seller, Chapter 7 provides some general information about the practice of writing and selling curses. The following chapters (8–11) examine the body of published curse texts, identifying the circumstances in which men and women created curses; what or whom they selected as the targets of their curses, and why. The chapters are, for the most part, organized according to the taxonomy of curse tablets currently in use. However, within this structure I question both existing interpretations of particular tablets and the boundaries and/or current descriptions of these categories of cursing. In particular, I examine those curses for which no context is immediately apparent or for which the current popular explanation of competition as the motivation for composition does not work. Instead, with some support from comparative studies of witchcraft in other cultures, I suggest that in many cases *phthonos*, or envy, often lies behind the creation of such *katadesmoi*.[17] These texts are testimony to a particular social environment, in which contact with the gods was frequent and occult violence was a reality; a world in which other people's envy, fuelled by gossip, helped nurture intense spiritual insecurity.[18] In such an environment, cursing was both an essential explanation of, and a weapon against, misfortune, while oracular consultation seemed to offer crucial insurance.

Usually, the project of ancient history cannot hope to capture the richness of events as they were experienced. These texts bring us vividly into contact with daily life in ancient Greece, especially Athens.[19] Dug up from graves, and wells, found nailed to temple walls, or discarded in the rubbish pits of long-abandoned temples, they record the voices of ordinary, sometimes anonymous, Greek men and women, voices that are rarely, if ever, found in the polished *bons mots* of the usual historical sources. These tablets record the unselfconscious emotional responses of ancient Greek men and women, from all levels of society, in fervent, sometimes ferocious, appeals to the gods.

Here are plotting politicians, and those conspiring against them; young noblemen who ran drunk and dissolute through city streets, and the women who danced, played, and otherwise entertained them at parties. Here are artisans who carved the pediments of great temples; farmers selling wood or sowing land; tradesmen anxious to set sail; chorus boys with crushes; shopkeepers and publicans, doctors and actors, net makers and silver workers, flour sellers and seamstresses. The tablets in these two collections take the reader on a journey across the teeming ancient city—to the docks, the theatre, the lawcourts, brothels and garrisons, markets and workshops, private parties, political meetings, international festivals. In these texts, women plead with the gods to stop their men from deserting them, and call down supernatural vengeance on those who have stolen their partners. Men question the paternity of their children; merchants try desperately to corner the market. Slaves beg to know how to escape their masters, while male and female prostitutes are both desired and detested for the potency of their charms.

Hope, lust, jealousy, envy, love, the sickening stab of fear, the festering irritation that grows into loathing—across thousands of years the intense emotions of the writers of these texts still resonate.

As this suggests, working with this material has involved an inescapable process of re-creation. First, of course, there are the problems of translation. Many of these tablets are fragmentary; the Greek is illegible or illiterate, or just impossible to make sense of.[20] When there is a text to work from, a second process of re-creation inevitably takes place, that of piecing together its meaning. Most of the oracle and curse texts provide some information: perhaps about the writer (named or anonymous), with more or fewer details about his or her context; the setting (perhaps just the name of a city, perhaps a specific institution like the Athenian lawcourts); particular relationships (with mortals and/or with the supernatural); or circumstances (experiences undergone, problems to be faced). When we read a curse or oracle text as a document of social history we inevitably try to extract what it can tell us about the circumstances in which it was composed. Usually, that means not just the sequence of events that have occurred, but the motivation behind the writing of the text. However, what we glean from this information will depend, in large part, on how we, as readers, put it together.[21]

The problems of how we 'read' a text have been much discussed elsewhere. To make my point without entering the dense thicket of literary theory, I will turn to E. M. Forster and his explanation of the difference between 'plot' and 'story', which I briefly quoted at the beginning of this chapter.[22] The full quotation reads:

'The king died and then the queen died' is a story. 'The king died and then the queen died of grief' is a plot. The time sequence is preserved, but the sense of causality overshadows it. Or again: 'The queen died, no one knew why, until it was discovered that it was through grief at the death of the king.' This is a plot with a mystery in it, a form capable of high development. It suspends the time sequence, it moves as far away from the story as its limitations will allow. Consider the death of the queen. If it is in a story we say: 'And then?' If it is in a plot we ask: 'Why?' That is the fundamental difference between these two aspects of the novel.

Using Forster's terms, this book is about the plots behind these two bodies of texts: it sets out to find out 'Why?' specifically, 'Why did he or she write this text?' Two levels of answer to that question—two plots—can be supplied, and I am interested in both of them. The first is about the motivation of the writer in the process of creation: why did he or she need to write a curse or question the oracle, what was his or her concern? This first plot is about the circumstances of composition. The second has a larger purview: it concerns the collective cultural understanding that meant that choosing to write a curse or oracle made sense and appealed to an individual. In this way, considered both individually and together, these two collections of texts help us to reconstruct certain aspects of the ancient Greek imagination. These tantalizing glimpses of everyday life reveal ancient expressions and perceptions of risk and the discourses and institutions it helped to shape. As we explore this culture's attitudes to risk, we also gather insights about its perceptions of identity, power and authority, cause and responsibility.

The Greeks were like us; they were unlike us. The challenges this presents for trying to understand their cultures have been discussed expertly elsewhere, and I will not attempt to describe them again here.[23] Suffice to say that in most cases discussed in this study, a multiplicity of possible plots may emerge from each of the texts. In making my choices, and trying to understand what this environment was like, I have turned to comparative anthropological work, including studies of witchcraft in twentieth-century England and explorations of the role of occult violence in South Africa.[24] I am not claiming any kind of unique insight into the meaning of these tablets. The fragmentary nature of the remains of this ancient culture demands that we remain flexible and creative in how we approach it.

This leads me to my final point: my interest in exploring the management of risk and uncertainty in ancient Greek society grew out of my work as a scenario writer, helping businesses and organizations to think about their long-term strategies, by writing stories about the different ways in which the future might play out. From multinational energy companies investing in emerging economies to international organizations looking at the tragedy of HIV and AIDS in Africa, these projects have drawn my attention to the various ways in which different cultures conceive of risk and uncertainty— and the crucial importance of taking account of them in cross-cultural projects. As the world becomes increasingly interconnected, how will people think about risk, and how will they manage it? My hope is that this book will not only shed some light on the ancient Greek experience, but also prompt thought about our own.

1

Exploring Uncertainty

> Cattle, Absence of, ... 17
>
> Entry in the index of E. E. Evans-Pritchard 1937: 547[1]

Two anecdotes from ancient Greek literature to start us off: one concerns the precarious nature of everyday life; the other a situation in which the dangers are more immediate. Together, they frame a spectrum of attitudes to the unknown future. The first occurs early on in book 1 of Herodotos' *Histories*. It describes the visit of the wise Athenian ruler, Solon, to the Lydian King Kroisos.[2] The monarch arranges for his visitor to take a tour of his treasures and then, obviously expecting this to sway his guest's response, asks him to name the most fortunate man he has met while on his travels. Much to the sovereign's dismay, Solon replies with a series of anecdotes about individuals who have lived humble lives, seen out their days contentedly and managed to die before suffering any great disaster. In response to the king's surprised and increasingly vexed interrogation, the wise man describes the instability of human life: no man can be judged to have been fortunate in his life until it is finally over.[3] At any point, an individual may have to confront deformity and disease, experience evils, or endure childlessness.[4] These unpredictable catastrophes are the party favours of the gods, who like nothing better than to tantalize a man with light and laughter, and then push him out into the cold.[5]

Herodotos' subsequent account of the downfall of Kroisos goes on to demonstrate the truth of Solon's conclusion. Kroisos consults the oracle at Delphi and is told that he 'will destroy a great empire'. It never occurs to him that the empire might be his. He invades Persia, is defeated in battle, and is captured and held prisoner by the Persian King Kyros. When he later sends to Delphi to complain that the gods misled him, he is told:

> Not even a god can escape his ordained fate. Croesus has paid for the crime of his ancestor four generations ago . . . Loxias wanted the fall of Sardis to happen in the time of Croesus' sons rather than of Croesus himself, but it was not possible to divert the Fates. However, he won a concession from them and did Croesus that much good: he managed to delay the fall of Sardis for three years . . . Croesus has no grounds for

complaint as regards the oracle. Loxias predicted that if he invaded Persia, he would destroy a great empire. Faced with this, if he had thought about it he would have sent men to enquire whether the god meant Cyrus' empire or his own. Because he misunderstood the statement and failed to follow it up with another enquiry, he should blame no one but himself for what happened.[6]

The second anecdote is from book 3 of Xenophon's *Anabasis*, or *Persian Expedition*, probably written in the 360s BCE. The author is trying to raise the morale of the officers of the Greek mercenary army with which he is serving. They are in desperate straits: betrayed by their Persian escorts, most of their generals and captains have been captured and put to death. They are far from home and surrounded by hostile tribes. That night, Xenophon has a vivid dream that prompts him to call a meeting of the army's remaining officers. They discuss the situation, the condition of their men, their low morale and how difficult it will be for them to fight. 'But,' Xenophon says, 'there will be a great rise in their spirits if one can change the way they think, so that instead of having in their heads the one idea of "What is going to happen to me?" they may think, "What action am I going to take?"'[7] His advice fires up the officers in his audience. They, in turn, appoint new leaders and rally the troops.

Both stories concern mortal ignorance in the face of supernatural knowledge. Both emphasize the importance of caution in dealing with information about the future. But the conclusions they lead to are quite different. Solon's account describes the everyday experience of living in a world where inexplicable catastrophes happen suddenly, reversing fortunes, toppling kingdoms. It stresses mortal impotence, although its vision of man is that he is not wholly helpless: information about his future is available, if he can keep an open mind. The oracular priestess, the Pythia, seems to suggest that if Kroisos had checked his assumptions about the first oracle by consulting her once more, he might have learned the truth. The possibility of a different outcome seems to hang in the air, yet Herodotos makes it abundantly clear here, and, in fact, throughout his history, that man cannot escape his fate. Mortals are helpless in the face of supernatural power: a man may consider himself lucky, but that is because he has, on the whole, no idea of what is in store for him. To that end, he may seem blind and foolish in how he chooses to behave—not just that he chooses wrongly, but that he thinks that his choices count at all. The story of Kroisos' fall raises a theme that recurs throughout the *Histories*: the inevitability of fate and the fragility of fortune, usually cast into high ironic relief by man's blatant misapprehension of what the gods have told him.[8]

A similar contrast between the helplessness of humans in the face of questions about what to do, and the omniscience of the gods, occurs in the

Anabasis. An almost programmatic statement of this occurs at 6.1.21, as Xenophon is considering taking up the position of leadership he has been offered.[9] He describes how he realizes that, 'It is unclear to all men what the future holds' and decides to sacrifice to the gods, in the hope that this will tell him what to do.[10] This pattern—an admission of helplessness followed by divine intervention—occurs in other key places: for example, Xenophon's divinatory dreams each follow an explicit reference to a state of ἀπορία, that is of 'being at a loss' about what to do.[11] However, Xenophon, in contrast, advocates action and engagement: it matters dreadfully how he and his companions choose to act. He clearly believes that the gods know what the future holds, and gaining access to this divine data is a crucial part of his campaign strategy. As was customary on military campaigns, he repeatedly makes sacrifices on the battlefield in an attempt to glimpse the future and divine his army's likely success; and, as we see from this example, he also interprets dreams and watches for omens.[12]

The narrative reveals that his concern to garner supernatural support continued off the battlefield: at home, too, oracle consultation was an important element of Xenophon's decision making. However, this does not mean that he abandoned his autonomy to divine mandate—far from it. As an example we can examine the question he put to the Delphic oracle as he contemplated joining Kyros' expedition and going to war: 'To what god shall I pray and sacrifice in order that I may best and most honourably go on the journey I have in mind, and return home safe and successful?' The phrasing of his question suggests that, in fact, Xenophon had already made up his mind to join the campaign, since his question seeks divine protection rather than divine guidance. This is underlined by the reaction of his friend, Sokrates, who observes that it would have been better to ask the oracle a series of questions, starting with the question whether it was better to go on the expedition or stay at home.[13] It obviously pays to be cautious: after all, Sokrates' final comment to Xenophon is that 'Since this was the way you put your question, you must do what the god has told you.'

These two stories provide complementary perspectives on the attitudes of the Greeks to future uncertainty. In both cases, the gods possess knowledge about the future and mortals must try to engage with them if they are to work out the right course of action, either in response to imminent misfortune, or to gain an advantage. Herodotos's tale of Kroesos' downfall vividly sketches the gulf separating bewildered mortals from the tricky gods. Advocating submission, if not resignation, this story sets the stage for the rest of Herodotos's programme.[14] For Xenophon, the gods are still distant, but not so devious. His suggestion that the Greek mercenaries make the decision to take action could be described as a psychological ploy, but Xenophon's personal divinatory activities suggest that it is backed by belief that it is possible for mortals, with supernatural support, to shape their own future. They may even obtain that support without asking directly—piety is helpful in this regard.[15] For Herodotos, piety is also important, but the tale of Kroesos demonstrates how a mortal's attempts at (and certainty about his own) piety may simply not be enough to save him from his fate.

These examples describe some situations in which mortals might seek divine intercession, but the information they provide is, of course, limited and mediated by their literary form. We are left wondering about the day-to-day activities and beliefs of ordinary ancient Greek men and women. The glimpses we are given of the behaviour of Xenophon and his fellow officers on and off the battlefield suggest that some Greeks, at least, did not assume the kind of passive stance of acceptance towards the uncertain future that Solon seems to suggest. But if you were not facing the immediate dangers of war, how did you think about and guard against the hazards of an uncertain future? In an environment bristling with threats of many different kinds, which ones merited your particular attention? Did your perception and expression of risk differ according to your position in society?

RISK, ABSENCE OF?

My argument is that the values of ancient Greek culture prompted its members to focus their anxiety about the uncertain future on specific situations in their lives, situations that were felt to present significant potential for great danger or opportunity. Oracles and cursing were used in response to such situations: these were the 'risks' of an ancient Greek community. But is my juxtaposition of 'ancient Greeks' and 'risk' coherent, or merely an inappropriate projection of modern ideas onto another—in this case, ancient—culture? Am I just (to return to the quote at the beginning of the chapter and anthropological misapprehension of which it is a reminder) looking for meaning in all the wrong places?

Similar and related problems frequently emerge in anthropological, as well as historical studies. A particularly prominent and useful example is the debate around use of the term 'magic', and I will draw on recent forays in this area to illuminate this question of cross-cultural comparison. This digression has particular relevance, since 'magic' is one of the categories that has been, and continues to be, used to describe oracle consultation and cursing.

First stop must be the long-appreciated anthropological concepts of 'emic' and 'etic', which have recently been used to frame this question of definition with regard to ancient ideas about magic.[16] Emic and etic approaches deal starkly with the semantic problems inherent in examining the values, beliefs, and practices of another culture from within the mindset and language of one's own. Emic approaches describe those internal to a language or culture, while etic are intended to provide a neutral reference language, to be used to make objective cultural comparison. The problems presented by such a simple approach have long been recognized by anthropologists: the ambition to get inside the minds of those of another culture, as the emic approach suggests, is particularly troubling in the case of ancient history where any fieldwork is obviously impossible. But the aspiration for neutrality of the etic approach is also flawed: a single, all-purpose definition of magic is just too blunt a tool to be able to distinguish variations between different societies across time and place, or different groups within a single society. And it raises the question of how this objective quantity is to be constructed: in the attempt to assemble a reference language, the chances are that any commentator will necessarily import his own cultural bias.

Another way of casting this disagreement has been in terms of essentialist vs. linguistic approaches.[17] Whereas the former seeks a single (modern) definition (of, for example, magic as the opposite of religion), the latter involves tracing the use of particular terms and how they change over time or place. We have just observed the kinds of problems inherent in trying to create a single definition. There are particular difficulties in using 'Greek religion' as a comparative quantity with which to define other activities, since, to quote John Gould's succinct summary, 'Greek religion was fundamentally improvisatory': there was no single ancient Greek religion, no central church, no liturgical canon.[18] Ritual activities were shaped by the different circumstances of their practice and the (changing) experiences of their practitioners.[19] Nor can we point to the divine personnel involved: the 'chthonic' gods associated with, say, a practice like curse-writing—and, as we shall see, with some necromantic forms of divination—may be associated with darkness or the underworld, but they are not a force of evil, standing in a simple opposition to what is good, as the devil does in modern conceptions of black magic.[20]

This brings us to the linguistic approach: the idea of tracing a term's development at first sight seems more promising. However, for Greek culture during the period under discussion it also raises questions. For example, the Greeks seem to have had no directly translatable term for, or concept of, magic—and certainly not subcategories of good, bad, or black magic.[21] The possibly relevant terms come down to us filtered through a variety of different discourses. What might seem like useful contemporary descriptions of particular activities must be treated with caution and in context: we have to ask who is making the observation, what motives they might have, and whose views they represent. As an example, briefly consider the charges made by the writer of the Hippocratic text 'On the Sacred Disease' against those priests who attribute a sacred origin to the onset of what has been identified as epilepsy, and claim to be able to cure it through ritual means.[22] He lambasts them for false religiosity and attacks the activities as based on deceit, fraudulence, and ignorance. It is wrong to accuse the gods (who are perfectly holy and purify mortals) of defiling the human body and wrong to claim to be able to coerce them. Instead he offers the argument that disease is naturally caused, not supernaturally, and must be treated accordingly.

At first sight this might seem like an early example of the identification of a set of magical activities. The speaker seems to be motivated by beliefs and knowledge we understand, a seemingly scientific approach that abhors the theocratic blunderings of the so-called holy men. However, although as modern readers we may appreciate this writer's more rational-seeming approach, we should not forget that he was also likely to be an itinerant professional, selling his skills in the same way and to the same market as the 'charlatans' that he attacks. Although he puts forward his own theories with great confidence, a number of them are fanciful, based on imagination, rather than evidence, and would have been easily disproved. As for his competitors, the beliefs they espoused, that disease was a result of supernatural intervention or a particular wrongdoing, were deeply rooted in their culture. This is demonstrated in the writings of the time, as well as by the established traditions and institutions of healing.[23] His rivals had a ready audience: moreover, it seems that a number of them were selling both physical approaches to disease (diet, etc.) as well as divine intervention. They had both aspects of the market covered, not only addressing the gods and performing purifications and incantations, but also recommending natural solutions that the scientific writer knows something about.[24] Where we see rationality should we suspect competition? Is this seeming scientific treatise closer, in fact, to an early marketing tract?[25] If we are still convinced that this account gives us a glimpse of early magic, this still leaves questions. If the basis of their activities, at least as attacked by this writer, is a belief in divine intervention as a cause and cure of disease, then should we accuse these itinerant healers of using magic or religion?

Perhaps it is not surprising that some modern commentators have stepped to one side of this debate about magic and refused to engage at all, while others emphasize the muddy nature of a concept that has built up over thousands of years of semantic accretion. The question remains—indeed, it may have reached something of an impasse—but in many ways the conflict itself has proved fruitful. The radical de- and reconstruction of the definition of magic (and its relationship with religion) has shed light on, for example, societies (both those we study and our own) in terms of the construction of power and its subversion, the use of language, understandings of morality, and perceptions of mortality and divinity. The archaeology of 'magic' may offer no clear strata, but it is worth sifting: it does indeed prove 'good to think (with)'.[26]

If we return to risk, can this prove as 'good to think with' as magic? Scholarship on the origins and development of science has long pursued philosophical concerns with uncertainty as they can be traced in ancient Greek literature.[27] However, the question of how the Greeks managed their uncertainty in the practical sense of how they lived day to day in anticipation of future events has received less consistent study.[28] Research in this area has tended to focus on situations that we in the modern world would perceive as risky, and then interpreted ancient Greek culture and behaviour in the light of this apprehension. This has resulted in work that has enriched our understanding of ancient life, but has had variable success in refining our apprehension of the significance or definition of risk among the ancient Greeks, or in modern cultures.

To give some examples: uncertainty and risk frequently appear, almost as technical terms, as topics for analysis in discussions of how ancient Greek communities and individuals coped with fluctuations in food supply caused by climatic or other changes in the natural environment, or disturbances in the social environment.[29] In extant Greek literature, there is little explicit comment on this topic, or on the related questions of how to tackle the challenges involved in ancient Greek agricultural practices, and so scholars have pieced together a picture of ancient Greek practice from archaeological remains, scattered literary references, and the probable context for institutional and administrative documents.[30] Gaps in the evidence have been filled with observations about what is known of rural farming practices in modern Greece[31]—though recent work on Greek agriculture stresses the caution that is necessary in this approach—and emphasizes the diversity of possible strategies available to ancient Greek farmers, seeing agricultural practices as the results of specific decisions they made.[32] Such approaches also discuss how the constant threat of subsistence crises and responses to it were both a product of, and an agent in, shaping social and cultural structures. For example, the emergence of the *polis* is seen as a response to the need to harness human and material resources more efficiently. The obligation for citizens of different social classes to give and to receive between themselves can then be seen as a form of 'interpersonal risk-buffering behaviour'.[33]

On the whole, risk-management in this account means 'elaborate strategies for survival, subsistence and collective security' developed by Greek peasants, and a risk is the result of a natural or man-made event that endangers any or all of these three elements and necessitates these strategies.[34] In this context, 'risk' describes aspects of everyday life that were managed automatically through daily activities and surrounding cultural institutions that were built into the fabric of society.

A second notion of risk in ancient Greek society offers a fundamentally different view. De Ste. Croix and Finley have both argued that maritime loans should be viewed as a response to risk, that is, as a form of insurance.[35] De Ste. Croix argued for this element insofar as the process of borrowing recognized 'that the loan is repayable only if the voyage ends safely', and that the system had an important social function, in that it '*spread the considerable risks of commerce* over the much larger and richer landowning class, [allowing] it to provide the initial capital the merchant needed to buy cargo, and in effect to insure him (in return for a high rate of interest) against the risks of sea-trading'.[36] Finley also argued for it as a form of insurance because it shifted risk from borrower to lender (explaining the high rate of interest involved).

However, these conclusions have been challenged: for a start, traders always sailed with their cargo, so if the ship and cargo went down, it is difficult to see how such a system of insurance would be of benefit. If the trader was lucky and only lost his cargo, but survived himself, such a system of insurance would still cover only part of the loss: sources suggest that the security (that is the cargo) offered in a maritime loan must be twice the value of the sum borrowed.[37] The trader who had lost his goods would still bear considerable costs.[38]

As Millett suggests, it seems more likely that these loans worked in a similar way to certain loans made to retailers in the agora, who 'operated on the margins without reserves'. Traders and retailers were, in general, extremely poor and depended on loans just to preserve their way of life—be it retail or trade—rather than to increase either wealth or productivity. This would make maritime loans closer to the modern financial arrangement of venture capital, rather than insurance. This kind of loan was quite different from the usual credit transactions that took place between family, friends, and neighbours in ancient Greek cities (so-called *eranos* loans). These carried an almost moral obligation, creating a network of reciprocal lending and borrowing, and the notion that it was somehow not acceptable to make financial gain from such a situation by charging interest.[39] It has been suggested that it was because maritime loans had a productive element that the charging of interest was justifiable, but this does not explain how they differed from other forms of business loan. Perhaps the charging of interest reflected an acknowledgement of the dangers involved in putting to sea—a sort of risk premium for the lender.

These more detailed considerations aside, the idea of risk that is being applied in this context clearly differs from that already discussed above. In the first example, risk management concerns the ways in which societies and cultures are structured to ensure basic survival. The idea of risk with regard to trade loans describes specific calculations by those involved in the realm of commerce. It concerns a transaction made in the knowledge of the possibility of losing cargo, while the introduction of the term 'insurance' even implies the suggestion of a technical understanding of hazards.[40]

Although they do shed light on ancient activities, what these two examples clearly demonstrate is the ambiguity of the modern term 'risk'. Each offers an acceptable contemporary use, but each comprises quite different nuances. To recall the debate on the definition of magic, it is unclear whether those discussing risk have taken an emic, etic, essentialist, or linguistic approach. This raises not just the question of what the ancients meant by risk, but also what we mean when we talk about risk.

This frames the question of the imposition of terms in a different way: the task is not to describe a distant culture in terms we understand, it is about negotiating understanding across two systems of meaning. The question is not about which set of terms we should use, theirs or ours, since neither alone will provide clear, objective reference points for cultural comparison, but how to move effectively between the two. As other disciplines concerned with this problem have found, a self-conscious process of translation will be needed, involving a series of dialogues between both mediator and subject, and mediator and reader, in which it is an essential part of the process to examine not only the terms and meanings of the culture of the subject (in whatever medium is relevant), but also those of the mediator and the reader.[41] Ancient historians, obviously, cannot participate literally in dialogue with representatives of the culture on which they are working, but this model of translation, and the self-examination that it encourages, is still of considerable use.[42]

INVENTING RISK

Tracing the evolution of 'risk' explains some of the confusion we see about its modern meaning. Although not as long-lived, it is almost as difficult to define as 'magic'. The etymology of the word 'risk' is unknown; it first appears in medieval documents and then spreads across Europe. Those who discuss its origins seem agreed that it emerged, and was most frequently used, with reference to maritime activity.[43] Slowly it acquires definition, shaped, first, by the Enlightenment spirit of empirical exploration and the quest to establish the laws that governed nature; then by increasing interest in and use of statistical data, and the development of the idea of 'normality'; finally, by the gradual erosion of determinism by the science of probability.

In terms of our ideas about risk, a key step in this process was the idea that just as there were laws governing the natural world, there were 'regularities' that governed human behaviour. It became apparent that statistics could help man understand—and manipulate—not just the natural world around him, but also the behaviour of populations (usually sub-populations, such as those involved in crime or vice). As a result, 'the first half of the nineteenth century generated a world becoming numerical and measured in every corner of its being'.[44] As the nineteenth century advanced, this plethora of statistical studies produced the ultimate weapon against uncertainty, the science of probability.

And with this, 'Moderns had eliminated genuine indeterminacy or "uncertainty" by inventing "risk". They had learnt to transform a radically indeterminate cosmos into a manageable one, through the myth of calculability.'[45] Risk was no longer a wild incomprehensible force of nature. Now it was a product of a world whose elements—human and non-human, concrete and intangible—were controllable because they could be measured. Risk could be described, predicted, and managed, as Knight's frequently quoted definition describes: 'If conditions are such that the probability estimates of an event are able to be known or knowable then that is a situation of risk; but when the probabilities are inestimable or unknown, that is a situation of uncertainty.'[46]

In the last couple of decades, the concept of risk has received increasing attention—and its ambiguity has increased. Technico-scientific approaches regard risks as pre-existing in nature, identifiable through scientific measurement and calculation, and controllable using this knowledge. In this schema, individuals are represented as rational information-processing units, who need only be presented with the scientific probabilities of an event to be able to make a decision to act. Where an individual does not behave rationally, individual psychology is looked to for an explanation. The fact that people in the real world often use, what this approach would view as, 'inferior' sources of knowledge (such as intuition) means that, in these terms, it becomes necessary to draw a distinction between an objective measurable risk and people's responses to it.[47]

Meanwhile, in colloquial use, although the quantifiable element of risk remains and the language of probability (for example, 'a one in one hundred chance') is still prevalent, we no longer seem sure just what such statistics prove or how we can apply these apparently objective statements to our everyday lives.[48] Although the technical understanding of risk has for a long time rested on the idea of quantifiability, in common use it has certainly lost its precision, while in academic discussions, the complexity of defining or calibrating risk is increasingly being recognized.[49] It is hard to believe that, until the end of the nineteenth century, the term had a neutral sense such that a risk could be either good or bad. Nowadays, it is invariably used to relate only to negative or undesirable outcomes: as the anthropologist Mary Douglas puts it 'the language of risk has become the language of danger'.[50]

This goes some way to clarifying why the two examples above demonstrate such a range of meaning. But looking beyond this semantic ambiguity, this overview raises further questions about the role played by risk—its perception as well as its management—within a community. In both the examples above, it is clear that the perception of risks is shaped by culture, by both the specific hazards of an environment and the particular relationships and institutions that structure a community. In the agricultural realm, risks arise from the vagaries of an unpredictable climate and its effects on subsistence farming. In the world of shipping, they emerge from the expense of being a merchant, at sea or in the agora. But we can also see this influence working in the other direction, so that the perception of risks, in turn, plays a part in shaping culture, informing relationships, and influencing the development of institutions, even creating the potential for further risk. In the first case, risks are described as prompting the creation of 'risk-buffering' behaviours, for example, the development of the *polis* and the cultural strategy of *xenia* or guest-friendship. In the second, the risk of trading at sea seems to have helped to shape a cultural strategy around loaning money. For sea traders there were additional risks, and it may be that the risks involved in financing such expeditions prompted the unusual (in the context) development of an interest-bearing loan.

Consideration of these cultural perceptions and responses, in turn, suggests that although there are risks that are probably common across most societies, it is likely that different social groups may perceive quite different risks, depending not just on their different environments—and the particular natural hazards that they present—but also on the values and beliefs they and others hold. This indicates, in turn, that knowledge about risk is bound to the socio-cultural contexts in which this knowledge is generated. This idea has been explored and developed by anthropologists and sociologists, occupying a range of positions between a more realist and more relativist viewpoint. Three basic approaches can be identified: those with a cultural-symbolic perspective, risk-society theorists, and 'governmentality' theorists whose work is much influenced by Foucault.[51] All three groups agree on the same central insights: the increasing importance of the concept of risk; the notion of risk as crucial to human subjectivity; risk as something that can be managed through human intervention; and the association of risk with notions of choice, responsibility, and blame.

The theories of the risk-society and 'governmentality' approaches are rooted in observations about the modern Western state and its members, and are therefore inappropriate frameworks for analysing societies in other cultures or times. In contrast, the cultural-symbolic approach of Mary Douglas, although largely concerned with the phenomenon of risk in modern society, is rooted in observations about the structures of, and interactions within, communities. A group will select some dangers from others for particular attention for reasons that make sense according to its shared values and concerns. What communities and individuals perceive as a significant disruption to their security—and what action they take to pre-empt it—will vary according to their specific vision of the world, their comprehension of time and space, their values and beliefs, and, in particular, their conceptions of blame, accountability, and responsibility. In any particular culture, where 'probable dangers crowd from all sides, in every mouthful and at every step' the risks that receive most attention are those that are connected, on the one hand, with legitimating moral principles and, on the other, with explaining misfortune.[52] So individuals are able to calculate risk—that is, to understand mutual obligations and expectations—and, in turn, the individual's understanding and acceptance of these mandates help to support and maintain the values and institutions of that culture.[53]

In almost all her publications on risk, Mary Douglas's concern has been to use this approach to explore the comparative prevalence of discourses of 'risk' in Western society, locating our modern obsession with risk in the end of Western civilization's love affair with science, examining the way in which, nowadays, forensic uses of risk have become commonplace in political discourse.[54] In modern Western society these selections become, literally, 'risks' and, of course, such analyses are not relevant to discussions of an ancient culture. However, at a theoretical level, the use of a specific term is not necessary to identify the dangers selected to play this role in other cultures. In fact, in her own work Mary Douglas herself illustrates, if only briefly and by example, the relevance to non-Western societies of the basic theory of the cultural selection of risks, citing how the Lele of Zaire with the presence of 'all the usual devastating tropical ills', focus on the risks of being struck by lightning, barrenness, and bronchitis.[55] It is worth stressing that the social-constructionist approach does not deny that a risk or danger in question is real, despite the cultural diversity of the responses and reactions it provokes; it just aims to describe how and why those perceptions and responses occur.[56] In turn, by examining which disruptions generate particular anxiety and/or disorder for a society or groups within a community, and by exploring their attempts to assert control over these potential threats we can gain insights into the workings and world-view of their culture.

Following on from this, my aim in introducing the term 'risk' into an analysis of aspects of ancient Greek culture is not to argue that the Greeks had a concept of risk that maps directly onto ours; this is clearly not the case. Indeed, as demonstrated, it is far from clear that contemporary modern society can offer a single neutral definition of the term for use in such a project. Instead, I will attempt to bring to bear an anthropological theory developed expressly to explain how and why perceptions of risk, and techniques for managing it, vary according to different contexts, and which encourages the exploration of those contexts. In its modern setting, the theory of the social construction of risk attempts to explain the modern prevalence of certain discourses of 'risk', but at its conceptual level it provides a way of describing how societies and individuals engage with the unknown future. In the context of this study, it raises a useful structure within which to think about risk and uncertainty among the ancient Greeks. More specifically, it provides a new approach for examining the function of certain ancient activities that we in the modern world have found difficult to comprehend.

RISK AND THE GREEKS

My intent is to try to access the views of ordinary ancient Greek men and women and their everyday experience, using two collections of epigraphic materials.[57] This apparently simple statement of intent contains a number of ideas that demand some elaboration—and disclaimers—from the idea of 'everyday experience' to the conception of 'ancient Greece'. The latter first: I must emphasize that this study is not setting out to unearth a rigid code of call and response that holds true for some unvaried geographical and temporal space. Just as our society comprises many different groups with different perceptions of risk over time and place, so did 'ancient Greece'. However, the nature of the evidence means that a detailed knowledge of the communities in which these texts were created is impossible: for example, the provenance of many of the curse tablets is unknown and, as mentioned earlier, for most of them, the date of their creation must remain approximate.

In the case of the oracular texts, although they were all excavated in one spot, little may be known about the community or individual who posed a question.[58] The tablets at Dodona only occasionally record the ethnic origin of a consultant, although surviving state consultations can also be of some help in suggesting likely locations, as can the form of alphabet or dialect used in the tablet.[59]

I am not claiming that the anonymous tablets can reveal the inner thought processes of individuals. The aim of this project is not to psychoanalyse the writers of this material. Nevertheless, these texts do allow us to focus on individual expressions of emotion enabling us to explore examples of specific behaviour, beliefs, relationships. As I have said, the two collections of texts show us the responses of men and women to two particular kinds of risk. The questions posed at oracles reveal situations of uncertainty that are, to an extent, self-motivated: each consultant has decided to make a choice. Those who wrote the questions we find inscribed on lead strips at the oracular sanctuary of Dodona had time to weigh up the possible consequences, as they gathered further (divine) information. In contrast, the harsh pleas of most curses suggest circumstances of imminent danger—danger, moreover, that is out of the curse writer's control.

This brings us to the question of what is meant by 'everyday experience'. To begin with, we are not discussing the kinds of community experiences, and attendant risks, that helped to forge the day-to-day fabric of city life, as, for example, maintaining a food supply in an unpredictable climate helped to prompt the development of the *polis*. The risks under discussion here were those that provoked particular anxiety and demanded specific management techniques. Individuals confronted these risks alone, or in small groups, within the context of city life and certain *polis* institutions. In the case of cursing, we can identify some of the situations that provided a context for this activity, and that it was often other individuals or groups of individuals that personified, literally embodied, risk. Oracles tend to provide more information about circumstances, since this is often the stuff of the inquiry itself.

As far as possible, I have tried to set these documents, the situations they describe and the activities that created them, in the culture in which they were embedded. This process of contextualization involves not just the tablets themselves, but also elements within the texts. For example, traditional interpretations of lists on Greek curse tablets have assumed that they were just a way of exhibiting or exerting power—either a way of attempting to be exhaustive lest the force of the magic escapes, or a way of alluding to an unstated claim of total efficacy. Gordon, however, has examined them in the context of Greek, specifically Athenian, culture. This was a time when the spread of literacy was encouraging the development of written laws and official, public lists. Particularly relevant to the question of lists on curses, within Athens, seems to be certain lists of shame, some of which were displayed on the Akropolis. These included the names of public debtors, deserters, or those condemned of homicide. Gordon suggests that the columnar lists of curse tablets form an example of magical practice usurping tokens of authority in the dominant world for its own ends. Because this form alludes to the lists of names used by the state to refer to its enemies, lists of names found on curse tablets acquired greater authority. The gods of the underworld, to whom the curse was directed, were being invited to react to the list of names as Athenian citizens reacted to the lists of names in the dominant world, by condemning them.[60] This kind of contextualization is, of course, not always possible. In such circumstances, comparative material may help stimulate insight and deepen understanding.

Next the question of time: the evidence is drawn from over a long time period with material dating from the sixth to first centuries BCE.[61] However, since the source material in each area of study appears unevenly, and since it is my intention to gather sufficient evidence to be able to explore developments in the way risk was expressed and responded to over time, the length covered seems appropriate. Moreover, this period appears to describe a discrete phase for both collections. With regard to Dodona, the sixth to first centuries BCE include the period during which the oracle flourished—although it was restored after 219 BCE by the Aitolians, it never really recovered from the Roman ravaging of Epiros in 167 BCE. As for the practice of writing curse tablets, from approximately the first century BCE onwards this spreads to much of the Mediterranean world; burial sites change; the formulae and content become highly syncretistic, showing influence from Jewish and Egyptian culture in particular.

Now, some disclaimers: as I noted above, this study is not setting out to establish systemic rules of behaviour that governed the practices of oracle consultation and cursing across time and place. This is not an attempt to prove that, either prescriptively or descriptively, oracles and curse-writing were used only as tools for minimizing or avoiding the risk of a particular situation. This is put forward as one possible motivation for both these practices, but examining and cataloguing the evidence in order to explore this approach also helps to elaborate and clarify other reasons for oracle consultation and cursing.

Where risk-management does seem to be the motivation for these activities, this study will attempt to explore how individuals varied in their approach, and why. This is difficult because in many oracular consultations we know only the name of the writer, nothing more, while the curse tablets do not usually reveal even that. Something of each writer's background can sometimes be assembled from the contextual detail of the text—for example, that he was a trader, or a farmer, or that he had a wife and a child—but, often this is very sketchy and, in the case of the curse tablets, usually impossible.

This, in turn, means that in describing the creators of these texts as 'ordinary men and women', I am making an assumption that because we cannot identify most of them, they are unlikely to belong to the intellectual, political, or cultural elite of their cities, whose names and writings we have inherited. This assumption is probably accurate in cases where we know the text was written by individuals who belong to groups that are systematically under- or unrepresented in literary and historical texts, women or slaves, for example. Of course there are exceptions: since political figures have been identified among the targets of a few curse tablets, there is a possibility that these individuals also wrote curses. However, lack of evidence precludes definite judgement.

As will become apparent, part of the reason these tablets are so intriguing is their very lack of completeness, the room they offer for speculation, and thus for exploration. What they offer is a starting point: as such they remain a valuable addition to information from other sources, helping to refine our ideas about core values and social relationships within the ancient Greek community.

2

A Lapse into Unreason

> I, too, used to react to misfortunes in the idiom of witchcraft, and it was often an effort to check this lapse into unreason.
>
> Evans-Pritchard 1937: 99

When the news reached Athens, for a long time people would not believe it, even though they were given precise information from the very soldiers who had been present at the event and had escaped; still they thought that this total destruction was something that could not possibly be true. And when they did recognise the facts, they turned against the public speakers who had been in favour of the expedition, as though they themselves had not voted for it, and also became angry with the prophets and soothsayers and all who at the time had, by various methods of divination, encouraged them to believe that they would conquer Sicily.[1]

The most famous sources of oracles—and the focus of this study—were of course the oracular sanctuaries, but before turning to those I want to set them in context. A first glimpse of that context can be provided by Thucydides' description of Athens in 413/412 BCE, and the final throes of the Peloponnesian war. News of the defeat of the Athenian navy in Sicily has reached the city, and with a few brief sentences Thucydides evokes the Athenians struggling with the realization of a disaster, of hopes betrayed. In the process, he shows us a city teeming with dealers in divination: *chrēsmologoi* were literally 'oracle-collectors', usually found selling verse oracles from collections attributed to early prophets and poets, including Homer, Mousaios, Bakis, the Sibyl, even occasionally Apollo himself.[2] But the word is also translated as 'oracle-monger' and, as this suggests, 'oracle-mongers' are also found working more generally with oracular material, offering interpretations of oracles supplied by others, and, occasionally, supplying oracles from their own inspiration.[3]

Mantis, in turn, is usually translated as 'seer' and sources show them offering a range of services related to seeing or manipulating things that are hidden, especially, although not always, 'signs of the future' ($\tau\grave{\alpha}\ \sigma\eta\mu\epsilon\hat{\iota}\alpha\ \tau\hat{\omega}\nu\ \dot{\epsilon}\sigma o\mu\acute{\epsilon}\nu\omega\nu$) as Nikias in Plato's *Laches*, puts it.[4] In the *Republic*, Plato describes how some *manteis* would go from door to door offering services that included sacrifices and incantations that could expiate and cure misdeeds by an ancestor, or spells and enchantments with which to harm an enemy, or oracles from oracle collections of Mousaios and Orpheus, which they use in their rituals.[5]

This is not the first or only time that Thucydides mentions such characters or the oracles they peddle.[6] As this suggests, diviners and their guidance were a crucial aspect, even weapon, of warfare. But they were also involved in most aspects of daily life. Once we are alerted to their presence, we find them everywhere throughout our sources. They hawk oracles in the histories of Herodotos, offer guidance to pious Xenophon, make ponderous pronouncements in the tragedies. They are mocked in the comedies of Aristophanes, abused by medical writers and philosophers, but lauded in city inscriptions.

Altogether, whether these voices are raised in praise or blame, they evoke a picture of ancient life in which events were accompanied by a persistent, prescient commentary, sometimes barely audible, sometimes the focus of attention, but never completely fading away. *Chrēsmologoi* and *manteis* are just two of the terms given to those involved in maintaining this constant hum of divine communication. There were also *magoi*, *goēteis* (male, singular *goēs*) and *goētides* (female), *pharmakeis* (male, singular *pharmakeus*) and (female) *pharmakides* (s. *pharmakis*), and *epōdoi*, *tetraskopoi*, *thaumatopoioi*, and *rizotomoi*. In general, all these characters can be described as 'sorcerers', and their activities, be they *mageia*, *goēteia*, or *pharmakeia*, are usually roughly translated as 'sorcery', denoting ritual activities that involve elements of the supernatural.[7]

Attempts have been made to understand just what specific set of skills or ideal type may lurk beneath each label or each category. In some cases, tracing the roots of each term may be of some help: for example, *epōdoi* were singers of incantations; *tetraskopoi* were 'interpreters of wonders'; *thaumatopoioi* were 'performers of wonders'; *rizotomoi* were probably herbalists, literally 'rootcutters'. The fact that the word *goēs* almost certainly developed from *goos*, a cry of lamentation used at funerals, has suggested that the *goēteis* specialized in raising souls from the dead; while the root of *pharmakeus* implies that those known by this profession were chiefly concerned with creating potions or poisons.[8] However, the ancient writers themselves seem not to have used these terms with any noticeable consistency, but suggest a much more flexible approach, with each practitioner likely to be able to offer his or her client a grab-bag of supernatural skills and services. These might range from predicting the future (from books of oracles, perhaps, interpreting wonders or myriad other means),[9] to purification, healing, summoning and laying the dead, harming an enemy through unnatural means, initiation into mystery cults, or miracle-working. We might sum them up, as one fourth-century source (the Derveni Papyrus) does, as those who 'make a profession out of rites'.[10] The word translated as profession is τέχνη—a term that carries both the sense of a craft or an expertise, and a profession or trade; the 'rites' in question are described collectively as τα ἱερά ('hallowed, sacred, consecrated things').

Some of these professionals may have come from families or associations of *manteis*, or, at least, claimed this heritage.[11] Of these prophetic lineages, a number seem to have managed oracular sanctuaries (for instance, the Branchidai at Didyma and the Iamidai and Clytiadai at Olympia).[12] Other practitioners were itinerant: some could claim a useful clan connection, for example, that they belonged to the Telmessoi in Lykian Telmessos,[13] the Galeotai (a clan of Sikel prophets),[14] the Melampodids (descendants of the mythical seer Melampos, the earliest of Greek prophets).[15] If you were without such an association, then you could probably find another story to legitimize your skills: for example, Herodotos describes Deiphonos, a seer who went on the Greek expedition to Mykale in 479 BCE. He claimed to have inherited his gift of seer craft from his father, the shepherd Euenios, who, in turn, had received it directly from Apollo, in return for being ill-treated by the citizens of Apollonia. Herodotos tells us the full story and then slips in: 'I have also heard it said that Deiphonos was not really Euenios' son, but usurped his name and used to travel throughout Greece, offering his work for hire.'[16]

Others simply acquired the tools of the trade and set themselves up.[17] One man who did this was Thrasyllos, a Siphnian, who was penniless when he inherited a set of oracle books from a friend. He managed to acquire a great fortune as an itinerant diviner—evidence for us that there was ample demand as well as supply, and also an indication that these activities were not limited, as much of our evidence is, to Athens.[18] The material we will examine in this book, including evidence for the creation of curses in Sicily and Makedonia and for magic workers in Dodona, will also help us gain a fuller picture of this market. But we can also bear in mind some of the factors that may have helped to develop such a market. By this I mean the turbulent political events of the late fifth–fourth century and the growing community of outsiders (those without a city-state) that it created. These people needed to produce an income, and this seems to have prompted an increase in a variety of itinerant skilled professionals, including mercenaries and doctors.[19]

As well as widening our vision to look beyond Athens, we need to deepen it, and look down through the social strata. Our evidence introduces mostly men (unsurprisingly, since a large number of these *manteis* turn up on battlefields, using their skills to guide commanders), but there were also women in this profession. Other than the mythical Kassandra, we have evidence for at least one named female seer, Satyra, and a number of female so-called *engastrimuthoi* or 'belly-talkers'.[20] Some of these are likely to have been on the road: in Aeschylus' *Agamemnon* Kassandra herself refers to wandering beggar women, either seers or priestesses, so-called *agyrtriai*. Theophrastos' *Deisidaimōn,* or 'superstitious man', also calls for priestesses to purify him after he has seen a shrine at a cross-roads.[21] These are surely referring to figures familiar to their audience.

As well as those who roamed, we should not forget those who practised their arts locally, making charms for members of their household or neighbourhood. Something of these women can surely be glimpsed in literary creations, for example, Phaedra's nurse in Euripides' *Hippolytos,* or Plato's Diotima, although, of course, it is hard to mine these representations for reality. Plutarch relates a story about Perikles, ill with the plague, showing a friend an amulet that had been hung around his neck by 'the women', probably the women of the household.[22] The figure of the maidservant skilled in eliciting supernatural help is a familiar one, but there is also some dramatic evidence from the lawcourts that raises the social stakes: Theoris and Ninon, two women immortalized for being put to death in Athens, probably under the charge of impiety, but with overtones of supernatural activities of other kinds. These were not the only cases of women being brought to court on such charges: as well as Theoris and Ninon, there is evidence to show that the famous *hetaira* Phryne was charged with impiety.[23] In addition, there are a number of stories that suggest that the figure of a woman standing trial for supernatural activities may have been common enough to become a stock figure of fable and model speeches.[24] I will discuss these stories in more detail, later.

The expectation of and need for divine guidance was deeply interwoven throughout all aspects of life, not only the daily needs of individuals, but the structure and functioning of major civic institutions and policies. Thucydides' brief description makes it clear that they pronounced on weighty matters of state policy and were taken seriously. He mentions them almost cursorily as if they were a fact of daily life, and other evidence, both literary and epigraphic, demonstrates that it was indeed usual practice to involve oracular evidence and its interpreters in political decisions, both before and after this date. For example, oracle-mongers seem to have been important to the Pisistratidae; while in Herodotos, they are pictured in Athens, arguing the significance of Delphi's pronouncement about the city's 'wooden walls', before the Persians invade. Aristophanes' portrayal of mantic characters flinging oracles at each other in the *Peace,* suggests that oracles and their interpretation may have been used in Assembly debates.[25] We find *manteis* entrusted with important political assignments, the butt of Aristophanes' political satire; and Bowden has argued for a link between *chrēsmologoi* and state sacrifices.[26] Moreover, we need to be cautious about what the term indicates: obviously some who used it were specialists of some sort, but it was also possible to attain the status of being a *chrēsmologos* or a *mantis* just by interpreting an oracle. Moreover, there is some evidence that suggests that this was a skill that leaders in and out of battle were expected to have—and not just leaders.[27]

To stay with the evidence from classical Athens, among the officials of this city were oracle interpreters, who recorded and worked with great books of oracles collected from sanctuaries and seers across the ancient world; city honours were given to seers for their work; individuals in high office had personal seers that worked with them, helping to design policy.[28] Indeed, if we return to the events surrounding the Sicilian campaign, Plutarch's *Life of Nikias* intimates how this may have worked. In addition to the seers and oracle-mongers apparently foretelling the future in the city, there was more partisan divination going on. Plutarch tells us that there was opposition to the expedition from amongst the priests, but that Alkibiades 'had a number of other *manteis* who introduced certain other old oracles that proclaimed great fame for the Athenians from Sicily'. His use of 'other' suggests that they were at some level considered to be equivalent in terms of their occupation. The contrast that Plutarch has set up here is surely deliberate: the priests occupy an official position, in comparison to those *manteis* employed by Alkibiades, but both clearly have their say. (A personal consultation used for official city business: does that count as magic or religion, as licensed or unlicensed activity?) It suggests that, in Athens at least, supernatural information was introduced, as a serious, compelling matter, into political debate, and that it was regarded as an area of expertise in which a politician must be skilled.[29]

Altogether, what this description offers is a glimpse of a city in which the majority believed that gods spoke to mortals every day and that they could, and did, offer guidance. Divine communication was as prevalent as advertising is now—and sometimes just as intrusive. Omens could be perceived everywhere: in the pattern of a bird's flight, in a dream, in the remains of a sacrifice, even in the timing of a sneeze.[30] Any of these signs, it was believed, might, just might, reveal the gods' will, if you could read it properly. Those who offered to do so comprised a motley crew—men and women, from across society, selling a range of supernatural products and services, providing informed guidance, or advantage, for the future, operating at every level of society, knit into almost all aspects of ancient life.

Of course, I am not asserting that all members of society simply believed what they were told by such *manteis*, or even that there was anything to tell. There was, without doubt, at any one time, a spectrum of attitudes to divination throughout society. There were certainly individual Greeks who voiced particular misgivings, but we need to be careful how we judge their concerns. For a start, this may not be a simple binary question of belief or no belief: it is quite possible for a person to hold, at the same time, apparently contradictory beliefs. Sometimes this can be justified through reference to a higher order belief, but usually it is less coherent than that.[31] As Luhrmann has argued, after studying the experience of twentieth-century witches: 'Beliefs do a job; they are not always disinterestedly asserted because they are felt to be true in themselves. Ideas and beliefs drift, in a complex interdependency of concept and experience.' We can compare Plato's succinct description of the difficulties (even for himself, perhaps) of taking a sceptical position in an environment of strong belief: 'In respect of all such matters it is neither easy to perceive what is the real truth, nor, if one does perceive it, is it easy to convince others. And it is futile to approach the souls of men who view one another with dark suspicion if they happen to see images of moulded wax at doorways, or at points where three ways meet, or it may be at the tomb of some ancestor, to bid them make light of all such portents, when we ourselves hold no clear opinion concerning them.'[32]

People are likely to have had quite particular motives for their criticisms. Thus, as we have seen, the vociferous protests of the writer of the Hippokratic text *On the Sacred Disease* were probably voiced as much from a sense of competition with those who sold supernatural healing, as a belief that their methods were inferior to his own. When Plato criticizes the wandering *manteis* whom he describes in the *Republic* (see above), he is concerned that their promises of purification might encourage wrongdoing. Although he seems to have felt a profound unease, sometimes deepening to indignation, at some of the activities of some of these itinerant professionals he concentrates on, and designs legislation against, those activities that are used to cause harm.[33] Similarly, the attitude of the writer of the Derveni Papyrus, referred to earlier, who described those who make a profession out of rites, also needs to be handled with care. When he describes how those who consult these individuals are to be pitied 'because it is not enough for them to have spent their money in advance, but they also go off deprived of their judgement', he seems not to be finding fault only with those individuals who offer the service or profit from it. Rather the criticism is of those who think that they can gain wisdom by simply paying for such services rather than seeking further understanding by undergoing more intense study and ritual activity.[34]

Robust social criticism is to be found in drama, both tragedies and comedies. In tragedy, mythical seers are regularly charged with corruption of the mantic art for personal profit.[35] Nevertheless, episodes also draw attention to the fact that just as it was possible for a seer to be guilty of corrupting his art for profit, it was also likely that he (or she) might be abused for giving an unwanted response. Thus, in Sophocles' *Oedipous the King*, Oedipous greets the famous Tiresias with respect as a 'sacred seer', but when he finds his pronouncements unpalatable, praise turns to abuse, and he denounces Tiresias as a charlatan, only concerned with making a profit.[36]

The comedies of Aristophanes famously prickle with abuse of grasping oracle-mongers, but his selection of targets is politically rather than religiously motivated, attacking characters that we know were, at the time, either in office themselves, or close to those who were.[37] Aristophanes' mockery draws our attention to the fact that this was a culture in which an oracle-monger—or the use of oracles—could become very powerful. His attacks revolve around a stock complaint (greed), and do not necessarily indicate a widespread scepticism of the practice as a whole.[38] Moreover, he limits his attacks to the oracle-mongers, and through this to the demagogues who used them, leaving other forms of divination alone.[39] Although Aristophanes makes at least a couple of references to the complexity of Delphic pronouncements, he never attacks the oracle for telling lies or for being out to enrich itself.[40]

ORACULAR INSTITUTIONS

This brings us back to oracles—sanctuaries and sites where you could directly consult a supernatural entity, be it a god or the dead. These were considered to be the receivers, *par excellence*, of the supernatural signal, thought to deliver the most significant and reliable of all divine messages.[41]

The most famous of all these oracles was, of course, in the temple of Apollo at Delphi, whose long-standing fame places it firmly amongst the ranks of the proverbial, even now. It would be easy to assume that this was the focus of all ancient Greek oracular activity, with perhaps the oracles at Dodona, Ammon, or Didyma running a distant second place. However, Trevor Curnow's gazetteer of oracle sanctuaries lists 49 oracular sites that were operating in Greece, and details of oracle sites that were probably in operation until the fourth century CE across many other countries.[42] Obviously, in many cases, when and how these oracles operated is unknown and some of these interpretations should be treated with caution.[43] It is clear, however, that oracular consultation was both widespread and long running. The earliest evidence for oracular activity dates to the fifteenth century BCE. It is a pronouncement about Hatshepsut's claim to the throne of Egypt and was made by the oracle of Ammon in Egypt. Of course, this is just the earliest we possess—there may have been oracles in operation before this period. In turn, the end of many oracles is hard to pinpoint exactly. Some lasted until the edict of Theodosios the Great in 385 CE, which ordered all remaining oracles in the Roman Empire to be closed down. But this did not necessarily mark the end of all oracular activity: for example, some oracles in Egypt were still operating at the end of the fifth century, while others did not so much stop functioning as carry on working 'under new management', adopting a Christian saint, in place of the original god.[44]

Delphi has received most academic attention and the temptation is to assume that all oracles worked in roughly the same way, in terms of both their mechanism and role within society. But this is a temptation we should resist. General explanations of 'oracular production' have shifted over time: since the late nineteenth century the scholarly focus has moved from explanations of the practical operation of oracles, through attempts to rationalize oracular consultation, to more nuanced functionalist explorations of the role of oracles in different societies. For example, at the operational end, some have argued that oracles, visited by key statesmen from all over the Graeco-Roman world, would have been singularly well placed to gather and disseminate information for political purposes or to help guide international travellers. In the attempt to rationalize what went on at Delphi, others have suggested that the priests were highly skilled in psychological techniques and 'must have found it comparatively simple to satisfy the interrogator by giving him the answer he hoped for, or even, in the case of barren women to have induced a state of psychological relaxation conducive to the fulfilment of the prophecy of childbirth'.[45]

Recently, more sophisticated explanations have gained immensely from work done on non-Western divinatory systems: the poison oracle used by the Azande in southern Sudan described by Evans-Pritchard, for example, or Ifa divination practised among the Yoruba of West Africa.[46] In addition, techniques of modern psychotherapy have helped modern Western observers come to terms with what may otherwise seem an essentially incomprehensible practice of an alien culture. Such an approach has challenged the mysticism cloaking oracular consultation, lessening the distance between Them and Us, and emphasizing the idea that this practice may play a variety of roles within its particular cultural system. This has drawn attention to the power of an external neutral authority in a community decision-making process and prompted exploration of how oracles participate in local understandings of causation in order to manufacture epistemological and sociopolitical harmony.[47] This, in turn, has brought different emphases to ongoing analyses of the oracle's operation. For example, where once the Pythia was condemned as a poor, gullible, uneducated woman, she has benefited from both cross-cultural and feminist approaches. Recently it has been argued that 'Neither a raving hysteric nor a prop of priests who duped the public, the Pythia at Delphi produced utterances that are a genuine expression of a cultural system which believed in and codified behaviour and speech that it understood as indicating the presence of the divine.'[48]

But if travelling seers and oracle-mongers have had to side-step a reputation for dishonesty and acquisitiveness, oracular sanctuaries, above all Delphi, retain a reputation for poetic, but problematic, if not positively tricky, responses. Many of these stories of ambiguity are surely the moral icing on the cake of literary parables: oracular confections that demonstrate the inevitability of fate, the arrogance of mortals, or which provide useful aetiologies for events or places. After all, various recent oracle compilations have demonstrated that many oracular responses comprised simply 'yes' or 'no' and were, in general, simply used to approve decisions that had already been made, helping to build consensus around difficult decisions.[49]

Some scholars have argued that any trace of an aetiological subtext, folkloric elements, proverb, riddle, or ambiguity indicate that an oracle should not be counted as historical.[50] But others have suggested that what looks like confusing detail to us may have had its uses, to either consultant or oracle. For example, being forced to debate the meaning of an oracle will compel a group of people to work out for themselves what they want to do.[51] Moreover, it allows consensus to be reached on the basis of an authoritative neutral, external source, a useful mechanism for those who might otherwise find it difficult to back down. In turn, ambiguity or obfuscation may at times have been a helpful, indeed, crucial tool for an oracle, allowing the institution to escape from politically sticky or threatening situations, a reminder that oracles were institutions that existed in time and place.[52] Others have suggested that some of the early, seemingly baffling oracles given to colonizers may have offered 'signs' that we no longer understand, but that helped the *oikist*, or leader of a colonizing expedition, to identify the site for which he was searching.[53] There may be some truth in a number of these explanations. Perhaps, as Plutarch suggests, actual oracular responses tended to grow simpler over time, responding to the needs of the period. Or, perhaps what had originally been quite simple responses became much more elaborate in the telling, gaining authority and narrative power as they grew more poetic. In the end, as Amandry noted in 1959, however much we disbelieve that an oracle was communicated in a certain form, it doesn't necessarily discount the reality of the consultation it reports.[54]

Meanwhile, we must be careful not to confuse a reputation for ambiguity with one for deceit. Oracles seem to have maintained a position as truth tellers, despite evidence that they were occasionally the victims of determined efforts at bribery and corruption.[55] In fact, the Greeks themselves seem to have developed techniques for checking doubtful oracles: either through discussion or by consulting another oracle. A number of examples, some historical, some not, describe what sound like serial consultations, the second used to verify the first.[56]

However, although a number of these explanations of how Delphi worked are useful for understanding oracles in general, they should not hide the fact that there were crucial differences between oracular sanctuaries—in their internal structure, in their operation, and in their social role. Among the most obvious is each sanctuary's supernatural personnel. There were oracular sanctuaries dedicated to a variety of different gods: as well as Apollo and Zeus, we find oracles of Ares, Herakles, and Demeter, among others.[57] Asklepios was a particularly popular oracular divinity, consulted using methods of incubation, the healing god appearing to the sick in dreams to tell them what was wrong and how to find a cure. There were sanctuaries belonging to heroes, such as the oracle of Trophonios at Lebadaea. Consultation of this particular oracle involved a journey underground (Trophonios was said to have been swallowed by the earth), which was apparently so terrifying that there was a proverb, 'He has consulted the oracle of Trophonios', which apparently meant that someone could no longer laugh.[58] There were also *nekuomanteia*, or oracles of the dead, where, it seems you could contact those who had died and ask them questions.[59] Plutarch tells how the Spartan commander Pausanias visited the *nekuomanteion* at Herakleia Pontika on the south coast of the Black Sea. He wanted to speak with, and somehow appease, the ghost of Kleonike, a young woman whom he had murdered and whose ghost was, as a consequence, driving him to distraction. Kleonike's reply—that he would find peace in Sparta—actually foretold his death.[60]

Divinatory mechanisms were also various: the oracle of Demeter at Patrai in Achaia, consulted by the sick as to whether they would live or die, made its pronouncement via a mirror that was lowered into a spring that flowed outside the temple.[61] Nearby, in the market-place at Pharai, was an oracle of Hermes: the consultant presented a coin and burned incense before an image of the god, then whispered it his question. He then kept his hands over his ears only removing them once he had left the market-place. The first thing he heard after that was considered to be a divine oracular utterance.[62] There were dice oracles, like the one at Termessos, in Pisidia in southern Turkey, where the consultant threw seven dice, and then matched the result to the corresponding verse, inscribed on the wall. At Olympos in Lykia, in south Turkey, visitors chose letters that matched verses inscribed on the walls of tombs—suggesting some kind of interaction with the dead.[63] At Olympia, they were said to use sacrifices, 'reading' the splits in the skins of victims.[64] Consultants at the oracle of Amphilochos and Mopsos at Mallos in Kilikia spent the night there, hoping to see the answers to their questions in their dreams.[65]

The most well-known method of ancient Greek oracular consultation is, of course, the raving Pythia at Delphi: much has been written about who she was, the ways in which she may have reached a state of oracular frenzy, how she managed to compose her baffling hexameters, whether and how they were interpreted by others. And yet, as we have seen, a number of the oracle responses suggest that her answers were far simpler—a choice made between options presented by the consultant. Some commentators have urged that these kinds of responses were probably answered by a lot oracle functioning at Delphi, in addition to the Pythian verse oracle.[66] Evidence includes late stories about lot oracles;[67] a collection of images interpreted as being of Kassandra prophesying the fate of Troy to Priam using a system of lots that may have been in use at Delphi;[68] the use of the verb *anairein* (to take up) in oracular speech;[69] and the question formulation 'Is it better that I do x or y/x or not?' which would be particularly susceptible to this divinatory treatment.[70] Some commentators have found this particularly appealing on the grounds that it may have provided a cheaper, more frequently available alternative to consultations of the Pythia, more suitable for those who were not state representatives, for example. In the end, the evidence is inconclusive, but even if there was no official lot oracle both historical and fictional accounts of consultation at Delphi suggest the use of mechanisms that resembled the selection of lots, rather than inspired prophecy.

Among the historical, we can point to the immensely careful consultation process described in the second part of an inscription of Eleusis from the fourth century, the so-called Sacred *Orgas* ('Land') decree. This describes the action taken by the Athenians to resolve questions about the boundaries and cultivation of certain areas of sacred land at Eleusis. These questions had political as well as agricultural or religious ramifications, since the land was on the long-disputed border between Megara and Athens. The first part of the decree describes how a panel of Athenians would be chosen to delineate 'the disputed boundaries of the sacred land'. It goes on to explain the process to be used to ask the god about whether or not to cultivate the land:

The secretary of the council is to write upon two pieces of tin which are equal and alike, on one 'If it is preferable and better for the Athenian people that *basileus* should rent out the parts of the sacred *orgas* currently being cultivated outside the boundaries, for the building of a colonnade and the equipping of the sanctuary of the two goddesses' and on the other 'If it is preferable and better for the Athenian people that the parts of the sacred *orgas* currently being cultivated outside the

A Lapse into Unreason 37

boundaries be left to the two goddesses untilled'. When the secretary has written, the chairman of the *proedroi* shall roll up each piece of tin and tie it with wool and cast it into a bronze water jug in the presence of the people. The *prytaneis* are to see to these preparations and the treasurers of the Goddess are to bring down forthwith two water jugs, one gold and one silver, to the people, and the chairman is to shake the bronze water jug and then take out each piece of tin in turn and put the first into the gold water jug and the next into the silver water jug, and the chairman of the *prytaneis* is to seal the jugs with the public seal, and any Athenian who wants can apply a counter seal.

The jugs are then placed in the Akropolis, and the Athenians send a delegation to the Pythia to ask her to choose between them. Note how the question is carefully posed so as to ensure that the options are constrained. The lot process not only ensures that no Athenian can exert undue influence over the outcome, but it also protects the oracle from being put in a situation in which she must speak explicitly for or against Athenian or Megarian interests. The revelation of the god's answer was to be read out to the people. As Parker has observed: 'There is a strong element of theatre about the transaction ... It is an ostentatious acting out of incorruptible procedure, and the climax of the drama is performed in Athens itself, in front of the people.'[71]

A probably fictional example of a lot mechanism is found in the story of the election of the Thessalian king Aleuas the Red, when the Thessalians are said to have taken lots (actually beans) to Delphi, with the candidates' names written upon them, for the Pythia to make a selection.[72] A similar process to this may have actually taken place when the Athenian political reformer Kleisthenes asked the Pythia to choose ten tribal eponyms from a pre-selected list of a hundred founding heroes. Granted no such process is mentioned in the literary descriptions, but then nor is there any such detail in the descriptions of the Athenian consultation about sacred land at Eleusis.[73]

Further contested evidence may be found in an inscription from Skiathos, dating to 350–340.[74] This document, broken in parts and difficult to read, seems to list the charges that individuals from Skiathos must pay for sacrificial cakes and victims when they visited the Delphic oracle. Depending on how the term *phruktos* is read, one line of the text may offer information about either a particular charge for consultation by lot or arrangements for the use of sacrificial cakes.[75] Whichever way we read these details, this document does provide evidence, albeit slim, for something of the bureaucracy of divination—that such arrangements might, at least in some instances, be made on behalf of individuals between oracle and state. It may be that something similar occurred at Didyma: it has been argued that the presentation of *phialai* to the shrine at Didyma by some cities (especially Milesian colonies) may be taken as an indication that they were clients of the oracle. As one inscription seems to suggest the non-payment of these *phialai* does seem to have been a serious matter, meriting negotiation.[76] But what bearing the payment of the phiale had for city or individual consultation is not mentioned in the relevant documents. Does this mean that individuals from those cities could only consult the oracle when their city had paid what was due?

Our inability to answer this question points out an interesting lacuna in our understanding of oracle use: the question of state versus individual consultation. Different patterns of use may have characterized different oracles, and may have influenced their modes of operation. About what areas of life did people visit an oracle, and at what point in their decision-making process did they seek divine guidance? What kind of help did they ask for and how was the request for that aid constructed? The specific activities of individuals (not historical figures, such as the *oikists*, or 'founders', of colonies, or tyrants) at oracle sites and the kinds of concerns about which they chose to consult an oracle, have received relatively little attention from scholars. In fact, after acknowledging Plutarch's, admittedly cursory, observations about the topics of individual questions at Delphi, most scholars have assumed that the behaviour of individuals at oracles mirrors state activity: the oracle provided a way of resolving uncertainty about religious or civic affairs, often helping to build consensus around difficult decisions. This conclusion is largely a result of the nature of the distribution of the evidence: as we will see, literary accounts of oracular consultations tend to comprise reports of state consultations. But the material does exist for us to begin to compile and explore the context, events, and experience of individual consultation. In particular, the body of epigraphic material from Dodona provides remarkable insight into the kind and range of topics about which individuals came to consult an oracle, an index of mundane anxieties that illuminate the daily relationship between man and gods.

Finally in this list, although it should be a primary consideration, we must consider the changing socio-political circumstances and context in which each oracle developed and functioned, as Catherine Morgan has shown in some detail.[77] For example, she compares the development of the oracle at Delphi with that of the oracle at Didyma during the eighth century BCE. This was a time of major changes in the economic, political, cultural, and social landscape of Greece, when emerging cities were dealing with unprecedented problems of state formation. At the same time there were significant changes in the material expression of religious beliefs across Greece, for example the development of new expressions for old cult practices, the founding of new sanctuaries and construction of temple buildings, and increases in votive offerings.[78]

During the eighth century, the community at Delphi appears to have been playing an increasing role in a developing local settlement system, boosted by expanding trade with Korinth and links north with Thessaly. In the sanctuary at Delphi, Korinthians, Thessalians, and Spartans are making dedications, although there is no temple building. During the last quarter of the eighth century, dedications increase in number and kind, indicating cult activity: bronze votives and imported pottery from far and wide.[79] Many of the dedications are on themes of warfare: there are little bronze warrior figurines, for example, and helmeted horse drivers. There are few rustic images. This suggests something of the character of those who are coming to Delphi: they're probably not farmers, with agricultural questions on their minds. They're more likely to be warriors, involved in the shaping of the new states. And this conclusion is supported by the record of early inquiries.[80]

During the seventh century, the sanctuary expands, gaining its first temple building, while the greater part of the settlement is abandoned.[81] The establishment of the temple may indicate the beginning of oracular activity on the site. Suddenly, sometime in the early sixth century the sanctuary is removed from local control; Delphians become sanctuary servers; and an inter-state league is created—the Delphic Amphiktiony (a kind of league connected with sanctuaries and the maintenance of cults)—to regulate cult activity. The victory is marked with the celebration of a major interstate festival.[82]

Delphi has undergone a process of transformation: removed from local control, it has become a neutral, interstate oracular sanctuary. New founding myths will develop that tell the story of its early foundation and panhellenic status. One example is the *Homeric Hymn to Pythian Apollo*, probably written around the time of Delphi's emancipation in the sixth century BCE. It describes how Delphi was founded when Apollo killed the great she-dragon Pytho on the site of the oracle, how the god travelled throughout Greece, trying to find the right location for his oracle, how the different parts of the Greek world were involved in the oracle's foundation. It manages to weave together both themes of religious celebration and divine ordinance and a strong political message—that the oracle is no local foundation, but a panhellenic sanctuary that precedes other Apolline cults.[83] In this sense, the substance of this foundation poem reflects the reality of Delphi's activities. It reminds us not to be seduced or put off by the aura of mystery that for centuries has surrounded Delphi. This may have been a powerful religious institution, but it existed in and played a significant role in a dynamic social and political context.

The same conflict of founding myth and archaeological evidence exists for the sanctuary of Didyma, situated just outside the city of Miletos, in western Turkey. Despite stories of the foundation of oracle and sanctuary before the Ionian migration, it is extremely unlikely that the oracle pre-dates the establishment of the sanctuary in the late eighth century. But this is where the similarity between Delphi and Didyma ends: whereas Delphi developed into a panhellenic sanctuary, Didyma seems to have been consulted chiefly by Miletos and Milesian colonies.[84]

There are stories of earlier use that seem to imply an international reputation: for example, in 608 BCE, the Egyptian Pharaoh Necho made dedications in thanks for his victory at Megiddo, which suggests that the temple was known, even if the oracle was not. Didyma received offerings from Kroisos and is said to have been one of the oracles he infamously tested. We should note that the story implies that Didyma gets the answer wrong, so was probably, as Fontenrose argues, part of Delphi's publicity package. Herodotos provides a story about the Kymaeans asking if they should surrender their suppliant Pactyes; when they are told to do so, their representative Aristodikos goes to inquire a second time and receives the response 'Yes . . . that is my command. Why? To hasten the impiety and consequent destruction of Kyme, so that you never again come to consult me on the issue of the surrender of suppliants.' Although the equivocal answer of the oracle in response to the Kymaeans seems credible, bearing in mind the current political circumstances, the episode quickly devolves into a cautionary tale.[85]

In 494, city and sanctuary were sacked by the Persians, and, in the years that followed, although the city was rebuilt and the sanctuary slowly returned to life, the oracle was not revived. This would makes sense if the oracle had primarily existed for Miletos' political use: under Persian rule there would be few internal civic conflicts. Over the next hundred or so years, Miletos remained a subject city: after Persian defeat, it became a part of the Athenian empire, then it was taken by the Spartans and handed over to the Persians. According to Kallisthenes, the oracle was revived (the sacred spring restarted along with oracular activity) at some stage between the recovery of Miletos and Alexander's arrival in Memphis in 331.[86] Morgan argues compellingly that this was because it was needed again, not only to resolve internal city disputes, but also to help expedite the relationship between a Greek/Asiatic city and its Hellenistic ruler. She contrasts this with Delphi's waning star and the role that Delphi had played in a world of autonomous Greek city-states, a world that was now taking on a different kind of political structure.

When we examine the oracle of Dodona, we find that it provides rich, if often puzzling, material to explore in all three of the categories considered so far. It has been suggested, with relation to Delphi, that the decision-making structures of *ethnē* (tribes) might not have been suited to oracular consultation, but this does not appear to hold regarding the relationship between the oracle at Dodona and its surrounding *koina* (alliances of tribes).[87] In fact, both oracle question tablets and the recent excavations at Dodona suggest that the sanctuary played both a significant religious and political role for the region, as well as being a crucial resource for individuals.

3

Individuals and Oracles

> Any culture which admits the use of oracles and divination is committed to a distinction between appearances and reality. The oracle offers a way of reaching behind appearance to another source of knowledge.
>
> Mary Douglas 1999*b*: 119

The superstitious man is the sort who washes his hands in three springs, sprinkles himself with water from a temple font, puts a laurel leaf in his mouth—and then is ready for the day's perambulations. If a weasel runs across his path, he will not proceed on his journey until someone else has covered the ground or he has thrown three stones over the road. When he sees a snake in the house he invokes Sabazios if it is the red-brown one, and if it is the holy one he sets up a hero-shrine there and then.[1]

Theophrastos' *Characters*, set in Athens in the late fourth century, comprises portraits of sixteen types of men. The frantic Superstitious Man (*Deisidaimōn*) lives in a world overflowing with supernatural signals, each one prompting a flurry of activity from him, intended to appease divine discontent and ward off misfortune. There can be no doubt that Theophrastos intends the superstitious man to provoke derision, but for the modern reader he also prompts fascination, consumed as he is by a host of everyday rituals and responses of a kind rarely described in ancient literature.[2] Moreover, he also directs us to a crucial question: in a context of constant divine communication, a world in which the gods are constantly providing signs to those who can read them, why, when, and how would an individual engage with the supernatural?

In this chapter, I will examine how the Greeks represented oracular consultation to themselves, in terms of both explicit instructions about consultation and the stories they told about it, and the literary evidence for individual consultations, with reference to the oracles of Didyma, Delphi, and Dodona.[3]

INDIVIDUAL INSTRUCTIONS

Starting with evidence for self-conscious instructions about how to use an oracle: What did people think one could ask about and what was not allowed? Xenophon's account of Sokrates' approach to divination in the *Memorabilia* provides a useful beginning:[4]

ἔφη δὲ δεῖν, ἃ μὲν μαθόντας ποιεῖν ἔδωκαν οἱ θεοί, μανθάνειν, ἃ δὲ μὴ δῆλα τοῖς ἀνθρώποις ἐστί, πειρᾶσθαι διὰ μαντικῆς παρὰ τῶν θεῶν πυνθάνεσθαι· τοὺς θεοὺς γὰρ οἷς ἂν ὦσιν ἵλεῳ σημαίνειν.

In short, what the gods have granted us to do by help of learning, we must learn; what is hidden from mortals we should try to find out from the gods by divination: for to him that is in their grace the gods grant a sign.

The following parameters for oracular consultation emerge: Sokrates believed that a clear course of action made an oracle unnecessary, but if one was dealing with something unseen or unclear then one could seek oracular aid.[5] Xenophon elaborates that Sokrates is saying it is wrong to question the gods about what can be known by the use of our own wits, by reckoning, measurement, or weighing up.[6] However, although carpentry and metalwork, activities involved in farming or government, proficiency in mathematics, estate management or military science are all, up to a certain level, within the scope of human judgement, the most important aspects of these subjects are areas of knowledge reserved by the gods for themselves. He gives the following examples: the man who has sown a field well cannot know whether he or someone else will reap the harvest; a general cannot know whether it is to his advantage to hold a command, or a politician if he should take an important office; a man with a beautiful wife cannot know if she will cause him pain; while a man who has secured influential connections in his native land cannot know if these will result in his banishment.

Insofar as these are all questions about what will happen in the future, they all seem to be typical of what we might expect to be asked at an oracle. As Xenophon describes it, these are not questions from men who are surrendering everything to divine will. They have already progressed in their decision, tackling the aspects that they can know about.[7] But man can only work things out so far for himself. The future provides a boundary, beyond which man cannot go; after that, it's up to divine will. Similar ideas appear in other parts of Xenophon's writing, and in the speeches of the orators.[8] Emphasis should also be laid on another aspect of this explanation, one that fits with the attitudes to uncertainty that were raised in the Introduction to this book. The examples that Xenophon has provided are all about good things—well-sown fields, beautiful wives, influential connections—and the things that might go wrong with them. Part of Xenophon's instructions about oracular consultations concerns a mortal's expectations about his or her life and fortune. Good things cannot, should not, be taken for granted: even, or perhaps especially, seemingly favourable situations carry risks.

At the other end of the period of this study, some similar lessons can be gathered from the instructions of the second-century Greek historian Polybios in his history of the rise of the Roman Empire. As he reflects on the role of fortune, he observes, regarding the use of oracles:

ὧν μὲν νὴ Δί᾿ ἀδύνατον ἢ δυσχερὲς τὰς αἰτίας καταλαβεῖν ἄνθρωπον ὄντα, περὶ τούτων ἴσως ἄν τις ἀπορῶν ἐπὶ τὸν θεὸν τὴν ἀναφορὰν ποιοῖτο καὶ τὴν τύχην ... πέμπομεν ἐρησόμενοι τοὺς θεοὺς τί ποτ᾿ ἂν ἢ λέγουσιν ἢ πράττουσιν ἡμῖν ἄμεινον εἴη καὶ γένοιτο παῦλα τῶν ἐνεστώτων κακῶν. ὧν δὲ δυνατόν ἐστι τὴν αἰτίαν εὑρεῖν, ἐξ ἧς καὶ δι᾿ ἣν ἐγένετο τὸ συμβαῖνον, οὐχί μοι δοκεῖ τῶν τοιούτων δεῖν ἐπὶ τὸ θεῖον ποιεῖσθαι τὴν ἀναφοράν;

As regards those phenomena which it is impossible or difficult for a mortal man to understand, it is reasonable enough to escape from the dilemma by attributing them to the work of a god or of chance ... we then send to ask the gods what we should say and do to produce a change for the better and to obtain a respite from the evils that oppress us. But as for those events whose causes we can discover and given an explanation as to why they happen, we should certainly not in my opinion regard them as acts of God ...[9]

Polybios' explanation conveys the same division between reasonable and unreasonable questions as was used by Sokrates. Fundamentally, he agrees with Xenophon that the subject matter of a consultation must concern what is not 'clear', and this explicitly includes what has occurred in the past. But those matters that are obvious or the efficient and final cause of which it is possible to discover should not be put down to divine action, nor should we send to the gods to find out what to do or say about them. However, Polybios' notion of what is reasonable carries a different nuance. His questions focus not so much on specific decisions to be taken by individuals as on the unknown environment of the natural world. So he states, 'if anyone had proposed that we should consult the gods to find out what we should say or do so as to increase our numbers and repopulate our cities, his advice would have been quite futile since the cause of this situation was self-evident and the remedy lay within our power'. But, in contrast, it is reasonable to ask about 'exceptionally heavy and continuous rain or snow, or on the other hand, the destruction of crops by severe drought or frost or a persistent outbreak of plague or other similar things of which it is not easy to detect the cause'.[10]

These kinds of question were indeed topics of consultation, according to Plutarch, who records that questions asked by states during his priesthood at Delphi concerned 'the yield from crops, the increase of herds and public health'.[11] However, in Polybios' opinion, it would be absurd to consult an oracle about the childlessness and population shortage of the Greece of his day when their causes were all too clear. And yet we know that this was a subject of consultation for many individuals at oracles certainly in the centuries before he was writing, and certainly during and after his lifetime. It draws our attention to a useful, if not startling, idea that we might sum up with the phrase: obviousness lies in the eye of the beholder. Indeed, we will see when we turn to the epigraphic material, that this is one of the most frequent topics of inquiry made by individuals at Dodona.

Plutarch also gives us examples of the kinds of questions that he, as a priest at Delphi, saw individuals asking the oracle. These include such inquiries as 'if they will win, if they will marry, if it is to their advantage to sail, to farm, to go abroad'.[12] Some of these questions are phrased as if the consultant need take no action, but can just wait for events to turn out, for example, '*if* they will win, *if* they will marry'.[13] Others emphasize the idea of an advantage: for example, '*if it is better* to sail, if (it is better) to farm, if (it is better) to migrate'.[14] At 408c, the questions described are phrased more uniformly, but their grammatical form gives a sense of inevitability. Consultants ask: '*if I must* marry, if I must sail, if I must make a loan'.[15] All these questions are concerned with ventures or decisions that offer great opportunities for prosperity if they go well, but also carry obvious risks. When we turn to the records of oracle consultations at Dodona, we will find differences and similarities in both subject matter and style.

INDIVIDUAL CONSULTATIONS IN THE LITERATURE

Further information about what it was thought appropriate to ask an oracle can be gathered by exploring stories scattered across Greek literature about individual oracular consultations. In what follows, since I want an overview of the kinds of questions asked by individuals that the Greeks themselves would have credibly attributed to these oracles, I do not try to distinguish between those oracles that were probably asked or delivered elsewhere and then later attributed to these oracles, nor do I exclude those oracles that are not conclusively historical.[16] However, I do omit those questions that seem to have been asked by individuals about plague or famine or other events on behalf of a community, or other situations where the individual is acting as an ambassador for a larger group of people.[17]

Herodotos' *Histories* is a famously rich source of stories about and including oracle consultations, particularly those made at Delphi. Most of these accounts concern communities and offer aetiologies for both historical and legendary events, such as the founding of cities, deaths of famous persons, outcomes of battles, etc. These stories provide examples of a range of attitudes to oracles, along with, implicitly, instruction on how to approach consultation. Many of these concern a consultant being so blinded by his own desires that he misunderstands, or takes too literally, the riddling instructions of the oracle. Herotodus' story of the fall of Kroisos, described at the beginning of this book, provides one famous illustration of this trope; there are plenty of others. For example, Kambyses, King of Persia, warned by the oracle at Buto that he will die at a place called Ekbatana, avoids the town of that name in Media. He dies instead at Ekbatana in Syria.[18]

Other lessons concerning how one should not behave towards an oracle include the angry response of the god of the oracle at Branchidai to the Kymaeans' inquiry about killing the suppliant Pactyes, and the story of the Spartan Glaukos daring to ask Apollo for permission to perjure himself so that he can keep a sum of money entrusted to him.[19] However, in addition to these morality tales, across Greek literature, there are numerous stories that reveal the more everyday concerns that individuals might take to an oracle, although often, in these accounts, these mundane inquiries lead to extraordinary results or are part of a narrative concerning a significant historical event.

In this context, we find individuals asking questions about their lack of children, especially heirs: for example, Teisamenos, from Elis, consulting about his lack of children receives a response which sets in motion his appointment as a diviner for the Spartans; while a man from Petra, Eëtion, asks about an heir by his wife, Labda, a member of the Bacchiadai family who ruled Korinth (his child will become the tyrant of Korinth, Kypselos).[20] Decisions regarding new responsibilities or possible professions are brought to the oracle: the Athenian general, Miltiades the Elder asks whether he should take on the affairs of the Thrakian tribe of the Dolonkoi, as they have asked.[21] Individuals make inquiries about sickness and health, illness or physical problems, their own or other people's. For example, the Lydian King Alyattes, fearing punishment for sacrilegious acts, asks about his illness, and, in one version of the story of the foundation of Kyrene, Polymnestos, a nobleman of Thera nicknamed Battos because of his stutter, is asking about his speech impediment when he receives the instruction to found a city in Libya.[22]

People also ask about borrowed, lost, or hidden objects: for example, Herodotos relates how Glaukos asked about returning money that had been entrusted to him.[23] Other examples include the legendary founder of Boiotian Thebes, Kadmos, seeking his sister Europa (who has been abducted by Zeus); and Polykrates of Thebes wanting to find the buried treasure of Mardonios, the Persian general. Other literary references provide the following additional topics of inquiry: marriage,[24] omens,[25] and travel, in particular colonizing expeditions, for example, Dorieus consults Delphi before he sets sail to Libya (along with the clear implication that this is expected of a *ktistēs*).[26] Generals are often described as asking about the likely success of their military campaigns—both Philip II and his son Alexander are said to have consulted the oracle about the success of their campaigns.[27] There are also inquiries about living a pious life, including questions about who is most fortunate, or who offers the best sacrifice.[28] Some of these questions concern illegal acts. It might seem surprising to find these asked of an oracle, suggesting that these stories are firmly in the realm of the fictional, indeed, might even be seen as morality tales. However, as we shall see later, questions concerning illegal acts do seem to have been put to the oracle at Dodona, albeit rarely.[29]

Sometimes, it is possible to make a guess at the likely phrasing of the original question asked at an oracle from the style of the answer it seems to have received. In most of the stories about oracle consultations at Delphi, the questions start with 'about' ($\pi\epsilon\rho\acute{\iota}$) and their topic: so requests about children are described as 'about the birth of children' ($\pi\epsilon\rho\grave{\iota}$ $\pi\alpha\acute{\iota}\delta\omega\nu$ $\gamma\epsilon\nu\acute{\epsilon}\sigma\epsilon\omega\varsigma$—Menelaos' inquiry; or $\pi\epsilon\rho\grave{\iota}$ $\tau\acute{\epsilon}\kappa\nu\omega\nu$ $\gamma\epsilon\nu\acute{\epsilon}\sigma\epsilon\omega\varsigma$ from Myskellos of Ripai; or $\pi\epsilon\rho\grave{\iota}$ $\tau o\hat{v}$ $\gamma\epsilon\nu\nu\eta\theta\eta\sigma o\mu\acute{\epsilon}\nu o\nu$ $\beta\rho\acute{\epsilon}\phi o\nu\varsigma$—Karkinos' question). Meleos is described as making his inquiry 'about dwelling' ($\pi\epsilon\rho\grave{\iota}$ $o\iota\kappa\acute{\eta}\sigma\epsilon\omega\varsigma$); while Alexander's is 'about the campaign' ($\pi\epsilon\rho\grave{\iota}$ $\tau\hat{\eta}\varsigma$ $\sigma\tau\rho\alpha\tau\epsilon\acute{\iota}\alpha\varsigma$). In a number of examples, what sounds like the question itself is included in the narrative: for example, Glaukos asks the god 'if he might purloin the money by swearing an oath';[30] Miltiades asks the Pythia 'whether he should go along with the request of the Dolonkians'; Dorieus asks 'if he will capture the land to which he is travelling'; and Damagetos' question is reported as 'whether (or not) it is necessary to marry a woman'. It is likely that these questions would be phrased in a way that would seem acceptable to the story's ancient audience, but, of course, we cannot rely on these narratives to provide us with the actual words of any individual's question.

Xenophon's own oracle consultations, reported in the *Anabasis*, are likely to offer a more reliable guide to actual practice. As I have described in Chapter 1, in the third book of the *Anabasis* Xenophon provides us, not without some humour, with examples of two typical question formulations.[31] When Xenophon visits the oracle, he phrases his question so that he asks to which god he should pray in order to make the best and safest journey. On his return, Sokrates corrects him, telling him that he should have asked the oracle whether he should go on the expedition or stay at home. 'Which god should I pray to?' And 'Should I do *x* or should I do *y*?' Descriptions of other consultations in literature and in the dedicatory inscriptions suggest that these two formulations sum up the most common question types for both individuals and communities. This example also clearly illustrates one of the functions that an oracle could play in the decision-making process: formulating the question to be asked meant framing the risk in question. It forced the consultant to select the specific aspect of his uncertainty for which he was seeking divine help, and this selection, in turn, shaped the outcome of the oracle consultation—especially if, as Sokrates notes, one considered the resulting instruction of the god to be binding.

During the campaign, Xenophon's inquiries to the gods are also consistently phrased in such a way that his initial decisions are already built into the questions that he puts to the gods: 'Should he do *x* or not?', or 'Should he do *x* or *y*?' or 'Which god should he pray to in order that . . .?' His questions are phrased so that they will shape the answer he receives.[32] Another oracular consultation coming, fittingly, at the end of the campaign, is only briefly mentioned and is much less informative.[33] Xenophon receives back the deposit of money pledged to Artemis that he had left with a friend in Ephesos before setting out on the Persian campaign. It appears that he consults an oracle about what he should do with it, but the exact phrasing of the question is not reported. The response is that he should buy for Artemis the indicated estate, which is at Skillos on the Selinous river. Xenophon gives some details about the similarity, of name and wildlife, of two locations—one near his new home, the other in Ephesos. From this, we can perhaps speculate that the question concerned where he should buy the estate (a similar question is asked by Timotheos of Anaphe, listed below). Although this oracle has been attributed to the oracle at Delphi, Xenophon is at this point living near Olympia, so it seems more likely that he would have consulted the oracle there.

In terms of literary evidence for the consultation of Didyma by individuals, we find questions on subjects similar to those brought to Delphi: Lyrkos, son of Phoroneus, a significant mythical figure in the history of Argos, asks about his lack of children; Neileos, mythical founder of Miletos, asks where he should settle; Seleukos I is recorded as asking about whether he should return to Makedonia and how he will die.[34] The original phrasing of each of these questions is, as with the examples above, obscured by the literary tradition, but the majority still contain the 'about ($\pi\epsilon\rho\acute{\iota}$) + subject matter' structure: Lyrkos asks 'about the birth of children' ($\pi\epsilon\rho\grave{\iota}\ \gamma o\nu\hat{\eta}s\ \tau\acute{\epsilon}\kappa\nu\omega\nu$); Neileos asks 'where is it necessary to found (the city)?' ($\pi o\hat{v}\ \delta\epsilon\hat{\iota}\ \kappa\tau\acute{\iota}\zeta\epsilon\iota\nu$); Seleukos asks 'about the journey back to Makedonia' ($\pi\epsilon\rho\grave{\iota}\ \tau\hat{\eta}s\ \grave{\epsilon}s\ Ma\kappa\epsilon\delta o\nu\acute{\iota}a\nu\ \grave{\epsilon}\pi a\nu\acute{o}\delta o\upsilon$) and 'about death' ($\pi\epsilon\rho\grave{\iota}\ \tau o\hat{v}\ \theta a\nu\acute{a}\tau o\upsilon$).

The ancient literature about Dodona offers even fewer insights into individual consultations, far fewer than the number of state consultations reviewed in the previous chapter. The few stories we possess usually concern historically significant figures starring in apocryphal events which most likely have little to do with, or provide little information about, an actual consultation. Those few consultations that are mentioned in the ancient Greek tragedies are not very illuminating. For the most part, Dodona seems to be used because it is wild and far away, a mysterious site for characters to visit. Most references revolve around the talking oak, although there is a little more detail in Sophocles' *Trachiniae*.[35]

References to individual consultations of Dodona in other genres provide little more insight. Odysseus visits the oracle to ask whether he should make his return 'secretly or openly'. A number of authors report an oracle from Dodona warning Alexander, the young king of the Molossi, that he should beware the Acheron and the Pandosia (the ambiguity of the oracle lies in the fact that there is not only an Acheron river in Epiros, but also a river Acheros in Lucania, where Alexander died in 330 BCE). Perhaps unsurprisingly, the story slowly develops until in Livy, and later, Justin, Alexander is killed on an expedition that he planned in order to avoid the very place that he thought would be the scene of his death. Similarly, Plutarch relates how Themistokles arrived at the court of Persia, apparently at the behest of Dodona, which had told him to travel to him who had the same name as the god. Dodona is connected with one *oikist* myth, that of Aletes' founding of Korinth; but is also said to be responsible for settling two prophetic families, the Galeotai in Sicily and the Telmessians in Karia.[36]

These are too few examples on which to base any definitive conclusions, but this brief overview suggests that references to oracles in literature can provide some idea of the kinds of topics that individuals, as opposed to communities, brought to oracles, and a limited idea of the ways in which such inquiries might be phrased. They suggest that the questions posed to the oracle were circumscribed both in their phrasing and their content. In the case of the content, these questions were focused on a specific situation or concern of the questioner, usually around a particular decision they were facing or action they had to take. In terms of phrasing, it appears that the questions were phrased in one of three ways: either requesting a 'yes or no' answer, or presenting two alternatives for the god to rule between.

Occasionally they asked for a specific piece of information, usually to do with ritual activities, and the identity of suitable gods to worship.

DELPHI: EPIGRAPHIC EVIDENCE FOR INDIVIDUAL CONSULTATIONS

How does the epigraphic material compare to the literary evidence? From Delphi and Didyma, the remains are sparse. At Delphi, some if not most, of the many dedications may have been made by individuals on private business, in return for the oracle's services, but only one offering carries a dedication (κατὰ χρησμόν) that suggests this is the case.[37]

(i) Dealing with the examples in chronological order, the first relevant record is a question by one Isyllos as to whether or not he should inscribe a paean:[38]

>Ἴσυλλος Ἀστυλάιδαι ἐπέθηκε μαντεύσασθα[ί] οἱ
>περὶ τοῦ παιᾶνος ἐν Δελφοῖς, ὃν ἐπόησε εἰς τὸν Ἀπόλ-
>λωνα καὶ τὸν Ἀσκλαπιόν, ἦ λώϊόν οἵ κα εἴη ἀγγρά-
>φοντι τὸν παιᾶνα. ἐμάντευσε λώϊόν οἵ κα εἶμεν ἀγ-
>γράφοντι, καὶ αὐτίκα καὶ εἰς τὸν ὕστερον χρόνον.

Isyllos asked Astylaidas in Delphi, to prophesy to him about the paean which he wrote for Apollo and Asklepios, whether it would be better for him to inscribe the paean? And an oracle was given that it would be better both now and in the future if he inscribes the paean.

(ii) The second dedication is that of a husband, whose name is lost, in gratitude for the children/child born. The dedicator describes Apollo as hearing his prayer/question and responding to it not only with favourable oracles, but also with the gift of the child.[39]

>[- - - Φοῖ]βος γενεὰμ μαντεύμασι δῶκεν
>εὐχῆς ἐξαΐων, κομίσαι τε κόμας προσέταξεν

Phoibos granted me children with his oracles, heeding my prayer; he instructed me to bring a hair-offering.

(iii) Poseidonios of Halikarnassos is anxious that his children worship the right gods in order that they might prosper. He receives a list of gods and details of worship. The rest of the inscription includes the will of Poseidonios and a resolution of Poseidonios and his heirs. It is possible that the oracular god is an Apollo of Telmessos in Karia, but no such oracle has been recorded there, and Daux has argued that this pronouncement was made by the Delphic Apollo.[40]

Ἀπο[στ]είλαντος Πο[σ]ειδ[ωνίου χρ]ησα[μέν]ου
τῶι Ἀπόλλωνι, τί ἄν αὐτῶι τε καὶ τοῖς ἐξ αὐτοῦ,
γινομένοις καὶ οὖσιν ἐκ τε τῶν ἀρσέων καὶ τῶν θ-
ηλείων εἴη λῶϊον καὶ ἄμεινον ποιοῦσιν καὶ πράσ-
σουσιν, ἔχρησεν ὁ θεὸς ἔσεσθαι λῶϊον καὶ ἄμεινον αὐτοῖς ἱλασκομένοις καὶ τιμῶσιν καθάπερ
καὶ οἱ πρόγονοι Δία Πατρῶιον καὶ Ἀπόλλωνα Τελε-
μεσσοῦ μεδέοντα καὶ Μοίρας καὶ θεῶν Μητέρα,
τιμᾶν δὲ καὶ ἱλάσκεσθαι καὶ Ἀγαθὸν Δαίμονα Ποσει-
δωνίου καὶ Γοργίδος, τοῖς δὲ ταῦτα διαφυλάσσουσιν
καὶ ποιοῦσιν ἄμεινον ἔσεσθαι.

Poseidonios of Halikarnassos consulted Apollo 'What would it be better and more good for him and his children (both male and female) to do?' The god pronounced that it will be better for them if they worship and sacrifice to Zeus Patroos and Apollo, guardian of Telmessos, the Moirai and the Mother of the gods, and honour and worship Agathos Daimon of Poseidonios and Gorgis, even as their ancestors did. It will be better for them if they make sure they perform these duties.

(iv) Timotheos of Anaphe wants to ensure that the temple they are building is situated in the right spot.[41]

ll. 1–4
[― ― ― ― ― ― ― ― ― ― ― ― ― συντελε]-
[λεσ]θέντο[ς δὲ τοῦ ναοῦ ἔστω δαμόσ[ια]-
θότι καὶ ὁ θεὸς ἔ[χρ]ησε[ν· τ]ᾶς δ'ἐπερωτάσ[ε]-
ως καὶ τοῦ χρησμοῦ ἀντίγραφά ἐστι τάδε·

ll. 24 ff.
ἐπερωτᾶι Τιμόθεος [τὸ]ν θεόν, πότερον
αὐτῶι λῶιον καὶ ἄμει[νό]ν ἐστιν αἰτήσασθαι
τὰν πόλιν ἐν ⟨τ⟩ῶι ἐπινοεῖ τόπωι, ἐν τῶι τοῦ
Ἀπόλλωνος τοῦ Ἀσγελάτα, ὥστε ναὸν τᾶς
Ἀφροδίτας οἰκοδ[ο]μῆσαι, καὶ ἦμεν δαμόσιον,
ἢ ἐν τῶι ἱερῶι τοῦ Ἀ[σκ]λαπιοῦ ἐν ὧι ἐπινοεῖ
τόπωι. Ὁ θεὸς ἔχρησε, αἰτήσασθ[α]ι ἐν τῶι το[ῦ]
Ἀπόλλωνος· τελεσθέντος δὲ τοῦ ναοῦ ἀνα-
γραφῆμεν τό τε ψάφισμα καὶ τὸν χρησμὸν
καὶ τὰν ἔφοδον ἐστάλαν λιθίναν.

Once the temple was completed, the people let it be granted as the god decreed. About the inquiry and the oracle it was inscribed thus: Timotheos of Anaphe asked the god whether, for him, it is better and more good to ask the city for the place he has in mind, in the shrine of Apollo Aigletes, so as to build a temple of Aphrodite for the people or in the temple of Asklepios? The god pronounced an oracle, that he should ask for a place in the sanctuary of Apollo, and when the temple is completed inscribe the decree of the city and the oracle and the expense on a stone stele.

(v) Although we do not possess the question of Mnesiepes of Paros, the response is, again, a detailed list of gods and how to worship them, so it may have been similar to that of Poseidonios.[42] The structure of the text suggests that the inscription records three separate but related inquiries and answers by the same consultant—a pattern of consultation also found among the individual oracular consultations at Dodona. Mnesiepes was founding a sanctuary to honour the Parian poet Archilochos. He consulted the oracle first, in order to get his sanctuary approved, then (twice) to find out which gods should receive cult.

> Μνησιέπει ὁ θεὸς ἔχρησε λῶιον καὶ ἄμεινον εἶμεν
> ἐν τῶι τεμένει, ὃ κατασκευάζει, ἱδρυσαμένωι
> βωμὸν καὶ θύοντι ἐπὶ τούτου Μούσαις καὶ Ἀπόλλ[ωνι
> Μουσαγέται καὶ Μνημοσύνει· θύειν δὲ καὶ καλλι-
> ερεῖν Διί Ὑπερδεξίωι, Ἀθάναι Ὑπερδεξίαι,
> Ποσειδῶνι Ἀσφαλείωι, Ἡρακλεῖ, Ἀρτέμιδι Εὐκλείαι·
> Πυθῶδε τῶι Ἀπόλλωνι σωτήρια πέμπειν :
> Μνησιέπει ὁ θεὸς ἔχρησε λῶιον καὶ ἄμεινον εἶμεν
> ἐν τῶι τεμένει, ὃ κατασκευάζει, ἱδρυσαμένωι
> βωμὸν καὶ θύοντι ἐπὶ τούτου Διονύσωι καὶ Νύμφαις
> καὶ Ὥραις· θύειν δὲ καὶ καλλιερεῖν Ἀπόλλωνι
> Προστατηρίωι, Ποσειδῶνι Ἀσφαλείωι, Ἡρακλεῖ·
> Πυθῶδε τῶι Ἀπόλλωνι σωτήριαι πέμπειν [:]
> Μ̣νησιέπει ὁ θεὸς ἔχρησε λῶιον καὶ ἄμεινον εἶμεν
> τι]μ̣ῶντι Ἀρχίλοχον τὸμ ποιητάν, καθ᾽ ἃ ἐπινοεῖ :

The god gave an oracle to Mnesiepes that it would be better if he set up an altar in the temenos, which he is constructing, and sacrificed on this to the Muses and to Apollo Musagetes and Mnemosyne. And he should sacrifice to and obtain good omens from Zeus Hyperdexios, Athena Hyperdexia, Poseidon Asphaleios, Herakles, Artemis Eukleia and he should send thank offerings to Apollo at Pytho.

The god gave an oracle to Mnesiepes that it would be better to set up an altar in the temenos, which he is constructing, and sacrifice on this altar to Dionysos and the Nymphs and Hours. And he should sacrifice to and obtain good omens from Apollo Prostaterios, Poseidon Asphaleios, Herakles and he should send thank offerings to Apollo at Pytho.

The god gave an oracle to Mnesiepes that it would be better for him to honour the poet Archilochos, according to what he has in mind.

In terms of question formulae, most of the questions are phrased, or their responses suggest that they were phrased, in terms of alternative courses of action 'Is it better to do *x* or *y*?' or 'Is it better to do *x* or not?' Timotheos' inquiry is a clear example of the former (although we can observe that the response provides more information than merely an indication as to which

Individuals and Oracles 53

course of action the god prefers); while Isyllos asks 'Is it better . . .?' (implied is the alternative '. . . or not?'). 'It is better' appears three times in the response to Mnesiepes of Paros, which suggests that his question may also have been formulated as an inquiry as to what course of action was preferable. The inscription ends with an instruction to 'honour the poet Archilochos, according to what he has in mind', an interesting formulation, which suggests that sometimes consultants only asked about what they were thinking—a suspicion that will be confirmed when we come to the Dodona question material. However, the question posed by Poseidonios appears to have been a request for instruction (which gods to worship) rather than an attempt to gain sanction for a particular course of action, so perhaps Mnesiepes' question was similar in structure to that. Unfortunately, we cannot tell how the husband's request for a child was phrased, although it looks from the response as if it was a question (perhaps combined with a prayer) as to whether or not it was likely that he would have children.

DIDYMA: EPIGRAPHIC EVIDENCE FOR INDIVIDUAL CONSULTATIONS

If the material from Delphi seems limited, what survives from Didyma is even sparser: two responses and a dedication, all dating to the sixth century, and another dedication from around 100 BCE.[43]

(i) In the first, the god seems to be confirming a previous proclamation made to an individual.[44] Parke, drawing on the evidence of a later oracle consultation, suggests that the prophet was asking about a command he had heard from the god in a dream. However, as we have seen, it was not unusual for a consultant to make serial inquiries of an oracle: there is no reason to assume that 'the previous night' does not just refer to a previous consultation.

$$[-\dot{α}π]ομυθέομ[αι·τ]ῆ[ι]αρ -$$
$$-τεως τῆι προτέρηι$$
$$νυκτὶ εἶπον· καὶ [τῶι μὲν πειθομέ$$
$$νωι λῶιον και ἄ]μεινον ἔσται, τῶι$$
$$δὲ μὴ πειθομένω[ι τοὐναντίον.]$$

I dissuade—I said on the previous night. On the one hand, for him who obeys, it will be advantageous; for him who disobeys, the opposite.

(ii) Copies and a 'squeeze' transmit this next fragmentary text; the original is lost. The exact form and content of the question is unknown: the inquiry has been interpreted as a request for permission to plunder or take something as booty, but could equally be about fear of being the victim of such activities.[45] The consultants could be a community or group of people or an individual. The response of the god survives:

> .....σοι̣[σι]
> ληϊστοί· θε̣[ὀ-]
> [s] δε ἔπεν· δίκ-
> αιον ποιεῖν
> ὡς πατέρες.

... plunderable? But/and The god said: 'it is right to do as your fathers did.'

(iii) Likely to be the earliest of these three inscriptions, this dedication is inscribed on a giant knuckle-bone.[46] Details of the text, along with the handle on the side of the surviving bone, suggest that the original offering may have comprised two bones joined together by a chain (hence the references to 'these offerings').[47]

> τάδε τἀγάλματα̣
> [ἀ]π̣ὸ λείο Ἀριστόλοχο[s
> [καὶ] Θράσων ἀνέθεσαν τ[ὠ-
> πόλλωνι δεκάτην· ἐχά[λκευε
> δ' αὐτὰ Τσικλῆς ὁ Κυδιμά̣ν̣δ̣[ρο.

Aristolochos and Thrason dedicated these offerings as a tithe from the booty; Tsikles the son of Kydimandros cast it.

Although there are clearly two individuals making this offering, I include it here since it appears to be a private rather than community consultation. *Astragaloi* or knuckle-bones were widely associated with games of chance throughout the eastern Mediterranean and Near East, the bones taking the place of dice. They seem to have been burned as part of votive offerings at this site, as at many ritual contexts throughout this geographical area.[48] It may be that the shape of the dedication indicates Aristolochos and Thrason's acknowledgement of the oracle's role in the lucky outcome of some game of chance, an ex-voto embodiment of future uncertainty.[49] Alternatively, it may have had much more immediate relevance if the knuckle-bones were used in the procedure of the oracle itself. As we have seen there were other such lot oracles in Asia Minor—in which a throw of dice provided the answer to a 'yes or no' or '*x* or *y*' question—and there may indeed have been such a procedure in operation at Delphi, and, as we will see, at Dodona. Here, the dedication of the bones may suggest that a similar process was used at Didyma, at least during the Archaic period. The two other sixth-century oracular responses, both of which are prose and can be easily fitted to questions constructed around alternative options, would support this.

(iv) The final dedication is evidence of an oracular consultation, but reveals nothing of the details of the inquiry.[50]

> Ἀπολλωνι [Δα]λίῳ Καλύμνας
> μεδέοντι κ[ατ]ὰ χρησζμὸν
> Διδυμέως Λό[χο]ς Λόχου, φύσ[ει]
> δὲ Ξενοκράτους . . .

To Delian Apollo, ruler of Kalymna, according to an oracle of (Apollo) Didymeus, Lochos Lochos' son, by birth Xenocrates' son (made this dedication) . . .

In contrast, the epigraphic material from Dodona offers a vast number of examples of questions posed by individuals, as well as some examples of oracular responses. The inquiries cover a wide range of different subject areas concerned with aspects of everyday life.[51] But before turning to that material, I want to give some idea of the setting of oracular consultation at Dodona, in terms of both its physical location and socio-political context, and the possible methods of divination used at the site.

4

The Dwelling of the Spirit

> While it intersects with religion, a divination system involves far more than religious belief. Divination is essential in providing a repository of cultural values as well as facilitating adjustments to a changing world.
>
> Philip Peek 1991: 69

What might a pilgrim like Lysanias have seen as he made his way towards the oracular sanctuary at Dodona, set in a high, narrow valley beneath the towering Tomaros mountain? By the second century BCE, thanks to the expenditure of the Molossian kings, the sanctuary was quite splendid. The late Sotirios Dakaris, who became Ephor of Antiquities at Epiros in 1959, and excavated the site extensively, wrote that its plan is reminiscent of a theatre: the precinct as if set on a *proskēnion* or a raised stage; its two gates to the east and west, like *parodoi*, the side entrances of an ancient theatre, between the performance space and the auditorium. From whichever direction he approached, a pilgrim's attention would have been slowly drawn, past the other ornate buildings and rippling colonnades, to the locus of oracular power, the *Hiera Oikia*, or holy house, and the sacred oak tree.[1]

But it had not always been like this. For centuries before King Pyrrhos of Epiros raised these magnificent buildings during the early third century BCE, the holy site had remained remarkably bare, with little to adorn the sacred oak tree that was its focus. The *Hiera Oikia* was built in the fifth century. Before this, some sources report, the site was marked with bronze tripods, dedications to Zeus from the oracle's many visitors, piled so high that they became like the walls of a temple. It was said that these were set so close together that if you touched one, they all vibrated, creating a tremendous sound.[2]

As the excavations have slowly revealed, during its hundreds of years of operation, probably thousands of people made the journey to Dodona from all over the Greek world. It is sobering to realize how easily and thoroughly time obliterated any visible record of the site. By the nineteenth century, the sanctuary of Dodona had all but disappeared. Christopher Wordsworth,

Bishop of Lincoln, who in 1832 set out on a tour across Greece, knew that finding it would pose a challenge: 'To ascertain the site of Dodona would seem now to require a response from the Oracle itself. The former dwelling of the spirit, which once guided half the world is lost . . . Still we do not believe that the search for Dodona is hopeless. The ruins of a large capital are easily distinguished from those of a dependent city; the ruins of a city again from a mere fortress; but the ruins of an oracular city will have something very different from both.'[3]

We can imagine Bishop Wordsworth perched on his donkey, pockets bulging with much-thumbed, leather-bound ancient texts. The problem was not a lack of literary evidence. On the contrary, there were almost too many clues in the literature, as the bishop noted. 'There are so many conditions to be satisfied, that to satisfy them all is impossible' he complains, and lists some of the confusing detail: 'A lake, a high mountain, a hundred springs, a miraculous fountain which extinguishes lights and rekindles them; a forest of oaks and beeches, a wide plain of excellent pasturage: these characteristics are all put together, as in the hue-and-cry of a military deserter; these are the attributes and features by which Dodona is first to be recognized, and then brought back to the post which it has deserted in the maps of Greece.'[4]

He finally recognized the site because of the remains of Pyrrhos' magnificent theatre, one of the largest in Greece, capable of holding an audience of around 17,000.[5] He remarks on the confidence of a city that is located in a plain, rather than on a hill. So small a settlement would have lacked any real military power—and yet, its theatre! 'Now the existence of a theatre at all, especially in this district, is a very singular circumstance; but the existence of so grand a theatre, in so insignificant a place, is without a parallel in the whole of Greece.'[6] Ironically, the final proof that he had found the right place rested on evidence that was not mentioned in any of the ancient sources: the multitude of inscribed lead oracular question tablets that were first dug up at the site by Konstantine Karapanos, and have continued to be excavated since then.[7]

THE PLACE AND PEOPLE

Dodona is in Epiros, north-west Greece, an area of fertile upland plains, between the Adriatic Sea and the Pindos mountains to the east; it is 11 miles south-west of what is now the city of Ioannina. Epiros enjoyed early and plentiful trade across the Adriatic Sea with cities in southern Italy. Along the Adriatic coast, there were Greek colonies that were said to date back to the period just after the Trojan war, as well as foundations more reliably settled during the eighth to sixth centuries.[8] However, as the archaeological evidence suggests, topography meant that the inhabitants of the inland areas more easily formed links with the Makedonians to the east and Illyrians to the north. Although the evidence shows that the Greeks were travelling inland to visit Dodona from the eighth century, and there was plentiful trade, especially with the Korinthians and Keryraians, a certain cultural and physical distance seems to have been maintained until the late fifth/early fourth century.[9]

For a long time the term 'Epiros', literally 'mainland', described the geographical area as seen by the Greeks in Kephallenia, Ithaka, and Kerkyra, rather than any sense of territorial identity shared by its inhabitants.[10] During most of the period under study, the urban and political landscape of Epiros and southern Illyria comprised *ethnē*, or tribes. The Epirote *ethnē* are the basic unit in any observations about both urban and political structures, but even this entity raises questions that are illustrative of the intriguing and complex organization of this area. For example, it is not clear whether an *ethnos* was a sort of family name or the label of a constituency.[11] Strabo (probably drawing on the sixth-century historian Hekataios) reports fourteen tribes, the most prominent being the Chaonians, Molossians, and Thesprotians, but many more have now been traced.[12] The system of governance of these *ethnē* varied between each other, and over time. Some, like the Molossian dynasty, had a system of monarchy, apparently based on a regularly renewed contract between king and people, others something of a more federal composition.[13]

The tribes lived, for the most part, a semi-nomadic life, in networks of smaller towns or villages, κατὰ κώμας, as one of our sources reports.[14] Different settlement patterns are found in the various regions of the area, according to their particular topographical, political, and cultural characteristics. Larger settlements developed slowly, sometimes, where it was available, following the model set by the Greek colonies. Some were a result of synoikism; others developed from fortified centres used as places of refuge or locations for meetings. These gradually became permanent sites of habitation, acquiring, over time, administrative, economic, or religious functions for the community that they served. A very few sites, for example Passaron, seem to have developed in the late fifth century, but most of the urbanization of this region took place in the fourth century, happening faster along the more cosmopolitan coastal areas, for example Chaonia, than inland, in Molossia or Thesprotia.[15]

If we are looking for a trigger for these political and cultural developments, the most likely seems to have been the emergence of the Molossian dynasty during the late fifth and early fourth centuries.[16] 'Emergence' sounds organic, but the ascendance of the Molossoi appears to have comprised a carefully calculated push for predominance, involving, as Davies has described, both cultural schemes (for example, the 'discovery' of Pyrrhos, son of Achilles, as dynastic ancestor)[17] and political policies (including a series of alliances with various Greek powers) that would combine 'to lock Epiros inescapably into the power struggles of Balkan Greece'.[18] Among the earliest Molossian strategies was the acquisition of Dodona from the Thesprotoi (c.400 BCE), followed by the construction of the first temple building (the *Hiera Oikia*), which was then enlarged around the middle of the fourth century by a stone wall surrounding the temple and sacred tree.[19]

A trail of inscriptions allows us to glimpse the development of a federal system in which the many tribes of the area combined in groups of various sizes, which joined together to form political *koina*, or alliances, whose exact nature, leadership, and membership, changed fluidly over time.[20] The inscriptions indicate a gradual change in the way the federation describes itself, from the expansion of the Molossian state (τὸ κοινὸν τῶν Μολοσσῶν) (370–c.330 BCE); to an Alliance of Epirotes, an alliance primarily for military purposes (from around 330 until some time after 232 BCE); to the gradual weakening of the Molossian monarchy and the formation of the Epirote League, in which the members had common citizenship (233/2–168 BCE).[21]

Certainly these developments demonstrated some kind of 'genius for incorporation', as Hammond describes, but it was a genius backed by effective force, as Davies has appended.[22] But this should not lead us to think that it was a unilateral, top-down process: a more fluid, collective process of gradual cohesion is more likely. The documents suggest that, throughout this period, individual tribes or smaller *koina* did not lose their autonomy. Even after the annihilation of Molossia by the Romans in 167 BCE, epigraphic evidence suggests that neighbouring peoples continued to enjoy a dynamic, independent political life.[23] All of this provides us with a useful political context for considering the role of the sanctuary at Dodona and the significance of state and individual consultations.

THE SANCTUARY

Foundation stories for the sanctuary of Dodona are a heady folktale mix: quaint narratives full of thieving shepherds and talking trees, solemn doves and pious wood-cutters.[24] One story attributes the founding of Dodona to Deukalion, a Noah-like figure who is said to have escaped Zeus' angry flooding of the world by living in a chest for nine days and nights, before setting about repopulating the earth.[25] It describes how he went to Epiros, to the oracle, consulted a dove sitting in the oak who told him to settle there, married a daughter of Zeus, an Oceanid called Dodona, and named the place after her. For modern readers, it is hard not to see this story as a blatant attempt to establish an insurmountably early foundation for the oracle, earlier than any other. We have seen how the foundation stories about Delphi also gradually pushed back the date of its origin, attaching the foundation of that oracle to Zeus. It seems likely that the motive for these stories was competition. An older oracle was no doubt considered a more authoritative oracle. It comes as no surprise to find traces of another story, albeit in a late source, claiming that it was Delphi that Deukalion visited for guidance after the floodwaters had receded.[26]

Unlike Didyma and Delphi, the material evidence at Dodona does provide evidence of prehistoric habitation—probably nomadic peoples, since there seems to be no evidence of dwellings—and contact with peoples to the north, in what is now the Central Balkans. Material from the Mycenaean period follows (possibly from as early as the fifteenth century BCE), then fibulae, tripods, and bronze figurines dating to the eighth century.[27] It is not clear when Dodona started functioning as an oracular sanctuary. Dakaris argued that the cult of Dodonaean Zeus began in the Early Bronze Age period (2600–2000/1900 BCE) or a little later (2000/1900–1600/1500 BCE). Parke and others have thought it more likely to have begun in the eighth century, when the material record is more suggestive of dedications to the god, and reveals first signs of contact with the mainland Greeks.[28]

In literature, references to the practice and process of consulting Dodona start with Homer. In book 16, Achilles prays to 'Lord Zeus', calling him 'Pelasgian, dwelling afar', and goes on to describe the officials of the oracle, 'the Selloi, your interpreters, with their unwashed feet, who sleep on the ground'. But these Selloi, known in some authors as the Helloi, are missing from the oracle's next appearance in Homeric literature. In the *Odyssey*, Odysseus describes how he 'had gone to Dodona to find out the will of Zeus from the great oak tree that is sacred to the god, and to discover how he should approach his own island of Ithaca after so long an absence, whether to return openly or in disguise'.[29] Homer's Dodona sounds distant and wild. In contrast, the Dodona that Hesiod describes in a fragment from his lost epic, the *Eoiai*, is quite different. He calls it 'Hellopia', perhaps explaining those Helloi, according to some of the Homeric scholiasts, but any definitive connections are lost in time. He describes it as being 'of much cornland and of good meadows, rich in flocks and shambling cattle, and in it dwell men of many sheep . . . many themselves in number'. His version of the oracular function is difficult to read, but the text seems to say: 'And they dwelt in the stock of the oak where those who live on earth fetch all their prophecies.' Unfortunately it never becomes clear who 'they' are. So in these three passages alone we find three different methods of oracular delivery: in the *Iliad*, there are male priests with dirty feet; in the *Odyssey*, a magic tree; and in Hesiod there's something or, rather some divinity, living in the oak.[30]

The oracular oak and dove remain significant throughout the sanctuary's history. In fact, as mentioned earlier, for a long time, the oak appears to have stood alone, the sole focus of the sanctuary, possibly surrounded by walls of bronze tripods dedicated to Zeus.[31] If so, then tripods gave way to the so-called *Hiera Oikia*, or holy house, the temple of Zeus, around the end of the fifth century. This was probably erected by the Molossians as part of their ongoing attempt to establish regional predominance.[32] When a precinct was added to the holy house at the end of the fourth century, a large empty area was left on the east side of the temple. Similarly, when the courtyard was enlarged later, during Pyrrhos' reign, with an elaborate colonnade, the east side of the inner colonnade was omitted. All this, it is suggested, was to leave space for the sacred oak.[33] Dakaris reports that when that area was excavated, a deep hole and hewn stones were found—probably those of an altar.[34]

Most of the rest of the monumental buildings at the sanctuary were raised in the Hellenistic period. Nevertheless, despite its lack of architectural splendour, the evidence suggests that Dodona was a flourishing sanctuary long before this, gaining in regional religious and political significance, and attracting plenty of international attention. By the sixth century, there are imports from southern Greece (Peloponnesian and western Greece); but other influences can be traced, including Attic and south Italian. As we would expect, considering the patterns of extensive trade and settlement that were already well developed along the coast, Dodona drew an international crowd.[35] In the latter half of the fifth century the number of dedications made at the site seems to have declined, perhaps as a result of the Peloponnesian war. Control of Epirus, and/or alliance with its various tribes, seems to have been sought by both Sparta and Athens.[36] Once the war was over, Dodona was consulted by both Sparta and, particularly in the fourth century, Athens.[37]

During this period, the growth of public buildings indicates the increasingly important role Dodona was playing in the religious and political life of the region. Excavations have revealed the remains of a *prytaneion* and *bouleuterion* (council chambers, parliamentary and executive, respectively) in the south-west part of the sanctuary, both constructed at the end of the fourth/beginning of the third century, replacing the older enclosure of the sanctuary.[38] Among the oracular lead tablets found at the site, there is one dating to the second half of the fourth/first half of the third century that asks

Zeus Naios and Dione whether the *diaitioi* (arbitrators) should allocate to the *prytaneion* the money received from the city. As has been observed, the fact that there is no city named suggests that it must be something obvious, like Dodona itself.[39] The presence of these buildings, indicating the functioning of government bodies, draws our attention to the simultaneous political and religious role that Dodona seems to have played during the period of the Epirote Alliance. Representatives of the Alliance (and later the League) would have met in the *bouleuterion* to discuss and vote on decisions and laws.[40] The fact that some of these public decisions were put on public view (imitating practice at other sanctuaries) suggests that the sanctuary was a site of display for local, regional, and international visitors.[41]

This was surely part of the intention of Pyrrhos, king of Epiros 297–272 BCE, who clearly saw Dodona as an important centre for his empire. During his reign the sanctuary was adorned with a number of temples and the sanctuary of Zeus was enlarged; a vast theatre was built, probably for the *Naia*, the four-yearly festival held in honour of Zeus Naios. In the years that followed, the evidence suggests that as the alliance of the Epirotes expanded, so did the role of Dodona, growing in importance as a religious and administrative centre of Epiros and the headquarters of the Epirote League. At the end of the third century BCE, the *prytaneion* was enlarged, combined with an extension, a complex for boarding and lodging government officials.[42] Around the same time, a stadium was built west of the theatre. The sanctuary offered a site for the public display of regional achievements and honours.[43] Meanwhile, numismatic and archaeological finds reveal that, as the region flocked to the sanctuary, the cult of Zeus Dodonaios and Dione spread to almost all tribes of Epiros, from the Ambrakian Gulf to the region of the lower Aous. Evidence suggests that the cult spread further as Dodona grew in regional significance.[44]

But the success of the sanctuary also made it a target. In 219 BCE, Dodona was sacked by the Aitolians; an attack later avenged by the Makedonian king Philip V's attack on Thermion.[45] The site was rebuilt in even grander style: this was when the stadium was built and the *Hiera Oikia* extended and enlarged. But in 167 BCE it was attacked again, this time by the Romans in retribution for the Epirotes' alliance with Makedon. Seven towns were razed, 15,000 people enslaved.[46] In 88 BCE, Thrakian tribes allied with Mithridates VI sacked the sanctuary again.[47] Nevertheless, the oracle continued to function: an inscription on an iron strigil seems to indicate that one Zeniketes, possibly a Lykian tribal chief, had sought and received divine guidance.[48]

But this was something of a last oracular gasp. Sometime at the beginning of the reign of Augustus, Strabo wrote of the region: 'At the present time, desolation prevails in most parts, while the parts that are still inhabited survive only in villages and in ruins and even the oracle at Dodona, like the rest, is virtually extinct.'[49] By the end of the second century, the Christian writer Clement of Alexandria can note how the silence of the oracle at Dodona is an example of the collapse of pagan oracles.[50] The worship of Zeus may have continued, but by the end of the third or fourth century, the sacred oak of Zeus that stood in the sanctuary had probably been cut down on the order of an Illyrian bandit chief called Arkes.[51] The ancient oracle was finally extinguished.

STATE CONSULTATIONS

From the literary evidence, it would be easy to assume that the oracle had greater international than regional significance and far more importance for states than individuals. However, the published oracular question tablets reveal only 14 questions from states or groups (listed in Appendix 1, in date order), although, of course, it is possible that only a fraction of the evidence for state consultation has survived.

The neighbouring Kerkyraians (modern Korfu, just across the Adriatic) have left a series of questions spanning a couple of centuries (if the dating of the tablets is right) asking to whom they should make sacrifice, so that they should do well. The tablets reveal some striking differences in the ways in which communities used the oracle. The first is dated to the late fifth century: 'God. The Kerkyraians ask Zeus Naios and Dione by sacrificing and praying to which god or hero may they live in the best and finest way now, and in the future.' The second, dated around 10 or more years after the first,[52] seems to be more specifically about the need to create consensus in the group: 'God. Good Fortune. The Kerkyraians ask Zeus Naios and Dione by sacrificing and praying to which god or hero can they be in agreement on a good course of action.'[53] The third question, dating to the third quarter of the fourth century, suggests the Kerkyraians have made an alliance with the Orikians. Orikos (Pascha Liman) was an important port of the Chaonians, situated at the head of the Gulf of Valona: 'God. The Kerkyraians and the Orikians ask Zeus Naios and Dione, by sacrificing and praying to which of the gods or heroes they may live most fairly and safely, and may there be fine and fruitful crops for them and enjoyment of every good fruit.'[54]

Chronologically, the next inquiry is a request from the city of Taras (now Taranto) in Apulia, Italy, which dates from the last quarter of the fourth

FIG. 1. Oracle question tablet from Dodona: 'God. The Kerkyraians and the Orikians ask Zeus Naios and Dione, by sacrificing and praying to which of the gods or heroes they may live most fairly and safely, and may there be fine and fruitful crops for them and enjoyment of every good fruit' (third century BCE) © C. M. Dixon/The Ancient Art & Architecture Collection

century. It starts off with a general concern about good fortune 'To the gods. With good fortune. The city of the Tarentines ask Zeus Naios and Dione about every good fortune and concerning the . . .'.[55] There the tablet breaks off, but the second half looks as if they were going to follow up with a more specific request, and some of the other community question tablets may give us ideas of how to fill in the gap.

So far, these questions all originate from the other side of the Adriatic. But the locals are also making inquiries. For example, in the middle of the fourth century, the inhabitants of the city of Byllis or Bylliake use the same basic formula ('to which god should we pray') to ask about how to do really well with regard to possessions.[56] There are also a series of questions from a number of different communities relating specifically to internal community affairs. In a way that recalls Herodotos' story about the consultation by the Apollonians when their land was stricken by barrenness, we find the Dodonaeans wanting to know why they are suffering: 'whether it is because of the impurity of some man that god sends the storm'.[57] The other question by the Dodonaeans asks, more intriguingly, about 'a sign in the oak', but it provides no more information, either about the subject of inquiry or the mechanism of oracle delivery.[58] A very fragmentary question by the Onchesimoi may be along similar lines to the first Dodonaean inquiry. This dates to the first half of the fourth century, is the only question on a tablet that has been folded twice, and is very difficult to read. It is possible that the third line may mention *limos*, which would suggest an inquiry about the causes of—and/or what to do about—a famine.[59]

Questions to do with appeasing the gods are not the only subjects of inquiry. Some have more political ramifications. For example, in the late fourth/early third century, in a period when the Molossian state dominated the area, the Chaonians were asking whether they 'should transfer the building of the temple of Athena the city goddess'. The site of such an important temple may well have had political significance, but the very posing of a question at this inter-ethnic sanctuary by the Chaonians about their internal affairs may also have been intended to raise their regional political profile.[60] Internal political/religious affairs are also the topics of two other tablets. On a tablet already mentioned, a group of *diaitoi* from an unknown city (but probably Dodona) 'ask Zeus Naios and [Dione whether if they spend the ... money] on the council chamber which he has justly received from the city [it will be better and more good for them]'.[61] The 'Mondaeans' (unknown provenance, on an undated tablet) came to ask about the money of Themis, and whether it was permissible and better to put it on loan for the goddess.[62]

More obviously concerned with regional politics is the question that was asked sometime in the late second or early first century BCE, by an unknown *koinon*: if 'they join the federation with the Molossi, it will be safe for them'.[63] As noted above, this question suggests that even during the period in which politics was dominated by the larger Epirote Alliance, another, smaller alliance of tribes—a *koinon*—was independently consulting the oracle about its political choices. There are also a couple of inquiries (both dated to the early/mid-fifth century) that are likely to come from the Chalkidian colony of Rhegion, in south Italy, although this cannot be certain, since both tablets are fragmentary and very difficult to read.[64]

The questions cover a range of concerns, from the desire for a community simply to do better, to the need to find group agreement, to internal community matters (pollution, the need to move a temple, the need to build a council chamber), to quite specifically political decisions, such as the successful creation of alliances. Greek colonies, tribes, and representatives of alliances are all visiting the oracle for guidance.[65] The inquiries made by communities in south Italy suggest how easily and often the inhabitants of these two coasts were in contact with each other. This is borne out by material evidence from the Bronze Age, the harbours along the coast of Epiros, as well as further up and down the coast, and literary evidence for the presence of small boats in these waters. Moreover, as we will see, many of the individuals who came

FIG. 2. Bronze coin from Dodona with oak tree and three doves, 300 BCE © Archaeological Receipts Fund, Athens

to Dodona were asking about journeys that they were planning to make down the coast or across the Adriatic. This suggests that, although common, such expeditions were scarcely risk-free. Apart from the hazards of being on water, there was always the threat of piracy, especially it seems from the Illyrians and, later, the Aitolians.[66]

As for those inquiries made by Epirotes, they are too sparse to use as evidence for significant developments in consultation practices over time. Nor can we use them to probe far into the hierarchy of local tribes and alliances—beyond observing the continuing apparent independence of different *koina* and *ethnē* within what we know was a larger federal organization. Nevertheless, they add to our understanding of how oracles were used during the Classical period. At Dodona, the oracle was consulted to resolve disputes or settle questions within alliances or larger tribal groups, while the sanctuary itself seems to have helped to reinforce a sense of cohesion amongst the different regional political groups, both symbolically and actually, in its role as a meeting site. Supporting this idea are coins minted by the Epirote League at the end of the third century BCE which feature the heads of Dodonaean Zeus and Dione, and the dove and sacred oak tree of Dodona.[67]

QUESTIONS OF DIVINE COMMUNICATION

This brings us back to the question of the method of consultation. Like the hunt for the site itself, there are plenty of clues about oracle delivery in the literature, but, unfortunately, as yet, no firm answers. Unsurprisingly, the oak and dove of the foundation stories remain a recurring theme. Turning to the oak first: in the *Odyssey*, as discussed above, it sounds as if the god somehow spoke through the oak, or was thought to be located in it, while the fragment of Hesiod seemed to say that Zeus was dwelling under the oak itself (most un-Olympian and, in fact, probably just the result of a lacuna in the text). The Servian commentaries on Virgil suggest an oracular spring rising from the roots of the oak—the spring that featured in Wordsworth's list of clues. This was a spring that extinguished torches that were plunged into it, but also, apparently, lit them when they were brought near it. But, unfortunately, there is little if any evidence for such a spring, inflammatory or not, although some ancient trace may remain in the epithet of Zeus 'Naios', explained by some ancient authors as deriving from the Greek for 'to flow'.[68]

Some ancient authors seem to say that responses were given through the rustling of the oak's branches and leaves that were then interpreted by oracle priests, perhaps Achilles' Selloi/Helloi, but this is likely to be a less than dependable later reconstruction. The same, unfortunately, is true of the various stories found about the tree and the Argonauts. These relate how the hero Jason and his team of fellow heroes set sail in a ship, the *Argo*, on their quest for the golden fleece with a beam from the oak tree at Dodona fitted into the keel—a structural addition that had the useful feature of being able to speak, guide, or warn the Argonauts, rather like a sort of early form of GPS. Such accounts suggest that it was the oak itself that was pictured as speaking. However, as noted, these are from late sources and tend to suggest that ancient writers were as much in the dark as we are.[69] As we have noted, there is one oracle tablet, a state consultation by the Dodonaeans, that mentions 'a sign in the oak'. But this tantalizing snippet reveals little if anything about the mechanism of oracle delivery, what kind of sign was expected, how it was given, or just how the oak was involved.

Doves were, as we have seen, a significant part of the story told at Dodona, at least from the time of Herodotos. In the *Histories*, Herodotos reports two stories, one told to him by the priests of Theban Zeus, which reports how two priestesses from that temple were taken prisoner by some Phoenicians. One was sold in Libya, where she founded the oracle of Zeus Ammon, and the other was sold in Greece, in Dodona, where she also founded an oracle. The other story is told in Dodona:[70]

The Dodona oracle's prophetesses say that two black doves took off from Thebes in Egypt, one of which flew to Libya, while the other came to them in Dodona. It perched on an oak-tree and spoke in a human voice, telling the people of Dodona that there ought to be an oracle of Zeus there. The people of Dodona realized that they were hearing a divine command, and they therefore did what the dove had told them to do. The story goes on to say that the dove which went to Libya told the Libyans to construct the oracle of Ammon—another oracle of Zeus. This is the story told by the priestesses of Dodona (who are, from oldest to youngest, Promeneia, Timarete and Nikandra), and it is supported by what the other Dodonaeans connected with the shrine say too.

The scholiast to Sophocles' play *Trachiniae* knows something like this founding story from Herodotos and implies that Pindar, the early fifth-century lyric poet, had also written on a similar theme as part of a long Hymn to Dodonaean Zeus which is unfortunately now lost.[71] The association stuck: later, in the second century CE, the word πέλειαι could mean both 'doves' and the women who worked as prophetesses at Dodona. Strabo explains it as developing from a related word used by the Molossians for 'old woman'.[72] Herodotos himself expresses decisively rational views about this confusion between women and doves:[73]

I would suggest that this is what happened. If the priestesses really were abducted by Phoenikians and sold in Libya and Greece, it really was the Thesprotians, in my opinion, who bought the one who came to what is now called Greece (though it is the same place that was in those days called Pelasgia). Since she was working as a slave for the Thesprotians, she built a shrine of Zeus under an oak-tree that was growing there, which is only what one would expect her to do: after all, she had served in the sanctuary of Zeus in Thebes, and one would expect her to think of Zeus when she came to her new home. Then she subsequently founded an oracle when she had learnt to speak Greek, and she told people about how the same Phoenikians who had sold her had also sold her sister in Libya.

But his sceptical reflections shed some inadvertent light on the method that the priestesses may have used—or not—to prophesy. He goes on:[74]

I think that the women were called doves by the people of Dodona because they were foreigners and when they spoke they sounded like birds. They say that after a while the dove spoke to them in a human voice, because that was when the woman could make herself understood by them. As long as she spoke a foreign language, however, they thought she sounded like a bird. After all, how could a dove speak in a human voice?

Herodotos' final emphasis on the intelligibility of the priestesses gives no hint of a suggestion that they fell into the same kind of frenzy as the Pythia at Delphi; nor that their oracles were in any way confusing or ambiguous. In fact, there are no such suggestions of this at all in the sources until

Plato categorizes the priestesses at Dodona alongside the Pythia at Delphi as examples of divine possession. After Plato, we find this image only, briefly, in Pausanias, and in the Christian writers, where it was most likely created in the service of forging a usefully horrifying stereotype of pagan practices.[75]

In favour of prose, we have evidence on some of the tablets from Dodona, among which, as we will see, there are almost certainly responses, although these are hard to trace, and often maddeningly brief. In Sophocles' *Trachiniae*, we find Herakles describing how, after his visit, he wrote down the words of the oracle himself, once he had heard them from the priest (which suggests that maybe what has survived from the site are only the notes of much longer responses, left behind by a few consultants who had no more need of them).[76] However, in support of prose responses, we can also point to the fourth-century politician Demosthenes as he exercises his persuasive powers in court, underlining his enemy Meidias' irreligious behaviour. He quotes two oracles that instruct the Athenians to establish choric dances for Dionysos: one is a poetic confection from Delphi, the other is an oracle of Dodona, which is in prose. And we can finish with the slightly less straightforward evidence of Strabo, who denies that the oracle used words at all and that Zeus 'gave out the oracle, not through words, but through certain symbols, as was the case at the oracle of Zeus Ammon in Libya'.[77]

This takes us to a third possibility: that oracles were given at Dodona through some non-verbal mechanism. This might be the bronze tripods that were said to have taken the place of walls for the sanctuary in its early years.[78] As we have noted, these vessels were famous for the noise they made. Other sources argue, however, that we should be thinking not of many vessels but of a single bronze statue, a boy with a whip that stood on one column, facing a cauldron that stood on another, a dedication by the Kerkyraians according to Strabo.[79] Later, Christian writers would state that it was this statue (as one described it, one of the 'godless instruments of pagan oracles') that facilitated the process of divination, relating how, in a variety of ways, but chiefly through the machinations of demons, the boy's whipping of the cauldron in turn beat the priestess into an oracular frenzy.[80]

But if this explanation does not appeal, the statue may yet provide us with a useful clue to the oracle's divinatory method. Strabo describes the whip that the boy wielded as made up of three strands, each one made up of *astragaloi* or knuckle-bones. As observed about the large *astragalos*-shaped dedication at Didyma, perhaps the appearance of knuckle-bones was a conscious comment on the precariously uncertain nature of the future—some kind of representation of the 'cruel blows of fate'. Alternatively, it may be that it was deemed an appropriate feature for a dedication at Dodona because, as

Strabo's 'tokens' suggest, the oracle used *astragaloi*, or something similar, in its method of divination.

In favour of this final prophetic possibility, the fourth-century historian Kallisthenes provides the most explicit literary evidence.[81] His account appears as part of a story about the omens that foretold the Spartan defeat at Leuktra by the Boiotians in 371 BCE. Ambassadors from Sparta are seeking an oracle about their chances of winning from Zeus of Dodona. It goes on to say that 'after their messengers had duly set up the vessel in which were the lots, an ape, kept by the king of Molossia for his amusement, disarranged the lots and everything else used in consulting the oracle, and scattered them in all directions'. Perhaps unsurprisingly, the priestess goes on to suggest that the Spartans should not expect victory.

This picture of written lots collected in a pot being presented to a priestess/prophetess for her selection brings to mind some of the divinatory processes described above as occurring at Delphi. These seem to have worked in two distinct ways: in the stories about the selection of Aleuas or that of the ten tribes, the Pythia's choice was (probably) made from a jar containing a number of tablets inscribed with a variety of names; in the case of the consultation on the Sacred *Orgas*, in contrast, each vessel presented to the Pythia contained one option. In Kallisthenes' story about consultation at Dodona, it is possible that the lots were all on the same subject, so that the priestess was choosing from among, for example, an equal number of lots marked 'yes' and 'no'.

However, Parke suggests a further possibility, drawing on a decree of the Thessalian city of Korope that prescribes the process of submitting questions to its local oracle of Apollo.[82] The text describes how, following a procession of oracle officers, each potential consultant's name is written on a board, then each one is summoned before the officials and submits his question tablet. 'Once the consultation has been completed' the tablets are sealed in a jar overnight. The following morning, the sealed jar is opened, and each consultant is called back to receive his tablet. Quite how and when the response was given to the consultant is far from clear. The phrase 'Once the consultation has been completed' may indicate that the entire oracle process—both question and answer—was completed in a day, and consultants simply stayed over night because it had got too late. Alternatively, it may indicate that the consultation itself took place overnight, which raises the possibility that some form of incubation process was involved.

Could a similar process have occurred at Dodona? Is this, perhaps, the implication of that puzzling detail about the Selloi 'who sleep on the ground'? Unfortunately, as Parke observes, there is only one literary excerpt that can possibly be taken as an indication that incubation took place: a passage of

Eustathios quoting another author who mentions the prophet of Dodona and then immediately afterwards mentions prophecy in dreams.[83] This juxtaposition is far too shaky to provide firm evidence for incubation at Dodona.

There is some evidence from the oracle tablets themselves that suggests that a lot oracle may have been in use. The consultant of one text (listed in this volume in Chapter 5 as 'Work 3'), kindly provided and analysed by Christidis, seems to be asking 'Whether it will be better and more useful if I farm this place'. The final lines may refer to the system of allotment that provided the consultant with his land. However, it is also possible, as suggested by Christidis, that they refer to a lot oracle. Christidis reported a number of questions that began with the phrase: περί κλήρου ('about the lot'), which could support either explanation. In fact, it is also possible that these tablets refer to some other kind of civic lottery system altogether. Without sight of the tablets themselves it is hard to make a judgement.

Talking doves and rustling oaks, erratic springs and men with dirty feet, women who may or not twitter like birds, echoing vessels and crowing demons, and finally tokens picked from a jar, possibly guided by dreams: in the end, as we said at the beginning, all that we know for certain is that consultants wrote their questions down on lead tablets, which they then rolled up. Occasionally some kind of identifying mark was scratched on what would have been the outside of the tablet, either the initials of the consultant or a reference to some aspect of the question. This may suggest that the tablet was handed over to a sanctuary official, or perhaps consultants marked their tablets before they took them into the presence of a priestess. Did they wait breathless for her wisdom, or leave their question tablet with her, looking back over their shoulders, biting their lip with anxiety as they left the inner sanctum? Or perhaps they were told to keep their tablet close by them, while they spent the night in the shade of the rustling oak tree, listening intently for some token from the god.

5

A Catalogue and Summary of Published Questions by Individuals and Responses from the Dodona Oracle

> The diviner's analysis transforms uncertainty into a conditional certainty and his instructions ... enable the consultor to move from inertia to purposeful activity.
>
> Jackson 1978: 134[1]

The organization of the catalogue is described and explained as part of the overview of its contents in Chapter 6.

INQUIRIES

Future concerns

Travel

This is the largest category among the published questions found at Dodona. It might well have been even larger, since many of the other categories contain questions that relate somehow to travel. In particular, there is a great deal of overlap between the tablets in this category and the next category, Work, but there are also tablets in the categories of Prosperity/Safety, and Health that concern travel. In sorting questions between Travel and Work, I have placed those questions that name their destination or place of departure under Travel; if the emphasis of the tablet is on a specific type of work, I have placed it under that category.

This concentration of questions around problems and concerns relating to travel supports an emerging historical picture of the peoples of the Mediterranean being consistently on the move: trading—or stealing—skills and goods, making religious pilgrimage, or migrating in order to find work.[2] The many questions in this category (see also those questions in the category of

Work that focus on matters directly or indirectly concerned with working on the sea), suggest that such travel, although common, was a cause of considerable anxiety. I have created three subdivisions in this category: (i) those tablets that mention their locations; (ii) those that do not; and (iii) those questions that are concerned with the desire not to travel, whose consultants want to remain at home.

Most of the inquirers seem to be consulting the god solely on their own behalf. In six of the 28 questions, the consultant mentions himself by name (9, 11, 14, 17, 19, and 27). Question 17 provides an example of a tablet with the question on one side, and the name of the consultant inscribed on the reverse. But a few more personal details appear in a couple of questions: question 5 mentions the inquirer's concerns about his possessions (περὶ παντασίας) and that his family do well; question 15 gives the name of the consultant's prospective business associate (and travelling companion?) and the consultant of question 26 asks about returning to his brother.

The questions reveal a variety of different reasons for travelling. Some just raise the idea of a journey. Of these, some name their destination (for example, question 19, specifying the Adriatic as part of the destination); others do not even do that (23). It's possible to read some uncertainty about the method of travel in a few questions. Two may be asking if he should make the journey by land (4, with a note on translation of the phrase, and 25); another (24) includes the phrase 'by sea' but it may just be a detail of his larger inquiry and not the focus of his question. Safety is an explicit concern in question 12, which asks something about conveying something or someone safely (κομίζοντι [- -ἀ]σφαλέως). However, looking across the category, the journeys about which Dodona was most commonly consulted were those made by sea, and most people were concerned with how they were likely to prosper if they made the trip, that is, they wanted to know if it was worth it. Most consultants included detail that allows us to infer their reason for travel. I have mentioned the overlap between travel and work. Those tablets that make these concerns specific include: questions 1, 20, and 24, which are most likely asking about travel for the purposes of trade; ἐμπορίας (1) means 'commerce' usually conducted by sea, the related verb ἐμπορεύεσθαι (20, 24) means travel, usually for business. Tablet 20 also has Ευπορα on its reverse, a partial single word that could be either a shorthand reference to the question or part of a response from the oracle. Question 18 brings up 'selling' (πωλοῦντες) although the tablet is too fragmentary to tell us what is being sold. The consultant of question 15 is contemplating moving to Megara in order to work (ἐργαζομένωι Μεγαροῖ).

A number of the inquiries seem to be about the advantages of moving to new places to live, using a variety of verbs. For example, question 6 uses ἀπιών to describe going away (although it doesn't say from where); question 14, οἰκοντι ἐμ Φάρωι ('for him, if he lives in Pharos'; this tablet has the question on one side, and seems to have some kind of shorthand reference to it, Φά short for Φάρωι, on the reverse); question 5 is about whether it is better or not for him and his wife and family to live in Kroton (περὶ Ϝοικέσιος ἰς Κρ⟨ό⟩τονα), and the oracle seems to have responded with a succint 'in Kroton'. The consultant of question 4 wants to know if he should move to Orikos or is better off staying put. Question 22, although very fragmentary, might be similar: the tablet is very difficult to read but seems to concern moving residence (ἀπουικέοντες), but the response on side B, μένε[τε ('Stay!')—if, indeed, it is the answer to this question—implies that this may have been the gist of the inquiry. Among these questions we often find the formulae λώϊον καὶ ἄμεινον, that is, literally, 'better and more good', or some form of it.

Some time in the early third century BCE, Ariston asked if it would be better to join a colony (but it is not clear which colony) of Syrakuse (17). He asks about being able to join it 'later, a phrase that may indicate some anxiety about the dangers of being in a first wave of colonizers or, perhaps, that he will miss out if he is not in that initial group.[3] Question 14 seems also to be connected with a problem to do with the process of emigration, this time to Pharos, the colony of Paros.[4] Nikomachos' question (11) may also concern the details involved in moving to a colony. He asks about the advantages of changing his registration of something—from the use of the middle form of the verb, it is probably the consultant himself that was meant—from Herakleia to Taras. It could be that Nikomachos was a metic, a free person who lived temporarily or permanently in a *polis* without becoming its citizen, simply moving from one city to the other, who would need to register himself as liable for a metic tax of some sort. Alternatively, it may be that he is a citizen of the colony of Herakleia moving back to the mother city of Taras under some kind of system of shared citizenship.[5] On this subject, note also tablet 6 in the category of Women below.

As for where they are travelling: two consultants (13 and 18) seem to offer the god a choice of destinations from which to select, but both questions are very fragmentary, so these readings cannot be certain. Most of the questions seem to have been posed by people who knew where they wanted to go, and how they intended to get there. Sometimes they talk in terms of larger regions (Elis, in question 18, may mean the region, rather than the town; Karia in question 21; Messene in question 13; Sicily in question 9); sometimes they pinpoint a particular town. Otherwise, a wide range of destinations emerges. People are travelling along the coast to Ambrakia, Apollonia, Chemara (a colony of Kerkyra), Epidamnos, and Orikos.

Others are headed towards mainland Greece, for example to Alyzea in

Acarnania, and Hermion in Argolis, one perhaps to Elis in the Peloponnese (but see previous paragraph). Some are setting sail for cities in south-east Italy: for example, Sybaris, Herakleia, Hipponion, Atria, Kroton, Ergetion, and Taras; one is heading for Syrakuse. One questioner (7) identifies his destination by its inhabitants rather than its name. There was a group of helot-like serfs in Thessaly called *penestai* and this question may refer to them, or indicate that there was a similar group in Epiros.[6] Another (18) included some detail about his route, using the verb περιέρχεσθαι, 'to go around' or 'end up in'. As the material evidence has suggested, for a long time, Epiros was part of a trade network that spanned the Adriatic and spread south to mainland Greece. Although we know that trade was conducted into Illyria and Makedonia, these areas are not mentioned in the questions that have survived.

I have discussed above how questions were structured to express the desires of the consultant. This was not only a question of content, but also nuance, as questions 27 and 28 illustrate. In both of these questions the consultant asks whether he should stay at home: not everyone, it seems, was eager to travel. Question 26, difficult to read, appears to be asked by someone anxious to return to their brother.

Location identified

1. *SEG* 43.335; Dakaris, Christidis, Vokotopoulou 1993: 58; M-4; archaic Korinthian alphabet; 550–525 BCE

[- -] ἐμπορίας ἐς Ἐπίδαμνον

... of a journey for trade into Epidamnos

2. *SEG* 43.323; Karapanos 1890: 157/8; Vokotopoulou 1992: no. 6; shortly before 510 BCE

Αἴ κα μέλλι ἐς [Σύ]βαριν ἰόντι λόϊον
ἔμεν [κ]α πράτοντι ταῦτα

Whether it would be better for me if I go to Sybaris and if I do these things?

3. *SEG* 43.321; Vokotopoulou 1992: no. 4; M-768; c.450 BCE; inscription on side B of left part of lead question

ἦ Ἱππονίο[ι - - - - -]

(If I go or sail) to Hipponion ... (would it be better for me?)

(Trans. Vokotopoulou 1992)

4. Dakaris, Christidis, Vokotopoulou 1993: 60; M-526; Korinthian alphabet; first half of fifth century BCE

Θεός . Τύχα .
Ἐν Ὀρικôι κα
λôιον πράσοι-
μι κατά χôραν ἐ
hôσπερ νῦν
Ϝοικέων

God. . . . Luck. Would I fare better in Orikos in the countryside, or as I am living now?

(This depends on translating κατά χόραν with a meaning more usually found later than the early Classical period. The alternative would be to take it as belonging to the second clause of the question: 'If I would fare better in Orikos, or in this place, as I am living now?')

5. *SEG* 43.325; Vokotopoulou (1992: no. 8); *Ep. Chron.* 1935; M-47; *c*.400 BCE; ll. 4–6 at right of ll. 1–3; both sides in same hand

Side A:
Θεός · τύχα ἀγαθά ·
περὶ πανπασίας καὶ περὶ Ϝοικέσιος
ἰς Κρ⟨ό⟩τονα ἐ̂ βέλτιον καὶ ἄμεινο⟨ν⟩
αὐτοῖ καὶ γενε-
ᾶι καὶ γυναι-
κί

God . . . Good Luck. About possessions and about a place to live: whether (it would be) better for him and his children and his wife in Kroton?

Side B (probably the response to A):
Ἐν Κρότονι

In Kroton

6. Parke 23; *SEG* 15.393; *BE* 1956: 143; *PAE* 1952: 300, 3; fifth to fourth century BCE

θέος · Ζεῦ, Διώνη, ἠ ἀπιὼν
ἐς Ἀλύζεαν βέλτιον
πρήξει;

God, O Zeus, Dione! Whether he will do better if he migrates to Alyzea?

(Evangelides notes that there are two letters on the reverse of this plate, which probably indicate the name of the questioner. Parke tells us that on the reverse of this plate is a response, listed below at 29, but *SEG* 15.393 gives this as being on the reverse of 24, below.)

7. Christidis; 400–380 BCE

Ἠ ἀ]ντρ{ι}οδιαίτοι[ς]
[Πε]νέσταις ἐὸν

Whether he/I should go to the cave-dwelling Penestai?

8. *BE* 1996: 226, 11; *SEG* 43.328; Vokotopoulou 1992: no. 11; M-122; early fourth century BCE
(*Side B* of tablet with no. 12 on side A.)

Ἠ μετὰ τῶν Παρίων ἐς Πάρον
[πόκα ἱ]κέοντι ἐς τὸν Ἰόνιον
κόλπον λώϊον καὶ ἄμεινον

Whether, when he arrives in the Ionian Gulf, to Pharos, with those from Pharos, it will be advantageous for him?

(Vokotopoulou: Paros is Pharos, a colony of Paros (cf. Strabo 7.5.5) founded in 385/384 BCE)

9. *SEG* 43.329; Vokotopoulou 1992: no. 12; M-1366; *c.*375 BCE; inscription on side B, partially readable

Θ[ε]ό[s] · Τύ[χα] ἀγαθά · Ἀρχω[ν]ίδας
[ἐρωτᾶι] τὸν θεὸν
πότερον πλέω εἰς Σικ[ελίαν]

God . . . Good Luck. Archonidas asks the god whether I should sail into Sicily?

10. *SEG* 43.338; Dakaris, Christidis, Vokotopoulou 1993: 59; M-718; *c.*350 BCE

Περὶ τᾶς οἰκήσις τᾶς
ἐγ Χεμαρίων πότερον
αὐτεῖ οἰκέωντι

About the residence in Chemara, whether it would be (good) for him to live (there)?

11. *SEG* 43.326; Vokotopoulou 1992: no. 9; *Ep. Chron.* 1935; M-1052; 340–330 BCE

Νικόμαχος ἐρωτῆ τὸν Δία [τ]ὸν Νάϊον ἠ ἀπογραψάμ[ε]ν[ος]
κα ἐς Τάραντα ἐξ Ἡρακληίας ἄμεινον

Nikomachos asks Zeus Naios whether he will fare better by having moved his registration from Herakleia to Taras?

12. *BE* (1996: 226, 11); *SEG* 43.328; Vokotopoulou 1992: no. 11; 330–320 BCE; M-122; *PAE* 1967: 48–9, 4; *BE* 1969: 348
(*Side A* of tablet with no. 8 on side B.)

[- - πε]ρὶ Ἡρακλέας
[- -]σα κομίζοντι
[- -ἀ]σφαλέως καὶ οἱ φύ
[λακες - -] Ἡρακλεωτᾶν

Concerns Heraklea (πε]ρὶ Ἡρακλέας) and conveying something safely κομίζοντι [- -ἀ]σφαλέως). Guards (οἱ φύλακες) are also mentioned.

13. *PAE* 1973: 94–6, 2a; fourth century BCE

- - -] . σατ [- -
- - -] δων π [- - -
- - -] ειτωι κα [- - - -
- - -] ιευμαρ [- - - -
- -π]ρὸς ἡμᾶ[ς - - -
- -] σιης καὶ εἰ π[ορευόμε - - -]
θα ἐς Μεσσήνην [⁷⁻⁸ - - -]
που ἤ ἐν Ἀμπρα]κίαι - - -]
ωμεν καὶ εἰ πρ[- - - - - -]
νεωμεν ἄν ἤ . [- - - -
- - -] ἤ τὰν [- - - - -
- - - -] κα [- - - - -

Something to do with a group (l. 5 π]ρὸς ἡμᾶ[ς) travelling to Messene (ll. 6–7 εἰ π[ορευόμε - - -] θα ἐς Μεσσήνην) or Ambrakia (l. 8 ἐν Ἀμπρα]κίαι).

14. *BE* 1969: 348, 6; *PAE* 1967: 33–54, 6; fourth century BCE

Ἐξακῶν ἐρωτᾶι τὸν Δία καὶ τὰν Διώναν
εἰ λώιον αὐτῶι οἰκοντι ἐμ Φάρωι

On the back in large letters: Φά

Hexakon asks Zeus and Dione if it will be better for him if he lives in Pharos?

On the reverse: *Pha*

15. *SEG* 24.454b; *BE* 1968: 318; Parke 1967c: 133(2); fourth to third century BCE

Καὶ ε⟨ἰ⟩ ἄμενόν
μοι μετὰ Διο-
[τί]μο ἐργαζομέ-
νωι Μεγαροῖ   Parke: Μεγάροι[σι]

And if it would be better for me to work with Diotimos, in Megara?

Parke: *Megaroisi* 'among the Megarians'

16. *SEG* 43.333; Dakaris, Christidis, Vokotopoulou 1993: 55; M-234; 300–275 BCE

[- - -] Ἀπολλωνίαν πλεύσας ἧι ἀλαστῶν τη-
[- - -] ε ὄντων πυνθάνοιτο

ll. 1–2 DCV suggest τῆ[ιδ]ε to balance ἧι in an où . . . là arrangement. However, Pleket comments that in this text we really need ἧι = ἤ = 'whether'.

Something to do with: 'having sailed to Apollonia where' (Ἀπολλωνίαν πλεύσας ἧι) and, possibly, 'learning some news' (ὄντων πυνθάνοιτο). . .

17. *BE* 1996: 226, 13; *SEG* 43.330; Vokotopoulou 1992: no. 13; M-46; early third century BCE

Side A:
Θεός · Ἀρίστων ἐρωτᾶ τὸν Δί-
α τὸν Νάϊον καὶ τήν Δηό-
νῆν εἰ λόϊόν μοι καὶ ἄμε-
νον καὶ δυνήομαι
πλὲν εἰς Συρακόσας
πρὸς τὴν ἀποικίαν ὕστερο-
ν

God, Ariston asks Zeus Naios and Dione whether it is better and more good for me and if I will be able to sail to Syrakuse, to the colony, later?

Side B:
Ἀρίστωνος
Of Ariston

18. *SGDI* 1561c; Karapanos 1878: pl. 35; reverse of plate

Ἦ εἰς Ἐλίναν περιέλ(θ)[ωμες......
ἢ εἰς Ἀνακτόριον [..........
ἢ πωλοῦντες τὸν [...........

Whether we should go around to/end up in Elis ... or into Anaktorion ... or selling the ...

19. Parke 1967a: 24; *Ep. Chron.* 1935: 252, 9

Θεός. Τύχη. εἰρω-
τᾶι τὸν Δία τὸν
Νάιον καὶ τὴν Διώ-
νην Αἰσχυλῖνος εἰ
μή αὐτῶι ἄμενον
πλὲν ἐς Ἀδρίαν
ἐς Τισατες

God. Luck. Aischylinos asks Zeus Naios and Dione whether it would not be better for him to sail to the Adriatic to Tisates (?)

20. *SEG* 15.387; *PAE* 1952: 301–2, 7

Side A:
Ἐμπορευόμενοι
ἐς ΕΠΙΛΟΜΙΧΟΝ
Making a voyage to Epilomichos

Side B:
Ἐνπορα ...
A voyage/business

21. *PAE* 1958: 105

Αἰ Συπτ. . . αι
ἐστὶν κάθοδ[ος
εἰς Καρείαν
ἐφ᾽ οἷς αὐτὸς
βόλεται

Whether . . . it is better to journey into Karia on the conditions he wants?

Unspecified location
22. *Ep. Chron.* 1935: 259, 35; fifth century BCE

Side A:
Περὶ τοτιμιονιο
ἦ ἀπουικέοντες
ἄμεινον τοῖς
εονιαυας

Starts with 'About' (περί) then goes on to ask 'whether by migrating it would be better for those' (ἦ ἀπουικέοντες ἄμεινον τοῖς)

Side B:
μένε[τε

Stay

23. *Ep. Chron.* 1935: 258, 26; fifth to fourth century BCE

περὶ τᾶς ὁρμᾶς

About the enterprise

24. *SEG* 15.394; *BE* 1956: 143; *PAE* 1952: 300–1, 4; fifth to fourth century BCE
(*Side B* of tablet with no. 28 on side A.)

(a kappa in reverse)
ἐπερωτεῖ τυα. . .
. . κατὰ θάλασσα[νπο]-
[ρε]υομένωι
. να
. . ικ πράσσοιμι
. . κα λαβὼν
. σ . . . γα

He asks (ἐπερωτεῖ) . . . for him/me travelling or doing business by sea (κατὰ θάλασσα-[νπο][ρε]υομένωι probably κατὰ θάλασσα[νἐμπορε]υομένωι) . . . I would fare better (πράσσοιμι) . . . if/and taking (κα λαβών)

25. *Ep. Chron.* 1935: 260, 38; fourth century BCE

Θεὸς
τύχα· ἦ καὶ ἔβην κατὰ χώραν

God. Fortune. Whether I also travelled by land/in the same place?
(See no. 4 for questions about translation.)

26. *SEG* 24.454c; *BE* 1968: 318; Parke 1967c: 132 (3); dialect of the consultation is not Attic; fourth to third century BCE

ἤ ἀφέρπης οἴκαδε πὸτ
τον ἀδελφεόν

Whether you(?) may return home to your brother

Remaining at home

27. Parke 22; *Ep. Chron.* 1935: 255, 13; fifth to fourth century BCE

ἀγαθᾶι τύχα[ι]
ἐπικονῆται Παρμενίδ-
ας τῶι Δὶ τῶι Νάω καὶ τᾶι
Διώναι λῶον καὶ ἄμει-
νον οἴκοι μένοντι

Good luck. Parmenides asks Zeus Naios and Dione whether he will fare better if he stays home?

28. *SEG* 15.394; *BE* 1956: 143; *PAE* 1952: 300/1, 4; fifth to fourth century BCE
(Side A of tablet with no. 24 on side B.)

αὐτεῖ οἰκεῖ-
ν καὶ ἐξέχεσθ-
αι

For him to stay at home and put up with it

For other tablets relating to travel, see also:

Work 4: *SEG* 43.331; *PAE* 1932; Vokotopoulou 1992: 86, 14; M-545; 340–330 BCE
Work 7: *Ep. Chron.* 1935: 254, 12; fifth century BCE
Work 9: Parke 19; *SGDI* 1568a; Karapanos 1878: pl. 37
Work 10: *SEG* 43.341; *BE* 1993: 346; *PAE* 1968: 53–4; Salviat 1993: 61–4; c.350–320 BCE
Work 11: *SGDI* 1583; Karapanos 1878: pl. 37, 3
Work 13: *SEG* 23.475; *PAE* 1958: 104–2
Women 6: *SEG* 24.454a; Parke 1967a: 132(3); *BE* 1968: 318; fourth to third century BCE
Prosperity/Safety 4: *PAE* 1967: 50, 7; *BE* 1969: 348, 7; third century BCE
Health 6: *SGDI* 1587b (a response to 1587a)

Women

The questions in this category are περὶ γυναικός that is, about women. Five questions begin with or include this formula (1, 8, 9, 16, and 19), while question 11 varies the formula to fit the circumstance of a father asking about his daughter, beginning [πε]ρ[ὶ] τῆς κόρ[ης], 'about the girl/my daughter'). The usual form of questions in this category appears to be 'whether' the consultant will 'do better' if he marries a particular woman. This seems to be the only area of life related to relationships that occurs, at least in such number, amongst the questions, published and unpublished, although Christidis reported one example of a question in the unpublished material that asks about a young man and calls him ὡραῖος, which may suggest an erotic feeling on the part of the consultant.

Three questions are specifically about marriage with a named woman (questions 1–3); six about marriage with an unnamed woman (questions 4–9). We also see fathers asking whether they should marry off their daughters; siblings asking if they should marry; and inquiries that appear to be about second marriages or additional relationships of some kind. In question 6, Isodemos seems to be considering marriage as only one in a series of life changes about which he asks, including whether it would be better for him to live among the Athenians as a citizen. (Since it was not a simple matter to become a citizen of Athens, it seems likely that he was either a citizen of Athens who was thinking about moving away, or that he was not an Athenian, but was contemplating moving there as a metic—although the verb in question means political rights, not freedom.)

Seven of the consultants name themselves (2, 3, 4, 6, 9, 15, 18); the rest remain anonymous. For most of the other tablets, we can tell that the gender of the consultant is male (for example, question 5 asks something like 'would it be better if I took a wife . . .'), but a few are less clear (for example, question 16 seems to ask 'about a woman' and then something to do with safety; it is possible that this question is about the safety of the women it mentions, but there is so little information in the text that this must remain in the realm of speculation). We should not automatically assume male authorship: Professor Christidis found a number of questions in the unpublished material inscribed by women asking about the marital prospects of their daughters. The questions suggest that marriage was considered to be a decision best guided by the gods. That marriages might turn on the outcome of a session of divination can also be seen from other sources.[7]

Other themes also shape these questions about marriage. Question 3, with or without the gloss offered by Christidis, is clearly concerned with gain. It appears to have been put to the oracle by the guardian of a girl who hoped to profit from his relationship with her. Apparently, some of the unpublished questions show that the chance of a dowry was an important consideration for a man contemplating marriage. There are at least two examples of questions concerning τίμασις γυναικός (literally, 'the estimation of the value of a girl'), both, apparently, posed after a divorce. Question 15 also seems to be about the reliability of some kind of gain, but it is unclear what this refers to—it could be the relationship or some material acquisition. Another significant factor for men and women to consider before marriage was whether or not a woman would produce children—as the next category of questions, Children, suggests.

Two questions seem to show the consultant concerned about changing his woman. Question 14 appears to be asking about marrying another woman. What may be a response (20) may be instructing the protagonist to 'put up with' his wife.[8] The very brief inquiry of question 13 may also be about a woman (although it could be about another feminine noun, perhaps land). Unfortunately, the rest of the text is missing and we cannot know the context or motivation behind the question.

Question 10 may concern marriage between siblings. Such a relationship would have horrified most Greeks, although Athenian law did allow the marriage of half-siblings from the same father, but not the same mother, and Spartan law from the same mother but not the same father.[9] There does not seem to have been a tradition of sister-marriage among the Molossians (at least not among their royal family, although Olympias did marry Alexander, her half-brother (king of the Molossians 272–240 BCE). I can find no particular evidence for sibling marriage among the Epirotes, although, of course, our knowledge of the culture of the area, let alone each individual tribe, although growing, is still relatively slim. But perhaps it is precisely a lack of precedent, and fear of breaking a cultural taboo, that drove the consultant who asked this question to the oracle.

Question 11 seems to be asking about the chastity of the consultant's daughter, a unique concern among the published questions. I have included it in this section under the assumption that the question was posed because it affected her chances of marriage. However, the question could have been posed regarding some other venture, perhaps, for example, the chance of gaining a priesthood—although the requirement of chastity for such a position seems to have been extremely rare.[10]

Marriage inquiries about specific women
1. *Ep. Chron.* 1935: 257, 18; side b, ii

περὶ γυναικὸς
πότερον κα τ[υγ-

χάνοιμι λαμβάνων
Κλεολαϊν

About a woman, whether I will be fortunate taking Kleolais as a wife?

2. *SEG* 19.431; *PAE* (1955: 172, a)

Ἐρωτῆ Κλεμήδης τὸν Δία καὶ τὰν Διώναν ἢ 'πιτύχοι κα- - - - -
θυγατέρα Ὀλυμπιάδα τῷ Νικάρχου ἢ δέδασται τουτ - - - - -

Klemedes asks Zeus and Dione whether it will happen that . . . Olympias, daughter of Nikarchos, will be given to him . . . ?

3. Parke 10

αἰ τύχαια μοι ἁ ἐπι-
τροπεία τὰν ἔχω
γαμῶν Λυκκίδας;   Christidis l. 3: τᾶμον

Whether the guardianship, which I, Lykkidas, gain by marrying, will bring me fortune?

Marriage inquiries about unidentified women

4. *Ep. Chron.* 1935: 255, 14; fifth century BCE

Ὀνασίμοι ἄμει-
νον τὰν γυναῖκα
κομίδεσται

And on the other side of the tablet: μελιχ

Will it be better for Onasimos to marry the woman?

5. *SEG* 15.396; *PAE* 1952: 306, 24; fifth to fourth century BCE

Βέλτιον τιταυ. . γαν . .
. κομένωι γυναῖκα
πράσσοιμι

Would I do better . . . if I took a wife?

6. *SEG* 24.454a; Parke 1967*a*: 133(1); *BE* 1968: 318; fourth to third century BCE

αι εἰ λ[ώ]ϊον γυναῖκα λαμβάνοντι   Parke: καὶ ἐ
[κ]αὶ ἄμενον καὶ παῖδες ἔσονται
[γη]ροτρόφοι Ἰσοδήμωι
[κ]αὶ Ἀθήνησι ἐπιδημοῖντι
[κ]αὶ πολιτευομένων Ἀθήνησι

And if I will do better by taking a wife, and whether there will be children for Isodemos, who will take care of him, and if he should live in Athens and become a citizen among the Athenians?

7. Kekule and Winnefeld 1909: 40

Ob die Frau zu nehmen, die er im Sinn hat, er sich wohler und besser befinden wird

Whether he will do better if he takes the woman he has in mind.

8. *Ep. Chron.* 1935: 256, 18, side b, i

περὶ γυναικὸ-
ς ἦ τ'ἄμυννο τε
λῶον πρᾶμι

About a woman whether. . . and I would do better

9. Parke 1967*a*: 6; *Ep. Chron.* 1935: 260, 37

Θεός. Γηριότον Δία ἐπ-
ερωτῆι περὶ γυναικὸς
ἦ βέλτιον λαβόντι

God. Gerioton asks Zeus about a woman, whether (he would do) better if he married (her)

Inquiry concerning marriage between siblings
10. Christidis; 400–390 BCE

[- - -] καὶ πότερα κασι[γνήται]
ἐάσσαι συνϜοικέω
αὐτος ἁ γυνὰ

l. 3 Christidis believes ἁ γυνα may belong to another inscription

And whether I myself should live with her, my half-sister

Fathers concerning their daughters
11. Christidis; 325–300 BCE

[Πε]ρ[ὶ] τῆς κόρ[ης] ἀγνείαν πῶς κα ταύ
[τα] λ[ώ]ιον καὶ ἄμεινον πράσοι

About the chastity of the girl/my daughter how would s/he do these things better and more well

12. Kekule and Winnefeld 1909: 41

Offenbare, O Zeus, ob es mir nützt, meine Töchter dem Theodoros und dem Tessias zu Frauen zu geben

Reveal, O Zeus, whether it is more serviceable to give my daughter to Theodoros or to Tessias as a wife

Taking another woman
13. *SGDI* 1570; *Ep. Chron.* 1935: 259, 28; fourth century BCE

ἦ ἄλλαν μαστεύων

Whether I should seek another (woman or land)?

14. *Ep. Chron.* 1935: 260, 39; fourth century BCE

ἒ ἀτέραν ἄγομει

Whether I should marry another woman?

A secure future
15. *SGDI* 1568b; Rhodes or Rhodian colony

Θεό(ς). Τύχα(ν) ἀγαθάν. [Ἐρωτ]ᾶι Πο(λ)έ[μα]ρ(χ)ο(ς) [τὸν]
(Δ)ί[α τὸν Ν](ά)ο(ν καὶ) [τὰ]ν Δ(ιώ)ν[αν· αἴ] τι ἀγαθὸν τᾶς γυναικὸς ταύτας παραμό[νι]μον ἐν.έχει καὶ. . . . . . .

God. Good fortune. Polemarchos asks Zeus Naios and Dione whether he will have a share in a something good and trustworthy from this woman . . . ?

16. *Ep. Chron.* 1935: 260, 36b

πὲρ τᾶς γυν-
αικός·αἰ τιαῦτα[ι] εἴει
ἀσφαλ . ως

About the woman, whether she will . . . safely?

Unspecific inquiries about specific women
17. *Ep. Chron.* 1935: 256, 17; beginning of fifth century BCE

Θορακίδα θυγατέρα
Θεαρίδαι

His daughter Thorakis to Thearidas

18. Kekule and Winnefeld 1909: 40

Eukrates fragt den Zeus und die Diona seine Frau Theuxena, die Tochter des Theuxenos

Eukrates asks Zeus and Dione (about) his wife Theuxena, the daughter of Theuxenos

Relevant fragments
19. *Ep. Chron.* 1935: 257, 22; Korinthian letters; fifth century BCE

περὶ τᾶς γυν-
αικὸ[ς] νουματοι(;)

About the woman (the rest is illegible)

20. *BE* 1998: 202; *Poikila Epigraphika* 1997: no. 4; M-189; Doric; mid-fourth century BCE

τὰν ἔσσαν ᾳ
στέργιν

l. 1 Parker: ἔσσαν for οὖσαν

As noted above, this tablet could be translated as: 'Bear with your defeat' or 'Put up with her'

For other tablets relating to women, see also:
Property 1: Parke 3; *Ep. Chron.* 1935: 253, 10; fifth century BCE.

Children

These inquiries all concern the birth of children. The word most frequently used to describe offspring in these consultations is γενεά. The word occurs 14 times out of 18 questions; the phrase περὶ γενεᾶς appears in five questions (2, 5, 7 (qualifying it as a male child), 11, 16). LSJ describes γενεά as rare in prose, a poetic term for descendants, often used in Homer. Perhaps it was used by the consultants to invest their inquiries with greater significance. Other terms found are: παῖς (question 8) and τέκνα (question 9). Professor Christidis told me that in the unpublished material περὶ γενεᾶς is most common, but other formulae are found, such as εἰ τέκνον εὐτοκία (*sic*) which translates as something like 'whether she will bring forth children easily'.

Only seven of these questions are concerned with the likelihood of having children from a particular woman (although a number of the tablets are very fragmentary, so there may be more). This is often phrased in the questions as ἐκ or ἀπὸ τῆς γυναικός that is, literally, 'out' or 'from the woman', and in most cases the woman is named. Five of the questions ask about how a child might be obtained, that is, to which gods the consultant must pray for this favour to be shown (questions 1, 6, 7, 16, and Christidis argued for question 15); in question 13 the parents just ask what they should do. This is a rare example of a question in which the inquiry was made by both parents, although this does not necessarily mean that both were physically present at the oracle. Men ask most of the other questions. In seven questions the consultant names himself (or, in the case of 13, himself and his wife) (1, 2, 5, 6A and B, 7, 10, 11, 16), while on others the phrasing of the question suggests a male (for example, question 12 asks: 'Zeus and Dione, will there be children in the future for him?' where the pronoun surely refers to the consultant).

There is one example of a question that we know is definitely asked by a woman (question 15, from the gender of the participle of dedication) in the published material. Others do not indicate the gender of the consultant: for example, question 8, which simply says 'for the sake of the birth of a child'. Question 9 may be a question asked by a woman, since the participle of the verb for consulting is feminine. Christidis told me that in the unpublished material, women do appear, asking about their own prospects of having children, albeit infrequently.

Only two phrases include the idea of 'doing better': question 11 asks: αι λώϊον] κα(ὶ) ἄ(μ)[εινο](ν) πρ⟨α⟩άσσοί, literally 'if he might do better and more well', while question 7 casts it in terms of superlatives: πράξαιμι λῶστα καὶ ἄριστα, literally 'if I might do best and excellently'. This latter tablet is the only one that makes a specific request for male children. Two other possibilities are question 2, which asks for περὶ γενεᾶς πατροιόχο, that is, 'a child to inherit' (although the adjective in other literary examples, is used of an heiress);[11] and 13, which asks for γενιὰ κ' ἀνδρογένεια, meaning literally children 'of descent from their father'.[12] This could mean 'like their father', but it may indicate concerns about paternity, in which case it is similar to the question in which Lysanias asks whether Annyla's child is his. This concerns a current, but concealed fact rather than a future plan, so I have placed it under the category of present concerns.[13]

Professor Christidis told me that in the unpublished material there are also questions showing concern about having few children or about the survival of offspring, and questions about the chances of begetting male children. Christidis suggested that questions 17 and 18 in this category are about abstaining from sexual intercourse and indicate problems with having children.

This category of questions, which includes the oldest of the questions among the published tablets, suggests how important children were in this society. In most cases, it is men who bring this matter to the oracle, formulating their questions one of two ways: 'Will I have children from this woman (named or unnamed)?' and 'To what god should I pray in order to have children?' This gender bias of the material evidence fits with the bias of literary accounts, in which it is, on the whole, men who visit oracles to find out about children. This bias might be explained by a tendency in Greek society to attribute the crucial ingredient for conception to men, but although we know some medical authors held this view, we also know others did not (in fact, they ridiculed it).[14] Probably, we should look for an explanation in more widely held cultural beliefs, for example, as shown in the language of the Athenian betrothal ceremony in which the father of the bride gives away his daughter to her future husband with the words 'I give you this woman for the plowing of legitimate children'. This imagery of woman as receptive earth that needs to be worked, and man as the tamer/farmer/

ploughman, etc. is repeated throughout Greek literature. In this light, the gender bias of questions about the chances of having children 'from this woman' make sense. It is likely that any visit to a doctor to resolve problems of conception through natural rather than supernatural methods was likely to have been accompanied with a visit to the oracle for divine guidance.[15] It is surprising, considering how dangerous childbirth was for mother and child, that there are no questions concerned with the details of birth.[16]

An incidental detail of the texts in this category is the repeated phrase 'the wife I have now' (see questions 2, 5, possibly implied in question 6). The implication may be that the inquirer regarded his relationship with the woman in question as temporary, especially if children were not forthcoming.

Inquiries about children from a particular woman

1. Parke 5; *PAE* (1931: 89–91); Boustrophedon; end of sixth/beginning of fifth century BCE

Ἕρμων τίνα
κα θεὸν ποτθέμ-
ενος γενεὰ Ϝ-
οι γένοιτο ἐκ Κ-
ρεταίας ὀνά-
σιμος ποτ τᾶ ἐ-
άσσαι·{*}

Hermon (asks) by aligning himself with which of the gods will there be from Kretaia offspring for him, in addition to those he has now?

* This last clause is difficult to read: does *ὀνάσιμος* agree with the children that Kretaia will have or is it Hermon himself? Or is Onesimos the name of another man? Does *τᾶ ἐάσσαι* mean existing children or is it the Doric form of the feminine dative participle ('a delight for Kretaia')?

2. *Ep. Chron.* 1935: 255, 15; fifth to fourth century BCE

Κλεάνορι περὶ γενεᾶς
πατροιόχο ἐκ τᾶς νῦν
Γόνθας γυναικός

For Kleanor, about offspring to inherit, from Gonthe, the wife he has now?

3. *Ep. Chron.* 1935: 259, 34; fifth to fourth century BCE

Πὲρ Μύδρας πιτα . .
σάνδρο γενεᾶς
ἔσσεται

About Mydra . . . will there be children?

FIG. 3. Oracle question tablet from Dodona: In this tablet, a man called Hermon asks to which of the gods he should turn to in order to get children from a woman Kretaia (end of sixth/beginning of fifth century BCE) © G. Garvey/The Ancient Art & Architecture Collection

4. Karapanos 1878: pl. 35, 1; Athenian or Ionian (Kyklades)

[τὸν] Δία καὶ τὴν Διώνην
..... τὸν θεὸν ἐπερωτᾷ
..... ἐκ τῆς γυναικός

l.3 Christidis in conversation suggested ἐούσας γυναικός

Zeus and Dione ... the god he asks ... from the woman

5. Parke 7; *SGDI* 1561a = Pomtow 24; puts two inscriptions together (Karapanos 1878: pl. 38, 4 and pl 35, 1)

Ἡρακλ[ε]ίδας αἰτεῖ τὸν Δία καὶ τὴν Διώνην
τύχην ἀγαθὴν καὶ τὸν θεὸν ἐπερωτᾶι
περὶ γενειῆς · ἦ ἔστα[ι] ἐκ τῆς γυναικὸς
– Α[ἴ]γλης τῆς{*} νῦν ἔχει

Herakleides asks Zeus and Dione for good fortune and asks the god about offspring. Will there be any from Aigle the (wife) he has now?

 * The sense of the genitive pronoun is unclear. I have read it as an accusative pronoun that has been attracted into the genitive.

6. Parke 1967a: 8; *SEG* 19. 426; *PAE* 1955: 171, a

Side A:
Καλλικράτης ἐπερωτᾶι τὸν θεὸν ἦ ἔσται μοι γενεὰ ἀπὸ τᾶς Νίκης
τῆς γυναικὸς ἧς ἔχει συμμένο-
ντι καὶ τίνι [θ]εῶν εὐχομένῳ

Kallikrates asks the god whether there will be offspring for me from Nike, the woman he has, if he shows allegiance and prays to which of the gods?

Side B:
Ἀγάθων ἐπερωτεῖ - - - - - - - - -
Νικώνδαι ΕΥΝΑΩΛ - - - - - - -

Agathon asks . . . to Nikondas . . .

7. Parke 9; *BE* 1959: 231; *BCH* 1957: 584

Θεὸς τύχα ἀγαθά · Ἀνάξιππος τὸν Δία τ-
ὸν Νάον καὶ τὰν Διώναν ἐπερωτᾶι περὶ ἐρσεντέρας γενεᾶς ἀπὸ Φιλίστας τᾶς γυναικός, τίνει κα θεῶν εὐχόμενος πράξαιμι
λῶιστα καὶ ἄριστα

BCH: ἐρσεντέρας is the Ionic form of ἀρρεντέρας

God, good fortune. Anaxippos asks Zeus Naios and Dione about male children from Philiste his woman. By praying to which of the gods would I do best and excellently?

No specific woman mentioned

8. *Ep. Chron.* 1935: 257, 19; beginning of the fifth century BCE

Γενεᾶς ἕννεκα παιδὸς

for the sake of the birth of a child

9. *Ep. Chron.* 1935: 258, 27; fifth century

Πότ[ερ]ον ἐμ[οὶ]
χρωμένη γίνεται
αὐτῆι τέκνα

Whether there will be children for me, if I consult the oracle?

10. Karapanos 1878: pl. 35, 3

. . . . . . Διὸς τοῦ Νά-
[ου] . . . . . ησασθαι εἰ μή
. . . . . . [αὐτ]ῷ καὶ τᾶ οἰκήσει
. . . .[πό]τερα Φιλόταν καὶ
. . . . γένειαν καὶ Θη-
. . . . ὁ πατήρ ἐν παν-

[τί] . . . . . ν γενέσθαι τῷ
. . . . μεν ὅτι σελ-
. . . . . .

Of Zeus Naios . . . if not . . . to him and there he will live . . . whether Philotas and . . . offspring and . . . the father in every . . . to be to . . . that . . .

11. *SGDI* 1572b

[θεός . τύχαν ἀ](γ)α(θ)ά(ν). Ἐ(ρω)τᾶ Μέν-
[ων Δία Νάον καὶ Διώνα](ν) περὶ (γ)[ε]ν[ε]ᾶς · [αἴ κα] συν-
[οικέων. . . . . .αι λώϊον] κα(ὶ) ἄ(μ)[εινο](ν) πρ⟨α⟩άσσοι

God. Good luck. Menon asks Zeus Naios and Dione about offspring. If by living with . . . he would fare better?

12. *SGDI* 1577b

[θε]ός
κα(ὶ) τὰν [Διώναν]
[γε]ν[ε]ᾶι αὐτ[οῦ]
[εἰς τὸ]ν ἔπ[ειτα χρόνον]

Zeus and Dione, will there be children in the future for him?

13. Christidis; 450–425 BCE

Θιὸς τύχα ἀγαθὰ : Βōκόλō κὴ Πολυμνάστη
τί κα δράοντοιν hυγία κὴ γενιὰ κ' ἀνδρογένεια
γινύο[ι]το κὴ παραμόνιμος ἰοιό[ς] κὴ χρε̄μάτων
ἐπιγγ[ύ]ασις κὴ τῶν ἰόντων ὄνασις

God, good luck. Bokolo and Polymnaste (ask) what they should do for there to be health and offspring like their father and a male child that will survive and security of things and enjoyment from things to come.

14. Christidis; 400–390 BCE

Ὀλίγα γενεὰ

A few children

15. Christidis; 400–350 BCE

Ἄλλει Ε[- - -]
θεμένα
[ἔσσ]εταί μοι
[γ]ενεὰ

If I . . . dedicate to another (?) will there be children for me?

16. *SEG* 43.332; Dakaris, Christidis, Vokotopoulou 1993: 55; M-38, (not *PAE* 1958: 104, no. 3 as recorded in *SEG*); c.350–320 BCE

Ἐπηστορεῖται Δεινοκλῆς Ἀπολλωνιάτας τὸν Δία καὶ
τὰν Διώναν περὶ γενεᾶς τ[ί][ι] κα θεῶν θύων καὶ εὐχόμενος
ΦΥΗΤΕΒΟΙ καὶ γένοιτο κ' ἄρα γ[ενεά - - -]

John Chadwick: ΦΥΗΤΕΒΟΙ = φυτεύοι

Deinokles of Apollonia asks Zeus and Dione about offspring, whether by sacrificing and praying to which of the gods . . . would there be children

Concern about intercourse
Christidis suggested that these two texts are about abstaining from sexual intercourse (taking θίγō as part (possibly a corrupt aorist form?) of θιγγάνω) and indicate problems with having children.

17. Christidis; 500–480 BCE

Ἐ̄ μὲ̄ θίγō [- - -]

Should I not have intercourse?. . .

18. Christidis; 450 BCE

θίγō
Ἀγη̄σαρέτα

(If) I have intercourse with Agesareta.

For other tablets relating to children, see also:
Women 6: *SEG* 24.454a; Parke 1967c: 132–3, 133(1); *BE* 1968: 318; fourth to third century BCE
Property 1: Parke 3; *Ep. Chron.* 1935: 253, 10; fifth century BCE

Work

As we have seen, many of the questions about travel are closely related to concerns about work. As I have said, where the specific type of activity is included in the tablet (including mention of a τέχνη, 'craft') I have placed it in this category, but both categories are also cross-referenced.

In the majority of questions in this section, the inquirers name themselves (questions 1, 4, 6, 10, 11, 12, 13, 14, 15, 16, and 17) and all are male. Most of these questions are concerned with very specific courses of action: herding, farmwork, bronze work, fishing, running a ship, and, possibly, working as a doctor. The consultants either name the activity involved, or they clearly have one in mind (for example, when they mention τὰν τέχναν). Only one of these questions (14) possibly makes an open-ended inquiry to the oracle about what the consultant should do for work—and, as I've described above, this may, in fact, be less open than it appears. Question 10, one of three questions that involve taking a share in a boat, gives us some idea of how closely the oracle might be involved in day-to-day decisions. The consultant, Timodamos appears to be using divine guidance with some care as he plots his career path: the tablet mentions a previous instruction, suggesting that the consultant had already described his situation in some detail to the oracle in a previous visit. This question shows him returning to ensure that his subsequent activities were still going to do him good. Nevertheless, for all his concern to get oracular instruction, it is apparent that he retains his autonomy: despite the oracle's previous instruction to stay home and give up his share in a boat, he returns to ask about doing business by land and by sea. Question 13 may provide us with a model of the earlier question and answer between Timodamos and the god: Lysias asks the oracle, if he should put up with the sea and take a share in a boat. On the back of the tablet is what looks like the oracle's response, but it is difficult to be sure of the translation. It seems to say 'it is necessary to do nothing by land'.

Most of these questions concern doing well (λώϊον καὶ ἄμεινον 'better and more good'). A few mention profit explicitly (1, 14, 15). The consultant of question 15 shows some ambition, wanting to do well 'for all time', [ἐς τὸν] ἄπ[α](ν)[τα] (χρ)[όνον].

In the unpublished material, according to Professor Christidis, there are general questions about employment. Other *technai* are named or implied, with phrases including σκυτικά (skill in shoe-making), χαλκεύς (smith's work or smithy/forge), πέλεκαν (an axe, so something to do with timber?), μάγειρος (butcher or cook), πατρῷα τέχνη (my father's craft), and ὀρυχχειν (*sic*, possibly from ὀρύσσω and relating to mining). These terms appear in such questions as 'Should I choose another craft or should I stick to my father's craft?'[17]

There are also specific questions about how a task is to be conducted, for example, about the allocation of timber: for example, 'Will I get the timber?' which Christidis suggests was asked by contractors in competition with each other. He also indicated the presence of other topics related to work, especially farming, including the state of the weather; the likelihood of a good harvest; and irrigation (φρέαρ), for example, 'Should I dig a well?'

Finally, I have included here question 17, by one Porinos, who identifies himself fully with patronymic and provenance. The phrasing of this question, written neatly in accurate Greek, gives a strong impression of its creator. It seems to be concerned with a career move, that is, whether Porinos should serve a satrap and hyparch (the two titles seem to describe the same individual here, even if not the same office). But the verb θεραπεύω 'to serve' or 'attend to' could also mean 'to treat medically', raising the possibility that this neat request is written by a doctor, one of the itinerant professionals of this period, summoned by the satrap from Kymai, unsure of what to do, and seeking a prescription from the oracle to help with his uncertainty.

Herding

1. Parke 17; *SGDI* 1559; Karapanos 1878: pl. 37, 1; Thessalian dialect; Karapanos suggests that the inscription on side B is probably a summary of the contents of the inscription on side A.

Side A:
Ἐρουτᾶι Κλεούτ(ς) τὸν Δία καὶ τὰν
Διώναν, αἴ ἐστι αὐτοῖ προβατεύοντι
(ὄ)ναιον καὶ ὠφέλιμον

Kleouts asks Zeus and Dione if it will be better and more profitable for him if he keeps cattle

Side B:
πὲρ προβα
τείας

About cattle herding

Farmwork

2. *Ep. Chron.* (1935: 258, 24); fifth century BCE

Ζεῦ Νάιε καὶ Διώνη καὶ σύννα[οι αἰ-
τῶ ὑ]μᾶς ἀγαθεῖ τύχει δοῦναι ἐ[μοὶ τὰν
γᾶν ἐργαζομένωι καὶ ἐν . . . .
. . . . ε ι λ .

O Zeus Naios and Dione and those dwelling alongside, whether you will give me good fortune as I work the land and in . . .

3. Christidis; 375–350 BCE

[- - -]λλωνίδαι
[- - -]οι μέλλει βέντι
[ον] καὶ ὄναιον ἦμεν
γαοργέοντι τὸν χῶρον
τοῦτόν μοι τὸν κλᾶρο
ν ἐξενθἕν

The first line may contain the remains of the name of the consultant (λλωνίδαι), then the question seems to be 'Whether it will be better and more useful for me if I farm this place', and then there is reference to the *kleros* (κλᾶρο) or lot, which might, it was suggested by Christidis, refer to a lot oracle. However, it is also possible that it indicates the system of allotment that provided the consultant with his land. The verb ἐξενθἕν could be related to τίθημι and be about putting or placing, providing something like 'the land which was allocated to me …'.

4. *SEG* 43.331; Vokotopoulou 1992: no. 14; *PAE* 1932; M-545; 340–330 BCE

Ἀγελόχῳ ἐξ
Ἑργετίω hο
ρμημένωι
ἄμεινόν ἐστι
γαοργῆ[ν]

Will it better for Agelochos (from Ergetion) if he sets out to be a farmer?

Bronze work

5. *SEG* 15.403; *BE* 1956: 143; *PAE* 1952: 304, 18; fourth century BCE

Side A:
Πότερα μ- - - - κα τὰν τέχναν ἐργαζομένῳ
ὄναιον ει- - - -αν χαλκηαν - - - - -

Whether it will be useful for me, if I work as a bronze smith (literally, 'working the bronze craft')

Side B:
- - - - - -ας τέχνα - - - - -

… craft …

Fishing (his father's skill)

6. Parke 18; fourth century BCE

Θεός. Τύχαι ἀγαθᾶι. Φαινύλωι θεμιστεύει ὁ
Θεὸς τὰμ πατρῶιαν τέχναν ἐργάζεσθαι, ἁλιεύεσθαι
καὶ λώιον καὶ ἄμεινον πράξειν;

God. Good Luck. Does the god rule that Phainylos he should pursue his father's craft, should fish and do better?

Unspecified skills

7. *Ep. Chron.* 1935: 254, 12; fifth century BCE

ἐ ἀποδαμον τύ-
χοιμί κα
ἐπὶ τὰν τέχναν

Whether if I went abroad I would do better at my trade?

8. *PAE* 1973: 94–9, 3; fourth century BCE

Θεός τύχα ἀγαθά, Ζεῦ Νάϊε κ[αὶ Διώνα]
ἐπερωτῆι τὸν Θεὸν ἦ τὰν τέχναν [λώϊον]
καὶ ἄμεινον πράσση(ι) καὶ ἦ [- - - -

God. Good fortune. O Zeus Naios and Dione. He asks the god whether he will do better at this craft, and whether . . . ?

9. Parke 19; *SGDI* 1568a; Karapanos 1878: pl. 37, 4

Τύχα ἀγαθά. Ἦ τυγχάνοιμί κα ἐμπορευόμενος
ὅπυς κα δοκῆι σύμφορον ἔμειν, καὶ ἄγων, τῆι κα δοκῆι,
ἅμα τᾶι τεχναι χρεύμενος

Good fortune. Whether I would do better travelling to where it seems good to me, and doing business there, if it seems good, and at the same time practising this craft.

Ship-related work

10. *SEG* 43.341; *BE* 1993: 346; *PAE* 1968: 53–4; Salviat 1993: 61–4; *c*.350–320 BCE

Side A:
Θεοί· Τύχαν ἀγαθάν·
ὦ Ζεῦ, ἀναίρει Τ[ι]μοδά-
μοι ἐμπ[ο]ρεύεσθαι
καὶ κατὰ γ[ᾶ]ν καὶ κατὰ θάλασσαν
τἀπὸ τῶ [ἀ]ργυρίο, ὅσσον
καὐτὸς [h]έληται χρόνον
ταῦτα κράτιστα;

l. 4 added later in smaller script; *side B*, ll. 5–8 are a reaction to this insertion; l. 5 τἀπὸ τῶ [ἀ]ργυρίο a reference to a silver mine owned by Timodamos, ed. pr. who connects this with B, l. 4—as the toponym indicating the location of the mine. Salviat prefers to interpret [ἀ]ργυρίο: 'engager de l'argent dans le négoce'. In B, l. 4 he restores γαύ[λοι], a *gaulos* being a merchant ship.

Gods. Good luck. O Zeus, will you tell Timodamos that these things are best: to do business by land and by sea, using money/his silver mine, for however much time he chooses?

Side B:
Θεοί· τύχαν ἀγαθάν· Ἐν τῶι
ἄστει οἰ[κ]ῆν καὶ καπηλεύ-
ην καὶ ἐμ[π]ορεύεσθαι, τὰ δ' ἐ-
ν τῶι γαυ. . ἐγδιδόμεν ·
ἐμπορε[ύ]εσθαι δὲ χρήματα
ἄγοντα [καὶ] κατὰ γᾶν καὶ κατὰ θάλασ[σα]ν, πωλῶντα καὶ
ὠνόμ[ε]νο[ν]

ll. 3–4: 'et céder ta part du gaulos,' i.e., 'louer, donner à bail ta part,' according to Salviat who points out that a ship was commonly owned by several partners, and quotes various literary parallels. He suggests translating χρήματα ἄγοντα (ll. 5–6) as 'en faisant circuler des marchandises'.

Salviat believes this question contains a question and a response, followed by a question and a response: Timodamos asks Zeus first of all if it would be good for him to do business with regards to his silver. The god's first response advises him to live in the town and set up his workshop there, do business there, and give up his share in the boat. The consultant returns to find out if he should conduct his business by land or by sea and the oracle instructs him to do business on both land and sea, in selling and in buying.

Gods. Good fortune. Dwell in the city and work as a trader and do business, and give up the share in the boat. Trade on land and sea, selling and buying

11. *SGDI* 1583; Karapanos 1878: pl. 37, 3

Θεός. Τύχαι ἀγαθᾶ[ι. Ἐπι]κοινῆτα[ι] Ἱππόστρατος τῶι Δὶ τῶι Νάωι καὶ
τᾶι Διώναι· ἦ μὴ ν[α](υ)κλαρη(ν) λώϊογ καὶ ἄμμεινομ πράσσοιμι

God. To good fortune. Hippostratos asks Zeus Naios and Dione whether he would not do better if he became a shipowner?

Profit: no specific task
12. *SEG* 15.398; *BE* 1956: 143; *PAE* 1952: 301, 5; fourth century BCE

Θεός · τύχα ἀγαθά· ἐπερωτᾶ Λοχίσκος
τὰν Διώναν περὶ ἐργασίας εἰ κατὰ
θαλα . . . ζόμενος εὐτυχοῖ
καὶ βέλτιον πράσσοι

BE: E. thought it could be θάλα[τταν πλα]ζόμενος but there is only space for 2 or 3 letters, for the sense it needs: ἐργαζόμενος

God. Good fortune. Lochiskos asks Dione about work, if by sea . . . by [doing something] he would have good fortune and fare better?

13. *SEG* 23.475; *PAE* 1958: 104–2

Side A:
Θεός, τύχα · ἐρωτῇ Λυσίας τ-
ὸν θεὸν ἦ τυγχάνοι κα τᾶς θαλ-
λάσσας ἀντεχόμενος καὶ πε-
δέχων ναός

God. Fortune. Lysias asks the god whether he will do better by sticking with the sea and taking a share of a ship

Side B:
γῆ οὐθὲν δεῖ τελεῖν
You should do nothing by land

14. Parke 25; *SEG* 15.405a; *BE* 1956: 143; *PAE* 1952: 305, 21; fourth century BCE

Θεοί · τύχη ἀγαθή ·
Ἀρίζηλος ἐπανερωτᾷ τὸν θεὸν
ὅ τι δρῶν ἢ ποιῶν λῷον καὶ ἄμεινον
ἔσται αὐτῷ καὶ χρημάτων κτῆσις ἀγαθὴ ἔσται

Gods. Good fortune. Arizelos asks the god by doing or making what thing, if he will fare better and more well, and acquire good (acquisition of) property

15. *SGDI* 1560a; Karapanos 1878: pl. 37, 9

Ἐπερωτᾷ Κράτ[υλος Δία]
Νάον καὶ Διών[αν · αἴ ἐσ-]
τ(ι) α(ὐ)τοῖ οι ΜΡΗΑΦΙ [. . ὄναιον]
καὶ ὠφέ(λιμον) [καὶ τοῦ ἐ-]
(π)ιόν[τος] κ(α)ὶ [ἐς τὸν]
ἄπ[α](ν)[τα] (χρ)[όνον]

Kratylos asks Zeus Naios and Dione if there is for him... useful and profitable, both in the near future and for all time?

16. Parke (1967a: 16); *SGDI* 1575; Karapanos 1878: pl. 35, 2a

[Θεός. Τύχαν ἀγαθάν. Τῶι Δὶ τῶι Ναΐ]ωι καὶ τᾶι Διώναι Σωκράτης ἐπικοι-[νῆται,
ἦ. . . . .] ἐργαζόμενος λώϊον καὶ ἄμεινον
[πράσσοι καὶ νῦν καὶ τοῦ εἰσιόντ]ος καὶ αὑτῶι καὶ γενεᾶι

God. Good Fortune. Sokrates asks Zeus Naios and Dione whether... by working, he will fare better both now and in the future, both for himself and his descendants

Service
17. Christidis; 340–320 BCE

Θεός τύχαι ἀγαθᾶι καὶ Διὶ Προνάωι καὶ Διώναι· Πόρινος
Κυμαῖος Εὐάνδρου εἰρωτᾶ τὸν θεὸν εἰ τὸν ξατράπην
καὶ ὕπαρχον θεραπεύοντ[ι] λώιον καὶ ἄμεινον ἔσται

God. To good fortune and Zeus Pronaios and Dione. Porinos of Kymae, son of Euandros, asks the god if he would do well if he served the Satrap and Hyparch

For other tablets relating to work, see also:

Travel 1: *SEG* 43.335; Dakaris, Christidis, Vokotopoulou 1993: 58; M-4; archaic Korinthian alphabet; 550–525 BCE

Travel 12: *BE* 1996: 226, 11; *SEG* 43.328; Vokotopoulou 1992: no. 11; 330–320 BCE; M-122; *PAE* 1967: 48–9, 4; *BE* 1969: 348

Travel 15: *SEG* 24.454b; *BE* 1968: 318; Parke (1967c: 133(2)); fourth to third century BCE

Travel 18: *SGDI* 1561c; Karapanos 1878: pl. 35; reverse of plate

Travel 20: *SEG* 15.387; *PAE* 1952: 301/2, 7

Travel 24: *SEG* 15.394; *BE* 1956: 143; *PAE* 1952: 300–1, 4; fifth to fourth century BCE

Slavery

Most of these questions are from the unpublished material, and were kindly supplied to me by Professor Christidis. They include questions by both slaves and masters and, for the most part, concern a slave's freedom, particularly the question of obligations following manumission. There are also less coherent questions that concern a court case (11); 'about the price of a slave' (10) and 'some kind of servant' (9).[18] What kinds of slaves are present at Dodona is not clear from the questions: for example, were they public slaves, perhaps locally employed, or domestic slaves who had arrived with their owners at the sanctuary? Tablet 12, which may be a response from the oracle, suggests that they might be χωρὶς οἰκοῦντες (the editors suggest that Δίχα οἰκέσιος is a west Greek equivalent for this phrase). These were privately owned 'slaves who lived apart', living and working outside the home of their owner, often in a workshop set up with their owner's capital, and paying their owners all or some of what they earned. Some of these slaves enjoyed a high level of freedom, even of income, and it does not seem inconceivable that they might make their way to Dodona, even if it meant travelling quite a distance.[19]

In question 5 an unnamed slave asks about freedom from his master, specifically about continuing in service after manumission (παραμονή); question 1 also includes the phrase, περὶ ἐλευθερίας and so its protagonist may have had the same intent, and it may be the inquiry of a slave (the name Ἄνθρōπος certainly suggests that this is so). Kittos in question 6 asks if he will obtain the freedom that his master Dionysios has promised him. The questions of these slaves, in contrast with those asked by their fellow free inquirers, tend to be formulated in terms of 'Whether *x* will happen' ('... or not', understood); Will it be something good? (7); 'Will Kittos get the freedom from Dionysios that Dionysios promised him?' (6). The exception to this is Leuka's question (3), which uses the comparative, 'Whether Leuka would do better if she stays put?' This seems to suggest that, unless they were consulting about breaking the law, these slaves came to the oracle not to find out how best to craft a route between several possible options, but merely to find out from the god what fate (and their masters) held in store for them.

Those consultants who intend to run away are, on the whole, quite straightforward about their plans, making no attempt to conceal them. It is not difficult to imagine the motivations behind these questions, but to find them asked at an established oracle implies that the gods could be asked to sanction acts which pitted slave against citizen. This raises questions about the kinds of situations in which it could have been considered culturally legitimate for a slave to seek to escape from his or her owner,[20] perhaps when the slave had been ill-treated, for example, but there is no evidence for this from the questions themselves. And it was not just the slaves who were contemplating illegal action. The person who asked question 8 wanted to re-enslave an individual who had been freed. It may provide another example of the god being asked to sanction what was probably an illegal action—although, again, there may have been mitigating circumstances.

We may have some idea of how the oracle reacted to such questions: the phrases either side of question 4 could be construed as a question by a slave about his possible fortune if he ran away ('what will happen if I leave?') and a response. The grammar of the question implies that it was asked by a man, although it is always possible that this is an inaccuracy of the inscription. The oracle's answer, if that is what it is, is succinct. It seems to say 'the woman stays', but $\mu\acute{\epsilon}\nu\epsilon$ may be an imperative, in which case it says something like, 'the woman, stay!' If the consultant was a man, this might refer to a partner; if a woman, perhaps this should be read as an order not to leave. As noted above, tablet 12 may provide another example of a response.

In the unpublished material, Professor Christidis told me there are many questions that come under this category, posed by both slaves and masters. The theme of $\pi\alpha\rho\alpha\mu\text{o}\nu\acute{\eta}$ is common. There is also a question about runaway slaves ($\phi\epsilon\acute{\upsilon}\gamma\text{o}\nu\tau\epsilon\varsigma$) and a couple of questions where the master is interested in the price he will get in the context of manumission. In addition, there are a number of questions about ransoms, which are likely to be connected to relatives who have been captured in war and enslaved.

Questions by slaves
1. Christidis; 450 BCE

$\text{Ἄ}\nu\theta\rho\bar{\text{o}}\pi[\text{o}\varsigma]$
$[\pi]\epsilon\rho\grave{\iota}\ \grave{\epsilon}\lambda\epsilon\upsilon[\theta\epsilon\rho\acute{\iota}\alpha\varsigma$

Anthropos, about freedom

2. Christidis; 420–400 BCE

Θεὸς τύχα ἀγαθά
Ραζία ἐπέθετο
αἰ διαλλαγὰ μέλλει
γενέσθαι ἀπο Τει
τύκō ζόοντος
καὶ ἀποχώρησ⟨ις⟩.

God, good fortune. Razia asks whether she will attain an agreement from Teitukos while he lives and a place of safety?

3. Christidis; 420–400 BCE

Λε
ύκα πότερα με[ί]
[ν]ασα ἢ βέντιον εἴη

Whether Leuka would do better if she stays put?

4. *SEG* 15.389; *PAE* (1952: 303, 10); Korinthian letters; fifth century BCE; A and B could be construed as a question and a response.

Side A:
ἦ ἰϝὼν τυνχάνω

What will happen to me if I leave?/Shall I make it happen?

Side B:
ἁ γυνὰ
μένε

The woman remains/O woman stay!

5. Christidis; 375–350 BCE

[- - -]ν ἐπερωτῆ τὸν θεὸν τί κα ποι
[έων] περὶ ἐλευθερίας ἔστι αὐτῶι
[παραμο]νὰ πὰρ τὸν δεσπότα

... asks the god what he should do about his freedom and whether he will gain *paramone* from his master?

6. Christidis; 350 BCE

Κίττωι εἰ ἐστὶ ἡ ἐλευ
[θ]ερία ἡ παρὰ Διονυσίου
ἣν οὖν ἔθετ' αὐτῶι
Διονύσιος

Will Kittos get the freedom from Dionysios that Dionysios promised him?

7. *PAE* 1931: 89–91, 3; fourth to third century BCE

Ἠ απιοῦσα ἄλλ[ο] τι μοι αγαθον
ἐσσειται
Διοι . . . τ . τκ .

Whether, by leaving, there will be something else that is good for me, Zeus. . . ?

Questions by masters

8. Christidis; 475–450 BCE

Ἐ ἀμδόλō
μα μὲ ἄγσō
ΠΑ [- - -]

Whether I should re-enslave *PA*

(Taking Christidis' suggestion that ἀμδόλōμα is a mistake for ἀναδουλοῦμαι, I re-enslave)

9. Christidis; 420–380 BCE

[- - -] . . . . Α Υ . . . [- - -]
καλαπαίδω[ν]

. . . of a servant

10. Christidis; 400–375 BCE

Θεὸς τύχαν ἀ[γαθάν· περὶ ἀνθρ]
ώπου τιμᾶς

God. Good fortune. About the price of a slave

11. Christidis; 350–330 BCE

Τοῦ ἀνδραπόδου {ου} τὰν δίκαν δικα
ξοῦμαι Σκιδάρκας ὦκα τού[τ]αν

Shall I, Skidarkas, proceed quickly with this private legal case of the enslaved captive?

(This seems to be about a man who had been illegally enslaved. This was a serious crime in Athens, at least, and a range of procedures were available against it: see Din. 1.23; Lys. 23.9–10; cf. Todd 1993: 187)

Possible response

12. *BE* 1998: 202; *Poikila Epigraphika* no. 3; M-163; beginning of fourth century BCE

Δίχα οἰκέσιος

Slaves living apart

For other tablets relating to slavery, see also Parke 26; *SEG* 15.385; *BE* 1956: 143; *PAE* 1952: 298–300; fifth century BCE (listed in this catalogue under Crime: Kidnapping 1).

Health/Disease

The majority of these questions concern which god(s) the consultant should pray to (e.g., question 1: τίνι θεῶν θύουσα) in order either to be released from sickness (νόσου or νοσήματος, for example 1, 2, and 3) or to retain his/her health (ὑγιεία for example, 4, 5); or both (3). A number of these inquiries are made on behalf of others: question 6 is a request for health on behalf of the consultant, his father and brothers; the consultant of question 7 makes a longer-term inquiry both for himself and for his descendants; and question 9 appears to be about the (male) consultant's son.

Questions 1 and 2 are both inquiries by women: questions 5 and 8 give no indications of the gender of the consultant; the rest of the questions are by men. Among the more general references to disease or health, the eyes occur explicitly in two of these questions (8 and 10), and the foot (a supplement in the text) of a child is mentioned in question 9. Professor Christidis told me that in the unpublished material there are further questions specifically related to the eyes, and also to hearing, skin disease, tumour, jaundice, and paralysis. There is also apparently a question about what we might call a mental or emotional state—περὶ ἀθυμίας—but at the time of writing no more is known.

One final point: question 6 appears to have been answered—and the response is intriguing. The question asks to which god the consultant should sacrifice in order to gain health for himself and various members of his family. But the god's answer appears to be a directive to travel. It is possible, of course, that this is actually a fragment from, or an answer to, another question. It may also be that the text, if complete, included information about a particular god or sanctuary that the consultant should visit. Even so, it suggests that sometimes the answers from the oracle did not simply comprise 'yes' or 'no' or the name of a god, nor, perhaps, were they predictable.

Disease
1. Karapanos 1878: pl. 35; side B

[Ἐπερωτᾷ . . . .]α τίνι θεῶν θύουσα
[καὶ εὐχομένα ἄμεινον] πράσσοι καὶ τᾶς νόσου
[ἀπαλλαχθειή]

She asks by sacrificing and praying to which of the gods would she do better and be released from this disease?

2. Parke 15; *SGDI* 1561b (put together from two separate tablets, cf. Children); Karapanos 1878: pl. 38

Ἱστορεῖ Νικοκράτ[ει]α τίνι θεῶν θύουσα
λώιον καὶ ἄμεινον πράσσοι καὶ τᾶς νόσου
παύσα⟨ι⟩το

Nikokrateia asks by sacrificing to which of the gods would she do better and be relieved of her disease?

Health

3. Parke 13; fourth to third century BCE

Θεός . τύχα . ἱστορεῖ Λεόντιος περὶ τοῦ υἱοῦ
Λέοντος ἦ ἔσσεται ὑγεία τοῦ νοσήματος τοῦ ἐπιμ . . . του ὅ λάζεταί νιν

God. Luck. Leontios asks about his son Leon, whether he will be healthy and (cured) of the disease which has gripped him?

And on the back: Λεοντίνου Π Ε

Of Leontinos

4. *SGDI* 1566a; Doric dialect

[Ἐπικοινῆται . . . .] ασσχ .
[Δὶ καὶ Διώναι, τί]νι κα θεῶ-
[ν ἢ δαιμόνων ἢ ἡρ]ώων εὐχ[ό -]
[μενος καὶ θύων] ὑγιὴς εἴη

l. 1 Hoffman: [Ἀν]άσσχ[ετος]

He asks . . . by praying and sacrificing to Zeus and Dione and to which of the gods or *daimons* or heroes might he be healthy?

5. *SGDI* 1577a

[τύχ]αν [ἀ]γαθάν. [Ἐ](ρ)[ω]τῆ . . . . .
ὑγιε[ίας]

Good fortune. He/she asks. . . about health

6. *SGDI* 1587a and b

Side A:
Θεό[ς· Τύ]χα ἀγα-
θά· Ἐρ[ωτ]εῖ Ἀντίο -
χο[ς τὸ]ν Δί(α) καὶ τὰν
Διών[α]ν ὑπὲρ ὑγι -
είας [α]ὐτοῦ καὶ πα-

τρὸς καὶ ἀδελφ -
ᾶς· τ[ί]να θεῶν
ἢ ἡρ[ώω]ν τιμᾶν-
τι λ[ώ]ϊον καὶ ἄ -
μεινον εἴη

God. Good Fortune. Antiochos asks Zeus and Dione about his health and that of his father and brother. By honouring which of the gods or heroes will he be better?

Side B:
Εἰς Ἑρμι
όνα
ὁρμά
σα
⟨α⟩ντι·

To/for him setting off to Hermione (probably a response)

Kekule and Winnefeld (1909: 41) note that Demeter Thermasia had a sanctuary at Hermione

7. Parke 12; SGDI 1564; Karapanos 1878: pl. 36, 5

[ἐπικοινῆται Σωκράτ -]
(η)ς Ἀμβρακιάτ[ας]
Διὶ< Νάωι καὶ Δη [ώναι]
Περὶ ὑγιείας αὐτοῦ [καὶ]
τῶν ὑπαρχόντων
καὶ εἰς τὸν ἔπειτα [χρ -]
όνον, τίνας θεῶν [ἱ -]
λασκόμενος λώϊον
καὶ ἄμεινον πρά[σσοι].

Sokrates, from Ambrakia, asks Zeus Naios and Dione about his health, both current matters and into the future. By appeasing which of the gods will he fare better?

Specific parts of the body

8. *PAE* 1973: 96, 4; fourth to third century BCE

περὶ τῶν ὀφθαλ -
μῶν

About the eyes

9. *SGDI* 1588; Karapanos 1878: pl. 37, 8

Ἐπερωτεῖ Ἀμύντας
Δ[ία Νά]ϊον καὶ Διώναν·

ἦ λώϊον καὶ ἄμει-
[νον το]ῦ παιδὸς
[πόδα] παγάσασθαι

l. 5 Karapanos: . . . . . . .ἀγάσασθαι (?)

Amyntas asks Zeus Naios and Dione whether it would be advantageous to [verb uncertain] his child's foot?

10. Parke 14

Θ]ρασύβουλος τίνι κα θεῶν θύσ[ας]
καὶ ηιλαξάμενος τὸς ὀπτίλ[ος]
ὑγιέστερος γένοιτο;

Thrasyboulos (asks) by having sacrificed to and appeased which of the gods, would I become healthier with regard to his eye?

For other tablets relating to health/disease, see also Work 17: Christidis; 340–320 BCE (if θεραπεύοντ[ι] indicates 'cure' rather than 'serve' or 'attendance on').

Property

In this category I have included three questions which contain, as an introductory phrase περὶ πανπασίας (questions 1, 2, and 3), which I take to mean property of all types (a phrase that is also found in question 5 of the Travel category, in which the consultant is asking whether or not he should move to Kroton). Question 1 mentions property as part of a general request to prosper in all areas of life. The second two questions are too fragmentary to supply much beyond this, although question 2 seems to have received an answer, which gives us some idea of the question's formulation, at least. The response comprises directions for making libations, including a list of gods and heroes, which makes it likely that the consultant asked the oracle to whom he should make sacrifice in order to achieve his desires.

The rest of the questions in this category focus on specific aspects of property. Question 4 appears to be a consultation about the advisability of living in a newly built, or another, house. The following four questions are all concerned with the wisdom of specific real estate ventures: question 6 about purchasing a house and land in the city; question 7 seems to be about whether it is a good idea to sell a property to one Aristophantos; and question 8 is about buying a particular pond. These all seem to be questions by the consultant in his own interest, but Alkinoos asks on behalf of someone else (5): 'Would it be better and more good for Nikeas to build a workshop?'

The majority of the questions are demonstrably written by men. Four include their names in their question (2, 3, 5, 7); the others mention a wife (1) or use masculine forms of participles to describe their actions (4, 6, 8).

Requests concerning *panpasia*

1. Parke 3; *Ep. Chron.* (1935: 253, 10); never folded; irregular grammar; fifth century BCE

περὶ πανπασίο αὐτοῦ
καὶ γενεᾶς καὶ γυναικὸ-
ς τίνι θεῶν εὐχόμενος
πράσσοιμι ἀγαθάν

About all my property, my children and my wife's, by praying to which god would he fare well?

2. *SEG* 15.391c; *BE* 1956: 143, 22; *PAE* 1952: 305, 22; fifth century BCE

Side A:
Δᾶμυς περὶ παμπ[ασίας --]
ε...ν----------------
περὶ γαεν--------------

l. 1 Damys, about all my property

Side B:
Θεὸς . Διὶ πατροίωι περὶ . . . ιο
Τύχαι λοιβὰν
Ἡρακλεῖ Ἐρεχθε⟨ῖ⟩
Ἀθάναι Πατρόια[ι]

On the back of the tablet on the left; possibly a response and something to do with libations:
God ... to Zeus the father, concerning ... to Fortune a libation, to Herakles Erechtheis, to Athena Patroa (of our homeland)

3. *Ep. Chron.* 1935: 254, 11; fourth century BCE

Θεός· τύχα ἀγαθά· ἐπ-
ιστορεῖ Γλαυκίας τὸν Διώναν περὶ πανπασίας ἦ ἐστι. . . .
τε καὶ περὶ ανοσκαια. . .

God. Good fortune. Glaukias asks Dione about possessions, whether it is ...
And about [...]

Housing

4. *SGDI* 1569a

[Θεός· τύχαν ἀγ]αθάν. Πότερα τυνχ[άνοιμι τὰν]
[νεωστὶ οἰκοδο](μ)ητὰν ἢ ἄλλαν οἴκησ[ιν ἔχων]

God. Good luck. Whether I will meet with advantage by having the structure recently built, or by another dwelling

Business ventures

5. Parke 21; fourth century BCE

Θεός. Τύχη. ἐπικοινῆται Ἀλκίνοος τῶι
Διὶ τῶι Ναίωι καὶ τᾶι Διώναι εἰ λ[ώιον]
καὶ ἄμεινον Νικέαι κατασκευάζ[ειν]
τὸ ἐργαστήριον

God. Fortune. Alkinoos asks Zeus Naios and Dione if it will be to the advantage of Nikeas to build the workshop?

6. Parke 20; *SGDI* 1573; Karapanos 1878: pl. 37, 1

Ἦ αὐτὸς πεπαμένος τὰν ἐ(μ) πόλι οἰκίαν καὶ τὸ χωρί-
ον βέλτιομ μοι κ' εἴη καὶ πολυωφελέ(σ)τε(ρ)ον.

Whether, by having acquired the house in the city and the piece of land, it would be better for me and more profitable?

7. *SGDI* 1581; Karapanos 1878: pl. 37, 7

[Θεός . Ἐπι]κοινῆ[ται Θέμις τῶι]
[Διὶ τῶ]ι Ναίωι κ[αὶ τᾶι Διώναι · ἦ]
κα (λ)ώ(ϊ)ο(ν) Θέμι ἔ(σ)[ται καὶ ἄμεινον]
τὸ ἀνώγεον, τ[ὸ ἔδωκε Ἀριστοφ -]
άντωι, ἀπ(ο)δ[όμεν . . .]
. . . (ὕ)στερον δ[ὲ μή]

God. Themis asks Zeus Naios and Dione whether it will be better for him to return the rope, which he gave to Aristophantos . . . later or not at all?

8. *SEG* 19.432; *PAE* 1955: 172, b

ἦ τὸ λίμνιον τὸ πὰρ τὸ Δαμάτριον πριάμενος πράξω τι
ἀγαθὸν κὰτ τοῦτον Φ Ρ Ε Λ . Σ ⟨ Ι Ι

Whether by buying the marsh by the Damatrion [temple of Demeter?] I will do a good thing and this . . .

See also Travel 5: *SEG* 43.325; Vokotopoulou 1992: no. 8; *Ep. Chron.* 1935; M-47; *c.* 400 BCE.

Prosperity/Safety

The first and last questions in this category concern how to 'do better and more well' as an end in itself. The first consultant (the participles suggest he is male) limits his inquiry to this, without relating it to any specific area of life. Question 6 posed by one Euandros on behalf of himself and his anonymous wife makes the same inquiry, but in much more detail. As with many of the oracle questions, he sets up his question using the formula that is often found opening city decrees Θε(ο)ί. Τύχαν ἀγαθάν ('Gods; Good Luck'), and suggests a range of supernatural personnel to whom he is willing to make sacrifice. He seeks prosperity not just now, but καὶ νῦν καὶ ἰς τὸν ἅπαντα χρόνον that is, 'both now and for all time'. The unpublished material apparently contains a range of similar questions about how to ensure prosperity, often phrased as 'Which god should I pray to in order that . . . ?'

Questions 3 and 4 explicitly concern σωτηρία or ἀσφάλεια ('safety' or 'security'). Question 3 offers little beyond this. In contrast, question 4, which appears to have been written by a trader anxious for his ship, is much more detailed. The consultant, Archephon, had apparently been to consult the god on a previous occasion: the ship he owns was made in accordance with Apollo's previous instruction. Tablet 5 appears to be a response of some kind, denying the possibility of safety, although there will be good business.

Professor Christidis told me that in the unpublished material ἀσφάλεια or σωτηρία are popular subjects for questions. Often they provide little indication of the particular danger involved, but a number were clearly written by people concerned about the state of family members who had been taken prisoner.

1. *SEG* 15.395; *BE* 1956: 143; *PAE* 1952: 303, 13; fifth to fourth century BCE

[τ]ίνι κα θεῶι εὐ-
χόμενος καὶ θύ-
ων βέλτιον πράσ-
σοι;

To which god should he pray and sacrifice so that his fortunes might improve?

2. *SEG* 15.402; *PAE* 1952: 303, 14; ὕστερον (third line) is in Korinthian letters; fourth century BCE

[Θε]ὸς . τύχα . [ἦ] ἐπιμ . . νάσας
λῶον καὶ ἄμινον πράσοιμ-
ι αὐτίκα καὶ ἰς τὸν ὕστερον χρόνον;

God . . . Luck . . . whether . . . would I do better and more well, now and into the future?

3. *PAE* 1967: 49, 5; *BE* 1969: 348, 5; fourth century BCE

[Ζεῦ Νάϊε καὶ Διώνα να]ῖα Θέμι καὶ Ἀπολλ[ον - - -]
[- - - σωτ]ηρίας καὶ τύχας ἀ - - -

Zeus Naios and Dione Naia and Themis and Apollo ... of safety and of fortune ...

4. *PAE* 1967: 50, 7; *BE* 1969: 348, 7; third century BCE

Ὠ Ζεῦ καὶ Θέμι καὶ Διώνα Νάϊοι | Ἀρχεφῶν
τὰν νᾶ | ἂν ἐναυπαγησατο⟨ν⟩, κελο-
μένο το Ἀπόλλωνος, ἔχω κατὰ χώραν · καὶ σωτηρία μοι ἔσσεται καὶ ἐμὶν
καὶ τᾶι ναΐ, αἰκα καὶ τὰ χρέα ἀποδ(ώ)σω

να = Dorian form of ναῦν

Zeus and Themis and Zeus Naios, I, Archephon have the ship in place, built according to the order of Apollo. Will there be safety for me and the ship, and will I pay back what is needed?

5. *BE* 1984: 231–3; *PAE* 1982: 29; bronze tile; response of the oracle; fourth century BCE

οὐκ ἐστι ἀσφάλεια ἀλλ'ἀπωλέωντι πάντα

It is not safe but for the man destroying everything

6. Parke 1; *SGDI* 1582a; Karapanos 1878: pl. 34, 3

Θε(ο)ί. Τύχαν ἀγαθάν. Ἐπικοινῆται Εὔβαν-
δρος καὶ ἁ γυνὰ τῶι Διεὶ τῶι Νάωι καὶ τᾶι Διώναι, τίνι κα θεῶν ἢ ἡρώων ἢ δαιμόνων
εὐχόμενοι καὶ φύοντες λώϊον καὶ ἄμεινο-
ν πράσσοιεν καὶ αὐτοὶ καὶ ἁ οἴκησις καὶ νῦν
καὶ ἰς τὸν ἄπαντα χρόνον

Gods. Good luck. Eu[b?]andros and his wife ask Zeus Naios and Dione by praying to which of the gods or heroes or daimons and sacrificing will they and their household do better both now and for all time.

For other tablets relating to prosperity/safety, see also:

Travel 12: *BE* 1996: 226, 11; *SEG* 43.328; Vokotopoulou 1992: no. 11; 330–320 BCE; M-122; *PAE* 1967: 48–9, 4; *BE* 1969: 348
Women 15: *SGDI* 1568b
Women 16: *Ep. Chron.* 1935: 260, 36b

Ritual activity

The text of question 1 is fragmentary to the point of non-existence, but the accompanying drawing on the tablet may have a magical implication, which could imply that the consultant was asking 'to which of the gods' he should pray in order to have a child. Question 2 asks about hiring one Dorios, a ψυχαγωγός or spirit-raiser, one of the men or women, already discussed, who travelled from place to place offering supernatural services. It looks as if this could be about a situation facing a group of people, perhaps a community, and this brings to mind stories of other communities that are reported to have hired such characters. *Psychagōgoi* start appearing in literature in the fifth century, although they are described as being active in late seventh/early sixth-century events.[21] Their primary activity seems to have been to lay angry ghosts who were causing trouble for communities or individuals, but some may also have been involved in ritual activity designed to harm.[22] Again, on the back of this tablet, there is what seems to be an abbreviated reference to the question.

Question 3 is extremely brief: the editors suggest that this is a new ritual term, related to τριθῦται found on another tablet (unpublished, M-1098 in the Ioannina museum). They associate this with a triple sacrifice known in Attika as τρίττοια or τρίττοα βόαρχος.[23]

See also the mention of a curse in Judicial Activity 2; and there are a number of questions that may be about supernatural ways of doing harm (depending on the translation of *pharmakon* as something involving supernatural activity or simply as poison) in Past/Present: Crime: Murder.

1. Christidis, Dakaris, Vokotopoulou (C–D–V) 1999: no. 2; M-269; second quarter fifth century BCE; Under line 2 there is a drawing that resembles the so-called 'clé sur la matrice' (the womb together with a key), which is found on later Graeco-Egyptian intaglios. C–D–V suggest that it may be related to a φυσικλείδον ('key to the vagina'), a much later spell intended to unlock the womb. Here it may be intended as a 'magical reinforcement' of the question being asked.

- - - - - - - - - - - - - - - - - - - -
[- - - - - - -]ας πὲρ [- - - - - -]
[θεῶν τίν]ι εὐχό[μενος - -]
- - - - - - - - - - - - - - - - - - - -

l. 3 Praying to which of the gods?

2. Christidis, Dakaris, Vokotopoulou 1999: no. 5; *BE* 1938: 153; *Ep. Chron.* 1935: 257, 23; fourth century BCE C–D–V: *c.*420–410 BCE

[- - -Διὶ] τῶι Νάωι καὶ τᾶι Διώναι· ἦ μὴ χρηῦνται Δωρίωι τῶ[ι] ψυχαγωγῶι;

To Zeus Naios and Dione, whether or not they should hire Dorios the spirit-raiser?

On the outer side of the question the name Dorios apparently recurs in an abbreviated form: Δώρι(–).

3. *BE* 1998: 202; *Poikila Epigraphika*: no. 1; *SEG* 1997, 819; M-89b; beginning of fourth century BCE

Ἡ τριθυτικόν

Whether (to make) the triple sacrifice?

For other tablets relating to ritual activity, see also:

Future Concerns: Judicial Activity 2: C–D–V 1999: no.3; M-186; mid-fourth century BCE

Past/Present Concerns: Crime 7: C–D–V 1999: no. 1; M-257; very early fourth century BCE

Crime 8: C–D–V 1999: no. 4; M-433; *c*.340–320 BCE

Military campaigns

There are two questions in this category. The second asks whether 'it would be better and more good' for the consultant to set off on an expedition against Antiochos, possibly, but by no means certainly, King Antiochos I, who ruled the Seleucid empire *c*.281–261 BCE.

The first question asks whether the inquirer should campaign by land: the consultant could be asking about whether the expedition should happen at all or whether he should join an existing land expedition. Since the other side of the tablet contains a response from the oracle to 'stay on land', it is most likely that he was asking about the route for the campaign. Professor Christidis noted that there are a number of questions regarding mercenary service in the unpublished material.

1. *BE* 1998: 202; *Poikila Epigraphika*: no. 2; *SEG* 47.820; M-96; first quarter of fourth century

Side A:
Στρατεύομαι
κατὰ γᾶι

Shall I go by land?

Side B:
Ἐπὶ γῆι σχέθε | τέλεος

Stay on land: completely (on the back, possibly a response)

2. *SEG* 15.407; *BE* 1956: 143; *PAE* 1952: 304, 15; fourth to third century BCE

Ἀγαθὴ Τύχη· ἐπερωτᾷ Ἀργει . λ [Δί]α Νᾶον καὶ Διώναν
εἰ λῷον καὶ ἄμεινον ειτονι ἀνελθόντα στρατεύ-
εσθαι ἐπ' Ἀντίοχον

SEG: l. 2. ἔσται

Good Fortune. He [Argei . . . ?] asks Zeus Naios and Dione whether it is advantageous to set off on campaign against Antiochos?

Judicial activity

There are two inquiries in this category. The first question seems to concern a court case against a neighbour and/or over a dwelling place. The inquiry specifically mentions victory. Although this is an example of a question genre given by Plutarch in *Moralia* 386c, this explicit request to win is rare among the published questions. The second, difficult to read, seems to concern the advisability of going to court (l. 3 δικαζόμ[ενος]) and, if one accepts the translation of ἐπάρασιος as something to do with a curse, is about how a curse would affect the outcome of a court case (and so I have also listed it under the category Ritual Activity).[24] Professor Christidis reported that in the unpublished material there are also questions about who will win a court case; whether or not to go to court; and arbitration, including conciliation (δίαιτα and ὁμόνοια).

1. *SEG* 15.391a; *BE* 1956: 143, 22; *PAE* 1952: 305, 22; fifth century BCE

BE: It is difficult to decipher, but without doubt has something to do with a judicial situation.

Θεός · τύχα · Διαι ται ικ
εὐμενος νικε ὑπὲρ τοῦ χο
εου τοῦ Ἀριστογειτοσα
πεδοιοχι τὸς ἀντιδίκος
καὶ τὰς Ϝοικίας

God. Fortune. If he beseeches Zeus for victory on behalf of . . . the judicial opponents and the households

2. Christidis, Dakaris, Vokotopoulou 1999: no. 3; M-186; mid-fourth century BCE

Ἐπικοινῆται Σώσανδρος [πὲρ]
τᾶς ἐπαράσιος τᾶς Ἀλε [max. 4]
ἦ τυγχάνοι "μι"* κα δικαζομ[ενος;]

  * The μι appears to have been added by the writer after that line of text was completed. The editors observe that the τ of τυγχάνοι has two verticals.

Sosandros asks about the curse of Ale ... whether I would do well if I went to court?

For other tablets relating to judicial activity, see also Slavery: Questions by Masters, 11.

City affairs and politics

The first question in this section asks about the advantages of citizenship both now 'and into the future'. I have also included references to four questions in other categories, which appear to show their protagonists paying attention to details of their citizen status (see Women 6 and Travel 11, 14, and 17, respectively); see discussions under the relevant categories. Professor Christidis told me that in the unpublished material there are a number of questions about taking up citizenship in another city.[25] There are also questions asking whether the protagonist is going to be selected as θεωρός. This word can indicate the title of a magistrate, and sometimes the envoy sent to consult an oracle; the precise meaning in these texts is not clear.[26]

Although the second tablet is fragmentary beyond reading, I have included it here because of its mention of Arybbas (side B, l. 2), which appears to have been a name in the Molossian royal family.[27] The subject matter of the consultation seems to have been stated at the beginning of the question, in the usual περί clause, but unfortunately is broken off mid-way, leaving us to speculate about what the second word might have been.

1. *SGDI* 1589; Karapanos 1878: pl. 35, 3

Ἠ αἰτέωμαι *T A N I*
πολιτείαν ἐπὶ ταύτὶ
ἢ τοῦ εἰσιόντος

Shall I request citizenship this year or next?

2. *SEG* 23.476; *PAE* (1958: 104, no. 3)

Side A:
περὶ ὑποσυγι- - - -πηωνεωμλ (?)

About ... (unclear)

Side B (possibly a response?):
οὗτος δὲ εἰμὴ πέμπω
ποτ' Ἀρύββαν, ἀλλ' αὐτεῖ μένη - - -

But if I do not send to Arybbas, but it stays here ...

For other tablets relating to city affairs, see also:

Travel 17: *BE* 1996: 226, 13; *SEG* 43.330; Vokotopoulou 1992: no. 13; M-46; early third century BCE

Travel 11: *SEG* 43.326; Vokotopoulou 1992; no. 9; *Ep. Chron.* 1935; M-1052; 340–330 BCE

Travel 14: *BE* 1969: 348, 6; *PAE* 1967: 33–54, 6; fourth century BCE

Women 6: *SEG* 24.454a; Parke 1967c: 133(1); *BE* (1968: 318); fourth to third century BCE

See also Work 17: Christidis; 340–320 BCE (if θεραπεύοντ[ι] indicates 'attendance on' rather than 'serve' or 'cure')

Past/Present concerns

Crime

Most of the questions dealing with events from the past are concerned with crimes—and most of these are direct questions about stolen property, asking for confirmation of a suspect's guilt. There are some exceptions: question 1 offers a number of suspects, and it is possible that this is a description of a gang; while in another (4), the question is aimed at establishing the fact of foul play, but no suspect is named. Objects mentioned as stolen include: silver, wool, blankets and pillows, clothing, and possibly, Parke suggests of question 5, a horse.[28] Professor Christidis told me that in the unpublished material, sacred property is also mentioned.

Under the subheading Murder, questions 7 and 8 inquire about responsibility for the past application of what may be natural or unnatural ways of doing harm.[28] Question 10 is fragmentary and hard to make sense of, but seems to be about somebody that has died (τέθνακε). Professor Christidis told me that in the unpublished material there are a number of questions about murders. As with stolen property, these are usually concerned with identifying the perpetrator (ὁ αἴτιος).

Kidnapping

1. Parke 26; *SEG* 15.385; *BE* 1956: 143; *PAE* 1952: 298–300; fifth century BCE

[Θ]εός · τύχα ἀγαθά · -οὐκ ἀνδρ⟨α⟩ποδίξατο Ἀρχωνίδας
τὰν Ἀριστοκλέος ἄοζον οὐδὲ Ἀρχέβιος ὁ Ἀρχωνίδα υ-
ἰὸς οὐδὲ Σώσανδρος ὁ Ἀρχωνίδα δοῦλος τόκα ἐὼν
ἢ τᾶς γυναικός;

God. Good fortune. Did not Archonidas enslave the son of Aristokles, and Archebios the son of Archonidas and Sosandros who was then the slave of Archonidas or of his wife?

Stolen/lost property

2. *SEG* 15.400; *BE* 1956: 143; *PAE* 1952: 303, 11; fourth century BCE

Βοστρύχα ἁ Δόρκωνος ηδυκε κι [. . . . ἀ] -
ργύριον τὸ Δίων ἀπώλεσε ξ . . . .
τοῖς νῦν Ἀκτίοις, ὦ Ζεῦ Νᾶε κ[αὶ Δίωνα - -]

Seems to be asking about Bostrycha, the (wife) of Dorkos (l. 1 Βοστρύχα ἁ Δόρκωνος) and something to do with the silver which Dion lost (ll. 1–2 ἀ]-ργύριον τὸ Δίων ἀπώλεσε) ... Something is said about Aktion, and the question ends with an invocation of Zeus Naios and Dione (l. 3 τοῖς νῦν Ἀκτίοις, ὦ Ζεῦ Νᾶε κ[αὶ Δίωνα - -])

3. *Ep. Chron.* 1935: 259, 32; fourth to third century BCE

ἔκλεψε Θωπίων τὸ ἀργύριον;
Did Thopion steal the silver?

4. Parke 27; *SGDI* 1586; Karapanos 1878: pl. 36, 1

Ἐρωτεῖ Ἆγις Δία Νάον [καὶ Διώναν]
ὑπὲρ τῶν στρωμάτων κ[αὶ τῶν προσ -]
κεφαλαίων, τὰ ἀπώλολ[ε . . . . ,]
ἦ τῶν ἔξωθέν τις ἀνέκ[λεψεν]

Agis asks Zeus Naios and Dione about the coverings and pillows which he lost, whether someome from outside stole them?

5. Parke 28; *SEG* 19.428; *PAE* 1955: 171, c

Ἀγαθᾶι τύχαι · ἐπικοινῆται Σάτυρος τῶι Διὶ τῶι Ναίωι
καὶ τᾶι Διώναι οὐκ ἀνεθέθη ὁ Σατύρου Σκύθος. ἐν Ἐλέαι
ἂν τὸν κέλητα τὸν Δωριλάου ὁ καὶ Ἀκτίου ἀπέτιλε

Good fortune. Satyros asks Zeus Naios and Dione whether, if Satyros' Skythian (horse) was not packed up, in Elea he would have 'plucked the hair off' the horse of Dorilaos, alias Aktios?[30]

6. Parke 29; *SEG* 19.429; *PAE* 1955: 171, d

ἔκλεψε Δορκίλος τὸ λᾶκος·
Did Dorkilos steal the cloth?

7. *BE* 1962: 173–4; *BCH* 1960: 751; fourth century BCE

Side A:
. . . ηπιστος (
ἄν ἔκλεψε τὰ ἔρια
ἀπο τοῦ κλισμοῦ τὰ αὖα

FIG. 4. Oracle question tablet from Dodona: Someone called Pistos is named in the first line—he may be asking the question or be the subjet of the question, which is 'if he stole the dry fleeces from the couch' (fourth century BCE) © G. G. Garvey/The Ancient Art & Architecture Collection

(l. 1) Perhaps name 'Pistos'; (l. 2) If he stole the dry fleeces from the couch?

Side B:

... περὶ τῶν λύκων τῶν θηρίων

... about the wild wolves

Murder

8. Christidis, Dakaris, Vokotopoulou 1999: no. 1; M-257; very early fourth century

Ἐπήνεικε φάρμακον
ἐπὶ τὰγ γενεὰν τὰν ἐ⟨μ -⟩
ἀν ἢ ἐπὶ τὰγ γυναῖκα [ἢ ἐ -]
π'ἐμὲ παρὰ Λύσωνος;

Did he (or she) introduce a poison (or potion) to my children, or to my wife or to me from Lyson?

9. Christidis, Dakaris, Vokotopoulou 1999: no. 4; M-433; Evangelidis 1929: 126, no. 5, fig. 15; *c.*340–320 BCE

Κατεφάρμαξε
Τιμώι Ἀριστο-
βούλαν;

Evangelidis: l. 2 Τίμων ?

Did Timo bewitch/poison Aristoboula?

10. *Ep. Chron.* 1935: 259, 29

ἦ τέθνακε

Whether he died

11. *SEG* 15.406; *PAE* 1952: 305–6, 23; fourth century BCE

Θεός · τύχα ·

Λυκόφρων . ἀτεκανο
αμυλαντοτανασριγγα κι
ε παι τιωντι καὶ . . . . πλαγᾶς
τᾶς Λυκόφρονος τέθνακε

Christidis: l. 4 ἐπαιτιων from ἐπαιτιος

Something to do with Lykophron (l. 2) and mortal blows that he delivered (πλαγᾶς τᾶς Λυκόφρονος τέθνακε).

Requests for truth

There are two questions in which the consultants seem to be asking to be told the truth, along with a related fragmentary and puzzling question that seems to concern wrongdoing in an oracle consultation. On the basis of Hoffman's translation, it appears to be an inquiry about a previous oracle consultation made by one Aristolaos apparently on someone else's behalf, which the consultant had expected Aristolaos to bring back sealed. The current consultant, a man called Sokrates, suspects that the previous consultation has been somehow perverted on the orders of a certain Sosias.

1. *SGDI* 1575b; Karapanos 1878: pl. 35, 2

. . . ιοι καὶ ἄμα τι λέγομες
. . . . [ἄ]μες γνῶμεν τὸ ἀλαθές

(l. 1) . . . at the same time what we say; (l. 2) . . . we know the truth

2. Karapanos 1878: pl. 35, 6

[τῷ πι]στεύοντι τί ἀ[λ]αθές

. . . he is believing something true

Wrongdoing in an oracle consultation

1. *SGDI* 1578; Karapanos 1878: 38, 2

[Θεός . Τύχα ἀγαθά · Ἐπικοινῆται Σωκράτης]
[τῶι Διὶ Νάωι καὶ τᾶι Διώναι περὶ τᾶς τοῦ]
[θεοῦ ὑποκρί]σιος καὶ τῶν σαμηῶν, τὰν Ἀρ(ι)σ -
[τόλαος οὐκ ἐ]σαμάνατο οὐδ'ἐπανέθετο · αἰ Σ -
[ωσίας ἐλθὼν ἐ]ς Δωδώναν περὶ τοῦ πινακίου
[τὸν Ἀριστό]λαον ἐκελήσατο οὐδε τεχνᾶ -
[σθαι σαμῆα οὐδ]ὲ γραφθῆμεν καὶ σαμανθῆμεν.

God . . . Good fortune. Sokrates asks Zeus Naios and Dione about the response of the god and the omens, which Aristolaos did not seal and did not set down. If Sosias having come to Dodona about the tablet, ordered Aristolaos not to produce it, and that the omens were not to be written down and not to be sealed.[31]

Treasure

SEG 15.408a; BE 1956: 143; PAE 1952: 304, 16; fourth to third century BCE

Ἀγ[α]σίων ὑπὲ⟨ρ⟩ τοῦ θησαυροῦ
ἢ λανομαι φανον

Agasion about the treasure . . .

The meaning of λανομαι is unclear, but enough of the question remains to suggest that this was an enquiry about the whereabouts of hidden treasure.

Children

Parke 11; SGDI 1565a; Karapanos 1878: pl. 36, 2; Doric dialect; second century BCE

Ἐρωτῆ Λυσα-
νίας Δία Νάον
καὶ Δηώνα(ν) · ἢ οὐ-
κ ἐστὶ ἐξ αὐτοῦ
ΘΙ τὸ παιδάριον
ὃ Ἀννύλα κυεῖ

Karapanos: At the beginning of the fifth line, is a sign that could be taken for an ithyphallic symbol, or it might be nothing more than the two letters *oi* written by mistake and then rubbed out.

Lysanias asked Zeus Naos and Dione whether the child with which Annyla is pregnant is not from him?

There is a further question concerning the paternity of children born outside wedlock in the unpublished material.[32]

For other tablets relating to children, see also Future concerns: Children above.

Health/Disease

Christidis; 340–330 BCE

Αἰ ⟨κ⟩α Φιλίσστας ἀξίωτο νοσέματος

If Philistas deserved his disease

The consultant seems to have been asking if an individual was deserving of his or her affliction, although the full meaning of the question is difficult to decipher.

For other tablets relating to health/disease, see also Future concerns: Health/Disease, above.

Death

SGDI 1569b; Karapanos 1878: pl. 36, 4

Λυσίας Δαμολ(ά)[ω περὶ του . . .
Πασία σάματος . . . .
αἰ πόμπα τιὰ[. . . . .

Possibly asked by Lysias (l.1), the question is something to do with a body (l. 2 σάματος) and burial (l. 3 πόμπα)

FORMULAE OF INQUIRY

What I have in mind

1. SGDI 1580; Karapanos 1878: pl. 36, 6

Ἠ συμπείθον[τι]
αὐτῶι ὑπὲρ [το -]
ὖ πράγματος, ὅ[ν -]
τινά κα τρόπο[ν
[φα]ίν[η]ται (δ)[ό -]
κιμον, βέλτιο[ν]
καὶ ἄμεινον
Πυστακίωνι (ἐ) -
σσεῖται

Whether it will be advantageous for Pystakion, if he acts as a joint advocate of this matter, in whatever way seems reliable?

2. *Ep. Chron.* 1935: 258, 25; fifth century BCE

ἦ καιαγκα αὐτὸ -
ς ἐπὶ γνώμαι ἔχ -
ηι καὶ χρήηι

Whether . . . what he has on his mind (l. 2–3 αὐτὸς ἐπὶ γνώμαι ἔχηι) you also foretell as an oracle (l. 3 καὶ χρήηι)

3. Parke 4; SEG 15.386; BE 1956: 143; PAE 1952: 301, 6; beginning of the fifth century BCE

τίνι κα θεὸν εὐξάμενος πράξαι
ἁ ἐπὶ νόοι ἔχε;

To which of the gods must he have prayed so as to achieve what he has in mind?

Demands for oracles

1. *SGDI* 1558; Thessalian dialect; Karapanos 1878: pl. 35, 5; Ionian lettering

[τό](δ)ε τὸ μαντήϊον ἐγὼ χρήω
κὲ αλάες

I want an oracle on the following subject: Whether I am on the wrong track?[33]

2. Christidis; 450–425 BCE

Ἒ ἀλλê μαντεύ[εσθαι]

Whether to seek an oracle consultation elsewhere

Prayers

1. *SGDI* 1597; Karapanos 1878: pl. 38, 7; Attic dialect

Ζεῦ Νάϊε [καὶ Διώνη αἰτεῖ ὑμᾶς καὶ
ἱκετεύει Ἐ[τεοκλ](ῆ)s αὐτῶι κ[αὶ τῆι γενε-]
âι, δοῦναι ε[ὐχὰs] αὐτῶι Ἐ[τεοκλ]εῖ καὶ τῶι]
ἑ[α](υτ)οῦ (υ)ἱεῖ κ[αὶ] τοῖs αὐτοῦ (ἐ)[κγ -]
ό[νοιs ἄ]πασι[ν] . . . .

Karapanos:

Ζεῦ Νάϊε [καὶ Διώνη αἰτεῖ ὑμᾶs καὶ
ἱκετεύει Γ . . . . [κ] -
âι, δοῦναι ε[μαυτῶ . . . . [καὶ]
θ[υγατρὶ καὶ] πᾶσι . . . .

(At the end of the fourth line of the tablet, the inscription is hidden by a fragment of another lead tablet, as if a larger tablet had been wrapped around the smaller one. On the smaller fragment can be read twice the word αὐτῶι, 'to him', and also τοῖs αὐτοῦ γ[ονεῦσι, 'to his children'. It looks as if the larger tablet held the question while the smaller tablet held the answers. This is one of three such examples mentioned by Karapanos.)

O Zeus Naios and Dione, Eteokles asks you and beseeches both for himself and his children, to grant his prayers, and those of his son and of all his grandchildren . . .

2. Parke 2; *SGDI* 1596; Karapanos 1878: pl. 38, 3; Attic dialect

[Θεόs . Τύχη] ἀγαθή
Δέσποτα, ἄναξ, Ζεῦ Νάϊε καὶ Διώνη
καὶ Δωδωναῖοι, αἰτεῖ ὑμαs
καὶ ἱκετεύει Διόγνητος Ἀριστομή -
δου Ἀθηναῖοs δοῦναι αὐτῶι

καὶ τοῖς ἑαυτοῦ ἐ(κ)[γό]νοις ἅπασιν
καὶ τεῖ μητρὶ Κλεαρέτει και

God. Good fortune. O lord and master, Zeus Naios, and Dione, and Dodonaeans, Diognetos, the son of Aristomedes, of Athens, asks and beseeches you to give to him and to all his grandchildren and to his mother Klearete and . . . .[34]

RESPONSES FROM THE ORACLE

Most of the possible responses have been discussed within the relevant category. A few remain: the first, a response to one Leton, is concerned with a disintegrating relationship (μὴ διαπιστεύοντι, 'not putting full confidence in . . .') with someone from Thourioi, the Greek colony in southern Italy, founded in 444/3 (τῷ Θουρίῳ, 'the Thourion') or a dative of location, in or to Thourioi.[35] Vokotopoulou suggested that this is a response, in which case, the phrase λώϊον καὶ ἄ[μεινον may indicate the structure of the original question. However, it also could indicate that this is a question, especially considering that the majority of the other responses are so brief in comparison. The second entry is a possible visual response, as suggested by Karapanos.

1. *BE* 1996: 226, 7; *SEG* 43.324; Vokotopoulou 1992: no. 7; *PAE* 1932; M-413; 330–320 BCE

Λήτωνι λώϊον καὶ ἄ[μεινον - -]
μὴ διαπιστεύοντι ἀ[- -]
τῷ Θουρίῳ πόκα ἔθη [- -]

For Leton, it was advantageous . . . not having confidence . . .in the man from Thourioi when he placed . . .

2. Karapanos 1878: pl. 37, 6. Includes some letters scrubbed out and the head of a serpent.

See also (discussed in the relevant section):

Travel 5: *SEG* 43.325; Vokotopoulou 1992: no. 8; *Ep. Chron.* 1935; M-47; *c.*400 BCE
Travel 22: *Ep. Chron.* 1935: 259, 35; fifth century BCE
Woman 20: *BE* 1998: 202; *Poikila Epigraphika*: no. 4; M-189; Doric; mid-fourth century BCE
Work 13: *SEG* 23. 475; *PAE* 1958: 104, 2
Slavery 4: *SEG* 15. 389; *PAE* 1952: 303, 10; Korinthian letters; side B; fifth century BCE
Slavery 12: *BE* 1998: 202; *Poikila Epigraphika*: no. 3; M-163; beginning of fourth century BCE
Health/Disease 6: *SGDI* 1587b

Property 2: *SEG* 15.391c; *BE* 1956: 143, 22; *PAE* 1952: 305, 22; fifth century BCE

Prosperity/Safety 4: *PAE* 1967: 50, 7; *BE* 1969: 348, 7; third century BCE

Prosperity/Safety 5: *BE* 1984: 231–3; *PAE* 1982: 29; bronze tile; response of the oracle; fourth century BCE

Military Campaigns 1: *BE* 1998: 202; *Poikila Epigraphika*: no. 2; *SEG* 47.820; M-96; first quarter of fourth century

City affairs and politics 2: *SEG* 23.476; *PAE* 1958: 104, 3

Fragmentary 9: Karapanos 1878: pl. 37, Ib

FRAGMENTS

1. *SGDI* 1564b; Doric dialect
2. *SGDI* 1572a
3. *SGDI* 1574a
4. *SGDI* 1574b, c
5. *SGDI* 1579
6. *SGDI* 1582b; Doric
7. *SGDI* 1584; Karapanos 1878: pl. 36, 3; Doric
8. *SGDI* 1585a
9. Karapanos 1878: pl. 37, Ib
10. *Ep. Chron.* 1935: 256, 18a
11. *Ep. Chron.* 1935: 259, 33; fifth century BCE
12. *SEG* 15.388; *BE* 1956: 143; *PAE* 1952: 302, 8; fifth century BCE
13. *SEG* 15.390; *PAE* 1952: 305, 20; fifth century BCE
14. *SEG* 15.392; *PAE* 1952: 306, 26; fifth century BCE
15. *SEG* 15.404; *PAE* 1952: 304, 19; fourth century BCE
16. *SEG* 15.408b; *BE* 1956: 143; *PAE* 1952: 304, 16; fourth to third century BCE
17. *SEG* 15.409; *PAE* 1952: 306, 25
18. *SEG* 19.430; *PAE* 1955: 172 e
19. *SEG* 43.322; *c.*350 BCE; inscription on side A
20. *SEG* 43.324; *BE* 1996: 226, 7; Vokotopoulou 1992: no. 7; *PAE* 1932; M-413; 330–320 BCE
21. *PAE* 1932; Vokotopoulou 1992: no. 5; M-818; first quarter of the fourth century BCE
22. *PAE* 1952: 302/3, 9b; *BE* 1956: 43, 9; fourth century BCE
23. *PAE* 1952: 303, 12
24. *PAE* 1952: 306, 25
25. *PAE* 1967: 48–9, 3
26. *PAE* 1973: 94–96, 3; fourth century BCE
27. Christidis, Dakaris, Vokotopoulou 1999: no. 2; M-269; second quarter fifth century BCE
28. Christidis; 410–400 BCE : Πὲρ σ / ōμά / τōν Π / ενεσ / τ[ôν

6

Oracles and Daily Life

> As both my Zulu diviners told me after, to be sure, some very recondite discourse: 'Spend some money on your fellowman and don't forget to call home.'
>
> Fernandez 1991: 220[1]

Collecting the published tablets in one catalogue provides an overview of the patterns underlying individual consultation at Dodona. In the previous chapter the tablets were grouped by category and discussed in detail. This chapter will discuss four themes relevant to the catalogue of curses as a whole: the subject matter and timing of the questions; the identities of those who visited the oracle; the language and behaviour of inquiry; and, finally, how these tablets deepen our understanding of the use of oracles by individuals between the sixth and first centuries BCE, including the evidence provided by responses.

SUBJECT MATTER AND TIMING

Clarity is seldom the most salient characteristic of these tablets. Often it is difficult or even impossible to decipher what they contain. This may be because of the state of the tablet or inscription, or it may be a result of the way the question is expressed: the subject matter left mysterious, the phrasing oblique, and the vocabulary unguessable. I have done my best to provide translations, but in many cases, these must remain uncertain. Those tablets whose contents have proved largely impenetrable can be found under 'Fragments'.

Among the others, I have identified 16 question topics, a number of which I have further divided into subcategories. These categories are not wholly mine: many of the questions themselves start with an indication of the general area of concern—so uniform in some cases that one wonders if it indicates official terminology, or some form of filing system in use at the oracle. For example, we find questions about children beginning περὶ + γενεᾶς, that is, 'about descendants', or questions about wives that start περὶ + γυναικός, 'about a woman', while general property concerns often begin περὶ παμπασίας. Amongst the questions on work we find the phrase περὶ ἐργασίας, while in travel matters the consultant sometimes asks περί followed by the intent of the consultant with reference to the journey (for example, περὶ ϝοικέσιος and περὶ τᾶς οἰκήσις, 'about a place to dwell'; or περὶ τᾶς ὁρμᾶς, 'about a voyage'). Where a consultant has been this clear about his or her subject matter, I have used his or her own categorization. In most cases, the questions found on the tablets cover areas of life that are also indicated as being subjects for consultation in literary sources.[2]

The categories of consultation in order of size are as follows: Future concerns: Travel (28 questions), followed by questions about Women (20), Children (18), Work (17), then Slavery (12), Health/Disease (10), Property (8), Prosperity/Safety (6), Ritual activity (3), Military campaigns (2), Judicial activity (2), City affairs and politics (2). Past/present: Crimes (11), Requests for truth (2), Treasure (1), Children (1), Health/Disease (1), Death (1) and Wrongdoing in an oracle consultation (1).[3] Professor Christidis told me that he had also found the following categories of questions among the unpublished tablets: (i) Competitions, in which the questions are usually about whether the individual will win a victory in the games (an inquiry as to whether it will be ἀκονιτί, 'without an effort', occurs three times; questions about αὐλός, 'flute' contests also occur); (ii) religious matters, which includes questions concerning priesthoods, for example, 'Are we going to get the priesthood of . . . ?'; what it would be appropriate to dedicate; the nature of sacrifices; and the cutting of trees in sacred places, such as in a *heroon* (in one case, concerning a sacred wild olive, the oracle supplies a negative answer); and inheritance, details of which were not clear for Professor Christidis at the time of our communication.

After the subject categories, I have included a number of questions grouped and arranged according to their formulae of inquiry. These include three questions in which the consultant conceals the subject matter of his question, referring to it only as 'What I have in mind'; two questions in which there is a demand made for an oracle; and two questions that are structured like prayers.

In what follows, I shall refer to the tablets by this catalogue system, using the name of the category, and subcategory where appropriate, followed by its number. Within the categories, I have listed the questions by date first (if it is known) and then by the date of its source, with the oldest that I have found first. Questions that appear on the reverse of a tablet with a question that has already been listed have been given a separate entry. If the reverse of the tablet carries what seems to be a reference to the original question or a response from the oracle I have not given them a separate entry in the catalogue, but left them as part of the original question.[4] The responses to the oracle are all listed under a separate heading.

These category headings might at first suggest a simple division of concerns, but, in fact, this is far from the case. For a start, each category represents a range of daily circumstances, while many of the tablets, for all their apparent brevity, contain a wealth of detail that illuminates specific anxieties that afflicted individuals. As an example, consider the kinds of questions that appear in the category of Travel. An individual might simply ask about the journey he is planning: one question we possess simply asks περὶ τᾶς ὁρμᾶς, literally, 'about the journey'. Alternatively, he might ask about how he should make the journey, should it be, as one question puts it, κατὰ χώραν, that is, 'by land'.[5] He might name the general area to which he is thinking of going or pinpoint the actual town.[6] He might say both where and how he is travelling, or he might include details of what he intends to do when he reaches his destination.[7] He might ask just about himself or (although rarely in the extant material) he might include his hopes for his family.[8] Or consider the contents of Women 6 in which one Isodamos asks if he will profit by taking a wife, having children who will look after him in his old age, moving to Athens, and living as a citizen among the Athenians: this tablet could be filed under any of, at least, four categories (e.g. Women, Children, Travel, or City Affairs).

The detail of and difficulty of interpreting these tablets means that these categories should be regarded, not as a strict taxonomy, but as a heuristic device intended to prompt our thinking about which areas of life people came to consult about at Dodona. When a tablet might fit under several different category headings I have listed it according to what seems to be its main emphasis, and cross-referenced it under other category headings. Particular overlaps between certain categories stand out: for example between some of the questions in the categories Women and Children, and between the categories Travel and Work. Of course, it is dangerous to draw any conclusions from the number of questions we find in each category: although it would be satisfying to build a more nuanced picture of risks and their relative importance from the distribution of questions, the nature of the evidence and the subjectivity involved in categorizing it makes this impossible. However, bearing this in mind, it is still striking how many of the questions across the different categories are concerned, at some level, with travel, usually by sea.

Turning to the timing of questions, although all the questions deal with matters that are unseen, not all of them are about the future. Consultants also asked the oracle about events that had already occurred, or that were current but hidden from them (see under Past/Present Concerns). I have divided the categories into Future Concerns and Past/Present Concerns: certain categories of questions are all about future events, for example, the published questions about travel or property; others (e.g. crime) are all concerned with past events. Two categories, Children and Health/Disease, include questions in both time categories. The questions in the additional subject categories that Christidis has supplied (Competitions, Religious Matters, Inheritance) are, he told me, concerned with what will happen in the future, rather than asking about past events. The timeframe of questions about mental states and dowries (noted in the discussions of the categories Health/Disease and Women respectively) were not clear to Christidis at the time of our correspondence.

THE IDENTITIES OF THE CONSULTANTS

Before we start exploring the subject matter of the questions, are there some more general observations we can make about the people who asked them? From among this welter of crumbling lead tablets, whose are the voices we hear and what kind of people does this corpus of ancient material represent?

Let us start with a brief consideration of where the consultants come from. Across the tablets, only a handful of tablets give information about origins. Three consultants come from relatively nearby: two (Deinokles is one, but the other remains anonymous) state that they came from the Corinthian colony of Apollonia;[9] one, a certain Sokrates, is an Ambrakiot. Three demonstrate Dodona's contacts with south Italy and Sicily: Nikomachos is from the colony of Herakleia and asks about registering himself in Herakleia's mother-city, Taras; Archias comes from Metapontion—nothing remains of his question, only the inscription on the outside of the tablet, with his name and origin, survives; a third, one Agelochos, has come all the way from Ergetion from the interior of Sicily; Porinos from Kymai writes a very elegant hand. Finally, there is an impassioned plea from Diognetos, an Athenian.

For some further assistance, we can turn first to the language of the tablets themselves. These are overwhelmingly in Greek, although the level of literacy varies enormously. Different dialects are in evidence: Attic, Ionian, Doric, and Thessalian, but nothing that we can identify as Illyrian.[10] Among some tribes in Epiros, Greek appears to have been an official language: the Thesprotians and the royal family of the Molossians seem to have spoken Greek; by the fourth century official documents are written in Greek, and they list officials with Greek names. As for Dodona itself, it seems to have been regarded by Herodotos as Greek-speaking.[11] In his story of the oracle's foundation, as we have seen, the priestesses learned to speak Greek: in fact, until they learned it, they twittered like birds.

As for the majority of the population, Hammond argues that Greek had been spoken in this area since the Middle Bronze Age.[12] But, perhaps the oracle tablets themselves are our best evidence, since they show individuals, involved in a wide range of activities, which place them across the sociopolitical (and geographical) spectrum, all writing in Greek. This still leaves open the question of an exact origin for each consultant: for example, the use of Doric Greek on a tablet might indicate the presence of a Corinthian colonist from one of the coastal *poleis*, or a local person whose family had always spoken this language, or one who had learned a new dialect.[13]

It is hard to know how much weight to put on names as indications of origin, considering how frequently people travelled, especially between west Greece, Sicily, and Magna Graecia. However, tracing the names that appear in the questions about women and questions about children provides some insights. For example, there are a number of names that only occur in the corpus of Dodona question tablets, including Thorakis, Geris, Kretaia, Mudra; the provenance of some names, for example Philotas, may even suggest attachment to a particular tribe. Other names suggest an Adriatic connection, for example, Aigle and Boukolos seem to have been names common in south Italy. Herakleidas, Nike, and Onasimos also appear to be names relatively common to this area.[14] Once all the tablets are published, a fuller examination of all names might help to build a more complete picture of patterns of consultation.

There are a number of tablets where the Greek is incomprehensible. The explanation for these may be that their writers were not literate, or were not Greek speakers. The same possible dual explanations may cover those few tablets that contain nonsense texts (so-called 'abecedaria') or have pictures scratched on them, in place of words.[15] This, in turn, might suggest that what was written on a question tablet was also communicated to the oracle verbally. Alternatively, perhaps it was generally accepted that the god would simply comprehend the consultant's question, whatever form it took. Unfortunately, in addition to those tablets that are incomprehensible, there are many tablets that are either too brief or too fragmentary to tell us anything about the person who wrote them. I have listed these at the end of the catalogue. Those writers must remain anonymous: only this expression of their anxieties survives.

As for those tablets that do supply more ample information, many simply state the name of the consultant: in the category of Travel, Ariston's inquiry to the oracle reads 'Ariston asks Zeus Naios and Dione whether it is better and more good for me and if I will be able to sail to Syrakuse, to the colony, later?'[16] so it is clear that this is Ariston's own concern. In others, we have to work with pronouns (αὐτοῦ or αὐτῷ) or verb forms to identify the gender of the inquirer. For example, in a question that simply asks 'to which god should he pray to so that his fortunes might improve?' the form of the verb to pray tells us the (male) gender of the nameless consultant.[17]

In sum, this evidence shows that the majority of consultants were men involved in, or contemplating, many different activities, with a range of concerns on their minds. It is obviously impossible to make definitive assessments of their social position or character, but with a few of the texts it is hard to avoid speculating about the nature of the consultant or his state of mind. The anxiety of the consultants is most obvious in those tablets that lapse into pleading vocatives (see the subcategory 'Prayers' in the section Formulae of Inquiry). More individually, the neat, grammatical inscription, careful vocabulary, and comprehensive information given by Porinos in Work 17, contrasts strongly with the wild grammar and spelling of most of the tablets.

The fact that most of our tablets were written by men is not a great surprise: the constricted lives of women in certain parts of ancient Greek society, especially Athens, is much discussed. However, it appears that women in Epiros, at least in the fourth to first centuries BCE, may not have endured the kinds of limitations that we expect when we draw on the traditional Athenian model. Inscriptions from the area, including records of manumissions from Bouthrotos and awards of citizenship from Dodona, show women either acting alone or taking a surprisingly prominent role in legal activities, and being recognized for their civic contribution.[18] This is not to suggest that such freedoms were society-wide, or that they imply a total equality with men. Nevertheless, the material intimates that although social conventions would likely have meant fewer women at the oracle, and limited the areas of life that they might ask about, the presence of single women at Dodona, asking questions on their own and others' behalf, is not wholly surprising. In some examples, couples attended together: for example, Eu[b]andros, who came to Dodona to find out how to ensure he and his household would do well forever and ever (the Greek is καὶ ἰs τὸν ἅπαντα χρόνον—that is, literally, 'and into all time') is an exception. He starts his question 'Eu[b]andros and his woman/wife ask . . .'.[19]

In the published and readable material, we can definitely identify seven women who posed questions to the oracle about their own concerns, although we do not know all their names.[20] Four of them are concerned with disease or sickness. Nikokrateia came to find out how she could do better and, more specifically, how to put a stop to her disease.[21] Like many of the people who presented questions to the oracle, she wants to know 'to which god she should make sacrifice' in order that these things might happen. A similar question is asked by an anonymous woman whose gender we know from the feminine form of the verbs that she uses. The gender of the consultant asking whether or not Philistas deserves the sickness he is suffering is not clear: it may have been Philistas who asked, it may have been someone else who posed the question on his behalf. This idea that somehow disease is deserved or at least brought upon oneself is also apparent in some of the questions asked by communities.[22]

The next two women whose names we know introduce us to an unexpected constituency of oracle visitors: Razia and Leuka are both slave women. It is hard to imagine that slaves would have the opportunity to visit the oracle, but the questions give us clues that suggest specific situations. For example, Razia looks for separation from her master and asks about her chances of leaving him while he is still alive.[23] It sounds as if she had already been manumitted and was looking for an end to her obligations when she consulted the oracle.[24] Leuka, in contrast, appears to be asking, 'if it would be better for her to stay'—suggesting that she was contemplating running away. As we shall see, this was often on slaves' minds when they came to the oracle. It is a surprising avenue of inquiry: individuals are seeking divine sanction for what was, essentially, an illegal action. Here may be historical examples of this strange genre of question, which we have already seen in the literary sources. On the other hand, Christidis argued instead that Leuka was probably concerned to remain long enough to fulfil her obligations to her master after manumission.

The same explanation may work for similar questions asked by two other anonymous slave women, also contemplating the advantages (or not) of leaving their masters. One can be translated: 'If I leave, will I find some other thing that is good?' The other, more difficult to make sense of, seems to say, either 'What will happen to me if I leave?' or 'Shall I make it happen?', but it rewards its reader with what appears to be a clear and concise answer from the oracle itself. The apparent response is: either, 'the woman remains' or 'O woman, stay!' The other answers (or tablets that seem to be answers) tend to be similarly pithy.[25]

The last question that we know was asked by a woman is about her chances of having children, preceded by a phrase that may mean 'if she dedicates to another', although it is not clear what other thing is meant here.[26] We do not know the woman's name because of the way the tablet has broken. But this combination of gender and concern is rare: among the published questions that were asked about children, this is the only one asked by a woman (although Christidis reported more among the unpublished tablets). It is surprising, because the number of questions posed to the oracle on this matter by men does suggest that it was an area of considerable concern.

THE LANGUAGE AND BEHAVIOUR OF INQUIRY

Exploring the ways in which they asked their questions helps us to understand the way consultants thought about the risks ahead: what kind of divine guidance they sought, what this indicates about their understanding of their relationship with the gods and its potency in different parts of their lives, and their perception of their own autonomy.

On the whole, when they came to consult the oracle ancient Greek men and women did not come with general questions about the course of their lives, hoping for glimpses of their future; nor did they ask about areas of their life that did not contain options, such as growing food; nor did they ask open-ended questions, for example 'What shall I do?', which would allow almost any response. Instead most questions they asked comprised two closely related formulae. First of all, there are closed requests for information, in which the context of the question is very specific. Possible answers are limited by the structure of the question itself, which is one that essentially asks, '*x* or *y*?' or '*x* or not?' For example, 'Did Thopion steal the silver (or not)?' asks one anonymous consultant, while another (probably female) asks about children 'Will there be children for me, if I consult the oracle?'[27]

Even more common are questions that combine this structure with an inquiry about good fortune. In these questions, the commonest opening phrase is 'Will it be better and more good if . . .' often introduced by 'whether' or 'if'. For example, 'If I pray to such and such a god?' or 'If I take this woman to be my wife?' or 'If I travel to this destination' or '. . . buy that piece of land'. Obviously, in response a simple yes or no will suffice. For example, in the category of inquiries about travel, the location has, in the majority of cases, already been decided upon and the question shows the consultant inquiring about his likely destiny if he sets that choice in motion. In the category of inquiries about marriage, the questions are either formulated about the intent itself ('Is *x* a good idea or not?') or about a particular woman ('Is this a good one or not?').

More open requests for greater direction from the god only rarely appear in the published tablets, and even then I have my doubts that they are as open as they first appear. One is a question about stolen bedding and pillows, in which the protagonist asks if one of the outsiders (literally, 'one of those from outside') committed the crime.[28] The phrasing suggests to me that the person asking the question had a suspect in mind, and was asking the god for confirmation. The other is a question in which the consultant asks what he should do in order to do better and make a profit.[29] It appears to be a remarkably unfocused question, in which the consultant seems to have no particular plan for getting what he wants. This may be so, but this would make it a very rare question type indeed, at least among the published tablets. In fact, I suspect that it is an example of another typical question asked at the oracle, in which the consultant has a particular situation in mind when he asks his question, but does not write the details on the tablet. I have listed other examples of this kind in the catalogue.

The closest to an open question formula that this leaves is the frequently occurring phrase 'To which gods shall I sacrifice and pray, in order that . . . ?'. This is most often found in questions belonging to the categories Health/Disease, in which there are five questions phrased like this, and Children, in which there are five. There may be an additional question in this category; it is largely indecipherable, but includes the phrase 'to which god shall I pray. . .' alongside an image of a key, which may be a magical drawing, intended to prompt the unlocking of a woman's womb.[30] Among the other categories, there are two examples of this formula in the category about Prosperity/Safety, and a single example in the category about Property. This latter, although it does begin with the phrase περὶ παυπασίο, 'about belongings', goes on to ask explicitly how to ensure that the protagonist's family will flourish.[31]

The pattern of use of this phrase, appearing in certain categories, suggests that certain areas of life—the birth of children, continued good health, and prosperity—were considered to be more dependent on divine will than others. This is in line with evidence from ancient literature: for example, we have seen at the beginning of this book some of the tropes in ancient literature about the uncertainty of good fortune; while the medical writers themselves describe, and some espouse, traditional views about the role of the divine in healing.[32] The distribution of oracle tablets adds further evidence for the nature of traditional practice: in these mysterious and crucial areas of life, it was essential to keep the right gods on one's side.

By far the majority of the consultants at Dodona whose questions have been published asked about key decisions they were about to take. For the most part, they wanted to know the likely outcome of their current plan, hoping to ensure that, whatever action they finally took, it would edge them closer to good fortune. Consequently, they visited the oracle with a good idea of what they intended to do, and that comprised the substance of their question. To us it might seem a very limited approach: after all, given the opportunity to consult about the future, wouldn't most of us ask more probing questions?

In fact, comparative anthropological studies of divination suggest that such limited questions are typical.[33] One explanation for this approach among ancient oracles is that it provided the oracle with a way to manage consultants' expectations: 'Their service could only survive and retain credit at this practical level by setting limits to the suitable forms of a question and answer. The gods were prepared to consider a choice between alternatives, but if mortals asked for too much, they risked provoking a god's displeasure. . . . The god then could not be refuted. If he advised action and the result was disastrous, questioners were left to reflect that the alternative would have been much worse.'[34] Such an analysis certainly makes sense from our vantage, as we examine the behaviour of this culture through the long lens of time. It even makes sense as a description of the attitudes of those who managed the oracle—if we impute a certain level of cynicism to them. But how to make sense of that stricture from the point of view of those who believed in the vision of the oracle?

To start with, we might turn the explanation of advantage around. Certainly it served the oracle well if it need not deliver the impossible. But it also surely suited the consultants to have their needs so specifically served. After all, there were plenty of traditional stories about oracles which emphasized the ways in which their flair for future focus could seriously disrupt one's plans. Consider, for example, Herodotos' story of poor Battos, visiting the Delphic oracle to get some help with his stammer, and suddenly told he must found a colony.[35] An example of this kind of spontaneous response may exist among the Dodona tablets (side b of Health/Disease 6) where, in response to a question about which god the consultant should worship in order to gain health for himself, father, and brother, the oracle appears to instruct him to go to Hermion. Perhaps, as a consultant, it was important to try to limit, or at least manage, the involvement of the gods in your decision.

So, carefully planning one's questions might have been related to a fear of finding out too much, and/or allowing the gods too much room for creativity. But not only were inquiries restricted in this way, they were also restrained in the way they asked for a successful, final outcome. Of course, there are tablets on which we find specific requests, for example, for children or health, or profit. However, among all the published tablets, there is only one mention of victory. This occurs on a tablet that is difficult to read but appears to be about a court case against a neighbour and/or over a dwelling place.[36] Even in this instance, the consultant asks *about* victory, not for it.[37]

Moreover, it is striking how often the consultant clothes his desire for good fortune in vague and formulaic phrases about 'doing better and more well'. The most common phrase in this context is λώϊον καὶ ἄμεινον 'will it be better and more good if . . .', 'I pray to such and such a god?' . . . 'I take this woman to be my wife?' . . . 'I travel to this destination or buy that piece of land?' We also find the verbs τυγχάνω or εὐτυγχάνω (here in the sense 'to go right' rather than just 'happen'), or the adjectives ἀγαθόν (good) or βέλτιον (better). Superlative forms also occasionally appear: these are rare and tend to be in requests that in other ways appear to suggest strongly felt emotion. For example, in question 10 of the category Work, Timodamos begins his plea for guidance about his commercial plans by calling on Zeus, as if in prayer. He goes on to ask whether things will work out κράτιστα, the very best for him.³⁸ At the end of his request for a child, Anaxippos asks to which god he should pray in order that he might do λῶστα καὶ ἄριστα 'best and excellently'. The strength of emotion in this request is also suggested by the language in the rest of the tablet, for example, the poetic term used for 'male child', ἐρσεντέρας.³⁹ Aorist forms of verbs are used in inquiries about specific events such as birth or recovery from disease, while present tenses cover more long-term prosperity. Occasionally reference is made to the very long term, in such phrases as as [εἰς τὸ]ν ἔπ[ειτα χρόνον in Children 12 and καὶ ἰς τὸν ὕστερον χρόνον in Prosperity/Safety 2, but there does not seem to be any particular pattern to their use.

Perhaps the fear was not so much that you might ask for too much, and be punished for greed, but that you might be given what you want. Other writers suggest that it was important to be vague about good fortune precisely for this reason. Perhaps the answer lies in instructions we find in other writers about how one should address the gods, and why. Artemidoros, for example, who wrote a book about the interpretation of dreams in the second century CE, tells his readers to be careful both in the way one makes a request for dreams and in one's attitudes to the dreams that one has. It is crucial not to fixate on a particular thing or message in your hoped-for communication with the gods or, when you do receive a divine dream, you will probably misunderstand it.⁴⁰ Similar concerns, but explicitly about prayer, are found in Plato's *Alkibiades*, where it is explained that one might conceivably pray for a thing that one thought was good, but which, in fact, was bad.⁴¹ These warnings bring to mind the moralistic fables about oracles that we find scattered across ancient literature, especially liberally in Herodotos' *Histories*. In these stories the oracle tells the consultant a crucial truth, but the consultant is too blind—too fixated on his own goals—to understand the warning he has been given.

On the subject of specific requests, there are a small number of questions that ask directly (δοῦναι) for help and safety, and one example that asks for good fortune while the consultant works the land. However, these requests are also unusual because they are phrased like prayers, calling on Zeus and Dione with emotional, demanding vocatives. In those that request help, the consultants don't just ask, they beseech (ἱκετεύει).⁴²

In this context, a number of the questions asked by the slaves compare interestingly with those asked by their fellow, presumably free, inquirers. Rather than seeking to find out 'What is better and more advantageous?' they are phrased 'Whether *x* will happen?' ('... or not?' understood). The exceptions to this are those questions asked by slaves who are considering 'not staying'. This suggests that these slaves consulted the oracle to find out what lay ahead, rather than in order to discover what they should do. Apart from those cases where a slave was contemplating breaking the law, the limited forms and subjects of the slaves' questions seem to reflect the limits on their ability to make autonomous decisions.

As for the behaviour of inquiry: a number of tablets suggest that the person asking a question may sometimes have been consulting the oracle on another's behalf, particularly, it seems for a family member. There are a number of such questions concerning health: for example, in the fourth or third century, one Leontios came to ask about his son. After addressing the gods, his question begins 'Leontios asks about his son Leon, whether he will be free of his disease . . .'.[43] Similarly, Amyntas came to the oracle to find out about his child's foot.[44]

It is obvious why people might visit an oracle on behalf of those too sick or too young to come themselves, but such visits also happened in other circumstances. There is, for example, a question, difficult to read, about an oracle consultation that seems to have, somehow, gone wrong. This seems to be an inquiry about a previous oracle consultation made by one Aristolaos but for someone else, the answer to which Aristolaos was meant to bring back sealed. The current consultant, a man called Sokrates, suspects the previous consultation of having been perverted by the orders of a certain Sosias.[45] As well as providing an example of a consultation made on behalf of another (in fact, it could have been made on behalf of a group, since there seem to have been several parties interested in its response), it raises a number of other themes. First, it provides further support for the point that oracular responses were significant communications, otherwise, why bother to corrupt it or care if it was corrupted? Second, it is another example of an oracle being used to find out about hidden past events, rather than explore the likely outcomes of the future: Sokrates was attempting to get at the truth of what happened and trying to ascertain if his suspicions were correct. Finally, it gives us a brief but vivid glimpse of the intrigue and secrecy that must have surrounded some oracle consultations. As we will see, some of the questions asked of the god had potentially extremely serious consequences. It is no wonder that consultants might have wanted to keep the answers secret.

But it was not just the answers they concealed: in the section Formulae of Inquiry, I have collected a number of tablets in which the consultant refers to his concern with the oblique phrase 'what I have in mind' as if trying to keep the matter concealed, and I assume that this is because the god is thought to know what is going on. After all, as other questions show, the oracle was thought to be able to see what was hidden, past, present, and future. In the meantime, the evidence suggests that, although it was not common, it was acceptable to consult an oracle on another's behalf.

It was also possible to ask the oracle a series of questions: tablet 2 in the Demands for Oracles category may indicate that the consultant intends to visit another oracle for further instruction. Others seem to have chosen to return to Dodona for a series of instructions (as Timodamos in Work 10; and the consultant of tablet 4 in the category Prosperity). Alternatively, it might mean that the previous oracle was, in some way, not satisfactory (as seems to be the case in the situation described in the question categorized under Wrongdoing in an Oracle Consultation). Either way, these oracles add historical examples of second consultations of the same oracle to those we find in literature, for example, the second consultation of the Delphic oracle by the Athenians on the eve of the Persian invasion; or the Kymaeans' consultation of Didyma, about the suppliant Pactyes, and, of course, the second consultation that was urged by Sokrates on Xenophon.[46]

INDIVIDUAL USE OF ORACLES

It has been argued that oracles were used chiefly by city-states or other communities to sanction decisions that had already been made, and so to prevent indecision or conflict in a group. Is something similar true of individual oracular consultations? It is possible that for individuals, whose concerns often focus on basic structural factors of their lives, there could have been a need to justify certain decisions to their communities and/or families, and to themselves. Such group contexts are perhaps represented in some of the questions asked at Dodona, apparently on behalf of others (e.g. Health/Disease 3, 6, and 9; and in the question asked on behalf of several members of a family in Travel 5). There may be further evidence of this aspect of individual questioning at Delphi where a number of requests, while seeking divine approval, were also probably intended to ensure group consensus.[46] Consultants such as poets composing paeans, and priests who were anxious to obtain the god's approval about the placement of their altars, could also be described as seeking validation of their professional activity in the eyes of society. However, it is likely that any number of the inquiries made at Dodona were made by individuals who had no other party to persuade and did not seek to build consensus, but wanted to acquire a sense of certainty about particular situations for themselves alone.

Exploring this evidence can help us to move beyond the broad descriptions found in ancient and modern literature that ascribe to oracles a simple role of resolving uncertainty and offering general reassurance to consultants. This material not only provides further information about the place and role of oracles in Greek society, but also gives a rare view of ancient Greek culture from the level of ordinary individuals, as they confront an unknown future and deal with the risks they perceive. It provides sufficient detail to illuminate for us both the circumstances that demanded an oracular consultation, and how individuals approached these events: at what point in their decision-making process they sought divine guidance and what kind of help they wanted; what they considered to be their responsibility and what part of a decision they allocated to the god.

Examining and cataloguing these tablets has illuminated how people used the oracle in different ways to frame and manage the uncertainty inherent in everyday life. For example, as well as questions directly about the future, they might ask about hidden past or present events whose future impact was less immediate, for example, about the paternity of a child or the identity of a criminal. They might ask for instructions about how to do better, and thus gain a sort of blanket coverage for future action or, if they had embarked on a course comprising a number of key decisions, they might use the oracle serially, to check each decision as it came up. Both examples of the latter concern seafaring and this, along with the number of questions concerning travel and commerce by sea (both in the category Travel and across the rest of the catalogue), may indicate that this was an activity that raised particular anxiety.[48]

THE RESPONSES

The individual responses are discussed, in detail, under each category, and I have also discussed some of the literary evidence for the oracle's method of response in Chapter 4. The records of the oracle's responses are brief and concise (sometimes to the point of impenetrability as far as the modern reader is concerned). However, they do not consist simply of a single word — for example, 'yes', 'no', the name of a god or a destination — so even if the method of consultation was by lot, these answers suggest that there was some attempt to create a more elaborate response. That the inquiry was simply conducted by lot is made less likely by one, unpredictable response: as noted, in Health/Disease 6 the consultant asks which god he should worship in order to gain health for himself, father, and brother. In reply (side B), the oracle appears to instruct him to go to Hermion.

Of course, as noted, we have no idea how these answers were given: it is possible that they are short notes of longer answers, taken down by oracle officials or by the consultants themselves. Although none of the texts seems to offer traces of poetry, and the literary evidence suggests a prose format, the possibility still remains that the answers were given in verse.

7

Curses!

> These . . . lines of approach lead to the final goal . . . This goal is, briefly, to grasp the native's point of view, his relation to life, to realize *his* vision of *his* world.
>
> Malinowski 1922: 25

*Being thrown out of Anthemion's tavern was the last straw. Philistas wrapped his cloak around him and sat in a doorway to nurse his pride and contemplate his next move. This bustling city was surely full of opportunities for a man of his mantic talents. Look at Lampon and Diopeithes—*manteis *whose skills had been recognized at the highest level, who held important civic positions. Granted, as a foreigner, these careers weren't open to him, but there were plenty of other roads to success. He just needed a chance . . . Perhaps Thrasyllos of Siphnos had given him good advice; perhaps he should abandon taverns and try private houses. Thrasyllos had certainly sounded as if he knew what he was talking about: 'Get a man on his own, away from the distractions of wine and girls and jeering friends, and he's far more likely to consider his spiritual needs. Make him think about the unseen dangers that surround him—the misdeeds, either his own or his ancestors, which might come back to haunt him. Offer him rituals of purification and sacrifices. Ask about his enemies. In a busy city like this, with everyone anxious to get ahead, it's inevitable that rivalries will develop, resentments fester and escalate. Perhaps he is going to court or has a business interest to protect? Perhaps someone has stolen his girl? An amulet can help protect a man from the hostility of others. Or he might choose to strike first: a simple binding spell, a* katadesmos, *for a reasonable price, will soon get dangerous situations back under his control . . .' He fingered the strips of lead in his bundle, cold as the corpses with whom they were destined to lie, and took careful note of the flight of a bird in the sky above. Thrasyllos was surely right: he hoisted his bundle onto his shoulder and set out towards the quieter streets that housed the wealthier citizens.*

We return to the itinerant, door-to-door salesmen of supernatural services—and one, in particular, of their products. As with the practice and relicts of oracle consultation, the creation of *katadesmoi*, 'binding curses' often called *defixiones* by modern scholars,[1] and the surviving texts, can give us profound insights into the daily difficulties faced by ancient Greek men and women. But unlike oracles, binding curses dealt not with the risks inherent in making decisions, but with more imminent dangers that arose from troubled relationships between the living.

When we talk about 'cursing' we are more used to thinking of the conditional model: 'if a certain offence is committed then may a certain punishment follow'. Conditional curses are intended to discourage those who are planning to commit a crime: they gain their potency from being seen or heard. In the ancient Greek world, the use of conditional curses was both popular and respectable: embedded in various aspects of ancient Greek civic life. For example, individuals would inscribe them on a variety of objects, from prized personal possessions to gravestones; some cities issued communal curses to protect their citizens from harm; and the Athenian Assembly regularly started its meetings with just such a curse. The evidence suggests that this conditional form of curse probably has a long history: as early as the eighth century BCE, it appears, the formula was so familiar that it could be turned around to become the basis for a joke, as in the jovial graffito that appears on the 'Cup of Nestor': '. . . Whoever drinks from this cup, may desire for fair-crowned Aphrodite seize him'.[2]

In contrast, binding curses usually aim to 'immobilize' their victims (although very occasionally, they ask for something nastier).[3] Often they target particular aspects of a person—his or her body parts, spirit or mind—sometimes they focus on relevant objects or locations. Exactly what 'binding' means in this context we will discuss in more detail later in this chapter, but for now I would argue that in each case the substance of the text, the objects of binding, reveal the writer's deepest fears—be it a person, a situation, the loss of something precious or desired, the achievements of others. From this perspective, the corpus of curses sheds a startling light on the nexus of values and relationships that underpinned life and death in the ancient Greek city.

Neither the creation nor the idioms of *katadesmoi* or 'binding curses' appear to have entered the public realm. The ritual of their creation appears to have involved equal amounts of mystery and secrecy. They were usually written on a small sheet of lead or lead alloys, which was sometimes moulded into a particular shape, for example, a tiny figurine; there is also evidence that, as well as lead other less robust materials were used. You might curse many people on one curse, or use several to curse a single victim.[4] The lead sheet was then folded, often pierced with a bronze or iron nail and buried underground.[5] Popular locations included wells, the sanctuaries of deities associated with the underworld, and graves, sometimes in the hand of a corpse itself.⁶ It may be that the practice of writing binding curses grew out of existing oral traditions: literary evidence hints that binding songs were being intoned, in Athens at least, around fifty years before the date given to the first Attic tablets.⁷ Aeschylus' *Eumenides* may provide an example of the first known oral binding curse, issued by the Furies in a scene that pits them as prosecutors in court, against the defendant Orestes, on trial for the murder of his mother. The curse they utter was intended to strike him dumb in court, according to the Hellenistic scholiast who commented on the play.⁸ But the appearance of written curse texts does not mean that the oral aspect disappeared from the rituals of either curse composition or the deposition of tablets—as some of the curses themselves suggest. There are curses in verse form and, in the Greek Magical Papyri, instructions for creating curses that include both oral and written techniques.⁹

In either form, the existence of *katadesmoi* is barely acknowledged in ancient literature. The fullest descriptions are found in two passages of Plato. In the *Republic*, binding curses are one of the services touted by travelling salesmen who knock on the doors of the wealthy offering to expiate current and ancestral sins, or cause harm to an enemy. In this text, Plato calls curses $κατάδεσμοι$, a term also found in the *Greek Magical Papyri*, which seems to originate from the verb $καταδέω$, 'to bind down', a term that, as we shall see, appears frequently across the curse corpus. The same intimation of binding is found in the other term for curses, $καταδέσεις$, which he mentions in the *Laws*. Alongside sorceries and incantations, he gives this as one of the ways to harm someone by supernatural methods, in contrast to poisons that are administered physically, causing harm, $κατὰ\ φύσιν$, that is, 'according to nature'.¹⁰ In addition to these two references, there is also an indirectly attested mention by the orator Dinarchus (in Harpokration's *Lexicon of the Ten Orators*, entry under $καταδεδέσθαι$).¹¹

Despite the scanty nature of the literary evidence, the archaeological record attests the popularity of these curse tablets: over 1600 have been found all over the Graeco-Roman world, dating from around the end of the sixth century BCE to the eighth century CE.¹² The earliest tablets date to the early fifth or late sixth century BCE and were found in the Greek colony of Selinous, Sicily. By the mid-fifth century, they begin to appear in Athens; a little later in Olbia, by the Black Sea. A century or so after that, curse-writing begins to spread gradually across the rest of the Graeco-Roman world.¹³

Since most pre-Imperial curses hail from Attika, it may be that Athens became the hub of the practice, the city's inhabitants adopting this practice from the Sicilians, along with the arts of rhetoric, and becoming the source for its development elsewhere.¹⁴ Alternatively, there may have been oral traditions of binding in other areas, and it was simply the technique of writing

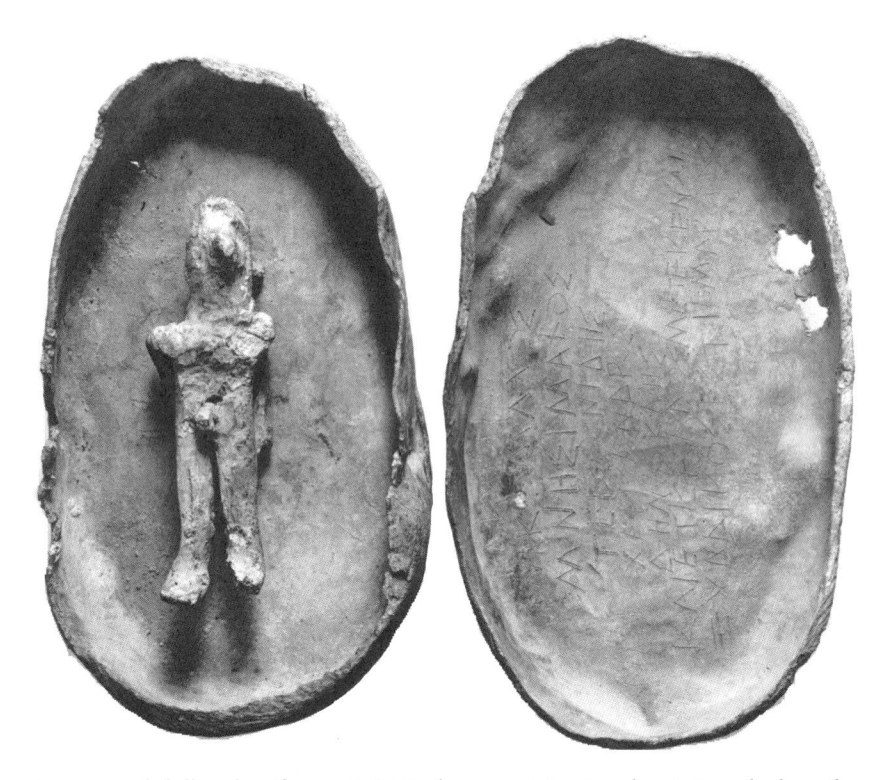

FIG. 5. Lead doll and coffin set: SGD 9, the name Mnesimachos is inscribed on the doll's right leg as well as in the curse text on the coffin lid. Photographs DAI, Athens, doll in coffin and lid Neg. NR. D-DAI-Athen-Kerameikos 5879; front of doll Neg. Nr. D-DAI-Athen-Kerameikos 5880; back of doll Neg. Nr. D-DAI-Athen-Kerameikos 5881. (All rights reserved).

that spread; or perhaps neither is the case and this apparent progression is just an accident of survival. Whichever explanation we prefer, the material evidence suggests that people were writing curse tablets for around 1500 years.[15] What was it about this activity that appealed to so many, for so long?

THE LANGUAGE OF BINDING

I will start with some more general information about the language of curse texts, and the identity and intention of their creators. A few curses actually include the names of those who composed, even if they did not write, their own texts, but for the most part, across the corpus, the authors of these curses

FIG. 5 *continued.*

remain anonymous.[16] Of course, the author of the curse was not necessarily the same as the person who actually inscribed the text. The use of repetitive formulae and the discovery of caches of curse tablets written, or tiny dolls shaped, by the same hand, suggest the activities of the salesmen Plato describes in the *Republic*.[17] But not all these writers were professionals: some tablets betray a more amateur approach through the use of less fine or near-illiterate inscribing; others a more personal style, by their use of particular expressions.[18] Consider, for example, *DT* 86, which is quoted at the beginning of the Introduction to this book. This curse is directed against a *hetaira*—a high-class sex-worker—called Zois and targets parts of her body and aspects of her behaviour, including her buttocks, her laughter, and her eyes. These targets are unusual, not found amongst the common cursing formulae, and evoke the sexual power of this woman, a power that someone was obviously desperate to disable. In another example, a text from Makedonia, a woman called Phila curses first the (imminent?) marriage between Dionysophontos and a woman called Thetima, then widens her hit list to include 'any other woman'. As the curse continues, the writer's language becomes increasingly desperate, and she begins to plead: 'Let him not marry any other woman but me ... Have pity for [Phila?] dear *daimones*, [for I am indeed bereft?] of all my dear ones and abandoned'. Unfortunately, such explicit and detailed expressions of need are rare; the tablets seldom tell us so much about their writer. In *DT* 72, the target of the curse is the 'hopes from the gods and heroes' of the victims: Audollent suggests that these might be the hopes of the victims for their afterlife.[19]

In comparison, information about the targets of these curses abounds. In fact, most of our information about the kinds of people who might be writing curses draws on what can be gathered from the texts about their targets. Over time, this ill-wished regiment draws its members from all parts of society, including women, children, and neighbours, husbands, wives, and lovers, pimps and sex-workers, soldiers, and slaves, politicians, litigants, and craftsmen.[20] The earliest tablets, from Athens at least, tend to comprise only a name or list of names in the nominative. The significance of such lists—and the way in which they may draw on public documents—has been discussed in detail by Gordon.[21] Over time the lists of names continue, but, alongside, a highly formulaic idiom rapidly develops. Three basic spell formulae can be identified: (1) a simple verb (of restraining or consigning or handing over) plus target(s); (2) an appeal to the gods, direct or indirect, to perform or witness an act of binding; and (3) the use of persuasive analogies to render a change in the victim of the curse. However, these are not chronologically sequential, and it is possible to find all three appearing at the same time, even on a single tablet.[22]

The first usually uses a verb of binding or restraining, which is often repeated, sometimes many times. The targets of binding may include people, sometimes singling out specific parts of their bodies (including, sometimes, the 'spirit'), their words and deeds (a common formula). Occasionally a curse aims the locations a victim works in and the tools he/she uses. They may target events or circumstances, such as marriage; even thoughts and hopes.[23] καταδῶ 'I bind'[24] is the most frequently used of these verbs, but we also find καταδεσμεύω meaning 'I bind up', and κατέχω, 'I immobilize or restrain'.[25]

What was this meant to achieve? Later stories, particularly related to court cases, help us to understand what 'binding' was intended to achieve: the doctor and medical writer Galen, for example, ridicules people who are taken in by the claims of magicians, but in the process he preserves evidence of their beliefs and notes that the verbal powers were the target of those who attempted to bind an opponent in a court of law, so that they could not plead their case.[26] Another example of how binding might be expected to work—

although, again, there is no tablet mentioned—is seen in an inscription composed in epic hexameters, dating from the third century BCE. It commemorates the foundation of the cult of Serapis on the island of Delos, despite a lawsuit that attempted to stop it.[27] The inscription describes how the god responded to the desperate prayer of his priest for help by striking his opposition dumb, by binding their tongues. Evidence for binding being used in a similar way in judicial settings is also found in the writings of both Cicero and Libanius.[28]

Among the tablets themselves, the meaning behind this verb of binding is vividly symbolized by the curse tablet in the shape of a doll with its limbs bound which was found in a grave in the Athenian Kerameikos cemetery.[29] Alongside the creation of bound dolls, the act of nailing a tablet may have provided a ritual reinforcement of this idea of control.[30] An Attic text from about 300 BCE (*DT* 49)[31] lists a series of verbs, including both binding and 'nailing down', which it aims at its targets' tongues, spirit, words, hands, feet, eyes, and stomach: καταδῶ ἀφα[ν]ίζω κατ[ο]ρύττω καταπατταλεω, 'all these things, I bind, I make disappear, I bury, I nail down'. Fritz Graf has asked whether we should conclude that καταδῶ describes a ritual done to the lead that includes the actions described by the three verbs that follow it, concluding that the order of the list makes it unlikely, since nailing occurs after burial; instead the phrase is almost certainly part of the rhetoric of an oral rite.[32] The opening phrase of another tablet (*SGD* 48; a fourth-century tablet) supports his conclusion. This curses a vast number of people, beginning its imprecation with the phrase: καταδῶ, κατορύττω, ἀφανίζω ἐξ ἀνθρώπων, 'I bind, I bury, I make disappear from among men'. Similar to that of *DT* 49, it omits the act of nailing, suggesting that in these opening statements καταδῶ is not a summary term for a series of actions, but one of a number of words describing the intent of a curse agent, in this case possibly part of a common formula. The intention that these additional verbs convey, of wiping something out or making it disappear, and therefore making it become useless, is one that, as we will see, is expressed, in various ways, throughout the corpus.

Other cursing verbs add further nuances to the initial notion of binding. Some use compounds of γράφω, 'I write', meaning something like 'I register';[33] we also find compound verbs of τίθημι and δίδωμι, 'I place' and 'I give' respectively, which seem to mean something like 'I consign'.[34] In some cases, the victim is sometimes registered or consigned πρός certain gods or the dead, where πρός seems to mean 'in the presence of', echoing its use in fifth-century BCE legal and business transactions.

The same echo of business language is found in those texts which seem to be concerned with the 'handing over' of the victim to the will of the god, in an arrangement that resembles something like a business transaction.³⁵ For example: *DTA* 102 describes itself as a letter (to the daimons and Persephone) that conveys (κομίσας) the victim, Tibitis; similarly, *DTA* 103 Ἑρμ[ῆ] καὶ Φερσεφ[ό]ν[η] τήνδε ἐπιστο[λ]ὴν ἀποπέμ[πω 'I am sending this letter to Hermes and Persephone ...'.³⁶ All these expressions seem to show the Greeks drawing on public and legal language, perhaps to add authority to their curses and it is possible that the development of curses in written form happened alongside, and was influenced by, the growing use of writing for commercial and legal purposes.³⁷ The use of written contracts in Athenian daily life may have shaped ideas about how best to make an effective arrangement even with the supernatural.³⁸

However, it is difficult to gauge the exact sense in which these terms are being used in the curse texts. Even within single or related texts there seem to be no hard and fast rules: so, SGD 88 registers its targets ἐπὶ δυσπραγ[ίαι] that is, 'for misfortune'; *DT* 87 registers (καταγράφω) its targets 'to him' (although the fragmentary nature of the text means we cannot be sure who this is); SGD 107, from Sicily, registers its victims πὰρ τὰν ἁγνὰν θεὸν 'in the presence of the holy goddess'. In SGD 91, ἀπογ]αράφō 'I register' seems to encompass a range of slightly different meanings: in l. 3, it is used to 'register all *chorēgoi* for failure in word and deed (ἐπ' ἀτελεία<ι> κ' ἐπέον καὶ ἔργον). However, in l. 6 it takes on a different nuance: the ἀπο (meaning 'from') of ἀπογ]αράφō seems to take on a stronger sense so that the verb seems almost to mean 'to register as separate from': Καλεδιαν [ἀπογ]αράφō ἀπ' Ἀπέλλιος, meaning 'I register Kaledias away from Apellios'.³⁹ Its next use 'I curse Sosias from the shop' could mean 'away from' or, more simply, 'hailing from'. However, neither meaning is easy to sustain in l. 10, which reads 'I curse [list of names] ... away from their sons and their fathers.'

As for assigning: *DT* 69 (a very fragmentary Attic curse) appears to assign his victim πρὸ] τὴμ παρὰ Πε[ρρ]εφά[ττηι ('in front of her, she who is near Persephone').⁴⁰ *DTA* 42, another curse from Attika, 'assigns' (καταδίδημι) a list of names, but without a witness being mentioned. In contrast, *DTA* 55 mentions the medium and destination, but not the witness, and 'consigns' (καταδίδημι) its targets ἐν μολύβδωι καὶ ἐν κηρῶ(ι) καὶ ἐμ [πο]τῶι καὶ ἐν ἀργίαι καὶ ἀφανί(αι) κα(ὶ) ἐν ἀδοξίαι καὶ ἐν ἥττ(η)ι καὶ ἐμ μνήμασιν καὶ αὐτοὺς καὶ οἷς χρῶνται ἅπαντας παῖ[δας καὶ] γυ[ναῖκας, that is 'I consign in lead and in wax and in water (?) in unemployment, obscurity, ill-repute, in defeat and in remembrance both these and all the children and wives with whom they live.' On the other side of the tablet, the fragmentary text uses the same structure, but with a straightforward verb of binding καταδῶ: 'I bind these in graves, in distress and in tombs'. Compare *DT* 86, the tablet from Boiotia that curses Zois, consigning (παρατίθομαι) its target, one Zois, to the gods, Earth and Hermes.

The gods are also called on as witnesses: the term πρός is used to invoke the presence of a god in formulae that use the verb καταδῶ.[41] They may also be pleaded with, or even ordered, to act. A number of texts call on the gods in the vocative and then use the passive third person singular perfect imperative, to request that their target 'be bound'—a plea perhaps rather than an order to the gods to perform an act of binding. For example, in *DTA* 105, a third-century text from Attika, we read 'O Hermes of the underworld, let so-and-so be bound in the presence of Hermes of the underworld and Hekate of the underworld' for a number of different targets. *DTA* 106, repeats this 'let so-and-so be bound in the presence of . . .' formula, although it does not include the call to the gods.

In formulae using the verb κατέχω, 'I immobilize', to call on the gods there is no mistaking the use of the imperative. In *DTA* 88, a curse from Attika dating to the third century BCE, the text begins by addressing Hermes Katochos, and instructing him: κάτεχε φρένας γλῶτ(τ)αν τοῦ Καλλίου, 'bind Kallias' mind, tongue'. In *DT* 50, a fourth-century curse from Athens, both Hermes and Persephone are invoked to bind the target, a woman called Myrrine, and her body, spirit, tongue, feet, deeds, and wishes until she goes down into Hades, wasting away: κατέχω Μυρρίνης . . . σῶ[μα καὶ ψυχὴν καὶ γλῶτταν καὶ πό.]δας καὶ ἔργα καὶ βου[λάς ἕως ἂν εἰς Ἅιδου καταβῆι . . .]. Although the verb κατέχω commonly appears as part of instructions to the gods given in the imperative, it is rarely found as describing a first-person action by the mortal agent of a curse. The exception is *DTA* 109, which starts Μανῆν καταδῶ καὶ κατέχω 'I bind and immobilize Manes'.

This kind of formula that appeals directly or indirectly to the gods or other supernatural powers for their assistance is the second style of binding spell. It appears as early as the fifth century, becoming much more common by the early fourth century, when it is found frequently in Attic curse tablets.[42] Of these tablets, some as already noted, directly address gods and ask them to act; others only invoke them as witnesses or overseers; others do both simultaneously. The gods in question are often called 'chthonian' in the sense that they are associated with the underworld, and there are tablets that bind their victims πρὸς τοὺς χθονίους.[43] But before we assume that these provide examples of 'evil' aspects of these gods, we must ask how these curse tablets were perceived by the society that created them. As we will see, there is evidence that some of these curse tablets were created by agents who felt that they had right on their side: either they had been hurt and were seeking justice, or they desperately needed help, in which case, these gods are manifestly imparting benefits to some (albeit through the deprivation of others). Moreover, while the gods—or aspects of the gods—that are named in the tablets may be 'chthonian' they are not necessarily simply 'gods of the dead' except in the loosest sense; for example, Hermes *Chthonios* does not rule over the dead, but presides over the journey between the underworld and the world of the living.

Gods involved include Hermes *Katochos* ('who holds down'), Hermes *Chthonios* ('of the earth'), Demeter, Persephone, Hekate *Chthonia*, and Ge (sometimes *Ge Katoche*).[44] *Daimones* are mentioned on Phila's tablet from Pella in Makedonia, on *DTA* 102 (as recipients of the curse, described as a letter), while on SGD 170 from Pantikapaion in southern Russia they are mentioned as a group that must not be allowed to loose the curse. There are also a number of rare supernatural figures or divine aspects mentioned: for example, on an Attic tablet from the third century, *DTA* 108, we find the *Erinyes*, famous vengeance-seeking goddesses, and on *DTA* 109 the *Praxidikai*, three vengeance-dealing goddesses, are invoked to bind one Manes. Equally rarely, this tablet goes on to offer εὐαγγέλια or thank-offerings to the goddesses and to Hermes *Katochos*, if Manes fares badly. NGCT 14 (later fourth century; sanctuary of Pankrates, Athens) addresses the sea-god Palaimon and requests καὶ δέομαί σου, ὦ Παλαῖμον, τιμωρὸς γένοιο 'I beg of you, O Palaimon, become their punisher'.[45] SGD 170 binds its victims before a range of goddesses rarely found among *katadesmoi*, including a *Praxidika*, the 'white goddess',[46] and Artemis *Strophaia*.[47] Both SGD 170 and *DT* 72 bind their victims 'in the presence of the heroes' (underworld heroes in the case of SGD 170), which presumably are references to the recipients of hero cult.

This last citation leads us neatly into consideration of the role of the dead on these curses. It has been argued that curse tablets are directed at the dead—in particular, the untimely dead—and that they were the entities intended to carry out the binding requested by a curse.[48] However, close examination of the texts of this period suggests that although the dead are addressed, and may be expected to act as witnesses, they are not expected to act.

First, let us consider those that address the corpse with which a curse is buried. There are two, possibly three, of these: *DTA* 100 may address the dead by name, but an alternative reading makes this the name of the writer of the curse (discussed in n. 16 above). More clearly, in a curse from Pella, Makedonia, Phila, the woman who wrote the curse, entrusts her intentions to Makron, who is presumably the person in whose grave the curse was buried, and the daimones. However, later in the curse, when she pleads for pity, pity that will lead to the carrying out of the curse, Phila addresses only the *daimones*.[49] *DT* 43 is addressed to one Pasianax and reads: ὅταν σύ, ὦ Πασιάναξ, τὰ γράμματα ταῦτα ἀναγνῶς· ἀλλὰ οὔτε ποτὲ σύ, ὦ Πασιάναξ, τὰ γράμματα ταῦτα ἀναγνώσει 'Whenever you, O Pasianax, recognize these letters—but neither will you, O Pasianax, ever recognize these letters' as if asking the corpse to read the curse, then realizing that the corpse cannot do this. The name is attested as an epithet of Zeus.[50] Wünsch suggested that Pasianax was a name belonging to Pluto, which, once transferred to a corpse, also carried power. Voutiras has suggested that such 'euphemistic appellations' as Pasianax may actually have been intended to soothe the anger of the dead with whom the curse was buried, lest it be turned on the curse-maker. He argues that later, similarly phrased curses suggest its use is likely to be formulaic.[51] Whichever way we read it, the text is hardly emphasizing the corpse's power to carry out the binding of the curse. On the contrary, having made it clear that the corpse is unable to read, the curse draws attention to its lack of capacity by drawing a hopeful analogy between its weakness and the way in which the man bringing the lawsuit will be unable to take action.[52]

Two, possibly three, curses invoke the general dead. The uncertain example is SGD 20, found in the Athenian Agora, and dated to the fourth century, which binds its victim πρὸς τοὺς κάτω 'in the presence of those below', a phrase which might be intended to describe either the dead or the underworld gods. More explicit is DT 52, a late fourth-century Attic text, which binds its victims before those youth who died before marriage (παρὰ τοῖς ἠϊθέοις). However, the power of their curse turns on their lack of power: the curse states that only when they read the curse will its main victim (Kerkis) be allowed to speak. The instruction to restrain or bind, that is, to carry out the intention of the curse, is given to Hermes. When the writer of DT 68, an early fourth century Attic text, asks to bind its victim πρὸς τοὺς ἀτελέσ[τους, he or she may also mean the unmarried dead. 'Unmarried' is just one of the many theories proposed for the meaning of this word. Whether we plump for 'unmarried', or 'uninitiated', or 'unfulfilled', it is likely to belong to a cluster of terms that indicate the dead who are, in some way, incomplete—if so, it may be the earliest appeal to the dead.[53] The curse attacks a woman called Theodora, asking that everything to do with her be ἀτέλεστα, just like the corpse with which the curse is buried is ἀτελής, and echoes these terms in its use of ἀτελέστοι to call on the dead. This play on a family of words that mean unsuccessful, uninitiated, and unfulfilled may be the earliest example of analogical magic among the curses.[54] Even if the exact meaning of each term is hazy, the intention of the curse is clear: it intends Theodora to experience a lack of success in both her business as well as her relationships (or, possibly, the business of her relationships, if she is a *hetaira*).[55] The same term ἀτελέστοι is possibly also found in NGCT 79 (included as a supplement), a curse found in a grave in Lilybaion, Sicily, and dated to the third century BCE. Here the dead are also described as ἀπευχομέ[ν]α[ισ]ιν or 'despised'.

So, across the curse corpus, on a few occasions, the dead, both the corpse in the grave and the pale throng of the underworld, are invoked as witnesses to, sometimes even expected to read, a curse. They are occasionally, although not always described as, in some way, dead 'before their time'. However, these tablets do not yet show the concentrated focus on invoking 'the untimely dead' that we find in later tablets and formularies.[56] Nor is it conclusive that these curses were usually buried with those who had died young.[57] Nor is there, in the material of this period, any tablet that directly addresses the dead—individually or generally—and asks them to carry out the instructions of the curse, as found in later material. Curse-writers of this period have not yet reached the ease of interaction with the dead that we see in later materials. In these curses the dead may be invoked as witnesses, occasionally even envisioned as reading a text, but it is their corpse-like qualities that are emphasized—their coldness and stillness, their inability to speak. If you sought to have something done to an enemy, then you were more likely to turn to the gods, not the dead.

The last but one example described above, against Theodora, brings us to the third and final style of spell, which uses wishes, for example, 'may the words of those listed here be useless', often in conjunction with persuasive analogies (so-called *similia similibus* formulae) to ask that the target should take on salient characteristics of something mentioned in the spell. For example, *DTA* 67 (an Attic text that has been dated to the third and fourth centuries) asks that the target's words be as cold (ψυχρὰ) and backwards (ἐπαρίστερα) as the words written in the curse. Three Attic curses, *DTA* 105, *DTA* 106 (dated to the third century), and *DTA* 107 (dated to the fourth century), all ask that the victims and their doings resemble the lead of the curse tablet, in slightly different ways. *DTA* 105 requests that the words and tongues of his victims become as cold (ψυχρὸς) and passionless (ἄθυμος) as the lead tablet; *DTA* 106 asks that the words and deeds of the target become as useless (ἄχρηστα) as the lead tablet; while *DTA* 107 describes the lead of the tablet as worthless (ἄτιμος) and cold, and asks that the doings of his victim be the same.[58]

On some tablets these wishes are reflected in more concrete ways. Twisting or scrambling the text may reflect what the author hopes for his victim. For example, in *DTA* 67, as well as requesting that the target's words be cold, the curse asks that they resemble the backwards way the curse is written, and the author has written some of the words in the text backwards. The writer of *SGD* 99, a curse text from Selinous, written on a round tablet, wanted the tongue of his victim to be twisted to the point of uselessness, and has written this part of the curse in a spiral.[59] In *DTA* 65 no particular wish is expressed, but the letters of the victim's name are twice written upside down at the end of the spell.[60] In some cases, the curse-writer's wishes are expressed in the very shape of the tablet: some of the Sicilian curse tablets may actually have been intended to represent the part of the body—a foot or a tongue—at which they were aimed. More sinister are the flat figurines or 'voodoo dolls' that have been found, sometimes buried in tight-fitting boxes resembling miniature coffins. In some cases, the doll's limbs are bound, its head, feet, or torso distorted. The curse may be written on the doll or inscribed on a surface of the coffin.[61]

Some have argued for a fatal subtext lurking beneath some of the *similia similibus* formulae, and when confronted with a curse inscribed on a coffin, complete with tiny, twisted corpse, it is hard not to conclude that the curse-writer had deadly ambitions for his victim. Nevertheless, in the majority of cases, the emphasis seems to be on creating weakness, not death in the victim. The few tablets that do ask for death tend to be quite explicit: for example, SGD 89, a curse from Sicily, dating to the second century BCE, gives a list of names and then asks 'and whoever else is a witness for Aristomachos, and is inscribed on this tablet, may both they and he, Aristomachos son of Ariston, perish'.[62] *DTA* 75, a fourth-century tablet from Athens, appears to ask that one of its victims perish, along with his workshop; while a third-century tablet from the Black Sea (*DT* 92) ends with the wish for its targets, 'may they and their children perish'. It may be that asking for children to be bound is an indirect way of asking for the destruction of a family line. There are also curses that target the genitals, which may be an indirect way of wishing someone childless.[63]

The idea that destruction is the intention is made less likely again by the intimation found in a number of tablets that the curse could be lifted, if the agent wished, or just by the passing of time. So, for example, in SGD 18, a curse dating to the fourth century, the agent states 'I bind all these men in the presence of Hermes of the underworld, the Trickster, the Binder, Erionios and I will not loose them', an expression that does suggest that it was in his power to do so. Other tablets include time phrases that seem to imply the possibility that a curse could be released. For example, in the text found at Pella, Phile says 'And were I ever to unfold and read these words again after digging (the tablet) up, only then should Dionysophon marry, not before';[64] while *DT* 50, as we have seen, wishes its victim bound 'until she goes down to Hades and withers away' and *DT* 52 asks that Hermes Chthonios 'bind these things and read (these words) for as long as they are living'. On SGD 170 the curse asks that no god or daimon be able to release the curse, 'not even if Maietas begs this as a favour, not even if they offer thigh meat as a sacrifice' μήτε Μαιήτας παραιτήσαιτο μηδὲ μηρία τιθ(έ)ντες.⁶⁵

This idea that it was possible somehow to loosen a binding spell is also found in later stories that describe how particular binding spells have been removed. For example, the fourth-century CE orator Libanius explains that for a period he was mysteriously prevented from speaking, writing, or reading in front of his students.⁶⁶ He wished only to die; could not talk of anything else; was unable to study; was plagued with gout. These disabilities only came to an end when the mutilated body of a chameleon was found and removed from his lecture room. The creature had its 'head tucked in between its hind legs, one of its forefeet missing and the other closing its mouth to silence it'. The removal of one foot may have been directed against the hand the orator used for gesticulation, but he had been suffering from gout, so it may be that the curse was perceived to be the cause of this disease. The removal of the other was surely intended to silence him. Two centuries later, the writer Sophronios describes how Theophilos, an Alexandrian man paralysed in both arms and legs, follows the instructions of a dream. He buys the next catch of his local fishermen, and finds in the nets a box, which is opened to reveal a bronze figurine with nails in its hands and feet. As the nails are removed from the statue, Theophilos regains the ability to move his limbs.⁶⁷

SUSPICION NOT CONDEMNATION

It is easy to understand why, even if their intention was not fatal, this kind of activity may have been regarded with dread, as various sources suggest.⁶⁸ However, there is no direct evidence that proves, unequivocally, that the practice itself was illegal.⁶⁹ Among the curses themselves, any concerns voiced in the curse texts themselves about possible repercussions concentrate on avoiding the anger of the dead, and on justifying the curse-maker's actions; they do not mention mortal punishments if caught by fellow citizens. Fifth- and fourth-century legal actions (see chapter 2: 29 and nn.) that do involve charges of using *pharmaka* (meaning spells or drugs, or both) preserve a distinction between means and intent. In each case, the defendant's use of supernatural methods is not censured, if she can argue that she intended to charm rather than harm. (Although even this defence had its limit: in Antiphon I, the unlucky concubine of Philoneas, unknowingly involved in a poisoning plot, rather than the administration of a love philtre, was immediately executed.) Plato himself may have been reflecting on such cases when he suggests in the *Laws* that in cases of non-fatal injury caused by *pharmaka*, professionals should expect the death penalty, but punishment for private citizens should be decided by the court.[70] It appears that at this point, the civic reaction to these activities has not yet crystallized into explicit condemnation. Although they might be criticized, it seems that supernatural activities were only condemned as dangerous if they actually proved fatal. Plato in his discussion in the *Laws* also picks up this distinction: making a distinction between fatal and non-fatal injuries, and then a further distinction between non-fatal injury caused by natural means and that caused by supernatural techniques, including binding. This was a period in which, as noted, cursing seems to have been becoming not only increasingly popular, but also more professionalized: it may be that Plato is expressing something of popular sentiment about the dangers posed to society by the growing numbers of professional curse salesmen.

One final point to observe, the legal cases under discussion are remarkable for all being made against women who were, at least as far as we can tell from the charges made against them, socially disruptive, in one way or another. Trying to commit a murder is very obviously socially unacceptable, but the associated charges of the other cases shed interesting light on the nature of social tolerance. Alongside possible charges of poisoning and/or impiety, we find that Theoris was thought to be teaching slaves to deceive their masters; Ninon was charged with holding *komoi*; and Phryne was holding unruly gatherings of both sexes. It may be that suspicions about the activities at these celebrations were made worse because of these women's social status: we know that Phryne was a prostitute; Ninon's name ('dolly') may indicate a similar profession. But perhaps it was simply enough that these women were interfering with established traditional religious practices, and that after the religious crisis of the late fifth centruy, Athenians were still capable of feeling extreme concern over the question of what was appropriate religious behaviour.

These cases bring to mind the social dynamics involved in other accusations of occult violence, made in later times and places. These also often involve the singling out of individuals who threaten existing social structures: for example, those on the margins of society or who do not conform to accepted social roles. Often, accusations are fuelled by local or family jealousies and resentments.[71] We do not know much of the circumstances of most of the Athenian cases, but it is not hard to imagine how similar dynamics may have played a part in the formation of those charges.[72]

WHY CURSE?

I will have more to say about these cases, but in this chapter they bring me to my final question: what role did cursing play for people in ancient society? Various factors that might have influenced the development of cursing have been raised throughout this chapter, including: the example set by Sicilian practice; the spread of the use of writing, especially for commercial purposes; gradual shifts in beliefs about the dead. All may have played a greater or lesser part—it is, of course, impossible to judge this with any great precision. But whatever importance we allot these different factors, we are still left asking why people turned to cursing: why might ancient Greek men and women find cursing an attractive solution to a problem?

In response, scholars are gradually abandoning the temptation to describe these tablets simply as evidence for primitive or black magical practices—partly, no doubt, because of the widely acknowledged difficulties of defining magic at all. Instead, more functional explanations have emerged: for example, that the tablets should be viewed as weapons in situations of rivalry and competition between individuals, providing vivid illustrations of the agonistic nature of ancient society; or that they were a way for people to regain the initiative in a situation of essential powerlessness.[73] Although more than three-quarters of published Greek *katadesmoi* offer little beyond a list of names, or are so laconic that they give no hint of the context of their creation, in many cases it is possible to use the contextual detail, vocabulary, and formulae of a curse to suggest the circumstance of its creation.[74]

In his 1904 collection of curses, Audollent identified five categories under which to classify the curse material: (1) *iudiciariae et in inimicos conscriptae*; (2) *in fures, calumniatores et maledicos conversae*; (3) *amatoriae*; (4) *in agitatores et venatores immissae*; and (5) *causa defixionis obscura*. These continued to provide the basic classification for curse tablets until 1991, when Faraone chose to exclude Audollent's second category from his overview of the material, and added two new categories.[75] Most scholars who work in this field gravitate to these five categories to describe the content and presumed context of curse tablets:[76] judicial, theatrical, commercial, love curses, and border-area curses (a category introduced by Versnel, for tablets that combine the formulae of prayers for justice with those of curse tablets).[77] Judicial is the largest category for the Classical period. Commercial curses (concerned with trade) along with curses related to the theatre are found dating from the fifth century BCE. Love curses can be divided into two subcategories, separation curses intended to drive lovers apart, and 'attraction' curses, intended to bring them together. This study will mostly be concerned with separation curses, which start to appear in the material record from the fourth century BCE. (Attraction curses, with a few exceptions, tend to date from much later.) Tablets in the 'border-area' category of curses also first appear in the fourth century BCE.

The categories can be useful insofar as they provide a general overview of the kinds of situations that might prompt an ancient Greek man or woman to use a curse tablet. But the neat boundaries of such a taxonomy may prove too much of a temptation, leading us to tidy up or overlook ambiguities within the texts. The validity of the categories must itself remain an object of inquiry and the use of these categories should be conditioned by close observation of the detail of the individual tablets, rather than relying on any expectations or preconceptions about the sentiments they express.[78] Although I will use the existing categories as a starting point to organize this case study, within this structure my re-examination of the data leads me to question existing interpretations of particular tablets and to challenge the boundaries and/or current descriptions of these categories of cursing. It will become clear how many of the tablets can be described as belonging to several different categories.

Without providing a comprehensive and detailed overview of each area of Greek life in which curses appear, I will explore the circumstances in which men and women created curses; what or whom they selected as the targets of their curses, and why. I believe that the ways in which curse tablets cluster in particular areas of life tell us about the lived experience of ancient Greek men and women, reflecting concomitant cultural values and their shifts. From many of these texts we can learn fascinating details about the operation of public institutions. Alongside, we see a darker, more vicious, side of ancient daily life: the unspoken resentments that smouldered beneath the surfaces, which the Greeks themselves explicitly recognized as threatening the harmony of their city.

I will start this journey, with the category of theatrical curses. This category of only four curses contains one of the earliest curse tablets (SGD 91, from Sicily, dated to 450 BCE), along with three tablets from the heyday of Athenian curse creation (late fourth or third century BCE). The tablets contain erotic, political, and hostile aspects; together they provide a useful first set of texts with which to get acquainted with some of the larger questions that emerge from the corpus of curses.

8

Urban Drama

> The act, in witchcraft, is the word.
>
> Favret-Saada 1980: 9[1]

I start with the smallest category of curses for this period: curses directed against public performers. There are only four of these: three (SGD 91, *DTA* 33 and 34) directed against various personnel involved with festival choruses, while the fourth targets an individual whom it identifies as an actor (*DTA* 45). Their estimated dates distribute them over a period of approximately three centuries.[2] I have chosen to begin with this category because its texts provide a usefully succinct introduction to the kinds of problems and questions raised by the corpus as a whole: from the basic difficulty of reading highly fragmentary texts, to the frustrations of trying to piece together the stories of their writers or targets.

In particular, this category challenges current theories about cursing. If we agree that curses were ideal weapons for use in a competitive environment, then why are there so few that concern public competitions?[3] These events must be the most obviously 'agonistic' of contexts, and yet for the period stretching from the sixth to first centuries BCE, the theatre is the only public competition for which there is evidence of cursing, and these few are the only curses that have been found. An accident of evidence, perhaps, but it contrasts markedly with the plethora of later Athenian curses that target various athletes, and the myriad Roman curses aimed at rival charioteers.[4] In turn, although the later material includes curses against individual public performers, there are no curses written against chorus members, trainers, or chorus leaders.[5]

As we have seen, one of the theories used to explain the creation of so-called circus curses argues that by targeting particular charioteers, curse writers were hoping to further their political ends. It could be argued that the writers of the four curses discussed here had similar ambitions: the curses were written by the competing *chorēgoi* of Classical Athens who were hoping to manipulate the political power of rival liturgists, by attacking particular performers on their teams.[6] However, closer examination of the texts reveals that these tablets have difficulty fitting the Classical Athenian context of choregic conflict, although they do reveal other information about the particular fears and aspirations of those who wrote them. This in turn suggests a new context for their creation.

The first curse in this category is from Attika, and dated probably no later than the second century BCE:[7] *DTA* 45 binds Euandros 'the actor', and, on its other side, as far as is decipherable, it binds things or people belonging to Euandros ('and all the . . . of Euandros . . .'). The fragmentary nature of the tablet makes it impossible to tell the role of Euandros' son, Asteas, whose name appears in the nominative: he could be another target of the curse; he could even be its agent. The occasion that has prompted binding is obscure, the only possible clue to context being that the primary target, Euandros, is twice identified by his profession. But this may be explained a number of different ways. First of all, it is possible that the text was written out of professional rivalry. After all, epigraphic evidence intimates that there was probably stiff competition between actors, an idea supported by literary references that emphasize their civic status.[8] Alternatively, it is also possible that the profession of the target was only included for identification purposes, in order to ensure that the powers invoked found and bound the correct individual.

SGD 91, found near Gela in Sicily, is written on the back of an earlier official document.[9] At the time of writing, there are two translations of this text to take into account: one by L. Dubois, the other by David Jordan who, on further inspection of the tablet, has suggested that Dubois' translation and other published versions require correction; and a revised text is planned.[10] In the meantime, I will comment on both Dubois's text, keeping the latter in French to avoid the risk of 'Chinese whispers', and Jordan's revised translation.[11] Dubois first:

Malediction d'Apellis pour l'amour d'Eunikos. Que personne ne soit plus appliqué qu'Eunikos, pas même Phintôn, mais, qu'il le veuille ou non, qu'on le loue, même Philêtas; pour l'amour d'Eunikos j'inscris tous les chorèges pour que leurs paroles et leurs actes soient sans effet, ainsi que leurs enfants, et leurs parents, pour qu'ils échouent dans le concours et en dehors des concours, ainsi que tous ceux de mon entourage qui pourraient me laisser tomber. Kalédia, je l'inscris pour la séparer d'Apellis et tous ceux qui sont là . . . Sôsias, je l'inscris pour l'arracher à sa boutique; Alkiadas, pour l'amour de Mélanthios; Pyrrhias, Muskelos, Damophantos et le . . . je les inscris pour les séparer de leurs enfants et de leurs parents, et tous les autres qui arriveraient ici. Que personne ne soit plus appliqué qu'Eunikos, ni chez les hommes ni chez les femmes. Que tant de tablettes de plomb, que le prix du plomb (qui est considérable) sauvegardent à tout jamais et partout la victoire pour Eunikos . . . C'est pour l'amour d'Eunikos que j'écris.

Jordan/Miller:

Luck. (I) Apelles (am writing) because of (my) love/friendship for Eunikos. Let no one be more successful/eager than Eunikos, or more loving/friendly, but that he should praise (Apelles?) both willingly and unwillingly and should love (him). Because of (my) love/friendship for Eunikos, I register all *chorēgoi* for failure in word and deed—and their children and fathers—and to defeat both in the contests and outside the contests, (all those) who would outstrip me. Kaledias I curse, away from Apelles, and all those there . . . Sosias I curse, away from the shop of Alkiadas because of his love/friendship for Xanthios, Purrhias, Musskelos, Damaphantos, and the (name missing . . .) I curse away from the children and fathers, and all others who arrive here so that no one be more successful with men or women than Eunikos. As this lead tablet (is inscribed) so let . . . preserve victory for Eunikos everywhere . . . Because of (my) love/friendship for Eunikos I write (this).

As the variations and questions in the translations suggest, this is a profoundly obscure tablet from which it is difficult to extract a coherent meaning. The agent of the curse, one Apelles, appears to have been strongly motivated by his feelings for a man called Eunikos, and he started and ended his curse with a statement about this. At the beginning of the text, according to Dubois, he followed this with a request that Eunikos be more successful than one Phinton, a name which Jordan/Miller read as a comparative form of the adjective 'loved'. Jordan/Miller's translation continues with Apelles' request that Eunikos' praise and love should be directed towards himself, 'willingly or unwillingly'; whereas Dubois reads these lines as Apelles asking that others share his admiration for Eunikos (whether Eunikos wants this or not), even Philetas. So far, so loved up: the next section gives us some clues about context. Apelles, 'for love of Eunikos', continues by cursing all other *chorēgoi* and their sons and their fathers 'so that their words and deeds are unsuccessful, both in the contest and outside it'. The cursing of other *chorēgoi* suggests that Eunikos was a competing *chorēgos* and the context was some kind of dramatic festival. This raises significant questions about the nature of the likely choral context, to which we will return.

The cursing of sons and fathers that follows may indicate that whatever the details of a *choregic* post, it is possible that it was an inherited position.[12] Alternatively, it may be intended to extend the reach of the curse (we have seen other curses aimed at targets' children, for example), or it may just be that this is a formula intended to emphasize the threatening nature of the curse. The latter may seem more likely if the repetition of the phrase near the end of the curse is taken to indicate a formulaic use. Apelles then curses οἵτινές με παρ' ἐμ' ἀπολείποιεν, another puzzling phrase. Jordan/Miller translate this as 'all those who would outstrip me (both within the contests and without)',[13] which could be about Apelles' fears about being beaten in any of three arenas: either in the choregic contest (assuming he was participating himself, presumably as part of Eunikos' team) or in his attempts to use a binding curse on behalf of Eunikos, or his fear of being outstripped by a rival in love. Dubois, in contrast, assumes that Apelles was in a choregic team and reads this line as indicating his desire to curse those on his team who might let him down. An alternative to both of these translations, taking $\mu\epsilon$ as $\mu\eta$, might read 'all those who do not desert and come over to my side', where 'coming over to my side' might refer to supporting Eunikos or changing allegiance to Apelles' team.

Abruptly, in between matters relating to Eunikos and the contest, the curse binds a number of others who do not seem to be involved in the choregic context—and introduces another puzzling phrase $\mathring{a}\pi o \gamma \rho \acute{a} \phi \bar{o}\ \mathring{a}\pi o$, which I have briefly discussed in Chapter 7. The verb $\mathring{a}\pi o \gamma \rho \acute{a} \phi \omega$ is not otherwise attested in curse tablets, although other compounds of the verb are common. Its use in this context seems likely to be of legal origin and mean something like 'denounce' or 'accuse'. The phrase is first used when Apelles curses ($\mathring{a}\pi o \gamma a \rho \acute{a} \phi \bar{o}$) Kaledias $\mathring{a}\pi$' $A\pi \acute{\epsilon}\lambda\lambda\iota o s$, literally 'away from Apelles'. This might be a renunciation of a former lover or the wish for a rival or enemy to be kept away from Apelles.[14] Sosias is cursed ($\mathring{a}\pi o \gamma a \rho \acute{a} \phi \bar{o}$), according to Jordan/Miller, with the intention of keeping him away from the shop [or tavern] ($\mathring{a}\pi \grave{o}\ \tau \hat{o}\ \kappa a \pi \bar{\epsilon} \lambda \epsilon \acute{\iota} \bar{o}$) of Alkiadas, because of this man's love/friendship for a certain Xanthios; but in Dubois's reading, it is simply to keep Sosias from ($\mathring{a}\pi \acute{o}$) the tavern, while Alkidas becomes a separate target, cursed because of his love for one Melanthios. Why these people should be cursed is not made clear and we can imagine many different explanations: they may have been members or supporters of a competing choregic team, for example, or Apelles may have feared that they were rivals for Eunikos' affections (though this is perhaps less likely, bearing in mind the relationships described among them). Alternatively, they could simply be other enemies of Apelles, whom he took this opportunity to curse (as with other curses that target a large disparate group of victims, for example those discussed in Chapter 10).

The curse goes on to target 'Pyrrhias, Mysskelos, and Damaphantos, using the same phrasing as before to 'register them away from' their sons and fathers, and 'all others who arrive here'. Dubois believes this is a separate sentence of the curse, unrelated to Eunikos. Jordan/Miller connect this sentence with the next and translate that these others are cursed 'so that no one be more successful with men or women than Eunikos'.[15] Whichever reading is preferred, the final intimation is that someone was arriving who was a threat and needed to be bound. The Jordan/Miller version suggests that these are contestants arriving from outside the city to participate in the choregic contest. The final part of the text, although very fragmentary, seems to show some traces of an analogical phrase 'just as the lead . . .' similar to those discussed earlier in Chapter 7. The curse ends with a final profession of the writer's love for Eunikos.

What can we gather from this difficult, obscure text, beyond a sense, centuries later, of the strength of one man's feelings for another? As sketchy as it is, it provides significant evidence that dramatic choral competitions of some form were held in cities in the Greek West. But what kind of dramatic competition provides the context here? What might it mean to be a *chorēgos* in Gela?

The *chorēgia* we know most about is that of Athens, where it was one of the city's 'liturgies', inextricably intertwined with the structure and values—and tensions—of the democracy.[16] It is worth briefly exploring some aspects of this institution, if only to get a firmer grasp on why a *chorēgia* might present a context of risk, attracting the creation of binding curses.

The Athenian *chorēgia* prompted reactions that were far from straightforward, even to the Athenians themselves. The fundamental problem was that when this institution demanded that the wealthy use their money in the service of the city, it drew attention to their good fortune. This could help engender harmony (the people calmed by the thought that the wealthy were channelling their funds towards the greater good) or it could stir up resentments—on both sides. We find many different representations of it (and the complex feelings it prompted) across ancient literature, especially in the forensic speeches, where persuading the judges of the real meaning of, or motivation behind, a man's performance of liturgies often takes on a pressing urgency. Some members of the elite argued that it was a breeding ground for *phthonos*, or destructive envy of another's good fortune, and was just a method of popular extortion.[17] Others argued that it offered them a path to pursue *philotimia* (literally, 'love of honour', itself a complex concept when constrained by the ideals of the democracy) and *lamprotēs* ('brilliance').[18] For any glory gained must be strictly civic not personal. This was not an opportunity for ostentatious personal display, and any such abuses of the role risked condemnation.[19] On the other hand, liturgical services might also be cited as proof that a person deserved the *charis*, or 'favour', of the Athenian people.[20]

As some of this might suggest, it was not just the taking part that raised concern—competition was high between *chorēgoi*. Plutarch relates how 'The result for the defeated *chorēgoi* was to be abused on top of it all and made laughing stocks'; and phyletic decrees do not show any interest in recognizing unsuccessful *chorēgoi*.[21] This idea of competition is supported by various anecdotes of attempted sabotage by rival chorus leaders. For example, there is Meidias' plot to ruin Demosthenes' *chorēgia*; or Alkibiades beating up his rival Taureas; and it may also be behind the emphasis which the speaker of Antiphon 6, *Concerning the Choreutes*, puts on the fact that his *chorēgia* was untroubled, which may be taken to indicate that this peaceful state of affairs was unusual. Antiphon 6 concerns an accusation of murder made against a *chorēgos* following the death of a young boy in his chorus, who dies after consuming a preparation intended to enhance his performance. The details of the case also suggest that *chorēgoi* might go to some lengths in pursuit of choregic victory.[22]

This last anecdote introduces another source of tension, apart from the political aspects, that the *chorēgia* seems to have raised: that is, the relationship between a chorus leader and his chorus members (*choreutai*). On the one hand, becoming a *choreutēs* was regarded as a significant part of the education of a young man. This was his opportunity to make a first public appearance and form relationships that could help his civic career.[23] On the other hand, the system of training young chorus members in Athens removed young men from their families and associated modes of authority, placing them in environments that provided different role models and possibly unwelcome relationships.[24] This potentially transformative process appears to have stirred up anxiety: parents were sometimes reluctant to relinquish their children to become chorus members.[25] Was it as a reaction to parental concerns or actual events that, in the fourth century, the city instituted a law that went some way to try to limit sexual relationships between a chorus leader and its members?[26]

Within Athens, we can see that these factors—political, social, sexual competition—might provide a suitable context for the writing of *katadesmoi*. If we accept that a competitive system existed in Gela, then this can help to suggest a context for the creation of SGD 91. But to what extent the *choregic* institution in Gela was similar to that in Athens—for example, whether or not it was a liturgy—is impossible to say.[27] Too little is known about the political system of this city, for example, whether it maintained its existing fifth-century tyranny or instituted a democracy; or the role of the *chorēgos* within that structure, for example who amongst its citizens became *chorēgos*; how the appointment was made; how it was regarded.[28] The structure of cultural institutions in mainland Greece often did provide a model for those in the West, but there is no reason to expect a slavish replication: different cities are likely to have developed their own particular roles and traditions, according to context, which itself was likely to be anything but static.[29]

In fact, apart from this, the evidence is sparse for any kind of dramatic competition: a few, brief statements in ancient literature, tell us how performances were judged, but even these are contradictory, two referring to the pronouncement of judges, one citing a show of hands by the audience.[30] We also know that Hieron, a fifth-century tyrant of Gela, sought to increase his reputation through patronage of the great festivals and of individual poets, including Aeschylus, who is reported to have been particularly honoured by Hieron and the inhabitants of Gela and spent the last three years of his life there.[31] It may be that our text refers not to full-blown dramatic performances but a competitive festival of choral poetry. Anne Burnett argues that it was this kind of event for which Stesichoros, and poets like him, were composing at the end of the sixth century, and that they were in great demand, at a time when 'colonies multiplied and rites and ceremonies proliferated'.[32] Colonies could call on Western precedent, but they must also establish new shrines, new rituals—and new choral songs.[33] As well as local festivals, there is also evidence for West Greek inter-city festivals: for example, Pausanias reports how a boys' chorus from Zankle, along with a *didaskalos* (a trainer) and *aulētēs* (a flute-player), were drowned while on their way by sea to a choral competition (prompting the Messenians to dedicate a set of thirty-seven bronze statues at Olympia in their memory).[34]

As for specific choregic functions: if Eunikos was a chorus leader following an Athenian model, then he would be expected to recruit his chorus along with a trainer; find a place for the chorus to train; provide maintenance, including food and sometimes a place to live; and furnish costumes for the performance. However, a brief reference in the lexicon of Pollux casts some doubt on the precise meaning of the term *chorēgos* in this context, describing how 'especially the Dorians' called their *didaskalos* (or chorus trainer) a *chorēgos*.[35] Dwora Gilula has suggested that the *chorēgos* that is labelled on an Apulian bell-krater should in fact be a *choragos*—a professional furnisher of props and costumes for theatrical performances (*choragium* being what they furnished).[36] On the other hand, we do have evidence for the existence of '*chorēgoi*' on Dorian Aigina in approximately the sixth century, as reported by Herodotos, which suggests that whether or not Aiginetans called it by this name, and whether or not it functioned as an Athenian *chorēgia*, it was sufficiently close to the Athenian institution for Herodotos to use the term.[37] The curse itself offers little further illumination: not too much emphasis should be given to the cursing of Eunikos' 'words and deeds' since this is, as we will see among later tablets, likely to be a common formula of ill-will, rather than indicating any particular activity of the victim.

There might be clues in the approbation that Apelles seeks for Eunikos. Does it make sense to seek the praise and love of others for a chorus trainer or director? Such rewards might seem more appropriate for a chorus leader: the stories from Classical Athens suggest that this was a role notorious for its public, if not publicity-seeking, side.[38] However, such a line of reasoning although provocative, cannot, in the end, be conclusive, partly because of our lack of knowledge about the historical context, partly because what information we have is given in the voice of a lover. However, it suggests that the combination of civic duty and sexual opportunity that may have formed the backdrop of Athenian choral competitions may provide some useful clues for reading SGD 91, where the erotic content of the text appears inextricable from its choral context.

THE CHOREGIC CONTEXT

If indeed the Athenian *chorēgia* was a locus of intense competition, both for honour and prestige and, possibly, for sexual or amorous relationships, it is surprising that there are only two Athenian curse tablets explicitly concerned with choral competition. The first, *DTA* 33 reads: 'Of these, Mantia, [and] all the *didaskaloi* in the team of Si- [the text breaks off here], and then continues 'all, all the youths (πάντας πάντας παῖδας)'. The other, *DTA* 34, curses 'all the *didaskaloi* and *hupodidaskaloi* in the team of Theagenes'.[39] We do not know what kinds of events form the background for these tablets, whether they are city festivals or local deme festivals, although the mention of youths in *DTA* 33 and 34 does suggest that for that text, at least, the context is a dithyrambic chorus rather than a tragedic or comedic event.[40]

The term *didaskalos* used in both texts probably indicates a professional trainer. Strictly speaking, the poet of a dramatic team was the *didaskalos*—the earliest generation of poets trained their own choruses—while a trainer employed by a poet might be termed a *hupodidaskalos*.[41] However, as the training of choruses became more specialized, the professional trainer usurped the title of *didaskalos*, with no sign of subordination.[42]

In these texts, the situation describes a number of trainers and sub-trainers 'attached to' or 'in the team of' a single man.[43] In their choice of target, these curses are surely aimed at disrupting a performance, rather than binding a particular individual. The use of the plural is puzzling if we assume that the tablets were aimed at the team—chorus, pipe-player, poet, trainer—hired by a rival *chorēgos* in a choral competition.[44] Although there is surely evidence for *sunchorēgiai* (two chorus leaders for one chorus) for Athens at least,[45] there is no evidence for one chorus leader taking on the costs of several choruses. It seems unlikely that *chorēgoi* would have hired several trainers for one chorus, or that they would have been in charge of two *choroi* (necessitating two trainers/assistant trainers). Could it be that they are likely to represent other officers of the *chorus*? (The speaker of Antiphon 6 mentions hiring a number of men to oversee the needs of his Thargelian chorus, but he does not use these official terms to describe them.)

A possible alternative explanation, which would fit the estimated dating and given provenance of the tablets, and explain the plural personnel targeted in these texts, could be that Theagenes, and the truncated 'Si-' of *DTA* 33, were not *chorēgoi*, but *agōnothetai*, an office created by Demetrios of Phaleron, probably during his time as Eponymous Archon in 309/8, to replace the *chorēgia*.[46] Drawing on public funds, which were never sufficient, and supplemented by his own wealth, an elected *agōnothetēs* managed all the theatrical performances at all the city festivals for a year. He would therefore have had several poets or trainers and undertrainers working for him.[47] These changes transformed the role of *chorēgos* into an official position of legitimized power in which the expenditure of great wealth was matched by the achievement of political power.[48] The establishment of the *agōnothesia* marked the beginning of euergetism and a new, unambiguous focus on the individual as a powerful benefactor of the people. The wealthy were recognized as a resource on which the city depended, and their largesse was something for which the citizens were explicitly grateful.[49]

Returning to the curse, we can posit that by binding those who helped to craft the spectacle, the ultimate aim of the curse was probably to disrupt the theatrical performances.[50] The focus of the curse was thus not on binding an individual holding office, but on disabling the service he rendered to the people—the source of his power. If this is correct, then the motivation behind these curses could be to hinder an individual's achievements, and hopefully obstruct his path to power, without committing any kind of explicit offence against him.

If this is right, then these are the only curses from this period that show a civic office under attack. This may be the result of an accident of evidence, or there may be a more complex explanation, for example, that their duties were thought too important for the survival of the city for competitive or hostile individuals to consider binding them or their activities.[51] However, this does not explain why binding curses seem not to have been used in straightforward competitive environments during the period under study here, if we accept the theory that cursing was prompted by the urge to compete.

The texts in this category give a sense of the problems inherent in reading, dating, or trying to explain the contents of binding curses, problems we will meet repeatedly over the course of this exploration. Nevertheless, despite these difficulties, they also demonstrate the kind of fascinating material that binding curses contain, the questions they raise and the challenges they present to our understanding of daily life in ancient Greece.

9

The Best Defence

> For the moral of the story is that no one escapes violence: he who does not attack automatically becomes the victim; he who does not kill, dies.
>
> Favret-Saada 1980: 122[1]

In Aristophanes' *Acharnians*, first performed around 425 BCE, the audience is told about the rhetorical embarrassment that befell Thucydides, son of Melesias, as an old man. Back in the 440s, Thucydides, son of Melesias, had been a political rival of Perikles, before he was banished from the city by ostracism. Ten years later, he returned to Athens and re-entered politics. He was prosecuted by Euathlos, son of Kephisodenos, on an unknown charge. But he was old now, and past his prime. During the trial, he broke down in tears and was unable to speak. The incident is explained in the text as the triumph of a speaker who was younger, more energetic, a 'faster-talker' than the old orator, who is now bent with age and unable to use the skills he once had against this 'glib-tongued advocate'.[2] The event is also referred to in the *Wasps*, performed three years later. Bdelykleon is defending a dog accused of pilfering cheese. The defendant takes the stand, but is unable to speak. To explain the sudden silence of his client—a dog famed for his barking—Bdelykleon reminds his audience of the 'sudden paralysis' that seized the jaws of Thucydides. However, the scholiast offers another explanation, stating that Thucydides was unable to plead his own defence, 'as if his tongue had been bound, and thus he was condemned'.[3]

Stage fright or sabotage? If we pursue the theme of 'sudden rhetorical incapacity' through ancient literature, we find this double explanation again and again. For example, just over four and a half centuries later, the great Roman writer and politician Cicero is writing the *Brutus*, one of his works on oratory. He lists the different aspects of public speaking which an orator must master, and holds up the consul Curio as an example of a speaker who was ignorant of and unskilled in all of them. He describes how, during a private courtcase, while he was actually rebutting a plea made by Cicero, Curio came to an abrupt halt, forgetting the whole case. Cicero puts it down to a feeble memory, but, in his own defence, Curio accuses the opposing litigant of using poisons and incantations to prevent him from speaking.[4]

As described above (Chapter 7), the fourth century orator Libanius claimed also to have suffered such an attack.[5] He describes how he found himself unable to study, or to speak, read or write in the classroom.[6] The effects of this episode were both debilitating and depressing—and fodder for gossip. Some people said he was dying, others were convinced he was already dead. Some of his friends suspected that his suffering was the result of a malicious spell: they even thought they knew who was responsible, urging Libanius to take the culprit to court. He restrained them, suggesting that they offer up prayers on his behalf, instead. However, their suspicions of foul supernatural play were confirmed when the twisted corpse of a chameleon was dicovered hidden in Libanius' lecture room: once it had been dug up, Libanius recovered. In turn, Libanius himself was perceived as the malefactor, accused of using similar tactics himself, specifically by a man whom he had beaten in a number of speaking competitions. The man becomes so convinced of Libanius' magical skills and hostility that he finally accuses him of using them to kill his wife.[7]

From the smallest category of curses we move to the largest: as the stories above demonstrate, the context of litigation is rich in examples of supernatural sabotage. In terms of curses, it provides both some of the oldest curses that have been found and the largest number for the Classical period. Judicial curse tablets for this period have also been found in Sicily, Spain, and southern Russia, but by far the largest number come from Attika.[8] Athenians regarded themselves as being significantly more litigious than other Greeks, and, although this may just be the result of the weight of current evidence, the distribution of curse tablets seems to support both this belief, and the competitive ethic often used to explain it.[9] This is a happy coincidence for the ancient historian, since this is the judicial context about which most is known. However, it does tend to mean that this becomes the model for the legal background to all these judicial tablets, regardless of specific origin—and we should not forget that this is far from certain; indeed, the evidence for Athenian legal processes may also, by its nature, provide only a partial understanding of that particular context.[10]

The judicial curse tablets offer us a further, unique, viewpoint on ancient Greek litigation: they reveal what those who were going to court feared most. At the same time, they add to our understanding of the legal process, the different roles played by its personnel, and the actual and symbolic significance of litigation within the city. For example, as this chapter will show, the curse texts indicate that litigation was seen as being fought in teams, suggesting that current versions of Athenian litigation as consisting simply of

The Best Defence 167

one-on-one power struggles between elite politicians is too limited. The range of personnel bound on the curse tablets suggests not only more people, but more kinds of people, were involved. For example, women and bystanders appear to have played a greater role—specifically, posed a greater threat—in court, than has, so far, been imagined. All this can help reshape our understanding of the social realities of litigation, creating a richer and more nuanced picture of this aspect of life in Classical Athens.

IDENTIFYING JUDICIAL CURSES

To begin with, how do we know which curses were written with a court case in mind? The curse texts, in general, seldom reveal anything about the identity of those responsible for creating the curses, so, for the most part, judgements about the context of a curse must come from an examination of its targets.[11] The most obvious clue is forensic vocabulary: this includes legal terms for people and their roles, such as οἱ ἀντίδικοι or οἱ δικασταί; or descriptions of legal action, for example, ἀγωνίζεσθαι; or more abstract terms describing legal processes or places, for example, δικαστήριον ('a court'), δίκη ('a private case'), or ἔνδειξις ('written accusation preceding summary arrest').[12]

On some tablets there are details that allow us to identify the likely role of target and agent. *DTA* 103 appears to identify one of the targets as someone who is pursuing a case (ll. 9–10: Δημοκρ[άτ]ης τ(ὸ)ν περὶ τῆ(ς) δίκη[ς δικαζ[ό]μενον, ('Demokrates (binds) the man pursuing a court case': this kind of mixing of cases, nominative followed by accusative or first person followed by third, is found across both oracle and curse tablets).[13] A *dikē blabēs*, a suit brought for personal harm, appears in two columns of NGCT 9. This is to be urged in the polemarch's court (according to the third column), suggesting that the defendant(s) was a metic.[14] Side A mentions: καὶ τὴν δίκην [βλάβης] τὴν [Ἀθηνοδώρο [τὴν πρὸς] ἡμᾶς δικάζεται ('and the case for damages, which Athenodorus is bringing against us') and the same tablet on the other side curses in a similar fashion: καὶ τὴν ... τὴν ἡμῖν ἐπ[ι]φέρ[ει] Σμινδυρίδ[ης] ('and the (suit for damages) which Smindyrides is bringing against us'). *DT* 43 and 44 both mention (l. 6 and l. 5 respectively) δίκαν ἐποίσει (literally, 'he has brought a case'). *DT* 60 curses τοὺς με[τὰ] Νερ-[ε]ίδ[ο]υ κατηγόρους ('the advocates with Nereides'). In these five (or six) cases, it seems likely that the writer of the curse is the defendant.

DTA 66b proclaims: καὶ ἐ(ἴ) τις ἐναντί(α) ἐ(ἴ) τὰ τούτων ἐσ(τ)ί ἄλλος πράττ<ι>ει ἐμοί ('and if there is anyone else who is also doing the hostile acts of these men against me'), which seems to imply that the agent of the curse considered himself to be the target of certain acts. Similarly, the text of *DTA* 94 (ll. 8–13) makes clear that the agent of the curse saw himself as being on the receiving end of others' machinations, since it shows him asking that the following be bound: καὶ τὰ δικαιώματα (ἅπαντ)α ἃ παρασκε(υ)άζεται ἐπ' ἐμὲ καὶ κάτε-<κα>χε αὐτόν· ἅπαντα τὰ δικαιώματ(α) Διοκλ(ῆ)ν τὰ ἐπ' ἐμὲ παρασκευάζεται. (In this phrase, it seems likely that δικαιώματα is being used to mean 'justification' or 'plea of right' rather than 'act of right' or 'duty':[15] 'and all the pleas of justification that are being prepared against me and bind him. (Bind) all the legal pleas that Diokles is preparing against me.') Both of these curses seem most likely to contain a description of the prosecution's preparation against the agent of the curse, but they could also conceivably describe the preparation of the defence.

The writer of *DTA* 105b l. 3 names the location: καὶ ἐν δικαστηρίωι, 'in the court', but we are none the wiser concerning his (or her) role. The first line of *DTA* 100 mentions what looks like ε]ὐθῦναί. A *euthynē* was an automatic procedure undergone by every public official, in which the record of his office was examined to ensure that he had fulfilled all his responsibilities and committed no misdemeanours, but it is not clear whether the agent is being cursed for the prosecution or the defence. The same applies to the mention of an *endeixis*, the written accusation preceding a summary arrest,[16] in SGD 49. If Jordan is correct in his translation, SGD 42 appears to target someone who is bringing a legal summons against the agent of the curse. *DT* 49 mentions events that might happen before the *diaitetai* ('arbitrators' l. 19), but it is not clear from this whether he is plaintiff or defendant.

This method of identification has produced a list of 67 published examples of judicial curses in the three major collections, of which 46 date from the Classical or Hellenistic periods.[17] A number of additions to, and some subtractions from, this basic list can be made. First, we can add tablets listed in Kagarow's analysis of texts that contain legal terms: *DTA* 79, 158; and *DT* 67,[18] and the latest collection of tablets, compiled by David Jordan, includes a further 8 tablets containing forensic vocabulary.[19] Gager includes a further 9 tablets in his section on likely judicial tablets, on the grounds that although they do not contain legal terminology, there may be other reasons for thinking that they were written by rivals who were fighting out their political differences in the Athenian lawcourts, for example, the identification of significant political figures.[20] He does, at least, distinguish them within the chapter; other commentators have suggested that the contexts in which the categories of political and judicial binding curses were created are essentially interchangeable.[21] Certainly, evidence for this approach can be securely gathered from tablets that contain both famous names and forensic

FIG. 6. Curse tablet (SGD 14) from the Kerameikos, Athens, naming Kassander, who succeeded Alexander, 319–297 BCE, his younger brother Pleistarchos, his general Eupolemos, and his governor Demetrios of Phalera. Photographed Hellner, DAI, Athens, Neg. Nr. D-DAI-Athen-Kerameikos 9862 (All rights reserved)

language.[22] Equally, there are tablets comprising lists of names, among whom no particular individual has been identified, which seem likely to be judicial. For example, SGD 107, the 'great defixio from Selinous'[23] binds 17 men who can be grouped together into seven interrelated families, a relationship that suggests a context of testamentary litigation for its creation, similar to that attested in cases in Attic law.[24] But although it is quite feasible that 'list' curses of this kind were created in a judicial context, there is no secure evidence that this is the case. Nor is the identification of famous figures in amongst a list sufficient evidence to place a tablet immediately in the category of judicial curses. As an example of the difficulties of categorization, compare the three 'doll and coffin sets', SGD 9, NGCT 11, and 13. The first two contain both identifiable names and forensic language.[25] The doll of the doll and coffin set SGD 9 has the name *Mnesimachos* scratched on its right leg. Mnesimachos has been identified as a *chorēgos* and a defendant in a lawsuit in which Lysias wrote the speech for the plaintiff.[26] In addition, the text binds καὶ ἔ τις ἄλλος μετ' ἐκένωιν ξύνδικός ἐστι ἔ μάρτυς 'and any other co-advocate with those men, or witness'. The technical language of this phrase suggests that a judicial context is right in this instance. Similarly, NGCT 11 is inscribed with five names, including that of Mikines. Jordan has argued that this is the defendant in a murder charge mentioned in fragments of a speech ascribed to Lysias

(Lys. frr. 170–8). Similar attempts have been made to identify some of the names inscribed on the miniature doll and coffin that comprise NGCT 13. The name Theozotides, which appears on the outer right leg of the doll, is comparatively rare[27] and may be identified as belonging to a particular political figure of the fourth century, who proposed a controversial decree, for which he was taken to court. Scraps of the speech written against him by Lysias survive, revealing an attack on two fronts: (1) for trying to restrict state stipends for orphans to γνήσιοι (the children of citizens) and excluding νόθοι (illegitimate) and ποιητοί (adopted) (the future tense of the speech suggests that this proposal has not yet been carried) and (2) for adjusting the pay of the ἱπποτοξόται (mounted bowmen, employed as police at Athens).[28] It may well be that NGCT 13 was written in preparation for a lawsuit, perhaps even that for which Lysias wrote his speech. But it is also possible that it was written in some other, non-judicial context of hostility. The two decrees described in the speech above, along with the speech itself, suggest that Theozotides exercised views that were likely to have made him enemies.[29] The identification of famous political figures among a curse's targets could indicate 'judicial' circumstances, but could also point us to a wider context of civic hostility.

If we discount the need for forensic language as a guide to the context in which the curse is created we risk making a number of assumptions that could distort our understanding of both the practice of cursing and particular civic institutions. First, a list of famous names on a tablet may indicate a battle conducted in the lawcourts; it may also, importantly, demonstrate to us that hostile activities took place in other contexts, illuminating our understanding of life in the Greek city. Similarly, it is a short step from assuming that a curse with a list of famous names must be judicial to assuming that any tablet that comprises a simple list of names (or names and parts of the body) is likely to have been written in a judicial context. In fact, it is easy to imagine plenty of other situations for which a curse comprising a list of names might seem appropriate, for example, the members of an unpopular club, a hated family, loathed neighbours, the slaves in a rival factory. Such lists may represent a selection of someone's enemies, among whom there are no obvious connections, except for this single factor of hostility. These conclusions may seem frustrating, but acknowledging that we do not know in what circumstances all these curses were being written allows us to manage our assumptions, while remaining open to ideas about other possible contexts and connections.

In a similar fashion, the binding of a victim's tongue is also sometimes given as a sign that a tablet is likely to have been written for a judicial context.[30] This is a sensible suggestion, but it should not be taken to mean that mention of a victim's tongue is always to be taken as a simple indication of a judicial context. In fact, the tongue is not that popular a target in this category of curses. Of the 67 curses identified as judicial by Faraone, 17 curse the tongue of a victim. Of these, only the early Sicilian curse tablets target the tongue specifically. Of the others, the tongue is mentioned in concert with other particular parts of the target—often the spirit, sometimes the hands, feet, perhaps the body—as if the curser might have wanted to prevent him, or her from being able to reach the court at all.[31] As a comparison, consider the 25 tablets categorized as 'commercial', of which eight include mention of a tongue.[32] These suggest that there were myriad situations in which cursing a tongue might have been considered appropriate: to dampen rivalry in the Assembly, for example, or, escaping the political context entirely, to stop the gossip of hostile neighbours. Sometimes the way in which a tongue is mentioned in a curse may provide a clue to the particular circumstances in which it was written. In *DT* 49, the cursed attributes of the male victims include tongue, spirit, and speech; of the female victim only her tongue and spirit. It implies that the context of the curse was one in which a woman would not have been making a speech. Beyond this observation, this tablet also offers a further, somewhat surprising insight, that is, that even though she might not be speaking publicly, the woman (and her tongue and spirit) still presented some kind of risk to the writer of the text. It suggests that this curse was aimed not just at events conducted by men in a public arena, but at a wider social network, which also included women. We will examine this aspect of the judicial curses in more detail later in the chapter.

A large number of texts include phrases or formulae that suggest conflict and hostility between groups and individuals of a type that could be found in judicial contexts, although no further detail confirms that these were the circumstances of creation. For example, in NGCT 66, a fifth-century text from Selinous, the writer binds the tongues of a series of people who 'might be useful to Mestor'. NGCT 79 includes the phrase 'so that he may not speak (?) against me'; NGCT 116, an early fourth-century tablet from Olbia on the Black Sea, comprises a list of names on one side, and, on the other, another three names preceded by the phrase 'and the others who oppose me'; a later fourth-century Italian tablet, NGCT 83, curses specific men and 'all the others opposed (by us) and anyone else who opposes us'. A fourth century text from Pydna (NGCT 40) asks that 'if there is anyone else, an enemy who is angry for any reason, let him not be able to say anything against me'.[33]

The idea that enemies might be teamed together in some way is found in a number of tablets that mention targets working with, or on behalf of, each other. Again, this could be about legal teams or supporters— or not. For example, of two unpublished lead tablets found near the banks of the Eridanos in the Kerameikos, one seems likely, from the phrasing, to belong to this category. The tablet reads καὶ ὅσοι με <τὰ> (Σ)ατυρινο(ῦ)

(*ΝΑΤΥΡΙΝΟΣ* tab.) εἰσι καταδῶ, 'And those who are with Saturinos, I also bind'.[34] SGD 133, a third-century text from Spain, curses those 'who are on Aristarchus' side'. NGCT 39 (Pydna, fourth century) targets a list of names and 'anyone else who takes his part'; two late fourth/early third-century texts from a sanctuary, probably of Demeter, at Mytilene, NGCT 49 and 50, both curse lists of names (NGCT 50 includes a woman's name, Aspasia) and end with the phrase 'and anyone else who is with them', while NGCT 48 (same date, same location) ends a list of victims with the phrase 'and whoever else is about to ask or act on their behalf'. SGD 171, a text from Olbia on the Black Sea, reinforces our questions about context: it offers a list of men's names followed by the phrase 'and all those in the city who stand alongside him'.

AN ELITE WEAPON?

Current interpretations of judicial curse tablets for this period draw on theories used to explain later curses found in the amphitheatres of Rome and Karthage. These target charioteers who, as mediators between their patrons in the social elite and their own mass of supporters, carried particular socio-political significance, investing the outcome of any chariot race with far greater meaning than a simple sporting event.[35] Judicial curse tablets are similarly seen as part of the armoury of the Athenian elite in their struggle for political power, prestige, and social and political recognition, fought out in the democratic courts of Athens. This interpretation draws on a particular model of the Athenian lawcourts, developed over the last three decades, that depicts the courts as a key resource in the perpetuation of conflict amongst, and control over, a group of wealthy Athenians.[36] On the one hand, the courts provided an arena in which the elite could pursue feuds and political goals, each litigant struggling to add 'to his own prestige the prestige lost by his unsuccessful opponent and the more the loser stood to lose, the more there was to be gained by the victor'.[37] On the other, the ideological constraints of Athenian legal process firmly maintained the collective values of the democracy: where we might expect appeals to legal precedent or the significance of political laws, speakers repeatedly ask the *dikastai* (judges) to decide cases based upon the life, character, and, of course, the civic merits of the litigants, invoking their sense of what is fair or good in the long term for the city.[38]

Such a view of the practice of Athenian law—essentially an endless zero-sum model of competition fought out by the elite—might seem the perfect setting for the creation and use of judicial curse tablets. *Katadesmoi* would have provided the ideal weapon for disabling one's opponent's rhetorical arsenal, without seeking the destruction of those involved in the competition. But this model of Athenian legal practice, although offering extremely valuable insights, has recently come in for criticism.[39] For example, it over-emphasizes honour as the major prize;[40] seems to suggest that the laws of Athens were irrelevant and all one had to do to win a case was impress the *dikastai* with an account of one's good character and services to the city;[41] and focuses on the individual feuds of a wealthy elite, whereas these famous contests may represent only a very few cases.[42]

This, in turn, raises questions about the earlier neat description of the function of cursing in this setting. Rather than assuming that the curse tablets reflect a particular picture of legal activity, what information do they provide for the context of their creation?

TARGETS: WHO AND WHAT IS BEING CURSED AND WHY?

Plato's report of wandering curse salesmen does suggest that they knocked on rich men's doors, but this does not mean that the wealthy, powerful, and politically involved were their only customers, or the only city dwellers to create curses.[43] Certainly, the targets of the texts come from a range of social levels, some of whom were unlikely to have had direct political interests. For example, a lengthy curse tablet from the late fourth century (SGD 48) includes in its list of targets politicians of the liturgical class, along with male and female prostitutes, and presumably indicates some kind of relationship between the two groups.[44] We have seen that a fourth-century text from Athens (NGCT 9) concerns two men and a woman who are about to urge a *dikē blabēs*, a private case brought for damage, in the polemarch's court, suggesting that the defendant was a metic.[45] Since we also hear of a metic who was possibly a prosecutor in this context, it would not be far-fetched for the agent(s) of the curse also to be metics.[46]

From the traditional model of elite legal activity and associated cursing, we might expect curses to target a single person—the one who initiates a case. In fact, it is extremely rare for any tablet to curse a single individual: most curses are concerned to eliminate a number of opponents. Moreover, these opponents are often accompanied by lists or groups of individuals described with terms that show they play official or unofficial roles of support. Among the former are fellow-prosecutors, witnesses, and informers, and different kinds of speakers. Among the latter, we have already noted those formulae that target 'those on so-and-so's side' or 'on behalf of so-and-so'. Other terms also appear, such as οἱ συμπαρόντες, οἱ βοηθοί ('those standing near by' and 'the helpers', respectively) and even φίλοι ('friends', in the phrase [ε]ἴ τις ἄλλος [φίλος α[ὐ]τοῖς 'if there is anyone else who is a friend to them').[47] The phrasing of the texts suggests that these are not merely further synonyms for other official terms, but it is not clear whether they are meant to indicate simply friends and family, or whether they have a more specific meaning. Similarly, a variety of phrases appear describing the enmity of those opposing the curser. These also tend to be groups of people rather than single opponents. Indeed, a number of texts are written to include everyone who might be hostile to the agent of the curse, even those not listed on the tablet itself. Below, I examine the different terms which appear on the tablets and explore why those coming to court might have felt it necessary to ask the gods to disable these targets.

Informers (οἱ μήνυται)[48]

There is only one curse which makes explicit reference to informing: it targets informers. In Athens, informers could include women and slaves, as well as citizens, who might bring information for reward, but information could also be brought to the Assembly or Council without these incentives being offered.[49] Osborne suggests that the general use of the word may have come to be associated particularly with slaves and Lysias (3.33) uses *mēnusis* to cover all slave testimony under torture. However, despite the frequency of challenges to torture slaves for evidence in the forensic speeches, it was rarely carried out—and so it seems unlikely to be what is at stake in this curse text.[50]

Does this mention of informers suggest what kind of case was at issue here? Information from *mēnusis* tends to be used in cases where third-party prosecutions are possible, usually extreme situations, where the offence is against the gods or against the state, or in cases of murder.[51] The evidence suggests that *mēnusis* by slaves for reward was restricted to cases where there had been an offence against the gods.[52] If this curse was written before events moved into the courtroom, the agent could have been cursing slaves and/or women. The mention of *dikastai* does not necessarily rule this out, although it may suggest that the agent was cursing informers who were to appear against him in the courtroom (and so were likely to be metics or citizens, and probably not slaves or women). The curse may have been aimed simultaneously at different groups of people involved in different stages of the legal process.

Judges (οἱ δικασταί)[53]

In an Athenian court, the *dikastai* played various official roles, encompassing activities that (for us) belong to both judge and jury, deciding not only the sentence, but also the meaning and applicability of the law, and the facts of the case. Although they were just as much 'at the mercy of their ears', as were those of the Assembly whom Kleon thus abused,[54] they were, similarly, not to be pictured as a silent and attentive body, sitting in neutral authority. In some ways, they could be described as taking on some of the activities of modern attorneys. Other aspects of their behaviour would simply get them expelled from a modern court: beyond their official duties, the *dikastai* might very well respond to what they heard in court, and could be highly vocal and demonstrative.[55]

The forensic corpus suggests that this rowdy behaviour meant they might themselves become part of a speaker's rhetorical arsenal: a prosecutor might prime the *dikastai* with information, telling them to demand answers from the defendant when he comes to make his speech; or he might just indulge in a question and answer session with them, in a sort of legal pantomime.[56] The laughter of the judges was also used by the litigants against each other, and was unlikely to be merely a ripple of amusement. Bear in mind that for public cases, there would have been 500 *dikastai* appointed to hear the case, for private cases, between 200 and 400.[57] But this does not mean they were simply passive props of the litigants. If they were not entertained or intrigued by what they heard, they might whistle or hiss,[58] murmur or boo disruptively, or just interrupt speeches to criticize their delivery.[59] They might grow angry or make demands.[60] The noise (or *thorubos*) this crowd made might be boosted with hand-clapping and foot-drumming.[61] As noted earlier, humiliation was a powerful weapon in this setting.[62]

Such a key role was obviously vulnerable to corruption and, indeed, there is some, albeit not much, evidence for specific instances of 'nobbling'—from individuals to entire panels. Our suspicions might also be raised by the wholesale reformation of the system for allotting *dikastai* to cases, which evidence suggests occurred some time before the late 390s. This seems to have meant *dikastai* were allocated to a court on a daily basis instead of being allocated to a particular court for a whole year.[63]

A few of the tablets also support these suspicions: there are three texts in which *dikastai* are cursed. In NGCT 14 the agent of the curse asks that his targets should seem to the judges to speak unjustly, which he justifies by explaining that they are saying and doing unjust things. However, *DTA* 67 curses the words of the informers and the *dikastai* 'with them'; and *DTA* 65 curses 'the witnesses or *dikastai* of Kallias'. It is one thing to try to influence the jury, it is another to suggest that they are partisan. The dating of these tablets is difficult to ascertain, but even after the system's reformation, the new process of allotment did not rule out the possibility that individual members of each panel, or powerful litigants, might wield influence over the judges—certainly the writers of these tablets seem to have thought it possible.

Witnesses (οἱ μάρτυρες)[64]

The relatively frequent binding of witnesses on curse tablets suggests that they posed a significant threat to litigants, and this is in accord with the importance of their role as implied by their frequent appearances in the speeches of the forensic corpus.[65] But in trying to understand why, we cannot just assume that the functions of Athenian *martures* are equivalent to those of our own modern 'witnesses'. The primary function of witnesses in an English court case is to tell the truth: they are called to provide testimony, they are then examined and this evidence is built into the case. In Athens, this does not seem to have been the same: the main focus of court action was not the examination of testimony, but the speech given by each litigant. Certainly witnesses gave information, since they were called to corroborate the points the litigant made, but they were very seldom cross-examined. Indeed, after 380 BCE, when a witness attested to a statement that had been written either by himself or by the litigant, he could not be cross-examined at all.[66] Unfortunately, it is extremely difficult to gain an objective understanding of the nature of their corroboration, since the majority of forensic speeches only indicate the point at which a witness gave a speech or a law was read out, and seldom include the testimony itself.[67] Instead we are left only with the comments of the litigants on the nature of their, and their opponents', witnesses, and the speculations of modern scholarship.

We might think that the techniques used by witnesses, as described by Philokleon in Aristophanes' *Wasps*, seem over the top (funny voices, stories, jokes, pleas for pity, dragging in their young children; *aulos*-recitals, set pieces from tragedies),[68] but witnesses do seem to have been involved in supporting litigants in a range of ways, from upsetting the process and timing of a case,[69] to enhancing the credibility of a litigant by testifying to his character and making clear his importance to the community or to his family.[70] It has even been argued that a witness could be expected to say whatever was needed to support his litigant.[71] Such allusions, although they may not give us an objective view of this evidence, do at least suggest that the *dikastai* paid attention to what the witnesses said.[72]

This is perhaps further supported by the existence of the *dikē pseudo-*

marturiōn, that is a prosecution brought for giving false witness. This was a private suit, since giving false witness seems to have been regarded as an offence against the opposing litigant, not the state, nor the gods (an Athenian witness was not normally on oath). But actions of false witness seem to have been brought for a variety of reasons in addition to challenging the truth of what was being said.[73] In most cases, it seems that witnesses took this risk voluntarily, since there did not exist anything equivalent to a modern *subpoena*.[74]

Turning to the tablets, we do find indications that the words of witnesses were a source of anxiety. The agent of *DT* 87 seems to have been concerned about what his opponent's witnesses might say, since he binds their tongues (and minds). As noted above, *DT* 49 suggests a similar concern, but raises questions about the relationship of witnessing to speech. We have already observed how tongue and speech seem to have different significance, insofar as the woman is cursed for her tongue, but not for her speech like the men on the tablet. A certain Pherekles stands out, in turn, amongst the male targets because Pherekles is the only one whose act of witness (*marturia*) is bound, while his speech is not. It suggests that some kind of difference was perceived between an act of witness and simply giving a speech (*logos*). If we accept that it might demonstrate a difference, then it could indicate that the other men might speak in court (for example as rowdy *dikastai* or as onlookers without officially testifying as witnesses. Alternatively, it might imply that they were to make speeches in an official capacity as fellow prosecutors or defendants, rather than as witnesses. *DTA* 94 binds the speech of Diokles (his *logos*) and then the acts of witnessing of him (or, which relate to him). This also suggests there was a difference perceived between speech and witnessing. Alternatively, it may, along with *DT* 49, suggest that the two terms comprise a hendiadys.

These last two tablets raise the possibility that the act of witnessing in each case was written rather than spoken. Written testimony is thought to have replaced spoken in the Athenian courts in the early fourth century (see above), so ascertaining whether the act of witness referred to on a tablet is written or spoken might lead to the possibility of dating each text slightly more securely. If we examine the tablets in the light of this possibility, then the two tablets above do seem to make some kind of distinction between written and spoken witnessing. Following this train of thought, we find two other tablets (*DTA* 65 and *DT* 89) that both mention witnessing without mentioning tongues: although, of course, we cannot be sure that this is not just an omission by the writer. In contrast, *DT* 87 includes a formulation which seems to imply spoken witnessing—binding the tongue of an individual's witnesses—so this curse is likely to date to a time before the reform. *DTA* 25 and 68 (one with no mention of a tongue, the other with many, but none directly associated with the *marturia* in l. 10, which is, in any case, largely a supplement) are both too fragmentary to be read accurately. It may be that there were other terms on the tablets that indicate people playing the role of witness. *DTA* 94 offers an interesting confluence of terms. On this tablet, among a number of tablets, we find the act of witnessing bound alongside the 'tongue and mind of those who are helpers of Diokles' (τὴν γλῶτ(τ)αν καὶ τὰ<ι>ς φρένας καὶ τοῖς Διοκλ(έου)ς Βοη(θ)οῖς πάντας). This may help shed light on the meaning of the term 'friends/helpers' when it appears on curse tablets: it may be that these are witnesses, although they are not specifically denoted as such. The idea of helper = witness might also help to define more closely the role played by those characters who are described on tablets as acting or being 'on behalf of so-and-so'.

A similar overlap of terms appears on *DT* 63, but this is, perhaps, less illuminating. If the restoration of the tablet is correct, then the targets here are described as 'fellow-speakers' who had been brought to court to be witnesses.[76] It may be that they were witnesses in a previous case, who are now coming to court as litigants in their own right, or they may have been litigants now called upon to testify: the overlap of terms, and the implications for legal process, are far from clear.

Supporting speakers, fellow prosecutors and defendants, and team players (οἱ συνήγοροι, οἱ κατήγοροι, οἱ ἀντίδικοι, οἱ σύνδικοι)[77]

The blurred relationship of terms for witnessing is a timely reminder that the use of forensic terminology on the curse tablets is probably not as precise as modern experience of law might lead modern readers to expect.[78] The terms in this next section comprise the most common targets of these curses, and reveal similar difficulties of definition. Other evidence suggests that they are all terms describing litigants: *antidikos* appears to mean an opponent in a suit, and can indicate either the plaintiff or the defendant; *sundikos* means generally an advocate, either a fellow-prosecutor or defendant in a private suit, but it was also used specifically to describe individuals who represented or, 'were the voice of' an association, such as members of *phratries*, *demes*, even the *polis* itself.[79] *Katēgoros* appears to mean accuser (and appears, in the plural, on only one tablet).[80] Although I will pay separate attention to the use of each term, distinguishing their different roles, and the kind of threat that each may have presented, is difficult.

(*a*) Of these terms, *sundikos* appears most frequently as the target of binding in the tablets. It usually appears in the plural without an indication of the number involved. Even more imprecise (or inclusive) is the phrase 'whoever is ...', which could indicate that the agent of the text was cursing one opponent, or several, or just did not know himself, and so was covering every possibility.[81] I cannot find the term used in the singular. On SGD 99 and 100, both from Selinous, Sicily, the phrase 'the foreign *sundikoi*' is used, which could mean that they are foreign residents (or metics) or perhaps meaning the advocate from another city in an inter-*polis* dispute.

As these examples suggest, on some tablets, the *sundikoi* appear to be a group targeted in addition and with equal force to the named individuals.[82] In some texts, they seem to represent the enemy: *DTA* 81 is fragmentary, but the text curses *sundikoi* alongside (and possibly as examples of) enemies (ἐχθρούς in l. 1 of the curse). *DTA* 103a l. 8/9 curses the *sundikoi* and anyone else who is a friend to them, and *DTA* 39 curses both *sundikoi* and friends. On others, this relationship is reversed, and they appear to be cursed because of their relationship with other targets named on the tablet; on these they are described as belonging (i.e., with or of someone) to another character.[83]

(*b*) *Sunēgoroi* tend to appear in the plural on the tablets, and both with and without indications of particular allegiances. *DTA* 38 includes four named individuals and whoever are their *sunēgoroi*. SGD 68 indicates that the *sunēgoroi* are those of Kallistratos. In NGCT 15, Theokles receives the epithet *sunēgoros* (co-speaker) alongside Menekrates, Kallistratos, and Nikostratos, along with three further men who are 'co-speakers with Menekrates'. *DTA* 63 names Pamphilos and the *sunēgoroi* equally at the top of the tablet, while *DTA* 65 includes *sunēgoroi* in a list that also includes relatives, *dikastai*, and witnesses, although the primary focus of the curse does seem to be one Kallias. *DTA* 95 appears, despite its fragmentary state, to include at least 10 named targets, one of them female, as well as the *sunēgoroi*. In SGD 176, those playing the role of *sunēgoroi* are indicated by a verb alongside 'those who stand around', and four named individuals. We know that non-citizen *sunēgoroi* were allowed—Boiotian and Phoenician *sunēgoroi* supported Aeschines in his defence speech against Demosthenes—but we find no explicit reference to foreign *sunēgoroi* being cursed.[84]

(*c*) Unlike the other terms, *antidikos* is used in the singular to identify named individuals: for example, on *DTA* 94, one Diokles, is identified with this term; SGD 51 where the opponent seems to be one Aristoboulos (he is supported by *sundikoi* 'with' him, who are also targets of this curse); and NGCT 24b, where the opponent is named as Dion (although there is at least one other named individual targeted).

It is also used in the plural, and, as with the other terms, appears both with and without indications of allegiance to other targets in the texts. On SGD 6 (in the phrase 'whoever are . . .') they appear in the plural and are identified as 'with Pytheas', who is the first of four named individuals in the text, but it is not clear whether the term is meant to describe those other individuals who are named in a list after Pytheas, or if they are to be regarded as an additional set of targets. In SGD 19, the use of *allos* clearly indicates that this group of *antidikoi* is being cursed in addition to the four individuals identified by name in the text. They are labelled as 'with him', where he seems to be Nikostratos, the last name in the preceding list.[85]

As we have noted, there are a number of curses where the arrangement of the names on the tablets does distinguish between an individual or individuals and his supporters, referring to 'him/those with so-and-so' or seeming to place a greater emphasis on a particular individual. These can be interpreted as closer to the conventional description of Athenian legal action as resembling a duel between two individuals, insofar as it suggests that there was a main speaker who was of greater importance than any others. Even so, it does suggest that whatever those fellow-speakers were saying, even if it was simply corroborating the main litigant's argument or adding to his status by expressing their support, they were still considered a significant part of the opposition, important enough to merit being bound.

But many cases raise a variety of difficult questions about the judicial context, especially if we imagine it structured according to this conventional model in which individual members of the elite do battle with each other for zero-sum supremacy. For example, in a curse tablet from Attika, over forty *antidikoi* are cursed: can these all be litigants in a court case? Although this seems a rare example, it is possible that just as many may be intended as targets on other tablets: the use of the plural terms *sundikoi/antidikoi* means we cannot tell how many are actually meant.[86]

On some tablets, as we have seen, there are a limited number of targets, but all with apparently equal weight given to each one and none of them distinguished as the main focus of the curse. The most obvious explanation is that these are all cases in which teams of prosecutors were elected, for example *apophasis*.[87] However, it has been suggested that it indicates a wholly non-judicial context and that when the terms *sundikoi* and *antidikoi* appear by themselves in tablets with lists of names and without any other allusion to judicial procedure, rather than having a legal significance they are likely to be closer in meaning to the terms *amicus* and *inimicus* found in Latin maledictions.[88]

Such a view depends on two assumptions: first, that the extant curse texts are complete, which is far from clear in a number of cases; and second,

The Best Defence 181

that the political structure of Athens was sufficiently similar to that of ancient Rome for there to have been a formal or, at least, organized system of patronage and political alliance. The latter assumption has been a subject of much debate: certainly there is evidence for both political alliances and the importance of financial generosity within the political structure of Athens, and, obviously, within lawcourts these terms represent members of judicial teams of speakers, but it is questionable how far this might be taken to indicate a widespread organized system that existed outside the lawcourts, and had a recognized terminology, such as at Rome.[89] Besides, there is no evidence from elsewhere to suggest that these terms, although technically (if imprecisely to our eyes) applied in the courts of Athens, have a separate meaning when they are not used in relation to judicial language. This is especially true of *sundikos*, which was also used, as noted above, to denote an advocate publicly appointed by the state.

An alternative suggestion is that the agent of this curse was comprehensively binding, in advance, any person who might possibly appear in court in any way as an opponent.[90] This suggestion finds support in the frequent appearance of various formulae at the ends of curse tablets, which seem to be trying to include, under a general phrase, any other individual which the curser might have forgotten or been unable to fit on the tablet. However, it still does not seem to explain those texts in which a small number of individuals have been selected, all cursed with apparently equal weight.

Rather than trying to fit all these curses into the existing model of court activity, it may be that this evidence suggests we need a more nuanced picture of the Athenian judicial context. As I have already mentioned briefly above, recent research has suggested that we should consider a wider spectrum of possible configurations of legal protagonists in Athenian courts beyond that of individual and supporter. One of the suggested alternatives is that there may have been situations in which, in effect, teams of litigants acted for the prosecution and defence and that the terms, *sunēgoroi, antidikoi,* and *sundikoi,* may have been used to refer to members of such teams in both *graphai* and *dikai*.[91] The tasks and self-presentation of some of these team-members may have differed markedly according to whether they acted for the defence or prosecution, and whether the action was a *graphē* or *dikē*.

For example, *sunēgoroi* pleading on the side of the prosecution in public actions often present themselves as supplementary *katēgoroi* in their own right, almost like expert witnesses with further important information about the case, rather than as offering support for the main litigant. This may be only a rhetorical ploy, in some cases, but in others their status is less clear: as Rubenstein has pointed out, the term is used to describe each member of a team of prosecutors, and supporting speakers, and prosecutors elected by the Assembly.[92]

In turn, it seems that a large number of defence *sunēgoroi* could appear on a litigant's behalf, each one making a different kind of contribution, their particular tasks depending on the nature of their relationship with the defendant.[93] Some will have made important speeches and perhaps even introduced their own witnesses, but not all such contributions need have been lengthy speeches. Some may have contributed only a few crucial paragraphs or focused on particular aspects of the defence. Some may not have spoken at all, but merely made an emotional contribution to the argument. From the forensic corpus it looks as if relatives and friends (and children and, perhaps, women—I examine the presence of women in court in more detail below) might be expected tearfully to bemoan the fate of the litigant.[94] The roles of these additional speakers were powerful in themselves and, in some cases, may have obscured the main protagonists of the case, distributing the perceived (and actual) responsibility for the conduct of a case as if across the members of a team.[95]

As for private suits, other than the *dike phonou*, the evidence of the forensic speeches is unclear as to whether a suit could be brought by more than one person at a time against more than one person at a time.[96] In terms of defence, a number of speeches indicate that demes, *gennētai*, and organizations could be sued by an individual.[97] As for prosecuting a group of private citizens, normal practice seems to have been to bring a set of separate suits, which were probably heard on the same day.[98] Nevertheless, there is evidence that both plaintiffs and defendants not only did sometimes represent a group or association, but also that in court, the presentation of the case might make the group nature of the prosecution or defence clear.[99]

Such an analysis of legal process has interesting implications for the tablets, making sense of some of the questions outlined above: for example, those curses that target small teams of co-speakers may indicate a private suit or public action in which a group of individuals had joined forces as plaintiffs, while choosing one of their number to carry legal responsibility. The curses targeting many fellow-speakers might be explained by expanding the current picture of the ways in which *graphai* were conducted and the possible variety of roles for fellow-speakers, and the types of people who may have filled them. If this were the case, the terms *sundikos* and *antidikos* might be used to indicate a range of activities, beyond the more traditional interpretation of them as 'opponent' or 'advocate'. The next two sections also suggest the need to expand our traditional picture of Athenian legal procedure.

Those who stood around[100]

In the last section I mentioned groups or individuals brought to court in order to exert some kind of emotional influence, and this may have some bearing on this next set of terms. The question to be tackled is why some curses target those 'standing around'. Chaniotis asks this question of a curse tablet thought to come from south Russia, in which the phrase ὅσοι συνηγοροῦσι καὶ παρατηροῦσι appears.[101] In the Attic orators the verb παρατηροῦσι preserves its literal meaning of 'watch' or 'look out for' without any judicial implications. Here, however, it seems to have had a specific sense that was somehow complementary to συνηγοροῦσι and describes 'someone whose presence, like that of the opponents' *sunēgoroi*, in a possibly fourth- or early third-century lawcourt north of the Black Sea was thought to be worth cursing'.[102]

Chaniotis suggests that one reason for this might be that these 'observers' were in fact supporters brought to court by the litigant in order to influence the judges, either by specific reactions or merely with their presence. As a parallel for this kind of activity, he cites a number of inscriptions recording events surrounding arbitrations at an international level.[103] In terms of individual legal activity, he suggests that this behaviour only refers to the practice of law in Olbia.[104] However, similar terms do appear in two Attic tablets (*DTA* 79 and *DT* 67), and there are other more common terms and periphrases (for example, friends/helpers, or 'those with so-and-so') that describe groups or individuals as supporters of the target of the curse. In support of this suggestion, there is plenty of evidence to suggest that the role of the spectator in the Athenian courts could be, in a number of ways, a powerful one. Using both literary and archaeological evidence, Lanni has argued convincingly for the crucial role played by the spectators (οἱ περιεστηκότες) who stood at the edges of the courtrooms in Athens (and indeed at other key political venues) watching and listening to the cases.[105] She points out that the presence of these spectators had 'an important effect both on the litigants' arguments and on the judges' decisions'.[106]

In terms of the effect on the litigants, evidence suggests that speakers thought about convincing the spectators in the courtroom as a task separate from convincing the judges; while during the case itself, it appears that the audience members were frequently encouraged by the speakers themselves to interrupt their opponents, often by means of appeals to their general knowledge of the law or the facts of the case.[107] With regard to the effect on the judges, the audience may have functioned (or, at least, this was used as a threat by the speakers) as a sort of informal *euthynē*. Speakers make reference to how the jury will be asked to defend their decisions when questioned by members of the audience as they leave the courtroom.[108] With the example of the Roman *contio* before us, we have to ask if it was likely that litigants might have gathered 'the right sort of crowd' to attend a case.[109] As we have seen above, in the discussion of *sundikoi*, the range of roles which friends and relatives could play as supporters of a litigant was wide. The semi-recognition of these activities in the texts—the fact that terms for 'friends/helpers', 'those who stand around', 'those with x . . .', appear with such frequency—is not undermined by the variety of terms used to describe such roles: this would be consistent with them not being official.

Women[110]

Finally, we return to the puzzle presented by women in these texts. Women seldom, if ever, appeared in court, even as supporters in the sense described earlier. And yet, women appear on a number of curse tablets that seem to have been created for legal contexts.

In those texts that indicate conflict, but which do not contain forensic language, they receive a spectrum of attention. Some comprise simple lists of names, in which the women appear alongside their male counterparts, with no qualification or explanation: for example SGD 10, an Attic text from a grave in the Kerameikos, or the early fourth-century Attic curse *DTA* 24, in which women are cursed alongside (possibly) famous male targets. NGCT 50, a fourth- or third-century text from Mytilene, binds a list of men and women 'and anyone else who is with them'. *DTA* 30, a third-century BCE curse from Attika, includes Ilara the *kapelis* or (female) innkeeper as the last in a list of ten names.

On SGD 48, we gather a little more information: the women appear to be identified as prostitutes; they appear alongside a number of possibly famous men.[111] SGD 46 consists of a list of names on side B, both men and women, but side A is devoted to a detailed attack on a woman called 'Mytis': '[I bind] her tongue and spirit and actions. May they all go against her.' The Attic curses *DTA* 84 and 89 also provide some more data about their targets: both curse their male and female victims with equal vehemence and detail, singling out parts of their body or aspects of their livelihood. The same is true of the lengthy vitriolic attack on the targets of *DT* 50 ('O Hermes Binder and Persephone, restrain the body and spirit and tongue and feet and deeds and plans of Myrrinē, the wife of Hagnotheos of the Peiraeus, until she goes down into Hades and withers away'). On *DTA* 87, a fourth-century Attic curse, Thraitta is targeted in the second line, but this may be just as part of an attack on her husband, Kallias. The curse also attacks 'Glykanthis, whom they call Malthake' and 'Mania, the inn-keeper'. On *DT* 61 (a fourth-century Attic curse) the woman, Plathane, appears to be leading a group of men and women. We have seen the formula 'with so-and-so' used on other tablets of those allied (officially or unofficially, we cannot tell) in a litigious team. These are all texts for which the context is uncertain, although some of them have been identified as having a political motive.

Women also feature in texts that are certainly litigious, appearing in a variety of formulae that indicate they may be playing a range of roles. Sometimes they are part of a list on a curse that also includes judicial terms: for example, the anonymous woman of NGCT 10, an Athenian curse found in the Kerameikos cemetery. On *DTA* 39, a third-century Attic text, we find Satura and her mother, Theodora, among a list of 19 names that ends with a final round-up of targets: 'and all those who are their *sundikoi* (fellow litigants) and their friends'. On a third-century Attic text, *DTA* 67, Aristylla appears at the end of a list of men who are targetted. The curse goes on to ask that the words of another man (one Krates) should be cold and nonsensical, and the same be true of all those informers and judges with them; no difference is drawn between the male and female targets. On *DTA* 68, the women are cursed in as much detail as their male counterparts. The same is true of *DTA* 106, a third-century Attic tablet, which uses the same formula for each victim 'Let him (or her) be bound in the presence of Hermes of the underworld and Hekate of the underworld!', rounding up, half-way through the curse with the phrase 'Let those who are the *sundikoi* to those inscribed here be bound before them.'

As mentioned before, with its use of bespoke formulae, *DT* 49, an Attic text dated by Audollent to around 300 BCE, may indicate a more specialized role for its targets, including the woman, 'Pyrrias' wife', who is one of the seven targets. Granted, the curse does not include such specialized instructions for her as are given for some of the other victims (for example, 'I bind Kineas, his tongue and spirit and speech that he is practising with Theagenes') but why mention her at all? And why bother to bind her tongue and spirit—what risk could they hold for the curse-writer? On *DTA* 95, a fourth-century BCE tablet, we find the women even more involved in the judicial events being described. It binds the actions and tongue and words and deeds of Menon, son of Aristokles, so that he may prove useless to the authorities, and then asks the same thing for Pithios and a woman called Neodike. The last line of the curse asks: 'The god who binds restrains the advocates Eukairos and Hedyle, the wife of Timokrates.'

Similarly puzzling is *DT* 87, a third-century text from Kerkyra, in which the first target, Silanos, has his tongue and mind bound, along with the tongue and mind of 'his witnesses'. Silanos is accompanied by three more targets,

Epainetos, Agenos, and Timareta, each of whom also have their tongues and minds bound. The set-up of the curse prompts us to ask in what way the victims are related. For example, if the last three targets are intended to be the witnesses referred to in the cursing of Silanos, what is the role of the woman, Timareta?

Indeed, although it has been argued that 'there was ... no objection to [a woman] being present in court if she chose',[112] it is unlikely that a woman would be physically present in an Athenian court. The courts were one of a number of civic spaces designed 'for the exercise of citizenship, where both to act before an audience and to participate in an audience are defining characteristics of democratic obligations' and so limited to male citizens.[113] We have examined, earlier, the possibility of women acting as informers. In cases of homicide, women and slaves could give evidence against, but not on behalf of, the accused.[114] However, most commentators seem to agree that there is no indication that women (or slaves) ever did this.[115] In all other cases, a woman's *kyrios* (male guardian) would present her evidence in court, and do this in his own name. Litigants would even go to some lengths to avoid mentioning respectable women's names, although it was acceptable to mention the names of the dead, of prostitutes, slaves, or female relatives of their opponents.[116] The apparent references to Neaira being present in *Against Neaira* serve as an exception which throws emphatic light on more usual behaviour since this woman is, in a number of ways, extraordinary.[117]

But are there other compelling reasons why women might be cursed in judicial tablets: were there ever situations where what they said could pose a threat in this context? Admittedly, women as litigants are extremely rare: there are a few famous examples, including the women mentioned earlier whose charges involved supernatural activity that threatened either individuals or the city. However, closer examination of the forensic corpus reveals court battles between men that seem to have begun as quarrels between, involving, or exacerbated by women.[118] The fact that the evidence supplied, directly or indirectly, by a woman was considered pertinent is supported by the number of ways in which, beyond using the *kyrios*, it could be brought before the court.[119] And a couple of examples of vicious attacks by litigants on women who have chosen to support their opponents suggests how much this mattered.[120] In turn, women could prevent their husbands from giving false evidence and their reaction to a verdict was important enough to the jurors for it to be brought up in forensic argument, as is spelled out in detail in Demosthenes' speech *Against Neaira*.[121]

Legal processes reflected life in the city: a trial would be only one stage of ongoing conflicts or alliances that were also played out in other arenas, such as the private realm of the family home or *oikos*. Women could play a significant, if unofficial, part in legal processes just as they could in the social and political spheres. Their appearance on the curse tablets suggests that this is true, and encourages us to look for evidence of women's involvement in these legal events, beyond what we know of the theoretical structure.

As part of building this larger social picture, some of the judicial curse tablets mention other parts of their targets' lives. For example, *DTA* 25 seems to include the victim's (victims'?) neighbours in the curse, while in *DTA* 87, Kittos, the target, is described as a neighbour. *DTA* 65 and *NGCT* 12 both mention some kind of connection by marriage, either to the curser himself or between his targets. *DTA* 68 and 87 repeatedly mention the professions (including male and female tavern-keepers, pimps and concubines, boxers, and housekeepers), work, and workplaces of their targets. *DT* 49 and *SGD* 42 (side b) each include details about the professions of some of their targets.[122]

This kind of detail sets the business of the law courts against a background of daily domestic life in the city, in addition to the usual picture of political machinations. In this context, we can also note that no curse in the current collection is directed explicitly at a *sykophant*, although it may be, of course, that they are identified by name rather than by role.[123] Since, presumably, the reason for writing these curses lay in their agent's belief that their opposition might have a compelling case, this absence might be seen to support Osborne's description of sycophancy in the Athenian court as an ad hoc, rather mild term of abuse, implying that the prosecutor did not have a very good case.

CURSING IN THE COURTS

Our understanding from the tablets of the precise situations in which these tablets were used can never be complete. The evidence from the tablets, and our more general knowledge about the courts, is such that, in many cases, we have to make our own judgement about the events each tablet records, the weight and reason with which each of the individuals or groups involved is cursed, and we must speculate about the exact role they played in court.[124] However, using our understanding of the historical context, we can draw some inferences about the way judicial binding curses were likely to be used; they, in turn, provide us with detail about the nature of the historical context.

The majority of Attic judicial curse tablets date from the period of the radical democracy, when the ideal of the citizen and his freedom of speech were dominant, however awkwardly realized.[125] The lawcourts of Athens embodied many of these ideas: offering a space in which citizens fought with rhetoric.

An inability to speak would have had direct consequences. At worst, it might lead to losing a case, the punishment of an individual, even the loss of life. At best, it could mean humiliation in, what we have seen was, an unforgiving environment.[126] The resulting ridicule, especially when exacerbated by ensuing gossip, would have been a serious matter.[127] This emphasis on the power of speech is a fitting context for these tablets. We might expect to find their writers trying to tinker with the truth, influence the judge, or simply destroy opponents. Instead, for the most part, they seek to bind, often invoking what was surely a well-known, and dreaded, affliction: the inability to speak, to perform persuasively, in court. The agents of these tablets seek to control their peers by inhibiting the words they might use against them.

In such a context, binding makes most sense as a pre-emptive strategy, reinforcing arguments that these curses were created either before, at the start of, or during, the trial process.[128] There is no evidence amongst the tablets, or in the associated anecdotes, that curses were used to exact vengeance after a defeat in court. The fact that penalties imposed on convicted defendants in *graphai* were more severe than for those convicted in *dikai*, and that an individual who prosecuted a *graphē* and failed to obtain 20 per cent of the votes faced (at least in some cases) a substantial fine, might lead us to suggest that curse tablets were more likely to be written in fear of the penalties of *graphai*. However, the evidence of the tablets indicates that they were written for both *graphai* and *dikai*. Cursing was a mechanism used by members of both prosecution and defence teams, in a range of different litigious situations, each seeking to increase their side's chances of success.[129]

In turn, the content of the tablets sheds light on the context of their use. In particular, the number and social range of people cursed in these texts suggest a broader and more inclusive picture of legal activity and its socio-political role than previous theories of judicial activity have suggested. It is no doubt the case that some curse tablets were written by individuals locked in one-on-one political struggles, but the evidence from these curse texts reveals far more about the nature of judicial conflict. The various personnel depicted across the curse texts surely reflects different configurations of conflict within the city: trials were not always simply legal duels, often groups of people faced each other in court, and court cases were sometimes conducted in teams. For example, the long lists of names that occur on a number of the tablets suggest that public actions may have been conducted by groups, providing an opportunity for a citizen, even if his financial resources were limited, to take part in litigation as part of a team.

Moreover, curses were aimed not just at one's opponent(s), but at a whole range of individuals, playing both official and unofficial roles, both within and outside the lawcourt, and not just citizens. Alongside lists of (potentially) famous political figures, judicial curse tablets offer glimpses of other individuals within the city, and of their lives: workshops are cursed, also networks of friends and allies, metics and slaves, prostitutes, wives, and neighbours.[130] Among the human targets are social groups we might not expect, such as women, who do not even appear at the trial, let alone speak in that context; while, in the courtroom, those who are cursed include *dikasts*, and individuals who were, as they are described in the texts themselves, just 'standing around'. This information suggests that the risks an individual confronted when he became a litigant were seen to arise not only from the behaviour of a single opponent, nor even just from events which occurred within the four walls of the court, but were affected by the networks of his relationships beyond in the larger community, and his standing within those networks.

So, in court, binding curses offered a way of trying to control the risks presented by fellow citizens. But this was not the only role they played: as the two stories at the beginning of the chapter demonstrate, the phenomenon of judicial cursing could also offer a redeeming explanation for those who had, for whatever reasons, found themselves suddenly struck dumb.[131] A new speaker might use stage-fright as an excuse, but this would not save more experienced speakers.[132] Instead, if you suffered this kind of paralysis, you might claim the malicious infliction of supernatural influence. Such explanations make even more sense when we recall that good oratory was itself regarded, by some, as possessing a certain supernatural power.[133] Such accounts might very well be accompanied by less charitable explanations— and the two might well coexist, without further elaboration. These anecdotes show the phenomenon of the binding curse in another light—they posed a risk themselves, and, as such, they were adopted as a compelling, perhaps even comforting, explanation for those who suffered, or witnessed, rhetorical misfortune. Together, these texts and tales offer complementary insights into the cultural understanding of risk and misfortune in the Athenian courts.

But not all the texts that have been placed in this category can be explained in this way: for a number of these binding curses the context is far from certain. Some of these texts comprise simply lists of names: a number of them consist of groups of individuals who, other evidence suggests, may have been associated by political beliefs or civic functions.[134] Others curse the tongues of their targets but include no legal terminology. It may very well be that these curses were written in anticipation of a court case, perhaps brought for political reasons, perhaps not. However, an alternative explanation may be that they were prompted by the need to control a group of associated enemies who were perceived as posing a threat to the writer of the curse. In some cases, again, this may be because of political affiliation, but for others there may well have been some other context of hostility, which we simply do not have the information to identify. The next two categories of curses will reveal further texts in which the hostility of the writer is plain, but clear information about the context of creation is frustratingly missing or ambiguous.

10

Business as Usual?

> I have yet to encounter anyone who accepts that his own poverty is inherently meaningless, that it represents nothing more significant than his own personal misery. . . .to questions about the inequitable distribution of good and bad fortunes, other answers are readily available. Suppositions informed by the witchcraft paradigm offer one of the most emotionally satisfying: 'We are being held back and are suffering because of other people's malice'.
>
> Ashforth 2005: 96[1]

For that night Homer slept there. The next day, as he went away, some potters, who were firing a kiln full of fragile ware, saw him and called him over, as they had heard of his skills, and encouraged him to sing for them, promising to give him some of their wares, and whatever else they had. Homer sang them these verses, which are called The Kiln:

> If you are going to pay for my singing, O potters,
> Then come, Athena, and hold your hand over the kiln:
> May the cups turn a fine black, and all the dishes,
> And be thoroughly baked, and earn the price they are worth
> As they sell in quantity in the market and the streets,
> And make good profits and benefit me as it does them.
> But if you turn to shamelessness and deceit,
> Then I will invoke all of the kiln gremlins,
> Smasher and Crasher, Overblaze and Shakeapart
> And Underbake, who does this craft much harm.[2]

In the ancient *Potter's Hymn*, we meet a terrifying crew: *Suntrips* (Smasher), *Smaragos* (Crusher), *Asbestos* (Overblaze), *Salaktes* (Shakeapart), and *Omodamos* (Conqueror of the unbaked). It is easy to imagine that these could be personifications of the destructive forces feared by potters, but are they evidence for supernatural methods of commercial competition? Did the ruthless businessmen of antiquity craft secret curses, launching such vicious powers against their rivals, in a desperate bid to gain control of the market?[3] Such an explanation has been put forward by a number of commentators in favour of creating a category of commercial curses.[4] The relevant tablets are almost entirely confined to Classical and Hellenistic Greece, and are included on the grounds that they seem to have been created by an ambitious trades/craftsman who is attempting to disable his business rivals in order to enhance his own success. It is understandable if current explanations for the motivations underlying these texts look for this kind of reckless competitive instinct and appetite for survival among their writers. This would bring them into line with judicial curses and the presumed motivations of their creators, which seem, at least at first sight, much easier to understand. In judicial curses, we have details in the texts that clearly locate the context of their creation, guiding our reflections on the nature of the risks that they were intended to allay. Once we explore the social circumstances surrounding that context, and the many different types of penalty it threatened, we quickly begin to understand why writing a curse might seem desirable.

However, the more closely we examine the texts themselves the more dubious this approach to the identification and description of commercial curses becomes. In fact, we find that across the tablets in this category, commercial detail receives a range of different kinds of attention from the writers of the curses, suggesting that an explanation that turns on a simple statement about commercial competition cannot adequately explain the contents of them all.[5]

THE LITERARY EVIDENCE

A number of literary passages are frequently adduced to support this picture of an environment of cut-throat commercial competition. They include some lines from Hesiod's *Works and Days*, the extract from *The Potter's Hymn* quoted above, a passage from Pliny's *Natural History*, and part of a definition from Pollux's *Onomasticon*.[6] But if we examine these passages in more detail, not all of them present the case for economic competition as strongly as has been suggested. Hesiod presents the clearest case: he makes a brief reference to the beneficial nature of the competitive strife between potters, joiners, beggars and singers:

> ἥ τε καὶ ἀπάλμόν περ ὅμως ἐπὶ ἔργον ἔγειρεν.
> εἰς ἕτερον γάρ τίς τε ἰδὼν ἔργοιο χατίζων
> πλούσιον, ὃς σπεύδει μὲν ἀρώμεναι ἠδὲ φυτεύειν
> οἶκόν τ' εὖ θέσθαι, ζηλοῖ δέ τε γείτονα γείτων
> εἰς ἄφενος σπεύδοντ'· ἀγαθὴ δ' Ἔρις ἥδε βροτοῖσιν
> καὶ κεραμεὺς κεραμεῖ κοτέει καὶ τέκτονι τέκτων
> καὶ πτωχὸς πτωχῷ φθονέει καὶ ἀοιδὸς ἀοιδῷ

[Strife] rouses even the shiftless one to work. For when someone whose work falls short looks towards another, towards a rich man who hastens to plough and plant and manage his household well, then neighbour vies with neighbour as he hastens to wealth: this Strife is good for mortals. So potter is piqued with potter, joiner with joiner, beggar begrudges beggar, and singer singer.'[7]

The picture this paints—members of the same profession competing with each other to make a better living—is realistic. However, it is a leap to argue that this must mean an environment of economic competition in which curse tablets and other magical techniques were the crucial weapons. It suggests rather that these individuals struggled to do better by vying about matters related to their 'pride in workmanship', such as the quality of their work, fabric, size of pot, etc. The passage from which this extract comes introduces a longer meditation on the need for each individual to work hard and honestly, and a reflection on the ways in which acquisitive and lazy men begrudge their fellows success. The range of professions Hesiod mentions does not focus solely on craftsmen and artisans, nor on competition, but seems intended to make a moral point about how individuals at every level of society need to work hard to make a living, from those who make luxury goods to those whose skills are needed on a more everyday basis, to performers who sell their poetic talents, even those who specialize in begging for their livelihood. The main intention of the passage seems to be to contrast those who do nothing to support themselves, like Hesiod's brother Perses, with those who know the importance, and so are able to acquire the benefits, of hard and honest work, like Hesiod.

No mention is made in the *Works and Days* of supernatural dangers to artisans or businessmen, let alone to supernatural methods of competition. However, the former do appear in the *Potter's Hymn*. As we have seen, this poem contains a list of what must be taken as either personifications of the destructive elements which potters feared, or the names of real *daimones*: 'names assigned to real powers in accordance with their particular "specialities"'. It has been asserted that this part of the hymn is 'almost certainly based on a once-extant formula for curse tablets against the kilns of rival potters'.[8] There is some doubt about this on grounds of dating, but if it is the case then we can observe that this appears to have comprised a quite different form of expression from the range of formulae found on the extant curse tablets.[9] For example, neither the names of those destructive elements nor similar entities described in the poem are invoked amongst the existing texts. This may be a matter of the survival of evidence, but we can also observe that, across all categories, none of the curses make any kind of reference to *daimones* that are specifically related to the area of life that they are binding. Nor do we find curses that aim to destroy the work of potters (or, indeed, the work of any craftsmen) in a way that focuses on different aspects of the creative process, as this description might suggest. In fact, most of the tablets focus on binding physical aspects of an individual before they go on (if indeed they do) to bind that individual's workshop or other aspects of his/her work. It seems more likely that these *daimones* were invoked by potters to account for what were otherwise inexplicable disasters in their workshops.

Later in the poem (ll. 15–16), the poet does call on πολυφάρμακε Κίρκη (literally, 'Kirke of the many potions') and invites her to ἄγρια φάρμακα βάλλε, κάκου δ'αὐτούς τε καὶ ἔργα 'mix your wild drugs, and harm them and their work'. He also invites Chiron, with his horde of centaurs, to destroy the kiln. Here indeed there may be a reference to the kinds of supernatural activities that we associate with those who also offered cursing, but none of the vocabulary of the poem suggests that binding is what the poet had in mind. And our primary point stands, that from the beginning of the poem, no mention is made of rival potters: the poet is threatening destruction if he is cheated by the potters, not because he is in competition with them.

Scholars have also cited comments by Pliny and Pollux as evidence that 'magic was popular among certain types of craftsmen, especially in those professions like bronze working where delicate heating and cooling processes were necessary to avoid breakage' and, more specifically, that curse tablets were particularly feared by such professions.[10] At first, it might seem that Pliny had binding in mind: he discusses how everyone fears being bewitched (*Defigi quidem diris deprecationibus nemo non metuit* 'Indeed, there is no one who does not fear being bound by fearful imprecations').[11] But by this he appears to be describing a more general sense of superstition since he goes on to talk about how, *Hoc pertinet ovorum quae exorbuerit quisque calices coclearumque protinus frangi aut isdem coclearibus perforari* ('this (feeling) makes us shatter the shells of eggs or snails immediately we have eaten them, or else pierce them with the same spoon'). Certainly Pliny is talking about the creation of maleficent magic, but he does not make specific reference to the creation or use of curse tablets, at least not the kind of curse tablet material under examination here. Rather, the passage offers an intriguing reference to generally held beliefs about the power of words. There is one reference to craftsmanship and the use of magic in this area of life, where Pliny describes how many people believe that pottery can be crushed by magic, but this appears to be in the text as part of an illustration of the range and extent of people's beliefs.[12] His exempla do not make reference to the type or origin of, or motivation behind, such supernatural attacks.

When Pollux describes the steps taken by bronze craftsmen to protect their work he does mention how they were created to 'ward off malicious envy', ἐπὶ φθόνου ἀποτροπῇ, but, again, he makes no specific mention of any aspect of the agent of this destructive magic and no reference to curse tablets.[13] The passage describes the activities of those who believe their work is somehow under threat from unseen forces and so seek to protect themselves, in turn, by supernatural means.

Viewed overall, the descriptions of the types of beliefs and *apotropaic* activities in these two passages focus on general responses to superstitions. They can be taken to demonstrate that among some craftsmen, perhaps particularly those in professions with a high potential for mistakes, supernatural powers were held responsible for inexplicable failures, but they make no specific reference to curse tablets.[14]

COMMERCIAL CURSES IN THE CORPUS

In turn, when we turn to the extant curse tablets, we find that relatively few potters and/or bronze workers are cursed. There are two relevant tablets. In a curse tablet from the fourth century (SGD 44), two potters, Demetrios and Demades, and their business are cursed, but it is hard to argue that they, or their commercial concerns, are the primary focus of attack. As well as their businesses, several other aspects of the potters are bound: for one, his hands, feet, and spirit and, for the other, his body and spirit. Far from being obviously commercially motivated, the arrangement of information in the text focuses on binding one Litias, who dominates the beginning and end of the text, while the potters hardly appear to be a main concern of the curse. In fact, the curse targets eight people in total, binding their tongues, hands, feet, heads, bodies, spirit, and work. That two of them are potters seems to be a detail intended to aid identification, rather than the main concern of the text. Moreover, the binding of their hands, feet, and even their business seems formulaic rather than having been rooted in any strong, focused sense of commercial competition on the part of the agent: the binding of their business just offers one more way in which to damage them.[15] It may be that the potters were being bound as a separate matter from Litias—although the structure of the curse suggests not—or it may be that the potters were somehow involved in the matter which motivated the agent to curse Litias (including his tongue).

The other relevant text is on a tablet found in the Athenian Agora (SGD 20). It may be directed against two bronze workers (among four possible others) on the grounds that they are identified as *ton chalkea*.[16] However, this could just be the writer's attempts to render the ethnic of the Euboean Chalkis (or less probably of the town Chalke near Larissa).[17]

Across the other tablets in the corpus, many other professions appear, for example: innkeepers, a miller, a boxer, pimps, and prostitutes (*DTA* 68); a helmet-maker (*DTA* 69); a scribe (SGD 48); a fabric seller, frame-maker or rope-maker and household slave (*DTA* 87); the bellows blower at a silver-works (SGD 3); doctors (SGD 124); a netmaker (SGD 52); stall-holder, household slave, innkeeper, and pimp (SGD 11); pipe-maker and carpenter (*DTA* 55); a leather-worker (*DTA* 12); and a seamstress (SGD 72). There is a helmsman mentioned in a tablet from Russia (SGD 170), the only mention in the extant curses of a profession related to shipping. Moreover, a number of tablets mention details about the workplace or bind aspects of work (tools or skills) without citing a specific activity, so we cannot identify the particular profession.[18]

As we have seen, there is evidence that artisans and craftsmen in occupations that involved a high level of risk did fear, and try to protect themselves against, the effects of malign supernatural forces, but it does not seem to be true that curse tablets were used primarily against those involved in such trades.[19] The most frequently mentioned profession in the tablets is that of the *kapelos* (and its female equivalent the *kapelis*). This term seems to indicate someone involved in retail at a low level, like a local shopkeeper or a tavern-keeper[20]—hardly the fiercely competitive artisan on which previous commentators have built their interpretation of commercial curses.

Moreover, it is crucial to remember that we are discussing the targets, rather than the writers, of curses. As mentioned before, ancient Greek curse tablets rarely offer any information on which to base statements about the nature and/or identity of any individual *making* a curse, and the texts grouped under this heading are no different in this respect. Two curses from among those listed above offer some slight information about their agents, but in neither case is it about their profession, and neither these two, nor any of the others, offer insights into the motivations (be they commercial competition or otherwise) behind the creation of the curse.[21] The nature of the evidence means that the basis for identifying a commercial curse must turn on details included in the curse about the *target*, usually descriptions of his/her profession or other details of those aspects of the target which the agent seeks to bind. And this approach leaves us with a number of questions about the nature of these tablets, the intention behind their creation and the identity of their targets and creators.

Professional identity

As I have mentioned above, there are a number of curses where the target's profession is mentioned. In some of these tablets, this detail appears to play an important part in the curse. A text from Athens (*DTA* 69) offers an example of this kind of spell: a man and his wife are bound and both their professions are mentioned (he is a helmet maker, she works with gold). Their household is also cursed, followed by their workshop, their work and their livelihoods, before the curse breaks off. There is no explicit information about the motivation that prompted the writing of the curse, but, in this case, the primary focus of this curse does seem to be the targets' professions.

But what about those texts in which a target or targets are identified by their profession (the so-called *technitikon*),[22] but there is no further detail about work or context? Can we assume that these curses are concerned with commercial competition, or is this information there for another reason? Consider the curse on a tablet found in a grave in the Athenian Kerameikos (*SGD* 11): the list of targets includes a number of their professions, including stall-holder, household slave, and pimp. Is the curse-writer competing in all these trades? One of them, Myrtale (l. 8), is described both as an innkeeper and as an old woman. Later in the curse, the ἔργα or work of the targets is just one element of several in a frequently found formulaic list. It seems more likely that, in this tablet, professional epithets are not provided because the curse is concerned with inhibiting commercial activity, but are included to secure identification of the intended victim(s).[23]

It may be possible to argue, that if a *technitikon* is being used in place of a patronymic and demotic, it may help to identify the social status of some victims. This might be the case in *SGD* 52, which identifies two individuals as netmakers, followed by two individuals who are identified by their fathers and their demes, suggesting that the netmakers were not citizens and so do not have a demotic that can be used in this curse. *DTA* 55 provides another example. This tablet includes details of the profession of some targets, but uses patronymics and demotics to identify others. However, an alternative and simpler explanation is that all the targets of a curse were citizens, but the writer of the curse was not systematic in his descriptions of them (indeed, in *DTA* 55 two individuals are described with patronymic, demotic, and profession (ll. 10 and 13)).

We are perhaps on safer ground in identifying non-citizens in the case of *DTA* 68, where the names of many of the targets suggest that they were of non-Athenian origin. (For example *Lykios* (l. 9) 'from Lykia'; *Lydes* (l. 10) 'from Lydia', and *Lakaina* (l. 14) 'from Sparta'.) On *DTA* 87, *Thraitta* is a typical name for a slave woman of Thrakian origin, and a number of texts note the owners of their targets, making it clear that they were slaves (for example, see *DTA* 68 and *DTA* 75). SGD 48 provides another possible example: this text begins with a vehement phrase asking for the binding, burial, and removal from the gaze of mankind, of three columns of mostly male names, some qualified with abbreviated demotics, one with his profession, and one with a description of his foreign origin. There are four female names in the final column, their owners described as Λαικάς, an abusive term for a prostitute.[24] This suggests that it is possible that the inclusion of a target's profession may have been, in some cases, a part of the curse-writer's attack, a form of ridicule or abuse. After all, it's well known that the comedy writer Aristophanes also found that one way of abusing powerful individuals was to mention their connections with certain occupations.[25]

As I have already suggested above, in some tablets the sheer number of professions that a curse mentions raises questions. For example, in the fragmentary Attic curse *DTA* 68 a number of the nineteen or so targets of the curse are identified by profession. In a repeated formula, each target's tongue, alongside his/her hands and feet, and his/her work and/or workplace are bound, including those whose profession is not mentioned. It is understandable that some scholars have argued that this is commercial competition, although clearly of an ambitious type.[26] But we have to ask, how could the agent of such a curse have felt he might profit from the lack of success of such a wide range of targets involved in making their living in so many different ways? Commercial competition could lie behind the agent's cursing of, say, the group of *kapeloi*, but surely not the other names and professions as well? Besides, in this case, there is the hint of another context: in line 10, a judicial term appears, *tous marturas*, 'the witnesses'. The repeated binding of the targets' tongues may also support the idea that this curse was written for a litigious context. It seems likely that, although the agent may *also* have wished to damage his targets' business activities, his primary focus was to disable some other threat. If this is the case, then the description of various individuals by means of their profession may have been intended simply to ensure their secure identification.

DTA 87 provides a similar example: it does bind a number of tavern-keepers,[27] but these appear alongside other individuals who are described as belonging to a number of different professions. Again, this suggests that the curse was not aimed solely at those who were competing to provide the same economic service as the agent. In all these tablets the professions of the targets were, for some reason, important enough to the agent for him/her to include them as salient detail in the curse, but commercial competition seems an inadequate explanation for these curses. Are there alternative contexts that might fit their content more readily?

DTA 87 might be able to help: it includes the information that the creator was a neighbour of its targets. This suggests that simple familiarity (and its proverbial offspring) might be one reason for the creation of this and similar curses. In these texts, it may be that the inhabitants of a local neighbourhood are brought to our attention, mapped by a curse-writer's feelings of hostility. Alternatively, as suggested in Chapter 9 on judicial curses, these 'saturation' curses, which target so many people at once, could have been written by disgruntled members of some form of association, a club or society.[28] This seems an appropriate explanation for the situation evoked on *DTA* 68, in which the agent pays particular attention to binding his targets' tongues. Such a context would provide an explanation for why the agents of these curses deemed it important to identify their targets by their profession, as well as for the assortment of professions named. Finally, it is possible that there is no connection between the individuals named on the tablet: if an individual was going to go to the trouble of creating a curse, it would be understandable if he just inscribed the names of everyone he wanted to bind, even if the motivation for each one was different.

Ultimately, there is no way to ascertain the agent's motivation for including certain details and not others. In some tablets the profession of a target is mentioned because his/her work and workplace appears to be the specific focus of the curse and the agent intended the target to suffer in this aspect of his life. In other tablets the inclusion of professional title(s) should be regarded merely as a way for the agent of the curse to ensure that the supernatural powers he/she was petitioning located the right individual. In some of these tablets, the sheer number of targets and their different professions suggest we need to think beyond an explanation of simple commercial competition to situations in which some targets were being cursed for commercial reasons and others not, and be open to considering other circumstances which might have motivated the creation of these curses.

The vocabulary of work

This brings us to the second method of identifying a commercial curse: the binding of some aspects of work. The relevant vocabulary in these tablets is wide-ranging, including skill or craft (τὴν τέχνην *DT* 52, *DTA* 73, 74, 87); profit (κέρδην *DTA* 86, *SGD* 75); equipment (σκεύη *SGD* 75, ὄργανα *DTA* 73); and livelihood (τὸν βίον *DTA* 69 and *DT* 92, ζόη and κτῆσις *DT* 92). In terms of locations mentioned, generic references to tavern-keeping or retail trade (τὸ καπήλιον *DT/DTA* 70, *SGD* 43, τὸ καπηλεῖον, τὰ καπήλεια *DTA* 87, τὴν καπήλειαν *DTA* 75) are common and the binding of workshops (ἐργαστήριον καὶ τὰ ἐν τῶι ἐργαστηρίωι ἄπαντα DTA 68, ἐργαστήριον DT/DTA 71 and SGD 124, κὴ ἐργασίαν κὴ ἐργαστήρια DTA 74, καὶ τὸ ἐργαστήριον DTA 84, τὸ ἐργαστήριο[ν] καὶ τὴν ἐργασία[ν] DT/DTA 71, τὴν ἐργασίαν καὶ τὸ ἐργαστήριον DTA 75, καὶ τὴν ἐργασίαν αὐτοῦ καὶ τὸ ἐργαστήριον SGD 52) is even more frequent. Tools, such as furnaces, kilns, and forges, appear more rarely. Across the tablets these work terms appear in a variety of ways, imparting a range of emphases. Sometimes the curser includes them as the main or sole focus of the binding verb, spelling out his or her wishes in elaborate detail. SGD 88 explicitly mentions a downturn in profit that the agent would like to see his targets suffer: δυσπραγί[αι [οἵ]δε γεγράβαται ἐπι τον] κέρδον 'these people are registered for a downturn/misfortune in their profit';[29] while SGD 124, a tablet from the cemetery at Metapontion in Italy, binds the workplace of a group of doctors, so that it will not work and will not be successful. The second part[30] of an Attic text (*DT* 52) is aimed at one Theon and his παιδίσκας (Theon is probably a pimp and these are his prostitutes).[31] The text binds Theon's skill (τὴν τέχνη), resources (τὴν ἀφορμὴν), and work (τὴν ἐργασίαν), alongside, formulaically, his λόγους καὶ ἔργα, his 'words and deeds'. In another Attic text, *DTA* 73, Timostratos is the fourth person bound, and the curse mentions his craft (τέχνην) and his tools (ὄργανα). In *DTA* 75, the curse lists and binds a number of individuals and their places of work—two workshops, one inn, and one shop—along with slaves and their masters.

More often, commercial terms appear in lists alongside, and without distinction from, the physical attributes of an individual, like their tongue, hands, or spirit.[32] These lists sometimes include more abstract elements (such as their spirit, mind, or their decisions); wives also appear and, occasionally, children. Binding the latter might be seen as a way of attempting to obstruct the target's future and, considering that children were often taught the trade of their fathers, could be interpreted as a way of cursing their current and future livelihood.[33] Such a common presentation of the commercial aspects of a person suggests that they were understood as located, almost embodied, in the individual. This interpretation fits current scholarly understandings of the ancient Greek use of the term for 'workshop' suggesting that it does not indicate a physical location so much as a space that took its identity from those who worked in it.[34] However, we also need some caution about assuming that these words automatically indicate a commercial concern. ἔργα ('deeds') for example, frequently occurs across the corpus of tablets in the common formula ἔπη καὶ ἔργα 'words and deeds', and does not always seem to have a specifically commercial meaning.[35] Even more often, the term ἐργασία [36] appears in the long lists of objects to be bound that are a feature of many of the curses, where it seems to indicate a general sense of activity or livelihood, rather than a specific commercial activity.[37]

In a number of these tablets, the combination of specific business expressions alongside these more general formulae exacerbates confusion about the intent of the agent and the context of the curse. For example, the phrase ἔργα ἐργασίας occurs four times in a curse from the Peiraieus, in Athens (*DT* 47, for example, in ll.1–2, 4, 7). But it appears to indicate just one of many aspects of the target's existence that the agent intended to damage, alongside other physical, spiritual, and emotional elements of the target, as well as his actions and various family members. The motivation behind the curse does not seem to be business rivalry so much as an intent to prompt bad fortune in every possible part of the target's life.[38] Two Attic curses (*DTA* 74 and 86) provide similar examples: *DTA* 74 binds somebody's (the tablet is difficult to read) spirit, tongue, and body before binding his or her ἐργασίαν, ἐργαστήρια, and τέχναν 'work, workshop' and 'skill'.[39] *DTA* 86 includes 'profits/income of work' at the end of a formulaic list of the usual targets (hands, feet, spirit, tongue). The commercial aspects of both these tablets seem to be included in a more general attack on the target, rather than focusing specifically on ruining his or her business.

A slightly different emphasis—although reaching the same conclusion—can be seen in three tablets from Athens. *DTA* 69 and *SGD* 3 and 4 all pay primary attention to binding their targets' commercial activities, before extending their ill wishes to other parts of their lives. For example, although the tablet is fragmentary and its text incomplete, *DTA* 69 starts by focusing on the work and products of its targets (this time a helmet-maker and his wife, a goldworker). The inclusion of detail about the household and 'life' of the couple that follows suggests that the agent of the curse intended to bind his targets' business with a specific emphasis not just on damaging their profits (in a competitive sense) or livelihoods, but on thoroughly destroying their lives.[40] Tablets *SGD* 3 and 4 are similarly constructed. These two curses, apparently aimed at the same blower from the silverworks,[41] identify him by his profession and curse whatever work he produces. They go on to mention other aspects of his life, including his wife and whatever possessions he has. It is as if the agent of the curse was anxious not just to harm his business or the products of his work, but also to ruin him in a number of other ways.[42]

In some cases, the appearance of commercial detail, even if it does not provide us with a clear context, can still lend interesting nuance to the apparent nature and focus of a curse's concern and its agent's intent. For example, as we have seen, the detail of the Attic curse *DT* 68 adds a commercial aspect to what otherwise might appear to be a curse intended simply to destroy the relationships of its target, Theodora. The targets of binding include (l. 6) both the 'deeds and words' of her work. This is perhaps a deliberate variation on the more familiar formula of 'words and deeds' intended to draw attention to the nature of her work. The curse appears to be intended to sever the relationship enjoyed by Theodora with two named men and with any other men with whom she has dealings. Dickie argues that Theodora was involved in the sex trade and builds on this assumption: 'It is to be surmised that the person responsible for the spell was a courtesan jealous of her trade.'[43] Although this is a possible explanation, there is no element of the text that indicates the gender, profession, or motivation of the creator of the curse, who might, in fact, have been male, and motivated by desire for either Charias or Theodora rather than by commercial rivalry (I will discuss these possibilities in more detail in Chapter 11).

In contrast, an Attic tablet (*DTA* 108) dated to the third century seems far more commercially focused. It targets a woman called Sosikleia, asking not only that her assets be bound, but also her great renown, and requesting that her friends come to hate her. But even in this case, the agent of this curse need not be a business rival, but someone fired by hostility for some other reason. Similarly SGD 75 targets the business affairs of a woman called Aphrodite, binding her equipment and profits, as well as her tongue, feet, and spirit, alongside aspects of her that are just and unjust.[44] Once more, commercial success is just one aspect of the target's life that the agent wished to control. In this instance, the mention of the target's tongue and the difficult phrase 'just and unjust' may indicate a litigious context, or it may simply tell us that whoever wrote the curse was moved to do so by a strong sense that he or she had been treated unfairly. There are a number of curses that reveal similar sentiments: they are discussed in the next chapter.[45]

This brief examination of the vocabulary of work demonstrates that it can offer another way to identify curses motivated by business concerns, but that this approach is far from straightforward. In some cases, the phrasing of the curse draws attention to these elements, emphasizing their significance. In others, an individual's work and workplace is one element in a list of other aspects, part of a general desire to see that individual suffer. In a number of cases, such formulaic lists seem to function like an all-purpose spray of ill-will on the part of the agent, this intent emphasized in some tablets by the inclusion of such phrases as 'and everything else belonging to them [the target(s)]', as if the agent were concerned that something might escape the destructive force of his attack.[46]

Unexpected rivalries and a range of risks

Looking back across the tablets in this category, the evidence for economic competition as a motivation for cursing is far more varied and nuanced than the initial description suggested. To begin with, only in a very few cases do the texts of commercial curses reveal anything about the identity, status, or detailed motivations of those who wrote these curses. Any suggestions on any of these fronts must, instead, depend on the information each curse provides about its target(s), and on our reading of the apparent emotional emphases of the text. When we turn to the targets, the evidence is confusing. As the passages at the beginning of this chapter suggest, we might expect business rivalry to be particularly rife between artisans in highly specialized crafts or with great potential for technical failure.[47] This would lead us to expect certain patterns of cursing to emerge across the tablets: for example, that these professions would be heavily represented in the tablets; that curses would either target several professionals who practised a single craft, or be focused on disabling a particular individual or workshop. But there are few curses that fulfil these parameters.

The relatively small number of curses aimed at those in highly skilled professions suggests to us that this was not an arena of great competition and other evidence supports this impression, even for the period after the Peloponnesian war, when there would have been few resources available to pay for such skills.[48] McKechnie argues that those with highly specialized skills (e.g., related to temple-building and sculpture) guarded them carefully, not passing them on easily. It was likely that numbers of highly skilled professionals probably remained low and there was enough work to go round, even that there was a seller's market, especially if craftsmen were used to moving from city to city for work.[49]

In contrast, the majority of individuals mentioned in the texts practise professions demanding a low level of skill and involving a high level of familiarity between target and agent: shop- or tavern-keepers, are particularly common.[50] Of course, business rivalry may still be the motivation for some of these tablets, or the selection of some of their targets. As an example, consider the group of *kapeloi* cursed in *DTA* 87. This may illustrate a case of economic competition: ancient literature suggests that taverns were widespread and popular,[51] which could create the right circumstances for an ambitious *kapelos* or *kapelis* to want to limit his/her colleagues' success and list all the local competitors on a single curse tablet.[52] But this tablet, as a number of others explored above, also attacks many other people, involved in a variety of different professions. Such indiscriminate rivalry, ignoring the specifics of profession, driving the desire to destroy anyone who might do better, is hard to attribute to commercial competition. Rather it suggests something closer to the zero-sum notion of *phthonos*, or envy, mentioned already in the chapter on theatrical curses, according to which another person's good fortune (in terms of honour, recognition, acquisition of material goods) was perceived as a threat to one's own. Indeed, the idea of *phthonos* helps to explain the emotional dynamics that Hesiod describes as prompted by competition, in the passage from the *Works and Days* quoted at the beginning of this chapter.

In addition, when we look at the type of commercial detail offered, we find that, in many cases, the nature of the arrangement of, and focus on, the commercial detail makes it difficult, if not impossible, to judge what kind of significance the agent was attributing to these factors, and the nature of the threat they presented to him/her. Their appearance in a list does not always indicate that inhibiting the commercial activity of the target was the main concern of the curse. The commercial activity might be only one aspect of an individual that was perceived as presenting a particular risk, which his/her enemy might seek to bind, control, and/or destroy. As mentioned at the end of the previous chapter, these curses may in fact concern a threat, perceived by the agent, about which there is no specific information in the text itself.

In conclusion, it may be more helpful to think about the commercial detail on these curses as playing a range of roles, indicating a range of commercially related risks. At the higher end of the range, we might group tablets in which the commercial activity of the target forms the focus of the curse: it seemed to pose a specific risk to the agent, which he sought to control.[53] Lower down the range might be a cluster of tablets that bind commercial aspects of their target, but do so in the course of binding many other parts of their life. Commercial aspects are included in a list of other targets intended to provoke general misfortune.[54] At the lowest end of this range are those tablets in which the commercial detail appears to indicate no commercial risk at all, for example those tablets where specific professions are mentioned only for the sake of identifying an individual.[55]

Nevertheless, even with the tablets at the lowest end of the range, managing risk of some sort is still a compelling explanation for their creation. The fact that such extreme action as writing a curse was taken, implies that the agent of the curse was in a desperate state: even if the agent's economic life was secure, he or she may have felt that other aspects of their life were at risk. We cannot hope fully to reconstruct the original circumstances in which these texts were composed, but the targets of binding suggest that the agent of a number of these curses perceived groups of local people as presenting some kind of threat. Whether this threat was commercially motivated, or the result of *phthonos*, or envy, stirred up by others' good fortune, or was prompted by specific acts of hostility, these tablets offer us a vivid glimpse into the breakdown of local relationships.

11

Love and Curses

> There be none of the affections which have been noted to fascinate or bewitch, but love and envy. They both have vehement wishes; they frame themselves readily into imaginations and suggestions; and they come easily into the eye, especially upon the presence of the objects; which are the points that conduce to fascination, if any such thing there be.[1]
>
> Bacon 1597 (Dick 1955: 23)

The other curse categories have raised the idea that curses were written in situations in which relationships had broken down. This final group of curses takes this as its central theme: the texts are concerned with hindering or encouraging the appetites of both genders for intimate relationships. Curse texts in this category appear for the first time in the historical record in the fourth century—later than the other types discussed above.[2] In addition, although across all these categories curses very rarely reveal their agents, it is likely that the majority of judicial, business, and theatrical curse tablets were written by or on behalf of men. Of the eight curses I will be discussing in this category, at least two are certainly written by women and, as I will show, it is quite possible that others were as well. There are a number of curses that others have included in this category, which I have not, and these are explored in more detail in Appendix 2. Among these are texts which appear to target individuals who make their living from selling sexual favours, their own or others, without demonstrating any evidence of desire or intimacy;[3] those which appear to be motivated by revenge, and so are strictly prayers for justice rather than *katadesmoi*;[4] and others which merely include the names of women or details of their family lives, or which mention particular body parts with no mention of an intimate relationship or other indications of desire.[5] However, it is possible that a few of these texts are concerned with inhibiting fertility, as well as binding sexual desire.

After examining extant treatments of this category of curses, I will briefly consider the historical context and possible circumstances for the creation of relationship curses. In my subsequent examination of the relevant texts,

I will, as before, be hoping to identify the nature of the risks that individuals were seeking to control through the use of these texts. My intention is to allow a full consideration of the different situations that could have prompted the creation of these curse texts, without any particular expectations of likely relationship models. The possible motivation for the appearance of these curses in the material record in the fourth century BCE has been much discussed; I will turn to this at the end of the chapter.

TAXONOMIES OF 'LOVE'

Previous treatments of the curses, usually grouped under the heading 'love', have generated a number of complex taxonomies. The curses have previously been divided into two basic subcategories according to the perceived intentions of their agents.[6] 'Separation' curses (*Trennungszauber*) are aimed at a rival in a love triangle situation, and occasionally at the object of affection, as well, in order to inhibit contact between the two. The main purpose of such a curse is to restrain erotic attraction and break any bond that may already have developed between the accursed and their partner. These curses have been compared to athletic and circus curses, since their basic aim is that any rival be made inert and unable to compete for the prize in question.[7] This kind of relationship curse is most prevalent in the Classical and Hellenistic period, and primarily found on the Greek mainland. Thirteen have been published: *DT* 68, 69, 85, 86, and 198; *DTA* 78, 89, 93; and SGD 30–2, 57, 154.[8]

The second kind of relationship curse is the *philtrokatadesmos*, which combines elements of later 'attraction' spells (*agōgai*), with the binding aspects of *katadesmoi*.[9] These seek to encourage the attraction of the target to the agent: the binding part of the curse can be seen either as an attempt to prevent the target from having sex with someone else or about tying down that individual's bodily functions, such as the ability to eat, sleep, move around, etc., thus causing unbearable suffering, until he/she succumbs.[10] Twenty-three of these curses have been published, but only one dates from the period under discussion here.[11]

Together, these two kinds have typically been described under one category heading as 'love' curses. But the use of such a culturally dependent (and subjective) term as 'love' may well prove misleading as we attempt to interpret this material. To confuse this issue further, the term 'love' in this field has acquired an almost technical sense: for example, the term 'love magic' is used by one scholar to describe the 'ritual techniques used by the Greeks to instil or maintain various forms of desire and affection', a definition that excludes curses that set out to bind or inhibit desire and affection—which comprise most of the material from this period.[12]

In fact, most of the work done on relationship magic has focused on the magical spells that seek to attract rather than separate lovers. In part, this is because the curse texts are discussed in conjunction with evidence from the Greek Magical Papyri (*PGM*). There is a strong case to be made in favour of such a synchronic approach, since there is evidence to demonstrate continuity in the tradition between Classical Athens and late-antique Egypt.[13] However, conflating this material is more likely to produce general conclusions about sexual dynamics in ancient Greek society, rather than allowing for more specific consideration of the evidence, and consequent insights into the likely lived experience of individuals at particular periods. I will review it briefly here, since it forms a significant backdrop for the rest of this chapter.

Much of this work on attraction magic is based on Winkler's compelling analysis of it as a powerful therapy for an individual (usually male) who is suffering the torments of *erōs* (which was regarded in ancient Greece as an invasion, a possession, and a disease). The agent of the magic sets in motion a process in which he imagines his target (usually female in this explanation) to be experiencing the agonies he feels instead of him, and thus he gains control of the situation.[14] Faraone describes curses as being a particular form of this attraction magic, intended to produce lust (*erōs*) and used generally by men to instil erotic passion in women, whereas spells designed to elicit affection (*philtra* for the creation of *philia*) were used generally by women or other 'social underlings'.[15] Like Winkler, Faraone still argues that attraction magic was used mainly by Greek males, but sees the motivation underlying it as being either the urge for sexual conquest, or the wish by the agent to advance his social position by arranging a profitable marriage for himself.[16] He argues that the violence of attraction magic is legitimized, indeed, normalized within a profoundly gender-divided culture. Men who practise less aggressive magic become socially constructed as female, while women described as practising attraction magic—such as *hetairai*—are socially constructed as male.[17]

This framework has been questioned by Matthew Dickie, who argues that the women of the Hellenistic period enjoyed a considerable amount of both the freedom and the will to practise attraction magic;[18] and that gender-based distinctions between spells to induce *philia* and those to invoke *erōs* are hard to maintain. *Agōgai* and *philtrokatadesmoi* spells in the formularies seek to create *philia* as well as *erōs*, while *philtra* are often designed to induce *erōs*.[19] In contrast, he focuses almost exclusively on women as agents of magic, assuming that the majority of curses are written by female sex-workers motivated by economic demands. However, although Dickie's view of curse tablets ostensibly challenges that of Faraone, it can be argued that, in fact, it subtly supports it, since he assumes that women active in this arena must be courtesans, that is, those whom Faraone would argue are socially constructed as male. Of the material under discussion here, Dickie assumes not just that many of the named characters of these curses are involved in commercial sexual activities, but also many of the unnamed agents—and that the motivations of all concerned are primarily economic.

The social construction of sexuality is, obviously, not an activity limited to the ancients. Faraone's descriptions of the typical behaviour and role of women appears to be based specifically around Classical notions of a 'normal' (i.e. not involved in trading sex for money) woman's sexual passivity, while Dickie emphasizes the figure of the sexually and economically powerful, even predatory, woman, more typical of the Hellenistic period. Both these approaches, however, elide the reality that many, if not most, women at all social levels would have been economically dependent on their husband/owner/purchaser, but this does not mean either that they were sex-workers, or that this was necessarily the only motivation for their wishing to maintain a relationship. In addition, in both cases, interpretations of these curse texts are by and large limited by an implicit assumption that they were composed in the context of heterosexual relationships.[20]

The opacity of this curse material means that it can be all too easy to treat it as a blank screen for the projection of contemporary constructions of sexuality. A brief examination of the recent work on these texts demonstrates how easily modern assumptions about gender roles and relations and the nature of sexual risk can influence and, indeed, have influenced how these texts are interpreted. Faraone's vision of the 'social construction of gender' in ancient Greece and the division of magical practice into male and female categories diminishes the complexity of sexual relations and reduces any kind of female presence in these texts to a simple reflection of male power.[21] Dickie's explanation of the likely identity of the curse writers, although at first sight espousing a view opposed to that of Faraone, in fact treads a similar path. If Faraone's women are virginal victims, Dickie's are greedy whores, based on the familiar stereotype of the acquisitive, independent, sexually active and dangerous woman—a sort of 'Gold Diggers of c.400 BC'.[22] Such explanations, although stimulating and provocative, still limit our insights into, and diminish the significance of, this evidence. It becomes important, therefore, to explore the historical context of these texts in order to widen our perspective on the possible circumstances of their creation.

LIVED SEXUAL EXPERIENCE AND RISK

Existing interpretations of these texts are based on analyses of relationships in ancient Greece rooted in the subject/object sexual discourse of the Greeks' themselves: those with control dominate those without control, male dominates female, penetrator dominates penetrated. Status becomes the key to understanding issues of ancient sexuality and only adult citizen males (or, at a reach, female sex-workers who are masculinized through their independent economic status) are expected to have had a capacity for sexual expression.[23] Such interpretations offer a clarity of the sort found in technical line-drawings, emphasizing the cultural significance of the adult male citizen's status, without venturing into what must have been the messier daily experiences of many individuals, both men and women.[24] As such, they have limited usefulness for exploring the possible contexts and intentions of these tablets, which are not mediated by the usual literary filter. Even if the evidence is lacking and we can only sketch possibilities, knowledge of the social complexity of the ancient city demands that we must, at least, acknowledge the possible range of sexual experiences and different needs of individuals expressed by these texts.

Just as an example, let us briefly consider the range of roles and diverse relationships possible for female sex-workers.[25] In this sphere, most attention has been paid to the figure of the *hetaira*. Here is a fantasy woman fine-tuned for the arts of love. She is witty and educated, beautiful and sexy, existing outside the constraints usually applied to women, yet warped by her economic independence so that she must also be judged, at best, wilfully capricious, at worst, greedy, cruel, and parasitic. As noted above, she is considered to be so far from a 'normal' woman (or from normative ideas of womanliness) that some modern commentators have argued that we must understand her as socially constructed as male.[26] For as long as she is beautiful, she poses an extraordinary temptation for respectable young men, who may spend all their wealth trying to win her affections. She is an indulgence, to be relished in the short period between childhood and marriage, or at parties, or saved for the retirement of old men who have paid their dues to the state by raising a respectable family. She prompts fear in fathers who cannot control their sons, shame in wives whose husbands cannot control themselves, and jealousy in men who want her.

This avatar has exercised a marked fascination not just for the Greeks themselves, but also for Classical scholars through the ages: the study of the *hetaira* provides an interesting overview of evolving attitudes in scholarship.

For a long time, modern commentators accepted a superficial reading of ancient literature's presentation of the *hetaira*, but even now that scholarship has dislodged its rosy spectacles, the figure of the *hetaira* all too often remains just that—a cipher, a social construct described in terms of male desire, even literally exhibiting it, according to some scholars.[27]

This example illustrates a specific danger for our considerations of the nature of relationships in the ancient city as context for reading these curse tablets. To begin with, there were clearly different, and sometimes quite complex, levels to the commoditization of sexuality in the ancient Greek city, which in turn would alter the types of relationships involved, and the concomitant risks they might present. The terms used to describe female sex-workers in fact cover many different activities—and thus different relationships and experiences—by which a woman who sold herself could subsist.[28] The language used by the Greeks to describe these roles was fluid, reflecting not only semantic imprecision, but also drawing our attention to its subjectivity. Unsurprisingly, the application of these terms tended to depend on the attitudes of the speaker or writer towards the woman in question, attitudes that could range between, at least, desire and contempt.[29] But, importantly, this semantic fluidity also reflects social actuality: it was possible for a woman to move between roles. She could certainly slide down the social ladder, for example, if she lost a partner on whom she depended for survival, or if she lost her looks. She might also advance her social status, managing to blend right into the realm of the respectable: Neaira's admittedly brief insinuation of herself into civic life is hardly likely to have been the only example of its kind. Indeed, there is also Aspasia whose son by Perikles was granted citizen rights and who herself, after Perikles' death, married Lysikles, another citizen; and a list of other women, supplied by Lysias, who were once prostitutes when they were younger, but then moved on and up.[30]

Even from this overview, it is clear that the potential relationships and experiences of a sex-worker were manifold. However, we can both broaden this picture, for example by including a greater range of the activities of sex-workers,[31] and deepen it, for example by invoking these women as individuals capable of a whole range of subjective emotions extending beyond those which accompany their portrayal as sexual objects. For example: what about their desires—for men, for women, too? What, in particular, would have threatened their ability to survive? What stresses and anxieties must have attended this way of living, and what pleasures? And, in particular for the purposes of this study, what risks confronted them? After all, if one's value (literally) in society arises from being a sexual object, then this can be a source of both strength and vulnerability.

Moreover, just as relationships overlap and interact in manifold ways, so must any study of gender and social roles in the ancient Greek city acknowledge this aspect of relationships, and not persist in exploring the genders in isolation, or only in certain configurations.[32] For example, we hear a great deal about the attitudes of men to sex-workers, but the curse texts prompt us to to go beyond this relationship. What about the attitudes of wives to the sex-workers their husbands enjoyed;[33] and how did wives or sex-workers in longer-term relationships feel about their husband's young male lovers, their *eromenoi*, and vice versa?

This brief overview is intended as an illustration and a prompt towards consideration of the multiplicity of possibilities of relationships that could potentially develop between individuals in the city, and might form the circumstances that compelled someone to compose a curse. I am not proposing to answer the questions it has raised here; my point is rather that it is important to ask these kinds of questions as we examine these curse tablets, since the nature of our questions is likely to shape the kinds of answers we find. Although I have focused on sex-workers, and in particular *hetairai*, this same point stands for representations of all women—so frequently left voiceless in ancient literature and therefore so much more malleable in modern scholarship—and also for the representation of certain men in the city: for example, male lovers of grown men, slaves, male sex-workers, etc. If we acknowledge the range of possible relationships in the ancient city, and the implicit and explicit risks which pervaded them, we have a broader and more diverse palette on which to draw as we seek to understand the material in these curses. And although exploration of the texts still might prove frustratingly inconclusive, this also provides a necessary reminder of the range of lived experience that these texts represent.

I will be referring to the curses in the rest of this chapter as 'relationship curses', since their content is the hopes and desires for future relationships between individuals, whether they are about fulfilling the wishes of the agent of the curse or obstructing the success of another, and I find, as I have described above, the existing terms confusing. For the period with which this chapter is concerned, I have identified eight curses as belonging to this category. This group comprises: two curses from Makedonia—one from Akanthos and one from Pella; two curses from Boiotia (*DT* 85 and 86); two curses from Attika (*DTA* 78 and *DT* 68 whose precise original locations are unknown); a curse from Knidos (*DT* 5);[34] and a curse from Nemea (*SGD* 57).[35] It is likely that *DT* 69 is correctly identified by Audollent as provoked by love,[36] because of certain terms found within the text that are similar to terms found in *DT* 68, but the curse is too fragmentary to yield any precise or overall meaning.

THE IDENTITY OF THE AGENT ... AND THE TARGETS

Of the eight curses under discussion in this category, three of them clearly state the identity of the agent. These are the curse from Akanthos in Makedonia, the curse from Pella in Makedonia, and *DT* 5, one of the curses excavated from the sanctuary of Demeter at Knidos.

The text from Akanthos written by a man called Pausanias, is the only formally erotic curse text in this group.[37] It contains the earliest surviving *katadesmos* that expresses an intention to bring the target to the agent of the curse (in this case, to summon a woman to a man). On one side of the tablet the agent of the curse, Pausanias, binds a woman called Sime, asking that she may not be able to perform a religious rite to Athena or have Aphrodite well disposed to her (or perhaps this means, 'enjoy the pleasures of Aphrodite') until she embraces him. On the other side of the tablet, Pausanias turns his attention to a person called Ainis, who is of unknown gender.[38] He asks that he/she not be able to sacrifice (although no deities are mentioned by name, as on the other side of the tablet) and that he/she not be the recipient of anything else beneficial until he/she has pleased/been gracious to Pausanias—the term he uses here seems to indicate an almost formal demand by Pausanias for atonement.[39]

It has been suggested that Sime was a sex-worker of some description.[40] This may be supported by the mention of her potentially enjoying the pleasures of Aphrodite. But presumably other women could enjoy these, too, and, I would argue, the fact that Pausanias chose to write a curse about this woman indicates that she was likely to be somehow unattainable. If she was a sex-worker who was not living in a stable relationship, he could presumably have negotiated a price for her, rather than go to the trouble of writing a curse. But she may have been owned by a violent pimp who would seek payment, or perhaps Pausanias could not afford her, or, of course, there is the possibility that whatever her status or price, Pausanias' fantasy of her surrender dictated such a method. If she was a married, sexually active woman or a *pallakē*, then this perhaps might explain both the mention of Aphrodite and the need to write a curse.[41] Winkling this woman out of seclusion by supernatural means would enable satisfaction of his appetites on a long-term basis, while lessening the chance that Sime might have reported his action to her husband (and Pausanias suffered the consequences).[42]

This text is particularly notable for containing two stipulations never seen together in one curse, nor, in fact, separately on a curse tablet of such an early date.[43] The second stipulation—that the target not enjoy the benefits (or pleasures) of Aphrodite—is reminiscent of the aggressively erotic spells known chiefly from the Imperial period, but is a great deal more restrained in its imposition of abstention.[44] The first stipulation—that the victim be unable to sacrifice—resembles an idea found in pleas to the gods for justice, prayers which appear in a variety of texts throughout the Mediterranean world and Asia Minor from the sixth century BCE to the second century CE.[45] The idea is that the target of the curse be put out of divine favour because he/she is prevented from being able to sacrifice, thus ensuring that they can never placate the anger of the gods or win their favor. Most texts which exhibit this formula are either prompted by some action which has been, or is feared likely to be, performed by the (potential) victim of the curse, or they are curses by individuals defending or addressing some kind of 'right' of that individual, such as the right not to have their possessions—including their slaves—pilfered, or their graves violated.[46] As such, they seem to have been used to support (or protect) what were generally felt to be the rights of a citizen.

In this context, the curse from Akanthos has several aspects worth noting. The agent names himself as well as his target, something which, as we have seen, rarely happens in more traditional *katadesmoi*. However, although the punishment invoked is explicitly aggressive and quite as damaging in its intention as those evoked for a sacrilegious act or the contravention of a social rule, the target appears to our eyes to have committed no specific crime. Rather, her 'sin' appears to have been one of omission—that is, of not (yet) yielding to the wishes of the curser. Is it possible that the agent of the curse may have seen the demands that he was directing towards Sime, and in which, it appears, she was not acquiescing, as some kind of a social right of which she was depriving him?[47] In this light, it is interesting to observe the use of the verb ἱλάσηται ('be gracious') by Pausanias to indicate what he wants of Ainis. Whatever it is that Pausanias expects from the two targets of his curse, he seems to have viewed it as some form of justified restitution.

The next two texts are, explicitly, written by women. Both express anger and outrage about the possible loss of their partner to another woman, although from different perspectives. The first is another text from Makedonia (Pella) dating from around the same period as the text from Akanthos and also including the name of the agent, this time a woman, identified as Phila.[48] I have mentioned this curse already, as an example of a text that comprises startling personal expression. Phila asks that an event, possibly a marriage, between another woman, Thetima, and a man, Dionysophon, should not take place (she binds the event rather than the individuals in question); that Dionysophon should not perform this act with another woman, widow or maiden (she binds the joy of any other woman or maiden); and, finally, that he should take no other women to grow old with him than herself.⁴⁹ She desires to grow old beside this man: this will make her happy and blessed.

The text can be viewed in two parts. The first resembles a straightforward binding spell in which the curse writer remains anonymous; the second comprises an outburst of emotional pleading by the agent, in which she names herself and beseeches the powers of the underworld to pity and help her, begging for misery and destruction on any rival, and for success and happiness for herself. The tablet differs considerably in its use of language from the large majority of simpler and often quite uncouth texts of Classical date. The mixture of very personal language and stock formulae suggests that Phila had sufficient education to write the text herself, although perhaps with expert advice.

Phila's curse binds the institution that threatens to remove Dionysophon— the man by whose side she says she would like to grow old. She does not curse Dionysophon himself; she does not curse Thetima directly, although she does mention later in the curse that she would like her to perish miserably; no children are mentioned. It seems unlikely, and there are no indications in the text (cf. *DT* 5), that she spoke from within an existing marriage. It may be more likely that she was in a relationship that she had hoped would provide her with some kind of security for the future. It is not clear whether this was emotional or financial security, and it could, of course, have been both.

In *DT* 5, a first- or second-century curse from Asia Minor, the agent of the curse, a woman called Prosodion, curses an unnamed 'other person' for seducing away her husband/lover. There is no listing of body parts to evoke physicality, no evocation of an emotion: the curse simply mentions the benefits Prosodion's husband brings and how their children will suffer because of his absence. There is a strong tone of indignation in this curse: he is shirking his responsibilities—which may suggest that Prosodion was the wife or *pallakē* (a concubine, or kept woman) of the man she is missing. If the reconstruction of the text at l. 6 is correct, then the curse was written at a time when the situation was not yet resolved and there was still a chance that the husband might return, and this may explain why the curse is not directed against her husband for his misdeeds.⁵⁰ Moreover, Prosodion may have been seeking more direct influence over the situation than possible divine intervention: if the curse was on public display as some have suggested, then it could have acted as a public statement of a threat, which might be seen by the seductress ('If you take away my partner, it'll be the worst for you . . .') or, indeed, by the husband.⁵¹

The agent of *DTA* 78, a fourth-century text from Attika, is probably also female. Although the agent does not appear by name in the text, the phrase ἄλλην γυναῖκα 'any other woman' confirms it. The curse is directed at any potential partner for Aristokydes, who is likely to be the curser's lover. In terms of the targets of the curse: the phrase τὰς φανομένας αὐτῶι γυναῖκας (meaning here the women 'who let themselves be seen by him') indicates that the women mentioned in this curse are unlikely to be 'respectable', invisible matrons.[52] They are more likely to have been *hetairai*.[53] Dickie's translation of that phrase as 'the women presented to him' even suggests a process of brothel prostitution in which women were lined up to be viewed and selected by clients.[54] The agent of the curse did not only fear the rival attractions of women: παῖδα is a gender neutral term and can be translated to mean either girl or boy. It is likely that there is a deliberate antithesis of gender terms in this phrase.[55]

Faraone originally assumed that the tablet was probably written by a jealous wife or fiancée. Later translations deem it more likely that the curse writer was a courtesan who was trying to stop her lover Aristokydes from engaging in a sexual relationship with any other woman or boy, and that the relationship that was the context of this curse comprised much more visibility than a traditional Greek marriage.[56] However, although it seems certain that the writer of the curse is female, there is nothing in the text that suggests the social status of the writer of the curse: women of any social status might fear the temporary distraction or permanent estrangement of the men with whom they were intimately involved.

The remaining five curse tablets provide far less information about the likely identity of their creators. The curse of tablet *DT* 85 (Boiotian; suggested dates ranging from the third to second century BCE, to the second or third century CE) uses an analogy between a dead person (Theonnastos) with whom, presumably, the curse was buried, along with the lead of the curse itself, to invoke the desired effect on the targets Zoilos and Antheira. It seeks to keep them away from each other.[57] The curse-writer provides a vivid picture of the events, the threat, which he or she is trying to avert: the juxtaposition of images of death, coldness, and burial contrast markedly with the vitality of and warmth between the lovers, who are brought to life through the intimate details, not just of their bodies touching, but, more whimsically, of their kisses and chit-chat. The text on side A provides a clear description of the couple's feared physical intimacy; the plea of side B that the god not find the two together τάνδε νύκτα, 'on this night', succinctly communicates the immediacy of the threat and the urgency of the curse.

There is no conclusive evidence for the gender of the agent (that Timokles mentioned at l. 6 of side B might be the agent is possible, but the text is far too fragmentary to prove this). This text provides a prime example of how wide-ranging the interpretations of relationship curses can become. Previous readings have argued both that the agent is a woman seeking Zoilos' affections, and the exact opposite, that the agent is a rival of Zoilos for Antheira's affections.[58] However, it is hard to see how this curse can be read as focused on the woman, Antheira, rather than the couple together.[59] Indeed, if anything, the focus at the end of side B of this text seems to fall on Zoilos. There the text curses a number of aspects of his life other than his relationship with Antheira, including his work, household, and friendships. The curse calls itself an ἀπορία, meaning 'a difficulty') which neatly sums up how the agent of the curse means it to work for Zoilos. Although the curse is aimed at destroying a relationship whose success was clearly keenly felt by the agent, the gender of the agent and whether or not he/she sought to have a relationship with Antheira is not apparent. It remains an unanswerable question whether the main motive of the text was to bring this relationship to an end for erotic reasons or as part of a more general attack on Zoilos.

The target of *DT* 86 (another Boiotian text, dated no later than the Hellenistic period) is Zois, an Eretrian woman, the wife of, or a woman in some kind of acknowledged relationship with, a man called Kabeira.[60] The listing of Zois' various attributes and charms creates a lucid image of her attractive qualities and her flirtatious behaviour, rather than comprising the more neutral listing of physical parts usually found in curse tablets. Nothing about Zois' sexuality remains hidden: the list provides a display of objects, and reduces her to the sum of her explicit parts. This is paradoxical, for although this description objectifies her and transforms her into a passive object, these areas are surely bound because the agent of the curse perceived them as being sources of her erotic power.

It is highly likely that Zois was a sex-worker. We are told that she is a cithara player (an occupation traditionally associated with this profession) and her eating and drinking is mentioned (eating and drinking with men who are not kinsmen is often presented in lawcourts as establishing that a woman is either a *pallakē* or *hetaira*).[61] However, she is also described as belonging to Kabeira. Is this a way of describing their relationship: was she some kind of *hetaira* with a long-term contract, or was he her pimp? The inclusion of this detail need not have been intended to serve any purpose other than identification, but it might underline the frustration of the agent of the curse, resentful of attractions displayed by an unattainable (because owned or somehow partnered) woman. However, if Kabeira really did present an obstruction to the curse-writer, we might expect him to be the object of the curse.[62] There is nothing explicit in the text that indicates the gender of the curse's agent or the motivation behind the curse, and the text is very fragmentary—a range of inconclusive possibilities remains. It could, for example, be the curse of a man or woman whose suit was rejected, seeking revenge, or even seeking to attract Zois: this may, in fact, be the remains of a *philtrokatadesmos*. In contrast, it may have been composed by a jealous or frightened girl- or boyfriend targeting the attractions Zois held for their partner. It is even possible that the curse was the work of an individual in pursuit of Kabeira, determined to remove Zois as a rival.

I have already discussed aspects of *DT* 68, a fourth-century Attic text, in the chapter on commercial cursing, so I will limit this discussion to the relationships that this curse depicts. In this text, a woman called Theodora is cursed in her words, deeds, business and her conversation with two men, of whom Charias receives most emphasis. As mentioned already, the focus is on Theodora being unsuccessful in her business, and her relationships—the two of which may be combined in a career as a sex-worker. We can add here that, if the reconstruction of the text is correct, the curse also asks that Charias will forget Theodora, and, possibly, that he will, in addition, forget her (not his) young (or dear) child.[63]

The status of Theodora's relationship with Charias is not clear, although it seems (from the repetition of κοίτη meaning 'the act of going to bed together') to have been more physical than with the other men mentioned. Some scholars have argued that Theodora and Charias were married; others have assumed that the curse just describes the relationship of a *hetaira* and a particular client.[64] The latter does seem more likely, especially considering the mention of other men, and the reference to her ἐργασία, a term that was used of a courtesan's trade.[65]

The main target of the curse—the risk it seeks to avert—appears to be the success of Theodora, in particular, but not only, in her relationship with Charias. However, the mention of κοίτη does not indicate that this intimacy with Charias had already happened at the time the curse was written, it could be the possibility of it that the curse is targeting. All we know is that Charias desired Theodora (side B, 1.11 ἐρᾶ[ι] ἐκε[ῖνος], 'he loves') and that was a source of anxiety for the agent of the curse. This provides little evidence for the identity of the agent of the curse. There is a range of possible explanations: the writer of the curse may have been a woman jealous of Theodora's trade—a wife, a *pallakē*, or a *hetaira*.[66] Alternatively, she may have been a sex-worker, owned by or contracted to all the men in question, who feared she was to be replaced by Theodora at the urging of Charias. On the other hand, it is possible that the agent of the curse may have been male, and motivated by desire for Charias. This might explain the agent's desire to make Charias forget his desire for Theodora.[67] Finally, it is also possible that the curse writer (male or female) may just have sought separation of the couple, rather than union with either of them.

In SGD 57 (a fourth-century text from Nemea) the text describes a man, body-part by body-part.[68] The details of the curse create a sexualized portrait of Aineas through a selection of largely physical constituents, though 'the spirit' is also mentioned. It appears that Aineas' physical charms exercised such sway over Euboula that a curse must be used to distract her attentions.[69] However, this enumeration of erotic elements suggests that the writer of the curse him/herself fully acknowledged the attractive power of Aineas' physical features. This might indicate that the writer was more concerned to free Aineas (and those corporeal components) for his/her own use, than because he/she was interested in Euboula, who appears in the curse only as a disembodied name.

RISK AND THE CONTROL OF DESIRE

The fact that the phrases within these curses are seldom repeated within or across the texts suggest that they are not merely formulaic expressions.[70] On the contrary, they seem to contain the personalized appeals of individuals trying to exert some influence over situations they found precarious and threatening. In most cases, the circumstances of these appeals must remain, at best, ambiguous, at worst, obscure. For just under half the tablets, the identity and motivation of the agent is unascertainable, and there is little evidence to describe the status or relationships of the individuals, named or unnamed, who appear in the texts, or the circumstances which prompted the creation of the curses.

However, it is possible in most cases to identify the focus of each curse, and this can assist our speculations about the context of and motivations behind its creation. For example, both Phila and Prosodion seem to have feared the risk of the loss of their male lovers: the target for Prosodion's curse is, specifically, the person who has stolen her man, while the targets of Phila's curse are more abstract—both the marriage of her man to anyone else, and the (presumably related) happiness of any other woman. The agent of *DTA* 78 also took aim at this level of abstraction: she wanted to keep her man from any possible couplings with any other women or youths. This curse appears almost like a pre-emptive strike rather than targeting any specific incident. The repeated mention of anonymous figures of either gender draws our attention to the nature of the anxiety haunting the agent of the curse.

In contrast, in *DT* 68 and 85, although specific relationships are targeted and are clearly significant, they appear alongside other aspects of a successful life that the curse is intended to harm. In *DT* 68 although the wish for her lack of success with Charias is particularly emphasized, Theodora is cursed in a number of other areas of her life (including her relationships with other men). The repeated mention of κοίτη emphasizes the idea of the couple's sexuality, but this is tempered by the formulaic cursing of the 'words and deeds' of Theodora. *DT* 85 seeks to separate a man and a woman, with a description of their imminent coupling that strongly evokes their sexual relationship. However, as is the case with Theodora, this appears to be part of a more general intention that Zoilos should suffer.

A number of these curses are identified as being about relationships because they include a listing of particular body parts, suggesting that these were the aspects of the target that were considered powerful and presented the greatest threat to the agent of each curse. Paradoxically, the technique of naming a target's physical or other charms in order to bind them and control them draws attention to them, almost increasing their apparent power. For example, SGD 57 evokes not just the individuals, and not just the individuals' physical parts, but displays them as sexualized bodies, actively involved with each other. Created in order to separate the two, the text actually reinforces the idea of their physical entanglement. In *DT* 86, the list of Zois' erotic qualities, included in order to be bound, actually leaves the reader with a sense of how overwhelmingly attractive they are, rather than an impression of the agent's control over them. As noted above, taken out of context, it could be a description of the key moments of a seduction: parallels for this kind of descriptive listing are found in other formats evoking and objectifying the sexual attractions of women in just such seductive contexts, for example, Hellenistic epigrams and the ancient erotic handbooks. However, it is not possible to ascertain the circumstances giving rise to the curse. We cannot even be sure whether it was intended to separate Zois from another, or to bind her as part of an attraction spell.

As with tablets in other categories, the creation of these texts appears to have been motivated by the need of their agents to exert some kind of control over others. The choice to use curses suggests that those who wrote them could not be sure of acquiring, or lacked the capacity to exercise, control in any other way. These curses do not refer to the conventions of marital relations (in fact, Phila actually seems to fear them), nor do they evoke the rules or transactions of commercial sex. Instead they evoke a context dominated by the power of desire. Although they never mention *erōs* explicitly, the way they target lists of parts of the body, describe sexualized behaviour, and observe the effects of desire on others, means that they deliver a very strong sense of its power and danger for both agents and targets.

In six of these curses, the targets are female. In *DT* 85 I think it likely that Zoilos is the main focus of the curse, but even here Antheira receives strong emphasis. In SGD 57, the attention of the reader is drawn more to the male half of the couple being cursed. Of the agents, however, we only know of one curse that was definitely written by a man—the curse from Akanthos. The creators of *DT* 68, 85, and 86 cannot be identified for certain. The curse from Pella, *DT* 5, and *DTA* 78 are all written by women seeking to control the behaviour of men. In order to do this, Phila, Prosodion, and the unknown agent of *DTA* 78 bind their rivals rather than binding the men in question. In Phila's case, this includes the joy of all women, alongside what is possibly a formal marriage between a specific woman and Dionysophon; the writer of *DTA* 78 binds youths as well as women. Are these examples of women practising 'aggressive male magic' as has previously been suggested? The curse form itself might imply this, but the curses themselves are, by and large, separation spells. It seems more apposite to observe that these women seem to have understood the erotic power of others as the risk they needed to control. This brings me, in conclusion, to consider the apparent timing and context of the appearance of this category of curses.

EROS AND RISK

These tablets begin to appear in the fourth century, at a time when the ways in which women were popularly represented were undergoing some changes. Evidence which is entirely independent of the curse tablets suggests that there was developing interest in the artistic representation of ordinary life, the role of marriage, and a more explicit recognition of female eroticism in these arenas. The fact that relationship curses appear at the same time as the evidence for these changes seems to beg exploration, even if we cannot achieve a conclusive explanation.[71]

On pots, the raw sexuality of images of heterosexual relations (rising to a crescendo of abuse and degradation of women on the symposiastic cups of the late sixth and early fifth century) is gradually replaced during the late fifth and early fourth century BCE with more romantic themes of courting, previously reserved for images of male homosexual couples. They are also now found on a range of other, larger vessels, the use of which is not confined to male-dominated spaces.[72] During the second half of the fifth century, iconography develops around the figure of Eros. Before this period, Eros had been associated with images of pederasty and prostitution, but shortly after 450 BCE, in the form of a graceful adolescent he starts to appear in the domestic sphere and then moves into nuptial scenes.[73] In accordance with what we might suspect from the changingiconography around women, in wedding scenes, Eros appears to be associated in particular with the bride. It is not clear if he is simply an attendant, or if he is to be taken as representing emotions felt by the bride or groom, or, alternatively, to be understood to be a force engendered by the bride or groom.[74] By the Hellenistic period, he also appears as a child or *putto*.[75] In later vases, Aphrodite herself eclipses her son, often in nuptial scenes adorning pot types associated with weddings.[76]

It appears, from the iconography at least, that by the end of the fifth century, female eroticism was acquiring a new significance, perhaps representing a respectable and desirable means of personal and civic happiness and stability.[77] It has been suggested that the style and subject matter of these pots reflect a need to escape from the horrors of the Peloponnesian war,[78] or a romantic reaction to general urban malaise.[79] Alternatively, the change in the content of these paintings may suggest that these new representations are aimed at a female audience that had previously been neglected, especially since the scenes are now found on pots for use in domestic settings.[80]

However, we need to be cautious: these changes do not necessarily tell us women's own experiences of their sexuality. It seems rather to express an idealization of respectable females, in contrast with sex-workers, which is also found in other media. These images of women as brides are accompanied, in Athens, by the open expression of male sexual power over female sex-workers, who appear mute and degraded in the more public forum of Old Comedy.[81] A little later, in the comedies of Menander, this dichotomy is more blatant. Both wives and prostitutes are represented as under male sexual control: sex-workers may never be redeemed and so remain at the mercy of male desire, while respectable young women are only raped and mistreated until they are discovered to be, by birth, wifely material. We can observe that throughout this period, and later, a more detailed examination of the individual and ordinary life was being pursued across the arts. However, from the Knidian Aphrodite caught unawares taking a bath, to the women of Theokritos' *Idylls*, to Lucian's *Conversations of the Hetairai*, these are male approximations—men describing to other men what it is that they imagine women want, what they desire. As Osborne puts it in describing the Aphrodite: 'The "ideal of the feminine principle" here ... is indicative of the way in which the "feminine principle" is constructed by male desire.'[82]

If these are male representations of women, then what might have been the underlying reality? This is a difficult question even to try to answer. As to what is actually happening to the status of women, the nature of the evidence is partial, fragmentary, and contradictory and the great majority of the sources are filtered through a male perspective. For the purposes of this chapter, the answer is further complicated by the wide geographical spread of the tablets in question and their distribution over time (datings which are, in any case, necessarily tentative).[83] A very few women may have acquired some greater freedoms: there is some evidence for a slow and tentative shift in certain aspects of women's role and status within society, and examples of women playing a more significant role in the lives of their cities.[84] However, this is not to argue that women were in any dramatic sense freed from the constraints of previous years.

It seems unlikely then, that these artistic changes, which place the eroticism of women so much more clearly in the public eye, directly attest changes in the lives of contemporary women, but they do seem to indicate some kind of change in attitudes to female sexuality during this period. Obviously, again, any attempt to describe this change must acknowledge the importance of individual contexts. For example, in Athens, some have posited a change in the environment from a focus on individualistic self-gratification to a period under the democracy when emotions were channelled towards the community's benefit.[85] There may be a specific link to Perikles' citizenship legislation, and the concerns that this engendered may have increased during the fourth century, as political events caused a more turbulent context. Certainly, Menander's concerns with rape, marriage, relationships, and the status of young women can be seen to reflect the concerns of a population for whom the preservation of the *oikos* was of the utmost importance.[86] In sum, it seems that this was a period in which the relationships between men and women (both sex-workers and respectable women) became a greater concern of art and literature. However, in most cases, we must note that the represented woman, although perhaps now gaining an extra dimension, is still an idealized creation, still usually portrayed as the object of male desire, and still, as such, does not speak for herself.

CULTURAL CHANGES AND CURSING

It is in such a context that curse tablets, which attempt to manipulate the desire of individuals, usually that of women, start to appear.[87] These tablets provide an interesting nuance to the male representations of women's sexuality and relationships that dominate other media. In contrast, the tablets reveal the details of stories in which desire is not a straightforwardly institutionalized exchange, and where women not only fear the power of others, but also seem to wield power themselves. Whoever bound Zois (*DT* 86) did so in the full knowledge of her attractions—this woman's sexual power is a threat which must be controlled. Pausanias clearly could not gain access to Sime, or he would not need to resort to this kind of control. The agent of SGD 57 who turned Euboula from Aineas, was presumably using a curse because he or she had no other recourse.

More remarkably, the curses by Prosodion (*DT* 5), Phila (the Pella curse), and the author of *DTA* 78 offer us access to the social expectations and fears of three women, expressed in their own words. Although we know little about these women, their status or their circumstances, and the evidence is sparse, these tablets do show us women asserting control over areas of their life that are threatened by the desire of the men with whom they are involved. We cannot know the exact circumstances in which these curses were written, but it does seem that these are women who could not invoke a marriage in order to strengthen their case (although Prosodion does mention her children), and were not upset about a simple economic transaction gone wrong. We can see that these women spoke from a context where male desire represented a rich vein of risk that, for them, extended into questions of sheer survival.

As with all the curse tablets discussed in this study, our preconceptions can severely limit how we read these texts. I have tried to show how the agents of all these texts, especially those where we have no indication of the gender of the agent, could have occupied a range of social roles and positions. These tablets may help to draw our attention to the rich variety of lived experience within the ancient city and how it was changing in the fourth century BCE.

12

Curses and Risk

> ... Where the philosophy of *ubuntu* proclaims that 'a person is a person through other persons', everyday life teaches that life in a world of witches must be lived in terms of a presumption of malice that adds: *because they can kill you.*
>
> Ashforth 2005: 1[1]

NGCT 24
Location: England, Oxford, Ashmolean Museum Inv. G. 514.3
Origin: Greece, Attika
Date: Very early fourth century BCE (Jordan 1999)
Text: Jordan (1999: 115–17)
Side A:

> Εἴ τις ἐμὲ κατέδεσεν
> ἒ̓ γυνὴ ἢ <ἀ>νὴρ ἒ̓ δ<ο>ῦλος ἒ̓ ἐ-
> λεύθερος ἒ̓ ξένος ἒ̓ ἀσ-
> ‛σ’τος ἒ̓ οἰκεῖος ἒ̓ ἀλλώτ-
> ρτος ἒ̓ ἐπὶ φθόνον τὸν
> ἐμεῖ ἐργασίαι ἒ̓ ἔργοις,
> εἴ τις ἐμὲ κατέδεσ-
> εν πρὸς τὸν Ἑρμέν τὸ-
> ν ἐριόνιον ἒ̓ πρὸ ‛ς’; τὸν
> κάτοχον ἒ̓ πρὸς τὸν δό-
> λιον ἒ̓ ἄλλοθι πο, ἀντι-
> καταδε ‛σ’μεύω τὸς ἐχ ‛ρ’θ-
> ὸς ἅπαντας.

If anyone has cursed me, whether woman or man or slave or free or stranger or citizen or household member or stranger, from jealousy for me, my work and deeds. If anyone has cursed me in the presence of Hermes the Erionos or in the presence of (Hermes) the Binder or in the presence of (Hermes) the Trickster or elsewhere, I curse in turn all my enemies.

NGCT 66 (Chapters 7, 9, 12)
Location: Germany, University of Würzburg, Martin-von-Wagner-Museum, inv. K2100
Origin: Sicily, Selinous
Date: Fifth century BCE (Weiss 1989)
Text: Weiss (1989: 201)
Side A:

    Τὰν Εὐκλέος τὸδειμάντō
    τὰν γλ{λ}ο̑σαν καταγ<ρ>άφō, hōς με̄-
    δὲν . . . Μέστōρι ὀφελέσ<ε>ι·
    τὰν Σιμία τō̑ Μιϙύθō γλο̑σα-
    ν καταγράφō, hōς με̄δὲν Μέ-
    στōρι ὀφελέσει· τὰν Πιθάϙō τ-
    ō̑ Λ---όō τὰν γλο̑σαν κατ-
    αγράφō, hōς με̄δὲν Μέστō-
    ρι ὀφελέσε[ι] · τὰν ---φō τō̑ ΡΛΙΛ-
    πō τὰν γλο̑σαν καταγράφō,
    hōς με̄δὲν Μέστōρι ὀφελέ̄σει·
    Φιλόνδαν τὸν Χοιρίνα κα̣{ι̣ χ̣}τα-
    {α̣}γράφō καὶ .ο..κλ[έ]α̣, hοὶ μ-
    [ε̄]δέν Μ̣έ̣στōρι ὀ̣φ[ελέσ-]
    ο̣ν[τι ·]

Side B:

    Τὰν Μέστορος τō̑ Ε̣-
    ικέλō τὰν γλο̑σαν κ-
    αταγράφō · τо̀ς ΟΙΙ..
    Εἰκέλō πάντας γλο̑σ-
    ας καταγράφō τὰ<ς> γλο̑σ-
    α̣ς, hōς μ<ε̄δ>ὲν Μέστōρι ὀ̣-
    φελέ̄σο̣ντι· κἀρχέστρα-
    τον͡τὸν Αἰσχίνα καταγ-
    ράφō, ἀντ' hο̑ν γλο̑σ̣α-
    ις Μ̣έ̣στōρι ὀ̣[φ]ελέ̣ι-
    λ[έ̄]σαν

Side A:

I register the terrible tongue of Euklēs, . . . let him not be useful to Mēstōr. I register the tongue of Simias, the son of Mikythos, let him not be useful to Mēstōr. I register the tongue of . . . Pitheus, (the son of?) . . . let him not be useful to Mēstōr. I register the tongue of . . ., the son of . . ., let him not be useful to Mēstōr. I register Philondas, the son of Choirinas, and I register . . ., let them not be useful to Mēstōr.

Side B:

The tongue of Mēstōr, the son of Eikelos, I register. The . . . of Eikelos, all their tongues I register, let them not be useful to Mēstōr. And Archestratos, the son of Aischinēs I register, because they have been useful to Mēstōr with their tongues.

I begin with two texts, both stinking with adrenaline even across the centuries: in side A of NGCT 66 someone is trying everything he can to stop a group of men from 'being useful' to one Mestor. We have no idea of the precise circumstances: it may be that the writer was going to face Mestor, and perhaps also these men, in court, or that he had committed a crime against Mestor and feared betrayal by associates or neighbours. We have only this historical splinter of events, a vivid cameo of a man desperate to prevent a situation he feared. On the second side of the tablet, we begin to understand that he feels justified in asking the gods to bind these men, because they already have been useful to this Mestor in just the way he is trying to prevent. In contrast, NGCT 24 was written in a welter of suspicion. The creator has probably been suffering some inexplicable misfortune, since he claims to have been cursed. And why would anyone do that? He puts it down to *phthonos*—simple, vicious envy towards him—and lashes out at anyone, from across society, who might be responsible.

The concerns of these two texts are typical of the curses of this period, when, my exploration of *katadesmoi* has suggested, curse-writing was essentially a pre-emptive practice, a defensive act of aggression against future danger, sometimes motivated by previous events, sometimes just prompted by fear and suspicion. Curse-writers wrote their texts because they wanted to direct future events in their favour by managing sources of risk: they aimed to weaken and incapacitate their targets and thus neutralize the threat that they presented.

This explanation directs our attention to the targets of these curses, and provides a theoretical framework within which to explore their significance: why and in what situations might a person need to bind another person, object, or institution? Such an approach allows the reader to acknowledge and explore the complexity and ambiguity of the relationships presented across the texts, something that the current popular explanation of competition, usually of a political nature, tends to constrain or ignore. If we examine these curses with the social construction of risk in mind, then a range of individual and cultural concerns emerge, illuminating surprising aspects of personal and social life in this period, providing insights into the nexus of values, relationships, and institutions that underpinned life in the ancient Greek city.

So, for example, judicial curses reveal groups or teams of people ranged against each other, including unexpected targets, such as women and bystanders. To understand them, we must look beyond the closed space of the courthouse, and a paradigm of duelling elites, and set them amongst a network of relationships reaching into the wider community. The evidence for theatrical cursing provokes questions about the nature and geographical spread of festivals, and about the attitude of the Athenians towards civic positions that combined wealth with power. Despite assertions to the contrary, none of the commercial curses can be proved to have been written by rival businessmen; in fact, many of them may not even be primarily concerned with commercial matters. Finally, relationship curses, precisely because of their ambiguity, provoke useful questions about the nature and conduct of relationships in Greek society. Moreover, in contrast with most of the evidence for this sphere of life, which is dominated almost completely by male expression, these tablets provide examples of women writing about their own situations. In a historical context that usually stresses the importance of marriage and female eroticism (by and for men), these tablets vividly draw our attention to the risks that confronted women, described in their own words.

Reading these texts under the rubric of risk offers a vivid glimpse of the individual citizens, non-citizens, metics, and women who were using curses, against their fellow citizens, to protect their own interests. The use of curses across these different contexts illuminates the experiences of individuals and how they felt about the civic group of which they were a part. In turn, grouping these curses reveals the concerns that ran throughout society, and how these concerns may have clustered and shifted over time.

For example, as mentioned, the appearance and nature of judicial tablets in the Athenian historical record may shed light on the significance and role of the Athenian lawcourts in the radical democracy, as experienced by its citizens. Here was an arena in which you were forced to struggle against your fellow-citizens for the approval of the *dēmos*: risk was embodied, concentrated in the activities of other people. Moreover, the distribution over time of curses on judicial matters corresponds to the distribution over time of surviving judicial orations.[2] I have raised the possibility that written tablets were connected with the move towards increasing specialization or professionalization in the fourth century, observed in other areas of civic organization and management.[3] Perhaps, in fact, the link is closer still, and the greater use of logographers helped to stimulate the use of curse tablets, and vice versa. Theatrical cursing offers another example, suggesting that writing binding curses may have provided an outlet for the competitive instincts of wealthy men that had previously been channelled through choregic competition. The appearance of curses concerning relationships,

Curses and Risk 229

seemingly at a time when other material evidence indicates that society was placing greater focus on the representation of relationships, may also indicate a shift in social anxiety towards this area of life.

Much of what I have said so far has been about the existing categories of curses. However, as I have tried to emphasize throughout, although we can guess at the circumstances and concerns that prompted the writing of a number of these curse tablets, we are far from being able to identify all. For example, a number of curses previously filed under the category of judicial curses have no forensic terminology in them, but comprise a list of individuals who may have shared political allegiance; for others not even these clues to circumstance are apparent. The same lack of context is true of many of the so-called commercial curses. Instead of a series of tablets slotting neatly into a tight taxonomy, we are left with innumerable vitriolic fragments. Working with this material is like straining to catch myriad, one-sided, slanderous conversations, whispered across a distance of thousands of years. All too frequently, there are only disconnected scraps—a roll-call of victims, a list of body parts, an intimation of deeply felt emotion.

What might have motivated the writers of these tablets? In answer, we can perhaps turn to NGCT 24 and 66 for some initial guidance. The writer of the NGCT 24 tablet assumes that the person who has cursed him has done so out of *phthonos* or envy—that is the risk he perceives—and so he curses them back, whoever they may be. The writer of NGCT 66 knows that the men he curses have acted against him. With these curses, we return to the doorstep offerings of Plato's itinerant salesmen: if you have an enemy, we have the technology to blunt his hostility. The aggressive act of writing a curse is justified by the need to act defensively; our enemies are bound to attack us, and we know we are/will be under attack (because we suffer daily misfortune/because we have seen them in action), so now we must attack them.

And these two tablets are not the only ones whose writers so overtly reveal their motivations. There are eight other curses that include a term or phrase specifically alluding to the unjust nature of the target and/or his actions, thus justifying the cursing action taken by the agent of the curse tablet.[4] In *DTA* 102, the act of injustice is described, simply, in the past tense: an event has occurred for which the curse writer seeks restitution.[5] In *DTA* 98, 100, 103, 158, SGD 58, NGCT 14 and 23, the act of injustice is described more vividly and immediately in the present tense, suggesting that the agent of each curse was still suffering this harmful action at the time of the writing of the curse.[6] In *DTA* 98, the agent of the curse describes how he is being wronged by the targets of the curse, ἀδικούμενος γὰρ ὑπὸ Εὐρυπτολέμου καὶ Ξενοφῶντος καταδῶ αὐτούς 'Since I am being wronged by Euryptolemos and Xenophon,

I bind them'. The rest of the curse demonstrates that its agent did not consider the danger posed by these individuals to be over and in the past: he used the curse to ask the gods to render useless any future plans of the targets: καὶ εἴ τι βουλεύονται καὶ εἴ τι πράττουσιν ἀτελῆ αὐ[το]ῖς γένοιτο 'and if they plan anything and if they do anything, let it be useless as far as they are concerned'. The writer of *DTA* 100, who appears to have been a woman,[7] also seems to have been concerned with an ongoing risk. The curse mentions anyone who is hostile to her (side A, l. 3) and binds not just their persons but 'their acts against' her (ll. 6–7: καὶ τὰς τούτων ἐπ'(ἐ)μοι πράξεις). This makes most sense if it is taken to mean acts that may still be to come.

In the case of *DTA* 103, the act of wrongdoing appears to be related to litigation. The targets of this curse are named and then described as (side A, l. 2) ἁμαρ[τωλο(ὐ)]s 'wrongdoers'. Later (l. 8) σύνδικοι 'fellow litigants' are mentioned and the phrase τ(ὸ)ν περὶ τῆ(s) δίκη[s δικαζ[ό]μενον 'he who is pursuing a private court case' follows the name of one of the targets (ll. 9–10). The use of the present tense to describe the conduct of the court case suggests that this curse was motivated by current legal events. It appears that the writer believed his opponents to be wicked because they were willing to prosecute him. By creating a curse, he may have been hoping to exert some force over those who would face him in the courtroom. *DTA* 158 is very fragmentary, but the words ἀδικο(υ)μ[ένοις (l. 7) and ἀ]δικο(ύ)μεν[οι (l. 9), suggest a similar situation of ongoing wrongdoing. SGD 58 binds those who have stolen τὸ δραύκι(ο)ν 'a necklace', along with 'those who know about it and those who took a share'. It looks as if NGCT 14 was written before a court case: the curse-writer pleads with the hero Palaimon to be his avenger, to ensure that the court judges think that his enemies are speaking unjustly, because they are saying and doing unjust things, presumably against him. NGCT 23 curses a list of people, ending with the protest that he has been wronged, without having done a wrong first.

These curses provide another view on the way cursing was understood to work in ancient society, being used not just to pre-empt a particular situation of risk (such as going to court), but also to manage the dangers inherent in a breakdown of social relations in which there was continuing hostility.[8] In eight of these curses, the writer pinpoints the wrongdoer and alludes to a specific act of enmity that has prompted the writing of the curse. NGCT 24 stands out because the author does not know the name of the person against whom he is writing his curse. He only suspects he has been cursed, and not for any particular wrongdoing, but because of someone's φθόνος, or envy, against him.

We can see this dynamic in action, and understand something of how it may have worked, by turning to recent work on witchcraft by the political scientist Adam Ashforth in Soweto, South Africa. He describes how 'while witchcraft is an endeavour predicated upon secrecy, the powers and possibilities imagined as its currency are also experienced as commonplace accompaniment of everyday life'.[9] At the heart of the practice of witchcraft is jealousy. Ashforth explains that this is 'premised upon hatred', drawing on Max Scheler's description of the emotional state of ressentiment 'where not only is the feeling of envy experienced as a nonfulfillment of a desire for something but the "owner is falsely considered the cause of our privation". The jealousy that is most dangerous is thus connected with a deluded sense of righteousness that allows an attack to be construed as defense.'[10] He describes how the knowledge—or just the suspicion—that someone is jealous of you can feed the suspicion that they are ready to attack you with invisible evil forces. These anxieties are fuelled by gossip within social networks; in fact, both gossip and witchcraft suspicions use the same circuits of gossip, since 'we gossip about those whom we suspect of malice and we suspect of malice those about whom we feel the need to gossip'.[11]

I plan to explore these dynamics of gossip, envy or jealousy, and explanations of misfortune in more detail in the future, but even now I find these parallels are stimulating and insightful, offering a new framework within which to view the corpus of tablets and its chorus of vitriolic but context-less voices. It offers a startling picture of a society riddled with rumour, beset by envy, suspicion, and rivalry, a society in which, to adapt Jean-Paul Sartre, risk was other people.[12]

We can observe that such a dynamic of generalized distrust might be deemed a startlingly suitable description of daily life in Athens during periods of the late fifth/early fourth century. It was a turbulent time, surely full of social and political uncertainty: the Athenians had lost the Peloponnesian war and endured two oligarchic revolutions, with attendant political, emotional, and physical horrors. The empire had been lost and the city drained of both men and resources. Plague had raised questions about the favour of the gods. Meanwhile, evacuations from the countryside into the city probably meant a more crowded, competitive urban population. We catch glimpses in the literature of the kind of hostilities such events may have fostered. Thucydides describes the atmosphere in Athens under the oligarchic coup of 411 BCE: 'it was impossible for anyone who felt himself ill-treated to complain of it to someone else so as to take measures in his own defense; he would either have had to speak to someone he did not know or to someone he knew but could not rely upon.'[13]

This is an appealingly appropriate context for the seeding of the use of *katadesmoi* in mainland Greece. In a time when men and women were vulnerable and, perhaps often, terrified, when anyone might turn out to be an enemy, curses would have offered a crucial means of self-protection. If such an explanation seems too simple, we can perhaps argue that it may not have been a necessary environment, but it seems to have been sufficient. Certainly, once the practice had taken root, it grew and developed. Binding curses continued to be used as a way of managing potential risks, but, with time, the idiom of the practice shifted, from a pre-emptive strike (used to stop something) to an act of aggression (used to get something). This is particularly well illustrated by the changes in relationship spells from the separation curses of the initial period under study here, to the erotic aggressive spells that developed.[14]

Later texts also reveal changes in the involvement of the dead: there is a massive expansion of ghostly personnel with a vast range of *daimons* and spirits of the dead adjured to carry out the instructions of curses, often focusing on a *nekuodaimon* (corpse-demon), the spirit of one who was dead untimely and is therefore angry and powerful.[15] The members of this new supernatural staff have a far more intimate relationship with the agent of the curse, having been awakened specifically to do his or her bidding.[16] The kinds of instruction they receive suggest that they were considered to be spirits of far greater power, expected to have far greater knowledge of local topography and to be able to follow detailed sets of instructions.[17] In the process, the agent now provides much more information about his or her intentions.[18] The contrast between these spells and the curses we have been studying is startling at first, but closer examination of the texts of the earlier period reveals intimations of these changes. As an example, consider the difference of expression in the tablets *DTA* 100 and SGD 21: in the former, the writer asks for the preservation of the woman who struck the lead; in the latter, written around 400 years later, the agent of the curse asks that the rage of the dead not be directed against him or her.[19]

Conclusion

> Wax image dolls: Code P63. Cure sickness, capture love, heal and hate with image dolls. Made from traditional formulae incorporating natural wax, herbs. By making an image you can work magic on that person perpetually. 6″ male or female dolls supplied ready to be personalised. Doll prepared with all accumulators, herbs, essences, ready to go. Natural wax colour. Some shamans keep shelffuls [*sic*] of dolls to control all their acquaintances.
>
> 1987 Sorcerer's Apprentice (UK mail-order occult store) mail-order form, reproduced in Luhrmann 1989: 5

In this book I have set out to explore some of the ways in which ancient Greek men and women constructed and responded to perceptions of risk and uncertainty in their everyday lives. In an attempt to describe the experiences of a wider section of society, I have worked primarily with non-literary material, investigating published oracle texts from Dodona and *katadesmoi* dated to the sixth to first centuries BCE. Often difficult to read, these texts preserve the individual voices of ordinary men and women, from among groups who are systematically under- or unrepresented in more traditional sources.

Using a theory of 'risk' that describes it as socially constructed, I have tried to bring to light some of the stories contained within these texts, setting out to identify when, how, and why ordinary Greek men and women used these technologies to seek supernatural aid. Oracles and curses show us different expressions of and responses to risk and uncertainty in everyday life. The Dodona oracle questions take us beyond the headlines of ancient history—consultations by states and historical figures—to reveal the everyday use of oracles by individuals. Here are men and women in the middle of making decisions with serious private or public consequences. They do not relinquish their autonomy: their questions are carefully structured to constrain the oracle's possible answers. When we turn to curses, we find ourselves exploring situations of more immediate danger, whose protagonists seem to have had little control over events. Examining the texts in detail, under the rubric of risk, encourages us to focus on the target(s) of each curse, and explore the possible reasons and circumstances for its selection.

Occasionally, the concerns of the two practices overlap: for example, a third-century curse from Attika (*DTA* 160) appears to mention *manteia* or 'sorcery' as one of its targets. Unfortunately, the text is very fragmentary and it is difficult to make out any more information, other than a number of names.[1] As mentioned in Chapter 5, there are a couple of oracle questions relating to curses. One seems to ask about the use of cursing in a trial, specifically the effect of a curse on the consultant—possible evidence that, at least sometimes, people knew when they had been singled out as targets. The other asks about using a *psychagōgos* or spirit-raiser, called Dorios.[2] As observed, in the literary sources these characters are primarily involved in laying ghosts that are causing trouble to communities, but Plato raises another, darker side of their profession. In the *Laws* he links *psychagōgēs* with those who practised *goēteia*, often translated as 'sorcery', who claimed not only that their practices could lead up spirits (*psychagōgein*) but also that they could persuade the gods. Other literary references suggest that the former must be the activity of ghost-laying. To understand the nature of the latter, 'persuading the gods', we can turn to the description Plato gives in the *Republic* of those spell salesmen who go from door to door offering on the one hand to expiate, cure, and purify, and on the other to create spells to harm an enemy. *Katadesmoi* themselves can provide the link between the two passages: these are spells to harm an enemy which, as we have seen, seek to 'persuade the gods', eliciting their help (rather than that of the dead) to activate the binding of the curse. It would be a logical development for these salesmen to offer to use their skills to harm as well as to cure.[3] Perhaps the writer of the oracle question wanted Dorios to rid his house or community of a troublesome ghost—or perhaps he wanted to hire him to write a curse.

Dorios takes us back to the largely itinerant men and women whom the Derveni Papyrus called 'those who make a living out of rites', the entrepreneurs of a society that believed in divine communication.[4] In this culture, people coped with the uncertainty of the future and particular risks by invoking supernatural help. Most of the curse and oracle texts that we can make sense of tell us stories of anxiety about particular risks and situations of uncertainty. Grouping the tablets (as far as possible) according to their context illuminates some of the dynamics underlying the institutions and relationships of the ancient city, and how they changed over time. Together, the information from these two collections helps us to build a fuller picture of the way ancient Greek men and women understood the world.

Attitudes to risk and uncertainty are only the beginning: if cultural perceptions of risk and danger are shaped by the pressures of social life and accepted notions of accountability, then examining the nature of risk within a culture can lead to a deeper understanding of how members of that culture tend to perceive the distribution of responsibility, the causes of misfortune, and the allocation of blame. Evidence from the texts in both collections illuminates the operation of these mechanisms among the ancient Greeks. The concerns of the oracle questions show which areas of life were perceived as particularly likely to be sources of misfortune—marriage to the wrong woman, travel, disease. The curse material, in turn, casts a harsh light on the perception of potential causes of misfortune within the Greek community. They demonstrate how in moments of particular crisis, other people were perceived as sources of risk: hence the constant attempts to bind them mentally, physically, even occasionally spiritually.

In addition to the material in the texts, the practices themselves also played a role in society's perceptions of the dynamics of risk and misfortune, and the relationship between them. Both oracle consultation and curse-writing concern the allocation of responsibility for an event before it takes place. The questions asked at the Dodona oracle, and their formulation, demonstrate general cultural understandings of the nature of the relationship between mortals and the supernatural: what kind of help it was permissible to seek from the god, what kind of responsibility one should take upon oneself, and what one could allocate to the supernatural.

An oracle consultation is both an attempt to secure the outcome of a decision, and an explicit acknowledgement that the power of the consultant to control this is limited. In many traditional stories about oracular consultation found in the sources, this lack of mortal power is explicitly demonstrated, as the consultant faces spontaneous, unexpected, or riddling oracle responses. In these stories, oracles become a source of risk, and sometimes even misfortune, as the, often uncomprehending, consultant tries to manipulate his future and is confused, tricked, or misled by fate. The idea of trickery is more common when the oracle is from a wandering *mantis*, rather than an oracular sanctuary, but Delphi's reputation for ambiguity cannot be over-emphasized. Perhaps this is why the historical consultations that have survived seem to have been so carefully phrased: these were conscious attempts to manage the scope of an oracle's possible response, in the light of its reputation.

As for curses, I have already noted above how envy, superheated by gossip, might lead to supernatural attack (or attack construed as defence). Here I want to emphasize the role that misfortune could have played in this dynamic. The writer of NGCT 24 must have experienced a misfortune of some kind in order to assume that he had been cursed and was at risk. In response, attempting to neutralize the source of risk, he resorted to a curse, and became a source of risk and misfortune for someone else—and not just in his own mind. The likelihood is that he was not the only one feeling threatened by the hostile relationships to which his curse alludes. Whoever he imagined as his enemy was no doubt thinking the same of him and taking action—and this pattern, stirred by suspicions, fuelled by gossip was being repeated across Greek society. NGCT 24 clearly demonstrates how curses themselves, and similar supernatural techniques, played their part in forging a relationship between perceptions of risk and causes of misfortune.

Of course, this curse text provides only the barest bones of a narrative, which we have to piece together. A fuller account of how experiences of misfortune might lead to perceptions of risk and the allocation of blame related to supernatural attack is told, centuries later, by the speaker, Libanius. As described above in Chapter 9, Libanius describes the increasingly wild behaviour of one of his professional rivals after he beats him in a series of competitions. The man accuses him of using sorcery in order to achieve those victories. He has obviously decided that Libanius is a manifest source of danger to him, because when he suffers further serious misfortune—the death of his wife—he also blames Libanius for this. Soon afterwards, Libanius himself becomes the victim of a supernatural attack. The perpetrator may well have been this man, or another who had perceived Libanius as a risk—a source of current or future misfortune.[5]

Sometimes, I believe, these dynamics of risk, misfortune, and blame exploded into public view in other ways. They are, I believe, lurking in the background of the fourth-century legal cases made against women involved in supernaturally related activities. As I have said, these cases bring to mind witchcraft accusations made in other societies in other historical periods, in which those who are socially marginalized or the focus of envy are blamed for the actual or potential misfortunes of others.[6] It is not hard to construct a plausible background to these cases in which the growth of gossip nurtured suspicions that led to allegations, until finally a case came to court.[7]

Supporting this picture of the social dynamics behind these cases are a number of intriguing inscriptions. Among the 13 or so curse tablets found at the temple of Demeter in Knidos, one (*DT* 4, side A) is written by a woman against a man who has accused her of giving *pharmaka* to her husband; the other (*DT* 1) is obviously written in similar circumstances of accusation and denial. In it a woman calls down a curse on herself if she has either administered a *pharmakon* to Asklapiadas, schemed against him, or summoned a woman to the temple and offered her three half-minae to curse him to death (note that the latter offers more evidence of female members of this profession). Before we scoff at this approach bear in mind the 'confession inscription' from Asia Minor set up by the descendants of one Tatias.[8] This woman had been accused of poisoning her son and so had gone to the nearby temple and set up a curse similar to those above. Unfortunately, soon after, her son had dropped a sickle on her foot and died as a result of the injury. Tatias' descendants took this as evidence of the curse having worked: she must have been guilty. They then, according to the stele, propitiated the gods and tried to loose the curse.

If rumour crystallized into an accusation and a case for damages actually went to court, one defence might have been to take refuge in the idea that you were not, at least, a professional. As noted above, Plato may have been considering such situations in his writings on suitable punishments for certain types of offences using *pharmaka*. The cases for which we have evidence may point to this defence being used: even when they are guilty of murder, the female defendants take refuge in saying that their intent was only to charm, that is, they were amateurs who just did not know what they were doing.[9]

Through the lens created by the evidence of these two bodies of texts—oracles and curses—a picture of life in the ancient Greek city can be developed. Alongside the more familiar vision of Athens, dominated by the great historians, philosophers, and dramatists, is another, more mundane, but no less fascinating. It shows us ordinary Greek men and women from every walk of life, dealing with everyday fears and uncertainty, in an atmosphere that was sometimes gripped by gossip, prickling with accusations.

Zois, Phile, Pausanias: in some ways we cannot imagine their lives at all, in others they are very familiar. The concerns they voiced to the gods so many centuries ago tell us something about how they saw the world, illuminating an implicit, inextricable web of connections between perceptions of risk, expressions of blame, and experiences of misfortune. It is not difficult to think of examples from our own time and cultures in which this web of connections has been manifest. I have introduced some parallels that have intrigued me; for some readers South Africa will be as exotic and distant as ancient Greece, for others less so. As I have explained in my Introduction, understanding how different people understand and manage risks differently must not remain purely an intellectual excursion. I hope that exploring aspects of the construction of risk and uncertainty in ancient Greece may prompt insights into the same process in our own societies, greater understanding of what constitutes risk for whom and why this is so.

Notes

INTRODUCTION

1. Parke 11, *SGDI* 1565a; Karapanos 1878: pl. 36, 2; Doric dialect; Second century BCE. Karapanos states that at the beginning of the fifth line is a sign that could be taken for an ithyphallic symbol, or it might be nothing more than the two letters 'oi', written by mistake and then rubbed out.
2. It is also, of course, perfectly possible that Lysanias is the lover of Annyla, who is someone else's wife (as Robin Osborne has observed; private communication).
3. Little is known about the goddess Dione, other than her appearance in the *Iliad* (5.370 ff.), when we are told she comforts her daughter Aphrodite after she has been wounded by Diomedes. See Simon 1986.
4. Side A of *DT* 86: found in Greece, Boiotia; dated to no later than the Hellenistic period (Dickie 2000: 576); text from Ziebarth 1934: 1040, no. 22.
5. The device of listing the attractive aspects of a lover is unsurprisingly a common motif of love poetry from many different periods, from the Song of Songs to Shakespeare's sonnet 130 and Marvell's 'To his Coy Mistress' to, more recently, 'Miss You Less, See You More' by the dance music group 'Faithless'. Versnel notes that it is a popular device in ancient and modern Near Eastern poetry (see Versnel 1998: 258 n. 113 for references). In Greek literature we find parallels in the amatory epigrams of the *Palatine Anthology* that date to a similar period to the curse tablet under discussion. These poems focus on the physical attributes of their male and female targets, aiming to invoke, presumably admiringly, the attractions of the individual described (compare, for example, the epigrams *AP* 5.129 and 131 with the text of *DT* 86). Such lists were likely to have been an essential feature of the ancient erotic handbooks—a literary form that seems to have developed around this time (H. N. Parker 1992). Partly the result of the urge to classify and systematize knowledge, characteristic of this era, these books manufactured a particular representation of the sexuality and carnal appetites of women, gaining authority through the use of the (doubtfully) female authorial voice.
6. 'Black magic': Versnel 1991*a*: 62–3; Graf 1997*a*: 22; R. Parker 2005*a*; Jordan 1988: 273. The idea of a dichotomy between rationality and irrationality has long been challenged. Where once it was enlightened to recognize that irrational behaviour could exist alongside rational (see Vernant 1974), now many argue that the use of such terms at all may be an imposition of modern categories of limited and limiting use when

applied to other cultures. So, for example, Lloyd (1999*b*: 4) observes that since Dodds's *The Greeks and the Irrational* it has become abundantly clear that the 'irrational' in one or other of its complex and diffuse forms is to be found at every period of Greek thought for which there is evidence. Discussions of rationality/irrationality are now moving towards more nuanced approaches, including consideration of the Greeks' own self-conscious approaches to these areas, with less emphasis on locating events in a schema of modern categories, and concentrating instead on their meaning for the culture concerned (see particularly Buxton 1999 and Gordon 1999*b*: 161). Those embracing this approach join a debate that has been raging in a wider context for a while, the focus of which is the question of whether discontent with making judgements such as rational/irrational means we must wholly embrace cultural relativism.

7. For a useful summary of the development of anthropological approaches to magic see Luhrmann 1989: 345 ff. She herself rejects an outright intellectualist approach (e.g. as Tylor and Frazer in which magic represents (wrong) beliefs about how the natural world functions), or a symbolist approach (e.g. as Durkheim, Douglas, Lewis, Tambiah which focuses on the expressive dimensions of ritual action) and argues instead for (353) 'ethnographies that describe the cognitive impact of cultural experience in its natural setting, rich detailed accounts that are sensitive to psychological theories and philosophical problems but which are neither experimentally based nor speculatively abstract'.

8. E.g. Morgan 1990: 16 ff.

9. For example, Whittaker (1965: 30), who uses the comparative material because in Africa 'different stresses have called forth the same response' or Price's discussion of some aspects of the Azande poison-oracle (used by individuals) in his discussion of city consultations at Delphi (1985: 143). Both approaches are valid and useful, but they do not compare with equivalent use of oracles across cultures.

10. Faraone 1985: 151.

11. Faraone (1991*a*: 16) cites Brown's work on magic in late antiquity and his observation that 'magic coalesces around areas of competition and uncertainty'. He takes up Brown's (1970: 25) suggestion that the use of curse tablets to bind the competitive power of the charioteer can be seen as more than an act of personal malice, but was also, indirectly, a political act.

12. Faraone himself admits there is no proof of this (1991*a*: 20): '[curse tablets] seem to have evolved from a special form of ritual (a symbolic gesture would have accompanied either incantation or prayer) that was primarily used by individuals involved in often-lopsided agonistic situations, to bind the power of their opponents. . . . The recurrence of what I have called a "defensive stance" in some of the texts discussed . . . suggests that the *defigentes* (curse-writers) may have perceived such activities as

protective in nature and not as aggressive magic at all. Indeed, it is a tempting but alas, completely unproveable suggestion that the person who would most often employ a binding curse is the one who doubted his or her ability to win without it, that is, that the *defigens* (curse-writer) was the perennial "underdog", who . . . was protecting himself against what seemed to be insurmountable odds.' (My additions in parentheses.)
13. Faraone 1985: 154.
14. Betz (*PGM* p. xliii): 'Magic was so utterly despised by historians and philologists that the announcement of the seminar [on the subject of the magical papyri at the University of Heidelberg in 1905] did not mention the word "magic"'. He reports a remark of Ulrich von Wilamowitz-Moellendorff: 'I once heard a well-known scholar regret that these papyri were found because they deprived antiquity of the noble splendour of classicism' (in *Reden und Vorträge*, Berlin: Weidmann, 1925–6: 254) also quoted by Graf (1997*a*: 11). Dodds (1951: 195) does describe the revival of incubation, the taste for orgiastic religion, the prevalence of magical attack as examples of 'regression taking an even cruder form' (as Graf 1997*a*: 290 n. 179) but qualifies this 'they were in a sense a return of the past. But they were, also, in another aspect, portents of things to come'.
15. For example, Douglas and Wildavsky 1982: 9; Douglas 1986: 59; 1992: 58.
16. An initial overview of its entry in Liddell and Scott's *Lexicon* suggests that it was used to describe something bad and imminent, but that it also sometimes indicated a more neutral sense of possibility.
17. For 'jealousy' as motive for witchcraft in South Africa, see Ashforth 2005: 70. 'Jealousy' in Soweto includes both envy of what another has, and fear that others will take away what you have.
18. Spiritual insecurity: see Ashforth 2005: 3–4.
19. Earliest tablets (early fifth or late sixth century BCE) from the Greek colony of Selinous, Sicily. By the mid-fifth century, in Athens, and late fifth–early fourth, Olbia, by the Black Sea. From here, the practice spread (see Chapter 7); a century or so later, curse-writing is spreading across the rest of the Graeco-Roman world; most pre-Imperial curses have been found in Attika.
20. The difficulty of getting hold of the tablets themselves means that I have not attempted to reread the tablets, but have worked with readings by other editors.
21. J. S. Bruner (1986: 25–6) has called this process, as it occurs in fiction, 'subjunctivising'. It comprises three features—presupposition, that is the creation of implicit rather than explicit meanings; subjectification, the depiction of reality . . . through the filter of the consciousness of protagonists in the story; and multiple perspectives. 'To be in the subjunctive mode is, then, to be trafficking in human possibilities rather than in settled certainties.'

22. The difficulties of defining the difference between plot and story are well known, but as Lowe (2000) has commented, despite a lack of academic rigour, Forster managed to capture much of what we instinctively understand by plot, as well as creating a sophisticated scholarly commentary.
23. In the fields of classics and ancient history, in particular see Sourvinou-Inwood 1991 and 1995.
24. See Luhrmann 1989, Philip Peek 1991, and Ashforth 2005.

CHAPTER 1

1. Luhrmann (1989: 382 and 438 n.) reports an anecdote of Ernst Gellner's: the philosophers Peter Winch and Alasdair MacIntyre, arguing about the limits of cross-cultural understanding, confused Evans-Pritchard's work on the Nuer, a pastoral people who live in southern Sudan and western Ethiopia, with that on the Azande of south-western Sudan, who do not keep cattle. They held a public debate on the meaning of cattle among the Azande, to which they invited Evans-Pritchard. 'At the debate's conclusion, Evans-Pritchard apparently remarked that he had little to add to the philosophical subtlety of the exchange, but that he wished to point out that there were no cattle among the Azande.'
2. Solon was archon of Athens in 594 BCE; Kroisos' reign began around 560 BCE.
3. Hdt. 1.32.4 ff.
4. Hdt. 1.32.6.
5. Hdt. 1.32.9.
6. Hdt. 1.91, trans. Waterfield; Loxias is an epithet of the god Apollo.
7. Xen. *An.* 3.1.41, trans. Warner.
8. Kroisos' story is followed by similarly themed stories: e.g., about Kyros (1.209.4) and his misinterpretation of his dream about Darios, although he claims to be shown everything in advance by the gods; Polykrates ignores his daughter's dream warning of his death (3.124–5). Xerxes' fate is sealed by a series of dreams that drive him onward, but the fact that this is a mistake is made clear in a series of conversations between him and his adviser, Artabanus, that echo the sentiments of Solon (7.10). Nor is this a view unique to Herodotos: the fragility of human fortune was a much-visited *topos* of ancient Greek proverbial wisdom, hymned and lamented across all genres of Greek literature (for further references and a thorough discussion of Herodotos' religious beliefs, including the role of fate and the gods, see further Harrison 2000, esp. 31 ff.).
9. Compare Xen. *Kyr.* 1.6.46.
10. Xen. *Oik.* 5.19–20. Jameson (1991) provides a comprehensive overview of the crucial importance of sacrifice and its significance for fortune throughout the different stages of military campaigns. The most frequent

form of divine consultation in the *Anabasis* is the sacrifice before battle. This was generally conducted by seers and/or by the generals themselves. It may be, however, that others in the army also trained in the mantic skill: at *An.* 6.4.15 Xenophon invites any man who might have trained as a *mantis* to come and read the sacrifice with him and we are told that many others were also present there. Ensuring such sacrifices were conducted was clearly part of the responsibility of a general and considered one of his strategic skills (Xenophon represents the father of the elder Kyros as having his son taught the mantic art so he will know what the gods counsel and not be at the mercy of seers or helpless without one *Kyr.* 1.6.2). It was also important to his soldiers (Xenophon defends himself to his troops by pointing out how often he has sacrificed on their behalf *An.* 5.6.28; soldiers rely on their general to read the signs correctly—it is important for their morale, *Eq. mag.* 6.6; Kyros tells the troops just before battle at *An.* 1.8.15, that the sacrifices have been favourable). Sacrifice was also used to make other strategic decisions (*An.* 2.2.3 after Kyros' death); when sacrifices are continuously unfavourable, these instructions are followed, however unwelcome (*An.* 6.4.15).

11. *An.* 3.1.11 and 4.3.8. Such salvation does not just occur to Xenophon personally. At *An.* 5.2.24 a divinity aids some Greeks who 'are in dire straits' ($αὐτῶν\ καὶ\ ἀπορουμένων$) during a plundering expedition.

12. Despite his obvious trust in divination, the interpretation, in advance, of a divine message is still clearly a difficult business, its truth only apparent in hindsight. Xenophon (*An.* 3.1.13) describes his own bewildered reaction after waking from a prophetic dream. His authorial self then comments: 'What is really meant by having a dream like this can be seen from what happened after the dream.' A number of signs reinforcing a message appear to make interpretation more certain—as we see when Xenophon is trying to work out whether or not to take up the leadership that has been offered him.

13. Xen. *An.* 3.1.5–8; Xenophon uses these formulations elsewhere in the *Anabasis*, see *An.* 6.2.15, 7.6.44; the answer, given at 6.1.24, indicates the nature of the question posed. As we shall see, it was not just Xenophon and Sokrates who phrased their questions in this way: 'To which god should I pray . . . ?' and 'Is it better and more good that I do x or y/x or not?' are the two most common question formulations used in both state and individual oracle consultations.

14. Belief in the instability of fortune is fundamental to Herodotos' historical enterprise, as he states: 'I will cover minor and major human settlements equally, because most of those which were important in the past have diminished in significance by now, and those which were great in my own time were small in times past. I will mention both equally because I know that human happiness never remains long in the same place' (1.5.4).

15. From his other writings we can see that in his view, the gods are under no

Notes to Chapter 1

compulsion to care for anyone unless they so choose. Throughout the *Anabasis*, references to the gods' involvement with a project are accompanied by reminders that this is dependent on their willingness. Acquiring this divine support, and trying to ensure some sense of security appears to turn on pious action. At *Kyr.* 1.6.4 Kambyses applauds his son and observes that since Kyros prays to gods regularly he can expect to obtain what he asks for—and this appears to apply to individuals, groups, and cities. As well as prayer, such pious actions appear to include sacrificing regularly (see advice to Xenophon at the end of the *Anabasis*) and keeping one's word (Klearchos makes a specifically pointed remark about this to Tissaphernes at 2.5.7; Tissaphernes in reply observes (2.5.21) that those who break their oaths must be 'without means and desperate and without any other way out and even then they must be villains').

16. These concepts are described in Harris 1968. The distinction is based on the established linguistic distinction between phonemic and phonetic. A recent disagreement in this field can provide us with an idea of how these terms are used: Dickie (2001: 324 n. 6) promotes the emic view, asserting that ancient historians must not abandon the attempt 'to see the world through the eyes of the members of the society studied'. He is challenging Versnel's argument (1991*b*: 184–5) that the past can only be discussed in terms understood by those in the present.
17. This distinction made in Ogden 2001: xviii.
18. Gould 2001: 210.
19. The title of Simon Price's 'Religions of the Ancient Greeks' (1999) sums up the situation very well.
20. Scullion 1994; R. Parker 2005*a*.
21. See Dickie 2001: 18 ff., especially his discussion of Graf 1996, p. 20.
22. Hippok. *Morb. sacr. passim*, II–III in particular.
23. Writings of the time, see Lloyd 1999*a*: 29; see also oracle questions asked by cities for guidance about suffering caused by divine punishment of mortal wrongdoing. On an oracle tablet the Dodonaeans ask 'whether it is on account of the impurity of some human being that gods send the storm' (Parke Public 7; *SEG* 19. 149, 427, discussed in Chapter 4). The Apollonians also ask about a curse of barrenness ravaging their land (Hdt. 9.93.4) and are told it is divine punishment. For questions asked at Dodona about divine intervention and individual healing see Chapter 5 of this book, under the category Health/Disease. It is surely connected to the popular oracular question formula 'to which god or hero should we/I sacrifice or pray in order to do better or more good . . .'. Divine healing: the *Iamata* (inscriptions describing miracle healings) at the temple of Asklepios, Epidaurus, include the stories of Hermon of Thasos (stele B, 22; T 3.11) who is cured of his blindness by Asklepios and then blinded again when he fails to show sufficient gratitude, and of Kephisias (stele B, 36) who laughs at the god's healing powers asking why he could not heal

the lame god Hephaistos, and is crippled by his horse; healing follows remorse. On the Epidaurian *Iamata*, cf. LiDonnici 1995 and Dillon 1994. Temple incubation: Van Straten 1976. Ancient medicine: Edelstein 1945, Gordon 1995, and Chaniotis 1995.
24. Lloyd (2003: 63): Hippok. *Morb. sacr.* III.2 'They forbade the use of baths, and of many foods that are unsuitable for sick folks—of sea fishes: red mullet, blacktail, hammer and the ell (these are the most harmful sorts); the flesh of goats, deer, pigs and dogs (meats that disturb the digestive organs) . . .'.
25. Competition: Lloyd 1999*a*: 69; Lloyd 1999*b*: 15 ff.
26. 'Magic, as a definable and consistent category of human experience, simply does not exist' Gager 1992: 24–5. Richard Gordon (1999*b*: 163) emphasizes that there was 'no single ancient view of magic . . . The notion of magic, at any rate in what I shall call a strong sense, was formed in the ancient world discontinuously and, as it were, with everybody talking at once.' Kotansky (1991: 123 n. 1): 'Many definitions . . . have been attempted: none, perhaps, is wholly satisfactory. The word connotes so much, the boundary line between it and religion is so hazy and indefinable, that it is almost impossible to tie it down and restrict it to the narrow limits of some neat turn of phrase that will hit it off and have done with it.' Good to think with: Gordon 1997: 67.
27. Examples include surveys such as Lloyd's studies of ancient Greek science (1999*a* and 1999*b*); while, more specifically, Thomas (2000) has examined Herodotos' *Histories* in the context of the late fifth-century Greek intellectual milieu and its pursuit of truth about the world.
28. Obviously the two concerns are related: specialized research which aims to create certainty will impact on day-to-day living (for example, the question of how to treat disease), while questions arising in a mundane context can inspire more specialized inquiry.
29. For example, Gallant 1991; Garnsey and Morris 1989; Halstead 1987, 1989; Halstead and Jones 1989; Halstead and O'Shea 1989*a* and *b*.
30. The best source for ancient Greek agriculture seems to be Theophrastos (*Enquiry into Plants*; *On the Causes of Plants*). Specific references to actual practices and recommendations concerning others occur throughout his work. Crop diversification is also referred to in a wide range of authors, including Galen, Athenaios, and Aristophanes, and is prescribed in some land leases. For the latter, there is a useful table showing the provisions of Classical and Hellenistic agricultural leases in R. Osborne 1987: 42–3.
31. Gallant (1991: 110) uses this information to create models with which he shows how 'with alarming regularity [the Greeks] would have found themselves running short of food in the face of climatically induced shortfalls in production'.
32. For example, Halstead (1987: 77) notes that although it is tempting to view both ancient and modern Mediterranean farmers as either generally

Notes to Chapter 1 245

'being in communion with nature' or, more explicitly, constrained by the natural environment of the Mediterranean in such a way that they experience an essential continuity in rural economy, 'it is clear that many aspects of traditional rural life are integrally bound up with elements of the contemporary natural and social environment which have not remained unchanged since time immemorial'. For the issue of Mediterranean continuity more generally, see Horden and Purcell 2000. Agricultural practices as results of specific decisions: Garnsey 1988 and Halstead 1987, while Gallant (1991: 35) describes the technology of ancient farming as 'a series of articulated production strategies chosen by individual households on the basis of their perceived subsistence needs, their labour product and the demands of extra-household claimants who had to be accommodated from the household's resources'.

33. The emergence of the *polis* from Garnsey and Morris 1989: 105; the nature of the gift and quotation from Gallant 1991: 143.
34. Gallant (1991: 1) quoting Arnold, *Famine: Social Crisis and Historical Change* (Oxford: 1988).
35. Detailed evidence for Greek maritime loans is found in Dem. 32, [Dem.] 34, 35 and 56, less detailed references are found in: Isok. 17.42; [Dem.] 33.4, 52.20. References to lenders: Lysias 32.6; Dem. 27.11; Hyp. *Against Demosthenes*, fr. 4, col. 17. See further Millett 1991: 188.
36. De Ste. Croix 1974: 41 and 43 (his italics).
37. [Dem.] 34. 6–7; 35. 18.
38. Millett (1983: 44) allows that it is possible to see maritime loans as a form of insurance policy 'because the mechanism of maritime credit gave the effect of insurance by shifting the risk of loss from the borrower to lender'. This then makes it impossible to argue that traders were forced to borrow through poverty—a view put forward by Hasebroek (1933). Millett suggests that there are elements of both productive and consumption capital in maritime loans, since the venture could make money, and yet it could not proceed without the initial investment. Finley (1999: 252 n. 82) states that he does not find Millett's arguments convincing, but he does not elaborate on the reasons for his disagreement. Reed (2003: 35) disagrees with Millett's emphasis on loans as being primarily a source of investment rather than insurance, asking 'Why cannot loans both serve as insurance *and* provide the capital needed by poorer *emporoi*?', arguing that 'Bottomry loans provided such good insurance that even some who were able to "put to sea without the help of lenders" might choose not to' (quoting Hasebroek 1933: 7 on Dem. 34.51). He cites Zenothemis and Hegestratos, who try to scuttle their ship (Dem. 32), and Artemon and Apollodoros, who lie to their creditors (Dem. 35), as examples of traders who have taken out a bottomry loan on the basis of the advantageous insurance purposes (since the terms of bottomry contracts mean they

need not repay the loan if the goods are lost), rather than in order to finance the expedition.
39. Interest-free loans to retailers: Hyp. 3. 1–12. Interest-bearing loans—and the contempt that the lenders incurred: Theophr. *Char.* 6. 9, also Dem. 37.52–4. For more on *eranos* loans, and the spectrum of lending behaviour, see Millett 1983: 48.
40. Finley (1999: 23) observes: 'Among the interest rates which remained stable were those of maritime loans, the earliest type of insurance, going back at least to the late fifth century BCE. A considerable body of legal doctrine grew up around this form of insurance, but no trace of an actuarial concept, and that may be taken as a reasonable symbol of the absence of statistics, and hence of our difficulty in trying to quantify ancient economic data . . .'. He is explaining how in thinking about the ancient economy 'the models we employ tend to draw us into a false account' of ancient society, its structure and institutions.
41. 'Interpretive anthropology . . . operates on two levels simultaneously: it provides accounts of other worlds from the inside, and reflects about the epistemological groundings of such accounts' in Marcus and Fischer 1999: 26, and 31 for ethnographer as 'mediator between distinct sets of categories and cultural conceptions that interact in different ways at different points of the ethnographic process'. See also Geertz 1973, Fischer 1977.
42. Hopkins (1965: 125) makes this point and Versnel (1991*b*: 184–5) quotes his initial statement in support of his own etic approach: 'Yet as moderns and as historians we have no alternative but to use our own concepts and categories to describe and explain other societies.' However, Hopkins continues in a fashion that suggests that such a straightforward imposition of terms is not his intention: 'Yet the existence of differences between our own and the Roman conceptualisation of the external world poses problems. We have to ask what are the limitations of using categories to describe and explain behaviour that was not conceived by the actors themselves in those terms. Certainly the differences are not solved merely by becoming aware of the problem, though this awareness certainly prompts questions and even suggests answers. Some systematic investigation of the differences and similarities in conceptualisation is surely necessary and it is surprising that so little of the efforts of ancient historians has been directed to this end.' It is still necessary to emphasize this point.
43. Commentators link the emergence of the word risk and its concept with early maritime ventures in the pre-modern period. According to Luhmann (1993: 9), it first appeared as a term in the 'transitional period between the late Middle Ages and the early modern era'. It is found occasionally in medieval documents, and spreads with the rise of printing, at first across Italy and Spain. To begin with it has a wide range

Notes to Chapter 1

of applications, many of which relate to navigation or trade. Giddens (1990: 21) suggested that the idea developed in the sixteenth and seventeenth centuries among Western maritime explorers; the word comes to England from the Spanish or Portuguese and described sailing into uncharted waters. See the introduction to Lupton 1999 and Hacking 1990 for a very clear overview of the concept of risk, to which I am indebted.

44. Hacking 1990: 61.
45. Reddy 1996: 237, also quoted by Lupton 1999: 7.
46. Knight 1921.
47. For example, the Royal Society's 1992 report on risk where a distinction is made between objective and subjective risk. Such studies tend not to consider the idea that the objective view itself may be filtered through a particular 'way of seeing'.
48. Lupton (1999: 9): 'Risk and uncertainty tend to be treated as conceptually the same thing: for example, the term "risk" is often used to denote a phenomenon that has the potential to deliver substantial harm, whether or not the probability of this harm eventuating is estimable.'
49. Adams (1995: 67) 'Any approach to risk that does not acknowledge the role of error and chance and culture in shaping attitudes, influencing behaviour and determining outcomes will be inadequate for coping, both in the insurance industry and in the casino of life.' In an attempt to capture this complexity, he describes what he calls 'the dance of the risk thermostats', in which a risk thermostat describes the system of variables that raise or lower a person's propensity for risky (i.e. hazardous) behaviour. They include an individual's propensity to take risks, his or her perception of danger, previous experiences, how all these factors are balanced. 'The setting of the thermostat varies from one individual to another, from one group to another, from one culture to another' (p. 15). The dance of the risk thermostats: 'However big and powerful you are, there is almost always someone bigger. However small and insignificant, there is almost always someone smaller. There are different, competing bands in each corner of the floor, playing different tunes with different rhythms. The dances form clusters; some prefer formation dancing, others individualistic jiving, some have flailing arms and legs and are given a wide berth by others, some are wall flowers lurking on the margins, some will loosen up after a drink or two. Some move about the floor, others tend to stay put. All human life is there, but no one on the dance floor can have more than a partial view of what is going on. Risk compensation and cultural theory provide a precarious imaginary vantage point above the dance floor, discern motives and pattern in all this activity. They provide a conceptual framework for making sense of this ever-changing order in diversity, and a terminology with which people can discuss how best to cope with it.' Slovic (2000: 392), describes risk as 'a game in which the rules must be socially negotiated within the

context of a specific problem'. However, it is worth pointing out that there is no mention of the work of the social constructionists in Slovic's discussion. Wilkinson, Elahi, and Eidinow (2003) use scenarios to explore the social impacts of different cultural conceptions of risk.
50. Douglas 1992: 40.
51. As distinguished in Lupton 1999. Cultural-symbolic approaches are discussed in the text. Of the other two:

 (I) Risk-society theorists include sociologists Ulrich Beck and Anthony Giddens, who have suggested that we are currently living through a new paradigm, where risk has emerged from the process of modernization as a central concern. They argue that ours is a 'risk society', or *Risikogesellschaft* as Beck describes it, and assert that risk is a universal controlling determinant of modern global culture, whether as a result of a greater number of risks (Beck) or a greater sensitivity to possibilities of risk (Giddens). The risk society is reflexive—that is, its members are able to reflect critically on the dangers of modernity, and this influences society in both public and private spheres.

 (II) Those who work with a governmentality approach to risk look at the way in which populations and individuals are monitored and managed in the neo-liberal states of the West in late modernity. The control of risk (understood as deviance from a statistically established norm) is managed by the state, but also by other agencies and institutions. In addition, individuals are expected voluntarily to engage with policies and strategies designed to regulate and safeguard the population.
52. Douglas 1986: 59.
53. For example, Douglas and Wildavsky 1982: 9; Douglas 1986: 59; 1992: 58. I will not use Douglas's model of grid/group since it is simply not possible to collect the data that would be necessary to make such an analysis.
54. Technology itself—and its manipulation by human forces—once thought to offer an instrument of objectivity, has become recast as a source of threats in the last 50 or so years. So, events such as floods, plagues, or famines are no longer blamed on acts of god or demons, but nor are they merely viewed as natural events which might be predicted and insured against or which technology might assuage. Rather, they become examples of inappropriate management by human forces—usually industrial or governmental. In this context, risk analysis has become a growth area, motivated by the need to avoid exposure to danger (and the penalties associated with responsibility for that exposure).
55. Douglas and Wildavsky 1982: 6–7.
56. As Douglas herself has stressed (1992: 29).
57. This approach is informed by the theories of New Historicism, which, insofar as it can be defined, insists on expanding its field of research to

include 'figures hitherto kept outside the proper circles of interest—a rabble of half-crazed religious visionaries, semi-literate political agitators, coarse-faced peasants in hobnailed boots, dandies whose writings have been discarded as ephemera, imperial bureaucrats, freed slaves, women novelists dismissed as impudent scribblers, learned women excluded from easy access to the materials of scholarship, scandalmongers, provincial politicians, charlatans and forgotten academics' (Gallagher and Greenblatt 2000: 9).

58. Although for excellent and detailed work on Epiros, see the four volumes in the series *L'Illyrie Méridionale et l'Épire dans l'Antiquité* edited by P. Cabanes.

59. Tzouvara-Souli (1993) suggests that evidence for the spread of the cult of Zeus Dodonaeus and Dione across almost all the tribes of Epiros (from the Ambracian Gulf to the region of the lower Aous) gives us some idea of who in the region may have used the oracle, while Vokotopoulou (1992) has collected a group of tablets which indicate use of the oracle by individuals and groups in Magna Graecia; see also Parke (1967*a*: 113). On the use of *ethnika* (added to the name of a person to indicate their origin, city, or region, usually when they are abroad), e.g. in sanctuary dedications, see Schachter (1994). It is possible that those in control of access to the oracle regulated visits from different *poleis*. Günther (1971: 126) in his discussion of clients at Didyma points out two documents (*Milet*. 1. 3. 141 and 155) that seem to imply that Miletos demanded gifts for Apollo of some kind from its colonies. Does this mean that individuals from those cities could only consult the oracle when their city had paid what was due? Did the city negotiate on behalf of its citizens or were these arrangements concerned only with rights of state consultation? And can we extrapolate parallel arrangements to other oracles? For example, we know that Delphi also made agreements with individual *poleis*. Unfortunately, there will not be room to follow up such questions here.

60. Gordon 1999*a*.

61. But it is essential to understand how difficult it has proved to date this material. Letter-forms, formulae, and the context of a tablet's discovery are all used to work out dates, but these criteria are necessarily inexact and the results often vary widely from scholar to scholar. (In the case of curse tablets, more precise dating can sometimes be achieved when it is possible securely to identify individuals on a tablet. For example: SGD 14, which seems to name a number of famous political figures in Athens during the time of Kassander; also *DTA* 24, whose personnel Wilhelm (1904: 115–22) identified as politically active in early fourth-century BCE Athens. In addition, unfortunately, a number of the earliest excavated curse tablets (for example, those in Wünsch's *DTA* corpus) have now disappeared, and so cannot benefit from more sophisticated modern dating techniques.

CHAPTER 2

1. Thuc. 8.1.1; trans. Rex Warner.
2. Although he distinguished these two types of diviner, Thucydides does clearly see them as constituents of a group that all 'practice divination', and he does not distinguish their different divinatory processes. Oracle collections: the *chrēsmologos* Onomakritos specialized in collecting the oracles of Musaios (Hdt. 7.6.3) and was banished from Athens by Hipparchos, son of Pisistratos, after he was caught slipping an oracle of his own into the collection; Herodotos also refers to collections of oracles by Mousaios at 8.96.2 and 9.43.2; cf. Ar. *Ran.* 1031–5 who describes Mousaios' poetry as about cures for disease and oracles; Orpheus is also sometimes found alongside Mousaios: Pl. *Prt.* 316d, *Resp.* 364b–365a; Ar. *Ran.* 1032–3 and Eur. *Rhes.* 941–7; and sometimes alone *Suda* s.v. Ὀρφεύς.

   Bakis (collections: Hdt. 8.20.1–2, 8.77.2, 9.43.1) had a number of popular personae: as a Boiotian from Eleon inspired by nymphs (Paus. 10.12.11), and in a frenzy (Cic. *Div.* 1.18.34); while others describe three Bakides, of whom the Boiotian is the oldest (Theopompos *FGrH* 115 F 77 = Schol. Vet. on *Av.* 962 (Philetas) ap. *Suda* Βάκις; Schol. Vet. on Ar. *Pax* 1071); or two Bakides (Clem. Al. *Strom.* 1.132, 398P; Schol. Vet. on Ar. *Eq.* 123). Sometimes Bakis is lumped together with the Sibyl, usually to indicate inspired prophecy (Ar. *Pax* 1095; Plato, *Theag.* 124d, Cic. *Div.* 1.18.34, Plut. *Mor.* 399a, Clem. Al. *Strom.* 1.132, 399P); it may also have been a title assumed by prophets. Sibyls originated from all over, including Erythrai, Marpessa, Samos, Kolophon, and Kyme; there was also said to be one at Delphi (Diod. Sik. 4.66.5–6, Paus. 10.12.2, and Plut. *Mor.* 398c). Oracles of Laios (carried by Antichares, Hdt. 5.43.1). Apollo himself, Ar. *Av.* 982. Fontenrose (1978: 163) also provides evidence for collections by Abaris, Mopsos, Amphiaraos, and others. For these references and others see Fontenrose 1978: 159 ff. and Bowden 2003.

   City collections: for example, we know that Athens had books of oracles (Hdt. 5.90.2, where they are described as being carried back to Sparta); the Spartans also kept books of oracles (Hdt. 6.57.2, 4 and Cic. *Div.* 1.43.95).

3. For example, see Dillery 2005: 169–70, who observes two meanings: 'compiler or purveyor' and 'one who "utters" oracles'; and Bowden 2003: 61, who distinguishes three meanings for the word: as speaker, collector, and interpreter of oracles. Interpreting oracles: most famously, those who try to translate the 'wooden walls' prophecy given to the Athenians by Delphi, as the Persians draw close to Attica (Hdt. 7.143.3). Creating their own oracles: spontaneous oracles spoken by the *chrēsmologos* Amphilytos the Acarnanian encouraging Pisistratos in his attempt to seize Athens (Hdt. 1.62.4,); Lysistratos foretells that 'the Kolian women will cook with oars'—which turns out to refer to the wreckage from the Battle of Salamis that ended up on Kolias Beach (Hdt. 8.96.2).

Examples such as those found in Thuc. 2.8.2 and 2.21.3 raise more detailed questions of oracular process. In these passages, *chrēsmologoi* are found λόγια ... ᾖδον and ᾖδον χρησμούς that is 'singing or intoning oracles'. LSJ informs us that *logia* and *chrēsmoi* can both mean oracles, although *logia* can also be variously translated as 'oracles from antiquity' or just 'verses'. According to LSJ, the scholion tries to make a distinction between the two, that *logia* are prose oracles, while *chrēsmoi* are verse, but the distinction does not hold. *Ēidon* can be translated as singing or perhaps chanting. This passage draws attention to the difficulties of deciding what may count as an inspired oracular performance: after all, even in choosing the right oracle from a collection, a process of (inspired?) interpretation may be occurring.

4. Hidden things and signs of the future: see Pl. *Lach.* 195e; Pl. *Men.* 92c Sokrates calls Anytos a *mantis* since he has not met a sophist but knows what they are. See discussion and further citations in Bowden 2003, Dillery 2005, Parker 2005*b*: 110; Dickie 2001: 61–74. The portents they interpret may be sought (Ar. *Pax* 1026 and sacrifices below) or unsought (Pl. *Leg.* 933c–d; Thuc. 7.50.4, advice to Nikias after an eclipse); cf. Bowden 2003.

5. Door-to-door salesmen: Plato, *Resp.* 364c. Overlaps: Hierokles and Lampon are described as both *manteis* and as *chrēsmologos* (Ar. *Pax* 1046–7 and Schol. Vet. on 1046; Schol. Vet. on *Eq.* 123, *Av.* 521; Paus. 1.34.4 and 10.12.1); Hierokles is a *chrēsmologos* (Ar. *Pax* 1047) and a singer of oracles (Eupolis F 231 K–A).

6. For example, at the beginning of the war as above; when Archidamos first invades Athens (Thuc. 2.21.3); after the plague, prophecies are recalled —an example of how interpretations are made in the light of events (2.54.2); throughout the war (5.26.4) and (8.1 as above). Dickie (2001: 69) states that these examples give us a sense of how 'soothsayers who traded on their possession of collections of oracles might intervene in public life and gain publicity for themselves'. This may be true, but these are also the kinds of crises that prompt people to try to find out the will of the gods, and on which they would expect some oracular insight. It is hard to imagine that a self-respecting diviner would not be working at such times.

7. See Liddell and Scott for translations and examples of each kind. For recent discussion and further bibliography, see Dickie 2001: 12 ff., 61; Parker 2005*b*: 111 n. 77. Bowden (2003: 257 n. 5) provides a useful overview of those who have argued for and against the identification of *manteis* and chresmologues.

8. Γοής: see Johnston 1999: 100 ff. for the idea of specialization (drawing on Burkert 1962, but differing from him in her conclusions about the role played by the *goēs*) and Dickie 2001: 13 for the case against. *Pharmaka* literally means potions, but there are plenty of examples, in which it seems to be used as an umbrella term that covers a variety of supernatural arts

used to exercise or acquire power over someone (Pl. *Meno* 80a2–3 and Xen. *Mem.* 3.11.7). This is spelt out by Plato (*Leg.* 933e), who distinguishes between *pharmakeia* ('methods of poisoning') that are *kata phusin*, that is, 'natural', in which the body is hurt by the action of another body, and those that work 'by incantations and binding spells'.

9. Other methods of divination are myriad. Examples include: sieve-seers Philippides fr. 38 K–A; mirror divination Ar. *Ach.* 1128–9; dream interpretation, Plut. *Ar.* 27.4 (see discussion Parker 2005*b*: 119); bird flight, Xen. *An.* 6.1.23; interpreters of portents Pl. *Leg.* 933c–d; dice oracles; skull-oracles: spells of Pitys in the *PGM* (see Faraone 2005).

10. A papyrus scroll found in a grave in Derveni, near Thessaloniki, and dating to the fourth century BCE, provides instructions for rituals that link *magoi* with mystery cults and the invocation of infernal powers (including the dead). See Janko 2002 and Betegh 2004. Col. 20, l. 4; for translation and commentary, see Parker 2005*b*: 116.

11. Men engaged in a common trade or activity were often organized as clans or *genē* 'families', claiming descent from a common ancestor: so physicians might claim descent from Asklepios (Pl. *Phdr.* 270c, *Prt.* 311b; called *genos* by Galen, *Anat. Adm.* 2.1, *Comp. med.* 9.4). The foundation myth of Didyma describes Branchos as the first oracle-speaker (Kallim. *Ait.* fr. 229 (Pfeiffer); Konon, *Narr.* 33, 44; Varr. fr. 252 (Cardauns) in Lact. Plac. *Theb.* 8.198; Strabo 9.3.9). See Fontenrose 1988: 76 for these and further examples.

12. Parke 1967*a*: 174 ff. There was a branch of the Iamidai who acted as diviners for the Spartan army (Hdt. 9.33.2).

13. Fontenrose 1988: 78, Hdt 1.78; Arrian, *Anab.* 2.3.3–4; Cic. *Div.* 1.41.91, 42.94. Fontenrose explains that the story told by Arrian of King Gordios' visit to Telmessos makes it clear that not all inhabitants of Telmessos were members of the mantic genos.

14. Parke 1967*a*: 178. The Galeotai and Telmessoi were both linked with Dodona by a late story (Steph. Byz. s.v. Γαλεῶται that describes how Telmessos and Galeotes were sent to found oracular sanctuaries. The story suggests that the three oracular sanctuaries were aware of each other—and either that the two sought legitimacy from a relationship with Dodona, or that Dodona sought to establish a self-serving hierarchy.

15. Parke (1967*a*: 165 ff.): Melampos (and other diviners, some his descendants) was hymned in the lost Hesiodic poem the *Melampodia* (frr. 270–9 MW), and appeared in the *Great Eoiai* (fr. 261 MW). In the *Odyssey* (15.225) he is first in a long line of seers. Parke raises the amusing but unanswerable question of whether Melampos 'Black foot' was somehow connected with the Selloi and their unwashed feet.

16. Hdt. 9.95.

17. In [Dem.] 25.80 Aristogeiton's brother acquires the tools of his girlfriend's mistress, Theonis.

18. Thrasyllos: Isok. 19. 5–9. His stepson proudly announces how Thrasyllos managed to father a number of children during his travels—was this a result of his charm, or a way for women to pay for his services, or both? At the battle of Plataea, *manteis* from Elis were working on both sides Hdt. 9.33.1 (Tisamenos of the Iamidai) and 37.1 (Hegesistratos of the Telliadae). There was also an Elean *mantis* working for Polykrates of Samos (Hdt. 3.132.2, *genos* not mentioned); fighting for the Krotoniates vs. the Sybarites (Hdt 5.44.2, Kallias of the Iamidai) and the Phokians vs. the Thessalians (8.27.3, Tellias—*genos* not mentioned, but likely to be from the Telliadae?). We hear of Symmachos from Achaia (*SEG* 28. 1245); while Hierokles came to Athens from Oreos in Euboia (*Pax* 1047, 1125). If it is the same man, then Diopeithes is in Athens (Ar. *Eq.* 1084–5, *Vesp.* 380, and *Av.* 988 with Schol. Vet.; Plut. *Per.* 32.1; *IG* i^3. 61.4–5) and in 399 in Sparta talking about the succession (Xen. *Hell.* 3.3.3; Plut. *Lys.* 22.5–6). Aristandros, seer to Philip II and Alexander the Great, was from the Karian city of Telmessos; Megistias, an Acarnanian, who was said to trace his ancestry to the legendary seer Melampos, died on the battlefield, was a seer for the Spartans (Hdt. 7.228); *SEG* 29. 361 shows us a seer from Argos.

19. See McKechnie 1989: esp. 22–8 and 142 ff.

20. Seers rewarded: Sthorys of Thasos (394 BCE) received a grant of citizenship from the Athenians to reward his prophetic activity in connection with a sea-battle at Knidos, see *IG* ii^2. 17; Osborne 1981: 43–51 and 1982: 45–8. The *Iliad* mentions a number of seers on the battlefield (Helenos, Polydamas, Chromis and Erinomos, Merops). Xenophon provides us with ample references to their continued important presence (e.g., *Anabasis* 5.6.29 and further, above), as does Aeneas the Tactician (10.4). And there is epigraphic evidence for seers who died or distinguished themselves in military service, for example Telenikos (ML 33), listed as part of the Athenian force that invaded Egypt in the mid-fifth century; and *SEG* 29. 361 for an Argive killed on campaign, and listed immediately under the king (all discussed in Bremmer 1996: 99).

Picking up on the theme of family trades raised earlier, note that Tisamenos' grandson Agias is seer at Aigospotami (Paus. 3.11.5; thanks to Simon Hornblower for bringing this to my attention). Satyra from Larissa, a third-century mantis, *SEG* 35. 626 (notes in Bremmer 1996: 103 n. 35); also Plato's Diotima in the *Symposion* (see Halperin 1990*a*: 113) and the Sibyl of Herakleitos B92. Belly-talkers: Hippok. *Epid.* 5.63, 7.28, Philochoros *FGrH* 328 F 78. (See Dickie 2001: 247 and Bremmer 1996: 107.)

21. Aesch. *Ag.* 1269–74 (see also Pl. *Resp.* 381d4–7); Theophr. *Char.* 16.13.

22. Plut. *Per.* 38.2.

23. **Theoris of Lemnos:** [Dem.] *Against Aristogeiton* 25.79–80 mentions Theoris in passing, describing her as a *pharmakis* and telling us that she

was guilty of 'poisons and incantations'; ii) Harpokration, s.v. Θεωρίς (= *FGrH* 382 F 60) cites this passage and calls her a *mantis*, explaining that she was condemned for impiety (*asebeia*), and executed according to the account given by Philochoros in the sixth book of his history; Plut. *Dem.* 14.4 calls her a priestess (*hiereia*), and then tells us that she was prosecuted for many criminal deeds and for teaching slaves how to deceive.

Ninon: Demosthenes (19.281) mentions Ninon during a discussion of Aeschines' mother, Glaucothea, whom, he says, brought together *thiasoi* (associations of people who worshipped a particular god—in the case of Glaukothea, the god Sabazios). He mentions that there was another woman who was executed for this kind of activity—Ninon, whom he calls a *hiereia*. One scholiast says that she was executed because her rites were thought to mock the mysteries. Another commentator links 'what Glaukothea did' to the creation of *pharmaka* and says she was actually accused of making love-potions (*philtra*) for young men. Her accuser was one Menekles, who is also mentioned as the accuser of Ninon at Dem. 39.2 and 40.9. Dionysios of Halikarnassos (*Din.* 11) tells us that Ninon's son later brought a case against Menekles and had a speech written for him by Dinarchos, although Dinarchos would have been too young to deliver the speech. Ninon may also appear in Josephus (*Ap.* 2.267) at the end of a list of men put to death by the Athenians because they 'uttered a word about the gods contrary to their laws', including Socrates, Anaxagoras, Diagoras, and Protagoras. Josephus mentions a priestess, who, if a textual emendation is right, could be Ninon. He gives the charges against her as initiating people into the mysteries of foreign gods.

Phryne: The charges against the *hetaira* Phryne are reproduced in an anonymous treaty on rhetoric (*Orat. Att.* Baiter-Sauppe II, p. 302): 'Phryne accused of *asebeia*. For she held a *komos* in the Lukeion. She introduced a new god and she organised *thiasoi* of men.' What follows tends to be taken as the authentic epilogue by the plaintiff Euthias: 'So I have now proven that Phryne is impious because she has participated in a scandalous revelry, because she has introduced a new god, and because she has assembled unlawful *thiasoi* of both men and women.' The new god was probably one Isodaites, of whom Harpokration says 'mentioned by Hypereides in his oration for Phryne. Some foreign daimon in whose honour women of the lower classes and particularly the ones that did not excel in virtue used to hold initiations'. It may be an epithet of Dionysos.

24. i) Aesop (Hausrauth = Perry 56) There are two versions of this fable: in the older version (the *recensiones Augustana*), the *gune magos* has an expertise in *epodai* (incantations); in the more recent version she makes a *kerdos* dispensing *epodai* to quell (*katathesis*) the anger of the gods. In the older version, she is taken to court on a charge of 'innovating in divine matters'; the more recent version, this has become a charge of *asebeia*.

ii) Antiphon I, the infamous prosecution of the stepmother for poisoning. The case concerns the poisoning of one Philoneos and his friend, during dinner at Philoneos' house in the Piraeus. At first, the murderer was assumed to be a slave woman, the mistress of Philoneos, who had served the two men poisoned wine after dinner. She was arrested, tortured for information and executed. But the case was reopened when an illegitimate son of Philoneos' friend, at the behest of his dying father, charged his father's wife, his stepmother, with the murders. This speech comes from that case, and in it the son argues that the slave woman was merely an accessory to his stepmother's plot to kill her husband, and had been persuaded by the stepmother's argument that the poison was a love philtre intended to restore love, not take life.

iii) *Magna Moralia* ([Aristotle] 16 = 1188b29–38): the writer explores the role of *to hekousion* 'the voluntary' in actions. He tells us about an anonymous woman brought before the Aeropagos for murder, on the grounds that she had administered a potion. She argues that she had only meant her target to fall in love, not to die—and so had acted without an understanding of the consequences of her actions. She is acquitted.

25. Pisistratos correctly understands the message of the diviner Amphilytos of Acarnania, Hdt. 1.62; the Pisistratidae retain the services of Onomakritos, Hdt. 7.6; the 'wooden walls' debate, Hdt. 7.143 ff.

    Hierokles and Lampon are described by Aristophanes and the scholiasts as *manteis* and *chrēsmologoi* (see refs. in n. 5 above). We see them in action in Ar. *Av.* 967–8, at the founding of a new city; Hierokles appears at Trygaios' sacrifice to *Eirēnē* in now peaceful Athens in *Pax* 1043–1126; a (probably typical) debate follows, each character in turn quoting from Homer, and from other oracles.

26. In the 'Chalkis decree' (probably dated to 423, see Bowden 2003: 266) Hierokles is commissioned by the people of Athens to arrange the sacrifices for Euboia, according to oracular instructions (*IG* i^3. 40. 64–9, ML 52); and is satirized for his gift: Ar. *Av.* 962, *Nub.* 332, *Pax* 1043–126. Lampon assisted in founding the panhellenic colony of Thourioi in 444–443, as head *mantis* with title of *exegētē* (Diod. Sik. 12.10.3–4; Plut. *Mor.* 812d; Aristophanic scholiast says he produced many oracles about colony, see Schol. Ar. *Nub.* 332, Schol. Ar. *Av.* 521); was the first signatory of the peace between Athens and Sparta in 421 BCE (Thuc. 5.19.2, 5.24.1); proposed amendments and new proposals to a decree about collecting first fruits from all of Greece at Eleusis (*IG* i^3. 78, ML 73); possibly honoured with free meals in the *prytaneion* (Schol. Vet. Ar. *Av.* 521b and *Pax* 1084; R. Parker 2005a: 117 n. 4 finds it difficult to pinpoint what service to the state might be deemed to deserve this, but acknowledges that 'in the case of religious specialists we do not know the level required'). See Bowden 2003: 267 for link between *chrēsmologoi* and state sacrifices.

27. Herodotos notes that Themistokles is better than the *chrēsmologoi*, when he joins the debate about the meaning of the wooden walls oracle (Hdt. 7.6.4); Kyros advised by Kambyses to learn mantic skills so that he cannot be misled (Xen. *Kyr*. 1.6.2); Xenophon has clearly learned to read sacrifices himself (Xen. *An*. 5.6.29, 6.1.22–4) and expects that others have as well—since he invites any soldier who 'happens to be a *mantis*' to attend a sacrifice (Xen. *An*. 6.4.14).

28. Personal seers: Plut. *Kim*. 18, *Nik*. 13, and for Stilbides, 23.5; cf. Ar. *Pax* 1026–32.

29. It has been argued by some (e.g. R. Parker 1985: 320; Bremmer 1993: 158, Price 1999: 74; Shapiro 1990: 345) that with the advent of democracy, oracles in general and *manteis* in particular fell into disrepute, but evidence suggests this was not the case (most recently, Bowden 2005). For example, oracles in state archives: Dem. 21.51–4; 43.66. But this raises a peculiar omission in Thucydides' account of events in 415 BCE: although he mentions the seers and oracle-mongers, he does not mention any kind of consultation at an oracle site. Granted Thucydides is not overly fond of the supernatural at any time, but this is a peculiar omission, bearing in mind his observations about the seers. It is hard to conceive of as an oversight; could it be deliberate? Certainly, as Dover (1965: 15) points out, when Nikias speaks to the assembly hoping to dissuade them from mounting the expedition he does use 'the language of oracular responses': Thuc. 6.9.1 'We still have this question to examine whether it is better to send out the ships at all' where 'it is better' is εἰ ἄμεινόν ἐστιν. However, this kind of phrasing is found elsewhere of situations in which there is no evidence for divination: e.g. 8.92.10.

Plutarch (*Nik*. 13.1–2) does report a consultation at the oracle site of Ammon, which may or may not have happened. He does not seem to suggest (as R. Parker 2005*a*: 113 n. 84) that this consultation was orchestrated by Alkibiades, only that he liked the result. He describes how the embassy hid the news on their return—frightened to spread words of ill omen. Why Ammon? Certainly we think of Ammon as a distant oracle, but evidence suggests it was well known to the Athenians. Parke (1967*a*: 212 ff.) suspects increasing connections between Athens and Ammon during the fifth and fourth centuries, drawing on evidence for trade and from literature (Eur. *Alk*. 112 ff. and *El*. 734; Ar. *Av*. 618 and 716; Plat. *Alk*. 148d, *Leg*. 738c). A very fragmentary inscription (*IG* ii^2. 16420) seems to suggest that the Athenians sent ambassadors to the oracle at Ammon a number of times before 360 BCE. These made offerings and, probably, consultations as well (Parke 1967*a*: 218, with A. M. Woodward, *BSA* 57 (1962), 8). (And not just the Athenians: Pausanias tells us that there were temples to Zeus Ammon in Lakonia at Sparta and Gytheion and notes 'The Spartans appear originally, most of all the Greeks, to have consulted the oracle in Libya' (3.18.3 and 3.21.8)—perhaps this would have made a supportive oracle from Ammon an even more powerful factor to have on the Athenian side.) Perhaps the distance the oracle had to travel made secrecy more important, and perhaps secrecy was necessary for reasons of morale, as Plutarch suggests. It echoes another secret consultation made by Kimon in 451, who 'sent to the oracle of Ammon men to make a secret inquiry from the god', Plut. *Kim.* 18.7, but then, as Thucydides shows, Kimon had detached a contingent from his Kyprian expedition and sent it to Egypt to aid insurgents against Persia. Thuc. 1.112.3.

30. From Xenophon's *Anabasis* as an example: bird omen: 6.5.2; dreams: 3.1.11 ff.; sacrifice: *passim*; sneeze: 3.2.8 ff.

31. A higher order belief: for example, there is a story about Niels Bohr, who is said to have hung a horseshoe over his door. On being asked if he believed that this would bring him luck, he apparently replied that he did not, but that, 'I am told that they bring luck even to those who do not believe in them': told by Luhrmann (1989: 353) who cites Elster 1983: 5, who cites Segrè 1980: 171. Veyne (1988: 54 ff.) describes a process of mental balkanization—the ability to hold contradictory views simultaneously—which he illustrates with Galen's different attitude to centaurs when promulgating his own ideas (that no one has ever seen one, e.g. *De Usu Partium,* 3.1) and when seeking to win new disciples (that Chiron the centaur was the originator of medical knowledge e.g. *Introductio seu Medicus* 1.1): 'when he was relying on popular belief in centaurs, Galen, for want of cynicism, must have been caught up in a whirl of noble and indulgent verbiage and no longer knew too well what he thought of it all. In such a moment are born these modalities of wavering belief, this capacity to simultaneously believe in incompatible truths, which is the mark of times of intellectual confusion.'

32. Luhrmann 1989: 353; Pl. *Leg.* 933b, trans. R. G. Bury.

33. Pl. *Leg.* 933d7–e5; as Dickie (2001: 45) observes, he describes those who perform such acts as displaying *tolmē* 'that is, as persons whose moral effrontery and audacity knows no bounds'. The term is also used in the *Laws* to describe 'the most heinous of criminal offences'; see *Leg.* 853e5–6, 866a5–6, 873a5–6, etc.

34. Betegh (2004: 363) of col. 20, 1–12: 'It is stated here explicitly that these people did in fact see and hear what is there to be seen and heard during the ritual. They even learned what they had to learn. Yet they have not acquired the crucial thing—understanding—and, as a consequence, they have been completely deceived. Moreover, it may very well be the case that Herakleitos' criticism of traditional religiosity and the Derveni author's criticism of the populace and rival practitioners come very close: it has been convincingly suggested that Herakleitos' scorn is directed not so much against the rites and cults as such, but rather against people who do not have a clue what they are doing when they partake in the cults.'

35. Soph. *Ant.* 1033–47, 1061, and 1055; *OT* 380–403; Eur. *Bacch.* 255–7.
36. Soph. *OT* 298–9 and 387–9.
37. Hierokles (Ar. *Pax* 1047, 1120, 1121); Diopeithes (Ar. *Eq.* 1085, *Vesp.* 380, *Av.* 988); Lampon (*Av.* 521, 988; probably *Nub.* 332); as above, Lampon's greed was not just related to his oracle-mongering—other comedy writers satirized his love of good living (*CGFP* 220. 98–103; Kratinos fr. 62 and 66 K–A; Lysippos fr. 6 K–A; Kallias fr. 20 K–A). Diopeithes (*PA* 4309) himself may have shared Aristophanes' concerns. According to Plutarch (*Vit. Per.* 32.2–5) he proposed a decree that 'those who do not recognize the divine or teach theories about the things on high should be impeached'.
38. Consider in comparison the vicar of English sitcoms—a stock character with particular comic attributes, and yet, simultaneously, a stalwart, respected figure of English society; see J. Mullan 'Ooh, vicar!' the *Guardian*, Tuesday 29 Nov. 2005.
39. As Smith (1989) observes, Aristophanes' anger is primarily political. See *Eq.* 116–49, 997–1089, 1229–53; *Pax* 1052–1126; *Av.* 959–91; *Lys.* 770–6. As Dickie points out (2001: 70), the favoured term of abuse is *alazōn* (used *Pax* 1045, 1069, 1120, 1121; *Av.* 983), meaning 'a man who lays claim to an expertise that he does not possess'.
40. Delphic oracle in Aristophanes: *Plut.* 1–55; *Vesp.* 158–60. Smith (1989: 152) also observes that none of the oracle-mongers suggest a visist to the Delphic shrine.
41. Cicero, *Div.* 1.19.37.
42. Curnow 2004.
43. As an example, the sanctuary of Poseidon at Onchestos in Boiotia is included by Curnow as an oracular sanctuary, with details of the oracular process based on a passage from the *Homeric Hymn to Apollo* 3.229–8. However, as Schachter explains in a detailed analysis of both this passage and the interpretations of previous scholars, it is highly unlikely that this describes a process of oracular consultation. See Schachter 1981 vol. 2: 219 and 1976.
44. Curnow 2004: 6–7.
45. Explanations of operation: e.g. Bouché-Leclercq 1880, Parke 1939, Latte 1940, Amandry 1950. Oracles as disseminators of information, in particular for colonization: Bouché-Leclercq 1879–82, Farnell 1909, and Forrest 1957. Psychological techniques: Whittaker 1965: 23; see also Jouan 1990; Malkin 1987.
46. Whittaker (1965) draws on Evans-Pritchard's work on the oracles of the Azande of the southern Sudan (Evans-Pritchard 1976, esp. 120–63 on poison oracles and 116 making comparison with Delphi) along with divinatory practices among a number of other African tribes. Price (1985) also refers to Evans-Pritchard's work. R. Parker (1985) cites Whittaker's article and the work of Evans-Pritchard and goes on to

compare divinatory practices among the Ifa (see Bascom 1969) and the Tiv (see Bohannon 1975); see also Maurizio 1995 (see further below). Mary Douglas (1999) uses a comparative approach to analyse oracles in Leviticus, comparing the use of oracles among the Yoruba. For difficulties of cross-cultural comparison, see James *et al.* (1997).

47. Douglas (1999: 115): 'One reason that oracles are authoritative is that the possible disasters and explanations are pre-packaged and also the possible answers so that a prior plausibility is built into the system ... Divination adjudicates between contested claims, and indicates the sacrifice that can make a truth for the people to live by. It works by pre-packaging all the important things that can happen. The diviners who work more complex oracles use the best understanding they can muster of the local situation, so as to select the right divinatory materials for casting the dice and to give the results of the throw a relevant reading.' Devisch (1985) provides a useful overview of the major approaches to studies of divination in Africa under the headings 'structural-functionalist', 'external cognitive', and 'internal, semiotic and semantic', usefully summarized by Philip Peek (1991: 11 ff.).

48. Maurizio 1995: 79. She uses a cross-cultural perspective to explore the role of the Pythia as a possessed, but coherent, authority as opposed to a more traditional view of her as ancillary to the male priests at the site. Compare Lloyd-Jones, who believed that the Pythia would produce incoherent gibberish, which was then reshaped by the priests of the sanctuary. He declared of that priestess that (1976: 67): 'If you tell an elderly peasant woman that on a certain day and at a certain time she will become the mouthpiece of Apollo, you do not need to be a hypnotist to get the desired result.' See also R. Parker's analysis of the relationship between oracle and consultant (1985).

49. Binary oracular responses: see, above all, Fontenrose 1978; the point is emphasized for responses to Athens in the Classical period in Bowden 2005: 22–4. Use of oracles by communities to create consensus: e.g. Bremmer (1994: 33): 'But in all cases, ancient oracles assisted in making choices and setting the seal on collective decisions rather than in predicting the future.' See also R. Parker 1985: 300. Morgan (1990: 176) describes the nature and function of the Delphic oracle as 'a non-interventionist mechanism for the sanctioning of pre-determined answers to difficult questions of state'. Parker (1985) provides a succinct and useful list of the kinds of decisions that communities took to oracles, including: how to obtain divine release from evils and prophylaxis against future evils (Polyb. 36.17; Plut. *Mor.* 408c); the establishment of shrines, sacrifices, and other forms of cult for gods, daimons, and heroes (Dem. 21. 51–3, 43.66); questions about the graves of the dead and the service that must be done in order to gain their favour (Pl. *Resp.* 427b–c; Hdt. 5.67); and colonization (Hdt. 5.42.2 and 4.155; Thuc. 3.92.5); warfare

(Hdt. 1.53.3 and 66.1, 6.76.1; Thuc. 1.118.3); arbitration between states and some other aspects of interstate relations (Thuc. 1.25.1; *SGDI* 1590).

50. Fontenrose (1978: 79–83): riddles are a sign of folkloric association and so indicate the probable inauthenticity of an oracle.
51. Price (1999: 73–6) notes that the authenticity of consultations has been doubted, but argues that they are supported by such historical examples as the Athenian consultation in 481 BCE. R. Parker (1985: 301) suggests that Apollo was 'forcing the client to construct, by interpretation, his own response'.
52. For example, Herodotos' story of Paktyes the Lydian (1.157–60ff.). Paktyes is put in charge of the treasury at Sardis by the Persian emperor Kyros. He takes advantage of his access to capital and organizes a revolt, but it's a failure and he is forced to take refuge in Kyme. The Persians ask for him back so the Kymaeans send to Didyma: 'What should they do?' They clearly can't give up a suppliant, but this is the Persians asking, not known for their patience with others' moral scruples. They are in serious danger. And Didyma pronounces: 'Give the suppliant up, and take the consequences.' The oracle squarely removes itself from the decision and gives responsibility back to the Kymaeans. This example given by Morgan (1989). This story has been analysed as illustrating the difficulties that confronted a Greek city that was unwilling to kowtow to the Persians (R. Osborne 1996: 319–20); at one level, it can be taken as illustrating the moral high-ground an oracle must take, in effect upholding the rights of the suppliant, letting the Kymaeans understand the wrongful nature of their question. However, bearing in mind that at the time the oracle at Didyma has the Persian empire breathing down its neck, as Morgan (1990: 157) suggests, it also illustrates how an oracle might choose to react to political pressures. Morgan discusses how ambiguity might have been useful to protect the integrity of an oracle consulted by a number of competitive and self-interested states, but stresses that this would have been more valuable in late Archaic and Classical times than earlier, and need not imply that this practice would have had a longer history. Plutarch (*Mor.* 407c ff.) raises the occasional need for ambiguity in oracular responses, allowing necessary secrecy.
53. Malkin (1987: 25) also notes, at the prompting of Plutarch (*Mor.* 407f–408a), that their folkloric nature may have helped the consultant to commit the oracle to memory.
54. Plutarch on poetic diction falling out of fashion: *Mor.* 406b ff. Amandry (1959: 412): 'La forme littéraire des oracles est une chose, la réalité des consultations en est une autre, la *teneur* des réponses et leur portée pratique en sont encore une autre.'
55. Examples of bribery: Kleomenes of Sparta bribes a Pythian prophetess called Periallas to say that the current king of Sparta, Demaratos, is illegitimate, in order to get him deposed (Hdt 6.66; *c*.491 BCE).

Kleisthenes of Athens persuaded the Pythia to tell the Spartans to free Athens from the tyranny of the Pisistratidai, when they had captured it (Hdt. 5.63 and 90; 6.123; *c.*510 BCE). At least in the first example, the Pythia is punished. Thucydides reports another rumour of bribery (Thuc. 5.16.2; 427 BCE) spread by the enemies of King Pleistoanax of Sparta—said to have been brought back from exile after he and his brother had bribed the Delphic oracle. That the oracle is medizing was brought up in 545 BCE (Hdt. 1.174) and has been described as the reason for the unhappy Athenian consultation of 481 BCE. The oracle is described as 'philippizing' by Demosthenes at Aesch. 3.130 (339 BCE). Of course, accusations of bribery were also useful in order to excuse not acting as the oracle suggested or, in hindsight, to explain why following an oracle may have had adverse results.

56. In Herodotos' explanation of Euenios' oracular gift (9.93.4), the Apollonians ask both Delphi and Dodona for their opinions. And there are other examples: in 388 BCE, according to Xenophon (*Hell.* 4.7.2), the Spartan king Agesipolis is involved in leading a campaign against Argos, and is offered a truce. He consults first Zeus at Olympia and then Apollo. He phrases his second question as follows: if 'on this question of the truce Apollo held the same opinion as his father . . .'.

57. Hdt 7.76 mentions an oracle of Ares; Gonzales (2005) assembles the evidence for the possible location of the oracle in Pisidia, southern Asia Minor, near the ancient city of Termessos. Herakles: Bura in Achaia, south Greece, see Paus. 7.25.6. Demeter at Patrai in Achaia, see Paus. 7.21.5.

58. Description of consultation of Trophonios: Paus. 9.39; Plut. *Mor.* 590–2; and Philostratos, *Life of Apollonius* 8.19. For life of Trophonios: see Schachter's entry of that name in Hornblower and Spawforth 1999. Proverb: Apostolius 6.82, Plut. *Mor.* 1.51, *Suda* s.v. Τροφωνίου. Ogden (2001: 24–5) observes that hero-oracles were never alluded to under the term *nekuomanteia*, although there are (and Ogden does give) ancient sources associating *nekuomanteia* with hero oracles: Plut. *Mor.* 109; Maximus of Tyre 8.2; Theodor. *Gr. Aff. cur.* 10.3.11.

59. In particular, when used of specific oracles, it refers to one of the following: Acheron in Thesprotia, Avernos in Campania, Herakleia Pontike (south coast of the Black Sea), and Tainaron at the tip of the Mani peninsula (Ogden 2001: 17). There were other oracles of the dead: some named for dead heroes, such as that of Trophonios and the oracle of Amphiaraos at Oropos. Unnamed oracles include the oracle of Ephyra, an oracle of the dead in Thesprotia in north-west Greece. There seem to have been many other *nekuomanteia*, about which very little is known, comprising caves or so-called 'birdless' lakes that either had an associated myth that linked them with the underworld, for example, that Herakles had dragged Kerberos up from the underworld, and/or had a suitable atmosphere (cf. Ogden 2001: 25 ff.).

60. Paus. 3.17; Plut. *Kimon* 6, *Mor.* 555c. A similar motive of appeasement may be involved in the story by Herodotos (5.92) about the Corinthian tyrant Periander, who visited the oracle of the dead at Ephyra, in order to find out the location of some hidden money from his dead wife Melissa. he ghost refuses to co-operate until she has been clothed: she says she is cold and naked, hinting at an improper burial. This demand for recompense, and its circumstances, suggests that Periander's visit to the oracle may also have involved appeasing the ghost of this woman, whom he had, in fact, murdered (3.50–3).
61. Oracle of Demeter: Paus. 7.21.5.
62. Paus. 7.22.2–4.
63. See Curnow 2004; also Lane Fox 1986: 209 for further examples.
64. Schol. Pind. *Ol.* 6.7 citing Dikaiarchos (*FHG II*, 239; fr. 14).
65. Plut. *Mor.* 434d tells the story of a suspicious Roman governor who sent a freedman with a sealed question tablet to test the oracle. The freedman sees the answer to the governor's secret question in his dream. This example from Parke 1967a: 106–7.
66. Amandry 1950 and 1959.
67. See Fontenrose 1978: 219 n. 33. *Suda* s.v. Πυθώ. Lot oracle: Philochoros *FGrH* 328 F 195 (= Zen. *Prov.* 5.75); Kall. *Hymn to Apollo* 2.45 (Pfeiffer) and Schol.; Hesych. θριαί (Θ 743); Steph. Byz. s.v. Θρῖα.
68. Apparently, three frescoes from Pompeii and a vase fragment, interpreted as showing a woman prophesying, thought to be copies of an earlier painting. Amandry argued that these are images of Kassandra, which seem to show her about to draw a lot from a vessel, and were based on contemporary knowledge of the Pythia's process. Parke argues that they could in fact represent the process of divination at Dodona. The frescoes also show a tripod mounted on a plinth in the background of the picture; in one, the vessel's mouth is too narrow to admit a hand, but Parke argues that this is a mistake, probably a result of careless copying. See Amandry 1950: 67–77, pls i–vi; Parke 1967a: 112; Fontenrose 1978: 219 ff.
69. For example Xen. *An.* 3.1.6 and 8. Fontenrose analyses the different responses which begin with this verb, noting that some would fit with the use of a lot oracle better than others, but goes on to suggest that the verb may have developed, from a previous or ongoing use with lots, into meaning 'proclaim' or 'ordain'. Of the eight historical responses that begin with this verb (H3, 4, 5, 10, 11, 12, 21, and 27), divination by a lot process certainly seems possible. The one described is Fontenrose H21.
70. However, as Fontenrose points out, the answers to these latter questions where they can be traced are all affirmative—and we would surely expect some negative responses if it was a simple lot oracle. Amongst historical questions and responses structured in this way he traces: H5, 25, 54, 61 (question and affirmative answer) and H2, 19, 27, 45, 47, 66, 74 (affirmative responses expressed with this formula imply the question).

71. 352 BCE: the Sacred *Orgas* decree *IG* ii². 204; translations from Rhodes and Osborne 2003: no. 58, 272 ff. Parker 2005*b*: 107, esp. n. 62, where he credits his observation of theatricality to Bowden 2003.
72. Plut. *Mor.* 4.492*a*.
73. Parke records it as fact (1939: 167), see [Arist.] *Ath. Pol.* 21.6; Paus. 10.10.1; Poll. *Onom.* 8.110. Historians on Eleusis: Philochoros *FGrH* 328 F 155 and Androtion *FGrH* 324 F 30.
74. Inscription *BCH* 63 (1939) 184 = Amandry 1950: 245, no. XVI. Fontenrose 1978: 220–3.
75. Lots: Amandry 1950. Cakes: Sokolowski 1949 argues that *phryktoi* mentioned are not lots but cakes similar to the kind (*eilytai*) offered to the dead hero Trophonios at his oracle at Lebadeia.
76. Günther raises this idea in his discussion of clients at Didyma (1971: 126; drawing on Robert 1959: 668). Negotiation about the payment of *phialai* in *Milet.* 1.3.141 (third century BCE) between Chians and Milesians. Evidence for the right of *promanteia* at Didyma is limited to one inscription, in which it is granted to Antiochos and his descendants (*Didyma* II, no. 479; 229/8 BCE; cf. Fontenrose 1988: 105; Morgan 1989: 41 n. 17).
77. See Morgan 1989 and 1990.
78. For example, some sanctuaries can be interpreted as intended to display the power of an elite group, either local or from across Greece; others were dominated by a particular social group; still others were built to signal control of territory. Of course, such categories are our own heuristic devices, but they can help us think about the different roles being played, sometimes by a single sanctuary. An example is the sanctuary at Perachora on the Korinthian Gulf. It was obviously important for Korinth to establish its claim to the harbour; however, the nature of the dedications that we find there (clay model bread-rings and exotic adornments) suggest that rather than being used to make any kind of pugnacious territorial statement, the cult activity at this sanctuary was dominated by women of the city. And this points up another role that some sanctuaries played: set on the edges of a territory, some seem to have provided places of cult activity for those who occupied a somewhat marginal place in the city. See R. Osborne 1996: Olympia, pp. 93 ff.; Isthmia, p. 96; Perachora, p. 95.
79. Morgan (1990: 134): Kretan tripods; imported pottery includes Achaian, Thessalian, Euboian, Attic, Argive, and Boiotian fabrics.
80. Morgan 1990: 138 and 141.
81. Settlement is not driven out completely, since it remains in the area; Pausanias reports that the city is on the hill just below the sanctuary (10.9.1).
82. It is said that it was the so-called First Sacred War that precipitated these changes—the historicity and details of which are difficult to untangle and have long been disputed (see Davies 1994 for a useful overview).

But whether the war happened or not, it indicates a crucial moment in Delphi's history.

83. There are many myths told about the foundation of Delphi—and the later they are, the earlier they tend to set the origins of the oracle. But by the fifth century, Apollo was said to have taken over an older oracle that had originally been run by the goddess Gaia and her daughter Themis. This is not surprising: the earlier the oracle was said to be founded, the more authority its pronouncements would have carried. Cf. Morgan 1990: 144 ff.

84. See Morgan 1989, especially p. 24; Fontenrose 1988: 104; Günther 1971: 126. Despite Herodotos' claim (1.157.3) that Didyma was consulted by Ionian and Aeolian cities of Asia before 494 BCE, there is little historical evidence for use of the oracle from this period of its operation. Morgan argues that it is most likely that Didyma's chief function was to sort out civic business, helping to smooth divisions between the many different groups within the city of Miletos and to sanction colonizing expeditions (although only one, late, inscription provides evidence, *Milet.* 1.3.155, mid-second century BCE, record by the Milesian colony of Apollonia in eastern Mysia, of a tradition that Apollo of Didyma guided the original foundation). The sanctuary's location, outside the city, and the fact that it was run by a single family, the Branchidai, rather than a civic official suggests that it was well placed, notionally and physically, to play this crucial civic role. The Branchidai's independence is demonstrated by the story of their refusal to allow entry to the city's oligarchs after they have covered the Gergithai (their lower-class opponents) with pitch and set them on fire, see Herakleides Pont., fr. 50 Wehrli (= Ath. 12.523f–524b); see further Parke 1976: 50–4 and 1985: 18–21. But cf. Fontenrose 1988: 209, no. 36.

85. Necho: Hdt. 2.159.3; Kroisos: 1.92.2 and 1.46–7; Kymaeans: 1.159 and see n. 52 for reflection on the political context; Fontenrose 1988: 212.

86. Kall. *FGrH* 124 F 14; cf. Strabo 17.2.43. There are no recorded oracle responses until 228 (Morgan 1989: 29), cf. Fontenrose 1988: 15–16 and Parke 1985: 35–6.

87. Morgan (1989: 36): 'The states who participated in sanctuary activity and those who consulted the oracle form distinct, if overlapping, groups, and it seems clear that oracular divination would have been largely irrelevant to the decision-making structures of most *ethnē* (insofar as we can reconstruct them).' However, this is further qualified in (1990: 85) where she emphasizes the role of state formation in the contrasting relationship between the Delphic oracle and developing *poleis* and the Delphic sanctuary and *ethnē*.

CHAPTER 3

1. Theophr. *Char.* 16, ll. 2–5, trans. Diggle 2004. Quite why *The Characters* was composed (performance, comedy, philosophy) has been much debated. Theophrastos seems to have been pursuing his mentor Aristotle's idea (*Nik. Eth.* 1108^{a}33–^{b}7) that it was possible to analyse the emotional aspects of a person's character, and that, ideally, each aspect should conform to a mean (avoiding an excess or deficiency). If this is the case, then *The Characters* seems to set out to examine what inappropriate extremes of behaviour might look like, but it is still not clear whether it is primarily intended to be an ethical, rhetorical, or comic exercise; cf. Diggle 2004: 12 ff. for an overview of the arguments for and against each genre. For the indeterminable date of composition see Diggle 2004: 27–37.
2. How widely were Theophrastos' views shared? The term *deisidaimōn* was originally used to indicate appropriate piety (Xen. *Ages.* 2.1–2, 8; *Kyr.* 3.3.58; Arist. *Pol.* 5.9.15, 1314^b.39–1315^{a}4), but after Theophrastos, derogatory meanings become more common. Diggle (2004: 350) observes of Theophrastos' unfortunate character: 'His actions and his attitudes, taken one by one, would probably not have seemed abnormal to the ordinary Athenian. What sets him apart is the obsessiveness and compulsiveness of his behaviour.'
3. This selection turns on the fact that only these oracles have left a significant material record for analysis from this period. Boiotia, for example, was an area famed for its oracles, but little material evidence survives (see Schachter 1981, vol. 1: 65–8). The oracle at Olympia has also not left any useful record of consultations—although Parke argues from the literary accounts that it was consulted on serious affairs of state (Xen. *Hell.* 3.2.22 and 4.7.2, Plut. *Agis.* 11; cf. Parke 1967*a*: 186) and was probably used by athletes anxious to gain reassurance about their future performances, see Chapter 4.
4. Xen. *Mem.* 1.4.15, trans. Tredennick and Waterfield.
5. Xen. *Mem.* 1.1.6: περὶ δὲ τῶν ἀδήλων 'about those things that are not clear', or, a few lines below, ἃ δὲ μὴ δῆλα τοῖς ἀνθρώποις 'the things which are not clear to men'.
6. This carries some idea of acting against what is naturally ordained to be right: τοὺς τὰ τοιαῦτα παρὰ τῶν θεῶν πυνθανομένους ἀθέμιτα ποιεῖν ἡγεῖτο, 'he thought those men who have learned such things from the gods, have done wrong'.
7. ἃ δῆλα τοῖς ἀνθρώποις 'the things that are clear to men'.
8. At *Oik.* 11.8, a similar idea is applied to prayer, where Isomachos states that the gods will not help those who cannot work out what steps to take to achieve what they want. See also Isok. *Or.* 15.246, Dem. 2.22.
9. Polyb. 36.17. 2–4, trans. Scott-Kilvert.
10. Polyb. 36.17. 6 and 2, respectively, trans. Scott-Kilvert.

11. Plut. *Mor.* 408c: φορᾶς καρπῶν πέρι καὶ βοτῶν ἐπιγονῆς καὶ σωμάτων ὑγιείας; 'public health', literally 'about the health of bodies'.
12. Plut. *Mor.* 386c.
13. εἰ νικήσουσιν, εἰ γαμήσουσιν.
14. εἰ συμφέρει πλεῖν, εἰ γεωργεῖν, εἰ ἀποδημεῖν.
15. εἰ γαμητέον, εἰ πλευστέον, εἰ δανειστέον.
16. Where they are known, I have included references to other oracle sites.
17. In what follows, the initials P/W followed by a number indicate an oracle in the catalogue of Parke and Wormell's *The Delphic Oracle*, vol. 2: *The Oracular Responses*; while the letters H, Q, F, or L followed by a number indicate an oracle recorded in Joseph Fontenrose's *The Delphic Oracle*, in either the Historical, Quasi-Historical, Fictional, or Legendary sections of his catalogue. See the bibliography for full details of these volumes.
18. This is Fontenrose's 'Jerusalem Chamber' type (1978: 58).
19. As observed by Crahay (1956: 50 on *avertissements incompris*), see also Harrison 2000: 122–57. Kambyses: Hdt. 3.64. 3–5; Kroisos: Hdt. 1.91; Q103, P/W 56. The Kymaeans' inquiry: Hdt. 1.159; Fontenrose Didyma 6C; Glaukos' inquiry: Hdt. 6.86 c2; Q92, P/W 35–6. Another example of the wrong kind of question: Diogenes of Sinope asks if he should debase the currency either because he was asked to do so by the workmen of the mint he was running, or once he had been charged and had escaped (Q201, P/W 180). According to Fontenrose, this is a proverb made into a response and attached to the philosopher; the consultation was also recorded as having taken place at Apollo's oracle in Sinope.
20. Many of these examples, and their references, drawn from Fontenrose 1978. Teisamenos: Hdt. 9.33.2; Eëtion: Hdt. 5.92 e2. Other examples: Myskellos of Ripai asks about children and is sent to found Kroton (Q28–31, P/W 43–5 and 229); Deinomenes of Syrakuse asks about his sons—who become tyrants (Q140, P/W 484); Karkinos of Rhegion asks about the child who is to be born of his mistress after suffering ominous dreams (Q225, P/W 275); Aigeus of Athens (L4, P/W 110) and King Erginos of Orchomenos (L5, P/W 111) both ask about their chances of having children; King Aipytos on his daughter Euadne's pregnancy (L10, P/W 141); King Laios of Thebes on his lack of a son (L17, P/W 148/372); Oidipous asks whose son he is (L18, P/W 149); King Akrisios of Argos asks about his lack of a son (L23, P/W 156); Xuthos of Athens on how to become a father (L28, P/W 190); Telephos on finding his parents (L34, P/W 198); Homer is reported to have asked about either (i) his homeland or (ii) the identity of his parents (L80, P/W 317–19); Kephalos on having sons (L82, P/W 322); Menelaos asks for children (L99, P/W 406); Charikles on his lack of children (F10).
21. According to Herodotos (6.34.6), Miltiades is asked by the Dolonkoi to become their founder when he fulfils an oracle that tells them to make this request of the man who first invites them into his house as they

return from the temple. Nepos (1.3) offers an alternative version in which the Athenians ask Delphi for sanction to appoint Miltiades as leader of a campaign to colonize the Thrakian Chersonese. Zeno of Kition asking about 'what he should do' provides another example (Q224, P/W 421).

22. Alyattes: Hdt. 1.19.1; Battos: Hdt. 4. 155. 2. Other examples include: Telesilla asks about sickness and is told to serve the muses (Q135, P/W 85); Orestes' madness (L8, P/W 602); Alkmaion on recovering from the madness caused by killing his mother (L40, P/W 202); Herakles' sickness after his murder of Iphitos (L109, P/W 445); Herakles after wearing the shirt of Nessos (L114, P/W 450); Periander (consulting the oracle of the dead at Acheron): Hdt. 5.92 b3.
23. Glaukos: Hdt. 6.86 c1. Other examples of questions about lost or stolen objects include Kadmos seeking his sister Europa (L11, P/W 142, 374, 481, 501); Lysippos and Straton ask where their children have gone (F13, P/W 517); Polykrates of Thebes asks about the buried treasure of Mardonios (Q162, P/W 109).
24. King Damagetos of Ialysos asks about a wife (Q21, P/W 368); Kydippe's father asks why his daughter falls sick whenever she is about to be married (L90, P/W 383); Paris asks about a wife (L99, P/W 406 with Menelaos asking for children).
25. Inachos asks about Io's dreams (L6, P/W 138; Aesch. *PV* 665–8); an example of an omen, the discovery of a skeleton in nets: Paus. 5.13.6.
26. Tlepolemos asks where he should go after killing his brother (L14, P/W 145); Teukros (L31, P/W 194); Melanthos the Messenian on where he should live in exile (L79, P/W 313); Demoklos the Delphian (L85, P/W 325); Meleos the Pelasgian (L87, P/W 375); Theseus looking for a place to settle (L102, P/W 411); Herakles (L107, P/W 442, 444); Mnesarchos of Samos went to the Pythia to inquire about a commercial enterprise and was told about a son (Q78, P/W 494; the child born was Pythagoras); Dorieus: Hdt. 5.42–3.
27. Philip II of Makedon asks if he will beat the Persian King (Q213, P/W 266); Alexander on his campaign against the Persians (Q216, P/W 270).
28. Who offers the most acceptable sacrifices: Theopomp. (115) F 344 (= Porph. *Abst.* 2.16); the most happy man: Val. Max. 7.1.2; the wisest man: Diog. Laert. 1.106; the most fortunate man: Plin. *HN* 7.151.
29. See later in Chapter 5, under the category of Dodona tablets labelled 'Slavery'.
30. Glaukos: εἰ ὅρκῳ τὰ χρήματα λῄσηται; Miltiades: εἰ ποιοῖ τὰ περ αὐτοῦ οἱ Δόλογκοι προσεδέοντο; Dorieus: εἰ αἱρέει ἐπ' ἣν στέλλεται χώρην; Damagetos: ὁπόθεν ἀγαγέσθαι χρὴ γυναῖκα.
31. Xen. *An.* 3.1.5–8, 6.1.22 (also Cic. *Div.* 1.54.122; Diog. Laert. 2.50).
32. For example, Xen. *An.* 6.2.15 and 7.6.44; while the answer given at 6.1.24 indicates the nature of the question posed.
33. Xen. *An.* 5.3.7 (also Strabo 8.7); Fontenrose H12; P/W 174.

34. Lyrkos: Parthen. 1.2; Neileos: Tzetzes on *Lyc.* 1385 and *Chil.* 13.111–12; Seleukos: App. *Syr.* 56 and 63.
35. Tragedy: Aesch. *PV* 829 ff.; Eur. *Erechtheus TGrF* fr. 367–88; Soph. *Trach.* 46 and 1159 ff.
36. Hdt. (1.46) describes Dodona as one of the oracles that Kroisos tests. Odysseus' visit to Dodona: Hom. *Od.* 14.327 ff. = 19.296 ff. Alexander's death is described by various authors: Strabo 6.1.5, Livy 8.24.1, Justin 12.2.3 and 14; Themistokles is described at Plut. *Them.* 28.5. Lysander is reported to have made an unsuccessful attempt to bribe the prophetess at Dodona in his endeavour to win the backing of the major oracles for a change in the Spartan leadership (Ephoros *FGrH* 70 F 206, Plut. *Lys.* 25; Diod. Sik. 14, 13, 4; Nep. *Lys.* (VI), 3, 1). On Aletes: Parke (1967*b*: 131) believes that although the legend connected with this oracle cannot contain authentic history, it is probably to be taken as evidence of ancient contact between Korinth and the Epirote oracle.
37. See Jacquemin 1999: 87–8, with n. 53. The dedication (dating to the second quarter of the third century BCE) was a statue of Audoleon, put up by Dropion (his grandson), king of the Paeonians.
38. Inscription of Epidauros, *IG* iv². 128 (= *IG* iv. 150 = Edelstein 1945: T594, ll. 32–6); Fontenrose H25; P/W 279; 338–335 BCE.
39. Inscription of Delphi, *FD* 3.1.560 (= *BCH* 80 (1956) 550, l. 3); Fontenrose H3; P/W 334; *c.*360 BCE.
40. Inscription of Halikarnassos, *AGIBM* 896 (= *Rev. Phil.* 15 (1941) 15, ll. 1–11); Fontenrose H36; P/W 335; 250 BCE?
41. Inscription of Anaphe, *IG* xii. 3. 248 = *Syll.*³ 977, ll. 1–4 and 24 Fontenrose ff. H54; P/W 427; *c.*110–100 BCE. For Apollo Aigletes, see *ad. loc. Syll.*³ 977.
42. Inscription of Paros, *Arch. Eph.* (1952) 40 (= *Philologus*, 99 (1955) 7, col. 2, ll. 1–15); Fontenrose H74; *c.*350–325 BCE. See also Amandry 1997: 206 f., who points out how this inscription records not only replies, in prose, to Mnesiepes, but also, as part of the inscription's account of the life of the poet Archilochos, verse oracles from 400 years earlier.
43. Later material from Didyma offers plenty of examples of individual consultations, for example, a poet (of the *Periegesis*) who wanted to visit a king of Bithynia (Ps.-Skymnos, *Perieg.* 50–64; probably some time in the reign of Nikomedes III of Bithynia 127–94); Appheion, also called Heronas, of Alexandria (*c.*130CE) who wanted to know if he would perform well in some sort of (circus? Parke 1985: 78) show (*Milet.* 1. 7. 250a); Karpos (*c.*130 CE) wants to know if he should fulfil his vow to Serapis (*Milet.* 1. 7. 205b). See further Fontenrose 1988: 177 ff.
44. *Milet.* 1. 3. 178; Jeffery, 1990: *LSAG* 33; Parke 1985: 29 ff. Parke compares it to another oracle asked centuries later, which also seems to concern the meaning of a dream. He is perhaps referring to *Didyma II* no. 505.6–10 (Fontenrose 1988: 234, A6), a fragmentary inscription from *c.*200 CE

recording a consultation in which the speaker seems to ask if he saw 'truly or falsely' although no explicit mention is made of a dream. See Fontenrose (1988: 180, no. 2) on lack of context for (the remains of) the question.
45. *Didyma II*, no. 11; Jeffery, *LSAG* 33; Parke 1985: 28 ff.
46. Curtis and Tallis (2005) give the dedication's dimensions as H 27.5 cm., W 39 cm., Th. 24.5 cm., Wt. 93.7 kg.
47. Parke 1985: 31 (restoration and suggestion: Haussoullier 1905: 155 ff.). *Didyma II*, no. 7.
48. Fontenrose (1988: 41) describes how, eight metres in front of the *krepidoma* of the (Hellenistic) *didymeion*, excavators found *astragaloi* amongst the remains of what was probably an altar composed of blood, the ashes of victims, vase fragments, and fuel, dating to the seventh and sixth centuries. He argues that it is an ash altar mentioned in Pausanias (5.13.11). For the frequency and possible significance of *astragaloi* bones in ritual contexts across the Levant and eastern Mediterranean see Gilmour 1997.
49. See Parke 1985: 31.
50. *ICos* 60.
51. On the original excavation, see Karapanos (1878). More recent excavations are described in Dakaris (1993) and reports by Dakaris and Evangelidis in the journals Ηπειρωτικά Χρονικά and Πρακτικά τής ἐν Ἀθήναις Ἀρχαιολογικῆς Ἑταιρείας. A large number of tablets from the excavations of Evangelidis during the period 1929–35 have not yet been published in their entirety, although the team working on them have published some of the tablets from this collection, with useful commentary and insights (see, for example Christidis, Dakaris, Vokotopoulou 1997 and 1999, and Vokotopoulou 1992). Before his death, Professor Christidis kindly shared some of the information with me and I am very grateful for his generosity. On oracular practice at Dodona, see Parke (1967*b*). Recently, the series *L'Illyrie Méridionale et l'Epire dans L'Antiquité* has provided archaeological explorations of Northern Epiros, helping to set the oracle at Dodona in its geographical and cultural context (see Cabanes 1987, 1993, 1999, 2004).

CHAPTER 4

1. Dakaris 1993: 31 ff.
2. Steph. Byz. s.v. Δωδώνη; Callim. fr. 483 (Pfeiffer). Tripods: Demon *ap.* Steph. Byz. s.v. Δωδώνη; *Suda* s.v. Δωδωναῖον χαλκεῖον; Schol. B, Hom. *Il.* 16. 233–5, p. 1057.61 ff.; Eust. on *Od.* 14.327 p. 1760. For these references and discussion, see Parke 1967*a*: 86 nn. 18 and 19.
3. Wordsworth 1840: 247.
4. Wordsworth 1840: 247. For further references to Wordsworth's clues:

Pind. fr. 57–60 (Maehler); Aesch. *PV* 829 ff.; Hekataios *FGrH* 1 F 168; Hdt. 2.52 ff.; Polyb. 4.67.3; Diod. Sik. 26.17.
5. Dakaris 1993: 30.
6. Wordsworth 1840: 250.
7. Karapanos (1878); since then excavations by G. Soteriades, D. Evangelidis, S. I. Dakaris. A. Ph. Christidis, and J. Vokotopoulou. See archaeological reports in Πρακτικά τῆς ἐν Ἀθήναις Ἀρχαιολογικῆς Ἑταιρείας *(PAE)* and Ἠπειρωτικά Χρονικά *(Ep. Chron.)*.
8. There were a number of cities that were said to have been founded during the *Nostoi*, the journeys home of the Greeks who had fought at Troy: Bylliake by Neoptolemus (Steph. Byz. s.v. βύλλις; Pindar, *Nemean* 7 and 4.51), Orikos by Elpenor (Ps.-Skymnos 442–3 and later authors); Bouthrotos by Helenos (*FGrH* 274 F 1); Argos Amphilochikon by Amphilochos (Thuc. 2.68.3). The histories of these foundations may have been described in seventh-century epic (see further Hammond 1967: 383 ff., 419 and 451 ff.). Later foundations: Chersikrates, one of the Korinthian Bacchiads, founded Kerkyra in 733 BCE; Epidamnos was founded in 626 BCE by Kerkyra and Korinth; Ambrakia by Gorgos son of Kypselos around 625 BCE; Anaktorion, on the south coast of the Gulf of Ambrakia, by Korinthians and Acarnanians, around 620 BCE; for Herakleia see Bakhuizen 1987: 192; Apollonia in 588 BCE, and Elea, of uncertain foundation date, but first minted coins between 360 and 355 BCE (Hammond 1967: 414 ff. 425–43, 542). The Eleans are thought to have been establishing colonies in south Epiros around the middle to late sixth century (Bouchetion, Elatria, and Pandosia): see [Dem.] 7.32, with Strabo 7.7.5 (Hammond 1967: 47; Davies 1981*b*: 239).
9. Cabanes 1987*a*: 20; Davies 1981*b*: 237 and 243; D'Andria 1987.
10. The name is found in Homer, *Iliad* 2.635 and *Od.* 24.378; Thucydides 1.5.2–3, 1.47.3, 3.94.3, 3.102.6, 3.114.4.
11. Davies (1981*b*: 255) lays out the question very clearly; longer discussion in Cabanes (1999*a*: 373 ff.), along with discussion of the other political terms of the region.
12. Hammond argues that Strabo is drawing on Hekataios via Theopompos (Strabo 7.5.6–12; Hammond 1967: 454–5). As Davies (1981*b*: 240) points out, the fourteen tribes may have been equivalent in stature or grouped around the big three. Cabanes (1987*a*: 22) notes 'Le nombre d'ethniques actuellement connu est sans cesse en augmentation'. He notes that he has found evidence for 55 from the inscriptions so far excavated at Bouthrotos.
13. See Hammond 1967: 487 ff. and Davies 1981*b*: 251.
14. Pseudo-Skylax (28–32) of the Chaonians, the Thesprotians, the Kassopaians, the Molossians: Dakaris points out (1987) that he is surely drawing on Hekataios (beginning of fifth century); see also Thuc. 3.94.4. For transhumant pastoralism as dominant pattern of land use see

Cabanes 1987a: 20, and Vokotopoulou 1987 on life in the Molossian settlement of Vitsa.
15. Dakaris 1987 with Cabanes 1987a: 22 and Corvisier 1993. Examples of urban development: Kassope, founded by synoikism, its development influenced by Greek colony of Ambrakia; Veliani (now Chrusauge according to Vlachopoulo-Oikonomou 2003: 187) (before the middle of the fourth century) and Gitana (now Goumani) in Thesprotia (fourth century) influenced by contact with Kerkyra.

This of course is a simplified description: e.g. Corvisier (1993: 87) describes how in Molossia alone, for example, four patterns of habitation have been suggested: larger cities that seem to have grown up around the fourth century, such as Dodona, or Kastritsa, which tended to become a focus for the development of the region; defensive sites, usually along the borders and created in the Hellenistic period, when the area had been absorbed into a kingdom; hill settlements for farmers; and, finally, then rural settlements. Even by the third century BCE, the territory of Molossia still mostly comprised small towns under 5 ha. in size (12 cities over 5 ha. out of 54 (8 between 5 and 10 ha., 3 between 10 and 30, and 1 over 30 ha.) housing 22% of the population).
16. With regard to the federal organization of much of Epiros, Cabanes (1999a: 382) has observed that we should not simply assume that every *koinon* had a federal composition. See his remarks on the Prasaiboi, the Bylliones, and the Balaites.
17. Full version: Justin 17.3.1–22, drawing on a third-century version by Proxenos (*FGrH* 703), which, in turn, probably drew on earlier sources (see Davies 1981b: 241–2).
18. See Davies 1981b: 243ff., quote p. 245.
19. As we will see, in its earliest period, Dodona was described as Thesprotian (see *Od*.14.327ff. = 19.296ff.; Hdt. 2.56.1; Pindar fr. 60 Maehler; Strab. 7.7.10); cf. Davies 1981b: 253–7. See Parke 1967a: 117 for a description of the precinct which is built asymmetrically, so as to make room for the tree. Evangelidis found a concentration of offerings in the south-east corner and suggested that this must be the site of the tree.
20. Cabanes 1999a: 377; fluidity of language of political organization, 253.
21. For a comprehensive overview (in translation) of the relevant inscriptions, see Davies 1981b: 246ff., with useful observations Cabanes 1999a: 376ff. and 1976: 151ff. This state development is outlined in Cabanes (1999a: 377) and Davies 1981b: 256ff. with further detail: Cabanes 1976: 151ff. and Hammond 1967: 636ff. The shift from Epirotan alliance (*SGDI* 1336: σύμμαχοι τῶν Ἀπειρωτᾶν) to κοινὸν τῶν Ἀπειρωτᾶν suggested by small bronze lamella, and a dedication from the late fourth century (Cabanes 1997: 103; *SEG* 47. 823). By the third century BCE documentation shows a decisive shift from 'Molossians' to 'Epeirotai' see Davis 1981b: 256ff. (An earlier date is supported by coinage labelled

ΑΠΕΙΡΩΤΑΝ, 'of the Apeirotai' dated to the 320s by Franke 1961: 116 ff. and Hammond 1967: 537, 560.)
22. Davies 1981*b*: 255, quoting Hammond 1967: 539.
23. See Hammond 1967: 654 for activities by smaller *koina*, e.g. under the Epirote Alliance, see state consultations at Dodona in Appendix 1 and later in this chapter.
24. Wood-cutters/admonitory doves: Philostratos, *Im.* 2.33; Schol. A. *Il.* 16.234. Thieving shepherds/talking trees: Schol. Hom. *Od.* 14. 327 = Proxenos, *FGrH* 703 F. 7. For a full discussion of these stories, see Parke 1967*a*: ch. 3.
25. Apollod. *Bibl.* 1.7.2, Ov. *Met.* 1.163–413.
26. Ov. *Met.* 1.379.
27. Evangelidis 1935: 208 ff.; see Parke 1967*a*: 97 ff. and Dakaris 1993: 6 ff.
28. Dakaris 1993: 7–8; Parke 1967*a*: 99; Tartaran 2004: 23.
29. Homer, *Iliad* 16.220 ff. Helloi: Schol. T, *Il.* 16.235; Schol. A, *Il.* 16.234 with reference to Pindar 59.3 Maehler. Homer, *Od.* 14.327 ff. = 19.296 ff., (trans. Rieu).
30. Hesiod fr. 240. 1 MW, translation, Parke 1967*a*: 46. For full discussion of these citations, see Parke 1967*a*: 1 ff. For Helloi–Hellopia connection, see discussion and references in Parke 1967*a*: 7.
31. See above, n. 3.
32. Davies 1981*b*: 257.
33. Parke 1967*a*: 117–19, summarizing the archaeological finds of Evangelidis and Dakaris.
34. Dakaris 1993: 16.
35. Bakhuizen 1987.
36. See Hammond 1967: 488 ff. for discussion of the activities of the various Epirote tribes during the war, and the strategic significance of Epirus to Sparta and Athens (including the tantalizing idea that control of this area would have meant control of the coastal trade routes with Sicily and Italy, rendering the Sicilian expedition unnecessary, p. 503). See their role in Ambrakia's attack on Argos in 430 BCE, Thuc. 2.68.
37. The Spartans are said to have consulted Dodona on at least two occasions: before the battle of Leuktra (Kallisthenes *FGrH* 124 F 22a and b; Cic. *Div.* 1.34.76 and 2.32.69) in 371—a visit that was somewhat upset by an ape—and then again sometime around 367 BCE (Diod. Sik. 15.17.3) before they fought with the Arkadians. They were told that the war would be 'tearless'. This was fulfilled in the 'tearless battle' when a Spartan army led by Archidamos was cut off by the enemy on their way back from an expedition into Arcadia. They managed to win their way through, without losing a man. Athenian consultations: Pausanias 7.25.1, set in the time of the Attic kings, an oracle prevents the Athenians from killing a group of Spartan suppliants. The story may have been created to contrast with the later treatment by the Athenians of Kylon

(Hdt. 5.71); or used by King Kleomenes in 508 BCE, when he and his Spartans were under siege in the Athenian Akropolis—and were allowed to leave unharmed (Hdt. 5.72). Dio Chrys. 17.17; Paus. 8.11.12; Plut. *Nik.* 13: the Athenians consult before the 415 BCE Sicilian expedition—the responses contain typical folktale ambiguities. In one version, the Athenians are told to attach Sicily to the city, in another to settle it with inhabitants. But the god meant a ridge of land near Athens not the island. Xen. *Vect.* 6.2 suggests sending to Dodona or Delphi to check his taxation reforms. Fourth century: Dodona oracles quoted by Demosthenes: 21.51 to emphasize the importance of the chorus in the Dionysiac festival; 19.29 about the dangers of politicians who grow too strong for the democracy (quoted Din. 1.78 and 98 against Demosthenes); 18.253 that 'the Tyche [or luck] of the city of Athens is good'. Hyp. *Eux.* 24 mentions that 'Zeus of Dodona had commanded the Athenians in an oracle to decorate the image of Dione . . .'. This was in the period between 330 and 324. It looks as if Athens may have been looking for help against Makedonia. . . But in 322, Munychia (steep hill behind Peiraieus) occupied by Antipater, the Makedonian governor. Plutarch (*Phok.* 28) suggests that Dodona had seen it coming—and had already warned the Athenians to 'guard the high places of Artemis so that others might not take them'.

Inscriptions: a decree of the Attic guild of worshippers of Bendis, indicating that the Athenians allow the establishment of the Thrakian goddess Bendis in Attika, which probably refers to the original founding in the late fifth century (*Leges Graecorum Sacrae* II.1.42; late third century BCE); *Syll.*^{3} 73, now lost, a dedication for a naval victory: 'the Athenians from the Peloponnese, having won a naval victory, made this dedication'. Parke (1967*a*: 136) suggests that this may have been to commemorate Phormio's victory over the Peloponnesian fleet at the mouth of the Korinthian Gulf (in 429 BCE).

38. The new precinct had Ionic colonnades on each side, except for the east side where the tree stood (Dakaris 1993: 14).
39. Parke State 9; Dakaris, Tzouvara-Souli, Vlachopoulou-Oikonomou, and Gravani-Katsiki 1999. *Diaitoi* were officers of the city; see Cabanes 1976: 154.
40. Perhaps as described for Athens at Thuc. 2.15.2.
41. Davies 1981*b*: 257. Hatzopoulos (2004: 509) remarks on the number of official documents collected by Cabanes (1976: 534–92) from Dodona (75) compared to those found at Passaron, the royal capital of the Molossi (2) and he observes that Passaron 'fait pâle figure' in comparison with the oracular sanctuary.
42. Tzouvara-Souli 1993: 73 and Dakaris, Tzouvara-Souli, Vlachopoulou-Oikonomou, and Gravani-Katsiki 1999. Dodona seems to have been of great regional political importance (Cabanes 1976: 377).
43. Dakaris (1993: 21) describes four stone pedestals excavated near the

bouleuterion, inscribed with honorary decrees granted by the League to those who had shown friendship to the Epirotes: e.g. the bronze statue of the Thesprotian cavalry general Milon, son of Sosander, commemorated by the League of the Epirotes for his friendship to the Epirotes and his bravery (*c*.230–220 BCE); a statue of the general Krison, son of Sabyrtios, of the tribe of the Molossian Kyesti, given by the League of the Bylliones (*c*. 230–220 BCE).

44. Tzouvara-Souli 1993: 78–9. Some of these indicate cult activity going back to the Archaic period, e.g. at Apollonia and Ambrakia. In other places, the cult seems to have spread later, e.g. in Amantia and Byllis.
45. Polyb. 5.9.2.
46. Polyb. 30.16; Strabo 7.7.3; Livy 45.34; Plut. *Aem.* 29.
47. Dio Chrys. 30–5, fr. 101. 2.
48. Zeniketes: Karapanos 1878: pl. 26, no. 8; W. Peek 1978. Parke (1967*a*: 123 ff.) translates the first lines 'To king Zeniketes a prophecy of Dione came: "Your goods and your handiwork will shine through all Greece." He himself having completed with skilful hand [dedicated me].' But a new reading of the inscription by Peek (1978) provides a very different translation; see Appendix 1. But Tzouvara-Souli (2004: 519) refers to 'the athlete Zenicetes'.
49. Strabo 7.7.9, trans. Jones.
50. Clem. Al. *Protr.* 2, p. 4.
51. Evidence for the celebration of the Naia in 243/4 CE: an inscription copied by Kyriakos of Ancona in the fifteenth century (*BCH* 1 (1877) 294; confirmed by Dakaris' discovery of part of the original (*BCH* 89 (1960) 744). Tree cut down: Servius on Virgil, *Aen.* 3.466.
52. Parke State 2; Dakaris, *PAE* 1967: 33–54; Karapanos 1878: pl. 39, 5 and Pomtow 1; 450–404 BCE (Pomtow).
53. Parke State 3; Karapanos 1878: no. 4, pl. 34, 4 and pl. 39, 7; Pomtow 2; late fifth century (Pomtow).
54. M-33 (these numbers beginning with 'M' indicate catalogue entries from the Museum of Ioannina and are provided where they exist or are known); Dakaris, Christidis, Vokotopoulou 1993: 60; Parke State 6; Corinthian alphabet; third quarter of the fourth century (Dakaris, Christidis, Vokotopoulou); Orikians in Hekataios *FGrH* 106, on the coast of Chaonia, and this seems to have been evidence of an alliance with Kerkyra. Site information: Stillwell (1976); Hammond 1967: 127 ff.
55. Vokotopolou 1992: 78; Parke State 1; Karapanos 1878: pl. 34; Pomtow 3; 325–300 BCE (Vokotopoulou).
56. M-827; 360–340 BCE; for Byllis or Bylliake, see Hekataios *FGrH* 104, Strabo 7.5.8. Bylliake by the sea (now modern Plaka, according to Hammond 1967: 137, 471, 691). Byllis (Hammond 1967: 225, Ceka 1987: 137) was on the right bank of the river Aous, in northern Chaonia. The provenance of the tablet depends on the foundation date of these settle-

ments: see Dakaris, Christidis, Vokotopoulou 1993: 57. The tablet literally reads 'regarding possessions' 'the Bylliones [ask] sacrificing to which god they will do best'.

57. Dodonaeans: see Parke State 7. Apollonia (Pojani; on the coast of northern Illyria). In Herodotos 9.93.4 the Apollonians consult the oracle about a curse of barrenness that was ravaging their land. The gods Apollo and Zeus (both oracles were consulted) attributed it to the fact that they had blinded the shepherd Euenios, punishing him because he had let 60 of the city's sheep, who were dedicated to the sun god, get killed. We know from the material evidence that the Apollonians did use Dodona, so to that extent the story is plausible. But it also serves as an explanation of how Deiphonos, Euenios' son, received his prophetic gift. Deiphonos went as a seer on the Greek expedition to Mykale in 479 BCE.
58. Christidis; 375–350 BCE.
59. M-177; first half of fourth century. Onchesmos was the principal port of Phoinike, the capital of Chaonia, and located on a hill near the modern village of Finiki; important for crossing the Ionian Sea to Italy (Strabo 7.7.5 and Cicero, *Att.* 7.2.1). Possible reconstruction of third line by Dakaris, Christidis, and Vokotopoulou (1993).
60. M-22; Evangelidis (*AE* 1953/4: 99–102) dated it to the fourth century; Robert (*REG* 1956: 134) to the end of the fourth century, beginning of the third. See also Parke State 5.
61. Parke State 9; Robert, *REG* 56 (1953), 146, no. 116; Wilhelm, *AfP* 15 (1953), 75 ff.; Evangelidis, *PAE* 1932: 52, no. 1. Wilhelm (1953) suggested that the last line of the tablet in fact contains the god's answer: 'To the arbitrators. Justly spend this on the council chamber' but Parke (1967*a*: 262, no. 9) is doubtful.
62. Karapanos 1878, pl. 34, 3; Parke State 4.
63. Karapanos 1878, pl. 39, 2; Parke State 8; dated to the late second or early first century BCE.
64. M-1099; first quarter of the fifth century, has been read as $A\dot{v}\tau o\acute{\iota}\ P(\epsilon\gamma\hat{\iota}\nu o\iota\ \ldots)$ but other solutions are possible. Vokotopoulou (1992: 80) argues that although it could be the dative of a first name, the larger letters mean it is more likely to be an official demand. The other (M-957) is written in a Chalkidian alphabet and dated to the second quarter of the fifth century.
65. These communities refer to themselves with a variety of expressions— *polis*, *koinon*, or just using the nominative plural of their people. There are some surprises: we might expect the Kerkyraians or Tarentines to refer to themselves as *poleis*, but why does the *koinon* of the Chaonians use the term, and why do the Bylliones not use it? I agree with Cabanes (1999*a*: 373) that the fluidity of such terminology means that the use of such terms is informal, even somewhat elastic. For example, the lack of use does not imply that the Bylliones were not present at the oracle,

requesting help as a *koinon*, as Dakaris, Christidis, and Vokotopoulou (1993) suggest, while its use to describe the Chaonians does not indicate that the community had adopted any particular socio-political structure.
66. Hammond (1967: 409 ff., quote 411), describing finds at Dodona dating to the last phase of the Bronze Age: 'the distribution of the flat axes with lateral projections in bronze and the affinities of the Epirote type of fibula show that the two coasts of the southern Adriatic Sea were in touch with one another'.

    Good harbours: Ps.-Skylax 28 and 30. Small boats: Diod. Sik. 15.14.2; Polyb. 4.16.6; Livy 45.43.10. Piracy: Pliny, *HN* 3.152; Polyb. 2. 8.4, 4.6.2 and 8; Thuc. 1.5.3; see Bakhuizen 1987.
67. Heads of Dodonaean Zeus and Dione on a silver didrachm of the Epirote League (end of third century BCE) in Archaeological Museum, Ioannina, inv. no. 35–6, picture in Dakaris 1993: 10; bronze coin with oracular oak-tree and three doves (*c*.300 BCE) in Franke 1961: ii. 318 ff.; cf. Parke 1967*a*: 76; picture in Dakaris 1993: 11. See Fig. 2.
68. Serv. on *Aen.* 3.466; the *Etymologicum Magicum* (s.v. ἀναπαυόμενον ὕδωρ) supplies some other key characteristics, including the fact 'that at midday and midnight [it] slacks off and ceases to flow; at other hours it comes constantly'. Zeus 'Naios': Dem. 21.53; Schol. B. Hom. *Il.* 16. 233. References and discussion in Parke 1967*a*: 67 ff.
69. Oracular rustling: Ov. *Met.* 7.614 ff. and the *Suda* s.v. Δωδώνη.

    As GPS for the *Argo*: in a fragment of a lost play by Aeschylus (*TGF* 20 = Philo Judaeus 2.468), where it seems to have spoken to prevent slaves coming on board. Also: on departure from Thessaly (Ap. Rhod. 1.525); at the climax of the voyage, a storm in the Adriatic (Ap. Rhod. 4.580); and when the ship was nearing the world of the dead (Orph. *A* 1160). Valerius Flaccus describes it speaking to Jason in a dream (1.302) and after the death of the helmsman, Tiphys (5.65). References and discussion in Parke 1967*a*: 27 ff. (rustling) and 35 (*Argo*).
70. Hdt. 2.55, trans. Waterfield.
71. A comment by the scholiast to Soph. *Trach.* 170 intimates that Euripides and Pindar may also have written about Egyptian priestesses. Euripides said there were three of them, and 'others say two, and that one of them came from Thebes to the oracle of Ammon and the other to the neighbourhood of Dodona, as also Pindar in the Paeans'. The scholiast is not clear whether he is discussing doves or women. Pindar's lost Hymn: frr. 57–60 Maehler, discussed by Parke 1967*a*: 53 ff.
72. Strabo 7, fr. 1a; Paus. 10. 12. 10; Hesych. s.v. πέλειαι and in the Servian commentaries on Virg. *Ecl.* 9. 11.
73. Hdt 2.56, trans. Waterfield.
74. Hdt 2.57, trans. Waterfield.
75. Pl. *Phdr.* 244b; Paus. 10.12.10 (see discussion Parke 1967*a*: 82); Clem. Al. *Protr.* 2. 11. 1 (followed by Euseb. *PE* 2. 3. 1 and Theodoret. *Gr. Aff. Cur.*

10.3.5, p. 243, 3) describes how the beating of the cauldron, inspires the priestess to prophesy. Use by demons: *Suda* s.v. *Δωδώνη* and Schol. B. Homer, *Il.* 16. 233 (see discussion Parke 1967a: 89). The use of hexameters in responses are often the sign of ecstatic prophecy, at least for Delphic responses, but the few examples that we have from Dodona are almost all fictitious (about Alexander's death: Scr. 6.1.5; Steph. Byz. s.v. *Πανδοσία*; on the Dorian invasion: Paus. 7.25.1; moments in Roman history: Dion. Hal. 1.19.3; Macr. *Sat.* 1.7.2874) (see discussion Parke 1967a: 82 ff.). Pausanias 10.12.10 offers two isolated hexameter lines, but this also seems unlikely to stand as evidence of manic manticism, since, as Parke (1967a: 82) observes, the priestesses are described as addressing Zeus in the third person and in the vocative, suggesting that the priestess 'even if in ecstasy, was not supposed to be stripped of her own personality'.

76. Soph. *Trach.* 46 and 1159 ff.
77. Strabo 7, fr. 1a. See discussion Parke 1967a: 84.
78. In Men. fr. 65 (K–A) *Arrephoros* there is the description of a nurse who was obviously a bit talkative: 'To stop the bronze vessel at Dodona, which they say sounds all day if a passer-by lays a finger on it, would be an easier job than to stop her tongue.' Earlier references: Kallim. *Hymn to Apollo* 286 refers to 'the Pelasgians, the earth-liers, the servants of the unsilenced cauldron'.
79. Strabo 7, fr. 3; Polemon and Aristides ap. Steph. Byz. s.v. *Δωδώνη*. Lucius of Tarrha tells us how, by his time, the whip had lost its lashes, although the myth of its sounding was preserved. For references and description of the bronze artefacts at Dodona see Parke 1967a: 88.
80. Clem. Al. *Protr.* 2.11.1, repeated in Euseb. *Praep. Evang.* 2.3.1 and paraphrased in Theodoret. *Gr. Aff. Cur.* 10.3.5, p. 243,3.
81. Kallisthenes (*FGrH* 124 F 22 (a) and (b) = Cic. *Div.* 1.34.76 and 2.32.69; trans. Falconer.
82. Parke 1967a: 104–5, c.100 BCE; LSGG 83 = *Syll.*³ 1157; 100 BCE; Robert, *Hellenika*, 5 (1948) 16 ff.
83. Eust. *Il.* 16: 233–5, p. 1057.61 ff. citing Lykophron 233 (van der Valk 1979: 844).

CHAPTER 5

1. Michael Jackson (1978: 134) describing one of the roles played by divination among the Kuranko tribe, Sierra Leone. Quoted by Susan Reynolds White in her analysis of divination among the Nyole in Eastern Uganda (1997: 81).
2. Horden and Purcell 2000.
3. Cf. the refoundation of Kyrene (Hdt. 4.159).
4. Vokotopoulou (1992: 84) argues that the Paros named on the question is Pharos, a colony of Paros (cf. Strabo 7.5.5), founded in 385/384 BCE.

5. Herakleia (modern Policoro) was a Tarentine colony founded in 433 BCE, close to the site of Siris (see Hornblower and Spawforth 1999: 683). Shared citizenship: Miletos seems to have had arrangements of isopolity with its colonies Olbia and Kyzikos (Graham 1964: 98 ff.), and there is evidence that the relationship between Lokroi Epizephyrioi and her colony Hipponion (ibid. 94) was one of double nationality or something similar. However, a variety of arrangements between colony and mother city were possible, and the arrangement under discussion here may not have been an official system of sym- or isopolity, but just an informal relationship close enough to allow for a fairly fluid movement between cities. That such arrangements existed can be seen in the arrangements found between Thasos and her mother city Paros, and Thasos and her colonies (see ibid. 71 ff.).
6. Thessalian serfs: Xen. *Hell.* 2.3.36, 6.1.11; Dem. 23.199; Theokr. 16.35 (cf. Schol. ad loc.); generally meaning slave or bondsman: Eur. *Her.* 639.
7. Ter. *Phorm.* 705–10: Geta runs through the omens that Phormio might offer to avoid being married. They include a black dog entering the house, a snake coming down through the skylight, and a hen crowing.
8. That is, if ἔσσαν is actually a west Greek form of οὖσαν as suggested by Robert Parker (private communication), but this question is elsewhere translated as an instruction to the consultant 'to bear with his defeat' (Christidis, Dakaris, Vokotopoulou 1997: no. 4).
9. See Hornblower (1982: 354, appendix 2) for Greek abhorrence of sibling marriage, in his exploration of sister-marriage among the Hekatomnids in Karia, and influences from Egypt and Persia. The Athenian law may offer some kind of understanding that the mother played a role in procreation, as Halperin (1990*b*: 279), who also notes that at Sparta the rule was the opposite (following A. R. W. Harrison 1968: 22–3). Dean-Jones (1994: 153 n. 20) points out that this was probably to do with regulating inheritance, preventing an *epiklēros* (a woman whose children inherit from her dead father) marrying a half-brother by her mother, and thus denying her agnate kin their inheritance. In early sources, *kasignētē*, seems to have been particularly used of half-siblings through the same mother, but this does not continue, see LSJ s.v.
10. See R. Parker 1983: 84 ff.
11. Hdt. 6.57.
12. In Hippok. *Ep.* 27; *Syll.*³ 1044.20 (Halik.): cf. LSJ s.v.
13. Obviously, it carries significant future risks, e.g. if the answer to Lysanias' question was 'no', then violence, questions of inheritance, lawsuits, are just some of the problems that might follow.
14. Halperin 1990*b*: 278 ff.; Dean-Jones 1994: 149 ff.; Lloyd 1999*a*: 86 ff.
15. Halperin 1990*b*: 282 ff.; for imagery of women as receptive in literature see Halperin 1990*b*: 283 n. 100.
16. Danger for mothers: Hanson 1991; Hippok. *Mul.*; Sor. *Gyn.*

17. Without the Greek we cannot tell if this is a verb in the present tense being used to indicate the future ('Will I ...?') or as a deliberative ('Should I ...?').
18. Christidis may have been drawing on a meaning given for καλαπόδιον in LSJ.
19. See Fisher 1993; Hansen 1991: 122 for slaves in various professions, including: a sea-captain, granting a loan of 1000 dr. to a merchant on board his ship Dem. 34.5–10; a banker Dem. 36. 13–14; a foreman Aeschin. 1.97; trusted to organize his master's goods Xen. *Oik.* 12.2–3.
20. A similar question is found among the *Sortes Astrampsychi* (Browne 1983: no. 89), a popular book of oracles from Roman Egypt, written in Greek on papyrus, dating to the first century BCE. The book contains instructions, a list of questions requiring answers of yes/no type, and then a list of oracular answers. The consultant used a complicated number system to find his or her answer.
21. Earlier community ghost-laying: in the Archaic period, Sparta summons Thaletas from Gortyn; he uses music to stay a plague (Plut. *Mor.* 1146b—was this a ghost-laying? Connections between *goēteia* and song Eur. *Hipp.* 1038–40, *Bacch.* 233–8, Pl. *Grg.* 483e6, *Meno* 80a2 and b6, *Leg.* 933a5; cf. Johnston 1999: 111 n. 71). In order to deliver inhabitants from a plague Athens summons Epimenides from Knossos after the sacrilegious murder of Kylon around 630 BCE; he purifies the city by propitiating the ghosts with a sacrifice (see *FGrH* 457). Plutarch (*Mor.* 555c) says that the Spartans summoned *psychagōgoi* from Italy to deal with the ghost of Pausanias in the mid-fifth century; Thucydides' version (1.134) describes a pollution not a ghost, and describes the Spartans consulting Delphi to resolve it, but the instructions that Delphi gives are very similar to ghost-laying rituals found elsewhere, e.g., in the Kyrenean *lex sacra* (*SEG* 9.72 = *LSS* 115) and the description of how the Orchomenians laid the ghost of Aktaion (Paus. 9.38.5).

    As Johnston (1999: 85 ff.) argues, fifth-century literature offers many examples of spirit-raising: Empedokles describes leading ghosts from Hades (fr. 101 Wr. = F 111 D–K); Aeschylus wrote a play called the *Psychagōgoi* or 'spirit-raisers', which dealt with Odysseus' invocation of ghosts, and showed an invocation on stage in the *Persians*, King Darios rising in response to rituals performed by the Persian elders (623–842). In Euripides' *Alkestis*, Herakles talks about the *psychagōgos* (1127–8). Plato uses *goēteia* and spirit-raising as a metaphor for sophistic language, *Soph.* 234c5–6 (Johnston 1999: 103).
22. See Chapter 12 for possible links between spirit-raisers and cursing.
23. See for example: Schol. Ar. *Plut.* 820; Epich. 187 K–A.
24. This is how it is read by Christidis, Dakaris, Vokotopoulou (1999: no. 3), who report that the verb ἐπαράομαι is well attested, but that the noun is apparently new: ἐπαρασις.

25. On the possibility of buying citizenship, see Robert, *Hellenica* 1, 37–42.
26. Magistrate: Thuc. 5.47; oracular envoy: Dem. 19.128.
27. Hammond (1967: 517) argues that Ἀρύββας, honoured by the Athenians in an Attic inscription *IG* ii². 226, 340 BCE (named after his grandfather), is King Θάρυψ or Θαρύπας, found with this name on *IG* iv². 95, the list of Epidaurian *Theorodokoi*, reigned 360–342 BCE. On the assumption that Ἀρύββας, Θάρυψ (Plut. *Pyrrh.* 1.3) and Θαρύπας (Thuc. 2.80.6) represent the same dynastic name, cf. Davies 1981*b*: 243–4 nn. 28, 30, and 36. However, it is not clear how the names are related—specifically how Θάρυψ or Θαρύπας would have dropped its first consonant.

    On the name, *LGPN* provides the following information:
    Vol. 1 (the Aegean Islands, Kypros, Kyrenaika): none
    Vol. 2 (Attika): one entry dated to fourth century BCE and likely to be an Athenian
    Vol. 3a (Peloponnese, Western Greece, Sicily, and Magna Graecia): five entries including one from Arkadia, fourth century BCE; three from Epiros (all from the fourth century and including this oracle tablet)
    Vol. 3b (Central Greece from the Megarid to Thessaly): eight entries all from Thessaly, ranging from the second century BCE to the first century CE
    Vol. 4 (Makedonia, Thrake, and the northern regions of the Black Sea): gives one from Makedonia, dating to the fourth century BCE.
28. Parke 1967*a*: 272.
29. For the possible meanings of *pharmaka* see Chapter 2, n. 8.
30. Based on Parke 28, which suggests that it is written in the jargon of the racing stables and translates ἀπέτιλε as 'stripped the hide off'.
31. Hoffman (*SGDI* 117): 'in Betreff der Antwort und der Siegel, welche (nämlich die Antwort) Aristolaos nicht mit Siegeln versehen und welche (nämlich die Siegel) er nicht daran gelegt hat: ob [Sosias sich] des Täfelchens wegen nach Dodona [auf den Weg machte und dem Aristo]lao den Befehl gab, er solle nicht einmal [die Siegel] verfertigen, [geschweige denn] (die Tafel mit ihnen) zeichnen und versiegeln.'
32. Further evidence that this was a 'constant concern for ancient men' occurs across Greek literature, as Versnel has discussed (2002: 119). As evidence, he lists the spell H. 216; Theokr. 3.31–3; *PGM* VII.411–16; Plin. *HN* 32.49 and 29.81.
33. l. 1: Hoffman interprets as 'I want an oracle on the following subject.'
    l. 2: Karapanos: κὲ αλάες; Karapanos says this is a response of the oracle; suggests that αλάες is a dialect form of ἀλάομαι.
34. Trans. Parke 2.
35. Vokotopoulou 1992: no. 7.

CHAPTER 6

1. James Fernandez describing his experience of consultation with Zulu diviners to show how they mediate between primary and secondary ways of knowing (that is, between figurative and linear ways of describing the world), as well as between the idea of different possible worlds and the troubled daily lives of their clients.
2. An exception is the category of literary questions concerned with a pious life. On the whole, these literary references date from later than the material under examination here. However, there is one earlier citation of a question on such a topic (Theopomp. *FGrH* 115 F 314 = Porph. *Abst.* 2.16); while Solon's instruction to Kroisos on the identity of the 'happiest of men', as described by Herodotos (1. 29–34), turns on the significance of a pious life, so this concern cannot simply be dismissed as irrelevant to this period. However, the catalogue of questions asked at Dodona suggests that oracular consultation was reserved for more mundane matters.
3. I note the general balance of the questions in each category because I am curious about what most consultants came to Dodona to ask about. However, obviously no definitive conclusions can be drawn on this matter since the nature of the evidence is constrained both by what has been found, and by what has been published; and, of course, I have imposed these categories.
4. See the catalogue for examples of the practice of labelling the reverse of question tablets with a reference to the consultant's name or question.
5. Travel 23 and 25.
6. Travel 21 and 3.
7. Travel 1, 2, and 15.
8. Travel 5.
9. Apollonian origin: Travel 16 and Children 16. Ambrakia: Health/Disease 7. Herakleia: Travel 11. Archias: Fragments 17; Ergetion: Work (Farmwork) 4; Porinos: Work 17; Diognetos: Prayer 2.
10. Ionian: Children 4 and Children 7; specifically Attic: Prayer 1 and 2; Doric: Health/Disease 4; Thessalian: Work (Herding) 1.
11. Hdt. 1.46.3; and nothing is said of the need for translation during Periander's consultation (Hdt. 5.92). See Hammond 1967: 414–24. He argues that the inscriptions are evidence for the relevant tribes speaking Greek in the fifth century, at least (p. 423).
12. Hammond 1967: 406 ff.: the material evidence suggests that there was contact between this area and Thessaly during the Bronze Age; and there are also the stories of colonization during the *Nostoi*.
13. Thuc. (2.68.3) probably describes such a process by the Ambrakiots, who were absorbed into Argos Amphilochikon and 'Hellenized'. Did they speak a dialect of Greek before? The evidence is inconclusive. Thucydides describes the following as *barbaroi*: those in the vicinity of Cheimerion,

282 Notes to Chapter 6

Chaones, Molossi, Atinates, Parauaei, and Orestae (2.68.9; 2.80.5; 2.81 and 82) but he does not specifically mention their language.

14. See *LGPN* vols. i–iv. Possible tribal origins of Philotas suggested by the fact that of 12 examples of the name, one hails from Italy, and 11 from Epirus, of which one is from Dodona (iv/iii BCE), and 10 from Bouthrotos, of the tribe of the tribe of Prasaiboi, all dating to 163 BCE.
15. For example, Ritual Activity 1 is a very fragmentary tablet containing a picture of a key. The only part of the text that can be read seems to be asking which god the consultant should pray to. Although the text is fragmentary the drawing on the tablet may represent the 'unlocking' of the womb.
16. Travel 17.
17. Prosperity/Safety 1.
18. See Cabanes 1983; also, on the Dodona inscription, Hoffman (1999).
19. Prosperity/Safety 6.
20. Professor Christidis reported that in his unpublished material he estimated that about 3 per cent of the questions were posed by women.
21. Health/Disease 2.
22. Anonymous woman: Health/Disease 1 (Future); Philistas: Health/Disease 1 (Past/Present).
23. Slavery, Questions by Slaves 2 (Razia) and 3 (Leuka). According to Christidis, Teitukos is an Illyrian name.
24. Different systems of manumission, civic or sacral, worked in different regions. Civic manumission basically comprised proclamation and registration, and was paid for by the slave. There were two forms of sacral manumission: (i) the slave was consecrated to a particular god, consecration to take place after a particular period of time during which the slave would continue to fulfil his or her duties; (ii) a master sells his slave to the gods for a sum provided by the slave. In Athens, the process of manumission involved a slave being charged in a *dikē apostasiou*, i.e. with the failure to fulfil his or her obligations. The slave won the case, gaining her freedom. Sacred protection was achieved by dedicating a 100 dr. *phialē* to Athena. Once the slave was consecrated, he or she could not be re-enslaved: the person who tried was open to a charge of 'theft of sacred objects'.
25. Slavery 4 and 7.
26. Children 15.
27. Crime 3; Children 9.
28. Crime 4.
29. Work 14.
30. Ritual Activity 1.
31. Children: 1, 5, 6, 7, 16; Health/Disease: 1, 2, 4, 6, 7; Prosperity/Safety 1 and 6; Property 1.
32. Lloyd 1999*b*: 39 ff.
33. See Whittaker 1965.

34. Lane Fox 1986: 214.
35. The founding of Kyrene: Herodotos 4.150–64.
36. Judicial Activity 1.
37. That said, according to Christidis, there are more examples of inquiries about winning competitions in the unpublished material. In addition, as we have already seen, this is put forward by Plutarch as an example of the kind of question that individuals asked (see Plut. *Mor.* 386c). It was surely the kind of question competitors would have put to the oracle at Olympia. (Evidence for future performance anxiety: Pind. *Ol.* 8.2; Olympia was probably the setting for Lucilius' short, satirical poems about athletes consulting the prophet Olympos, see *AP.* 11.161, and 163, cf. Parke 1967*a*: 184 and 189).
38. Work 10. This is a difficult question to understand. It is one of a pair—the other written on the other side of the tablet. Side A says: 'Will things be best for Timodamos if he does his business, by land and by sea, [from the silver] for as long as he chooses.' Dakaris (1968) suggested that the phrase '[from the silver]' referred to a mine; Salviat (1993) disagreed and argued that it meant 'use the money in business'.
39. Children 7.
40. Artem. 4.2.5 ff.
41. Pl. *Alk.* 148b.
42. Requests for help and safety, Prayers 1 and 2; for good fortune, Work 2. Versnel (1981: 7–8) has made the link between oracles and supplication explicit arguing that 'The wish, which forms the link with the prayer of supplication, is always in the background, usually implicit, but sometimes explicit …'. He suggests that the oracle question and the prayer of supplication are close to each other; and in support of this cites the emotional oracular question from Dodona (Parke 2) by Diognetos the son of Aristomedes of Athens. Of this he says we 'see clearly how asking for knowledge and asking for help are frequently two sides of the same thing … Does the anxious question of "whether my son will recover from consumption?" not imply the unspoken prayer that the reply be favourable?' He goes on to suggest that such examples from 'the domain of oracles … pave the way for true prayers of supplication'. It is not clear in what precise sense he means this, but since the two activities coexist, it seems unlikely that he is envisioning a literally evolutionary process.
43. Health/Disease 3.
44. Health/Disease 9.
45. Wrongdoing in an Oracle Consultation 1.
46. Hdt 7.139.5–143; 1.158; Xen. *An.* 3.1.5–8.
47. See Chapter 3, pp. 50–52. Delphi nos. 1 and 5.
48. Blanket coverage: questions in the category Prosperity/Safety. Serial questions: Timodamos' question, tablet 10 in the category Work, and Archephon's question, tablet 4 in the category Prosperity/Safety.

CHAPTER 7

1. Ogden (1999: 5) reports that *defixio* (from *defigo*, to 'nail down' or 'transfix') is probably the standard Latin term for a curse tablet. He notes, however, that this word is only found in a bilingual gloss, see LSJ s.v. ii. 40. Other possible Latin candidates include: *execratio* 'curse', *devotio* 'dedication/curse/spell', *commonitorium* 'memorandum', and *petitio* 'petition'. Tomlin (1988: 59) discusses the use of these terms and suggests that those who created the British tablets probably used the term *donatio*, meaning 'dedication/giving'. The British curses are mostly of the prayers-for-justice type, usually seeking redress for a theft. The 'dedication' in these cases refers to the giving over of the lost goods in question, or the thief him/herself. The verb *defigere* as found here is found in some British curse tablets (e.g., R. G. Collingwood and R. P. Wright, *et al.* (eds.), *The Roman Inscriptions of Britain* (Gloucester, 1983–91), nos. 6–7).

   Contemporary Greek terms include reference in one curse (*DT* 85, side B, l. 8) to κατάδεσμον but this may be a projection of Ziebarth (1934: 21–2, no. 23). This same curse culminates with ... καταγράφω κὴ ἀπορίαν κατὰ σφραγῖδα, which can be translated as 'I inscribe this "blocking spell" with a seal' (trans. Gager 1992: 8). Other possible terms are found on other tablets: for example, 'the lead' is found on *DTA* 55, side A, l. 16; εὐχά (a prayer or boast) on an early tablet from Selinous, *SGD* 91 (although other commentators have read this as an invocation to the goddess of luck or chance, *Tuche*, of a kind often found at the beginning of public documents, cf. *SGD* 19 and *DTA* 158). See further discussion of relevant terms later in the chapter.

2. Objects: for example, Middle Proto-Korinthian II aryballos, 675–650 BCE inscribed 'I am the lekythos of Tataoa; whoever steals me shall become blind (London, BM 1185. 6–13. 1(A 1054), in Oakley 2004: 234 n. 38; in Greek epitaphs of Asia Minor, found on grave stelai from the fourth century BCE (see Strubbe 1991). Civic language: at the beginning of meetings of the Athenian Assembly against any misdirecting speaker: Dem. 19.70, Din. 2.16; by plaintiffs against themselves before they enter the homicide courts of the Areopagos (Dem. 23.67–8) or Palladion (Dem. 23.71, although Aeschin. 2.87 describes an oath being taken by the winner of the case, after its successful conclusion); Aeschin. I.114 implies that curses might be taken before other court cases. Faraone argues for the use of conditional curses, especially in military circumstances, reinforced with rituals of sympathetic magic, e.g. Xen. *An.* 2.4; Herodotos 8.132.2; Aesch. *Sept.* ll. 43–54, parodied by Aristophanes *Lys.* 189. The citizens of Teos publicly cursed anyone who might wish them harm (*c.*470 BCE; ML 30); curses apparently made at Kyrene's foundation to protect the settlement agreements were reported by the fourth-century Theran embassy to Kyrene (ML 5). Nestor's cup (late Geometric; ML 1/*CEG* 454); see Osborne 1996: 116 ff. For an alternative view, see

Faraone 1996. For the early date of conditional curses, and evidence for them being part of the drift of religious technology from the East into Greece, see Faraone 1993 and Johnston 2004: 349 ff.
3. Among the judicial curses, SGD 89 provides a rare example of this intent from this period. Later curses more frequently describe more gruesome intentions (e.g. *DT* 93 and 129).
4. A series of seven tablets from Morgantina (SGD 116–1; three of which are too damaged to read) seem to have been written against a woman called Venusta, using a variety of expressions to hand her over to the underworld powers. There is some debate as to whether they are all to be counted as curses or some of them are better described as 'pious prayers' (see Nabers 1966: 67; SGD 179–80 and Jordan 1980: 236–8 and Faraone 1991*a*: 18–20). For figurines, see note 61 and discussion in the text.
5. Lead as appropriate for writing to the dead, because of its physical properties, see for example, Wünsch, *DTA*, pp. ii–iii, but now unlikely in the light of evidence that other materials were used (see Graf 1997*a*: 131 and Gager 1992: 31 n. 5 for examples of curses written on a variety of materials, including copper, tin, *ostraka*, limestone, talc, papyrus, and gemstones). Among the curse collections: *DT* 196 is made from bronze; *DTA* 55 describes the creation of tablets in lead and wax. The *Greek Magical Papyri* includes recipes using gold or silver (*PGM* x. 24–35) or iron (*PGM* IV. 2145 ff.); *Suppl. Mag.* 44 is written on a scrap of linen. Plato (*Leg.* 933a–c) mentions moulded images of wax left at crossroads or in graveyards. For lead as cheap and available, see Jordan 1980: 226–9 for an overview of ancient Greek texts inscribed on lead tablets, including private letters and financial documents.
6. Jordan 1988: 273–4 and SGD 1 and 2.
7. Evidence for oral practice includes the binding curse apparently uttered by the Erinyes or Furies in Aeschylus' *Eumenides* (l. 306 ff.; cf. Faraone 1985) and discussed more fully in Eidinow 2007. *DTA* 108 (Attika, second or third century BCE) and SGD 150 (Kyrene, second century BCE) are composed in hexameters; cf. Faraone 1995 and the use of the 'performative future' in ritual contexts, in particular binding curses.

Faraone also suggests that Pindar's *Olympian* 1.75–8, in which Pelops prays to Poseidon to bind the spear of Oenomaos, may be an even earlier example of a curse that impedes another's performance in a competition. However, this is unlikely to represent a binding curse of the kind found in *katadesmoi* since the verb used, πέδαω, is not found on curse tablets. It may suggest that earlier curses made in the context of sporting events were verbal in form, rather than written—but there are written judicial curses from this period and it is not clear why curses from sporting contexts might be different.
8. The Erinyes say (303): οὐδ' ἀντιφωνεῖς, ἀλλ' ἀποπτύεις λόγους; 'You do not reply, but spurn [my] words . . .' and go on (306) ὕμνον δ' ἀκούσηι τόνδε

δέσμιον σέθεν. 'You will listen to my song by which I will bind you' (see Sommerstein 1989: 136 for use of objective genitive σέθεν). The Furies may mean that Orestes is not listening to them, or that he is about to be unable to resort to words. The scholia vetera offer this explanation: οὐκ ἀποκρίνῃ. ἢ ἀντὶ τοῦ οὐδὲ ἀντιφωνήσεις μοι ἀλλὰ σοῦ βουλομένου λαλεῖν τὸ φθέγμα δεθήσεται ('You do not reply. Or in place of this: you will not reply to me, although you want to speak, your voice will be bound'). Faraone (1985) suggests that it represents either an early form of written binding curse, or an oral type of a sort that existed prior to the written versions. I would suggest that, as with the development of the use of writing in other areas of life, it is more likely that oral and written practice coexisted (as Thomas 1992: 45 ff.). This is supported by instructions for the creation and deposition of curse tablets found in the *Greek Magical Papyri* (e.g. *PGM* IV. 296–466) in which the practitioner is told to intone certain words as he or she deposits a curse tablet.

9. A curse composed in dactylic hexameters: *DTA* 108 (cited Johnston 1999: 76 n. 119). Cf. Faraone 1985 n. 21: lists the following spoken and written curses working simultaneously: *PGM* IV. 325–35, V. 314 ff., VII. 429 ff., XXXVI. 161 ff.. Faraone (1991*a*: 4–5 and n. 19) mentions a cache of blank curse tablets (listed at *DT* 109, but since disappeared) nailed through and buried, which might also indicate that, in some cases, the curse itself was delivered orally alongside a nailing/burial ritual. However, he notes David Jordan's suspicion of their original description—and the fact that they have now disappeared. The later *Greek Magical Papyri* continues to include instructions for the creation of curses that include both spoken and written ritual.

10. Pl. *Resp.* 364c–e; cf. *PGM* IV. 2176–7; *Leg.* 933a.

11. Thanks to Simon Hornblower for bringing this to my attention.

12. Most of the 1600 curse tablets are written in Greek, although there are ongoing discoveries of large numbers of late Latin *katadesmoi*, especially in Britain. These numbers from Ogden (1999: 4) and Faraone (1991*a*: 22). There are some problems of identification: for example, the 436 inscribed lead tablets listed in Audollent as *DT* 45 each comprise a single different name; they show little sign of manipulation or any nail holes. Although Audollent included them in his collection, other scholars believe they were probably used for counting or registration of some kind, and are not curse tablets. Of the Greek material, *DTA* has 220 examples (all Attic Greek); *DT* contains 166 tablets (and 137 in languages other than Greek); while 'SGD' lists another 189 published examples and reports the existence of a further 461 tablets which have not yet been published; 'NGCT' lists 122.

13. However, as noted in Chapter 1 n. 61, it is extremely difficult to date these texts so tablets tend to be dated very generally, and even then dates can vary widely between scholars. Moreover, a number of the earliest excav-

ated curse tablets have now disappeared, so they cannot be re-dated using modern methods.
14. For the theory that the study of the arts of rhetoric originated in Sicily (beginning with Korax and Tisias, then Empedokles, who taught Gorgias) and subsequently appeared in Athens, see Cic. *Brut.* 46–8; Radermacher 1951, sect. V ('Initia Vera'), pp. 11–27, and Kennedy 1994: 11 ff.
15. As noted, I will be focusing on those tablets dated to the period of the sixth to first centuries BCE. After this period, there is a change in both the composition and character of curse tablets: they show greater syncretism, much more aggression, and a wider remit. For a discussion of how curse tablets change over time, see Ogden 1999: 6 ff.
16. Other texts in which the writer identifies him- or herself (from these few examples we know of a number of women who wrote curses): for example, 'Pausanias' names himself on a tablet from Akanthos, Makedonia (see Jordan 1999, no. 3); 'Phila' on a curse found in Pella, Makedonia (see Voutiras 1998); in *DT* 5, 'Prosodion' curses the unnamed woman who has seduced her husband; Onesime may have written *DTA* 100, a curse text from fourth-century Attika. Wünsch(1897) thought so and Versnel (1991*a*: 65) agrees, but this is debatable, as Parker 2005*b*: 126 n. 42 observes). A number of judicial tablets seem to mention the names of those who wrote them—or at least, of those who are facing legal difficulties, e.g. *DTA* 88, SGD 6 and *DT* 44.
17. Cache examples: *DT* 18–21 are four of some 60 fragmentary Greek inscriptions inscribed on talc found at Hagios Tychonas (ancient Amathous) that seem to show the same formulae and share a writer; a further 200 fragmentary tablets (of which 16 have been published, erroneously ascribed to Kourion, Kypros, but actually from Amathous). See Aupert and Jordan 1981: 184, who date the tablets to the second century CE and report 'We now have more texts written by this scribe than by any other magician . . . They give us some idea of his working method: certain trivial errors in the texts imply that he was copying from a papyrus(?) formulary.' Further examples: see Jordan SGD 160 ff. (tablets) and 1988: 276 (dolls). Plato's professional curse salesmen: *Resp.* 364c–e; see above, p. 141.
18. More illiterate inscribing: *DT* 85, SGD 48, 173.
19. *DT*, p. 101; the target of *DT* 73, a curse found in the same location, also curses the victims' hopes.
20. Political figures: *DTA* 11, 24, 30, 42, 47–50, 57, 65, and 84; litigants: *DTA* 39, 66, 94, etc.; actor: *DTA* 45; chorus members, chorus leaders, and trainers: *DTA* 33 and 34; doctors: SGD 124; NGCT 24; neighbours: *DTA* 25; lovers: SGD 57; children: *DT* 47; sex-workers: SGD 48, 109; soldiers: *DTA* 55; slaves: *DTA* 75; craftsmen: potters, SGD 44; silver bellows-workers, SGD 3 and 4; a seamstress, SGD 72; a ship's pilot, SGD 170; a helmet-maker and his wife, a gold-worker, *DTA* 69; a cloth-maker

and what may be a wooden-frame maker or a rope-maker, *DTA* 87; a pipe-maker and a carpenter, *DTA* 55; *DTA* 68 provides a selection of professions including a pimp, sex-workers of various kinds, a boxer, a miller, There are a number of tablets that mention innkeepers, for example: *DTA* 30, 68, 87, SGD 11.
21. Gordon 1999a; see above, as discussed in Chapter 1.
22. Faraone 1991*a*; this is a simplification of his own four categories, which are, in turn, a simplification of Kagarow's five categories (1929: 44–9). Faraone (1991*a*: 5) suggests that Attic curses that mention only the name of the intended victim steadily decrease in frequency until they disappear in the first century CE, while complex formulae become more popular in later periods. The opposite appears to be the case with the older curse tablets from Selinous, where lists of names become more common towards the end of the fifth century, while more complex formulae appear earlier, see Curbera 1999: 165.
23. Names and body parts *passim*; workshop in *DTA* 68, 75 (and *emporion*), SGD 124; tools in *DT* 52, *DTA* 73; marriage in a curse from Pella, Makedonia (see Chapter 11); thoughts in *DT* 52; hopes in *DT* 73.
24. Wünsch, *DTA*, p. iii: short for (κατα)δῶ ἥλοις 'I fix with nails' (cf. Pind. *Pyth.* 4.71); noted by Faraone (1991*a*: 24 n. 24). But nailing the tablet was surely a symbolic action, intended to reinforce the larger intention of attempting to impose a restraint, some kind of disabling control over something the writer of the curse perceived to be a threat. See below, n. 32, for further discussion of the example of *DT* 49, which suggests that nailing and binding were two separate activities.
25. καταδεσμεύω NGCT 24; καταδηνύω *DTA* 75; κατέχω *DTA* 109.
26. Gal. *De Simplic. Medic. Temp.* 10.1.
27. *IG* iv. 1299; Powell 1925: 68–71. For direct parallels between this description and the texts of contemporary *katadesmoi* see Engelmann (1975: 53–4). For text and references, see Faraone 1991*a*: 19–20.
28. Cic. *Brut.* 217; Lib. *Or.* 1.245–9, explored in more detail in Chapter 9 on judicial curses.
29. See n. 4 above.
30. Later, the two reinforcing rituals merge, somewhat gruesomely, and there are myriad examples of stories, spells, and even actual examples, of dolls, and even animals, that are ritually nailed. Examples of stories include: Lib. *Or.* I. 243–50; *Narratio Miraculorum Sanctorum Cyri et Joannis* (cf. Faraone 1991a: 9). Of dolls, the most famous example is the Louvre figurine. (See SGD 152, *Suppl. Mag.* 47 for text; Kambitsis 1976, *SEG* 26. 1717.) This is a young woman on her knees, hands bound behind her back, and pierced with 13 nails. It was found together with a lead inscription bearing a curse similar to a spell in the Greek Magical Papyri (*PGM* IV. 335–84, which also seems to have been a model for a number of other curse tablets; see discussion in Gager 1992: 97, nos 27 and 28).

The instructions in the *PGM* spell probably provided the model for the creation of the figurine, although it is not inscribed as that recipe instructs (ll. 296–329; cf. Kambitsis 1976).

31. Cited by Graf 1997a: n. 56, but wrongly labelled there as *DTA*, no. 49; the tablet is no. 49 in *DT* and Wünsch 1900, no. 10.
32. See discussion on binding and nailing Graf 1997a: 135 ff. With regard to *DT* 49, he asks if binding indicates a separate physical action: 'Is this [binding] really a separate rite—perhaps the tablets were tied with a thread of organic matter that left no trace in the soil? Or is it only the summing up of the three following actions, so that "making disappear, burying and nailing down" together constitute the act of "binding"?'
33. These verbs are most usually found in early Sicilian tablets and only occasionally in Attic tablets (see Faraone 1991a: 24 n. 20).
34. These do not appear in judicial tablets of the period studied here. Graf (1997a: 124) also notes among later Greek tablets verbs meaning 'to adjure' ὁρκίζω and ἐξορκίζω (a rare early appearance in SGD 81?) and among tablets in Latin, the derivative *ligare*, *alligare*, and *obligare* and the verbs *dedicare* and *demandere* 'to dedicate' and *adiurare* 'to entreat'.
35. Versnel (1991a: 73) compares the use of verbs of similar sense on the Knidian tablets (*DT* 1–13); Faraone (1991a: 10) finds contemporary parallels in the inscriptions on two Attic grave *stelai* (*IG* ii². 13209–10) that hand over the two markers to the control of the underworld gods; and a Kretan tablet, dated to the Imperial period that also places a nearby gravestone under the gods' control.
36. See also SGD 54, location unknown, undated, which, according to Jordan's reading, mentions a gift. It may be, as interpreted by Faraone (1991a: 24 n. 15), that the victim is being offered to the gods of the underworld as a gift, or that the gift is intended to persuade the gods to do the agent's bidding. SGD 109, from Lilybaion, Sicily, second century BCE, uses a similar gift formula, but (as Jordan says 1985: 177) its significance is not clear from the published text.
37. Gordon (1999a: 257) discusses the significance of the use of lists, see above n. 21 and Chapter 1, n. 59. A further example of this mimicking of public documents is the use of the phrase Θεοὶ ἀγαθὴ τύχη, which is regularly used in public inscriptions and which opens at least one curse tablet (SGD 18) and, as we have seen, a number of the oracle tablets.
38. Athens' first city archive was built at the end of the fifth century, probably to organize the accumulated documents and inscriptons of the democracy. Evidence for the first written contract (Isok. *Trapez.* 17. 20) dates from the first decade of the fourth century. In the courts, changes in terminology indicate that complaints at the preliminary hearing (*anakrisis*) that were originally made orally were, by the time of Demosthenes, being made by the litigant himself, in writing; the earliest evidence for the reading out of written testimony in court dates to

around the late 390s (Isai. 5. 2); see Thomas 1992: 41–5. That alphabetic literacy is not a neutral skill that transforms a society, but is used to support cultural practice, see Thomas 1992: 26. She also argues (p. 31) that, from as early as the Archaic period, there was likely to have been a strong cultural association between public documents and communication with the gods (e.g. temple dedications and sacred laws). On commercial letters, see Thomas 1992: 73.

39. Cf. Dubois 1989: 152 ff., no. 134.
40. *Pherephattei, Pherrephatta, Phersephassa* are all versions of the name of the goddess Persephone.
41. Examples from among many: an Attic tablet of uncertain date (*DTA* 85) binds its victims *pros ton Hermen* 'before Hermes'; *DT* 68 binds its victims in the presence of Hermes of the underworld, the dead, and Tethys.
42. A couple of examples of the formula are: *DTA* 89, Attic, fourth century BCE, begins Δέσποτα Ἑρμῆ, κάτοχε κάτεχε Φ(ρύ)νιχ. *DTA* 105, Attic third century BCE, begins Ἐ]ρμῆ χθ[ό]νιε καταδε[δέσθω Πυθοτέ]λης πρὸς τὸν Ἑ[ρμῆν τὸν χθόνιον καὶ τὴν Ἑκάτην τὴν χθονίαν.
43. Examples: as above *DTA* 105; *SGD* 170 provides a splendid range of chthonian gods, including Hermes, Hekate, Pluto, the white goddess, Persephone, and Demeter. Regarding the debate on the existence or not of a group of specifically 'chthonian' (literally 'of the earth', but translated here 'of the underworld') gods, distinct from the 'heavenly or Olympian' gods, suffice it to say that distinguishing gods—or personifications of gods—with chthonian characteristics is obviously not a question of identifying evil or even sinister divinities from good, and the earth is associated not just with darkness and the underworld, but with growth and the natural cycle of fertility. Different gods have greater or lesser chthonian aspects that demonstrate different traits and demand different kinds of mortal attention. See Jameson, *BCH* (1965), 159–65; Scullion *ZPE* 132 (2000), 163–71; R. Parker 2005*a*: 126 and 424 for discussion and further references.
44. Hermes *Katochos*: *DTA* 100, *SGD* 75; Demeter: *SGD* 60; Persephone: *SGD* 42, 75; Ge: *DT* 69; Ge *Katoche*: *SGD* 75. On Hermes *Chthonios*: Parker 2005*a*: 296 and Sourvinou-Inwood 1995: 304 ff. Sourvinou-Inwood argues that this personification excapsulates a new role for Hermes that differentiates Homeric from fifth-century beliefs about the dead and access to Hades.
45. LSJ s.v. *Palaimon*, a child of Ino (and murdered by his mother), who according to Paus. (1.44.7, 2.1.3) and Apollodoros (*Bibl.* 3.4.3) was posthumously renamed Palaimon; the Isthmian games were established in his honour (see R. M. Newton, 'Ino in Euripides' Medea', *AJP* 106, no. 4: 496–502).
46. The name of the sea-goddess Ino, described by Homer as 'once a woman, but now living in the depths of the salt sea' and cited by the chorus in

Euripides' *Medea* as they search for a precedent for Medea's killing of her children. Ino, in this story, was driven mad by Hera, killed her children, and leaped into the sea (Newton: *AJP* 499 and above). LSJ s.v. *leukothea Od.* 5.334 and Pind. *Pyth.* 11.2.
47. Literally 'twister', usually used of Hermes to mean 'standing as porter at the door-hinges' but it could mean here 'who wears the girdle' coming from *strophēs*.
48. See Johnston 1999.
49. Voutiras 1998.
50. Gager 1992: 131 n. 35; also Voutiras 1999.
51. *DT* 44 uses much the same formula—and the same corpse—to target another legal team and Voutiras introduces for comparison another, later text that calls on the more familiar *daimon Abrasax* using a similar formula (Voutiras 1999: 78; *SEG* 40. 919).
52. However, Voutiras argues 'although they [the writers of these curses] treat them as lifeless corpses for the purpose of sympathetic magic that will render the *defixio* powerless, the operants must have felt that the spirits of the dead could become powerful and are potentially dangerous *daimones* of the nether world'.
53. Audollent (*DT*) drew on Ziebarth (1899, no. 16) to translate it as 'the uninitiated', relating it to the mysteries that some individuals went through to ease their journey in the afterlife and referring the reader to *Phaedo* 69c where Plato describes the suffering of those who arrive in Hades uninitiated. Audollent quotes Wünsch's justification of the inclusion of Tethys—whose chthonic nature was particularly suitable in the context of an appeal to the ἀτελέστοι. Graf (1997*a*: 150–1) holds that it means those who have not reached their goal of marriage and Gager 1992: 90, no. 22, drawing on LSJ, also translates both ἀτελής and ἀτελέστοι as meaning 'unmarried', but this meaning is not found elsewhere for either term (see Johnston 1999: 78 n. 127). Jameson, Jordan, and Kotansky (1993: 131) propose that it means those who have not received τέλη, or proper funeral rites, from the living after their death. Cf. Soph. *Ant.* 998–1032; Hom. *Od.* 11. 72–6 and a fourth-century gold tablet which assures the dead woman in whose grave it was found that 'you will expect beneath the earth what τέλεα the other blessed (dead) expect' (see Jordan, 'A Note on a Gold Tablet from Thessaly', *Horos*, 7 (1989), 129–30). Graf (1994, the French edition: 153) argues that the graves of the uninitiated would not have been marked; Johnson (ibid.) responds that 'this does not carry much weight, as we cannot assume that the graves of the untimely dead would have always been marked as such, either'. However, it is possible that the graves of unmarried men and women were marked with *loutrophoroi* (e.g. see Oakley 2004: 27 (Athens National Museum 1975) and 74 (Museum of Fine Arts, Boston, 03.800) for images on white-ground lekythoi that depict such a use of this vessel),

or with a stele inscribed with an appropriate poem (e.g. a young woman called Thersis is commemorated in a poem composed by Anyte, *AP* 7.649, which is likely to have been inscribed on the tomb, see Snyder 1989: 68, cf. *AP* 7.486, 490, and 646; for Attic grave markers for women from the late fifth century onwards, see Osborne 1998: 195 ff.). Local knowledge may also have provided information for a curse writer or salesman about graves suitable for curse burial.

54. Earliest form of analogical magic: Jameson, Jordan, and Kotansky 1993: 130. Earliest appeal to the dead: noted by Johnston 1999: 73. ἀτε[λ]ής also found in *DTA* 98, *SGD* 99.
55. Theodora as *hetaira* cursed by a rival courtesan: Dickie 2000: 576.
56. See, just for example, the erotic spells collected in *Suppl. Mag.* many of which begin by invoking a spirit of the dead, or *nekuodaimon*, to do their bidding; alongside chthonic gods and daimons, no. 45 calls on the 'untimely dead youths'; no. 46 invokes 'men and women who suffered an untimely death, youths and maidens'.
57. Jordan (1988: 273) does say 'in every period of antiquity when we have been able to estimate the ages of the dead who have curse tablets in their graves … those ages have proved to be young', but in *SGD* 152 he draws attention to the fact that 'In only a very few cases, however, has it been possible to test this theory, for the ages of skeletons with which *katadesmoi* have been found are seldom reported and the burials are seldom adequately described.' (This point also made by Parker 2005*a*: 128 n. 48.) Pl. (*Leg.* 933b2–3) describes how people are disturbed by seeing wax figurines left on the graves of their ancestors, which might suggest that some of the graves involved were of those who had lived long enough to have children (this point noted by Johnston 1999: 75 n. 118).
58. The similarity of their formulae may suggest that, despite the different dates once allotted to them, they were created by the same writer—either an extremely litigious individual who wrote his own tablets, or a curse salesman who created them for different clients. Either way, they seem to have been crafted from the same semantic model, so if the dating is correct, it is a neat example of the survival of particular formulae.
59. *SGD* 100, also from Selinous, is very fragmentary, but appears to have a similar shape and content (Gàbrici 1927, no. 13).
60. Examples of tongue-twisting analogies in *SGD* 99, 100, and 108. Moraux turned to the philosophical/scientific literature of ancient Greece to examine the significance of coldness, finding that it represented fear and lack of vitality (1960: 49): 'c'est également pour annihiler l'ardeur combattive de l'adversaire et le purer de ses moyens d'attaque que l'on prie les dieux de lui "refroider"'. Text written on a tablet shaped like a foot on *SGD* 87; on a tablet possibly shaped like a tongue, *SGD* 86. Scrambled text is found on *SGD* 95, and letters written backwards on *DT* 60.

61. SGD 9 (Athens, early fourth century); NGCT 11–13 (Athens, Kerameikos cemetery; early fourth century).
62. Appears to be middle (perish) of ὄλλυμαι, but the ending is puzzling. If plural it should be -νται, if singular -νται. If either are right, then the verb appears to be in the indicative, not the subjunctive or optative cases, usually used to express a wish. But *SEG* 4.31: 8/9 argues that [ὄλ]λυστα[ι = ὄλλυσθαι, in which case this is an example of an infinitive used as the second-person imperative.
63. Examples of the different ways in which wives and children may be cursed on these tablets: *DTA* 55 ('wives and children' added at the end of the curse); *DTA* 77 (Kallistrate, the wife of Theophemos, is the focus of the curse, as are her children); *DTA* 102 (the wife is the focus of the curse and her three children); SGD 91 (the fathers and children of the victim are cursed, discussed in detail, below, p. 157 ff.). Of course, in those tablets that mention *paides* in the context of work or a workshop, 'slaves' may be meant, for example, *DT* 52 (Theon's children cursed alongside his tools and workshop); *DT* 92 ('may they and their children be destroyed'). For curses that target women's genitals see Appendix 2.
64. Translation Voutiras 1998.
65. Is this name related to the name of the local tribe? LSJ s.v. *Maiotis* (Ion. *Maietai*) a Skythian tribe to the north of the Black Sea (Hdt. 4.123, Xen. *Mem.* 2.1.10).
66. Lib. *Or.* 1.245–9.
67. *Narratio Miraculorum Sanctorum Cyri et Joannis* (discussed by Faraone 1991*a*: 9).
68. Looked upon with dread: Plato, *Leg.* 933b1–4: see above, n. 57; also note the concerns of Theophrastos' Superstitious Man, Chapter 3 above.
69. Illegality: Versnel (1991*a*: 62–3) believes the secrecy surrounding this practice indicated that it was thought shameful; Faraone (1991*a*: 17) is not so sure, and argues that this secrecy was primarily about stopping victims from finding out and taking steps to avert the force of the curse. There is nothing in the Classical Greek law codes about *katadesmoi*. However, a citizen of Athens who believed that someone had used magic to harm him could presumably bring a *dikē blabēs* (Pl. *Leg.* 932e6–933a5 believes that damage caused by magic is a *blabē*); or if he believed that *pharmaka* (which can mean poison, but is also used of spells and curses) had been used to commit or attempt to commit a murder this could go before the Areopagos ([Arist.] *Ath. Pol.* 57.3; cf. the Teian curses, see n. 2 above) or he could presumably bring a *graphē asebeias* (for example, Gordon 1999*b*: 250 suggests that the case against Theoris, see above pp. 253–4, was a *graphē asebeias* (Plut. *Dem.* 14.4 and [Dem.] 25.79 f.)).
70. Pl. *Leg.* 932e6–a5.
71. Envy appears consistently across cultures in local explanations of bad luck caused by malevolent supernatural attack.

72. There are numerous descriptions in Greek literature of such vicious dynamics (see Pl. *Laws* 731a; Pind. *Pyth.* 11.28; Eur. *Supp.* 240–42, Eur. *Med.* 290–97, *El.* 900 ff. for a few examples). For the link between vicious gossip and charges of witchcraft made more explicitly, see the Conclusion.
73. Agonistic: Faraone 1991*a*; powerlessness: as noted, Faraone on the underdog, see above in the Introduction and n. 12 there. He argues that they were likely to have been a last defence of the 'perennial underdog . . . protecting himself against otherwise insurmountable odds' (1991*a*: 20) but himself admits there is no proof of this; also Graf 1997*a*: 157.
74. *DTA* 68 provides a good example of how difficult and tentative a process this can be. This curse tablet is concerned repeatedly with the hands, feet, tongues, and workshops of its targets, and becomes classed as judicial only because, in its tenth line, it includes most of the word μάρτυρας.
75. Faraone 1991*a*.
76. The following scholars at least divide the tablets this way: Jordan (at Versnel 1991*a*: 62); Faraone 1991*a*: 10 and 16, Gager 1992: 42–199, and Graf 1997*a*: 141–2.
77. Versnel 1991*a*: 64.
78. Cf. the remarks of Faraone 1991*a*: 17.

CHAPTER 8

1. The quotation is part of an explanation by the ethnographer Jeanne Favret-Saada of the power of words in the practice of witchcraft among the inhabitants of the Bocage (a term used to describe some of the countryside of western France, characterized by small fields divided by tall hedgerows).
2. SGD 91 is dated to around 450 BCE; *DTA* 33 and 34, which are thought to be by the same person, are dated to approximately the fourth or third century BCE; while *DTA* 45 is, according to Wünsch, from the third century BCE, although Gager (1992: 50, no. 2) expands on this and states that it is hardly likely to be later than the second century BCE. All appear to have been created in the context of theatrical performance.
3. Graf (1997*a*: 155) calls these agonistic spells, stating that he is using the definitions created by Faraone (1991*a*). Faraone uses this label to describe all *katadesmoi*, since, he argues (1991*a*: 11) that 'an essential feature of all four types is that they refer to agonistic relationships, that is, relationships between rival tradesmen, lovers, litigants, or athletes concerned with the outcome of some future event'.
4. For example: Jordan (1985: 211 ff.) lists six tablets targeting athletes, excavated from a Roman well (well V), in the Athenian Agora, and dated 'late Roman' (the well was in use from the second half of the first to the first half of the third century CE); *DT* 15 appears to be a curse against rival pantomime actors, dated to the third century CE; SGD 167, a late

second- or early third-century CE tablet, curses a long list of rival horses and their drivers. Later examples of curses against actors include: second-century CE curse against the mime Eumolpos (see Versnel 1985: 247–8, and 269); SGD 167 refers to an unpublished Korinthian curse which targets a 'retired(?) mimic actress'.
5. As mentioned, Pind. *Ol.* 1.75–8 may offer the earliest example of a curse impeding another's performance in a competition, but see discussion in Ch. 7, n. 7.
6. Faraone (1991*a*: 16) drawing on Brown (1972): 'This connection between athletic and political competition is not limited to later antiquity; in classical Athens intertribal competitions—albeit in a much less organized fashion—often provided arenas for intracity rivalries, where victories in theatrical performances and even athletic events could be interpreted as indicators of the waxing or waning of the political power of the liturgists involved ... by inhibiting the performance of actors and athletes, the *defigens* could conceivably restrain the political power of their backers and undermine their popularity with their fans, often their only source of political influence.' See also Gager 1992: 76.
7. Gager 1992: 50.
8. Inscriptions listing winning actors: the Fasti *IG* ii². 2318, the *Didaskaliai* and the Victor Lists; see Csapo and Slater 1995: 40 ff. Aristotle, *Rhet.* 1403^{b}31–5, mentions the budding status of actors in passing, as he protests about how 'just as in the theatre, the actors are now more important than poets, so it is in the political contests, because of the degeneracy of the citizens'. Much later, Hesychios and Photios (s.v. νέμεσις ὑποκριτῶν) and the *Suda* (s.v. νέμεσεις ὑποκριτῶν) tell us that 'the poets used to get three actors assigned by lot to act the dramas. Of these the winner was entered in the competition of the following year, bypassing the preliminary selection'.
9. W. C. West (1999: 206) reports, 'A likely scenario is that the tablet was first used as a document in a case in court, after which it was returned to the originator, who was either a litigant himself or someone who testified (by deposition) in behalf of the litigant.'
10. Dubois 1989: 152 ff., no. 134 and Jordan's revised translation supplied in Gager 1992: 76.
11. It is not clear how much of this latter text draws on the work of A. P. Miller 1973, no. 36.
12. Gager (1992: 77 n. 129) suggests that the post was probably inherited though he gives no evidence for assuming that there is a family tradition involved in this profession. However, as observed above, curses that target family members are common.
13. I find Gager's explanation of Jordan/Miller's translation difficult to follow. He notes (1992: 77) that what he provides is 'close to a translation proposed by Miller in her discussion but not included in the translation

proper' because she believes it raises problems of interpretation 'namely, the other *chorēgoi* might have known about the *katadesmos* and the literary contest might thus have been subject to "forcible persuasion or even, perhaps, sabotage"'. Gager concludes that there must have been some public knowledge of this (type of) curse tablet, and suggests that after all, a *katadesmos* is 'an attempt to change things by force, persuasion, and sabotage'. Dubois (1989: 157) suggests the translation: *Tous ceux qui dans mon entourage pourraient me laisser tomber.* Although in the text he translates: *tous ceux de mon entourage qui pourraient me laisser tomber* (p. 159).

14. This construction of the verb ἀπογράφω, which seems likely to mean 'to register', has prompted much discussion. Since the writer consistently uses it with this meaning here, could it simply be that he has made a mistake?
15. Jordan and Miller's interpretation of this section actually fits better with Dubois' interpretation of the first couple of lines that Apelles wants everyone to share in his feelings for Eunikos. It sits oddly with their own interpretation of the text that Apelles wants Eunikos to praise and love him.
16. Liturgies were tasks allotted to members of the elite that channelled their wealth into particular services for the city. *Chorēgoi* for (each of the men and boys') dithyrambic competitions were chosen by each of the ten *phylai* or tribes of Athens from among volunteers (Wilson 2000: 22); for performances of tragedy and comedy, they were appointed from among the wealthiest citizens. Other festival-related liturgies, included supplying a banquet (*hestiasis*) or producing a team for an athletic competition (*gymniasarchy*). The other type of liturgy was the *trierarchy*, which involved funding a ship in the navy. Davies (1981*a*: 9): 'Even the cheapest liturgy cost nearly as much as a contemporary skilled workman was paid in a year.' See Csapo and Slater (1995: 141) on the evidence for the cost of dramatic liturgies given in Lysias 19 and 21: 'The resulting figures show that Athens, at war, and fighting for its very survival, spent on a single dramatic festival an amount equivalent to the total annual expenditure on one-tenth of its navy.'
17. [Xen.] *Ath. Pol.* 22.5, Isok. *Antid.*, Theophrastos, *Oligarchic Man* 26.5–6, cf. Christ 1998, Fisher 2001: 187 ff., Davies 1981*a*: 96. Alkibiades explicitly states that his *chorēgiai* have aroused *phthonos* in his debate with Nikias (Thuc. 6.16). The idea that such *phthonos* was a real threat, not an elite fantasy, is seen in Dem. 20, in which the speaker argues against the Law of Leptines that proposed the abolition of immunity from festival liturgies on the grounds that the city must preserve trust and that this would be seen as the people indulging their *phthonos* (20.10). Definitions of *phthonos* are found in Arist. *Rhet.*: *Phthonos*, or 'envy', is 'a disturbing pain resulting from the well-being of another' (2.9, 1386^{b}18–19) not, however, out of a desire to have something oneself but simply that the other not have it (2.10, 1387^{b}23–4) (elaborated by Konstan 2001: 13).

18. The right kind of *philotimia*: see Lys. 16.18; 21 and 26.3. Speakers in court frequently refer to the idea that their performances in their liturgical duties have been undertaken with brilliance: see Antiph. 2.b.12; Dem. 21.159; 45.78. It is one of Aristotle's marks of a man who shows *megaloprepeia* (Arist. *Nik. Eth.* 1122^{a}34, 1122^{b}35, 1122^{b}23, 1123^{a}20; *Ath. Pol.* 27.3).
19. For example, Lysias (26.3) attacks Evandros' claim of exemplary public service.
20. There are many examples of the topos of *charis*, a sample include: Lys. 3.47, 6.48, 49; Dem. 18.257, 21. 151–9, 25. 76–8, 34.24; Isok. 16.35, 18.58; Isai. 4.27, Lyk. 1.139. It may even have played a part in enabling success in other spheres of leadership. Sokrates of Anagyrous was a candidate for ostracism in 443; but following his successful *chorēgia* for a tragic chorus (commemorated on *IG* i^3. 969), he was elected to high military office in 441/0. Wilson (2000: 133–4) thinks it likely that Sokrates performed the role of *koryphaios* himself.
21. Plut. *Mor.* 349b; *IG* ii^2. 1138; the two fragments *IG* ii^2. 1139 and *Hesperia* 22 no. 1; *IG* ii^2. 1147; *IG* ii^2. 1157, and perhaps 1158.
22. Alkibiades: Plut. *Alk.* 16, [And.] 4.20–1; Demosthenes and Meidias: Dem. 21; *chorēgos* accused of murder, Antiphon 6 (for a useful analysis, see Wilson 2000: 116–20).
23. Fisher 1998.
24. Wilson 2000: 174 ff.
25. This may be why the *chorēgos* was allowed to impose fines or levy distraint by force (Antiph. 6.11).
26. Aeschin. *In Tim.* 9 ff.: attests a law that a *chorēgos* in charge of a chorus of boys must be over 40 years of age 'in order that he has reached the more temperate period of his life' so that he is deemed able to resist the sexual temptations of his charges.
27. Dubois (1989: 156) states emphatically that this is not a question of liturgy. Miller suggests that the meaning of *chorēgos* here need not point to Eunikos being a wealthy patron (as the position of *chorēgos* at Athens would suggest), but might rather indicate that he was a trainer of the chorus (Miller 1973, cited by Gager 1992: 77). Wilson (2000: 357 n. 34) is undecided.
28. Kleandros set up a tyranny in 505 BCE, overthrowing the previous oligarchy (acc. to Arist. *Pol.* 1316^{a}37). He was succeeded by his brother Hippokrates, possibly after some difficulties. After his death (on campaign in Hybla in 491), the Geloans revolted against tyranny and there was a civil war (cf. Dunbabin 1948: 378). Gelon fought a victorious battle on behalf of Hippokrates' under-age sons, then overthrew them and set up as tyrant (Hdt. 7.155). In 478 he was succeeded by Hieron at Syrakuse and Polyzalos at Gela.
29. Greek settlers used familiar cultural institutions, in particular *choroi*,

to help establish the socio-political structures of their new cities and 'to stake their claims to the territory and its traditions through authorising aetiologies, to forge connections with and to delineate differences from the cults and traditions of their old homes', but the local culture may very well have developed its own independent tradition (Wilson 2000: 279 and 357 n. 34). We should be wary of a *post hoc propter hoc* treatment of our evidence that treats *chorēgia* as an Athenian export, and a democratic one at that. As Wilson (2000: 299) discusses, in the fourth century and later, there were many cities, with different political structures, which celebrated choral competitions sponsored by wealthy individuals.

The lead tablets found at Kamarina in 1987 (*SEG* 42. 846), which seem to suggest some kind of democratic reorganization around 460 BCE, include one that reads: '. . .keas Thrasys an Emmenid, the best in a song contest of the Dorystomphoi'. The Emmenids were a tyrannical family of Akragas; the Dorystomphoi were probably an elite military brotherhood. This may be a hangover from the older tyrannical regime (as Murray argues in 'Rationality and the Greek City: The Evidence from Kamarina', in V. Hansen (ed.), *The Polis as an Urban Centre and as a Political Community, Acts of the Copenhagen Polis Centre* 4 (Copenhagen, 1997)), or evidence of continuity under the new democratic arrangement (cf. Hornblower 2005: 191).

29. Gela: G. Nenci and G. Vallet (eds.), *Bibliografia Topografica della Colonizzazione Greca in Italia e nelle Isole Tirreniche*, 8 (Pisa, 1990), 5–65; Dunbabin 1948: *passim*.
30. We know that some forms of theatrical competition were being held in parts of western Greece, because of very brief statements about how they were judged. Some cite judges: Zenobios *Prov.* 3.62 (second century): ' "It lies on the knees of the five judges, proverbial for such things as are in the power of others. The proverb was used insofar as five judges judged the comic choruses, as Epicharmos says'; Hesych. s.v. πέντε κριταί (fifth century) 'five judges: so many judged the comic choruses not only in Athens but in Sicily'. (These references from Csapo and Slater 1995: 162.) Plato (*Leg.* 659a–c) cites a show of hands: 'The true judge should not learn from the audience nor be impressed by the noise of the many or by his own ignorance . . . It was possible for him according to the old Greek custom just as the present custom in Sicily and Italy to leave it to the majority of the audience and judge the winner by a show of hands' (Csapo and Slater 1995: 164). Aristotle, *Poet.* 1448^{a}28–40 discusses how the Megarians claim to be the inventors of comedy, and draws attention to the Megarians of Sicily, since the poet Epicharmos who was much earlier than Chionides and Mages came from there. As Csapo and Slater (1995: 3) suggest, the anecdotes found in Satyros, *Life of Euripides* (*POxy.* 1176, fr. 39, col. 19), that describe how the Athenians taken prisoner after the disastrous Syrakusan expedition of 415 BCE were saved by their

captors' love for Euripides, can scarcely be taken at face value, and are more likely to be an example of a trope 'culture saves the city' (e.g. Plut. *Vit. Lys.* 15). If we take it seriously it is not clear whether it is evidence of a great knowledge or a lack of tragic performance; cf. Plut. *Nik.* 29. Sicilian imports and local imitations of Attic terracotta figurines and vase paintings attest keen interest in Athenian drama from about 420 BCE (Csapo and Slater 1995: 4; Trendall 1991; Todisco 2002).

31. The number of trips made by Aeschylus to Sicily is uncertain. *Suda* s.v. Αἰσχύλος records his final visit, as does *Marm. Par.* The *Life of Aeschylus* (*Vit.*) 9–11 suggests three visits: (1) for the founding of the city of Aetna, for which he wrote *The Aitnaiai* (*Vit.* 9); (2) to produce a performance of *The Persai* (*Vit.* 18) and recorded as mentioned by Eratosthenes in the scholia to Ar. *Ran.* 1028; and, finally, to live, three years before he died and was buried at Gela (see further: Sommerstein 1996 and Griffith 1978).

32. A. Burnett, 'Jocasta in the West: The Lille Stesichorus', *CA* (1988), 107–54. Some of the festivals she lists include: Kroton, a lament for Achilles' sung by women dressed in black as part of a Hera festival, said to have been established by Thetis (Lyk. *Alex.* 856–8 and Tzetzes ad 856); mimed grief at Paestum (Aristox. ap. Ath. 14.632a = *FGrH* II 291 fr. 80 = 124 Wehrli[2]); Velia, a threnody sung for Leukothea (Arist. *Rhet.* 1400[b]); Lokrian women sing a funeral song for Ajax as they send off the maidens (Lyk. *Alex.* 1131 ff.); Taras, lamentations and rejoicing in honour of Hyakinthos (Polyb. 8.28.2); three-day celebration for Dionysos (Cass. Dio. 9 fr. 39.5; Pl. *Leg.* 637b). At Rhegion, for 60 days, male choruses sang paeans for Artemis Phakelitis. Aristoxenes of Taras explained that this was to thank Artemis for once curing the city's women of insanity. She demanded new songs each year: A. ends by saying 'This then is the reason why there are so many composers of paeans in Greek Italy' (*ap.* Apollon. *Mirab.* 40 = *FHG* II p. 282).

33. Representations of dancers that seem to allude to festival occasions include an Archaic bas-relief from the *temenos* of Demeter Malophoros at Selinous, where eight curse tablets have been found (see R. Ross Holloway, *Influences and Styles* (Louvain, 1975), 93 and fig. 123, noted by Burnett 1988: 145 n.).

34. Poets and dramatists: Miller 1973: 83–5 cited by Gager 1992: 77, n. 130; Aeschylus: *Life* 10 and 11; Pausanias: 5.25.2–5; on Gela, see Dunbabin 1948. Among the curse tablets found here is SGD 101, which includes one 'ἱστίαρχος'. Is this a name or does it indicate the holder of another liturgy, the *hestiasis*? Most commentators favour the name: the *LGPN* for Sicily lists five other entries, two on another curse tablet from the same site (SGD 103); another on a coin from Taras; and one more from Tauromenion *c.*154 BCE.

35. Wilson 2000: 338 n. 96 on Pollux 9.41–2 ('And they also called the *didaskaleion* "*khoros*", whenever they also used the word "*khoregos*" for

"*didaskalos*", and "to be a *khoregos*" for "to teach" (*didaskein*); and that was especially so with the Dorians, as Epicharmos shows in his *Odysseus the Deserter.*)' (referring to Epicharmos fr. 103 K–A).

36. D. Gilula in 'The Choregoi Vase—Comic Yes, but Angels?' *ZPE* (1995), 5–10; she argues that although the term is known to us from Roman comedy (she quotes Plautus, *Trinummus* 858 and *Persa* 159–60), it must have originated from Greek plays 'and the Greek performers from South Italy who transplanted them to Rome'. She quotes the use of the verb χορηγέω meaning 'I furnish and equip' as in Arist. *Triphales* 564.2 (K–A). Apulian krater: New York, Fleischmann coll. F93.
37. Hdt. 5.83; cf. Wilson 2000: 281. Wilson observes that Herodotos 'intended his audience to understand a leitourgical duty'; he notes that the Aiginetans had stolen their rites from Epidauros—but that although the Athenians had been involved in the early stages of this story, it was unlikely that the Epidaurians, and in turn the Aiginetans had copied the choregic liturgy from Athens. It was more likely to come from within their own rich choral tradition.
38. See Davies 1981*a*: 9; Wilson 2000: 98; Kurke 1998: 163–4 on choregic expenditure. The infamous *chorēgiai* of Alkibiades is a prime example of the publicity-seeking possibilities of the role of the *chorēgos*. Ath. 12.534c reports that when he entered the theatre he was gazed at with admiration by men and women; Thuc. 6.16 allows Alkibiades to justify his behaviour—although this is exceptional as pointed out by Wilson 2000: 154; cf. Fisher 2001: 189 ff. who points out that any expenditure by chorus-leaders on themselves would have been matched by equal if not additional expenditure on the chorus they supported.
39. Neither text includes a verb of binding: the cursed person or persons are simply cited (in the accusative case) as the direct object of an implied verb.
40. Dithyrambic competitions in Athens were held at particular city festivals, including the Great Dionysia. Each of the ten Athenian tribes would enter with one chorus of men and one of boys. In public inscriptions or forensic speeches they are referred to as 'the men' or 'the boys', e.g. *IG* ii². 2318, fourth-century BCE Victors' List; and Lys. 21.1–2. However, neither the age nor the socio-political category of the members of choruses of tragedies or comedies are specified in the literature, although Winkler has argued that the term *tragoidoi* is itself an age–class term (see Winkler 1990*a*).
41. *Didaskalos* could mean 'teacher', but Wünsch points out that *hupodidaskalos* is only used in the context of dramatic competition. See Phot. s.v. (discussed in Pickard-Cambridge 1988: 91 n. 6) and Pl. *Ion* 536a.
42. Except perhaps at Athens, where, in the production of an old play, they may still have been called *hupodidaskaloi* out of respect for the original composer (Wilson 2000: 83).

43. In both cases, the preposition indicating the connection between named individual and group is παρά + dative, which can be translated here to mean 'being on the side of' or 'in the team of'. It is used in this sense by Xen. *Mem.* 2.7.4; *An.* 1.7.4; Pl. *Phd.* 64b; and Dem. 15.19. See also the entry for παρά in LSJ.
44. Faraone identifies Theagenes as the *chorēgos*, and so he emerges as the focalizing figure of the performing ensemble and Wilson agrees that this is surely right. Wilson also sees the use of the plural as a problem for *DTA* 34, see (2000: 356 n. 33).
45. We find this in the festivals of the demes: see *IG* ii².3095, an inscribed marble base from Ikarion, dedicated by father and two sons, dated before mid-fourth century; *IG* ii².3098, an inscription on a small shrine found at Ikarion dated to the middle of the fourth century BCE 'Hagnias, Xanthippos, Xanthides, victorious, set this up'. (see Csapo and Slater 1995: 126). For the urban festivals, the only secure evidence for the *chorēgia* as a joint responsibility is the scholion to Ar. *Ran.* 405, who quotes Aristotle 'in the archonship of this Kallias (410 or 406 BCE) it was decreed that *chorēgoi* would jointly defray the costs of the tragedies and comedies at the Dionysia'. However, compare Demosthenes in *Against Leptines* 23 (355/4 BCE) who argues: 'But if indeed the numbers of those able to perform *chorēgiai* did fall short, by Zeus would it be better to have the cost of the *chorēgiai* defrayed by joint contributions, as we do the trierarchies, or to take back what we have given to our benefactors?' (Csapo and Slater 142–3). Capps (1896) argues that the dramatic *synchorēgia* was established for tragic and comic chorēgia for the City Dionysia in 406 BCE, between 399 and 394 it was repealed for tragedy, for comedy it was retained until about 340 BCE.
46. It is likely that all the city *chorēgiai*, across all the festivals, were reformed at the same time. See Wilson (2000: 271 ff.) for reasons for attributing this reform to Demetrios. 'The monument of Xenokles' an inscribed monument found in the Theatre of Dionysos at Athens, provides the first inscriptional record of this. Note that two choregic inscriptions survive from 319 BCE.
47. The only dates for these tablets are given by Wünsch, who labels them third century. As noted in Chapter 9, some of this corpus was redated by Wilhelm to the fourth century, although not these two tablets. Since the tablets in this corpus have since disappeared, there is no way to check the accuracy of this dating. However, even if Wünsch's dating is not accepted, the anomalies of the text must still be explained.
48. The evidence suggests that it was held by leading political figures of the day, e.g. Xenokles, who held the office in 307/6 (see *IG* ii².3073), was a major public figure, who seems to have occupied a key position in the supervision of the city's finances under Lykourgos, and been a *trierarch, chorēgos, epimelētēs* before being elected *agōnothetēs* (his 'euergetic'

302 Notes to Chapter 9

monument *IG* ii².749; Wilson 2000: 382 n. 41). Philippides son of Philomelos and *agōnothetēs* in 288/7 was also *stratēgos* (recorded in a decree of the people moved by Stratokles in 293: *IG* ii².649); another Philippides, a poet, seems to have had a similarly active role in politics along with an *agōnothesia* in 288/7 (*IG* ii². 657).

49. See Veyne 1990 for the rise of euergetism.
50. When Meidias wanted to damage Demosthenes' *chorēgia* he corrupted his *didaskalos* (Dem. 21).
51. Even *DTA* 103, described in Chapter 9, which appears to target a group of trierarchs occurs in the context of a court case. This tablet seems to date to a time when these trierarchs were under attack for negligent behaviour that was perceived as endangering the city. A curse tablet in such a situation might also have been motivated by serious concern for the welfare of the city.

CHAPTER 9

1. Favret-Saada, an ethnographer, explaining the violent beliefs underlying the practice of witchcraft among the peasants of the Bocage in western France.
2. Translation: Sommerstein 1980.
3. Sommerstein (1980: 192, notes to Ar. *Acharn.* ll. 703–18; Ar. *Vesp.* 946–8 Scholion): ὥσπερ ἐγκατεχομένην ἔσχε τὴν γλῶτταν, καὶ οὕτω(ς) κατεδικάσθη. However, this should not necessarily be taken as evidence that curse tablets were well known to the audience of the play: the information provided by the scholion differs in two important ways from the original text: it specifies the tongue (as opposed to the jaw) of Thucydides—and the tongue is a chief target of judicial curses—and it uses not the medical terminology of paralysis, but the participle ἐγκατεχομένην, a compound of κατέχειν which, we have seen, is a verb used to bind on the curse tablets. Since the language of the two sources is so different, it is quite possible that the scholiast is solely responsible for this technically correct introduction of the idea of binding, and that he is interpreting the passage in the light of his own understanding; cf. Faraone 1989: 158. However, as noted in Chapter 7, the *Erinyes*, or Furies, in Aeschylus' *Eumenides* appear to issue something like an oral curse against the φρένες, or mind, of Orestes (327–33), so it may be that the idea of cursing or binding was known, even if the technology of the curse tablet itself was less widespread at this point. See Faraone 1989 for discussion of all three examples.
4. Cic. *Brut.* 217: poisons and incantations are 'veneficiis et cantionibus'; the image of the speaker as a magician is also found in the work of Gorgias and in a number of Plato's discussions of rhetoric.
5. Lib. *Or.* 1.245–9, see further, Chapter 7.

6. Messing with his memory: a few curse tablets attack the memory ($\mu\nu\acute{\eta}\mu\eta$) of the target, e.g., *DTA* 68, 87; the mind ($\phi\rho\acute{\eta}\nu$) is more common (e.g., *DTA* 88, SGD 11). Directed against his rhetorical abilities: C. Bonner 1932: 34–44.
7. *Or.* 1.43: the rival speaker explains that he has been worsted by Libanius, because of his use of *goēteia* (Libanius is accused of hiring a 'man who could control the stars'). The charge is made again at Lib. *Or.* 1.71 when his rival succumbs to stage fright and argues that he has been bewitched. Libanius is accused of being a *goētēs* at *Or.* 1.62 After Libanius has beaten him in a rhetoric competition, the rival's wife dies and he accuses Libanius of having killed her through magical means.
8. Sicily: SGD 89, 95, 99, 100; NGCT 66, 78, 79; Spain: SGD 133 (third century BCE?); Russia: NGCT 116, SGD 171. Judicial curses are more widespread in later periods.
9 See Thuc. 1.77; [Xen.] *Ath. Pol.*; Ar. *Pax* 505, *Nub.* 206–8, *Av.* 32–41, 109–11, *Vesp.* 106–9, 158–60, 978–1008, and 1113. Todd (1993: 152) points out that 'the Greek competitive ethic may help us understand why Athenian litigants fight to destroy their opponents in situations in which we might have preferred to compromise, nevertheless it cannot explain why Athenians had a reputation for litigiousness ahead of other Greeks'.
10. Cartledge, Millett, and Todd (1990: 10): 'For those who accept the proposition that 'law' is an entirely autonomous activity, there is no difficulty here: it becomes perfectly legitimate to assume, in default of hard evidence to the contrary, that the function of a named institution in a democratic polis like Athens will have been essentially the same as its function in a dynastic state like Ptolemaic Egypt. But the moment we admit that law has an organic relationship with its social and political context ... then we must admit also that the practical differences between places and across time were probably greater than the continued use of the same legal vocabulary might imply.' Evidence for a common conception of the rule of law can be assembled (Gagarin 2004 and Chaniotis 2004), even so, this cannot be taken as evidence for shared procedure. That similar curse tablets occur in other parts of the Greek world may indicate that judicial cursing in Attika rests on elements of legal procedure likely to have been replicated quite widely.

Partial evidence for Athens: the forensic speeches we possess tell us only about some disputes which came to court in Athens and not those which were resolved, by arbitration or otherwise. We should consider the possibility that material from court cases is representative of a particular sector of society, insofar as rich, politically involved Athenians may have been more ready to pursue cases into the courtroom up to the point of a final decision than poorer members of society. However, as Rubinstein (2000) argues, the possibilities of participating in a prosecution as part of a team may have lessened this bias. Most judicial curse tablets seem to relate to activity in the courts, but, as explained below, this need not be taken as a blanket proposition.

11. On SGD 6, there may be a reference to the agent of the curse (ὁπόσοι ἰσὶν ἀντίδικοι Εὐόπηι μετὰ Πυθέο) and perhaps in *DTA* 88 (Mikion), but in neither tablet does this detail help to identify the context of the tablets.

12. Kagarow (1929: 53–4) lists examples for 16 different terms pertaining to a confrontation in the courts: οἱ ἀντίδικοι, οἱ σύνδικοι, οἱ συνήγοροι, οἱ κατήγοροι, οἱ μάρτυρες, οἱ συμπαρόντες, οἱ μηνυταί, οἱ δικασταί, ὁ διαιτητής, ἀντάδικα, δίκη, δικαστήριον, [ἔν]δειξις, πράξεις, ἀγωνίζεσθαι, μαρτυρία. To the tablets he has listed under these terms, we can add a number of further examples: ὁ ἀντίδικος -οι (SGD 6, 19, 42, 51, 61 (side b), NGCT 12, 24, 88); ὁ σύνδικος -οι (*DTA* 88, SGD 49, 51, 71, 95, 99, NGCT 1, 38, 46); οἱ συνήγοροι (SGD 68, NGCT 15); δίκη (*DT* 43–4); εὐθῦναι (*DTA* 100); [ἔν]δειξις (*ARW* 1911: 55. 5; SGD 49); οἱ δικασταί (NGCT 14). And some additional terms: ἐμαρτύρατο (*DT* 63); δικαιώματα (*DTA* 94); ἐπίτευξις ἀποσιμα, for ἀποσημα (SGD 82), which, according to Jordan, means 'treating of [serving?] a legal summons'; τ(ὁ)ν περὶ τῆ(ς) δίκη(ς) δικαζ[ό]μενον (*DTA* 103); συνηγορέω (SGD 176); τὰν κριτᾶν (NGCT 82). NGCT 9 contains the phrase δίκη βλάβης and appears to be aimed at a woman and two men who are about to urge their case in the polemarch's court (see above).

13. According to LSJ, δικάζομαι (in the middle form) is used of pursuing a private suit, although in the examples it provides, the verb takes either a genitive object (of the legal case) or an accusative with a dative of the person against whom the case is being made.

14. The *dikē blabēs* is one of the most frequently attested of private procedures in Athenian law and seems to have applied in a variety of cases. As Todd (1993: 279) explains, it has been suggested that it did not indicate a single action. Rather it represented either 'a group of procedures, each dealing with a separate and statutorily defined form of damage', or 'a rhetorical or generic term' held together by 'a unifying idea . . . action or inaction which causes (especially material) harm'.

15. Justification of a plea: s.v. LSJ: Thuc. 1.41, Isok. 6.25, Arist. *Cael.* 279 [b]9.

16. Todd 1993: 117, quoting Hansen 1976 '*Apagoge, endeixis* and *ephegesis* Against *kakourgoi, atimoi* and *pheugontes*: A Study in the Athenian Administration of Justice in the Fourth Century BCE' (Odense), argues that *apagōgē, endeixis,* and *ephēgēsis* were three parts of one procedure. *Apagōgē* is the term used to denote the action of the arrest by the prosecutor, *endeixis* the written accusation made beforehand, and *ephegesis* was used to describe the arrest when it is made by the magistrate instead of the plaintiff.

17. Faraone 1991*a*: 30 nn. 71–2. These are: *DTA* 25, 38, 39, 63, 65–8, 81, 88, 94, 95, 103, 105–7, 129; *DT* 39, 43, 44, 49, 60, 62, 63, 77, 87–90; SGD 6, 9, 19, 42, 49, 51, 61, 68, 71, 89, 95, 99, 100, 108, 133, 173, 176. Gager adds

another 9 tablets: *DTA* 24, 26, 47–50, 95; SGD 14 (see Jordan 1980: 234), 48, 107. Dating: Wünsch dated all the tablets in his *DTA* collection to the third century BCE, though he thought that 38 and 107 might be from the fourth century. Wilhelm redated *DTA* 65, 66, 95, 103 on prosopographical and epigraphic grounds to the fourth century BCE, and *DTA* 38 to the fifth century BCE. The tablets have since disappeared and so most have never been properly redated. Audollent has *DT* 49 (end), 60 (late), 62–3 dated to the fourth century BCE; 77 seems to have been regarded as undatable. SGD 9, 19, 42, 49, 51 are dated to the fourth century BCE; SGD 6 to the late fifth or early fourth century BCE.
18. On the grounds that πράξεις has a legal meaning in *DT* 67.
19. NGCT 1, 9, 10, 12, 14, 15, 24, 38.
20. Gager adds another nine tablets on these grounds: *DTA* 24, 26, 47–50; SGD 14, 48, 107. Wilhelm (1904: 115–22) argued that *DTA* 24, 47–50, and 57 reflect the turbulent political climate of the early fourth century when the war between Athens and Sparta had come to an end and Thebes was rising as a new threat to Athenian power. He believed these tablets were created between warring political factions within Attika. Wilhelm also offers notes on individuals listed in *DTA* 11, 24, 30, 42, 65, 84 and SGD 18; see Wünsch (1897) on *DTA* 28, 47–51, 87, 89, and (1900: 63) on *DT* 60. Ziebarth 1899 identifies many of the individuals on SGD 48 as belonging to the political circle of the fourth-century Athenian statesman, Demades; on this see also Habicht 1993. SGD 14 (see Jordan 1980) names the Makedonian ruler, Kassander, and members of his retinue.
21. This is not a new discussion: as we have seen, a number of the early Attic curses contain the names of renowned orators and politicians. This suggested to Preisendanz (1972: 9) that all such curses might be labelled 'political curses'. He had to admit, however, that since many cases in Athens were in fact political in nature, it would be difficult to separate judicial from political curse categories. Gager 1992: 119 and Faraone 1991*a*: 16.
22. SGD 42 was identified by L. Robert (1936: 12–13, no. 11) as containing the names of several politicians from the early fourth century. It also contains terminology indicating a legal context: ὅπως οἱ ἐνθαῦτα ἀντίδικοι τέλος λαβόντον τῆς [δίκ]ης. *DTA* 103 includes the phrases (l. 9 ff.), Δημοκρ[άτ]ης τ(ὸ)ν περὶ τῆ(ς) δίκη[ς δικαζ[ό]μενον· Μνησίμαχος Ἀντί[φιλος and was clearly created for a legal situation. It comprises a list of individuals who were associated with the naval affairs of Athens, mostly as trierarchs. The tablet has been dated to around 323 BCE, when Athens revolted unsuccessfully against the rule of the Makedonians. Athens' defeat was largely due to the bad condition of its navy, and this period saw a number of lawsuits involving trierarchs and naval affairs (see Wilhelm 1904: 122–5). NGCT 5 may include the orator Lykourgos

alongside other *diaitētai* (*arbitrators*); see Willemsen 1990 and Habicht 1993.
23. Calder 1963; Jeffery 1955: 73, no. 10.
24. E.g. lawsuits involving the Dikaiogenes family in Isai. 5 or the Hagnon family in Isai. 11.
25. NGCT 11 and 13 and 5 were all found in the Kerameikos in Athens, and date to the early fourth century. From the same find as NGCT 11: NGCT 10 (a tablet without any useful terminology and a list of names which lack both patronymics and demotics) and NGCT 12, a doll and coffin set which almost certainly comprises a judicial curse since its text refers to καὶ οἱ ἄλλοι ἀντίδικοι ('and the other co-advocates'). See Schlörb-Vierneisel 1964 and Jordan 1988.
26. Identified by Trumpf (1958): *chorēgos IG* ii². 3092; Lys. fr. 182 Baiter–Sauppe; see Jordan 1988: 275.
27. This identification made by Jordan (1988: 276). There are five Theozotides listed in the *LGPN* vol. 2. Of these: (1) is possibly (Stroud 1971: 297) the man we seek; (2) is certainly him; and (3) is likely to be his grandson.
28. On the speech, see *APF*: 222–3; information found in part of a papyrus (*PHibeh* 14), discovered in 1902 by the Egypt Exploration Society, which contained part of an oration by Lysias concerning a decree about state stipends proposed in 403/2; in 1970, a stele was discovered inscribed with this very decree (cf. Stroud 1971: 280–301). Opinions differ as to whether Theozotides raised or cut the pay of the *Hippotoxotai* (for the former Stroud 1971: 298–9, with further references in Loomis 1995: 232 n. 11; for the latter, see Loomis 1995).
29. If he did, then both measures can be interpreted as overtly pro-democratic. His success in reducing the pay of the *Hippeis* (the second property class) would be a blatantly hostile measure taken against a group that had supported the Thirty during their period in power in Athens. The decree to support the orphans of those Athenians who had fought at Phyle meant, in effect, providing for them as if their fathers had died in a foreign war, rather than a civil war. Moreover, by stressing the fact that support would go not to νόθοι and ποιητοί sons ('illegitimate' and 'adopted', respectively, as the speech tells us), but to the orphaned legitimate sons of Athenian citizens (this from the stele), Theozotides seems to have been showing support for the idea of limiting citizenship—which was surely a subject for debate in the months following the restoration of the democracy. However, Loomis argues that Theozotides was attempting to reduce the city's costs during a time of 'acute financial emergency' (p. 236). Either way, what matters to this argument is that Theozotides' political activities were likely to have generated controversy and hostility.
30. Ogden 1999: 27.

Notes to Chapter 9

31. SGD 95, 99, 100, and 108 all (seem to) target the tongue alone. *DTA* 65 asks for mindlessness ἄφρονες γένοιτο; *DTA* 66: τὴν ψυχὴν καὶ γλῶτταν; *DTA* 68 binds the hands and feet (χεῖρας πόδας) of most of its multiple targets, and then adds variously the tongue, memory, and/or workshop to this basic formula; *DTA* 79 binds the tongue; *DTA* 88 binds mind and tongue (φρένας γλῶτ(τ)αν); *DTA* 94 tongue and mind (τὴν γλῶτ(τ)αν καὶ τὰ<ι>ς φρένας); *DTA* 95 words and deeds (ἔπη καὶ ἔργα); *DTA* 105 tongue, words, and deeds (καὶ γ]λῶτταν καὶ ἔπη καὶ [ἔργα); *DTA* 107 spirit, mind, tongue, and desires (ψυ-χὴν καὶ νο(ῦ)ν καὶ γλῶτταν καὶ βο(υ)λὰς); *DT* 49 tongue, spirit, and speech (γλῶτταν καὶ ψυχὴν καὶ λόγον); *DT* 87 tongue and mind (τὰν γλῶσσαν καὶ τὸν νόον).

32. *DTA* 68 (note the overlap above); *DTA* 74 binds the tongue, body, work and workshop, and skill (γλῶταν κὴ σῶμα κὴ ἐργασίαν κὴ ἐργαστήρια κὴ τέχναν); *DTA* 75 binds the tongue (and possibly other parts) of one target, the work (τὴν ἐργασίαν) of one, the workshop of another (τὸ ἐργαστήριον); *DTA* 84 the evil tongue, evil heart, evil spirit, and workshop (τὴν γλῶτ(τ)αν τὴν κακὴν καὶ τὸν θυμὸν τὸν κακὸν καὶ τὴν ψυχὴν τὴν κακὴν καὶ τὸ ἐργαστήριον); *DTA* 86 feet, hands, spirit, tongue, profit of work (πόδας χεῖρας ψυχὴν γλώντας ἐργασίας κέρδην); *DTA* 87 work, mind, spirit, hands, tongue, feet (ἐργασίαν αὐτοῖς καὶ νο(ῦ)ν. ψυχὴν χεῖρας γλῶτταν πόδας); *DTA* 97 hands, feet, tongue, spirit (τὰς χεῖρας καὶ τοὺς πόδας καὶ τὴν γλῶσσαν καὶ τὴν ψυχήν); *DT* 47 action, spirit, work of workshop, feet, hands, tongue, heart (πρᾶξιν ψυχὴν ἔργα ἐργασίας πό[δας] χ[εῖ]ρας [γλῶτ(τ)αν θυμὸν); *DT* 52 words, deeds, tongue (λόγους καὶ ἔργα... μαὶ τὴν γλῶσσαν) for one victim, girls (probably meaning that he was a pimp and these were his prostitutes), skill, resources, work, words, and deeds for another (τὰς παιδίσκας αὐτοῦ καὶ τὴν τέχνην καὶ τὴν ἀφορμὴν καὶ τὴν ἐργασίαν αὐτοῦ καὶ λόγους καὶ ἔργα αὐτοῦ); SGD 75 tongue, and right and wrong, and feet, spirit, tools and profit (γλῶταν καὶ δίκαιον καὶ ἄ[δικον? [κα]ὶ πόδας κα(ὶ) ψυχὴ(ν) καὶ σκεύη τὰ κέρδη).

33. NGCT 22, although very difficult to read, seems to contain a similar 'if there is anyone else who ...' phrase lurking in its fragments.

34. SGD p. 157/8: note the backwards writing of the name of the target.

35. On circus curses: Brown 1972: 128–9. Faraone (1985: 153–5) extends these observation on the competitive context of the circus to the 'radically democratic courts in fifth-century Athens' which, he feels, 'provide an analogous arena of competition and uncertainty'. Some scholars place greater emphasis on their 'magical'—and, indeed, shameful—nature: e.g. Jordan (1988: 277): 'They were men of influence and leadership at the close of a century that is the most brilliant in human history. The leaden objects that we have discussed today suggest that some of these men also engaged in black magic.'

36. For this model of the lawcourts see Todd 1993, also Cartledge 1990,

Christ 1998: 35–7, Garner 1987, Ober 1989 and 1994, and Wilson 1991. Many attested and identifiable litigants were politically active and wealthy, see Hansen 1989: 34–72.
37. Cohen 1992: 106.
38. I have chosen to translate *dikastai* as judges rather than juries, on the grounds that their role was closer to the former modern role than the latter. See Harris 1994: 136 for a persuasive argument about the likely legal knowledge of the average *dikastēs*. On the grounds for judgements made by *dikastai* see Sinclair 1988: 153.
39. This account has been questioned by other scholars, including Carey (1994) and Rubinstein (2000), both of whom emphasize the difficulty of understanding a legal system which is both familiar in some ways and yet alien in others. As Carey (1994: 184) says: 'Implicit imposition of our own standards leads to confused and fruitless questions. Too great an emphasis on distance risks oversimplifying the Athenian system and turning the courts into an area for competition, a place for settling feuds.' He argues that the existing model rests on a misunderstanding of attitudes to the rhetoric of litigants in their presentation of their political and other services to the city as a part of their case, emphasizing that the Athenians had great respect for the law and that we should not underestimate the question of legality in most trials. Rubinstein examines the role of the *sunēgoroi* in Athenian courts, arguing that they held a greater role than has previously been understood, and that, in fact, this term refers to the members of teams of litigants who took part in *graphai*.
40. In a number of cases it may have figured alongside much more mundane concerns, such as the distribution of money. Certainly the many inheritance cases in which Isaios was involved, suggest that money, not honour, was the important issue for many who came to court.
41. Concerns about law still tend to focus on issues such as matching the action to the crime or equal access to the courts: Hyp. 3.5–6; Dem. 22.25–7.
42. Compelling arguments have recently been put forward (Rubinstein 2000) for a different view of *graphai* and possibly also of *dikai*, that is, that they were fought out by teams of people who could choose to share in the risk of going to court or not (and need not undertake the rhetorical burden in its entirety), rather than by competitive individuals, and that such teams could and did comprise ordinary citizens of Athens as well as wealthier members of the community. See also Rhodes 1986: 142, who brings up synegorial activity as one way for a non-elite individual to participate in politically prominent activity.
43. Pl. *Resp.* 364b–c. Jordan (1988: 277) emphasizes that in this passage the speaker refers to the hirers of these mendicants as being rich. He goes on to argue: 'It is obvious in curses against legal opponents, and I believe that it is safe to assume in other curses as well, that when a man is cursed,

it is by social, political and economic peers of his. [They] would have been powerful. They were indeed rich and could afford, as we have seen, to employ the best legal talent available.' Gager (1992: 119) argues against an assumption that the tablets must have been primarily used by the poor: 'The Greek and Latin *katadesmoi* demonstrate conclusively that the use of curse tablets was by no means limited to "unlettered and superstitious" members of the lower classes.'

44. Ober 1989: 149 n. 109. Politicians: Xenocles (*APF* 11234) and Deinomenes (*APF* 3188). A similar social mix is also found among the extant Sicilian curses, according to Curbera's survey (1999). The examples we possess include about 430 male names including their patronyms. The older texts are usually written against groups with more single targets among the later texts. Unfortunately, the Greek names do not specify social standing so it is difficult to know the status of the individuals who are named, but Curbera suggests that in the oldest tablets, the inclusion of places of origin may suggest the presence of slaves. Individuals of higher social standing may be indicated by the fact that a number of the names found on Sicilian curse tablets also appear in lists of magistracies of other cities and islands or (for later tablets) among the Sicilian nobles mentioned by Cicero in the *Verrine Orations*, so it seems as if there are politically involved persons from the higher levels of society on these tablets, as there are on the Athenian ones. Further to this, the names on the tablets offer evidence of the mobility of the population in Sicily (e.g. male names not of Doric origin in tablets from Kamarina and Selinous, and patronyms from Eretria and Euboia; the presence of Punic and Libyan names in tablets from Selinous and Lilybaion attest to contact between these parts of the island and Africa, from the end of the Archaic period through to Roman times). Curbera suggests that the curses offer evidence of internal conflict between members of an original Greek culture and Roman elements more recently arrived on the island.

45. Private cases involving metics were heard before the polemarch. Metics as defendants: [Arist.] *Ath. Pol.* 58.2–3 and the original summons issued against Pankleon in Lys. 23.2. A metic possibly a prosecutor in the polemarch's court: Dem. 32.29 (but the defendant may have been a metic). A wide variety of different cases were brought under *dikē blabēs*, see Todd 1993: 279 ff. for elaboration on the idea of damage underlying this category of procedure.

46. The legal status of metics is obscure. Free aliens could be witnesses in both public and private cases (public: Dem. 19.146, 25.162; Aeschin. 2.155; private: Dem. 35. 14, 20, 23, 33; Hyp. 5.33). There may be evidence for a metic prosecuting a public case (Dem. 59.66, *Against Neaira*, in which we are told Epainetos of Andros, only a visitor and not even a metic, indicts Stephanos for unlawful imprisonment). However, for several public procedures the statutes seem to imply the exclusion of

aliens (Dem. 21.47 regulating *graphe hubreos* and Dem. 59.16 regulating *graphē xenias*), so it is likely that they feature elsewhere in the forensic corpus; for this and further information see Todd 1993: 196.
47. See *DTA* 94 and 103.
48. οἱ μήνυται *DTA* 67.
49. R. J. Bonner 1905: 1939; MacDowell 1978: 181–3; Lys. 7.16 and 13. Rewards: in the case of the mutilation of the Herms (see Andok. 1.11–68 and Thuc. 6.27.2) the Assembly appointed investigators and offered rewards—slaves were to be rewarded with their freedom. Informers included a metic, Teukros; two slaves, Andromachos and Lydos; Agariste of the Alkmaeonid family (*APF* 382–3); a citizen Diokleides, who was convicted of giving false information and executed; and Andokides himself. Andok. 1.20 (400 or 399 BCE) implies that the law (of 415 BCE) that had offered an informer impunity if his information was true or death if it was false, was no longer in force and the terms were probably fixed for each informer by the decree of the Council or Assembly granting it. No reward is mentioned in Lys. 29.6 where the term *mēnusis* is used to describe the revelation of a breach in a private contract.
50. Thür (1977: 59–60) catalogues 42 examples of a challenge to torture a slave for evidence from the forensic corpus, none of which is accepted.
51. Against the gods: Andok. 1 and Lys. 7. Cases of: murder (Antiph. 5 and Lys. 13); *apographē* (Lys. 29 against Philokrates); *graphē astrateias* (Lys. 14 against the son of Alkibiades).
52. Osborne (2000: 83): this would mean that the political exclusiveness of the enfranchised was not threatened by this system: the state made sure that citizens did not face the disturbing prospect of being brought down by their own slaves, except in those cases where their actions had endangered the state by offending an even higher authority.
53. οἱ δικασταί *DTA* 65, 67; NGCT 46.
54. Thuc. 3.38/Ar. *Eq.* 837: Kleon, in his endeavour to dissuade the Assembly from reversing its decision about the punishment of Mytilene, charges its members with being at the mercy of their ears.
55. See Bers (1985: 1–15) and Hall (1995: 43–4).
56. Dem. 18.52, 19.75, 20.131, 23.95–9, 33.35–6; Aeschin. 1.159, 2.4 and 153, 3.205–6, 244.
57. Decrees survive that specify the number of judges to try a particular case (Rhodes and Lewis 1996: 34): *IG* i^3.71(=ML 69, 16, late third century) 1000 for cases to do with the Delian League; *IG* ii^2. 850 specified 501 for the confirmation of citizenship grants; *IG* ii^2.1629 (=Tod 200, 204–17, fourth century BCE) 201 to be enrolled by the *thesmothētai* to hear *skepseis*—exemptions pleas made by citizens nominated to be trierarchs. See also Todd 1993: 83.
58. Dem. 18.265, 21.226.
59. Hall (1995: 44) notes the verb κλώζειν is used by Demosthenes—and

found elsewhere to indicate a noise made by the audience when they wanted an actor to leave the stage (Dem. 21.226 with Harpocration s.v. κλώζετε); interrupting: Ar. fr. 101 K–A; murmuring: Alexis fr. 33 K–A.
60. Hall *loc. cit.* Angry: Dem. 58.31; and demanding: Dem. 23.18–19, Hyp. 1.20.
61. Hall *loc. cit.*, drawing on Plato's description in *Leg.* 700c1–4 and Pollux 4.122.
62. Plato's *Leg.* 876b1–6 with *Resp.* 492b5–c1 (cited Hall 1995: 43), describing *thorubos* the din from assemblies, theatres, military encampments, and lawcourts. See Dem. 18.138, quoted by Halliwell (1991).
63. [Arist.] *Ath. Pol.* 27.5 (Anytos); Isok. 18.11 (Xenotimos); Aeschin. 1.86 (Demophilos/Nikostratos): all involve jury-bribing scandals at the end of the fifth/beginning of the fourth century BCE. Aeschin. 3.1 and Dem. 19.1 suggest that supporters would try to influence the verdict before the beginning of a trial by approaching *dikastai* in the agora. Evidence for the reform of the procedure of allocation of *dikastai* can be observed (Todd 1993: 84) in the difference between descriptions in Aristophanes' *Wasps* (422 BCE) and the *Ekklesiazousai* (late 390s BCE) (681–90); *Ath. Pol.* 63–5 seems to suggest the daily allocation of individuals rather than panels.
64. οἱ μάρτυρες *DT* 87, *DTA* 25, 65, 68a, 94; μαρτυρία *DT* 49, 89b, *SGD* 173 (although this was published by Shkorpil as a personal letter offering to bribe a judge); μαρτύρω *SGD* 89; μαρτύρομαι *DT* 63.
65. Todd (1990: 27) notes that they are cited on 'more than 400 occasions in the 100 forensic speeches, at an average frequency of six sets of witnesses per hundred sections of text', but can only name one certain example (Dem. 33.30–1) and three further possible examples (Andok. 1.112–16, Dem. 27.8–9, and Lys. 20.26) when the discussion is preceded by testimony (ibid.: 23 n. 6). They are used far more frequently in private suits than in public actions (*ibid.* 32).
66. R. J. Bonner (1905: 46–8) suggests dating the change from spoken to written witness statements to about 380 BCE. The precise date of this reform is debated (Ruschenbusch 1989: 34–5 argues for a date in the very early fourth century, while Rhodes 1980: 315 prefers a later date in the 370s). However, such differences seem paltry when compared to the questions surrounding the dating of many of these curse tablets, often cast in terms of centuries, rather than decades.
67. Even with the exceptions, there are plenty of complications, as described by Todd 1993: 44 n.
68. Aristoph. *Vesp.* 562–70, 579–86.
69. Used tactically: Lys. 17.2 and Andok. 1.69; Rubinstein (2000: 72 ff.) suggests that witnesses were used to upset the level playing field of the courts since, during their evidence, the *klepsydra* timing each side's contribution was stopped. She suggests that this may have been one of the reasons why written evidence was introduced.

70. For example, it has been observed that witnesses are used far more frequently in the private suits for which we have evidence than in the public suits, and especially in speeches concerned with family property, see Todd 1990: 32. Humphreys (1985 and 1986) argues that witnesses were used to demonstrate crucial local (sometimes specifically family) support, in a time of socio-political change. Clearly, if this view is accepted, then the identity (and status) of a witness would have mattered as much as, if not more than, what he said. This aspect was acknowledged by theorists of the time: *Rhet. ad Alex.* 1437^{a-b} and Arist. *Rhet.* 1398^a. See Todd 1990: 27 ff.

71. As Todd (1990: 27) argues, the use of μάρτυς and its cognates to mean 'somebody (or something) which supports my arguments at this point' is found in both Thucydides and Herodotos, e.g. Hdt. 2.18.1 and Thuc. 1.8.1, that is, outside the context of legal rhetoric. Use of large numbers of witnesses: Todd (1990: 31) suggests that the reason why witnesses appear more than twice as frequently in Isaios 9 than in any other of his speeches, is to strengthen what is a weak case with support for points that are not actually contested. Expected to say anything: Cohen (1995: 110) cites Aeschin. 1.47–8 and Lys. 7.19 and observes that witnesses were usually drawn from among the litigant's friends and their opponent's enemies and were expected to say whatever was needed in support of their own side's case.

72. Todd (1990: 24) distinguishes between character assassination of witnesses and those which are really attacks on the litigant by means of his witnesses, when he states that there are only three examples of the former: Lys. 12.87, Dem. 34.18–20, 27.51 (not including *dikē pseudomarturiōn*). However, I am not sure of the success of this distinction (surely the accusation that witnesses are lying is a blight on their character as much as on that of the man who may have bribed them to lie). For the purposes of my point, however, there are plentiful examples of the topos of the untrustworthiness of witnesses (e.g. Dem. 19.216; 21.112, 139; 29.28; Xen. *Mem.* 4.4.11; Isok. 18.52–7; Lys. 19.7). These examples are cited by Cohen (1995: 107), who states that 'Athenian orations abound with specific accusations of false testimony and with comments about the frequency of this practice'.

73. Carey (1994: 184) argues that the possibility of *dikē pseudomarturiōn* proves the importance of what a witness said. Todd (1990: 37) reports that a fragment of Theophrastos' *Laws* (schol. Plato *Laws* 937) seems to suggest that if a *dikē pseudomarturiōn* was successful, it might overwhelm the plaintiff's previous conviction, but the evidence is inconclusive. However, cases were also brought by successful defendants, e.g. Theomnestos prosecutes Dionysios, a witness involved in Lysitheos' case against him (Lys. 10. 24–5), an action which suggests revenge. Moreover, Todd (1990: 38) suggests that in Dem. 45–6, Apollodoros prosecutes Stephanos for the

evidence he gave on behalf of Apollodoros' stepfather Phormion because he was incensed by the fact that Stephanos, his marriage relation, had chosen to back Phormion rather than him. Stephanos' testimony is clearly untrue, as Apollodoros claims, but, in fact, this makes no difference to Phormion's case.

74. There were ways to compel a reluctant witness to appear, but the details—and relationships between the different procedures—are unclear. As Todd 1990: 24: the litigant could ask that he give evidence or choose between taking an oath of denial (*exomosia*), testifying to a prepared statement, or being fined 1000 dr. He could issue some form of formal summons and if the witness failed to turn up, he could bring a private suit, the *dikē lipomarturiou*. But there is only one known case where it was brought—unsuccessfully (Dem. 49.18–21). See discussion in Harrison 1971: 140 ff. and Todd 1990: 25.

75. See NGCT 39, 49, 50, and 116; SGD 133.

76. *DT* 63, ll. 4–5: [... ... καὶ] το(ὰ)ς συνδίκ[ο(υ)ς ο(ὖ)ς | [ὁ δεῖνα ἐμαρτύ]ρατο, 'and those advocates whom that man called to testify'.

77. οἱ συνήγοροι: *DTA* 38, 63, 65, 95b, SGD 68, 176, NGCT 15. οἱ κατήγοροι: *DT* 60. οἱ ἀντίδικοι: *DTA* 94, SGD 6, 19, 42, 51, 61, NGCT 12, 24, 88. οἱ σύνδικοι: *DT* 39, 62, 63, 90, *DTA* 39, 66a, 81, 88, 103a, 106a, 107a, 129; SGD 49, 51, 71, 95, 99, 100, NGCT 1, 38, 46.

78. Reflecting what is already known of its use in the ancient Athenian forensic context: see Harrison 1971: 74 and Rubinstein 2000: 42 ff. This apparent lack of definition by the Athenians with respect to their laws has added to the increasingly debated view that Athenian legal interpretations and decisions were fairly arbitrary, depending on the manipulation of the *dikastai* by the speaker.

79. Dem. 29.23.

80. *Antidikos* as plaintiff: Lys. 7.13; as defendant: Antiph. 1.2. *Katēgoros* as an accuser: Andok. 4.16, Lys. 7.11; when acting as prosecutors on behalf of a group *IG* ii². 1205, and found in the plural in Antiph. 5.64 and 94, Lys. 19.2 and 61, and 21.20. *Sundikos* as advocate: Dem. 18.134, and meaning public advocate, elected to represent the *polis* in civic or inter-*polis* disputes: Dem. 20.146, 18.134; often applied to the representative of an association in court: [Arist.] *Ath. Pol.* 42.1, *IG* ii². 1196 and 1197, and used of elected *phyletai* in Dem. 23.206. *Sunēgoros* used in similar fashion: Dem. 24.36 (applied to a person elected by the Assembly to defend an existing law in a *nomothēsia* procedure); Hyp. 3.12 (to describe elected *phyletai*). Also used to describe private individuals appearing in court as advocates for friends or family. In addition, a board of *sunēgoroi* assisted the *logistai* with *euthynai*—possibly as prosecutors—while a board of *sundikoi* received confiscated property (Isai. fr. 12 Thalheim) and handled repayments of state loans owed by persons who had served in the cavalry (Lys. 16.6–7). Harrison (1971: 34–5) concluded that they

presided over, rather than pleaded cases (cf. Rubinstein 2000: 43–5). However, it is still possible that they could be the targets of cursing—just as the *dikastai* above.
81. References in the plural with no indication of number: *DTA* 39, 66a, 81, 88, 103a, 106a; *DT* 39, 62, 90; SGD 49, 51, 71, 100 and NGCT 46. The phrase 'Whoever are . . .' is found on *DTA* 106a; 'Whoever is . . .' on *DTA* 107a and NGCT 38. References in the singular: SGD 95, 99; NGCT 1.
82. On *DT* 39, one other name at least is mentioned, but the tablet is too fragmentary to read. *DT* 90 curses two others in addition to the *sundikoi*. On NGCT 1, they are (if Jordan's restoration is correct) 'other *sundikoi*', a phrase which may imply that the nine individuals who are named on the tablet are also to be considered *sundikoi*.
83. On SGD 49, the *sundikoi* are called 'his' (although the tablet, very fragmentary, does not include any names); on SGD 51 they are described as 'with Aristoboulos', the only named individual on the tablet, and seemingly the main focus of the curse. Kallias is similarly the only named individual among the targets on *DTA* 88, and the *sundikoi* are described as his; *DTA* 107a targets whoever may be a *sundikos* to Pherenikos, who is clearly the main target of the curse. On NGCT 38, the *sundikos* appears to belong to a team of three named individuals who are also cursed; and on *DT* 63, they appear to be connected to someone who has been involved in witnessing—but the syntax of the supplement is not clear and the text is fragmentary.
84. Aeschin. 2.142; Rubinstein (2000: 48) also adduces Dem. 49.22 with 49.10.
85. See also NGCT 12, which targets a group of *antidikoi*, who are being cursed in addition to the four named individuals on the tablet; NGCT 88, where the *antidikoi* appear in the plural, but their relationship to the individuals named on the text—whether they are a separate group or meant to denote the same people plus any others—is not clear; and SGD 61 (side b), where the term appears in the plural, but the state of the tablet makes it difficult to glean anything more.
86. The tablet in question is SGD 42. SGD 48 and 107 comprise similar numbers of names, but do not contain any legal language. Indeed, SGD 48 does not even refer to the binding of a tongue, though it does contain a reference to the 'words and deeds' of one target; SGD 107 does mention tongues, but no legal detail.
87. *Apophasis*: a procedure in which the Areopagos investigated any threat to the state, reporting their findings and recommendations to the Assembly. This power was probably added in the fourth century, around 350 BCE. See Todd 1993: 82 and 362.
88. Faraone 1991a: 16. However, it still leaves the question of how to explain them when they do appear on a text with other legal terminology.
89. See Rhodes 1986, Finley 1983: 76–84. For example, we know that men

would support members of their deme or tribe both within and outside the lawcourts: Andok. I.150, Hyp. 4.12, Lys. 27.12, Dem. 23.206. The system of liturgies provides myriad examples of the importance of personal financial expenditure in ensuring political allegiance. *Hetaireiai* were known to work for political ends (see Andok. I.61–4, Thuc. 8.54.4, Lys. 12.43–4, Hyp. 4.8, Pl. *Ep.* 325c5–d5 and *Theaet.* 173d4; the oath of a *xunōmosia* may be given in Arist. *Pol.* 1310^{a}7). Leading politicians were aided by friends and those whom they paid for their services in the courts, holding offices, and proposing measures in the Assembly: Dem. 21.139, Plut. *Dem.* 21.3. It has also been argued that there were subtle, but important changes in this system towards the end of the fifth century: a shift from working through friends and wealth, to appeals to the people and the exercise of skill: see Connor 1971: 87–198 and Davies 1981*a*: 114 ff.

90. Jordan in a letter to Curbera (quoted in Curbera 1999, n. 52): 'Let us admit that such huge numbers of persons would not be present as witnesses or judges at any one trial, but can we be sure that the writer of a curse tablet knew exactly who would be called as witnesses? He may as well name all the persons he could think of as likely possibilities. In this case, a hundred persons does not seem too large a number.'

91. Rubinstein (2000: 62): *sunēgoroi* appear in at least 28 out of 36 public trials and 21 out of 47 private suits for which we have evidence from the corpus of forensic speeches. In the public actions, *sunēgoroi* were employed by prosecutors in 19 instances, and by defendants in 21 instances, and this is spread across a range of different types of public action. In the private actions there is evidence for 15 employed on behalf of prosecutors and 14 employed by defendants.

92. Rubinstein (2000: 131 ff.): there are nine non-elected *sunēgoroi* supporting prosecutors in public actions whose speeches are preserved: Lys. [6], 13, 14, 15, 27, Dem. 20, 22, [59] and Hyp. 4. Of these, most prefer to concentrate on a specific claim of information about the defendant and do not mention their relationship with the main prosecutors, even if there may have been one, e.g. in Dem. 22, Diodoros does not mention long-standing joint political activities with Euktemon (described in Dem. 24). Only three refer to personal relationships with the litigants.

Rubinstein (2000: 94) draws attention to the similarities between the role played and the language used, by the supporting prosecutor in a public action, and the citizen who proposed a rider to a decree in the Assembly. She suggests that just as those in the Assembly would have carried responsibility for their contributions, *katēgoroi* in the courts may also have had to bear responsibility for their contributions to a case: 'The concept of multi-authored motions for which several individuals had taken responsibility, was not unknown to the Athenians.'

Examples of teams (all cited by Rubinstein 2000: 98 n.): Antiph. 5.64; Lys. 19.2, [20].7, 21.20–1, 25.5, 27.14, 30.34; Andok. 1.6; Dem. 21.64. Supporting prosecutor: Andoc. 1.92, Aeschin. 3.52. Elected: Din. 1.51, 58, 114, 2.6; Dem. 25.4.

93. See Rubinstein 2000: 149 ff. Considerable numbers: Aeschines (2.179 and 184) distinguishes particular individuals (Euboulos and Phokion) and also his father, along with brothers, brothers-in-law, friends, and contemporaries; Andokides (1.150) has elected supporters from his *phyle* and Anytos and Kephalos; see also Hyp. 3 and Lys. 5.

Different kinds of pleas: Ar. *Vesp.* 562–75. Lys. 14. 19–22 expects three groups of supporters to plead for the younger Alkibiades—friends, relatives, and an unrelated group with no affiliation but with some expertise (in this case, magistrates). This division of groups and types of pleading is also found in Lys. 30.31, [Dem.] 59.117; Lyk. 1.135 and 138, Aeschin. 2.179 and 184; Hyp. 2.10 (as listed Rubinstein 2000: 152 n.).

94. Emotional distraction, from children: Ar. *Vesp.* 568–75, Aeschin. 2.152, and 179; [Lys.] 20.35; from relatives, demesmen, and friends: Lys. 27.12, [Lys.] 20.35; Dem. 25.78, 57. 67–8; Isai. 12.5. See further Rubinstein 2000: 154 ff. and Hall 1995: 42.

95. Whether the names of fellow-speakers were on the decree or not, their performance in court might very well have meant that they were held responsible, at least in popular opinion, for a case's outcome. In Lys. 12.67, Theramenes is described as having caused the death of Antiphon and Archeptolemos, whereas in the decree quoted in [Pl.] *X Orat.* 833e–f, one Andron is described as having moved the decree, while Theramenes appears as one of a long list of co-prosecutors (see discussion by Rubinstein 2000: 177–8).

96. *Dikē phonou*: *IG* i^3.104.20–3, restored from [Dem.] 43.57; evidence for individuals only: Isok. 20.2, *IG* ii^{12}.1258 (in which the *Eikadeis* (possibly a *genos*, see Rubinstein 2000: 81 n.17) need an individual to challenge Polyxenos to a *dikē pseudomarturiou*. For (presentations at least of) joint interests: Dem. 34, 56, Isai. 5. For discussion of all these examples, see Rubinstein 2000: 87 ff.

97. Deme: Isai 12.11. Genos: Dem. [59].59–60. Organizations: *IG* ii^{12}.1258 (Rubinstein 2000: 81 ff.).

98. See Rubinstein 2000: 83 ff. Examples include: Dem. 47 (unknown speaker vs. Euergos and Mnesiboulos who gave similar testimony); Dem. 45.7 (Apollodoros vs. several witnesses who gave similar testimony); Aeschin. 1.62 (Pittalakos vs. Timarchos and Hegesandros); Dem. 27.12 (Demosthenes vs. his guardians).

99. *IG* ii^2. 1258; Dem. 34; 56.37; Isai. 5. In all of these it is clear that, although formally the case was the responsibility of a single individual, emotionally and rhetorically it was felt and presented as the concern of a group of people.

100. οἱ συμπαρόντες *DTA* 79; τοὺς μετ' ἐκείνο[υ σ]υνεστάκειν *DT* 67; καὶ τὸς αὀτῶι συνιόντας SGD 171; πάντας παρατηροῦσι SGD 176.
101. The tablet is SGD 176; the article is Chaniotis 1992: 69–73.
102. Jordan 1987.
103. Chaniotis 1992: 71–2: the first is a Hellenistic inscription (c.182–167 BCE) recording an arbitration by citizens of Patrai in a dispute about territory between Thuria and Megalopolis. The litigant tried to bring enough supporters with him, that he could sway the jury. The inscription commemorating Thuria's victory includes the names not just of the official participants but also those of the volunteers who had accompanied the arbitrators as supporters—111 names in total (Moretti 1967: 128). The second (*IC* III.4, 9.27 f) describes the arbitration by Magnesia on the Maeander between the Kretan cities of Itanos and Hierapytna (c.112 BCE). Each city's advocates were accompanied by supporters from allied cities, and these are included in the inscription as συμπαρόεντες. We might compare contemporary evidence for the same situation: Lord Justice Potter has expressed concern about members of the public who support the defendant and make their feelings plain by 'eyeballing' the jury (private communication).
104. He draws attention (1992: 73) to another Olbian *katadesmos* concerning a lawsuit (SGD 171), where the unique formula καὶ τὸς αὐτῶι συνιόντας πάντας appears. Though the precise meaning of the verb is not clear in this context, it is possible, as he sees it, that the term might imply that '"those who go with" the litigant might have been persons engaged by him to attend the trial, and, by their reactions or other unofficial methods, to influence the judges'.
105. Literary: at least 19 of the surviving real and imaginary speeches include explicit references to spectators: e.g. Antiph. 6. 14, 24 (referring to the spectators of previous trials not the current one); Pl. *Ap.* 24e–25b, 35b; Andok. 1.105; Aeschin. 1.77, 177, 173; 2.5; 3.8, 56, 207; Dem. 18.196; 19.309; 20.165; 25.98; 30. 32; 54.41; 56.48; Isai. 5.20; Din. 1.30, 46, 66; 2.19; Hyp. 5.22; Lys. 12.35; 27.7. Cf. Eubulos fr. 74 K–A and Plut. *Mor.* 580d–f.

For archaeological evidence of *dryphaktoi* (railings/fences) used to hold back the crowds in court locations: see Boegehold 1967, Thompson and Wycherley 1972, Travlos 1974, Boegehold *et al.* 1995, and Townsend 1995. Evidence for the crowds listening to the Assembly: Aeschin. 3.224; Din. 2.15, 3.1. See Hansen (1985) for further information on the arrangement of fences to control spectators in this location. The Council also drew a crowd: Dem. 19.17, Ar. *Eq.* 641, Pl. *Men.* 234a–b, Aeschin. 3.125. Possibly also at the Areopagus as well: Dem. 25.23 usually taken to indicate the exclusion of spectators from its meetings actually seems to describe an exception to usual practice. Lys. 10.11 seems to offer an indication that attendance at the court sessions of the Areopagos was common and perhaps even expected.

106. Lanni 1997: 183.
107. Convincing the jury: Antiph. 6.14 and Aeschin. 2.5. The audience interrupts: Antiph. 6.14, Aeschin. 2.5 again, also Din. 1.30, Dem. 30.32. Managing the noise of the mob, as opposed to the interruptions of the judges (cited Hall 1995: 44): *Rhetorica ad Alexandrum* 18.1433^{a}14–20.
108. Dem. 20.165, 25.98; Aeschin. 1.117, 3.247; [Dem.] 59.109; Lykoph. 1.14; Din. 1.22, 27, 2.19, 3.22; Andok. 1.140; Lys. 12.91, 22.19–21; Isok. 18.42.
109. On the peopling of the Roman *contio*—'the "informal," that is, non-voting, form of popular assembly where public speeches were heard'—see Morstein-Marx 2004: 119 ff., defined p. 3.
110. Of the tablets that include forensic terminology, women appear on: *DTA* 39, 67, 68, 95, and 106; *DT* 49 and 87; and NGCT 10. They also appear on *DTA* 24, 30, 84, 87, 89; *DT* 50, 61; SGD 10, 46, 48; NGCT 37, 50.
111. L. Robert (1936: 13–14) argued that the word *laikas* that follows each woman's name (ll. 16–19) should be read as 'prostitute'.
112. R. J. Bonner 1905: 32.
113. Goldhill 1994: 353.
114. Harrison 1971: 136.
115. MacDowell 1963: 102 ff.; Harrison 1971: 137 n. 1.; Todd 1993.
116. Schaps 1977: 323–30; see also Sealey 1990.
117. [Dem.] 59 *passim*. The speech climaxes in a demand that the audience look at the woman to make their own judgement about her character. In the forensic orators, there is a topos of women being 'exhibited' by a litigant in order to arouse pity in his audience. Just (1989: 112) points out, however, that in the references to this practice that are generally cited, there are only two examples where those placed before the jury include women: in one, the female is a little girl, and in the other, it is the aged mothers of the defendants. It seems likely that women who were exhibited tended to be in these categories, rather than those who were, as Just puts it, 'possessed of their full sexuality'; see Ar. *Vesp.* 568 ff. and Dem. 25.
118. As Todd (1993: 208), women could only be sued in cases for which they could pay the penalty. Because they (officially) did not own property, this meant that they could not appear as defendants in cases where the penalty was a fine or the payment of damages. However, they could still be executed or sold into slavery. Examples include [Dem.] 59, Antiph. 1, and Dem. 57.8. For women prompting or exacerbating court cases, see Foxhall 1996: 141 ff. Examples include Lys. 1; Dem. 41 and 55.23–5, 27; Isai. 3; [Dem.] 48; Demosthenes' recovery of his patrimony, encouraged by his mother, Kleoboule (Dem. 27–30); see also the role of the mother of the orphans who are fighting for their inheritance in Lysias 32 (Todd 1993: 203).
119. Although there is no evidence that women ever took evidentiary oaths in court, it does seem clear that a woman could swear an evidentiary

oath in an arbitration, which could then be proffered by a male litigant as evidence in court. See Todd 1990: 35 and 1993: 96; Foxhall 1996: 144. Just (1989: 38) raises the possibility, but denies its realization (see Dem. 40.10; Isai. 12.9). In two further cases, there is no express reference to an arbitration nor is an oath in court in any way implied, but both these cases were subject to arbitration, so they afford no support for the view that an oath could be administered to a woman in court (Dem. 29.26 and 33; 55.27).

Ways of bringing in female evidence: one method was just to incorporate it into the speech in question, demonstrating that the woman was in a position to know the facts; see for example Lysias 32, Dem. 27.40. The speaker might also offer an imprecation on his own head to emphasize his recital of what he had learned from a woman, Dem. 55. 24.

120. For example: [Dem.] 45.71–86 and Andok. 1 (see Foxhall 1996: 141).
121. Isai. 12.5; Dem. 59.110–11: 'And when each one of you goes home, what will he find to say to his own wife or his daughter or his mother, if he has acquitted this woman? When the question is asked you, "Where were you?" and you answer, "We sat at jury." "Trying whom?" it will at once be asked. "Neaira," you will say, of course, will you not? . . . And the women when they have heard, will say, "Well, what did you do?" And you will say "We acquitted her." At this point, the most virtuous of the women will be angry at you for having deemed it right that this woman should share in like manner with themselves in the public ceremonials and religious rights . . .' (trans. A. T. Murray: 1939).
122. DTA 25 γείτονας (ll. 7 and 10); DTA 65 Νουμηνίου κηδ(ε)σταί NGCT 12 Θοχάρης ὁ κηδεστής; DT 49 μάγειρος; SGD 42 κροκοπώλης; DTA 87 Καταδῶ Κίττον τὸν γείτονα τὸν καναβιο(υ)ργόν.
123. See Osborne 1990: against this view Harvey 1990.
124. Different court procedures offered different possible resolutions for different offences (see Osborne 1985). The question of which kind of procedure was to be utilized turned on the kind of risk the prosecutor was willing to run and, of course, how he could construe his case. I acknowledge that this is a brief glimpse of the ongoing scholarly discussion about the open texture of Athenian law. In its original use (Hart 1994: 123) this term described the ambiguity of the substantive aspect of law: specifically how a law that necessarily describes general categories of action should be applied to specific circumstances. It is applied by Osborne to the procedural aspect of Athenian law (observing this different use, see Harris 1994: 150 n. 16 and Rubinstein 2000: 221) to describe how and why an offence might be prosecuted under a variety of different procedures (both public and private), allowing litigants (surely only prosecutors) to choose a procedure that fitted their social and financial standing. The purpose of this chapter is to explore the

information provided by curse tablets, rather than the complexity of the legal and social function of Athenian law and procedure. Osborne (1985) argues that the situation of both prosecutor and defendant were considerations, and that this therefore helped to ensure a level playing-field; Rubinstein (2000: 222) is more critical, arguing that surely only the prosecutor made the selection, and that therefore this element of Athenian law was capable of constructing an 'extraordinarily *uneven* playing field'.

125. The majority date to the Classical period; in fact, the number of judicial curses far outweighs those from other contexts during the Classical period (although, of course, it is difficult to argue from a lack of evidence).
126. Halliwell 1991: 286; Bers 1985: 3.
127. Halliwell 1991; Chaniotis 1992. Exacerbating role of gossip: Aeschin. 1.127. As Versnel has commented (1999: 139): 'In a society that values honour and shame as perhaps the most fundamental elements of its cultural identity and hence as primary incentives to social action, this is indeed the worst thing that can happen.'
128. Ziebarth (1899) argued that these curses were written after the judgement given in a court case. Wünsch (1900: 62–85, in particular p. 68) argued that there was no proof supporting this opinion (Audollent agreed: *DT* pp. lxxxviii–lxxxix): all curse formulae seem to point to a future event and so were either written before the case came to court or before judgement was given. Most commentators accepted this view. Ziebarth (1934) raised the question again, arguing that the situation was between these two extremes. In many cases, the curse seems to have been written in advance of the case, but curses may also have been created to attack the tongue and/or intelligence of an adversary and that side's witnesses or the witnesses themselves during the trial itself, at the point when they had given evidence or given in written statements and the debates had been conducted, but before judgement had been pronounced (*DTA* 65, 4. Aud. *DTA* 94, 2.) However, Moraux (1960) observes that he cannot locate anywhere, either in the material that Ziebarth adduces or elsewhere, a single curse made which seems to have been created after a judgement was pronounced. Moreover, it is not absolutely clear that the curses against witnesses and advocates need to have been made after the evidence was given and the debates conducted. The fact that a witness is named means nothing, since those coming to court would probably know the names of witnesses ranged against them.
129. Gager (1992: 117 and 122 n. 8): 'By the very nature of the case, those who commissioned the tablets were prospective defendants.' He appends a list of legal vocabulary, though it is not clear if he is presenting this as evidence of his statement: σύνδικος cannot be taken simply to mean

prosecuting opponent as Gager translates it. Ogden (1999: 32): 'It is also believed, on the basis of technical legal vocabulary found in the tablets, that curses relating to criminal cases were only made by defendants' adding '(i.e. the people with something to lose).' He goes on: 'although there is no obvious reason why a prosecutor should not have used a tablet to secure a conviction, especially if the prosecution was, as so often, malicious'. Literary evidence also suggests that this was not the case: in Aeschylus' *Eumenides* (306 ff.), the Erinyes, that is the prosecution, appear to issue an oral binding curse against Orestes—who is in this context, in the role of the defence.

130. The corpus of forensic oratory does mention cases involving those with a low political or social profile. This usually happens when penalties for the wealthy are being discussed and these are compared to penalties that poorer citizens have endured (Rubinstein 2000: 228): e.g. Dinarchos 1.23, where the speaker contrasts the unknown offenders of a previous trial with the well-known Demosthenes; also Hyperides' description of the punishment endured by an Aristomachos for having borrowed a knife from the Academy, and a Konon of Paiania for having received a *theorikon* of five drachmae on his son's behalf. Hyperides is using these examples to illustrate his argument to the jury that these misfortunes could happen to them as easily (1 fr. VI cols. 25–6).

131. Brown 1970: 25 and Faraone 1989; also see Dover 1974: 133–56.

132. Eur. *Alk. TGF* 67; Cic. *Brut.* 217 and *Orat.* 128–9.

133. Pl. *Men.* 80a–b; *Euthyd.* 303a. Such allusions occur throughout the literature of the fifth century; see Derrida 1981.

134. Political affiliation: for example, Habicht 1993 on Willemsen 1990: 148–9; NGCT 5. Habicht points out that NGCT 5 along with SGD 48 and *DTA* 103 reveal to us that the citizens of Athens were far from united in their opposition to Makedon, as other sources, such as Hyperides' *Funeral Oration* in 323, might suggest.

CHAPTER 10

1. Ashforth on popular explanations of inequity in Soweto, South Africa.
2. Hom. epigram 14 (at [Herodotos], *Life of Homer* 32 = Hes. F302 MW). ll. 1–11, from *Hesiod, The Homeric Hymns and Homerica*, trans. West (2003; see also pp. 300–5). Preserved in a *Life of Homer* attributed to Herodotos where it is said to have been written by Homer, at the request of local potters, during his stay on Samos; Pollux (10.85) says some attribute it to Hesiod. It is generally assigned to the period around 500 BCE (see Noble 1965: 72–83; cited by Gager 1992: 155). If this is the case, Jordan points out there in private correspondence, then it cannot be right to think that it originated in the formulae of *katadesmoi*.
3. Faraone (1991a: 11): 'Tradesmen (and innkeepers as well), in their efforts

to stay ahead of the competition, employed *katadesmoi* to inhibit the success and profit of their rivals'. Gager 1992: 152: 'We should not be surprised to find individuals who were prepared to seek an advantage for themselves by cursing or binding the affairs of their nearby competitors.' Ogden (1999: 32) states: 'Trade curses appear to have been generally made between rival tradesmen.'

4. Faraone identifies the following tablets as belonging to this category (1991*a*: 27 n. 47): *DTA* 68, 69, 70, 71, 72, 73, 74, 75 and 84, 85, 86, and 87; *DT* 47, 52, 70, 71, 72, 73, 92; *SGD* 20, 52, 73, 75, 88, and 124. Gager (1992: 151 ff.) adds *DTA* 55, 97, 108, 109; *SGD* 3, 60, 44. Ogden (1999: 34) adds *SGD* 3, 48, 72, 124, and 170; *DTA* 12, 30. Lopez-Jimeno (1999) adds *SGD* 4, 11, 43, 81, and Kovs. 3. All these curses are discussed in this section except *SGD* 60 and *DTA* 85, which do not seem to me to be concerned with commercial activity. Kovs. 3 is curse 3 in Willemsen 1990: 145–7. This is not, as Lopez-Jimeno (1999: 305) lists it, I 518, but the previous tablet, I 513, and it does not include any commercial detail. Since she does not make reference to this in her commentary it seems likely that this is an oversight. A similar oversight seems to have been made by her with reference to *SGD* 81: this extremely fragmentary tablet makes no mention of any aspect of life connected to business matters and her own commentary on this text does not mention commercial interests.

The tablets date as follows. Fifth century BCE: *SGD* 88. Fifth or fourth century BCE: *SGD* 3, 4. Fourth century BCE: *DTA* 55, 75, 87; *DT* 50, 52, 68; *SGD* 11, 20, 43, 44, 48. No later than fourth century BCE: *DTA* 86. Third or fourth century BCE: *DTA* 95; *DT* 66, 72, 73; *SGD* 73, 75, 124. Third century BCE: *DTA* 12, 30, 53, 56, 63, 64, 72, 77, 94, 97, 104, 105, 106, 108, 109, 120, 137, 160; *DT* 47, 92; *SGD* 52. Classical/Hellenistic: *DTA* 68, 69, 72, 73, 74, 84, 85, *DTA/DT* 70, 71. No earlier than the second century BCE: *SGD* 60. Ogden (1999: 35) locates two reasonable Roman-period examples of trade curses: one from Nomentum dating from the first century CE or possibly even from the Late Republic (*DT* 135; Gager 1992: 80) and one from Karthage (second or third century CE; Gager 1992: 62).

5. E.g. Gager 1992: 151; Faraone 1991*a*: 11.
6. These texts cited in Gager 1992: 153 and 154 and Faraone 1991*a*: 11.
7. West 1978. Hes. *Op.* ll. 20–6; trans. West 1978 (used for all translations of this poem).
8. Gager (1992: 153–4, and 155 n. 14) cites these texts from Hesiod, Pliny, and Pollux.
9. See above, n. 2.
10. Plin. *HN* 28.4.19, Poll. *Onom.* 7.108. On Pliny, Faraone (1991a: 11): 'Immediately following his comment that no one was immune to the fear of curse tablets he [Pliny] states: "Many people (presumably potters) believe that the products of potters' shops can be crushed by this means" (i.e. curse tablets).'

11. The verb *defigere* as found here, is found in some British curse tablets (e.g. *RIB*, nos. 6–7). However, the detail with which Pliny continues suggests that he was not thinking of curse tablets.
12. Plin. *HN* 28.4.19: *multi figlinarum opera rumpi credunt tali modo, non pauci etiam serpentes, ipsas recanere et hunc unum illis esse intellectum, contrahique Marsorum cantu etiam in nocturna quiete*. 'They believe that many ceramics are broken in this way, and no few serpents as well; they are themselves able to undo the charm, this being the only intelligence they have.'
13. Poll. *Onom.* 7.108 describes the apotropaic talismen that bronze workers placed in their foundries in order to ward off the evil eye. The Greek is: πρὸ δὲ τῶν καμίνων τοῖς χαλκεῦσιν ἔθος ἦν γελοῖά τινα καταρτᾶν ἢ ἐπιπλάττειν ἐπὶ φθόνου ἀποτροπῇ followed by a fragment of Aristophanes βασκάνιον ἐπικάμιον ἀνδρὸς χαλκέως (fr. 607). Another possible reference to such an object may be found at Ar. *Aves* 436, where Tereus instructs two slaves to hang a suit of armour πλησίον τοὐπιστάτου. The scholiast to Ar. *Aves* 436 (Σ 436 A) gives three explanations for ἐπιστάτου, of which one is 'a clay image of Hephaistos set beside the hearth in order to watch over the fire'. Dunbar (1995: 303) observes that this meaning of ὁ ἐπιστάτης (as 'domestic hearth-god') is not found elsewhere, but suggests that it may be similar to Pollux's talisman. See also Sommerstein 1987: 224.
14. On a black-figure hydria from Etruria (Beazley Online Archive vase number 302031; Munich *Antikensammlungen* 1717) in a scene depicting artisans at work, a mask is shown hanging over a kiln. This may be an apotropaic device meant to protect the contents of the kiln from attack by supernatural forces; see the name vase of the Foundry painter (red-figure kylix, Berlin 2294).
15. Gager (1992: 162) in contrast: 'The context for the curse is business competition among potters in the Kerameikos district of Athens, although the basis for this conjecture is limited to the references to the business of two of the secondary targets . . .'.
16. ΧΛΑΚΕΑ (l. 1) and ΧΑΛΚΕΙΑ (l. 2), Curbera and Jordan 1988*a*: 215–18.
17. Curbera and Jordan 1988*a*: 215–18.
18. e.g., *DT* 47, 52, 71 (*DTA* 71), 72, 92; *DTA* 74, 84, and *SGD* 88. A flour-maker and a painter are also reported among the targets of *SGD* 48 (see Gager 1992: 152).
19. Gager 1992: 153.
20. See Davidson 1998: 53 ff.
21. The agent of *DTA* 87 tells us that two of his targets (Kallias, a shop/tavern-keeper and Kittos, a maker of wooden frames/rope-maker—depending on whether it reads τὸν καναβιουργόν [as Wünsch] or καναβιουργόν [an alternative offered by Gager]—are ἐγ γειτόνων. The text of *DTA* 55 includes a name that appears centred above the rest of the text,

in the nominative case. It appears to say 'Diokles, the son of ...'; the patronymic is lost. It may be that this Diokles was the author or originator of the curse.

22. Whitehead (1977: 63 n. 36) admits that the significance of the use of the *technitikon* is puzzling. He suggests that it might function as a 'poor man's *ethnikon* for freedmen', but notes that it is also found after the names of slaves and some citizens, the latter usually along with a demotic, the former with the name of his/her owner. In Rhodes and Osborne 2003: no. 4 ('Rewards for men who had fought for democracy at Athens, 401/0'), the names of those honoured are organized tribally and some are listed with their professions. Rhodes and Osborne (p. 27) seem to be saying that this indicates that these men were metics, probably of humble status, but they explicitly compare this form of identification with that of the manumitted slaves on the *phialai exeleutherai* of the late fourth century. In comparison, the official nomenclature of an Athenian citizen was probably tripartite (name, patronymic, demotic) with the demotic only coming into use a century or so after Kleisthenes' reforms (see Rhodes 1981: 254). This form of identification is very rare in the corpus of curse tablets, which usually include only the name of their target(s) and lack either patronymic or demotic, although there are exceptions (e.g., see NGCT 1, which gives the demotic of each of the seven supporters of its target, Eukrates, and *DTA* 11, which gives the demotic of some of its victims; while *DTA* 42 gives the patronymics of some targets).

23. The targets of *DTA* 12, 30, SGD 48, 72, and 170 include a leather-cutter, innkeepers, a scribe, a seamstress, and a ship's pilot, respectively. They are all identified by name and profession and then bound, without any further information about the work, workplace, or production of the target. Gager (1992: 152) has suggested that the fact that a profession sometimes occurs as a qualifier in these curses is an indication of 'the social importance of work', and likens it to the use of a patronymic or a demotic. But does this indicate commercial competition? It is hard to make a case that the targets of *DTA* 30 are the victims of commercial competition, when the tablet includes a list of (at least) 10 names, of which only two have their professions appended (one male tavern-keeper, one female tavern-keeper). In contrast, in SGD 72, several different professions seem to be bound simultaneously.

24. L. Robert 1936: 13 for interpretation of Λαικάς. Versnel (1991a: 95 n. 23) describes, as if for comparison, examples of *diabolai*—special types of *katadesmoi* that are based on the use of abuse—such as *DT* 155 and 188. *DT* 155: τὸν δυσσεβῆν καὶ ἄνομον καὶ ἐπικατάρατον κάρδηλον and *DT* 188: τόνδε τὸν ἄνομον καὶ ἀσεβῆ. However, the abuse found in these tablets is concerned with accusing the target of evil deeds against the god in order to provoke divine wrath against him/her.

25. For example, the statesmen Kephalos, Kleon, Kleophon, Anytos, and

Hyperbolos were all abused as *banausoi* for their connections with business: Kephalos as the son of a potter (Schol. Ar. *Eccl.* 253); Kleon as a tanner (Ar. *Eq.* 129 ff. and see Schol. Ar. *Eq.* 44); Kleophon as a lyremaker (Andok. I.146); Anytos as a tanner (Pl. *Meno* 90a); and Hyperbolos as a flaskmaker (Ar. *Eq.* 1315 and see Schol. Ar. *Pax* 692).

An examination of the names of those victims who appear in curses from Athens that seem most focused on commercial matters indicates that these individuals had at least some likelihood of being Athenian citizens, although they may be attested without demotic or ethnic. In the *Lexicon of Greek Personal Names* (*LGPN*) most of these individuals appear under the 'Athens?' category, which contains people who could be metics, but 'whose credentials support Athenian citizenship'. It is obviously difficult to make a secure judgement from the limited information in these texts, especially where a curse provides the only example of a particular name, for example Kerkis in *DT* 52. (But note Agathon and Karpos in *DT* 87, categorized under 'Athens?', are each described as *oikētēs*, or house-slave, in the curse text.)

26. Gager 1992: 161.
27. Gager (1992: 156): 'Here, the occasion is competition between small-scale merchants, mostly tavern-keepers.' He also suggests that there may be a further motive of erotic jealousy that underlies the creation of this text. Working from a manumission document of 330–320 BCE (*IG* ii². 1554–9, face A, col. 5, l. 493; see Lewis 1959: 219) he raises the idea that Thraitta was originally the wife of one Menedemos, from whom she fled and who was then prompted to create this tablet. However, it is unlikely that these two are the husband and wife of the curse tablet, since, according to that document they lived in different parts of Athens. Moreover, the verb which Gager reads as indicating that Thraitta 'fled' her husband ($\dot{a}\pi o\phi v\gamma\grave{\omega}v$) is actually a verb of manumission: Menedemos was the owner of Thraitta who freed her.
28. It is not easy to find evidence for such clubs at this level in Athenian society: most of the evidence we have is for upper-class bands (*hetaireiai*) organized for social and political purposes. However, it is possible that such clubs existed: a law of Solon's concerning Athens in the early sixth century (Gaius, *Dig.* 47.22.4) lists a number of social groups and organizations both sacred and secular, including *orgeones, sussitia, thiasoi*, and those who have joined together for the purpose of piracy or trade (see Whitehead 1986: 13–14 and Jones 1999).
29. Jeffery (1955: 67–84, no. 18) reads *KEPΔON* as the accusative form of a name, *Kerdos*. But Faraone (1991*a*: 27 n. 48) cites *DTA* 86 as containing another example of $\kappa\acute{\epsilon}\rho\delta o\varsigma$, meaning profit, as a target of a binding curse.
30. The two parts are divided between lines 9 and 10 by a horizontal line at the left.

31. As Audollent notes: a conclusion reached by Ziebarth (1899, no. 20).
32. e.g. *DTA/DT* 71, l. 2; *DTA* 75, side b, l. 8.
33. *DTA* 77a, l. 7, κ[α]ταδ[ῶ τὰς ψυχας καὶ τὰ ἔργα αὐτ[ῶν καὶ αὐτοὺς ὅλους καὶ τὰ τού[των ἅπαντα b, l. 4 (very similar formula); *DTA* 104, l. 6 καὶ ἔργα καὶ τέλος; *DTA* 120, l. 2 καὶ τὴν ψυχὴν ... κ[αὶ] τὰ ἔργα; *DTA* 160b, l. 2 ἔργα τὰ πάντα; 161a, l. 3 (largely unintelligible); *DT* 47, ll. 8–9 κ]αταγράφ[φ]ω Βιότην [χ]εῖρας πόδας ψυχὴ[ν] γλῶταν ἐργασίαν τέκνα καὶ τὰ ἐκεινης ἅπα[ντα.]; also ll. 4–5; *DT* 50, ll. 3, 6, 9, 13 in various combinations, l. 6 καὶ γλῶτταν καὶ ψυχὴ[ν καὶ ἔργα καὶ πόδας καὶ] β(ου)λάς; *DT* 66, l. 2 [γλ]ῶταν ἔ]ργ]α l. 5 πό<σ>δας ἔργα.
34. Burford 1972: 78–9 and Finley 1973: 65, who quotes the scholiast to Aeschin. I. I.24: 'That the appellations [of workshops] are not from the shops to the men but from the men to the places.' Rather than indicating the existence of a workshop as a distinct building, the term may be used to mean a group of slaves employed in one place in the production of goods (e.g., Dem. 27.9 where the speaker refers to two *ergasteria* because his father had two distinct sets of slaves). SGD 124 (ll. 7–8) appears to curse first the ἐργαστήριον of the doctors and then their slaves (listing their names) as if these people were what comprised the detailed aspects of the workshop. Possibly the people listed in *DT/DTA* 71 were the personnel of the ἐργαστήριον which appears in the curse; the same may be true of the lists of names in SGD 43. Possibly ἐργαστήριον should be translated as 'team' rather than 'workshop'.
35. Variously found as ἔπη καὶ ἔργα· *DTA* 56; 84b, l. 2; 95b, l. 6; 98, l. 3; 105a, ll. 2, 4, 6, 8, and b 2; 106b, l. 2; 137, ll. 7–8.
36. As part of a formula: along with spirit, work, hands, feet (*DT* 52, *DT/DTA* 71, *DT* 92, *DTA* 69, 87); τὴν ἐργασίαν καὶ τὰ ἔργα (*DTA* 69); ἐργασίας [ἁ]πάσας (*DT* 72 and 73); [τ]ούτων ἅπαντα καὶ τὰς ἐργασίας (*DT/DTA* 70, *DT* 73); ἐργασίας κέρδην (*DTA* 86, follows spirit); τὸ καπήλιον καὶ τὴν ἐργασίαν (SGD 43).
37. E.g. ἔργα γλῶτταν (*DTA* 53; 95, b3); or just as an expression of things the target may do (e.g. *DTA* 63, l. 3, καὶ] ἔργα μέλ(λ) ε[ι, and *DTA* 64, l. 6, καὶ ἔργα καὶ ἥντινα μέλλει Λ ...). The work of *DT* 72 and 73 may not be commercially related (see n. 42). It is possible that the business in which Manes is engaged (*DTA* 109) may also not be a commercial venture—the periphrastic text suggests that the agent is being secretive about the matter which concerns him and about which he seeks vengeance.
38. So also SGD 73 (which binds Nikos from Ephesos, his mind, his business, his house), and *DTA* 84, which curses five people, using list formulae that touch on many parts of the targets' lives, including their commercial activities.
39. This appears to be the significance of the final summary phrase of the curse which seeks to bind καὶ τὰ ἐκε[ίνου πάντα.
40. (ll. 4–7) καὶ τὴν [ο]ἰκ]ίαν αὐτῶν καὶ τὴν [ἐ]ργασίαν καὶ τὰ [ἔργ]α καὶ τὸν

βί[ο]ν αὐτῶ[ν 'and their household and their workshop and their deeds and life'.
41. Gager (1992: 163) says, 'probably a worker of bellows in a silver shop'.
42. *DT/DTA* 70 does include mention of one of the target's profession and does mention τὰς ἐργασίας, but the consistent binding of ἄπαντα suggests that the main intent of the agent of the text was to attack more than just the commercial activities of the targets.
43. Dickie 2000: 576.
44. It is not clear what αἵματι means in this context.
45. This same point can be made about *DTA* 97 which, although it does mention the business activities of its targets, focuses primarily on preventing them from speaking against a certain Philon, who may indeed be the agent of the curse.
46. *DTA* 77a ll. 8/9; 120, l. 7 (fragmentary); 160b, l. 2 (again fragmentary).
47. As suggested by Burford (1972: 65): 'Given the scale of the economy even in the larger cities of the ancient world, it is clear that craftsmen who worked in expensive materials and unusual techniques . . . had to face the problem at one time or another of finding adequate employment for their special skills.'
48. Burford (1969) analyses the nationalities of those who worked at different levels on the temple at Epidauros. McKechnie (1989: 144) suggests that this provides evidence that craftsmen usually spent months away from home, but on relatively close sites. See Burford 1965.
49. Burford (1969: 201 ff.) supports this suggestion when she discusses the shortage of skilled workers available to build the temple at Epidauros in the late fifth and early fourth centuries BCE. She goes on to argue (1972: 12) that the itinerant skilled worker was one of the few outsiders whom the early Greek community was always glad to see. See also McKechnie 1989: 142 ff.
50. Skilled workers: τὸν κρανοποιόν ('helmet-maker') and τὴν χρυσωτρίαν (gold-worker, *DTA* 69) and ἰατροί ('doctors', *SGD* 124). Less skilled: τὸ ἀργυροπίο φυσετές ('bellows worker at a silver works', *SGD* 3); τὸν καναβιουργόν or τὸν κανναβιουργόν (a rope or a frame-maker, *DTA* 87); τὸν στιγματίαν δικτυοπλόκον ('net-maker', *SGD* 52). For shop- or tavern-keepers, see, for example, *DTA* 30, 68, and 87, and *SGD* 11.
51. Popular: see Arist. *Rhet.* 1411^{a}24; Ar. *Plut.* 435, F285 K–A; Antiphanes 25 K–A; Nikostratos 22 K–A; Eubulos 80 K–A; Lys. 1.24.
52. I would prefer an explanation that turns on economic competition to the explanations advanced by either Ogden or Gager. Ogden's argument seems to turn on a view of the suitability of cursing to this social group (1999: 34): 'The innkeepers' profession predominates, which is gratifying in view of their ancient literary reputation for obstreperousness and vulgar abuses.' He goes on to quote *DTA* 87a, observing that it gives pride of place to innkeepers. In fact, we can observe that the term in question

can also mean shopkeeper (which he acknowledges in his translation). Gager (1992: 153): 'It would seem that the frequent use of *katadesmoi* in and around the tavern demonstrates that important issues were transacted there.' But it is not clear why it is necessary to argue for any further motivation than vindictive behaviour or economic competition.

53. *DT* 52, 70, and 71; *DTA* 72, 73, and 75; and SGD 52, 88, and 124.
54. Examples of these include: *DT* 47, SGD 75, *DTA* 74 and 86.
55. *DTA* 12 and 30; SGD 11, 48, 72, and 170.

CHAPTER 11

1. Francis Bacon 1597, *Of Envy*, in Dick 1955: 23.
2. Although SGD 91, discussed above under the category of theatrical curses, appears to have been created because of the love of the agent for Eunikos, I have not included it here because its primary concern appears to be to obstruct the performance of *chorēgoi* in the contest, rather than to instil or obstruct desire. Jordan/Miller's reading of the opening of the text as a plea by Apelles that Eunikos love him willingly or not is uncertain (Dubois offers a different interpretation) and sits oddly with their translation of the penultimate sentence, that 'no one be more successful with men or women than Eunikos'.
3. Dickie (2000: 576) has suggested that curses that are aimed against brothels and taverns be included in the category of amatory magic as magic designed to further or impede the interests of those who were making a living from selling sexual favours. Although he does not mention specific examples of the texts he means, I am assuming that he is talking about texts such as *DTA* 68, 75, and 87 and *DT* 52.
4. SGD 60, 109, and 118–21.
5. See Appendix 2 for examples and more details.
6. Described in Faraone 1991*a* and again 1999; also Graf 1997*a*: 178–9.
7. Faraone 1991*a*: 13.
8. In Faraone 1991a. Of these, *DT* 198 is from the second or third century CE, and SGD 30–2 and 154 are from the third century CE and so will not be discussed in this chapter. Two others have been reported from the Nemean excavations by S. G. Miller (1981: 64). These, seen by Jordan and included as 28 and 29 in his latest catalogue (NGCT), apparently contain a formula similar to that of SGD 57, but with different personnel.
9. The name *philtrokatadesmos* is a reference to the type of spell it is rather than the form it necessarily must take, for example *PGM* iv. 296–303 involves the creation of two wax or clay figures, a male and a female, and includes the following instruction: 'Make the male in the form of Ares fully armed, holding a sword in his left hand and threatening to plunge it into the right side of her neck. And make her with her arms behind her back and down on her knees . . .'.

10. Responsible for these two explanations: Faraone (1991*a*: 14) and Petropoulos (1988: 216) respectively.
11. Faraone (1991*a*: 13–14) originally argued that erotic attraction curses date from the second century CE and emerge in North Africa and Syria. These include curses from Karthage (*DT* 227, 230–1), Hadrumetum (*DT* 264–71, 304), and Egypt (*DT* 38; SGD 151–3, 155–6, 158–61); also texts from Egypt which are unpublished and not wholly read (SGD 191) and from Karthage (SGD 186–7) and Tyre (SGD 192). However, an attraction spell from Akanthos in Makedonia dating from the late fourth century or early third century BCE suggests that the tradition was longer-lived. Faraone was criticized for this opinion by Dickie (2000: 575 n. 37), but in fact had already pointed out his own error and considered the new evidence of the Akanthos curse (Faraone 1999: 143).
12. Faraone 1999: 18. He includes curses as a form of aggressive attraction magic (p. 30), where he is clearly concerned only with *philtrokatadesmoi*. He does also adduce examples of separation curses (p. 86 for a discussion of *DT* 86).
13. For example, the papyrus handbooks of late Hellenistic/Roman Egypt show marked similarities to papyrus fragments of handbooks dating to the first centuries BCE and CE (see Brashear 1995: 3413–14). Many other magical handbooks were probably burnt in the first century CE (see Acts of the Apostles 19: 19 and Suet. *Aug.* 31.1).
14. Winkler 1990b: 87–91.
15. Faraone 1999: 27 and 132.
16. Faraone 1999: 83. He argues that the majority of attraction spells were based on the model of bridal theft, that is, using violent means to extract a woman from her existing family or relationship and forge a new relationship. He suggests that they were used by young men looking for young women (secluded by their families) with whom they could settle down and live happily ever after. The pain they wish to inflict has everything to do with the cultural need to rape the bride-to-be violently as if she were 'a member of a hostile tribe' as 'a prelude to a settled and even happy relationship' with the man in question. He argues that attraction spells are a 'traditional and practical response to problems of access to woman of marriageable age'. Graf's approach to attraction binding spells has elements similar to Faraone's, insofar as it argues that curse tablets are a way for ancient Greek males to express a strong urge to compete. Graf (1997a: 186) suggests that attraction binding spells are all part of the competitive need to outdo one's peers, in this case expressed as the need to make a marriage better than that of their fellows. Again, the competitors in this interpretation are viewed as being, in the majority, male.
17. In addition, magic used in a domestic setting is described as a 'male' tool brought into the home and used as a 'frightening attack against privileged male power'. See Faraone 1999: 100.

18. Dickie (2000) argues that, although the formularies are often written as if they were designed for a man to cast against a woman, in fact it seems that these formularies could be and were adapted for different situations, involving men and women in the roles of both targets and agents (e.g. *PGM* xxxiia and lxviii both draw on one formulary, but the former is written by one man against another, while the latter is written by a woman against a man). Moreover, he points out that it is not at all clear that the majority of spells were written with the intent of achieving marriage, or that they were directed by youths seeking access to young women living in seclusion. The spells frequently ask that a woman come to a man, an idea which seems actually to negate the violent invasion of a household which bridal theft seems to require and, more practically, demands that the target in question not be a secluded, sheltered young female. A number of spells are aimed not at untameable young women, but at women who are already involved in marriages with someone else, e.g., *PGM* iv. 2740–58, 2755–66 and lxi. 29–30.
19. See *katadesmoi*: *PGM* xixb.53–4; xxxvi.81. *Agōgai* and *philtrokatadesmoi*: *PGM* iv.351–2, 396, 1502, 1533–5, 2910, 2931–3; xvi.3–8; xxxvi. 81, 147, 151–2.
20. Dickie 2000: 565 and Faraone 1999: 140, 147–8.
21. Faraone's expression of this fact is (1999: 149): 'Literary evidence beginning in the Classical period suggests that one special group of women regularly co-opted these traditionally male forms of magic: courtesans and prostitutes.' This statement raises the questions of how and when and in which literary sources (before the beginning of the Classical period, where we hear of their use by women) were these forms of magic established as 'traditionally male' before then being 'usurped' by women.
22. As in the Busby Berkeley 'Gold Diggers of 1933' (also '. . . of 1935' and '. . . of 1937'). To find such women accused of practising a dangerous, antisocial supernatural activity is neither surprising nor novel. See Ch. 7, n. 72.
23. Most scholars agree that in ancient Greece sex was not considered a mutual act, but an action which was done 'to' somebody: it was (as Halperin 1990*a*: 30) 'either act or impact'; see Dover 1978, Foucault 1985 and 1986, Keuls 1985, Halperin 1990*a*, Winkler 1990*b*. The significant action was that of penetration, and the nature of that act was polarizing and hierarchical. He who penetrated was considered active and dominant, while he or she who was penetrated was thought to be passive, submissive, and subordinate. Davidson (1998: 178), however, has argued that this position has been overstated and that it reflects modern anxieties collected at the 'endpoint of a long meandering Western tradition about making love'. He asserts that the Greeks did not see a gulf between a desire to penetrate and a desire to be penetrated. He argues,

that in fact, in Greece, it was not so much the fact of penetration which caused a partner to be considered unmanly, nor a stance of passivity, but the fact of a sexual appetite considered to be lewd and insatiable: Davidson (2001) explores the history of this emphasis on penetration in modern scholarship. Katz (1995: 21–43) provides a useful summary of the debate over status. Interestingly, the gender debate has arisen in this area of study itself. See Richlin (1991) for details of how male scholars such as Winkler and Halperin who follow the theories of Foucault fail to acknowledge the work done in this area by female and feminist scholars.

24. As a number of feminist scholars in particular have emphasized, much of the material we have represents the opinions of only a small sample of male individuals, which are then mediated via only a small sample of male individuals. See Richlin 1991 and Katz 1995.

25. I focus here on female sex-workers since the experience of being a male sex-worker would have brought with it some different, gender-specific experiences. This deserves more attention than there is room here to give, but just for example compare the experiences of and attitudes towards male prostitutes who worked in *oikēma* 'little booths', with female prostitutes who worked in *porneia* 'brothels'. As Davidson (1998: 91) observes, it appears to have offered a far more independent experience: indeed, in Pl. *Charm*. 163b 'sitting in an *oikēma*' is listed alongside 'selling salt-fish' and 'making shoes'.

26. Constructed as male: Faraone 1999 (in particular, p. 156) where he analyses the use of 'masculine' aggressive magic by Simaetha in Theokritos' Second Idyll. Faraone goes on to talk more generally about the 'peculiar "male-ness" of prostitutes and courtesans in circum-Mediterranean cultures'. Compare, however, the conclusions of Neils (2000) that the ancient Greek iconography of the *hetaira* deliberately echoes that of the maenad.

27. Feminist writers, such as Keuls (1985), reacted to the overly romantic vision of *hetairai* by dividing the female population into two groups: wives and sex-workers. However, this approach still describes women in terms of their value as sexual objects and ignores the experiences of the women themselves. See also Pomeroy 1975: 92 who, although she acknowledges different roles, summarizes her approach using the dichotomy of wife/*hetairai*; also Just 1989: 141 and Ogden 1996: 105. Cf. Brown (1990: 248–9), who warns of the inaccuracy of failing to recognize the degree of variation even within categories of sex-worker. Omitowoju (2002: 213) observes a division in status between types of women appearing in New Comedy, based on the attributes which would make her potentially marriageable. As an example of the more nuanced approach to *hetairai* as a distinct group, Davidson (1998: 109–36) explores the significance of the gift and the *hetaira*'s manipulation of visibility.

28. For example (drawing on Davidson 1998 and his marvellous overview of ancient Greek prostitution): the street-walkers (male and female) whose

names survive in the slang that was used to describe their status (Hesychios s.v. γεφυρίς apparently a prostitute who sold her wares ἐπὶ γεφύρας (probably meaning 'on a bridge'); Phrynichos 34 K–A; *Com. Adesp.* 192 K–A; Theopompos *FGrH* 115 FF 225 and 213; Timokles 24, 1–2 K–A; cf. Xen. *Mem.* 2.2.4, Ar. *Pax* 11, 164. The brothel prostitutes (Plaut. *Poen.* 34.1 and the threats made against the slave-girl in Antiph. 1, also Xenarchos 4 K–A, Eubulos 67 and 82 K–A, and Alexis 206 K–A). The *hetairai* (flute-girls, dancers, and escorts, usually owned by pimps) who survived by entertaining at *symposia*, although they could be hired for longer than just a single evening (Neaira began her career entertaining at parties [Dem.] 59, while in Menander's *Samia*, Chrysis is threatened with having to return to the life of a party *hetaira*, l. 390 ff.; also Plaut. *Asin.* 746 ff.). More long-term relationships between client and worker could also be arranged, either by making a contract with a *hetaira* if she was a free woman, or if she was not by buying her: in such situations the sex-worker's role was that of a mistress or *pallakē*. (Examples of longer contracts are found in Plaut. *Asin.* 746 ff., *Merc.* 536 ff., and *Bacch.* fr. 10 and 896 f.) Such an arrangement might be made by one man, but a woman could also be shared between several (as Neaira [Dem.] 59.29). Sometimes the owner might buy the slave's freedom as well, but this would entail the risk of not being able to recoup the cost later. In some cases, the sex-worker supported the household (as Stephanos seems to have lived off Neaira ([Dem.] 59; see also Lynkeus of Samos *ap.* Ath. 13.584b, 6.246b; Machon frr. 6 and 7 (Gow); Ath. 13.591de). Sometimes these relationships were conducted by men on the side of official marriages or they became a primary relationship after a man had enjoyed marriage with a citizen woman and produced legitimate children. (See Isaios' description (6.21) of the old man Euktemon who apparently kept a mistress during his marriage with whom he eventually moved in; and Hyperides, described by Idomeneus *FGrH* 338 F 14, who is meant to have kept three mistresses one of whom eventually moved into his house, presumably after the death of his wife.) Alternatively, a young man might shack up with a *hetaira* in the short time before he matured and married a respectable girl (e.g. the behaviour of Timanoridas and Eukrates with Neaira before they settled down). There are also examples of situations where these cohabitations seem to have taken on an unofficial marital status (Isai. 6, Dem. 48.53–5; see also the plots of Menander's *Girl with Her Hair Cut Short*, *The Man from Sikyon*, and *The Hated Man*). Finally, there were the great *hetairai* who set up in houses of their own, such as Phryne (Ath. 13.590d) who reputedly modelled for Praxiteles, as well as Lais the younger, Lais the elder, Sinope, Maniea, Gnathaena, Nais, Thais, etc., many of whose exploits are described in the anecdotes of Machon and Lynkeus of Samos.

29. For example, Apollodoros follows his clear tripartite division of the roles

of women at [Dem.] 59.122 with inconsistent use of his own taxonomy which intimates his contempt and anger that Neaira, 'a common whore', was actually living as a citizen of Athens; also *pornē* used as a term of abuse at Men. *Epit.* 794.
30. Neaira: [Dem.] 59; Aspasia: Plut. *Per.* 24.1–6, 32.1–2. Other women: Lys. 82, p. 365, no. 59 (Thalheim).
31. For example, Lucian's work shows that women could at least be imagined to, and surely did, patronize female prostitutes (the fullest description appears in Lucian's *Dialogues of the Courtesans*). Cf. Anakreon fr. 13; Asklepiades 7 (Gow–Page); or by considering the activities of male prostitutes.
32. On the development of this point in Classical scholarship, Katz 1995: 36.
33. For example, Hipparete sought her divorce from Alkibiades, it is alleged, because he introduced *hetairai*, free and slave, into his home: Plut. *Alk.* 8 and Andok. 4.
34. One of the 14 or so tablets found in the sanctuary of Demeter at Knidos, in Asia Minor, near the island of Kos. The fragmentary nature of the remains of these curse tablets mean that different editors have enumerated a different final number of tablets—the original editor, Newton (1862–3), collected 14. All the curses in this set are by women.
35. *DTA* 78, *DT* 68, the curse from the Kerameikos, and SGD 57 are all dated to the fourth century; the curses from Makedonia are dated to the late fourth/possibly early third century; *DT* 86 is dated to the Hellenistic era, while *DT* 85 is dated by most commentators to the third or second century BCE (although it has been dated by others to the second or third centuries CE); the date of *DT* 5 is probably second century BCE, according to Jordan (1980: 231 n. 23).
36. An Attic tablet of uncertain provenance, damaged and broken into two parts with writing on both sides of each part: in Audollent's index under *Genera et Causa: Amatoriae*.
37. Dated to the late fourth or third century by Jordan (1999, no. 3), except for the first line on side B which he thinks is somewhat earlier. A text has been published by Trakosopoulou-Salakidou, 'Κατάδεσμοι από την Ακανθο', in A.-Ph. Christidis and D. R. Jordan 1997: 161, no. 4; but Jordan (1999) includes an improved text.
38. Jordan (1999: 120) gives examples of male and female use: masculine at SEG 9.45.28, Kyrene, fifth century; feminine at *IG* ii². 9536, Athens, fourth century BCE.
39. The verb ἱλάσκομαι used in Homer, always of gods, to mean appease: see *Il.* 1.147, 386, and 472 and *Od.* 3.419; s.v. LSJ. Of mortal relations: Xen. *Oik.* 12–13. Of men to conciliate: Pl. *Phd.* 1c and Plut. *Cat. Min.* 61.
40. Dickie 2000: 575: 'Such indications as there are would suggest that Sime was sexually experienced and sexually available.'
41. Euphiletos (Lys. 1) claims that the 'justifiable homicide' statute (probably

Dem. 23.53) extends to those who kill because of offences to their *pallakē* as for those who kill on behalf of their wives. However, he does claim this in the context of having killed a man for *moicheia* (adultery) so it is likely that he was misrepresenting the law here; see discussion by Omitowoju 2002: 97 ff. It seems likely that the legal position of a *pallakē* was more complex than has often been assumed; see Sealey 1984.

42. We know most about legal actions to deal with sexual offences in Athens. However, even here the evidence is complex and inconclusive; Omitowoju (2002) provides a thorough and incisive path through it. She suggests that sex-workers probably had no recourse to legal help if they were raped; as for adultery or the rape of citizen women, it seems likely, at least in Athens, that such cases were settled out of court, either through arbitration or through more violent means (e.g. Lys. 1).
43. Jordan 1999: 120–3.
44. Martinez (1995) has discussed the theme of abstention in oaths and vows. He notes how in erotic magic, both the state of abstention and the conditions for releasing that state are imposed upon the victim. His discussions focus on the more detailed curses of the Roman and Byzantine periods, where food, drink, sleep, and peace of mind are all denied the target of the curse (see *DT* 265, 266, 270). But the sentiment in this text is more like those wishes which ask that the target not have intercourse with another, such as *DT* 85, SGD 31, etc. There is a continuum of deprivation that links the pains of renunciation inflicted on a target in an *agōgē* spell and those associated with the renunciations imposed in a separation spell.
45. Versnel 1985: 68 f. He includes in his survey: a Latin curse against Sosio dating *c*.200 CE; a curse on a tombstone from Mopsuestia, possibly third century CE; the Amphyktionic oath (Aeschin. 3. 110 f.); *Syll.*^{3} 1219—a *lex sacra* from Gambreion which decrees that those who infringe their rules of mourning should not be able to sacrifice; an inscription from Hierapolis which prescribes punishment for the *paraphylakes* who have abused their power; Plaut. *Poen.* 488 f.; an Oscan *defixio*, 'the curse of Vibia', dating from the second century BCE; ritual prescriptions from Sounion dating from the late second century CE; and SGD 60. More indirect expressions of ill-will include: *DT* 72 and a curse from Carnuntum (see R. Egger, 'Eine Fluchtafel aus Carnuntum', in *Römische Antike und frühes Christentum, i* (Klagenfurt, 1963), 81–97)—both of which beseech the god's anger in punishment. Wishes for the gods to be angry with those who violate tombs are commonly found on Greek grave curses, including J. M. R. Cormack, *MAMA* VIII (Manchester, 1962), nos. 544, 547, 550, 553, 555, 557, 559, 565, 568, and 578; *IG* IX.2.106; *Syll.*^{3} 1237. Versnel traces the idea to include wishes that the god be merciful (to one who atones), or not merciful or directly angry (to one who has committed a crime).

46. This category of curses breaks down into public curses, uttered by authorities to support social mores as well as religious sanctity: Versnel (1985: 264) cites K. Latte, *Heiliges Recht. Untersuchungen zur sakralen Rechtsformen in Griechenland* (Tübingen, 1920) and notes the kind of action which is often listed at a temple as reason for the imposition of a curse which prohibits its target from entering the temple and thus participating in the rite of sacrifice. The crimes committed include adultery, murder and treason, religious offences, including those against the sanctity of the temple itself; see R. Parker 1983, ch. 6. The curse on Sosio, mentioned above, is an exception to this general rule—it appears to be motivated by competition.

47. Versnel (1998: 264 n. 131) also comments on this matter: 'stealing, refusing to return a loan, poisoning, etc. are offences not tolerated by society, hence to be entrusted to gods whose concern is justice and retaliation. Rejection or abandonment of a lover, on the other hand, is a personal "affront", demonstrably assessed as an act of injustice by the lover, but not concerning society or the gods (with the occasional exception of Aphrodite).'

48. Presented by Voutiras 1998. Tablet dated from letter forms: Voutiras points out that the closest parallels to these letter types are provided by a group of Attic lead tablets containing judicial curses. These were securely dated by Wilhelm (1904: esp. 117–23) on prosopographical grounds between 368 and 343 BCE. Another recently published judicial *katadesmos* from Athens, shows writing style close to this one and has been dated to *c*.370 BCE on prosopographical grounds (see Willemsen 1990: 142–3).

49. Phila refers to the event she seeks to bind and thus prevent as τὸ τέλος καὶ τὸν γάμον. That ὁ γάμος can mean intercourse is indisputable, but the meaning of τὸ τέλος is less obvious. Voutiras (1998: appendix 1) argues that the two terms together comprise a formula describing 'the ceremonial meeting of man and woman and its result, i.e., marriage'. He bases his argument that this is a ceremonial formula on what he believes to be a parallel phrase ἡ σύμμειξις ... καὶ ὁ γάμος in [Arist.] *Ath. Pol.* 3. 5. The phrase in Aristotle appears to describe and is translated by Voutiras as describing two quite different actions—a meeting followed by intercourse. If it is used as a parallel to this curse, then it appears that the meaning of the term τέλος indicates marriage (in the Dorian dialect) and γάμος a subsequent act of intercourse. Similar phrases are found as follows to refer to the marriage rite: τέλος γάμοιο in Hom. *Od.* 20.74, cf. *AP* 6.276 (Antipat.); γαμήλιον τέλος in Aesch. *Eum.* 835; τὰ νυμφικά τέλος in Soph. *Ant.* 1241; τέλος ὁ γάμος ἐκαλεῖτο in Poll. *Onom.* 3.38. It seems possible, considering these, that the phrase in this curse tablet is a hendiadys, separating out two elements that together here describe a marital rite (although Voutiras disagrees, see 1998: 112). However, whether this is

strictly a reference to marriage or not, the idea of whatever it is occurring with another woman clearly poses an enormous threat to Phila.
50. We might compare it with the much more final phrasing of curse *DT* 5, where the lover has definitely removed himself. The reconstruction of this text is (l. 6): [εἰ τοὺς π]αρὰ Νάκωνος ὑποδέχεται ἐπὶ πονηρίαι τᾶι [Προσοδ]ίου, where τοὺς should be restored as τίς according to Jordan (private communication).
51. Newton claims that there were holes in the corners of the tablets (1863 vol. 2: 719–45) and suggested that this meant that the tablets were hung on a wall in the temple.
52. Faraone's original treatment of this curse (1991*a*: 14) as meaning 'Let him not marry another matron or maiden who has been seen about with him', has been criticized and corrected. See Voutiras 1998: 57 n. 23, Dickie 2000: 576, and Faraone himself 1999: 13 and 151.
53. As Voutiras 1998.
54. As described in Xenarchos 4 and Eubulos 67 and 82 K–A.
55. Voutiras 1998: 57 (and before him L. Robert 1967: 80). Such an antithesis also appears at Ar. *Ran.* 148.
56. Dickie (2000: 576) emphasizes the business aspect of this relationship arguing that the text was written by one who 'did not wish her livelihood to be threatened or destroyed'.
57. Third or second century BCE by Faraone (1991*a*: 13) and Dickie (2000: 576). I reject Gager's date to the second or third century CE (1992: 88).
58. Gager (1992: 88) interprets this text as primarily targeting Zoilos and therefore most likely written by a rival (male) suitor. Dickie (2000: 576) notes that there is a further man mentioned in the text and that this makes it likely that Antheira was a courtesan, and that the text was composed by a woman, a rival for Zoilos' affections. However, the text is so fragmentary that the role of Timokles and the nature (indeed, the fact) of Antheira's relationship with him remains a mystery.
59. As Dickie 2000: 576.
60. The original location is unknown and no date is given by the editor; Dickie (2000) suggests it is no later than the Hellenistic period.
61. e.g. Isai. 3.13–14; [Dem.] 59.24, 33, 48.
62. We might also expect this if, as Gager suggests, the curse concerns a love triangle, where the agent of the curse was a woman seeking to steal the affections of Kabeira from his wife.
63. Side B, ll. 10–11: Gager (1992: 90) translates it as 'May Charias forget the girl, Theodora, the very one whom he loves'. I reject Audollent's reading that this is a tablet *de* paiderastia *res igitur* which, as Petropoulos (1988: 220) suggests, 'makes for a bizarre (and unprecedented?) three-cornered relationship'. It seems more likely that the 'child' is Theodora's (but not Charias'?) and the curse tablet is citing a relationship between the child and Charias of a paternal sort, such as seems to be found in *DT*

5. Moreover, an overview of the conventions regarding erotic magic and memory suggests that mention of the child of a relationship may have been almost formulaic (see Petropoulos 219 ff., who refers to Sapph. fr. 16 and Alk. fr. 283. 5–9 Page). (By mentioning this, I am not of course meaning to imply that the text has simply inserted a non-existent child as part of a formula, but is referring to the real child of a relationship in formulaic fashion.) As Petropoulos notes, many papyri love spells work on the memory of the target, see *PGM* xv. 4 f; Theokr. 2.44 f; *PGM* iv. 327, 2756 f.; xixa. 56 f; and lxi. 29 f.

64. Gager concentrates in his summary of its content on the relationship between Theodora and Charias—a side effect of understanding it to be about a marriage. Faraone (1999: 86 n. 182) also seems to place this text in the context of marriage when he cites this curse in a footnote to his explanation of the use of binding spells to create forgetfulness in brides, showing how women were bewitched in order to be stolen away from their family homes, as part of the process of bridal theft. Faraone: 'In most *agōgē* spells, the various forms of torture and deprivation are applied for a limited time only to force the desired woman to shake off the many social constraints and obligations that anchor her to home and family.' However, he fails to point out that although the curse sets out to bind Theodora, it actually seeks to manufacture forgetfulness in the male half of this couple, and so cannot be explained in the traditional terms of bridal theft. In fact, if anything, it subverts Faraone's model, and perhaps suggests that the agent of the curse thinks of him—or herself—as stealing Charias away from an existing family arrangement. Perhaps this is a comment on the perceived power of Theodora in her relationship with men. Dickie, on the other hand, focuses on the idea that the curse appears to be trying to sever the relationship enjoyed by Theodora between two named men and any other men she has dealings with, and this leads him to suspect that the motive behind the curse is primarily economic.

65. Hdt. 2.135; Dem. 18.129; and of sexual intercourse: [Arist.] *Pr.* 876^{a}39; Dickie 2000: 576.

66. As Dickie (2000: 576): 'It is to be surmised that the person responsible for the spell was a courtesan jealous of her trade.'

67. *PGM* xxxiia is an erotic spell written by one man about another (this evidence is from late Roman Egypt, but the spells themselves are likely to be a great deal older). If we were to imagine such a scenario, would this tell us anything about the possible age of Charias? Literary evidence suggests both that young men who were sexually active with women were still admired and desired by other men, and that the perception of a young man as beautiful did not stop automatically when that young man reached a particular age, but rather as he acquired particular physical attributes of age (such as body hair). There is no question that Athens in the fourth century had a culture that emphasized the beauty of younger

men. However, even a brief glimpse of the evidence suggests that the lines of desire were not rigidly drawn. In Xen. *Symp.* (4.12–35) it is suggested that Sokrates has been flirting with Kritoboulos (who is just married, but appears not to have a beard), who, in turn, professes an extreme infatuation for Klinias. At 8.2 Kritoboulos is described as 'still having his admirers, and is already setting his heart on others'. Antigonos of Karystos reports how Persaios the Stoic philosopher bid for, and won, a flute-girl at a symposiatic slave auction. However, because he lived with his lover Zeno, he was afraid to take his prize home (Antigonos of Karystos 117 (Wilamowitz); Davidson 1998: 114).

There is also some evidence for relationships between men of the same age: Dover (1974: 86–7) notes male couples on Greek vases who appear to be of similar age, Hupperts also (1988: 255–68), and a male couple of equivalent age seems to be depicted on the Hellenistic Leiden gem (see Clarke 1998: 35 ff.). There is also literary evidence for male (rather than boy) prostitutes e.g. Aeschin. 1.74 (describes the men in the *oikēmata*); Pl. *Charm.* 163b (describes prostitution as a profession); and Aeschin. 1.158 (a prostitute called Diophantos who notoriously took a client to court—suggesting that he was over 18), all of which suggests that sex with older men was not an inconceivable practice among these citizens. We also find Euripides' love for the older Agathon being justified at Plut. *Mor.* 770c and Sokrates' love for Alkibiades at Pl. *Prt.* 309b.

I agree with Davidson (1998: 167 ff.) that those terms which have traditionally been thought to indicate a passive homosexual role, and so a homosexual male over the age of 18 (e.g. *kinaidos* and *katapugon*), are more likely to indicate general sexual excess. So, although relationships between older men are neither commonly represented in ancient literature, nor seem to have been culturally encouraged, there is evidence that older men may have enjoyed relationships with each other as well (although the evidence suggests that these were still constructed on a model of an older with a younger man). This offers further possible scenarios for the creation of these curses.

68. Found in a levelling fill at the south-western corner of the *Heroon* at Nemea, see S. G. Miller 1980: 196–7. Further curse tablets have been found in this area; noted in this excavation report are two more lead curse tablets 'which have so far resisted cleaning and deciphering' (IL 369 and 370). Three more were found in the following year (as reported in the subsequent archaeological report); these are IL 367, 372, and 373. IL 367 and 372 have apparently been read by Jordan. Letter forms suggest late Hellenistic date and seem to be inscribed by one person, and to have a formula quite like that of SGD 57. The texts are not provided in this report, but it is mentioned that, although the personal names and some anatomical details are different, both record curses very similar to that reported in *Hesperia* 1980: 196.

69. The tablet was originally thought to aim to separate one man from another, but Jordan has since expressed the opinion that Euboula should be understood to be feminine. He also doubts the early date: this in private correspondence with Versnel (1998: 231 n. 38) with no grounds for these opinions reported.
70. Compare the erotic spells in the surviving spell formularies from late Roman Egypt, most likely devised by professional magicians and then copied out for individual use by scribes/magicians. These are unlikely to provide much of a guide to the state of mind of the individual who commissioned the spell.
71. Ogden (1999: 1–90) states that this is 'because the binding idiom did not seem immediately useful for situations of love, and it was indeed the rather specific erotic circumstance of the presence of a rival (real or feigned) for the beloved's affections, an "enemy" in love, that first brought curse tablets into the erotic sphere'. However, such an explanation seems to turn on the idea that rivalry in relationships only started occurring in the fourth century BCE, which is hard to believe.
72. Sutton 1992. Extreme examples of violent heterosexual sexual activity: ARV^2 86a (cup by the Pedieus painter); ARV^2 372.31 (red-figure cup by Douris); ARV^2 444.241 (red-figure cup by Douris). The sexually explicit representations are chronologically restricted almost exclusively to the years 575–450, with a significant drop after 480, very few after 450, and only one from the fourth century; see also Clarke 1998: 22. The fourth century BCE marks the first appearance of the nude female figure—among the most famous is the Knidian Aphrodite of Praxiteles (see Pomeroy 1975: 145, Dean-Jones 1992: 86). Around the early fourth century the female nude also appears in large-scale painting (Pliny, *HN* 35.61 and Cicero *De Inv.* 2.1.1).
73. Hermary *et al.* 1986: 902–17 and 933–6; Sutton 1992; Boardman 1989.
74. A good example is on the red-figure *loutrophoros* (Boston 03.802) which shows the procession to the nuptial bed.
75. Eros as a child continues to be a popular theme among the Hellenistic epigrammatists: e.g. Asklepiades 15 (*AP* 12.46); Meleager 15 (*AP* 12.47); and 58 (*AP* 5.187). The huge power of this physically diminutive god is reflected in Theokritos' *Idyll* 4, which tells of a great wound inflicted by a tiny thorn (see Fowler 1989: 152, drawing on Onians 1979: 128).
76. See Burn 1987: 30 ff. A few examples: Lekanis, Naples, Museo Archeologico Nazionale Stg. 316; Lekanis, Naples, Museo Archeologico Nazionale 2296; squat lekythos, Oxford, Ashmolean Museum 1966.714 (all catalogued as 'Manner of the Meidias Painter, General' in Beazley's *ARV*); Acorn lekythos, Frankfurt, Liebieg-Haus 538 (painter of the Frankfurt Acorn).

77. Clarke (1998: 29) argues that the same romantic imagery was applied to male-to-male lovemaking.
78. Pollitt 1972: 123–5.
79. Burn 1987: 94–6.
80. Sutton 1992.
81. Zweig (1992: 84) argues that in addition to the portrayal of *hetairai* on the stage, the parts of female personifications such as Treaties (Aristoph. *Eq.* 1389), Abundance and Showtime (*Pax* 705, 842) were played by real women—*hetairai*—who appeared naked and were ill-treated on stage.
82. The 'feminine principle' here is a reference to Robertson's term for female sexuality (see Osborne 1994: 85). I am not implying that this is in any way part of a linear change in women's status; Semonides 7 is an example of the construction of the desiring woman from a much earlier period—although her description here portrays the female as uncontrollably sexual, rather than sexually autonomous. This is accompanied by the description of the always-about-to-be cuckolded husband. This poem, which sets out to convince men that they are indeed threatened by wives who will always turn out to be animals of one sort or another, is an example of the construction of sexual risk from a much earlier period.
83. An abundance of information suggests that women's status changed partly because of the pressures of political events (Euxitheos' defence that many Athenian women work on account of our city's misfortunes, in Dem. 57. 31–45), partly because of the example of the Hellenistic queens. This is perhaps especially true of areas newly Hellenized through Makedonian conquests: see Pomeroy 1975: 126, van Bremen 1983, Blundell 1995: 197 ff. However, Pomeroy (1975: 126–7) warns that we need to beware of making sweeping assumptions—there would have probably been less freedom for women in Athens under Demetrios of Phaleron, for example. Van Bremen sees the changes in women's status in the Hellenistic East linked to their increased wealth within the same traditional ideology rather than an evolution in their legal rights. Schaps (1979) concludes that he has not been able to detect any evolution in the status or legal freedom of women at this time.
84. Hellenistic queens provide the obvious examples, but, in addition, women making *epidoseis* or loans to the state and receiving honours in public decrees, e.g. Archippe at Kyme, second century BCE (Pleket 1969, no. 3 with *BE* 1968: 444–5); Phile of Priene a female magistrate (Pleket 1969, no. 5) or contributing to artistic or intellectual life (see van Bremen 1983 and Pomeroy 1975).
85. Effects of democracy: Sutton 1992; also Perikles' plea, as reported by Thucydides 2.43, that the citizens become the lovers (*erastai*) of their city.
86. See Omitowoju 2002.

87. It has been argued (Petropoulos 1988: 221–2) that techniques that appear later in Egypt must have been in existence long before Hellenistic and Roman times. Gager (1992: 79), basing his argument on Faraone (1991a: 15–16), observes that although 'love magic' may have been around for longer, the use of *katadesmoi* in this arena may still have emerged in the fourth century, 'adopted by nervous lovers on the basis of its reputation as a successful device in constraining the behaviour of other persons, most notably in legal matters'.

CHAPTER 12

1. Ashforth explaining his understanding of how community humanism (a principle known as *ubuntu*) in Soweto is undermined by spiritual insecurity, which assumes that we are all exposed to invisible forces, manipulated by our neighbours.
2. This is not to suggest that the frequency of surviving judicial curses offers a straightforward graph of the statistical risk of being a victim of litigation at Athens: evidence from Attic comedy suggests that litigiousness was an extremely prominent feature of Athenian life before the date of any surviving curse tablets. But there is also evidence to suggest that cursing itself was known about earlier than the material evidence indicates. As mentioned in Chapter 9, the description of Thucydides, son of Melesias, in Aristophanes' *Wasps* and the binding song of the *Erinyes* in Aeschylus' *Eumenides*, suggest that cursing may have been a recognized (oral) practice, even if written curse tablets were not themselves a widely used technology.
3. Rhodes 1980.
4. These are from Versnel's category of 'border area curses', proposed in 1991, which comprises elements of both *katadesmoi* and prayers for justice, which pray for divine justice to punish a crime, often a theft. The transaction that takes place between god and agent appears quasi-legal in nature. Versnel (1991a: 67): 'I do not plead for the complete elimination of the samples of our "border group" from the collections of the *katadesmoi*, provided that their specific peculiarities are duly recognized and appreciated.' In his original paper on this subject, he proposed 20 examples of 'pure' prayers for justice and 18 border area cases (Versnel 1991a: 64). Of these, 8 border area curses and 16 prayers for justice (SGD 60, *DT* 1–13; two bronze tablets, *DT* 212 and one from Asia Minor, see Dunant 1978) have been dated to the period relevant to this study. *DTA* 109 does not appear to have been dated so I have not included it in this section, although it does appear in Versnel's article as a hybrid curse. NGCT 23 and 24 also qualify for Versnel's category of border area curses; NGCT 89 includes both elements typical of prayers for justice (language of prayer and justification) and of binding curses (binding verbs, e.g.

paradidomi, spiralling text, invocation of the undead), but no description of ongoing acts of injustice against the curse-writer.

'Border area' curses tend to be older than prayers for justice and have been found over a smaller area. Border area curses: NGCT 24 dated to the early fourth century; *DTA* 100, 102, 103 to the fourth century; *DTA* 98, 120, 158 to the third century BCE; NGCT 23 to the second century BCE; SGD 58 between the first century BCE and the first century CE. Prayers for justice: *DT* 1–13 date to the first/second century BCE; SGD 60 to the second century BCE at the earliest; the bronze tablet from Asia Minor to 100 BCE to 200 CE; the bronze tablet from southern Italy to the third century BCE; NGCT 89 dates to somewhere between the first century BCE and first century CE. The provenance of the prayers for justice ranges from Italy to Asia Minor; 6 of the 8 border area curses originate in Attika, the other 2 are from the island of Delos and Oropos respectively.

5. *DTA* 102: l. 8 τὴν ἐμ(ὲ) ἀδικο(ῦ)σαν.
6. For example, in *DTA* 120 (a fragmentary curse), the target is described as (ll. 5–6) τὸ[ν] ἐμὲ ἀτιμοῦντα. In *DTA* 158, similarly difficult to read, little remains except the participles used to describe the actions of the target, but these are also in the present tense: (l. 7) το]ῖς ἀδικο(υ)μ[ένοις and (l. 9) ἀ]δικο(ύ)μεν[οι]. NGCT 23 offers little information, but it does yield the phrase: ἀξιῶι οὖν ἀδικούμενος καὶ οὐκ ἀδικῶν πρότερος which appears to be concerned with justifying the agent's choice to create this curse, and again describes the unjust act as happening in the present tense.
7. Side A, l. 5 names her with a feminine name; l. 13 refers to τὴ]ν μολυβ-δοκόπον, 'she who cut the lead', but this is a restoration.
8. SGD 58 is the only border area curse that gives a clear account of the crime that has been committed against the writer of the curse (the theft of a necklace). This tablet is opisthographic and Versnel suggests that the two texts provide examples of the two different kinds of recourse to divine help available to the victim of an injustice: side A offers a prayer for justice, side B seems to be closer in its formulae to a traditional *katadesmos*. It seems to me that there is a case to be made for suggesting that SGD 58 actually belongs to the prayers for justice category. The elements of side B that are similar, formulaically, to a *katadesmos* are the use of the verb καταγράφω in l. 4 and the list of body parts in the latter part of the text. However, formulaic lists similar to those found in traditional *katadesmoi* are found in SGD 60, which is categorized as a prayer for justice. Moreover, the term καταγράφω is one of Kagarow's second category of binding verbs (1929: 25–8), those 'with technical and legal connotations that either "register" the victims before an imagined underworld tribunal or those that simply consign the victims to the control of the chthonic deities' (Faraone 1991a: 24 n. 24). Verbs of the latter type (often compounds of τίθημι and δίδωμι, although not in this

instance) are the verbs found at the beginning of many of the prayers for justice of this period.
9. Ashforth 2005: 68.
10. Ashforth 2005: 70, quoting Scheler (1998: 35), who is explaining Nietzsche's views on Christian morality.
11. Ashforth 2005: 67.
12. 'L'Enfer, c'est les Autres' said by Garcin at the end of J.-P. Sartre's *Huis Clos* (originally published, 1944, as *Les Autres*).
13. Thucydides 8.54, 63 and especially 66 (translation: Warner, 1972). Thanks to Robin Osborne for drawing this to my attention.
14. That there is a change in approach is supported by Faraone (1995: 4): Archaic, Classical, and Hellenistic texts tend to be pre-emptive attacks, whereas after the first century BCE binding spells take on a different nuance, being used for more general magical purposes.
15. In the *Suppl. Mag.* I and II, *nekuodaimon*: 42.12 (3rd–4th century CE; Hermoupolis); 57.1 (fourth century CE; provenance unknown); untimely dead: 44.13 (3rd–4th century CE; provenance unknown); 45.4 (fifth century CE; north of Assiut), 49.12 (2nd–3rd century CE, Oxyrhynchus); cf. *DT* 15 (Syria, 3rd century CE). *Ataphoi*: *DT* 27 (Kypros, 3rd century CE); *et passim* Audollent index B (*Daimones*), p. 465. In 54.22, Chthonic Hermes, *Kore Ereschigal*, and other *daimons* are asked to deliver the target to the untimely dead, 'so that you melt his flesh, sinews, limbs, spirit'.
16. Spirits of the dead are usually roused in the imperative (*Suppl. Mag.* 45.4 and 47.18) but sometimes the present indicative is used: 39.1. Spirits of the dead are usually called anonymously, but see no. 37.47.
17. In *Suppl. Mag.* 42, l. 14, the demon is commanded to take on the form of a bath-house woman (*genou balanissa*). In 50.17–19 (2nd–3rd century CE; Oxyrhynchus) the demon is instructed to 'go into every place and into every quarter and into every house and into every shop'.
18. So, we find erotic charms that describe in detail what the agents want to happen: 'Through the entire night let her not be able to get sleep, but drive her, until she comes to his feet, loving with mad love and affection and intercourse' (*Suppl. Mag.* 45.6–7); or do not want: 'Drive, bind Matrona, whom Tagene bore. .. so that she not be fucked, not be buggered, not fellate, and not perform venereal activities with another, not go with another man than Theodoros, whom Techosis bore ...' (*Suppl. Mag.* 49.19–23). Against athletes: 'Bind, bind down the sinews, the limbs, the mind, the wits, the intellect, the three hundred and sixty five limbs and sinews of NN, whom Taeias bore, and of Aphous, whom Taeis bore, and company, foot-racing athletes, so that they cannot run (?) nor have strength, but let them be sleepless through the entire night and let them throw up all food to their distress and ... of them so that they do not have the strength to run, but let them come in behind ...' (*Suppl. Mag.* II 53.12–22, 3rd century CE; Oxyrhynchos).

19. SGD 21 dates to the first century BCE; *DTA* 100 to the fourth century BCE. In the magical papyri, *PGM* IV.449–56 includes a prayer to accompany an erotic spell that explicitly averts the wrath of the dead from the curser.

CONCLUSION

1. *DTA* 160, side A, l. 3 Εὐ]κολύν[ην] καὶ μαντεῖα.
2. For Dorios, see Christidis, Dakaris, Vokotopoulou (C–D–V) 1999: no. 5; *BE* 1938: 153; *Ep. Chron.* 1935: 257, 23; fourth century BCE (C–D–V: *c.*420–410 BCE); in this volume, Ch. 5, under catalogue subsection Ritual Activity 2. For the judicial curse, see Christidis, Dakaris, Vokotopoulou 1999; M-186; mid-fourth century BCE; this volume, Judicial Activity 2, also listed under Ritual Activity.
3. *Psychagōgēs* and *goēteia*: Plato, *Leg.* 909a–d. The *Suda* provides a definition of *goēteia* that includes a detailed description of how this was done. *Suda* s.v. *psychagōgias* 'They accomplish certain sorceries with regard to the dead . . .'
4. Derveni Papyrus col. 20, l. 4.
5. See above Chapter 9; Lib. *Or.* 1.43, 1.62, 1.71.
6. See Chapters 2 and 7.
7. Drawing on the hierarchical model of gossip, allegations, and accusations described by Goody (1970) in her work on witchcraft in central and eastern Gonja, Ghana, in the 1960s; outlined by Ashforth 2005: 65.
8. P. Herrmann, *Tituli Asiae Minoris*, vol. 5, pt. 1 (Vienna, 1981), 318; Versnel 1991*a*: 76.
9. Pl. *Leg.* 932e–933e; cases of Theoris and Ninon *et al.* discussed in Chapters 2 and 7.

APPENDIX 1

Questions Presented by Communities at the Oracle of Dodona

1. Parke State 2; Dakaris, *PAE* 1967: 33–54; Karapanos 1878: pl. 39, 5 and Pomtow 1; 450–404 BCE (Pomtow)

Θεός. ἐπικοινῶντ]αὶ Κορκ[υραῖοι τῶι Δὶ τῶι Νάωι
καὶ τᾶι Διώναι τί]νι κα θεῶν [ἢ ἡρώων θύοντες καὶ
εὐχόμενοι κάλ]λιστα καὶ ἄ[ριστα καὶ νῦν καὶ εἰς
τὸν ἔπειτα χρόνον] Ϝοικέοιει[ν

On reverse: Δ (Pomtow says this stands for *damou* or *damosion*)

God. The Kerkyraians ask Zeus Naios and Dione by sacrificing and praying to which god or hero may they live in the best and finest way now, and in the future.

2. Parke State 3; Karapanos 1878: no. 4, pl. 34, 4 and pl. 39, 7; Pomtow 2; late fifth century (Pomtow)

Θεόν. τ[ύ]χαν [ἀ]γαθ[άν]
ἐπ[ι]κοινῶνται τοὶ Κ[ο]ρκυρα[ῖοι τῶι Δὶ
Νάωι καὶ τᾶι Δ[ι]ώναι τίνι κα [θ]εῶν ἢ
ἡρώων θύον[τ]ες καὶ εὐχ[ό]μενοι
ὁμονοῖεν ἐ[π]ὶ τὠγαθόν

God. Good Fortune. The Kerkyraians ask Zeus Naios and Dione by sacrificing and praying to which god or hero can they be in agreement on a good course of action.

3. M-957; Vokotopoulou 1992: no. 2; *SEG* 43. 320; Chalcidian alphabet; 475–450 BCE

(. . . .) Ϝεγῖν (οι. . .)
(. . . .) Ηοδο (. . .)
(. . . .) χον (. . .)

4. M-1099; Vokotopoulou 1992: 3; 475–450 BCE

Αὐτοί Ϝ(εγῖνοι . . .)

Other restorations are possible, but Vokotopoulou suggests that the larger letters and atypical beginning to the question make it more likely that it's an official demand.

5. M-177; Dakaris, Christidis, Vokotopoulou 1993: 58; first half of the fourth century

[Θ]εοί. Ἐπερωτέοντι
['Ογχ]εσμαῖοι ἦ 'στι αὐτοῖς
[. . .]ός ἐν τάν αὐτῶν

Gods. The Onchesimoi ask whether there is . . . for them in their . . .

6. Christidis; 375–350 BCE

[Θε]ὸς τύχα ἀγαθά· ἐ[π]ερωτ[ῶ]ν[τ]
ι Δ[ι]ωδωναῖοι Δία Νᾳιον καὶ Δ[ιών]α[ν]
[ἦ ἐ]ν τῶι δρυί σαμῆον ἐστι.

God, good fortune, the Dodonaeans ask Zeus Naios and Dione whether there is a sign in the oak?

7. M-827; Dakaris, Christidis, Vokotopoulou 1993: 56; 360–340 BCE

περί παμπασίας
Βυλλίονες τίνε θε-
ῶι θύοντες βέλτισ-
τα πραξοῦντι

Regarding possessions, the Bylliones (ask) by sacrificing to which god will they fare best?

8. M-33; Dakaris, Christidis, Vokotopoulou 1993: 60; Parke State 6; Korinthian alphabet; third quarter of the fourth century (Dakaris, Christidis, Vokotopoulou)

[Θ]εός. Ἐπικοινῶνται τοι Κορκυ-
ραῖοι καί τοι Ὠρίκιοι τῶι Διί τῶι Ν[αί]-
ωι καί Διώναι τίνι κα θεῶν ἤ ἡ-
ρώων θύοντες καί εὐχόμενοι τά-
ν πόλιν κάλλιστα οἰκεύεγ καί ἀσφα-
λέστατα καί εὐκαρπία σφιν καί πο-
λυκαρπία τελέθοι καί κατόνασις παν-
τός τὼγαθοῦ καρποῦ

God. The Kerkyraians and the Orikians ask Zeus Naios and Dione, by sacrificing and praying to which of the gods or heroes they may live most fairly and safely, and may there be fine and fruitful crops for them and all benefit of the good crop.

9. Nafissi 1995: 314; Vokotopolou 1992: 78; Parke State 1; Karapanos 1878: no. pl. 34; Pomtow 3; SGDI 1567; 325–300 BCE (Vokotopoulou); end of fourth, beginning of third century (Nafissi)

(Θεός. τύχαι ἀγαθᾶι [ἐπερωτῆι]
ha πόλις ha τῶν Ταραν[τίνων]

τόν Δία τόν Ναῖον καὶ τ[ὰν Διώναν]
περὶ παντυχίας καὶ π[ερί- - -]
ταχ. . . ρωι˙ καὶ περὶ τῶν [- - -

To the gods. With good fortune. The city of the Tarentines ask Zeus Naios and Dione about good fortune and about . . . and about the . . .

* Pomtow: π[. . . ἐν; Hoffman: π[ερὶ χωρίων,] τα χ[η]ρῶι

10. M-22; Parke State 5; fourth century (Evangelidis, *AE* 1953/4: 99–102); end of the fourth century, beginning of the third (Robert, *REG* 1956: 134); *SEG* 15, 397

Ἀγαθᾶι τύχαι. αἰτεῖται ἁ πόλις ἁ τῶν Χαόνων
τὸν Δία τὸν Νάον καὶ τὰν Διώναν ἀνελεῖν εἰ λώιον καὶ ἄμεινον καὶ συμφορώτερόν ἐστί τόν ναόν
τόν τᾶς Ἀθάνας τᾶς Πολιάδος ἀγχωρίξαντας
ποιεῖν

Good Fortune. The city of the Chaonians asks Zeus Naios and Dione to answer if it is better and more expedient if they build the temple of Athena Polias, having moved it nearer(?).

11. Parke State 8; Karapanos 1878, pl. 39, 2; Pomtow 5; dated to the late second or early first century BCE (Pomtow)

ἐπερωτῶντι τὸ κοινὸν τῶν . . .
ων Δία Νᾶον καὶ Διώναν μα . . .
τι αὐτοῖς συμπολειτεύουσι[ν?
μετὰ Μολοσσῶν ἀσφαλῆ ἦι

The community of the . . . asks Zeus Naios and Dione whether . . . will it be safe for them if they join the federation with the Molossi.

12. Parke State 7: *SEG* 19. 149, 427; *PAE* 1956: 171b

ἐπερωτῶντι Δωδωναῖοι τὸν
Δία καὶ τὰν Διώναν ἦ δι᾽ἀνθρώ-
που τινὸς ἀκαθαρτίαν ὁ θεὸς
τὸν χειμῶνα παρέχει

The Dodonaeans ask Zeus and Dione whether it is because of the impurity of some man that god sends the storm.

13. Parke State 9; Robert, *REG* 56 (1953), 146, no. 116; Wilhelm, *AfP* 15 (1953), 75 ff.; Evangelidis *PAE* 1932: 52, no. 1

ἐπερωτῶντι τοὶ διαιτοί τὸν Δία τὸν Νάϊον καὶ [τὰν Διώναν ἀναλισκόντοις τὰ . . . nominis χρημα-]
τα ἰς τὸ πρυτανῆον τὰ παρ τᾶς πολιος ἔλαβε δικαίως [ἐσσεῖται αὐτοῖς λώιον καὶ ἄμεινον]

διαίτοις · ἀναδῶσαι ἶς το πρυτανῆον δικαίως τοῦτο

(Wilhelm supposes that the last line is the god's answer, but Parke expresses doubt.)

The arbitrators ask Zeus Naios and [Dione whether if they spend the... (a name) money] on the council chamber which he has justly received from the city [it will be better and more good for them].

To the arbitrators, it is just to spend this money on the council chamber.

14. Parke State 4; Karapanos 1878: pl. 34, 3; Pomtow 4. (There is an unexplained letter, possibly a sigma, at the end of l.1.)

Δὶ Νάωι καὶ Διώναι
ἐπικοινᾶται Μον[δ]αιατᾶν τὸ κοινὸν πὲρ το(ῖ) [ἀρ-
γύροι τᾶς Θέμιστος αἰ ἀ(ν)εκτ[ό]ν ἐστι τᾶ Θέμι-
(σ)τι καὶ βέλτιον ἐ(σ)κιχρέμεν

The community of the Mondaeans asks Zeus Naios and Dione regarding the silver of Themis, whether it is allowed by Themis and is better to put it on loan.

15. Reconstruction: Peek, *ZPE* 30 (1978), 247–8 (*SEG* 1979; 256), see also T. Gomperz, *AEM* 5 (1881), no. 36 ff.

Ζηνικέτῃ βασιλεῖ χρῇ δῶμα Διὸς να[ός τε Διώ]νας·
χρῆμα καὶ ἐργασία σᾶ˙ πᾶσ[α]ν [μίμν]ει 'ς ὥραν
αὐτὸς ἐπισταμένᾳ τελέσας χερ[ὶ πᾶν ὅταν ἀρκῃς]·
σχέσθα[ι δὲ θρασ]έων πέ[ρ]ας, ὦ ξένε, τίμ[ιον ἕξει]

* Peek reads σὰ ('your') but Gomperz's reading σᾶ ('safe') seems more appropriate for both sense and meter.

To king Zeniketes, the temple of Zeus Naos and shrine of Dione proclaims: Goods and business remain safe for all time, whenever you, having achieved everything with a skilful hand, prevail. Hold fast to your courage, O stranger, an honourable end will come.

APPENDIX 2

Texts Excluded from the Relationship Category

I have excluded three groups of materials from the category of relationship curses. First, I read the majority of those curses aimed at individuals involved in the sex trade, such as *DTA* 68, 75, and 87, and *DT* 52, as focused on the business aspect of this activity rather than focusing on specific relationships between the people they mention in this context. *DTA* 75 and 87 focus on tavern-keepers and only occasionally mention women belonging to these male targets. *DTA* 68 explicitly mentions a prostitute by profession, but without any detail beyond her name. *DT* 52 concerns Blastys, Nikandros, Glykera, and, in particular, Kerkis, who appears to be a pimp—and for that reason, Audollent says *non potest quin amatoria fuerit defixio*. However, this curse seems far more concerned with business arrangements than amorous or lustful concerns, and most specifically with preventing Kerkis from speaking (hence the concentration on cursing his tongue). On the whole, these curses do not describe, try to bewitch, or attempt to inhibit any elements of their targets which are significantly related to matters of desire, love, or lust.

However, this does not mean that those curses that target individuals and appear to concern an economic relationship cannot also have a component of desire. *DT* 68, which is aimed, at least at first sight, at a woman called Theodora, and which is discussed in Chapter 11, certainly seems to contain elements of both. It is worth bearing in mind that the line between being a sex-worker and using a sexual/loving relationship as a way also to ensure economic survival can be fine, especially if we try to draw it using such limited and fragmentary evidence as these curse tablets contain.

In the second case, I have excluded those curses which seem to have been composed in order to harm rather than bind, because they appear motivated by a past event, rather than with the possibility of enhancing or preventing a future connection between two people, and so read more like 'prayers for justice', as described in Chapter 12. So, for example, in *SGD* 109, the victim is handed over 'as a gift' to Hermes *Katochos*, which may be an elaboration of the idea of dedicating one's target to the infernal powers, as is found in a number of curses for justice and revenge, for example in the Knidian curses (*DT* 1–13), in *DTA* 100, *DT* 74 and 75. The identification of the motive behind tablets *SGD* 118–21 turns on the meaning of the verbs ποτιδέχεσθαι (a Doric form of προσδέχεσθαι which is rare among *katadesmoi*) and παραδέχεσθαι. It allows the texts to be read either as curses 'to the death' or as pleas that the target enjoy a swift admission to a proper afterlife. Nabers (1966: 68) has argued that the verb is not harsh enough to be used in a curse and so must mean that the texts—with the exception of one—are in fact prayers. He is supported in his observations about the use of this verb by Robert and Robert (1966, no. 518); Jordan (1980) argues against this interpretation.

In some of these cases, the motivation for revenge is clear: *DT* 10, for example, is aimed at Dorothea, who has stolen (or embraced?) the husband/lover of the writer of the curse, who remains anonymous. I would include SGD 60 in this subcategory of revenge, although other commentators have suggested that it is an erotic text, focusing on the maidservant and arguing either for an erotic attachment between her and her owner, or between her and her abductor. Homolle (1901) suggests that the client himself must have wanted or enjoyed the slave girl as his lover, so that jealousy would have added fuel to the sense of social and economic injustice, but there are no grounds for this argument in the text as it stands. Faraone (1999: 87) concentrates on the idea that the slave girl has been charmed away (perhaps by a love charm), seeing this as another example of how *agōgē* love spells are concerned with stealing the property of another man, subverting another man's claim to ownership, and attacking the patriarchal order. But is her removal achieved by means of an *agōgē*, as Faraone assumes? The verb used to describe how Epaphroditus stole her away is συναποθέλγεσθαι, based on the root θέλγ- which is used for charms and spells as early as Homer (e.g. Hom. *Od.* 5.47 and 12.40). But it is also used to mean to cheat (Hom. *Od.* 16.195 and 1.57) or, in a metaphoric sense, to beguile or charm (Hom. *Od.* 17.521). Perhaps any intimation that magical powers have been used should be seen as an expression of the shock and outrage of the agent of the curse (and apparently his wife), rather than an accusation of supernatural means. On the whole, this curse seems to be more concerned with the need for revenge and justice than erotic feelings.

SGD 109 does imply some kind of erotic motive, insofar as the writer of the curse seems to have been aware of the attractive aspects of his victim, even as he handed her over to a chthonic god. In this curse, the different parts of the target, Allia Prima, are enumerated and each separate part is described as beautiful. The 'two lovers', referred to on side B, l. 2, may be a reference to the earthly context, indicating a rival lover, and thus, perhaps, a motivation for the cursing or, as Gàbrici (1941: 298) observes, it may indicate that the curser was willing to share the object of his love with Hermes—that is, he wished her dead.

A text from Attika which dates from the end of the fourth century and was found in the Kerameikos at Athens, also seems to be concerned with revenge (see Willemsen 1990: 145; Kovs. 3). It seeks to bind the wife of Dion, a woman called Glykera, so that she may be punished and become [ἀ]τε[λ]ὴς γάμου. So, a woman, already a wife, is being wished a lack of success, which suggests that γάμος is some act or state further to the ceremony of marriage and may concern the success of the sexual relationship within the marriage and the couple's hope for children. However, it seems more likely that this curse was intended to punish its target—since no intimation is given that the curse-writer was attracted to the male half of the couple. It may be that the agent hoped to fulfil a future hope: after all, if Glykera could not have children, then her husband might seek a relationship with a woman who could.

Finally, the inclusion of women's names or lists of particular body parts does not necessarily imply a relationship curse and I have excluded those texts which in fact

Texts Excluded from the Relationship Category 351

seem to list these elements for other reasons. *DTA* 102 mentions women's names and has been described by Gager (1992: 201) as dealing 'with love affairs involving several women'. Two boxers are among the targets, and Gager goes on to describe how 'Wilhelm suggests that these two boxers may well be the source of the anguish that led to the commissioning of the curse. They may have won the affections of the women in question.' However, there is no basis for this reading in the text itself. Reminiscent of tablets *DTA* 68 and 85 above, *DTA* 77, 89, and 93 and SGD 58 and 136 include sexual parts of the body, seemingly as part of a more general wish for the target's lack of success. *DTA* 89 comprises curses on individuals and individual parts of the body, including genitalia. Again, it does not seem to be strictly an erotic curse, but more the tool of someone who wished an enemy general ill-will. Compare SGD 58 (an opisthographic tablet from Delos, date not given but probably between the first century BCE and first century CE from its letter forms), which lists all body parts, including the genitals of the target, but is clearly a curse written in revenge for the stealing of a necklace, rather than having a particularly erotic focus. *DTA* 77 also includes the private parts of some of the targets in the binding, with no obviously erotic overtones.

According to *LGPN*, the name of the accursed, Ἱερώ, in *DTA* 93 was a woman's name. She is identified by her status as a wife and as a mother (using a term μαμμία which we know to have been used by children). The curse then makes a list of body parts, but these do not seem focused in any way on matters erotic. Certainly, the emphasis of the curse is on the maternal status of the target, rather than casting her in an erotic role. In that case, it may be that the mention of sexual parts was intended to cause infertility rather than being an erotic challenge.

SGD 136 is undated, but some of the phraseology suggests a date after the first century CE, at least. Phrases of the type found in this tablet, e.g. 'now, now, now, quickly, quickly, quickly', and variations on this theme are characteristic of tablets from Africa and Italy e.g. *DT* 156, 159, 160, 161, 166, 174, 178, 187 (from Rome); 271 (from Hadrumetum); 238, 239, 240, and 248 (from Karthage). It is extremely common in the later erotic magical incantations, e.g. *PGM* I. 262; III. 35, 85, and 123; IV. 973, 1593, and 2037. Commentators (e.g. Roesch 1966–7: 233) have suggested that the writer of SGD 136 was either a man furious at losing Satornina to the benefit of another, or a woman jealous of Satornina whom she regarded as a rival. As this suggests, there is no information about the agent's motivation in the text. The instruction that she should be bound, ἐν τῇ εἰδίᾳ γονῇ may mean that the curse is directed at her fertility/womb, rather than her children. Either way, the intention may be similar to that of *DT* 84, which appears to be a curse against a whole family, and includes a curse directed against the daughter with the intention that she remain unmarried. There is no particular reason to assume that this curse has an erotic basis: the focus seems to be intended to bind the daughter's fertility and prevent her from continuing the family line.

Catalogue of Binding Curses

THE catalogue includes all the curses discussed in the book. These are found in the following collections: R. Wünsch, *Defixionum Tabellae Atticae Inscr. Gr.*, vol. 3, pt. 3 (Berlin, 1887), *DTA*; A. Audollent, *Defixionum Tabellae* (Paris, 1904), *DT*; D. Jordan, 'New Greek Curse Tablets (1985–2000), *GRBS* 41 (2000), 'NGCT'; and D. Jordan, 'A Survey of Greek Katadesmoi Not Included in the Special Corpora', *GRBS* 26 (1985), 'SGD'; W. K. Kovacsovics (ed.), 'Die Eckterrasse an der Gräberstrasse des Kerameikos', *Kerameikos*, XIV (1990), 145–7, 'Kovs.' In SGD and NGCT, Jordan has provided references to the texts, which I have followed up and reproduced below. Please see *SEG* for the editorial conventions; however, these may not apply to those texts produced before these conventions were fully developed.

DTA **11** (Chapters 7, 9)
Origin: Greece, Athens, Patissia
Date: Third century BCE (Wünsch 1897)
Text: Wünsch (1897); tablet folded with nail hole

Μοσχίω[ν
Λουσιεὺς   Δ   Ν
Πολύευ[κτ]ος   Μ   Μ
Ἡραιάδας Κρής Χάρ[ης
Καλλίας Λουσιεὺς Δεινόμαχ(ος)
Νουμήνιος Ἁλαιεύς

Moschiōn of Lousia ... Polyeuktos ... Heraiadas the Kretan, Charēs, Kallias of Lousia, Deionmachos, Noumēnios of Halai

DTA **12** (Chapter 10)
Origin: Greece, Attika
Date: Third century BCE (Wünsch 1897)
Text: Wünsch (1897)

Ὀνομακλέους
Θέα ἡ σκυτοτόμος
Μ[αλ]θάκη ἡ Εὐθυκρ(άτους).

Thea, the leather-worker, wife of Onomaklēs, Malthakē, the wife of Euthykatēs.

DTA 24 (Chapter 9)

Origin: Greece, Attika, Halai
Date: Early fourth century BCE (Wilhelm 1904)
Text: Wünsch (1897); retrograde

Side A:
Φυκίων Ἐργοκράτης
Τρυ]φ(ε)ρός Ἀριστοκράτης

Side B:
Μ]ήδεια Πιστοκλέης
Νικο[μ]ένης Εὐθήμων Σ[ύ]ρα.

Side A:
Phykiōn, Ergokratēs, Trypheros, Aristokratēs

Side B:
Mēdea, Pistoklēs, Nikomenēs, Euthemōn, Syra.

DTA 25 (Chapters 7, 9)

Origin: Greece, Athens, Patissia
Date: Third century BCE (Wünsch 1897); fourth century BCE (Wilhelm 1904)
Text: Wünsch (1897); ll. 1–8 retrograde

. . . . ς
Ἀ]λ[κα]μέ[ν]ης
Ἀ[ρι]στοκλέης
Ἀρι[στο]κλείδης
μάρ[τυρε]ς
. . α τ . . .
γ]είτο[να
σ . . . . . . σον
       δε
γείτ]ονα[ς
ὅ]σ[ο]ι [ε]ἰσίν

... Alkamenēs, Aristoklēs, Aristokleidēs, witnesses ... neighbour ... son and neighbours whoever they are

DTA 26 (Chapter 9)

Origin: Greece, Athens, Patissia
Date: Third century BCE (Wünsch 1897)
Text: Wünsch (1897); folded with nail hole; names written backwards

Κ[ρό]νιος
Σ(ω)κράτης
Κ]ρα[τ]ῖνος
Θεό]δοτος

Ἀλ]καῖος
. . . . .ης.

Kronios, Sōcratēs, Kratinos, Theodotos, Alkaios . . .

DTA 28 (Chapter 9)

Origin: Greece, Attika
Date: Fourth century BCE (Wünsch 1897)
Text: Wünsch (1897); names written backwards

Λυσίστρατος Ἵππων Χαι[ρε]φ[ά]νης
Φιλόδημ[ος] Νικ[ο]κ[λ]έης
Φιλιστ[ί]δης

Lysistratos, Hippōn, Chairephanēs, Philodēmos, Nikoklēs, Philistidēs

DTA 30 (Chapters 7, 9, 10)

Origin: Greece, Attika
Date: Third century BCE (Wünsch 1897)
Text: Wünsch (1897); retrograde

Ξενοφῶν
Τηλοκλῆς
Ἀγά[θαρ]χος
Ἀριστοκλῆς
Ποσείδιπ(π)ος
Λυσίστρατος
Μνη(σι)κλῆς
Μουσαῖος ὁ κάπηλος
Δημήτριος
Ἱλαρα ἡ κάπηλ(ις)

Xenophōn, Teloklēs, Agatharchos, Aristoklēs, Poseidippos, Lysistratos, Mnēsiklēs, Mousaios the innkeeper, Dēmētrios, Hilara the innkeeper

DTA 33 (Chapter 8)

Origin: Greece, Attika
Date: Third century BCE (Wünsch 1897); fourth or third century BCE (Gager 1992: 49)
Text: Wünsch (1897); l. 2 and parts of ll. 3–4 retrograde

Τ]ῶν
Μαντία
τοὺς παρὰ Σι-
δι]δασ[κ]άλους . . . . πάντας
πάντας παῖδας

Of these, Mantia, [and] all the *didaskaloi* in the team of Si- . . . all, all the youths

DTA 34 (Chapter 8)

Origin: Greece, Attika
Date: Third century BCE (Wünsch 1897); fourth or third century BCE (Gager 1992: 49)
Text: Wünsch (1897); once folded; ll. 2–3 written backwards

Το[ὺ]ς παρὰ Θε[α]γένει πάντας [δι-
δασκάλους καὶ ὑποδιδα(σκάλους)
καὶ διδασκάλο(υς)
καὶ ὑποδιδασκ(άλους).

All the *didaskaloi* (professional choral trainers) and *hupodidaskaloi* (assistant choral trainers) in the team of Theagenes, and the trainers, and the assistant trainers.

DTA 38 (Chapter 9)

Origin: Greece, Athens, Peiraeus; a grave
Date: Early fourth century BCE (Wünsch 1897); fifth century BCE (Wilhelm 1904)
Text: Wünsch (1897); tablet once folded; pierced with a nail

Φιλιππίδης
Εὐθύκριτος
Κλεάγορος
Μενέτιμος
καὶ το(ὺ)ς ἄλλο(υ)ς πάντας
ἢ ὅσοι συν[ήγο-
ροι αὐτο[ῖς

Philippidēs, Euthykritos, Kleagoros, Menetimos, and all the others, or whoever may be co-speakers with them

DTA 39 (Chapters 7, 9)

Origin: Greece, Attika
Date: Third century BCE (Wünsch 1897)
Text: Wünsch (1897); folded with a nail hole

Ἀρ]ιφράδης
Κ]λεοφῶν
Ἀρχέδαμος
Πολύξενος
Ἀντικράτης
Ἀντιφάνης
Ζάκορος
Ἀντιχάρης
Σάτυρα
Μίκα

Σῖμον
ἡ Σατίρας
μήτηρ
Θεοδώρα
. θο . . . . . ς
. . λο [υ]μένη
Ἄνταμις
Εὐκολίνη
Ἀμεινίας
καὶ τοὺς τούτων
συνδίκο(υ)ς πάντας
καὶ φίλους

Ariphradēs, Kleophōn, Archedamos, Polyxenos, Antikratēs, Antiphanēs, Zakoros, Anticharēs, Satyra, Mika, Simon. The mother of Satira, Theodōra . . . Antamis, Eukolinē, Ameinias, and all their co-litigants/co-prosecutors and friends

DTA 42 (Chapters 7, 9)

Origin: Greece, Attika
Date: Third century BCE (Wünsch 1897); fourth century (Wilhelm 1904)
Text: Wünsch (1897); names written backwards; tablet folded and pierced with a nail

καταδίδημι
τούτους ἅπαν-
τα]ς
Δημοτίων
Σκύθων
Φιλόμηλος
Δ[εξ]ιφάνης
Ἀκεσᾶς
Χοιρίνη
Κόνων
Εὐθύδημος
Τιμωρός
Κυδίας
Θαλλός
Γνιφωνίδης
Λέανδρος Φοίνικος
Κλέανδρος Γνίφω(νος)
Εὔξενος Κήτωνος
Εὔξενος Θοραιεὺς
Λεοτοφάνης

I bind all of them, Dēmotiōn, Skythōn, Philomēlos, Dexiphanēs, Akesas, Choirinē, Konōn, Euthydēmos, Timōros, Kydias, Thallos, Gniphōnidēs, Leandros, son of Phoinix, Kleandros, son of Gniphōn, Euxenos, son of Kētōn, Euxenos of Thorai, Leotophanēs

DTA 45 (Chapter 8)

Origin: Greece, Athens, Patissia

Date: Third century BCE (Wünsch 1897); no later than second century BCE (Gager 1992: 50)

Text: Wünsch (1897); folded and pierced with a nail

Side A:
Εὔανδρον [κ]ατα-
δῶ ἐν δεσμ[ῶι] μο-
λυβ[δίν]ωι καὶ . . .
. . . .
ότην · Εὔανδρ[ον
τ]ὸν ὑποκ[ρι](τήν).

Side B:
τοῦ καὶ σύμ-
πα[ντα] . . . .
. . . .
. . . . Ε]ὐάν[δ]ρου
Ἀστ[έ]ας Εὐά[ν]δρου
τοῦ ὑποκ(ριτοῦ).

Side A:
I bind Euandros, in a lead band and . . . Euandros, the actor

Side B:
Of him also everything . . . . of Euandros, Asteas son of Euandros, the actor.

DTA 47–50 (Chapters 7, 9)

Origin: Greece, Attika; (found all fixed together with one nail)
Date: Fourth century BCE (Wünsch 1897)
Text: Wünsch (1897); each tablet folded and all fixed together with one nail

DTA 47

Side A:
Φ[ιλ]οναύτην κα[τ]αδῶ

Side B:
τὸμ μετὰ Μενύλλο(υ)
ὄντα

Side A:
I bind Philonautēs

Side B:
(I bind) the man who is with Menyllos

***DTA* 48**

Side A:
Κηφισοκλέα κατα[δ]ῶ

Side B:
τὸμ Μενύλλου
κηδεστήν

Side A:
I bind Kephisokles

Side B:
(I bind) the in-law of Menyllos

***DTA* 49**

Side A:
Ἀστύφιλον
Ἀλ[α]έ[α] Φα[ν]ίαν
καταδῶ   καταδῶ

Side B:
τὴγ γλῶτταν
καὶ τὴν ψυχήν

Side A:
Astyphilos of Halai and Phanias, I bind . . . I bind

Side B:
(I bind) the tongue, and the spirit

***DTA* 50**

Side A:
Μένυλλον
Ἀλαέα καταδῶ
τὴγ γλῶτταν

Side B:
καὶ τὴμ ψυχήν

Side A:
Menyllos of Halai, I bind the tongue

Side B:
And the spirit

***DTA* 53** (Chapter 10)

Origin: Greece, Attika
Date: Third century BCE (Wünsch 1897)
Text: Wünsch (1897)

. . .ν οἶκον [κα]ὶ ἔργα γλῶ-

ττav .... θ]υμὸν ἔργα γλῶ-
ττav ... .β]ίον τὸν Δίωνος.

... home and work, tongue ... heart, work, tongue ... life of Diōn.

DTA 55 (Chapters 7, 10)

Origin: Greece, Attika
Date: Late fourth century BCE (Wilhelm 1904)
Text: Wünsch (1897); the names in brackets are scrambled

Side A:

      Διοκλῆς [Ξενοφῶ]ντος
Κι[μωνοκλέα Οἰν]έα συριν[γοποι]ὸν καὶ τέκτονα
καταδ[ῶ καὶ τὸν ἀμφορ]έα αὐτοῦ καὶ [τὸ κι]βώτιον οὗ αἱ σύρι-
γ(γ)ες φέ[ρονται καὶ Ἀθ]ηναγόραν. (Κιμωνοκλέα Οἰνέα).
Ξέναρχ[ος καὶ Πα]ταίκιον ἣν ἔφη Ἐπαίνετος θυγατέρα εἶναι[ι καὶ ἠγγ]ύησε γυναῖκα Ἐχεσθένει Τροζηνί-
ωι (Πα[ταίκιον Τροζη]νίωι) ἀράν. Δείνων Δεισιθείου Πειραεύς Δείνων ([Δεισι]θείου Πειραεύς) Οἰνι[ά]δης Ἀπολλο-
δώρου Ἐροιά[δης ὃ]ς στρ(α)τεύεται ἐν τοῖς Π[ει]ραϊκοῖς στρατιώ-
ταις (Οἰνιάδ[ης Ἀπο]λλοδώρου Ἐροιάδης). Τέκτονα.
Χαιρελείδ[ης Χαιρ]ελείδου Ἀναφλύστιος [ὃ]ς στρατεύεται
ἐν τοῖς Πει[ραϊκοῖς στρα]τιώταις (Χαιρελείδης Ἀναφλύστιος).
Δημόστρατ[ος] Ἀρχαμένους Μυρρινούσιος (Δημόστρατος
Μυρρινούσιος). Ἡρόστρατος [στ]ρατευόμενος ἐν τοῖς στρα-
τιώταις [Πειραϊκοῖς ἀπρο]φασί[σ]τ[α]τος.
Τούτους ἐγὼ καταδίδημι ἅπαντας ἐν μολύβδωι καὶ ἐν κη-
ρῶ(ι) καὶ ἐμ [πο]τῶι καὶ ἐν ἀργίαι καὶ ἀφανί(αι) κα(ὶ) ἐν ἀδοξίαι
καὶ ἐν ἥττ(η)ι καὶ ἐμ μνήμασιν καὶ αὐτοὺς
    καὶ οἷς χρῶνται ἅπαντας
     παῖ[δας καὶ] γυ[ναῖκας.

Side B:
Λυ[σιμ]ήδην Ν . . . .
Φιλόστρατος Κει[ριάδης.
Τὸν στρατευόμε-
νον ἐν τοῖς Πει-
ραϊκο[ῖ]ς στρατιώται[ς . . . .
Σ Ι Ε Α Τ Ṇ Ṛ (Κηφισό)δοτον
καταδῶ τοῦτο(υ)ς ἐμ μνή-
μασιν κα(ὶ) ἐν ἀπορίαι
καὶ ἐν τύμβοις.

Side A:
Dioklēs, son of Xenophōn, Kimōnoklēs, Oineus, pipe-maker and carpenter, I bind, and his jar and the box in which his pipes are carried and Athēnagoras, (Kimēnoklēs,

Oineus). Xenarchos and Pataikion, whom Epainetos says is his daughter and pledged as wife to Echesthenēs of Troezēn, on him (Pataikion of Troizēn) a curse. Deinōn, son of Deisitheios, from Peiraeus, Deinōn, (son of Deisitheios, from Peiraeus), Oiniadēs, son of Apollodōros, of Eroiadai, who is serving with the soldiers in the Peiraeus, (Oiniades son of Apollodōros, of Eroiadai). Carpenter. Chaireleidēs, son of Chaireleidēs, of Anaphlystos, who is serving with the soldiers in the Peiraeus, (Chaireleidēs of Anaphlystos). Dēmostratos, son of Archamenēs, of Myrrhinous, (Dēmostratos of Myrrhinous). Hērostratos, who is is serving with the soldiers in the Peiraeus, absolutely without apology. All these men I consign in lead and in wax and in water (?) in unemployment, obscurity, ill-repute, in defeat and in remembrance/ their graves both these and all the children and wives with whom they live.

Side B:
Lysimedēs . . . Philostratos, Keiriadēs. That man who is serving with the soldiers in the Peiraeus . . . Kēphisodotos, I bind them all in their memory/graves and into helplessness and in their tombs.

DTA 56 (Chapter 10)

Origin: Greece, Attika

Date: Third century BCE (Wünsch 1897)

Text: Wünsch (1897); names written backwards; tablet folded and pierced with two nails

Καταδῶ Μένωνα   . . A.   Καταδ[ῶ. . .]ον καὶ Λο. . . . . . καὶ
                                                   Φανία[ν] κ[αὶ
       Πα(μ)φίλου   A . . . P A   καὶ .A . . . . Δ I H . . Δ A I A . . T I .
                                                   A καὶ τὰ . . H I
καὶ ἔργα καὶ ἔπη τὰ ΠΡΗΧ . EAT <ΓAΠ   καὶ τὴν . . . . I H . . . . . . Θ Α καὶ
                                                   O . . . .
. ἐμοὶ καὶ γλῶτ(τ)αν   ψυχὴν καὶ πράξεις τὰς ἐκεί[νου] καὶ
τ]ὴν ἐκε[ί]νου καὶ ψυχήν καὶ   καὶ νύκτ[α] καὶ [ἡμέρ]α[ν

I bind Menōn . . . I bind . . . and . . . and Phanias and of Pamphilos . . . and . . . and . . . and words and deeds . . . and the . . . and . . . to me and tongue and spirit and deeds of that man and the spirit of that man both night and day

DTA 63 (Chapters 9, 10)

Origin: Greece, Attika

Date: Third century BCE (Wünsch 1897)

Text: Wünsch (1897); retrograde

Πάνφ(ι)λ[ο]ς οἱ συνήγορ[οι .
Πανφ(ί)λου αἱ πράξεις ὁπό[σας
. καὶ] ἔργα μέλ(λ)ε[ι .
A E . . . I I . E (Π)άνφιλ[ος.

Pamphilos, the co-speakers, the actions of Pamphilos, whatever . . . and the deeds he is about to . . . Pamphilos.

DTA 64 (Chapter 10)

Origin: Greece, Attika
Date: Third century BCE (Wünsch 1897)
Text: Wünsch (1897); once folded; ll. 3–14 written backwards

Κ]αταδέω τὸν Πελ . .
. . . Ι Α αὐτοὶ Π Ι Λ Ε . Ο Α Ι .
καὶ μήπο[τ]ε αὐτὸς εὖ πρ[άττοι
καὶ εἴ τις αὐτῷ πρόξεν[ος . .
αὐ]τῶι πάντα ἐναντία εἶναι . . . . . .
καὶ ἔργα καὶ ἥντινα μέλλει Λ . . .
ἐναντία γένοιτο · ἀλλὰ [. . . . . . γένοιτο καὶ οἵτινες εἰς ἂν[. . . . . ἐναντία γένοιτο· Μη(ν)όφιλος ἀλ . . . . . .
μονα· ἄγοι αὐτος Χαιρ(ε)στράτη[ν . . . .
Κ Ι θεοὶ Ν Ι Ν Μ Ι Σ Ε̣ Θ Ι Η Ν Α Ρ αὐτὸς κα[ὶ . .
σθαι Χαιρ(ε)στράτην· Μ Ι Σ̣ Ε Θ Α Ι αὐτὸ[ς
φιλ[ον] καὶ . . . Ε Ρ Κ . . . .

I bind the (name?) . . . they . . . and may he never do well and if anyone is a patron to him . . . let all things go awry for him . . . and deeds, and whatever woman he is about . . . Let it go awry. But . . . . let it be and those who into an . . . let it go awry. Mēnophilos . . . Let him lead Chairestratēs . . . gods . . . he also . . . Chairestratēs . . . he Philos and . . .

DTA 65 (Chapters 7, 9)

Origin: Greece, Attika
Date: Third century BCE (Wünsch 1897); fourth century BCE (Wilhelm 1904)
Text: Wünsch (1897); ll. 2–9 written backwards; tablet folded

ΑΡΟΣ Καλλ[ία]ς . . ΣΑ . Χ . . Λ Εὐκτήμονος
Χαρίας Καλλίας : ἐφ᾽ὑμῖ[ν . . . .
Καλλίας [Ἱ]π(π)όνικος: Ἱπ(π)ο(λ)όχης
Καλλίο[υ] μάρτυρες ἢ δικα[σταί?
Κ]αλλία[ν] ἐλαχίστου . . . .
Νουμηνίου κηδ(ε)σταὶ . . . . .
συ(ν)ηγόρ[ους] καὶ Καλ[λί]ας · Χ[α]ρίας . . .
ἄφρονες γένοιτο· Ἀμεινί[α]ς . . . .
Καλλίας (μάρτυρες) Κα[λλία]ς
Καλλίας
Καλλίου.

l. 10   Letters upside down
l. 11   In the right margin and written upside down

. . . Kallias . . . Euktēmonos, Charias, Kallias . . . against you . . . Kallias, Hipponikos: Hippolochēs, witnesses of Kallias or judges . . . Kallias, of the least . . . The in-laws of

Noumēnios, co-speakers and Kallias. Charias ... let them be mindless. Ameinias ... Kallias (witnesses) Kallias, Kallias, of Kallias

DTA 66 (Chapters 7, 9)

Origin: Greece, Athens, Peiraeus

Date: Beginning of fourth century BCE (Wünsch 1897); fourth century BCE (Wilhelm 1904)

Text: Wünsch (1897); Side A written backwards from the bottom of the tablet to the top; Side B written backwards

Side A:
καταδῶ Εὐάρατον·
καὶ ὅσοι σύνδικοι κ-
αὶ Τελεσῖνο(ν) τ[ὸ]ν Ἰδιώτο(υ) καὶ τὴν ψυχὴν καταδῶ Ἰδι(ώ)του, γλῶτταν κα[ὶ] αὐτὸν· μετ' Ε-
ὐαράτο(υ) σ(υ)νπράττωσι καὶ ὅσοι ἂν σ-
(ύ)νδικος μετ' Εὐαράτο(υ) καὶ το(ὺ)ς Εὐ-
αράτο(υ) καὶ τὴν ψυχὴν καὶ γλῶτταν

Side B:
καὶ ε(ἴ) τις ἐναντί(α) ε(ἰ) τὰ τούτων ἐσ(τ)ί
ἄλλος πράττ<ι>ει ἐμοί.

Side A:
I bind Euaratos and whoever are co-advocates and Telesinos, the son of Idiōtos, and the spirit of Idiōtos I bind. Tongue and him. And whoever is working with Euaratos and whoever is a co-advocate of Euaratos and those (sons/allies? of) Euaratos and the spirit and tongue

Side B:
And if there is anyone else who is also doing the hostile acts of these men against me.

DTA 67 (Chapters 7, 9)

Origin: Greece, Athens, Peiraeus

Date: Third century BCE (Wünsch 1897); fourth century BCE (Wilhelm 1904)

Text: Wünsch (1897); tablet folded; text retrograde

Ὀνητορίδης Ε[ὐη](θ)ίδης
.... Ἀρχέδικος Ναύκριτος
Φιλοξενίδης
Δημήτριος Αἰγυπτία
Φιλόδημος Προκλείδης
Ἀρίστυλλα
καὶ τοὺς μετ' ἐκείνων
ὥσπερ ταῦτα ψυχρὰ καὶ ἐπαρίστερα

οὕτως τὰ Κράτητος τὰ ῥήματα ψυχρὰ [καὶ
ἐπαρί]στερα γέν[οι]το κα[ὶ] τῶν μετ' ἐκ[εί]νων μη-
νυτῶ]ν καὶ τῶν δικα[στῶν
... σαι .... ἔχε το

On side B ΩΣΠΕΡ written backwards can be read and following ΚΑΙ also written backwards, appears twice.

Onētoridēs, Euēthidēs ... Archedikos, Naikritos, Philoxenidēs, Dēmētrios, Aigyptia, Philodēmos, Prokleidēs, Aristylla, and those with them. Just as these words are cold and written backwards, in the same way may the words of Kratēs be cold and backwards and those of the informers with them and the judges ...

DTA 68 (Chapters 7, 9, 10, 11)
Origin: Greece, Athens, Patissia
Date: Classical/Hellenistic (Faraone 1991a: 27 n. 47)
Text: Wünsch (1897); retrograde; folded and pierced with a nail

Side A:
Φιλέαν τὸμ μυλωθρὸν χεῖρας πόδας γλ[ῶτταν] ῥήματα . . Α Λ . . Ι Λ . . . Ο Γ Ι Ν Ι Κ
......
Ι . Σ Α Ν Α χεῖρας πόδας καὶ [ἐργ]ασίαν τὴμ [μνή]μην χεῖρας καὶ πόδας καὶ
ἐργαστήριον
Φύλ]λιδα Β . . φορον .... ἐργαστήρι[ον . . . . .]κλ[έους
γυνὴ χεῖρας πόδας γλῶτταν καὶ Η Τ .... ρίαν ....
Παρθένιον τὴν κάπηλιν χεῖρας πόδας· Λυ[δ]ὴν τὸ [ἐ]ργαστήριον πα ......
Ναυσ[ίπο-
ρον χεῖρας πόδας τὴν συνοικίαν πᾶσαν καὶ σύνοικα πάντα συ .... χαριτο-
πῶλιν χεῖρας καὶ πόδας καὶ ἐργαστήριον καὶ τὰ ἐν τῶι ἐργαστηρίωι ἅπαντα.
ΧΡΕΣ . ΚΙΣΕΑΗΝΑΛ ὀπίσω καὶ ΚΛΗΣ . . . χεῖρας πόδας [ἐργαστήριον καὶ τα ἐν
τῶι
ἐργαστηρίωι ἅπ[α]ντα . . . . Λυδ[ὸν] τὸμ . ΟΓ. . . . . ΙΝ τὸμ πύγ[μαχον καὶ] χεῖρας
πό[δας
τ]οὺς . . . α . τοὺς μάρτ[υρας] τοῦ Π . . ΣΤΑ .... ΙΜΗΝ ....
τὸ ἐργαστήριον καὶ ΠΟ .... ΤΟΝ............. ΜΙΓΟΤ . . . Α Ν [χεῖρας] καὶ
πόδας
καὶ ...... κάπηλο[ν. . . . .] Η . Ν ...... χεῖρας πόδας [ἐρ-
γαστήριον τὴν κάπηλιν χεῖρας πόδας τὸ ἐ[ργαστήριον καὶ τὰ ἐν τῶι ἐργαστηρίωι
ἅπαντα· Ἀρέσκουσαν τὴμ μαστρ[ο]π[ὸν] χεῖρας πόδας γλῶ[τταν] τὸν ΕΛΕ ......
ΡΩΤΑΝ
.. ΤΟΝ .... γυν]αῖκα χεῖρας [πόδας ....]αν Νικο[κλέους χεῖρας
κ[αὶ] πόδας.

Side B:
Διφίλην καὶ χ[ε]ῖρας καὶ πόδας καὶ γλῶτταν καὶ πόδα[ς καὶ ἐργαστήριον καὶ
τὰ ἐν τῶι ἐργαστηρίωι ἅπαντα · Πόσιν χεῖρας καὶ [πόδας καὶ γλῶτταν
καὶ τὸ ἐργαστήριον καὶ τὰ ἐν τῶι ἐργαστηρίωι ἅπαν[τα .... χεῖρας

καὶ πόδας καὶ γ[λῶ]τταν καὶ [τὸ ἐργαστήριον] καὶ τὰ ἐν [τῶι ἐργαστη]ρίωι [ἅ-
παντα. Λ(ύ)σανδ[ρ]ον χεῖρ[α]ς καὶ π[ό]δας καὶ ἐργαστήρι[ον καὶ τὰ ἐν τῶι] ἐ[ργα-
σ]τηρίωι ἅπαντα · Ἀνύ[τ]αν τὴν [κά]πη(λι)ν χ[ε]ῖρας καὶ [πό]δα[ς καὶ τὸ
ἐργασ]τήρι[ον
καὶ τὰ ἐν τῶι ἐ[ρ]γαστηρίωι ἅπαν[τ]α EPP .. EO νατον Λυ ....ον χε[ῖ-
ρας καὶ πόδας καὶ γλῶτταν καὶ ἐργαστήριον καὶ τὰ ἐν τῶι [ἐργαστηρίωι ἅπαντα.
Λύκιον χεῖρας καὶ πόδας καὶ γλῶτταν καὶ ἐργαστή[ριον καὶ] τὰ ἐν τῶι ἐργαστηρίωι ἅπαντα. Λυδὴν χεῖρας καὶ πόδας καὶ γλῶτ[ταν καὶ ἐργασ]τήριον
καὶ τὰ ἐν τῶι ἐργα[σ]τηρίωι ἅπαντα. Κίλικα Ν. . PMAKP [... χεῖρας πόδας
καὶ ἐργαστήρι[ον] καὶ τὰ [ἐν τῶι] ἐργ[ασ]τηρί[ω]ι ἅπαντα. Μέλα[να χεῖρας καὶ π]όδας
καὶ πό[δ]ας καὶ [γλῶ]τταν [κ]αὶ [ἐρ]γαστήριον κ[αὶ] τὰ ἐν [τῶι ἐργαστηρίωι
ἅπα]ντα.
Λάκαιναν τὴμ Μέλανος πάλ(λ)ακα χεῖρας πόδας καὶ ....
κα[τ]αδῶ τὸν [δ]ο[ῦ]λο(μ) Μέλανος ... ENIA χεῖρας καὶ πόδας καὶ ἐργαστή
[ριον ....

Side A:

Phileas the miller, hands, feet, tongue, speech ... hands, feet and work, the memory, hands and feet and workshop. Phyllida ... the workshop ... woman, hands, feet, tongue and ... Parthenios the (f.) innkeeper, hands, feet. Lydē the workshop ... Nausiporos, hands, feet, all those living together, all the household ... tart ... hands and feet and workshop and everything in the workshop ... backwards ... hands, feet, workshop and everything in the workshop. Lydos the boxer, and hands and feet ... witnesses ... workshop ... hands and feet ... and ... innkeeper (m.) ... hands, feet, workshop, the innkeeper, hands, feet, workshop and everything in the workshop ... Areskousa the pimp, hands, feet, tongue ... woman, hands ... hands and feet of Nikoklēs.

Side B:

Diphilēs, and hands, and feet, and tongue, and feet, and workshop, and everything in the workshop. Posis, hands and feet and tongue and workshop, and everything in the workshop ... hands and feet and tongue and workshop and everything in the workshop. Lysandros, hands and feet and workshop and everything in the workshop ... hands and feet and tongue and workshop and everything in the workshop. Anyta, the (f.) innkeeper, hand and feet and workshop and everything in the workshop ... hands and feet and tongue and workshop, and everything in the workshop. Lykios, hands and feet and tongue and workshop and everything in the workshop. Lydē, hands and feet and tongue and workshop and everything in the workshop. Kilix ... hands and feet and workshop and everything in the workshop. Melas, hands and feet, and feet and tongue and workshop and everything in the workshop. Lakaina, the concubine of Melas, hands and feet and ... I bind the slave of Melas ... hands and feet and workshop.

DTA 69 (Chapters 7, 10)

Origin: Greece, Athens
Date: No later than second century BCE (Gager 1992: 157)
Text: Lechat (1889: 77–80)

Καταδῶ [Δι]ονύσιον
τὸν κρανοποιὸν καὶ τὴν
γυναῖκα αὐτοῦ Ἀρτέμείν
τὴν χρυσωτρίαν καὶ τὴν [ο]ἰ-
κ]ίαν αὐτῶν καὶ τὴν [ἐ]ργα-
σίαν καὶ τὰ [ἔργ]α καὶ τὸν
βί[ο]ν αὐτῶ[ν, καὶ] Κάλλιπ-
[πον ?] . . .

I bind Dionysios the helmet-maker and his wife Artemeis the gilder, and their household, and their workshop, and their deeds and life, and Kallippos

DTA 70/DT 70 (Chapter 10)

Origin: Greece, Attika
Date: Classical/Hellenistic (Faraone 1991a: 27 n. 47)
Text: From David Jordan's autopsy (private correspondence)

Καταδήω τὰ Ὠφιλίων[ος] καὶ Ὠφιλίω-
να καὶ τὸ καπήλιον Ὄλομπον. Κ[α]ταδήω τὰ Με-
λαμβίου ἅπαντα καὶ τὸ καπηλιον Ἀγάθωνα ·
καταδήω τὰ Συρίσκος, ἅπαντα τὰ Συρεος .
Κα[τα]δήω τὰ Πιστίου ἅπαντα, Μανῆ καὶ Πι-
στ[ί]ου ἅπαντα. Καταδήω τούτων ἅπαντα,] τὰς ἐργασίας ἁπασ[ας] τούτων
[   ]ηρ[   ]
- -

2 Ὄλομπος Ὄλυμπος at Ὄλομπον: first ο corr. from κ   3 Ἀγάθωνα: first α corr. from another letter   4 Σύρισκος for Συρίσκου: second σ corr. from letter with vertical at left   Σύρεος genitive of *Σῦρις, truncated form of Σύρισκος
Μελαμθίου for Μελαν- at ll. 2–3.
Jordan: Olympos (l. 2) and Agathon (l. 3) are personal names rather than names of shops; and καπηλιον is a diminutive, rather than a spelling of καπηλεῖον.

I bind the (words?) of Ōpheliōn and Ōpheliōn and the innkeeper Olympos. I bind all the words of Melanthios and the innkeeper Agathōn. I bind the words of Syriskos all the words of Syris. I bind all the words of Pistias. Manēs and everything of Pistios. I bind all their words, all their workshops

DTA 71/DT 71 (Chapter 10)

Origin: Greece, Attika
Date: Classical/Hellenistic (Faraone 1991a: 27 n. 47)
Text: From David Jordan's autopsy (private correspondence)

Ὠφιλίων Ὠφίμη, Ὄλομπος.
Καταδέω τὸ ἐργαστήριο τὸ Ὠφιλίωνος καὶ τὴν ἐργ[α]σία[ν ·
Ἑκαταῖος Μανῆς, Φίμη, Ἐρήνη
καὶ τὴν ἐργασία τῆ[ν] Ἰρήνης
----

1 passim Ὠφιλίων for Ὠφελιών ε, η, ι = [i]   Ὄλομπος = Ὄλυμπος   2 η = ε. καταδήω / καταδέω   ἐργαστήριο τό, loss of -ν before τ   4 and 5 Ἐρήνη = Ἰρήνη

Ōpheliōn, Ōphemē, Olympos. I bind the workshop of Ōpheliōn and the work. Hekataios, Manēs, Phimē, Eirēnē and the work of Eirēnē

DTA 72 (Chapter 10)

Origin: Greece, Attika
Date: Third century BCE (Wünsch 1897)
Text: Wünsch (1897); found with *DTA* 73, pierced with the same nail

Φίλην τὴμ Μικίωνος Φρυγίαν
Μάλλιον τὴν Σωσιβίου Σ . . . . .

Philē, the Phrygian wife of Mikiōn, Mallion the wife of Sōsibios . . .

DTA 73 (Chapters 7, 10)

Origin: Greece, Attika
Date: Classical/Hellenistic (Faraone 1991a: 27 n. 47)
Text: Wünsch (1897); found with *DTA* 72, pierced with the same nail

Φίλην τὴ(μ) Μικίωνος Μάλιον τὴμ . . . P X A P I K E I
Δ]ιονύσιον τὸγ κάπηλον Τιμόστρατον τὸγ Κορίν[θ
ιον καὶ τέχνην τὴν Τιμοστράτου καὶ ὄργαν[α·
καὶ Μίτριν καὶ Κόμνον καὶ Θούας:

Philē the wife of Mikiōn, Malion the . . . the innkeeper, Timostratos the Korinthian and the craft of Timostratos and his tools; and Mitris and Komnon and Thouas

DTA 74 (Chapters 7, 9, 10)

Origin: Greece, Attika (near Boiotian border)
Date: Classical/Hellenistic (Faraone 1991a: 27 n. 47)
Text: Wünsch (1897); once folded

Λα . . λον καὶ Αεξ. καδδίδημι
κὴ αὐτὰν κὴ ψυχὰν καὶ αὐτὸν
κὴ γλῶταν κὴ σῶμα κὴ ἐρ-
γασίαν κὴ ἐργαστήρια κὴ
τέχναν καδδίδη[μι . . . .
Θεόξενον καδδίδημι κ[ὴ
αὐτὸν κὴ [ψ]υχὰν καὶ τὰ ἐκε[ίνου
πάντα.

La-...-lon and Aex- . I bind both her and spirit, and him and tongue, and body, and work, and workshops, and skills I bind .... I bind Theoxenos, both him and spirit and everything of his.

DTA 75 (Chapters 7, 9, 10)
Origin: Greece, Athens
Date: Fourth century BCE (Wünsch 1897)
Text: Wünsch (1897); tablet folded

Side A:
Κα[τ]αδηνύω Ἀνάχαρσιν
καὶ τὸ ἐργασίαν καταδηνύω α[ὐ]το[ῦ
Ἀρτεμί(ν) τὸν [..κ]αταδηνύω .. Μ Η Ε
κ]αὶ Ἀρτεμί(δ)ος δε[σπ]ότην καταδη-
νύ(ω). Ὑμνίδα τὴν Ε.. Ρ]οδίονα κάπ(ηλον)
καταδ(ην)ύω Ρό(δ)ων[α· ἀπ]όλοι[το
καὶ τὸ ἐργαστήριον . Ι Φ Ο Λ Ο Ο Ν
ἐργάζεται· καταδηνύω Ρό-
διον τὸν κάπηλον κατ[α-
δην(ύ)ω τὴν καπήλ[ειαν
κατα[δ]ηνύω (καὶ) τὸ ἐμ-
πόριον.

Side B:
Καταδην[ύ]ω Ἀ[ρ]ταμίν
καὶ Ο Ο Γ Χ Ο Λ Τ Η Ν . Ν Ε Ρ Λ Ο
καὶ Ν Ω Λ Ι Α Δ Υ Ω Ι Ν Ο Σ Δ Υ Ι Ο Ο
καὶ Ἀρτεμίδα δυνατὸς γέν[οιτο
Α Ρ Ο Μ Ω Δ Α Ρ Α Ω Α Ι Ἀρτεμιν
Ο Φ Θ Α Ι. τὴν ἐργασίαν καγα[δη-
νύ(ω) Α Ν Ι Ε Γ αν τὴν γ[λ]ῶτ(τ)αν ...
καταδηνύω Θεο[δό]την
καὶ τὸ ἐργαστήριον
τοῦτο· Ἀρταμ(ί)[ν] Κ Ι Τ Η ....
κα[τα]δ(ην)ύω Φίλον ἔργ[α] Η Ι
... ουρα ἀδ(ελ)φ[ὴ
... ρου φίλος.

Side A:
I bind Anacharsis and his work, and I bind his Artemis the ... I bind ... and I bind the master of Artemis. I bind Humnis the E- ..., Rodion the innkeeper, Rodon. Let him be destroyed and his workshop ... he works at. I bind Rodion the innkeeper, I bind the inn and I bind the shop.

Side B:
I bind Artemis and ... and ... and Artemis; let (?) become powerful ... Artemis ... the work I bind ... and the tongue ... I bind Theodotēs and this workshop. Artemis ... I bind Philos, deeds ... sister ... friend.

DTA 77 (Chapters 7, 10, 11)

Origin: Greece, Attika
Date: Third century BCE (Wünsch 1897)
Text: Wünsch (1897); some text, especially names written backwards

Side A:
Καταδοῦμεν (Καλλιστράτην)
τὴν (Θεοφήμου)· γυναῖκα καὶ
Θεόφιλον τὸν Καλλιστράτης
κα[ὶ] τὰ παιδία τὰ (Καλλι)στράτης
καὶ [Θ]εόφημον καὶ (Εὔστρατον)
      ἀδελφὸν ...... κ[α]ταδ[ῶ·
τὰς ψυχὰς καὶ τὰ ἔργα αὐτ[ῶν
καὶ αὐτοὺς ὅλους καὶ τὰ τού[τω-
ν ἅπαντα.

Side B:
καὶ τὰς ψωλὰς αὐτῶν καὶ τοὺς κύσθ-
ους αὐτῶν καὶ Κανθαρί[δ]α ⟨καὶ⟩ καὶ τὸν
Διονύσιον· (Κανθαρίδος)· καὶ αὐτοὺς
καὶ τὰς ψυχὰς αὐτῶν [καὶ ἔρ]γα καὶ
αὐτοὺ[ς] ὅλ⟨λ⟩ου[ς] καὶ τὴν ψωλὴν καὶ
τὸν κύσθον τὸν ἀνόσιον· (Τλησία-)
ς κατ]άρατος· (Θεόφημον Εὔεργον
Κανθαρίδα Διονύσιον).

Side A:
We bind Kallistratē, the wife of Theophēmos and Theophilos the son of Kallistratē and the children/slaves of Kallistratē and Theophēmos and Eustratos, brother. I bind their spirits and the deeds and their whole selves and everything of theirs.

Side B:
And their cocks and their vaginas and Kantharis ⟨and⟩ and Dionysios, son of Kantharis, both themselves and their spirits and deeds and their whole selves and the cock and the unholy vagina. (Tlēsias) accursed. Theophēmos, Euergos, Kantharis, Dionysios.

DTA 78 (Chapter 11)

Origin: Greece, Attika
Date: Fourth century BCE (Wünsch 1897 and Wilhelm 1904)
Text: Wilhelm (1904: 13); tablet folded

Ἀριστοκύδη καὶ τὰς φανομένας
αὐτῶι γυναῖκας ·
μήποτ' αὐτὸν γῆμαι ἄλλην γυναῖ(κα) μήτε παῖδα

(I bind) Aristokydēs and the women who let themselves to be seen by him. Do not ever let him 'marry' another woman or a youth

DTA 79 (Chapter 9)

Origin: Greece, Attika
Date: Third century BCE (Wünsch 1897)
Text: Wünsch (1897)

$$\text{Καταδ}[\hat{ω}$$
$$ψυχὴ[ν$$
$$γλ]ῶτ(τ)α[ν$$
$$αὐτ(ῆ)ς$$
$$(Ἑ)ρμῆ$$
$$τοῦ ὅστις Τ.Σ$$
$$περὶ [ἐ]μ[οῦ$$
$$...ΜΕ..$$
$$εἶν]αι καὶ$$

Δ	ἄπαν[τα		
καὶ ψυ-	ΜΕΤΕΘΕΣ	συμπαρόντας	
χὴν	ΩΙ	Μενό-	
καὶ	κατα-	κριτος	
γλῶτ(τ)αν	δῶ	ΤΩΙ	
	κατα[δῶ		

I bind tongue (and) spirit of that woman, o Hermēs, and of whomever ... about me ... to be and everything (column i) and spirit and tongue. (column ii) I bind (column iii) those standing around (who support) Menokritos

DTA 81 (Chapter 9)

Origin: Greece, Attika
Date: Third century BCE (Wünsch 1897)
Text: Wünsch (1897)

καταδ]έω τοὺς ἐ[μοὶ ἐχθροὺς
... π]ρὸς τὸν Ἑρμῆ[ν ....
συνδί]κους· καὶ τούτους κα[ὶ] τὰ α[ὐτῶν ἄπαντα
... Πάταικον Φρεαρρέ· οἰκοῦντ[α

I bind my enemies ... in the presence of Hermēs ... co-advocates, and those men and everything of theirs ... Pataikos Phrearre (of Phrearrhioi?), who dwells

DTA 84 (Chapters 9, 10)

Origin: Greece, Attika
Date: Classical/Hellenistic (Faraone 1991a: 27, n. 47)
Text: Wünsch (1897); folded and pierced with a nail. Side A: l. 3 written backwards and upside-down above l. 2; l. 4 written backwards and upside-down above l. 5. Side B: all lines written backwards.

Side A:
Ἀνδροκλείδη καταδῶ
καὶ τὴν γλῶτ(τ)αν τὴν κακὴν καὶ τὸν θυμὸν τὸν κακὸν καὶ τὴν
τὴν ψυχὴν κακὴν καὶ τὸ ἐργαστήριον καταδῶ καὶ τοὺς παῖδας.
Δ]ιονύσιον κατα[δ]ῶ καὶ τὴν γλῶτ(τ)αν τὴν κακὴν καὶ τὸν θυμὸν τὸν κακὸν
καὶ τὴν ψυχὴν τὴν κακὴ[ν.
κακὴν*
Side B:
Ἀφροδι<α>σία κατὰ Τ Η Ι Ω Ρ Μ Ν ου καὶ τὸ ἐργα(σ)τ(ή)ριομ καὶ τὰς
πα(λλ)ακάς·
Καταδῶ Τρύφ[ω]να πρὸ(ς) τὸ(ν) Ἑ(ρ)μ(ῆ)ν· (αὐ)τὸμ καὶ ἔργα [κ]α(ὶ) ἔπεα.
Δημέα (Δ)ημαιν(έτ)ου καταδῶ Μιαν . Ι Λ Ḥ Γ . . Α

* Wünsch combines with τὴν ψυχὴν at the beginning of l. 3.

Side A:
I bind Androkleidēs and his evil tongue, and his evil heart, and his evil spirit, and his workshop, and I bind his children. Dionysios I bind and his evil tongue, and his evil heart, and his evil spirit.

Side B:
Aphrodi(a)sia according to . . . and the workshop and prostitutes. I bind Tryphōn in the presence of Hermēs, him and deeds and words. Dēmeas son of Dēmainetos I bind . . .

DTA 85 (Chapters 10, 11)
Origin: Greece, Attika
Date: Classical/Hellenistic (Faraone 1991a: 27 n. 47)
Text: Wünsch (1897)

Βίαιον τὸν Φιλονί-
κου δοῦλον καταδ-
ῶ καὶ Ἀγάθωνα
πρὸ[ς τ]ὸν Ἑρμῆν
  τὸν κάτοχον

Biaios, the slave of Philonikos, I bind and Agathōn, in the presence of Hermēs the Binder.

DTA 86 (Chapters 9, 10)
Origin: Greece, Attika
Date: No later than fourth century BCE (Gager 1992: 160)
Text: Wünsch (1897); individual words in ll. 1 and 2 are written right to left; tablet folded and pierced with a nail

Ἰφεμυθάνην Ἀνδροσθένην καταδῶ
καὶ Σιμ(μ)ίαν Δρόμωνα· πόδας χεῖρας
πρὸς τὸ[ν] Ἑρ[μῆ]ν τὸν κάτοχον

ψυχὴν γλώντας ἐργασίας
κέρδη.

Iphemythanēs, Androsthenēs I bind and Simmias and Dromōn, feet, hands, in the presence of Hermēs the Binder, spirit, tongues, work, profit.

DTA 87 (Chapters 7, 9, 10, 11)

Origin: Greece, Attika
Date: Fourth century BCE (Wünsch 1897)
Text: Wünsch (1897); folded and pierced with a nail; beautifully inscribed (Wünsch)

Side A:
Καταδῶ Καλλίαν· τὸν κάπηλον τὸν ἐγ γειτόνων καὶ τὴν γυναῖκα αὐτοῦ
Θρᾶϊτταν· καὶ τὸ καπηλεῖον τὸ φαλακροῦ καὶ τὸ Ἀνθεμίωνος καπηλεῖον τὸ
   πλησίον Δ Α . Ο Η
καὶ Φίλωνα τὸν κάπηλον· τούτων πάντων καταδῶ ψυχὴν ἐργασίαν
χεῖρας πόδας· τὰ καπηλεῖα αὐτῶν.
Καταδῶ Σωσιμένην τ[ὸν] ἀδελφόν· καὶ Κάρπον τὸν οἰκότην αὐτοῦ τὸν
   σινδο[νο]πώλην καὶ Γλύκανθιν ἣν καλοῦσι Μαλθάκην· καὶ Ἀγάθωνα
   τ[ὸ]ν κάπηλον
τ]ὸν Σωσιμένους οἰκότην· τούτων πάντων καταδῶ· ψυχὴν ἐργασία[ν β]ίον
   χεῖρας πόδας.
Καταδῶ Κίττον τὸν γείτονα τὸν καναβιο(υ)ργὸν καὶ τέχνην τὴν Κίττου καὶ
   ἐργασίαν καὶ ψυχὴν καὶ νο(ῦ)ν καὶ γλῶτταν τὴν Κίττου.
Καταδῶ Μανίαν τὴν κάπηλιν τὴν ἐπὶ κρήν(η)ι καὶ τὸ καπηλεῖον τὸ
   Ἀρίστανδρος Ἐλευσινίου καὶ ἐργασίαν αὐτοῖς καὶ νο(ῦ)ν.
ψυχὴν χεῖρας γλῶτταν πόδας νο(ῦ)ν· τούτους πάντας καταδῶ ἐμ
   μνήματι ΑΣΦΑΡΑΓΙΑΙ
κ   πρὸς τὸν κάτοχον Ἑρμῆν.

Side B:
τοὺς Ἀριστάνδρου οἰκέτας.

Side A:
I bind Kallias the innkeeper in the neighbourhood, and his wife Thraitta,* and the inn of the bald man, and the inn of Athemiōn nearby . . . and Philōn the innkeeper. Of all these men, I bind spirit, work, hands, feet, their inns. I bind Sōsimenēs his brother and Karpos his servant, the fabric seller, and Glykanthis whom they call Malthakē and Agathōn the innkeeper, who is the slave of Sōsimenēs. Of all these I bind spirit, work, life, hands, feet. I bind Kittos the neighbour, the maker of wooden frames (ropes?)** and Kittos' craft and work, and spirit and mind and the tongue of Kittos. I bind Mania the innkeeper, the woman near the spring, and the inn of Aristandros of Eleusis and their work and mind. Spirit, hands, tongue, feet, mind. All of them I bind in the . . . grave*** in the presence of Hermēs the Binder.

Side B:
The servants of Aristandros.

* As well as a commercial motive, Gager (1992: 156) suggests an angry husband may have had other reasons for the creation of this text. Working from a manumission document of 330–320 BCE (*IG* ii². 1554–9, face A, col. 5, l. 493; see Lewis 1959: 219), he raises the idea that Thraitta was originally the wife of one Menedemos, from whom she fled and who was then prompted to create this tablet. However, it is unlikely that these two are the husband and wife of the curse tablet, since, according to that document they lived in different parts of Athens. Moreover, the verb which Gager reads as indicating that Thraitta 'fled' her husband (ἀποφυγών) is actually a verb of manumission: Menedemos was the owner of Thraitta who freed her.

** = καναβιουργὸς 'frame-maker' might be κανναβιουργὸς 'rope-maker' (Gager 1992: 157)

*** = Faraone has suggested that μνήματι ΑΣΦΑΡΑΓΙΑΙ should be read as the 'unsealed tomb', i.e., the grave in which the tablet is buried.

DTA 88 (Chapters 7, 9)

Origin: Greece, Attika

Date: Third century BCE (Wünsch 1897)

Text: Wünsch (1897); tablet folded and pierced with a nail

Side A:
Ἑρμῆ κάτοχε
κάτεχε
φρένας
γλῶτ(τ)αν
(τοῦ Καλλίου· δέω)
ἐ]ναντία εἶναι Καλλί-
αι πρὸς Μικίωνα ὅτι [ἂν εἴ-]
ποι καὶ τοιαῦτα Καλ-
λίου συνδίκοις κατὰ
Μικίωνος.
Καλλίαι
(πάντα ἐναντία)
εἶναι

Side B:
Ἑρμῆ
κάτοχε
κάτεχε φρέ(νας).

Side A:
O Hermēs the Binder, bind the mind, tongue of Kallios. I bind whatever he would say, let (the words) against Mikiōn be hostile to Kallias, and let such (words) of Kallias against the co-advocates on Mikiōn's side all be hostile to Kallias

Side B:
O Hermēs the Binder, bind the mind.

DTA 89 (Chapters 7, 9, 11)

Origin: Greece, Attika

Date: Fourth century BCE (Wünsch 1897)

Text: Wünsch (1897); folded and pierced with a nail

Side A:
Δέσποτα Ἑρμῆ
κάτοχε κάτεχε Φ(ρύ)νιχον κ[α]ὶ τὰ ἀκρω[τήρ]ια αὐτοῦ
το(ὺ)ς πόδας: τὴν κεφα[λὴ]ν
τὰς χεῖρας τὴν γαστ[έρ]α
ψυχὴν τὴν πιμελῆς
φύσιν Δέσποτα [Ἑ]ρμῆ
τὴν π[υ](γὴ)ν κάτοχε κάτεχε
Κίτ[τ]ον κα(ὶ) τὰ ἀκ[ρω](τήρ)ια
τὴν ψυχὴν
καὶ το(ὺ)ς (ὀ)φρῦς Σ Ι
καὶ τῆς Ρ Δ Ω
(ψυχὴν) Ω .

Side B:
Δέσποτα (Ἑ)ρμῆ
κάτεχε Χαιρύλ(λ)ην
κα]ταδῶ αὐ[τ]ῆς καὶ [τὰ] ἀκρ(ω)τήρια αὐ(τ)ης
κα[τ]αδῶ Χαιρύλ(λ)ης τοῦτο(υ)ς . . . . .
καταδῶ <τὰς χαῖρας> τὰς [χ]εῖριας
τὸν νοῦ] ψυχῆς τὴν κεφαλῆς
τὴν ἐργασίαν : τὴν καρδίας
τὴν οὐσια[ν
τὴν γλ[ῶ]τ(τ)αν.

Side A:
O Lord Hermēs, Binder, bind Phrynichos and his extremities, his feet, his head, his hands, his stomach, spirit, the stuff of his fat. O Lord Hermēs, bind his arse. Restrain Kittos and his extremities, his spirit and his eyebrows . . . and of her . . . spirit . . .

Side B:
Lord Hermēs, bind Chairyllē. I bind also her extremities. I bind these of Chairyllē . . . I bind her hands, her hands, the mind, the (stuff of) spirit, the (stuff of) head, the work, the (stuff of) heart, the stuff, the tongue.

DTA 93 (Chapter 11)

Origin: Greece, Athens, Patissia
Date: Classical/Hellenistic periods (Faraone 1991a: 28 n. 59)
Text: Wünsch (1897); folded

Side A:
Ἑρμῆ [χθόνιε· λά]βοι ψυχὴν
Ἑρμ(ῆ) δόλιε· τῆς Πύρρου γυναι(κὸς)
Ἑρμ(ῆ) κάτοχε· μαμμίας Ἱεροῦς
τὰ]ς χεῖρας καρδίας πόδας
. . μαμμί(α) Ἱερ(ώ) . . . .

... Τ Ι κάτοχ[ε ......
...... Τ Ι Ο ....

Side B:
Κα[ταδῶ ....]λια τὴν
Πύρ(ρ)ο(υ) γυν[αῖκα] ψυ[χ]ὴν πό-
δας χεῖρας σῶμα καρδίαμ
βίον τὰ ῥήματ[α] ει.
. Α Ε Σ . αὐτ(ῆ)ι ... αρα
.... Λ .....
.... Γ ....

Side A:
Hermes of the underworld; may you take the spirit, Hermēs the Trickster, of the wife of Pyrros, O Hermēs the Binder. The titties of Hieres, the hands, hearts, feet, titties of Hieres ... O Binder ...

Side B:
I bind ... -lia the wife of Pyrros, her spirit, feet, hands, body, heart, life, the words ... to her ...

DTA 94 (Chapters 7, 9)

Origin: Greece, Athens, Patissia
Date: Third century BCE (Wünsch 1897)
Text: Wünsch (1897); folded

Δέσποτα κάτοχε
καταδ(η)νύ[ω] Διοκλῆ (ὡ)ς τὸ(ν)
ἐμὸν ἀντίδικον· τὴν γλ-
ῶτ(τ)αν καὶ τὰ<ι>ς φρένας
καὶ τοῖς Διοκλ(έου)ς βοη(θ)οῖς
πάντας κα(ὶ) τὸν λόγον
αὐτο(ῦ) κ(α)ὶ (τὰ)ς μαρτυρί-
ας καὶ τὰ δικαιώματα
(ἅπαντ)α ἃ παρασκε(υ)ά-
ζεται ἐπ' ἐμὲ καὶ κάτε-
<κα>χε αὐτόν· ἅπαντα τὰ δι-
καιώματ(α) Διοκλ(ῆ)ν τὰ ἐπ' ἐμὲ
παρασκευάζεται μ(ὴ)
ἀνύσ<σ>αι το(ὺ)ς βο(η)θο(ὺ)ς το(ὺ)ς Διοκλέ-
ο(υ)ς καὶ ἡτ(τ)ᾶσθαι Διοκλ(ῆ)ν
ἀπ' ἐμο(ῦ) ἐν παντὶ δικα-
στ(η)ρίωι καὶ μ(η)θ' ἓν ἀντ(ῆ)ι
Διοκλ(ε)ῖ δίκαιον.

O Lord Binder, I bind Dioklēs as my opponent in court; the tongue and all the thoughts of those who are helping Dioklēs and his speech and the witnesses and all the pleas of justification that are being prepared against me and bind him. (Bind) all the legal pleas that Dioklēs has prepared against me and bind him down. All the pleas that Dioklēs has prepared, do not let those helping Dioklēs succeed, and defeat Dioklēs (from me) in every court and do not let one just thing come to Dioklēs.

DTA 95 (Chapters 9, 10)

Origin: Greece, Attika
Date: Third century BCE (Wünsch 1897); fourth century (Wilhelm 1904)
Text: Wünsch (1897); tablet folded and pierced with a nail

Side B:
καὶ Μένωνα
τὸν Ἀριστολκλ[έους
καὶ αὐτὸν κα(ὶ) τὰ ἔργα τὰ
Μένωνος καὶ τὴν
γλ[ῶ]τ(τ)αν καὶ . . . .
. ἔπη καὶ ἔργα
καὶ πρ(ὸς) το(ὺς) κυρίο(υ)ς
ἀχρε(ῖ)ον εἶναι
καὶ Πίθιον καὶ (Νεο-
δίκην) καὶ τὸν . .
αὐτῆς καὶ . . . .
Ἀναφ(λύστιον)
καὶ Ξενόκριτον
καὶ [(Σωσί)]νομον?
καὶ Ἀρισ . . . .
(Νικίαν Χαρίσιον) ?
το(ὺ)ς Διοφαν . . . .
. . . .
. . . . μάχου Φλυεύς
Λυσιμαχίδ<ρ>ης
Φιλίνου Περα(εύς)·
ἔχει θεὸς κάτο-
χος συνγόρου-
ς τὸν (Εὔκαι-
ρον) καὶ Ἡδύλη(ν)
τὴν Τιμοκράτο(υ)ς

And Menōn, the son of Aristoklēs, both him and the deeds of Menōn and his tongue and . . . words and deeds and (let them be) useless before those in authority; and Pithios and Neodikē and the . . . of her and . . . of Anaphlystos, and Xenokritos and Sōsinomos and Aris . . . . Nikias, Charisios(?), those Diophan- . . . -machou of Phyle, Lysimachidrēs the son of Philinos, from Peiraeus. God the binder holds the advocates, Eukairos and Hēdylē, the wife of Timokratēs

DTA 97 (Chapters 9, 10)

Origin: Greece, Athens, Peiraeus, tomb of uncertain location
Date: Third century BCE (Wünsch 1897)
Text: Wünsch (1897)

Μικίωνα ἐγὼ ἔλαβον καὶ
<καὶ> ἔδησα τὰς χεῖρας καὶ
τοὺς πόδας καὶ τὴν χλῶσσαν
καὶ τὴν ψυχὴν καὶ εἴ τι μέλλει<ε>
ὑπερ Φίλωνος ῥῆμα μοχθηρὸ
<καὶ τὴ>
ν φθέγγεσθαι, ἡ γλῶσσα αὐτοῦ
μόλυβδος γένοιτο. καὶ κέντ-
[η]σον α[ὐτ]οῦ τὴν γλῶσσαν καὶ
εἴ τι μέλλει ἐργάζεσθαι, ἀνόνητα αὐτῶι γίνοιτο καὶ ἄχωρα
καὶ ἄμοιρα καὶ ἀφανῆ αὐτῶι
ἅ]παντα γένοιτο. Ἱππονωΐ-
δ]ην καὶ Σωκράτην ἐγὼ
ἔ]λαβον καὶ ἔδησα τὰς
χε]ῖρας καὶ τοὺς πόδας καὶ
τὴ]ν γλῶσσαν καὶ τὴν ψυχ-
ὴν καὶ εἴ τι μέλλουσιν
ὑπὲρ Φίλωνος ῥῆμα μοχθ-
ηρὸν ἢ πονηρὸν φθένεγεσθαι
ἢ κακόν τι ποῆσαι, ἡ γ[λ]ῶσ-
σα αὐτῶν καὶ ἡ ψυχὴ μόλυ-
βδος γένοιτο καὶ μὴ δύναιντο
φθένεσθα[ι] μηδὲ ποῆσαι, ἀλλὰ
τὴν γλῶσσαν καὶ τὴν ψυχὴν
αὐτῶν κέντησον, καὶ εἴ τ[ι
αὐτοῖς ἐ[σ]τι ἢ μέλλει τι εἶνα[ι
χρήματα ἢ οὐσία ἢ ἐργασία
ἅπαντα ἀνόνητα καὶ ἄ-
χωρα καὶ ἄμοιρα πάντα
αὐτοῖς γένοιτο καὶ ἀφανῆ
αὐτοις ἔστω.
<Ἀροστὼ ἐγώ>
Ἀροστὼ ἐγώ ἔλαβον καὶ ἔδη-
σ]α τὰς χεῖρας καὶ τοὺς πόδας
καὶ τὴν γλῶσσαν καὶ τὴν ψυχὴν καὶ μὴ δύναιτο ὑπὲρ Φίλωνος φθένγεσθαι ῥῆμα πο-
νηρὸν ἀλλὰ ἡ γλῶσσα αὐτῆς μόλυβδος γένοιτο καὶ κέντησον
αὐτῆς τὴν γλῶσσαν.

I have seized Mikiōn and I have bound his hands and feet and tongue and his spirit. And if he is about to utter any wicked statement on Philon's behalf, may his tongue become like lead, and stab his tongue. And if he is about to do any work, let these things become unprofitable for him, and may everything be unresolved* and without benefit and destroyed. I have seized Hipponidēs and Sōcratēs and I have bound the hands and feet and tongue and spirit, and if they are about to utter any wicked or evil statement on Philon's behalf, may their tongues and their spirit become like lead, and may they not be able to speak or act, but stab their tongue and spirit. And if there are any possessions or matter or work going on for them, let these all be profitless and let these all become unresolved and without benefit, and let these all be destroyed. I Aristō, I have seized Aristō and I have bound her hands and feet and tongue and her spirit. And let her not be able to make evil statements on Philiōn's behalf, but let her tongue be like lead. Stab her tongue.

* Literally, 'homeless'.

DTA 98 (Chapters 7, 10, 12)

Origin: Greece, Athens, Patissia
Date: Third century BCE (Wünsch 1897)
Text: Wünsch (1897); folded and pierced with a nail

Εὐρυπτόλεμος Ἀγρυλῆ[θ]ε[ν·   Εὐρ]υπτ[όλ]εμον καταδῶ καὶ Ξενοφῶντα
Ξενοφῶν·   τὸμ μετ' Εὐρυπτολέμου καὶ γλώττας τὰς τούτων καὶ ἔπη καὶ
ἔργα τὰ τούτων καὶ εἴ τι βουλεύονται καὶ εἴ τι πράττουσιν ἀτελῆ
αὐ[το]ἶ[ς] γένοιτο. φ[ίλ]η Γῆ κάτεχε Εὐ[ρυ]πτόλεμον [κ]αὶ Ξενοφῶντα
καὶ ἀδυνάτους αὐτοὺς πόει καὶ ἀτελεῖς καὶ φθόην Εὐρυπτολέμωι
καὶ Ξενοφῶντι· φίλη Γῆ βοήθει μοι· ἀδικούμενος γὰρ ὑπὸ Εὐρυπτολέμου καί
Ξενοφῶντος καταδῶ αὐτούς.

Euryptolemos of Agrylē. Euryptolemos I bind and Xenophōn. Xenophōn.* The man with Euryptolemos and the tongues of those men and their words and deeds. And if they plan anything and if they do anything, let it be useless as far as they are concerned. Dear Earth, bind Euryptolemos and Xenophōn and make them powerless and useless. (Bring) decay to Euryptolemos and Xenophōn. Dear Earth, help me! Since I am being wronged by Euryptolemos and Xenophōn, I bind them.

* Gager (1992: 180) reports that Jordan observes that the names Xenophōn and Euryptolemos in the first lines are set apart and appear like a heading for the text.

DTA 100 (Chapters 7, 9, 11, 12)

Origin: Greece, Attika; a grave near Athens
Date: 360–330 BCE (Wünsch 1897)
Text: Wünsch (1897)

Side A:
.............ε]ὐθῦναι?
..........Σά]τυρ[ον] Σουνιᾶ

καὶ Δη]μή[τριο]ν καὶ εἴ τις ἄλλος ἐμοὶ ἐ[χθρὸς
καὶ τούτους πάντας· καταδῶ αὐτοὺς [ἐγὼ
Ὀνησίμη· πάντας τούτους
αὐτοὺ[s] καὶ τὰς τούτων ἐπ᾿(ἐ)μοὶ
πράξεις σοι παρακατατίθεμαι
τηρ(ε)ῖν, Ἑρμῆ κάτοχ(ε) κάτοχος
ἴσθι τούτων τῶν ὀνομάτων
καὶ τῶν τούτων πάντων.
Ἑ]ρμῆ καὶ Γῆ, ἱκετεύω ὑμᾶς τηρ(ε)ῖν
ταῦτα καὶ τούτους κολάζ(ε)τ(ε)
σῴζετε τὴ]ν μολυβδοκόπον.

Side B:
Ο Ι Δ . . . .
. . . .
. . . .
. . . .
. . . .
. . . .
. . . .
. . . . . Νίκων ἐκ
Κυδαντιδῶν . . . . . Ἀλωπεκεύς
. . νίκα Παρ[ν]. Θεῖος Παρν. Φιλοκλέης
Λα[μ]πτρ. Κ Ι Μ Ο Ρ Τ Ι Ω Ν Αἰξωνε[ὺς
. . . . . Δαμασικλῆ Ἀκρόποδος Ε Π Ι
. . . . Υ Ν Η Ι

Side A:
... euthynai ... Satyros from Sounion and Dēmētrios, and if there is anyone else who is my enemy and all of these men. I bind them, I Onēsimē. All of them and their actions against me I entrust you to watch over. O Hermēs Binder, bind these names and of all these men. O Hermēs and Earth, I beseech you to watch over these things and punish these men, and save the woman who inscribes the lead.

Side B:
... Nikōn from Kydanthenaion ..... of Alopeke .. -nika of Parnassos, Theios of Parnassos, Philoklēs of Lamptrai, ... of Aixone ..... Damasiklēs son of Akropous ...

DTA 102 (Chapters 7, 11, 12)

Origin: Greece, Attika, Athens
Date: Fourth century BCE (Wilhelm 1904)
Text: Wünsch (1897)

Side A:
Ἐπιστο<σ>λὴν
πέμπων
δ]αίμο(σιν)

καὶ Φρεσσεφών(η)⟨ς⟩
κομίσας
Τιβιτίδα
τὴν Χοιρίνης
τὴν ἐμ(ὲ) ἀδικο(ῦ)σαν
θυγατ(έρα)
ἄνδρα
καὶ τρία (π)αιδία
ἐκείνης
δύο θήλεα καὶ ἓν ἄρρεν·
Παγκράτη Μαντ(ίαν)
Διόφαντον
Μεταγένη.

Side B:
Κατόχ(ους) τὴν (Γῆν)
το(ὺ)ς πύκτας
τοὺς Ἀριστό-
μαχος καὶ Ἀρι-
στών⟨ν⟩υμο(ς)
κάτεχε τὴν δ[ύ-
ναμιν ἅπασ(αν) ἐκ[είκων.
Εὐανδρία ἡ Χαρι-
κλε(ί)δο(υ) θυγάτη-
ρ (τὸν) . . . .
. . . .
ἡ Ἀριστοκράτο(υ)ς
ταύτ(ην) ὅλην κάτεχε
Φερσεφόνη.
πάντας (τού)τους κατέ-
χε[τε Ἑ]ρμῆ Ἅιδη
ὦ [δ]αίμων παρὰ σ-
αυτῶι Γαλήν[η] ἡ
Πολυκλε(ί)ας θυγάτηρ.

Side A:
I am sending a letter to the gods below and Persephonē, conveying Tibitis, the daughter of Choirinē, who has done me wrong, and her daughter, her husband, and three children, two girls and a boy; Pankratēs, Mantias, Diophantos and Metagenēs.

Side B:
(Bind) the Earth (?), the bound boxers Aristomachos and Aristōnymos, bind all the power of those men. Euandria the daughter of Charikledēs, ... the daughter of Aristokratēs, may Persephonē bind all of her. Bind all of these, Hermēs, Hadēs. Demōn, (hold fast) Galēnē, the daughter of Polyklea by your own side.

380 Catalogue of Binding Curses

DTA 103 (Chapters 7, 8, 9, 12)

Origin: Greece, Athens, Peiraeus
Date: Third century BCE (Wünsch 1897); fourth century BCE (Wilhelm 1904)
Text: Wünsch (1897); tablet folded and pierced with a nail

Side A:
Ἑρμ[ῆ] καὶ Φερσεφ[ό]ν[η] τήνδε ἐπιστο[λ]ὴν ἀποπέμ[πω· ὁπ]ότε ταῦτα (ἐ)ς ἀνθρώπο(υ)ς ἁμαρ[τωλο(ὺ)ς φ]έ[ρω,
αὐτο(ύ)ς, Δίκη, τυχεῖν τέλο(υ)ς δίκης.
Καλλικράτης Ἀναξικράτους· Εὐδίδα[κτ]ος
Ὀλυμπιόδωρος . . . ος Θεόφι[λος
. . ρ[ο]ς Πλ . Ι . . Χαρῖνος Καλλένικος Κινείαν
. . . . . δωρος [Λυσί]μαχος Φιλοκλῆς [Δη]μόφιλος
        καὶ σύνδικοι καὶ [ε]ἴ τις ἄλλος [φίλος
α[ὐ]τοῖς· Δημοκρ[άτ]ης τ(ὸ)ν περὶ τῆ(ς) δίκη[ς
δικαζ[ό]μενον· Μνησίμαχος Ἀντί[φιλος.

Side B:
Λῦσις Δωροθέου Ἀρχῖνος Χαρῖνος
Μενεκλέους Νικοκρ[άτης.

Side A:
I am sending this letter to Hermēs and Persephonē. When I convey these things against wicked men, O Justice, may they pay the penalty. Kallikratēs, son of Anaxikratēs, Eudidaktos, Olympiodōros, . . . -os, Theophilos, . . . -ros, . . . Charinos, Kallenikos, Kineias, ... -doros, Lysimachos, Philoklēs, Dēmophilos and their co-advocates and if there are any other friends of theirs. Dēmokratēs (binds) the man pursuing the private court case. Mnēsimachos, Antiphilos.

Side B:
Lysis, son of Dorōtheos, Archinos, Charinos, son of Meneklēs, Nikokratēs.

DTA 104 (Chapter 10)

Origin: Greece, Attika
Date: Third century BCE (Wünsch 1897)
Text: Wünsch (1897)

. . . . . . Λ Ι . . .
. . . Α Ν Τ Η . . .
. . . Μ Α Ν . . . .
. χ]θονίαν καὶ | . . . .
. . . . . Η Ν Μ Α . Δ . . .
καὶ ἔργα καὶ τέλος Μ . .
δος καὶ Εὐεργέτην . .
καταδέω πρὸς τὴν [Ἑκά-
την χθονίαν . .
καὶ . . . .

... earthly and ... and deeds and success ... also Euergetēs. I bind before Hekatē of the underworld ... and ...

DTA 105 (Chapters 7, 9 10)
Origin: Greece, Attika
Date: Third century BCE (Wünsch 1897)
Text: Wünsch (1897)

Side A:
Ἑ]ρμῇ χθ[ό]νιε καταδε[δέσθω Πυθοτέ]λης πρὸς τὸν Ἑ[ρμῆν τὸν χθόνιον καὶ τὴν Ἑκάτη-
ν τὴν χθονίαν καὶ [γλῶτταν] καὶ ἔπη κ[αὶ ἔργα. . . . .
Ἑρμῇ χθόνι]ε· κατα[δεδέσθ]ω Πυθοτέλης πρὸς τὸ[ν Ἑρμῆν τὸν χθόνιον καὶ τὴν
Ἑκάτην τὴ]ν χθον[ίαν καὶ γ]λῶτταν καὶ ἔπη καὶ [ἔργα· Ἑκάτη χθονί-
α καὶ Ἑρμῆ χθόνιε· κ[αταδεδέσ]θω Τρου . . . [πρὸς τὸν Ἑρμῆν τὸν χθόνιον καὶ τὴν Ἑκάτην τὴν χθονίαν· [καὶ γλῶττα]ν καὶ ἔπ[η καὶ ἔργα . . . .
. . καταδεδέσθ]ω [Σ]ωσιγέν[ης] πρὸς τὸ[ν Ἑρμῆν τὸν χθόνιον καὶ τὴν
Ἑκάτην τὴ]ν χθον[ίαν καὶ γλῶτταν] καὶ ἔπη καὶ ἔργα .
. . . .

Side B:
Ὡς οὗ[το]ς ὁ μόλυ[βδ]ος ψυχρὸς καὶ ἄ[θ]υμος [οὕτως καὶ τὰ τῶν ἐνταῦθα γεγραμμένων ψυχρ[ὰ ταὶ ἄθυμα ἔστω] καὶ ἔπη καὶ ἔργα κ[αὶ γλῶττα . . . .
. . Α Ι . . . . . . Ε Κ Τ . . . . . . Σ καὶ ἐν δικαστ[ηρίωι . . . .
κ]αὶ γυναικῶν [. . . . τῶν ἐ]ν[ταῦθα] γεγραμ[μένων . . . .

Side A:
O Hermēs of the underworld, let Pythotelēs be bound in the presence of Hermēs of the underworld and Hekatē of the underworld, and his tongue and words and deeds. O Hermēs of the underworld, let Pythotelēs be bound in the presence of Hermēs of the underworld and Hekatē of the underworld, and his tongue and words and deeds. O Hekatē of the underworld and Hermēs of the underworld. Let Trou ... be bound in the presence of Hermēs of the underworld and Hekatē of the underworld, and his tongue and words and deeds. Let Sōsigenēs be bound in the presence of Hermēs of the underworld and Hekatē of the underworld and his tongue and words and deeds . . . .

Side B:
Just as this lead is cold and passionless, in the same way also, let the words and deeds and tongue of those inscribed here be cold and passionless ... and in a law-court ... and of women ... of those inscribed here ...

DTA 106 (Chapters 7, 9, 10)

Origin: Greece, Attika
Date: Third century BCE (Wünsch 1897)
Text: Wünsch (1897); once rolled up

Side A:
καταδεδέσθω. . . . . . .] πρὸς τὸν [Ἑρμῆν τὸν χθό]νι[ον καὶ τὴν Ἑκάτην τὴν χθονίαν
κατα]δ[εδέσθω. . . . . .] πρὸς τὸν Ἑρ[μῆν] τὸν [χθό]νιον [καὶ τὴν Ἑκάτην τὴν χθ[ονίαν
καταδε[δέ]σθω Ἀσπασία πρὸς τὸν Ἑρμ[ηῆ]ν τὸν [χθό]νιον κα[ὶ τὴν] ἑκά[την τὴν
   χθ]ονίαν
καταδε[δέ]σθω Σωκράτης π[ρ]ὸς τὸν Ἑρμῆν τὸν χθόνιον καὶ τ[ὴ]ν Ἑκάτην τὴ[ν
   χ]θονίαν
καταδε[δέ]σθωσαν οἵτινες πρὸς τούτων εἰσὶν σύνδικ[ο]ι τοῖς ἐνθαῦτα γεγραμμένοις
καταδε[δέ]σθω Ἀπιστία πρὸς τὸν Ἑρμῆν τὸν χθόνιον καὶ τὴν Ἑκάτην τὴν χθονίαν
κατα]δεδέσθω Λυδὸς πρὸς τὸν Ἑρμῆν τὸν χθόνιον καὶ τὴν Ἑκάτην τὴν χθονίαν
     καταδεδέσθω Μαν[ῆς] πρὸς τὸν Ἑρμῆν τὸν χθόνιον καὶ. . .
        τὴν [Ἑ]κάτην τὴν χθονίαν

Side B:
Καὶ ὡς οὗτος ὁ μόλυβδος ἄχρηστος, ὣς ἄχρηστα εἶναι τῶν ἐνταῦθα γεγραμμένων
καὶ ἔπη καὶ ἔργα
. . . . τῶν ἐντᾶθα γεγρα]μμέν[ων . . . .
. . . . καὶ ΕΚΤΟ . . . .

Side A:
Let . . . be bound, in the presence of Hermēs of the underworld and Hekatē of the underworld. Let . . . be bound, in the presence of Hermēs of the underworld and Hekatē of the underworld. Let Aspasia be bound in the presence of Hermēs of the underworld and Hekatē of the underworld. Let Sōkratēs be bound in the presence of Hermēs of the underworld and Hekatē of the underworld. Let them be bound, in their presence, whoever are advocates with those whom I have inscribed here. Let Apistia be bound in the presence of Hermēs of the underworld and Hekatē of the underworld. Let Lydos be bound in the presence of Hermēs of the underworld and Hekatē of the underworld. Let Manes be bound in the presence of Hermēs of the underworld and Hekatē of the underworld.

Side B:
And just as this lead is useless, in the same way may the words and deeds of those inscribed here be useless . . . of those inscribed here . . . and

DTA 107 (Chapters 7, 9)

Origin: Greece, Attika
Date: Beginning of fourth century BCE (Wünsch 1897)
Text: Wünsch (1897)

Side A:
Φ]ερέν[ικο]ς πρὸς τὸν Ἑρμῆν τὸν χθόνιον καὶ [τὴν Ἑ-

κάτην χθονίαν καταδεδέσθω· Γαλήνην, ἥτις Φερεν[ί-
κωι, καταδέω πρὸς Ἑρμῆν χθονικὸν καὶ Ἑκάτην χθονίαν κατα[δ-
έω· καὶ ὡς οὗτος ὁ βόλυβδος ἄτιμος καὶ ψυχρός, οὕτω ἐκε(ῖ)νος καὶ τὰ ἐκε(ί)νω ἄτιμα
[κ-
αὶ ψυχρὰ ἔστω καὶ τοῖς μετ᾽ ἐκε(ί)νο(υ) ἃ περὶ ἐμο(ῦ) λέγοιεν καὶ βο(υ)λευοίατο
Θερσίλοχος Οἰνο[φιλος] Φιλώτιος καὶ εἴ τ[ι]ς ἄ-
λλος Φερενίκωι σύνδικ[ος, πρ]ὸς τὸν Ἑρμῆν τὸγ χθόν[ι-
ον καὶ Ἑκάτην χθονίαν καταδεδέσθω· Φερενίκο(υ) κα[ὶ ψυχὴν καὶ νο(ῦ)ν καὶ γλῶτταν καὶ βο(υ)λὰς καὶ (τ)ὰ πράττει καὶ τὰ περὶ
ἐμο(ῦ) βο(υ)λε[ύ-
εται, ἅπαντ᾽ αὐτῶι ἀντία ἔστω καὶ τοῖς μετ᾽ ἐκε(ί)νο(υ) βο(υ)λεύο(υ)σιν καὶ
πράττο(υ)σιν.
καὶ ὅσον

Side B:
Ἑρμῆς χθόνιος
καὶ Ἑκάτη χθονία

Side A:
In the presence of Hermēs of the underworld and Hekatē of the underworld, let Pherenikos be bound. I bind Galēnē who belongs to Pherenikos, in the presence of Hermēs of the underworld and Hekatē of the underworld. And just as this lead is worthless and cold, so may that man and his doings be worthless and cold and for those on his side, whatever they say or plan about me. Thersilochos, Oinophilos, Philotios, and if there is any other man who is a co-advocate alongside Pherenikos, let him be bound, in the presence of Hermēs of the underworld and Hekatē of the underworld. Pherenikos' spirit and mind and tongue and plans and the things he does, and the things he is planning about me, let all these things work against him and against those planning and working with him. And whatever . . .

Side B:
Hermēs of the underworld and Hekatē of the underworld

DTA 108 (Chapters 7, 10, 12)

Origin: Greece, Attika
Date: Third century BCE (Wünsch 1897)
Text: Wünsch (1897)

Side A:
Δήσω ἐγὼ Σωσικλείαν κα[ὶ κ]τήματα | καὶ μέγα κῦδος
καὶ πρᾶξιν καὶ νοῦν, ἐ | χθρὰ δὲ φίλοισι γένοιτο.
Δήσω ἐγὼ κ | είνην ὑπὸ Τάρταρον ἀερόεντ[α
δεσμοῖς ἀργαλείοις σύν θ᾽ Ἑκάτ(η)ι χθο | νίαι.

Side B:
ΣΩΣΙΚΛΕΙΑ ΒΙΤΤΩ (written upside-down and backwards)
καὶ Ἐρινύσιν ἠλιθιώναις

Side A:
I will bind Sōsikleia and her possessions and her great fame and business and mind. Let her become an enemy to her friends. I will bind her beneath murky Tartaros in painful bonds, with Hekatē of the underworld.

Side B:
Sōsikleia Bittō. And to the Erinyes who drive their victims to distraction

DTA 109 (Chapters 7, 10, 12)

Origin: Greece, Attika
Date: Third century BCE (Wünsch 1897)
Text: Wünsch (1897); text written in reverse, from bottom to top of the tablet and from left to right

Μανῆν καταδῶ καὶ κατέχω· ὑμε-
ῖς δὲ φίλαι Πραξιδίκαι κατέχετε αὐτ(ὸ)ν καὶ Ἑρμῆ κα-
τοχε κάτεχε Μανῆν καὶ τὰ Μανοῦς καὶ τὴν ἐργ-
α[σί]αν ἣν [ἐ]ργάζεται Μ[α]νῆς ἅ[πα]σαν εἰς τἀναν-
τία καὶ ἐπαρίστερα γίνεσθαι Μανεῖ· ὑμῖν
ἐγὼ Πραξιδίκαι καὶ Ἑρμῆ κάτοχε Μανο-
ῦς] κακῶς πράξοντος εὐαγγέλια θύσω.

I bind Manēs and I restrain her. And you, dear Praxidikai, restrain him, and O Hermēs Binder, bind Manēs and the possessions of Manēs and the work that Manēs does, let all of it be awry and back-to-front. I will make a thank-offering for the good tidings, O Praxidikai and Hermēs Binder, when Manēs fares badly.

DTA 120 (Chapters 10, 12)

Origin: Greece, Attika
Date: Third century BCE (Wünsch 1897)
Text: Wünsch (1897); folded

...... (καταδέω?) καὶ τὴν ψυχὴν
..... κ[αὶ] τὰ ἔργα· καιροὶ
κ]αὶ τὴν............
Ἑρμῆ?
τὸ]ν (Κτησί[α]ν) τὸ[ν] ἐμὲ ἀτιμο-
ῦ]ντα...........
.. πάντα.

... I bind also the spirit ... and the deeds ... times and the ... Hermēs. The Ktesian has dishonoured me ... everything.

DTA 129 (Chapter 9)

Origin: Greece, Athens, Patissia
Date: Third century BCE (Wünsch 1897)
Text: Wünsch (1897)
(Difficult to make any sense of; included here because of the legal term *sundikos* or 'co-advocate'.)

$$\overset{\tau o \hat{\iota} s}{\overset{}{}}$$
ἄελπτα   οὐσια
καὶ   πάντα   σύνδικ[ο]ς

For those ... unexpected ... substance and ... everything ... co-advocate

DTA 137 (Chapter 10)

Origin: Greece, Attika
Date: Third century BCE (Wünsch 1897)
Text: Wünsch (1897); folded

.... ιπ(π)ον ....
. . . .
.... Ἰκ[ά]ριο[ς? ...
. . . .
ἐργασίαν] ἄπασ[αν
.. χεῖ]ρα ἔπ[η ...
. κα[ὶ ἔργ]α ....
...... Δ]ημο ...
Ἀφροδ[ίσιον   ....
Καλλίθ[ε]ο[ν   ....
... Ikarios ... all work ... hand words ... and deeds ... Aphrodision .... Kallitheon ...

DTA 158 (Chapters 7, 9, 12)

Origin: Greece, Attika
Date: Third century BCE (Wünsch 1897)
Text: Wünsch (1897); tablet once folded and pierced with a nail

... ος τύχῃ ἀγαθή ....
... νω τὰ φ(ε)ρόμ[ε]να ...
... ι κ(α)ὶ ἐναντί(α) ἐκ[είνοις
... ν καὶ Μενέστρ[ατον
. . . .
. . . .
.. το]ῖς ἀδικο(υ)μ[ένοις
. . . .
... ἀ]δικο(ύ)μεν[οι

....(κ)αὶ δίκ(η)...
....εἴ<τ>τις....
....
...η ἀδελφὸ[s...
....
...ἠτ(τ)ῶν[ται?...
....

... good fortune ... the things that are brought ... and oppose those men ... and Menestratos ... to those who are being wronged ... those who are wronged ... and justice ... if anyone ... brother ... they are defeated ...

DTA 160 (Chapter 10)

Origin: Greece, Attika
Date: Third century BCE (Wünsch 1897)
Text: Wünsch (1897)

Side A:
....
....
Εὐ]κολίν[ην] καὶ μαντεῖα ..
.. κ]αὶ τοῦ Νι .. καὶ φίλον
.. καταγ]ράφω καὶ ἅπ-
αντας [κ]αὶ ἐμὴν καὶ Εὐ-
... μετ' ἐκ[εί]νο[υ] Ε Ι Α
.. ΜΙ ἅπαν ἐμοῦ· κα(ὶ) τὸ
....
... ΗΔΟ καὶ Ἀπολλων[ί]ης

Side B:
καὶ ....
... ἔργα τὰ πάντα Ἀπ[ολ-
λό]δω[ρ]ον καὶ ......

Side A:
... Eukolinēs and prophecy .. and of Ni- ... and a friend ... I register both all of these and mine and Eu- ... with that man ... everything of mine. And the ... and of Apollōnia

Side B:
and ... all the deeds, Apollodōros, and ......

DT 1

Origin: Asia Minor, Karia, Knidos; one of 13 (Audollent 1904) or 14 (Newton 1862–3) tablets; near remains of a statue of Demeter
Date: First/second century BCE (Audollent 1904)
Text: Audollent (1904)

Side A:

    Ἀνιεροῖ Ἀντιγό-
    νη Δάματρι Κού-
    ραι Πλούτωνι θε-
    οῖς τοῖς παρὰ Δά-
5   ματρι ἄπασι καὶ
    πάσαις · εἰ μὲν ἐ-
    γὼ φάρμακον Ἀ-
    σκλ[α]πιάδαι ἢ ἔ-
    δ[ωκ]α, ἢ ἐνεθυ-
10 μήθ[η]ν κατὰ ψ-
    [υ]χὴν κακόν τι
    [α]ὐτῶ ποῖσαι, ἢ ἐ-
    κάλεσα γυναῖκ-
    α ἐπὶ τὸ ἱερόν,
15 τρία ἡμιμναῖ-
    α διδοῦσα ἵνα
    ⟨ι⟩αὐτὸν ἐκ τῶν
    ζώντων ἄρη,
    ἀναβαῖ Ἀντιγό-
20 νη πὰ Δάμα-
    τρα πεπρημέ-
    να ἐξομολοῦσ[α],
    καὶ μ[ὴ] γένοιτο
    εὐειλάτ[ου] τυ-
25 χεῖν Δάματρο[ς],
    ἀλλὰ μεγάλα-
    ς βασάνους βασ-
    ανιζομένα · εἰ δ'εἶ[-
    πέ] τις κατ'ἐμοῦ π-
30 ρὸς Ἀσκλαπιδα, εἰ κ-
    [α]τ'ἐμοῦ καὶ παριστ-
    άνετα[ι] γυναῖκα
    χαλκοῦς δοσα
    ιανασμουια
35 . . . .

Side B:
ll. 1–22 have vanished

    ἐμοὶ δ'ὅσια καὶ
    εἰς βαλανέον
25 καὶ ὑπὸ ταὐτὸ
    στέγος εἰσελ-
    θεῖν καὶ ἐπὶ τὰ-
    ν αὐτὰν τρπ-
    εζαν.

Side A:
Antigone dedicates to Demeter, Persephonē, Pluto, and all the gods beside Demeter, both male and female. If I have given a potion to Asklapiadas or conceived in my spirit of doing anything bad to him, or have summoned a woman to the temple, giving her 3 half-minai, so that she might take him from the living, let Antigonē come to the temple before Demeter, burning, and confess, and may Antigonē not find Demeter merciful, but may she be tormented with great suffering. And if anyone says anything against me to Asklapiadas, if (anyone) brings forward (as a witness) against me a woman giving her coppers . . .

Side B:
But let me go, innocent of any profanity, both into the baths, and under the same roof, and to the same table (as the person I am cursing).

DT 4

Origin: Asia Minor, Karia, Knidos; one of 13 (Audollent 1904) or 14 (Newton 1862–3) tablets; near remains of a statue of Demeter
Date: First/second century BCE (Audollent 1904)
Text: Audollent (1904)

Side A:

    [Ἀνα]τίθημι Δάματρι καὶ Κούραι τὸν κατ'ἐμο[ῦ . . . . .
    ε]ἴπ[α]ντα ὅτι ἐγὼ τῶι ἐμῶι ἀνδ[ρὶ] φάρμακα ποιῶ · ἀνα[βαῖ]
    παρὰ Δάματρα πεπρημένος μετὰ τῶν αὑτοῦ [ἰδίων]
    πάντων ἐξαγορεύων καὶ μὴ τύχῃ εὐειλάτου [μήτε
5 Δ]άματρος καὶ Κούρας μηδὲ τῶν θεῶν τῶν παρὰ Δά[μα-]
    τρος · ἐμοὶ δὲ ἦ⟨η⟩ ὅσια καὶ ἐλεύθερα ὁμοστεγησάσῃ ἢ ὧι πο[τε]
    τρόπωι ἐπ[ι]πλεκομένηι · ἀνατίθημι δὲ καὶ τὸν κατ'[ἐμοῦ]
    γράψαντα ἢ καὶ ἐπιτάξαντα · μὴ τύχοι Δάματρος καὶ
    [Κ]όρας μηδὲ θεῶν τῶν παρὰ Δάματρος εὐιλάτων, ἀλλ' ἀ[ν-
10 α]βαῖ μετὰ τῶν ἰδίων πάντων παρὰ [Δ]άματρα πεπρημένος.

Side A:
I dedicate to Demeter and Persephonē the man who spoke against me . . . that I made poisons for my husband. May he come to the temple of Demeter, burning, along with all his allies/family and publicly confess, and may he not meet with mercy from Demeter and Persephone and the other gods with Demeter. But let me be innocent

and free under the same roof, or whenever I have dealings with him in any way. I dedicate also the man who has written (accusations) against me or directed another man to accuse me. Do not let him find Demeter or Persephonē or the gods with Demeter merciful, but let him burn and come before Demeter with his allies/family.

DT 5 (Chapters 7, 11)

Origin: Asia Minor, Karia, Knidos; one of 13 (Audollent 1904) or 14 (Newton 1862–3) tablets; near remains of a statue of Demeter
Date: First/second century BCE (Audollent 1904)
Text: Audollent (1904)

[Ἀνιεροῖ Προσόδιο]ν Δάματρι καὶ Κόραι
[καὶ τοῖς θεοῖς το]ῖς παρὰ Δάματρι τίς τὸν Προσο-
[δίου ἄνδρα <τὸ]ν Προσοδίου ἄνδρα> περιαιρῖται
[Νάκωνα πα]ρὰ τῶν παιδίων · μὴ τύχοι εὐιλά-
[του] μὴ Δάμα<μα>τρος, μὴ θεῶν τῶν παρὰ Δάματρι
[εἰ τοὺς π]αρὰ Νάκωνος ὑποδέχεται ἐπὶ πονηρίαι τᾶι
[Προσοδ]ίου, Προσοδίοι δὲ ὅσια καὶ αὐτᾶι καὶ τοῖς παιδίοις
[κατὰ πᾶ]ν μέρος · καὶ τίς ἄλα Νάκωνα τὸν Προσοδίου
[ἄνδρα] ὑποδέχεται ἐπὶ πονηρίαι τᾶι Προσοδίο[υ],
μὴ τύχοι εὐιλάτου μὴ Δάματρος, μὴ θεῶν [τῶν]
πὰ Δάματρι, Προσοδίοι δὲ ὅσια
    καὶ τοῖς τέκνοις
    κατὰ πᾶν μέρος.

Prosodion dedicates to Demeter and the Maiden and the gods at Demeter's side, whoever is taking away the husband of Prosodion, ⟨the husband of Prosodion⟩, Nakōn, from his children. Do not let Demeter nor any of the gods at Demeter's side be merciful to her, whoever receives from Nakōn, adding to the misery of Prosodion, but let Prosodion be blessed, her and her children in every way. And any other woman who receives from Nakon the husband of Prosodion, adding to the misery of Prosodion. Do not let her meet with a merciful Demeter, nor the gods by Demeter's side, but let there be blessings for Prosodion and her children in every way.

DT 10 (Chapter 11)

Origin: Asia Minor, Karia, Knidos; one of 13 (Audollent) or 14 (Newton 1863) tablets found near remains of a statue of Demeter
Date: First/second century BCE
Text: Audollent (1904)

. . . .
[Δ]άματρι καὶ Κούραι καὶ τοῖς
ἄλ]λοις θεοῖς πᾶσι ἀνατί[θ-
ημι] Δωροθέαν τίς τὸν ἐ-

[μ]ὸν ἄνδρα εἶχε .
... μ . . . .

... To Demeter and the Maiden and all the other gods, I register Dōrothea, who has my husband ...

DT 39 (Chapter 9)

Origin: Greece, Achaia, Melos
Date: Fourth century BCE (Audollent 1904)
Text: Audollent (1904)

. . . . πον πάντας
. . . . Εὔφρονα
[. . . . . καὶ τοὺ]ς συνερ-
[γοὺς . . . . το]ῖς συνδίκο-
[ις . . . . π]άντας
[. . Ἑρμῆν] κάτοχον
. . . . νιον ἀλλὰ
. . ε . φορ . . . .
. . τὰ το[ῦ] Ρα . . . .
. . οδαμο . . . .

... all ... Euphrōn ... and his fellow-workers .... to his fellow advocates ... all of them .... Hermes the Binder ... but ... for ...

DT 43 (Chapters 7, 9)

Location: Greece, Athens, National Museum, inv. no. X 9369
Date: c.300 BCE (Voutiras 1998: 64)
Text: Voutiras (1998: 64 ff.)

ὅταν σύ, ὦ Πασιάναξ, τὰ γράμματα ταῦτα ἀναγνῶς - ἀλλὰ οὔτε
ποτὲ σύ, ὦ Πασιάναξ, τὰ γράμματα ταῦτα ἀναγνώσει οὔτε
ποτὲ Νεοφάνης Ἀγασιβώλω
δίκαν ἐποίσει· ἀλ' ὥσπερ σύ, ὦ
Πασιάναξ, ἐνθαῦτα ἀλίθι[ος]
κε[ῖ]σοι, αὗτ[ι] καὶ Νε[ο]φά[ν]εα
ἀλίθιον καὶ μηδὲ[ν] γενέσθαι.

Whenever you, O Pasianax, recognize these letters. But neither will you ever recognize these letters, O Pasianax, nor will Neophanēs, son of Agasibōlos, have brought a case. But just as you, O Pasianax lie, useless, here, may Neophanēs also be useless and become nothing.

DT 44 (Chapters 7, 9)

Location: Greece, Athens, National Museum, inv. no. X 9368
Date: c.300 BCE (Voutiras 1998: 64)
Text: Voutiras (1998: 64ff.)

ὅταν σύ, ὦ Πασιάναξ, τὰ γράμματα ταῦτα ἀν{αν} αγνῶς - ἀλλ'οὔ[τε] ποτὲ σύ ταῦτα ἀναναγνώσει οὔτε ποτὲ Ἀκέστωρ ἐπὶ Ἐρατ[ο]μέ-
νεα δίκα<ν> ἐποίσει [ο]ὐδὲ Τι-
μανδρίδας· ἀλ' ὥσπερ σὺ ἐνθαῦτα ἀλίθιος κεῖ[?]οι καὶ οὐ-
δέν, οὔτως καὶ Ἀκέστωρ
καὶ Τιμανδρίδας ἀλίθιος εἴη
καὶ οὐδέ[ν].

When you, O Pasianax read this letter. But neither will you ever read this letter, nor will Akestōr press his suit against Eratomenēs, nor will Timandridas. But just as you lie here useless and nothing, in the same way may Akestōr and Timandridas be useless and nothing.

DT 47 (Chapters 7, 9, 10)

Origin: Greece, Athens, Peiraeus
Date: Classical/Hellenistic (Faraone 1991a: 27 n. 47)
Text: Audollent (1904)

Μέλαν[α καταγράφω πρᾶξιν ψυχὴν ἔργα ἐφ-]
γασίας πό[δας] χ[εῖ]ρας [γλῶτ(τ)αν θυμ-]
ὸν καὶ τοὺ[ς ὑπ]ὲρ Μέλανο[ς π]ράτο[ντας · Ἑρμείην]
καταγράφω ἔργα πρᾶξ[ι]ν ψυχὴν χε[ῖρας τέκ-]
να ἔργα ἐργασίας καὶ ε[ἴ] τις : Ἐρ[μ]είει συ[μπράττει ·]
καταγράφω Εὐαγόραν χεῖρας πόδας ψυχὴν
γλῶταν ἔργα ἐργασ[ί]ας καὶ τὰ ἐ[κ]είνης ἅ[παντα ·
κ]αταγρά[φ]ω Βιότην [χ]εῖρας πόδας ψυχὴ[ν]
γλῶταν ἐργασίαν τέκνα καὶ τὰ ἐκεινης ἅπα[ντα.]

I register Melas, his business, spirit, work of his workshop, feet, hands, tongue, heart and those working on behalf of Melas. I register Hermeia, deeds, business, spirit, hands, children, work of workshop and if anyone is working for Hermeia. I register Euagora, hands, feet, spirit, tongue, work of workshop, and everything that belongs to that woman. I register Biotē, hands, feet, spirit, tongue, workshop, children and everything that belongs to her.

DT 49 (Chapters 7, 9)

Origin: Greece, Athens

Date: c.300 BCE (Audollent 1904)

Text: Audollent (1904); pierced five times with a nail

Καταδῶ Θεαγένην
γλττᾳ καὶ ψυχὴν καὶ λόγον ὅμ
               μαγείρου
μελετᾶι· καταδ[ῶ] δὲ καὶ Πυρρίου χεῖρας
[κ]αὶ πόδας
[γλ]ῶττᾳ καὶ ψυχὴν καὶ λόγον ὅμ με-
λετᾶι : καταδῶ δὲ καὶ [Πυ]ρρίου γυναῖκα : γλῶτταν
καὶ ψυχὴν ⁚ καταδῶ δὲ καὶ Κερκίωνα τόμ μ[ά]γει-
ρον καὶ Δόκιμον μάγειρον γλῶτταγ καὶ ψυχὴν καὶ λόγον ὅμ μελετῶσιν · καταδῶ δὲ καὶ
Κινέαν γλῶττᾳ καὶ ψυχὴν καὶ λόγον ὅν συμ-
μελετᾶι Θεα[γ]ένε[ι· κα]ταδῶ δὲ καὶ Φερεκλέους
[γ]λωτταγ καὶ ψυχὴν [καὶ μ]αρτυρίαν ἥ(ν) Θεαγέ[νε]ι
μαρτυρεῖ : καταδῶ δὲ [καὶ Σ]εύθου γλῶττᾳ καὶ ψυχὴν καὶ λόγον ὅμ με[λ]ετᾶι καὶ πόδας καὶ χεῖρας
ὀφ[θ]αλμοὺς [καὶ στόμ]α : καταδῶ [δὲ] καὶ Λαμπρίου
[γλῶττ]αγ καὶ ψυχὴν καὶ λόγομ ὅ(μ) μελ[ε]τᾶι χεῖρας
πόδας ὀφθαλμοὺς καὶ στόμα : τούτους ἅπαντας
καταδῶ ἀφα[ν]ίζω κατ[ο]ρύττω καταπαττα-
    ύ
λεῶ · καὶ ἐπ[ὶ δ]ικαστη[ρί]ου καὶ παρὰ
διαιτητεῖ [ἐὰν] ἀντιποιῶσ[ι] μηθα-
[μ]οῦ φαίνεσθαι μήτ[ε] ἐ[ν
λό]γωι μήτ[ε] ἐ[ν
ἔργ]ω[ι.]

I bind Theagenēs, the cook/butcher, tongue and spirit and speech, which he will make. I bind the hands and feet of Pyrrias, tongue and spirit and speech that he will make. I bind also the wife of Pyrrias, tongue and spirit. I bind Kerkiōn the cook/butcher and Dokimos the cook/butcher, tongue and spirit and speech that they will make. I bind also Kineas, tongue and spirit and speech that he is practising with Theagenēs. I bind also Phereklēs' tongue and spirit and act of witness that he will make for Theagenēs. I bind also Seuthēs' tongue and spririt and speech, which he will make, and feet and hands, eyes and mouth. I bind also Lamprias' tongue and spirit and speech that he will make, hands, feet, eyes and mouth. All these men I bind, I make disappear, I bury, I nail down. And in the lawcourt and before the arbitrator, if they act against me, let it be of no account, neither in word nor in deed.

Catalogue of Binding Curses

DT 50 (Chapters 7, 9, 10)

Origin: Greece, Athens
Date: Fourth century BCE (Audollent 1904)
Text: Audollent (1904); pierced with a nail repeatedly

Ἑρμῆ κάτοχε κα[ὶ Φερσεφόνη κατέχετε Μυρρίνης τῆς Ἁγνο-]
      Πειραιέως
θέο(υ) γυναικὸς σῶ[μα καὶ ψυχὴν καὶ γλῶτταν καὶ πό-]
δας καὶ ἔργα καὶ βου[λὰς ἕως ἂν εἰς Ἅιδου καταβῆι . . .]
φθίνουσα·
           καὶ Ἀπολλωνίο(υ)
Ἑρμῆ κάτοχε καὶ [Φ]ερσε[φ]όνη κα[τέχετε Παρθενίο(υ) τῶν παιδ-]
ίων τῷ[ν] Ἁγνοθέ[ο(υ) κ]αὶ γλῶτταν καὶ ψυχὴ[ν καὶ ἔργα καὶ πόδας καὶ]
β(ου)λάς ·
     καὶ Φε[ρσ]εφ[ό]νη
Ἑρμῆ κάτοχε κατέχετε Εὐξένο(υ) <τοῦ> Μυρρίν(ης) ο[ἰκέτου ψυχὴ-]
ν καὶ [σ]ῶμα κ[αὶ πόδ]ας καὶ χεῖρας καὶ ἔργ[α κ]αὶ βο-
[υλ]ὰς καὶ γλω[ττα]ν ἕως ἂν εἰ[ς] Ἅ(ι)δ[ου κ]α[ταβῆι·]
Ἑρμῆ κάτοχε καὶ Φερσεφόνη κατέχετε [Ἁγνοθέο(υ) καὶ Μ]υρρίν-
ης καὶ Παρθενίο(υ) καὶ Ἀπολλωνίο(υ) καὶ τῶν Ἁγνοθέο(υ) οἰκετῶν
πάντων καὶ των νῦν ὄντων καὶ τῶν προτερίων καὶ ἔργα
καὶ ψυχὰ[ς] καὶ γλῶτταν καὶ βουλάς, μηδ' ἀ[νι]ῆτε ἕως ἂν γ'
εἰς Ἅιδ[ο]υ καταβῶσι.

O Hermēs Binder and Persephonē restrain the body and spirit and tongue and feet and deeds and plans, of Myrrinē, the wife of Hagnotheos of the Peiraeus, until she goes down into Hades and withers away. And of Apollōnios. O Hermēs Binder and Persephonē restrain tongue and spirit and deeds and feet and plans of Parthenios of the children of Hagnotheos. And Persephonē. O Hermēs Binder, restrain his spirit and body and feet and hands and deeds and plans and tongue of Euxenos, the slave of Myrrinē, until he goes down into Hades. O Hermēs Binder and Persephonē restrain Hagnotheos and Myrrinē and Parthenios and Apollōnios and all the slaves of Hagnotheos, both those now and those who will be, and deeds and spirits and tongue and plans. Do not release them until they have gone down into Hades.

DT 52 (Chapters 7, 9, 10, 11)

Location: England, Oxford, Ashmolean Museum, inv. G.514.1
Origin: Greece, Attika, Menedhi
Date: Later fourth century BCE (Jordan 1999: 119); third/second century BCE (Audollent 1904)
Text: Jordan (1999: 119); once folded and pierced with a nail

Κέρκις
Βλάστος
Νίκανδρος

Γλυκέρα
Κέρκιν καταδῶ καὶ λόγους καὶ
ἔργα τὰ Κέρκιδος καὶ τὴν γλῶσσαν παρὰ τοῖς ἠϊθέοις καὶ ὁπόταν-
ν οὗτοι ταῦτα ἀναγνῶσιν, τότε
Κέρκιδι καὶ τὸ φθέγξασθαι .

———

Θέωνα καταδῶ, αὐτὸν καὶ τὰς
παιδίσκας αὐτοῦ καὶ τὴν τέχνη-
ν καὶ τὴν ἀφορμὴν καὶ τὴν
ἐργασίαν αὐτοῦ καὶ λόγους καὶ
ἔργα αὐτοῦ. Ἑρμῆ χθόνιε, ταῦτα
σὺ κάτεχε καὶ ἀνάγνωθι
ταῦτα τέως ἂν οὗτοι ζῶσιν.

Kerkis, Blastos, Nikandros, Glykera. I bind Kerkis, both his words and the deeds of Kerkis and his tongue, before those youth who died unmarried, and whenever they recognize these words, then will be the time for Kerkis to speak. I bind Theōn, him and his girls and his craft and his resources and his work and his words and deeds. O Hermēs of the underworld, bind these things and read (these words) for as long as they are living.

DT 60 (Chapter 9)

Origin: Greece, Attika
Date: Late fourth century BCE (Audollent 1904)
Text: Audollent (1904)

Νηρεΐδης
Δημοσθένης
Σωκλῆς
Λυκοῦργος
Εὐθυκράτης
Ἐπικλῆς
Χαρίσι[ο]ς
Βοηθός
Πολύοκος
καὶ τοὺ[ς] ἄλλο[υ]ς ἅπαν-
τας τοὺς με[τὰ] Νερ[ε]ΐδ[ο]υ
κατήγορους.

Nēreidēs, Dēmosthenēs, Sōklēs, Lykourgos, Euthykratēs, Epiklēs, Charisios, Boēthos, Polyokos, and all the others who are advocates with Nereidēs.

DT 61 (Chapter 9)
Origin: Greece, Attika
Date: Fourth century BCE (Wünsch 1900)
Text: Audollent (1904)

Θαλπαην
Μένων
Πλαθάνη
Σωσίας
Μνήμων
Εὐκ....
Ἀ[ρ]ιστομάχη
Σίμων
Μένιλλα
τοὺ μετὰ Πλαθά-
νης πάντας καὶ ἄν-
δρας καὶ γυναῖκας

Thalpaēn, Menōn, Plathanē, Sōsias, Mnēmōn, Euk-... Aristomachē, Simōn, Menilla, all those with Plathanē, both men and women

DT 62 (Chapter 9)
Origin: Greece, Attika
Date: Fourth century BCE (Audollent 1904)
Text: Audollent (1904)

. . .
Τ[ιμόξε]νος Ἀθεναῖος
Ἱπ[πίας] Ἀθεναῖος
Ἀμ[ήνιτ]ον Ἀθεναῖος
καὶ τ[ο(ὺ)ς σ]υνδίκο(υ)s

... Timoxenos of Athens
Hippias of Athens
... Amēnitos of Athens and all the other co-advocates

DT 63 (Chapter 9)
Origin: Greece, Attika
Date: Fourth century BCE (Audollent 1904)
Text: Audollent (1904)

. . . . Ἀθηναῖος
. . . . λίδης Ἀθηναῖος
. . . . Ἀθηναῖος
[. . . . . . καὶ] το(ὺ)ς συνδίκ[ο(υ)s o(ὺ)s
[ὁ δεῖνα ἐμαρτύ]ρατο

... the Athenian ... -lidēs, the Athenian ... the Athenian ... and those advocates whom that man called to testify

***DT* 66** (Chapter 10)

Origin: Greece, Athens, Peiraeus
Text: Wünsch (1900)

Side A:
[Εὐ]ήνιος ...
[γλ]ῶταν ἔ[ργ]α ...
καὶ ἄφωνοι, οὕτω ...
Ἀρκέσας. Καταδῶ Ἐφέ[στιον ..]
πό<σ>δας ἔργα καὶ τὸ ...
[γέ]νοιτο. Καταδῶ κ[...
...... γλῶ]ταν ἔ[ργα ...
δύ?]ναται σχτ̣   αδ
    αιτα   εσχε

Euēnios ... tongue, deeds ... and voiceless, thus ... Arkesas. I bind Ephestios .. Feet, deeds and the ... let it become. I bind ... tongue, deeds. he would be able ...

***DT* 67** (Chapter 9)

Origin: Greece, Attika
Date: Fourth century BCE (Audollent 1904)
Text: Audollent (1904); text begins on the right

Μένωνα καὶ Φιλοκύδην καὶ [Φ]ιλόστρατο-
ν καὶ Κηφισόδωρον καὶ τοὺς ἄλ[λ]ους τοὺς μ-
ετ' ἐκείνο[υ σ]υνεστάκειν ομ.ιον.σ.γ.μτ
..ς καταδῶ π[ρ]ὸς τὸν Ἑρμῆν τὸν κάτοχ[ον·]
μ. ..... ταῦτα ἐναντίον γέγραπται, ἐναντί-
αλ..ο..ς γείνεσθαι τὰς π[ρά]ξεις τὰ[ς ὑπὲρ Μ-
[ένω]νος καὶ [ψ]υχρὰ[ς] τὰς πράξεις · καταδῶ κατ[έχω]
πάσας.

Menōn and Philokydēs and Philostratos and Kēphisodōros and the others, those standing around with that man ... I bind before Hermēs the Binder ... has written hostile words against ... so that the actions, those on behalf of Menōn, the actions may become cold. I bind, I restrain all.

***DT* 68** (Chapters 7, 10, 11)

Origin: Greece, Attika
Date: Fourth century BCE (Jordan in Jameson, Jordan, and Kotansky 1993: 130)
Text: Audollent (1904) except for an improved reading of the first 8 lines of side B by Jordan (1993: 130)

Side A:
[κα]ταδῶ Θε[ο]δώρα[ν] πρὸς [τ]ὴ-
[ν] παρὰ Φε[ρρε]φάττηι καὶ πρὸς
[το(ὺ)ς] ἀτελ[έ]σ[το(υ)ς]· ἀτελὴς [ε]ἴ[η] α[ὑτὴ

Catalogue of Binding Curses

κα]ὶ ὅτι ἄμ πρὸς Καλλίαν διαλ[έγειν] μέλ-
[ληι καὶ πρ]ὸς Χαρίαν ὅτι ἄν διαλ[έγειν] μέλληι
καὶ ἔ]ργα καὶ ἔπη καὶ ἐργασίας· . α   πρ
   ἔπη λόγον ὃν ἄμ πο[τε] καὶ λέ[γηι · καταδῶ (?)
Θεο]δώραν πρὸς Χαρίαν ἀτελὴ αὐτὴ(ν) ε[ἶν]αι
[καὶ ἐπι]λαθέσθαι Χαρίαν Θεοδώρα[ς] καὶ τοῦ π]α[ι-
δί]ο(υ) τοῦ Θεοδώρας ἐπιλαθέσ[θ]αι Χαρί[α]ν
[καὶ τῆς] κοίτης τῆς [π]ρὸς Θε[οδ]ώρα[ν.]

   Jordan (1993): the opening of side A ([κα]ταδῶ Θε[ο]δώρα[ν] πρὸς [τ]ὴ[ν] παρὰ Φε[ρρε]φάττηι καὶ πρὸς [το(ὺ)ς] ἀτελ[έ]σ[το(υ)ς]·) is no longer tenable.

Side B:
[ὡς] οὗτος [ἐ]ντ[α]ῦ[θ]α ἀτε[λ]ὴς κ[εῖται, οὕ-]
[τως] ἀτέλεστα εἶναι Θεοδώρ[ας πάντα]
[κα]ὶ ἔπη καὶ ἔργα τὰ πρὸς Χαρίαν καὶ
[πρ]ὸς ἄλλος ἀνθρώπος· καταδ[ῶ Θεόδω-]
[ρον π]ρὸς τὸν Ἑρμῆν τὸ<γ> χθόνιον κα[ὶ πρὸς]
τὸς ἀ]τελέστος καὶ πρὸς τὴν Τῆθυν. ἀ[τελέστ-]
[α κ]αὶ ἔργα τὰ πρὸς Χαρίαν καὶ τὸς ἄλλος
[ἀνθ]ρώπος καὶ [τὴν] κοίτην τὴν π[ρ]ὸς Χαρίαν
[ἐπι]λαθέσ[θ]αι Χαρίαν τῆς κ[οί]της· [X]αρ[ίαν]
            καὶ. το(ῦ) παιδίο(υ) [Θ]ε[οδ]ώ[ρας ἐπιλαθέ-
σθαι ἧσ]π[ερ] ἐρᾶ[ι] ἐκε[ῖνος]
          γ   ο

Side A:
I bind Theodōra in the presence of the one beside Persephonē and the unhappy dead. May she be useless both whenever she is about to chat with Kallias and whenever she is about to chat with Charias and her deeds and words and business . . . Words, talk that, at any time, she may say. I bind Theodōra to be useless with regard to Charias and Charias to forget Theodōra and Charias to forget the child of Theodōra /dear little Theodōra˙ and sex with Theodōra

Side B:
Just as this man lies here, useless, in the same way may everything of Theodōra's be useless, both her words and deeds, those directed to Charias and those to other men. I bind Theodōra in the presence of Hermes of the underworld and in the presence of the unhappy dead and before Tethys. Useless the deeds directed at Charias and the other men and sex with Charias and Charias should forget sex; Charias should forget the child of Theodōra /dear little Theodōra, the woman he loves

˙ See discussion in Chapter 11.

DT 69 (Chapters 7, 10, 11)
Origin: Greece, Attika
Text: Audollent (1904)

Fragment 1: Side A:
. . . . τραι . . . τ . . . . .

```
. . . . . . . . . . οκ . . . . . . . .
. . . . . . . . ασες ικ αλμ . . . . .
. . . . . . [κατα]δίδημι Γῆι κ[αὶ
. . . . . . πρὸς]   Ἑρμῆν χθόνιον
[καὶ ὡς οὗτος ὁ νεκρὸς ἀτε]λὴς κεῖται ὡς ἀτελ[ῆ εἶναι]
. . . . . . . . . . κ . οιδοσατται
. . . . . . . . . ατο καταδίημι
. . . . . . . [πρὸ] τὴμ παρὰ Πε[ρρ]εφά[ττηι]
. . . . . . . .ης δ[ὲ] τῆς παρασ
. . . . . . . . .ιαν τῆς κοίτη[ς] τῆ[ς]
```

Fragment 1: Side B:
```
. . . . . . . . . μαν καταδίδ[ημι
πρὸς τὴμ] παρὰ Φ[ε]ρ[ρ]εφάττηι
. . . . . . γλῶσσαν καταδίδημι κ[αὶ
. . . . κα]ὶ τὸν νο(ῦ)ν καὶ τὰς φρ[ένας]
. . . . . ιατταβ.ν αὐτοὶ καὶ ἔρ[γα]
. . . . . . . . καὶ ὡς ο[ὗτος ὁ νεκρὸς ἀτελὴς
κεῖται] οὕτως ἀτελῆ εἶναι [. . . . . . πάντα
καὶ ἔ]ργα καὶ ἔπη
```

Fragment 2: Side A: *Fragment 2: Side B:*
```
. . . . . . . . . .                        . . . . . ρ
[κα]ταδίδημ[ι]                             . . . . . . η
. . . . . . . . . .                        [. . τ]ὴμ παρὰ [Φερρεφάττηι ?]
. . . . . . . . . .                        . . . το(ὺ)ς ἀτελ[έστους]
. . . καί . . .                            . . . νας καταδίδ[ημι]
                                           . . .α . αδ. . . .
```

Fragment 1: side A includes (l. 4) I bind to Earth and; (l. 5) in the presence of Hermes of the underworld; (l. 6) and, just as this corpse lies useless, in the same way useless may be; (l. 8) I bind; (l. 9) in the presence of Persephonē; (l. 11) of sex.

Fragment 1: side B includes (l. 1) I bind; (l. 2) in the presence of Persephonē; (l. 3) tongue I bind and; (l. 4) and the mind and the thoughts; (l. 5) they and deeds; (ll. 6–7) and just as this corpse lies useless, in the same way useless may be . . . everything; (l. 8) both deeds and words.

Fragment 2: side A includes the words I bind.

Fragment 2: side B includes the words (l. 3) in the presence of Persephonē; (l. 4) the unfulfilled; and (l. 5) I bind.

DT 70; see above *DTA* 70 (Chapter 10)

DT 71; see above *DTA* 71 (Chapter 10)

DT 72 (Chapters 7, 10)

Origin: Greece, Attika

Date: Third maybe fourth century BCE (Gager 1992: 165)

Text: Audollent (1904); see also *DT* 70–1, 73 (all from same source, with shared targets)

Καταδήω Ὠφιλίωνα
καὶ Ὠφιλίμη(γ) καὶ Ὄλυμπ[ο]ν
καὶ Πιστίαν καὶ Μάγα[δ]ιν
καὶ Πρ[ῶ]τον καὶ Κάδον, Θουκλείδην καὶ Μέλανα καὶ
Κῶμον
καὶ Βα(κ)χίδα καὶ Κίττον,
τούτων τῶν ἀνδρῶν καὶ
γυναικῶν καὶ ἐλπίδας
καὶ παρὰ θεῶν καὶ πα(ρ') ἡρώων καὶ ἐργασίας [ἁ]πάσας
καὶ πρὸς τὸν Ἑρμῆν τὸν
κατούχιον καὶ πρὸς τὴ[ν Ἑ-]
κάτην καὶ πρὸς τὴν Γῆ[ν κ]αι
<τὴν Γ[ῆ]ν>
πρὸς θεοὺς ἅπαντας
καὶ Μ[η]τέρα θεῶν.

I bind Ōphiliōn and Ōphilimē and Olympos and Pistias and Magades and Prōtos and Kados, Thoukleidēs and Melas and Kōmos and Bakchidas and Kittos. Of these men and women, (I bind) their hopes from both gods and heroes, and all their work, both in the presence of Hermēs the Binder and and in the presence of Hekatē, and and in the presence of Earth and the Earth, in the presence of all the gods and Mother of gods.

DT 73 (Chapters 7, 10)

Origin: Greece, Attika

Date: Classical/Hellenistic (Faraone 1991*a*: 27 n. 47)

Text: Audollent (1904)

Καταδήω Πάνφιλον και
ἐλπίδας τὰς Πανφίλου ἁ-
πάσας καὶ ἐργασίας πάσας ·
Θουκλείδην, ἐλπίδας
τὰς Θουκλείδου πρὸς . . .
. . . .
καὶ παρὰ τη . ισσινς ·
σὺ δ[ὲ] Ἑρμῆ κάτοχε

I bind Panphilos and the hopes of Panphilos and all his work all. (I bind) Thoukleidēs, the hopes of Thoukleidēs in the presence of . . . and from . . . And you, O Hermēs Binder

***DT* 84** (Chapter 11)

Origin: Greece, Boiotia, Thebes
Date: Second century BCE (Audollent 1904)
Text: Audollent (1904); once folded

Side A:

	Ζώπυρος κακὸν καὶ μέλεον
	Ζωπύρω μὴ γῆ καρπὸν μὴ
	Θύννω μὴ θάλασσα μόν[ω αὐ-]
	τῶ ὑγρά.
Καταδίδη-	Καταγράφω Νικόκλεαν
μι Νικο-	κακὴν καὶ νελέαν.
κλέας	Νικοκλέ μὴ γάμος
ιεστηνηλι	μηδ᾿ ὑμέναιος.
καν.	Καταγράφω Δαμαρῶν
Καταδίδη-	κακὴν καὶ μελέαν
μι Δα-	Πυθόκριτος Ζωπύζω
ματων	κακὸν καὶ μέλαιον
τὴν Θύνν-	ἑλκύσοι κάτω
ου κυναῖκα-	καὶ Νικόκλεαν Πυθόκριτος
ν. Δαμαροῖ	ἑλκύσοι κακὴν καὶ με[λέ]
μὴ ἔργος	αν.
ἀνησιφόρος	Ἀντίγονον καταγρά-
Πυθόκρι δὲ	φω κακὸν καὶ μέλαι-
Δαμαρῶν	ον στω . . θ . σιν τα της
κακὴν καὶ με-	ηλι . . . . . . ης ἀπλε-
λέαν	θεῖν ἑλκύσοι κάτ[ω .]
ἑλκύσοι κακὴ καὶ μελέα.	

Side B:

Μὴ κατ᾿ αἶαν
μηδὲ κατὰ θά-
λαταν,
μὴ ἔργο μὴ ἐρ-
γασίη,
Δαμαρὼ μὴ ἔρ-
γον μὴ ἐργασίη .
. . . . . . δε
. . . . ν
. ω . . . .
μὴ γῆ καρπὸν
Ἀν[τίγονον?]
Ζ[ώπυρον? μὴ]
ἔργο μὴ ἐρ-
γασίη .

Column 1:

I bind . . . of Nikoklea . . . I bind Damato the wife* of Thynnos. For Damaro, let there be no advantageous** work. And may Pythokritos drag down evil and useless Damaro, evil and useless Damaro

Column 2:

Zōpyros, (I bind) evil and useless Zōpyros, (let there be) no fruit of earth, nor for Thynnos, (let there be) no wet sea. I register Nikoklea evil and useless.*** For Nikoklea (let there be) no marriage and no bridal song. I register evil and useless Damaro. May Pythokritos drag Zōpyros down below, and may Pythokritos drag down evil and useless Nikoklea. I register evil and useless Antigonos . . . to come away, let her/him drag below

Column 3:

Neither by land**** or by sea, (let there be) neither work nor business, Damaro, neither work nor business . . . (let there be) no fruit of the earth, Antigonos, Zōpyros, (let there be) no work nor business

   * Assuming that κυναῖκα is a misspelling of γυναῖκα (Aud.) l.
   ** Misspelling of ὀνησιφόρος (see Aud.).
   *** Misspelling of μελέας.
   **** Misspelling of γαῖαν (Aud.).

DT 85 (Chapters 7, 11)

Origin: Greece, Boiotia

Date: Third or second century BCE (Faraone 1991*a*: 13); no later than the Hellenistic period (Dickie: 2000: 576); second or third century CE (Gager 1992: 87)

Text: Audollent (1904); round tablet

... ὑπὲρ τὺν θεὸμ ... δε τε ἀδύνατο[ν...] σοι χειρῶν ποδῶν σώματος ἐπάξῃ ... οικον ομεις η τι Φιλιμένη ... κακά .... κή Ζωΐλος ἀδύνατος Ἄνθειραν βαίν[ε]μεν κὴ Ἄνθειρα Ζωΐλο[ν?...] τὸν αὐτὸν τρόπον ... κή Ἑρμᾶν ... ψυχ[άν] ...

Text: Ziebarth (1934: 21–2, no. 23)

Side A:
Ὥσπερ τύν, Θεόνναστε, ἀδύνατο[ς] εἶ χειρῶν, πο[δ]ῶν,
σώματος πράξῃ τι ἢ <οἰ>κονομήσῃ τι, φίλμεν παργίνη κακά
ἴδεμεν, οὕτως κὴ Ζωΐλος ἀδύνατος μένει, δι' Ἄνθειρ(α)ν
βαίνιμεν κὴ Ἄνθειρα Ζωΐλον τὸν αὐτὸν τ<ρ>όπον·
φιλατα κὴ Ἑρμᾶ κατὰ φυλαατ χιπυτα
ἀλλαλοφιλίαν κὴ εὐνὰν κὴ λάλησιν κὴ φίλησιν
Ἀνθείρας κὴ Ζωΐλω κὴ ατο · ουναν τὰ [πὸ]τ ἀλλάλως
συναλλάγματα· ὥσπερ κὴ ὁ μόλυβδος οὗτος
ἔν τινι (τόπωι) χωριστῶ ἀπὸ τῶν ἀνθρώπων,
οὕτως Ζωΐλος (κε)χωρισμένο(ς) παρ' Ἀνθήρας τὸ σῶμα
κὴ ἄψιν (κ)ὴ τὰ φ(ι)λείματα κὴ τὰ (σ)υνουσιάσματα
τὰ Ζωΐλου κὴ Ἀνθείρας κὴ φ(ό)βον Ζωΐλω ἐνεγίνειν (?)
καταγράφω κὴ ἀπορίαν κατὰ σφραγίδα.

Side B:
γρ ... γ .. ακο τοιαύταν
μισ.ο...τες αλλα αλωσαι αν
κ(ο)ὐχ ἁλίσκοις, θιὲ, Ἄνθειρ(α)ν κὴ Ζωΐλο(ν)
...σ . τάνδε νύκτα κὴ ετινιταν
[μὴ] μετ' ἀλλάλων γίνεσθ(αι) κὴ αφ. .ας
ε Τιμοκλεῦν τὸ αὐτὸ εωθογεα · λατ
ως περιφιμμίσῃ ἀνθρώπους ἐνδέρσας·
... παμφοιρντο κατάδεσμον
.εδεμ.μμ.π.. τω, οὕτως κὴ Ζωΐ-
λ[ος] . κεει αμμρεπισωφιω κι..
μ .ν εἰ κὴ ἐπιτελεῖ π.εἰς α τετον
ο.. κατάδεσμον οὗτον κὴ λιτοψεξχ
    .τ .απαλοχ.........αὖτις ἔστω
        λαλῶντα [π]ονφό{γ}λυ[γας]
    .., [κ]η ἀμναστ(α) βαστ   εο
ὥσπερ ὁ μόλυβδος ὀρώρυχτ(αι) π[ά]ν-
παν κατορωρυγμένος πὴ οτει . α

αμ .νζμ, οὕτως κὴ Ζωίλωι
ἁ κατορύχοις κὴ ἐργα[σ]ία κὴ
οἰκονομία κὴ φιλία κη
τὰ λοιπὰ πάντα.

Side A:
Just as you, Theonnastos, are without power in any action or exercise of your hands, feet, body ... so let Zōilos remain powerless, to come[*] to Antheira, and Antheira to Zōilos in the same way. And beloved Hermēs ... love between them and bed and chat and love of Antheira and of Zōilos and ... and any other dealings between them. And just as this lead is in a certain place separate from men, in the same way let Zōilos be kept in another place from Antheira, her body, and touch and the kisses and the couplings of Zōilos and Antheira, and let fear spring up in Zōilos. And I register this spell of obstruction with a seal.

[*] Gager (1992: 88) translates this as 'screw' in a sexual sense from βινέω, rather than 'come' from βαίνω.

Side B:
Much of this is untranslatable: (ll. 2–3) But may you not catch, O god, Antheira and Zōilos (l. 4) ... on this night and ... (l. 5) let ... not become between them and (l. 6) ... Timokles ... (l. 7) ... thus ... men (l. 8) ... binding curse (l. 9) ... Thus also (l. 10) Zōilos ... (l. 12) ... this binding curse and ... (ll. 16–17) and just as this lead tablet is buried, utterly deeply buried ... (ll. 18–21) thus also may you utterly bury Zōilos and the works and household and love and all the rest.

DT 86 (Introduction and Chapters 7, 11)

Origin: Greece, Boiotia
Date: No later than the Hellenistic period (Dickie 2000: 576)
Text: Ziebarth (1934: 22, no. 22)

Side A:
παρατίθομαι Ζο-
ίδα τὴν Ἐρετρικὴν
τὴν Καβείρα γυναῖκα
- [τ]ῇ Γῇ καὶ τῶ Ἑρμῇ, τὰ βρώ-
ματα αὐτῆς, τὸν ποτὰ, τὸν ὕ-
πνον αὐτῆς, τὸν γέλωτα,
τὴν συνουσίην, τὸ κιθ{φε}άρισ[μα]
αὐτῆς κὴ τὴν πάροδον αὐ-
[τῆς], τὴν ἡδον<ὴν>, τὸ πυγίον,
[τὸ] (φρό)νημα, {ν} ὀφθα[λμοὺ]ς
- - ααπηρη(?) τῇ Γῇ.

Side B:
καὶ τῶ Ἑρμῇ τὴν
περιπάτη(σι)ν μοχθη
ρ[ὰ]ν, ἔπεα [ἔ]ργα, ῥήματα

κακὰ
καὶ τὸ - - -

Side A:
I assign Zois, the Eretrian wife of Kabeira, to Earth and to Hermēs. I bind her food and her drink, her sleep and her laughter, her meetings and her cithara playing, her entrance, her pleasure, her little buttocks, her thoughts, her eyes . . .

Side B:
And to Hermēs (I assign) her wretched walk, words, deeds, evil statements, and the . . .

DT 87 (Chapter 9)

Origin: Greece, Epiros, Kerkyra
Date: Third century BCE (Audollent 1904)
Text: Audollent (1904); diptych-style tablet, folded down the middle

. . . . ανα . . . .
    Σιλανοῦ τὸν νόον καὶ τὰν γλῶσ-
σαν τουτεῖ καταγράφω καὶ τῶν μαρ-
τύρων τῶν Σιλανοῦ τὰν γλῶσσαν κ-
αὶ τὸν νόον τουτεῖ καταγράφω · Ἐπαι-
νέτου τὰν γλῶσσαν καὶ τὸν νόον τουτεῖ καταγράφω · Ἀγῆνος τὰν γλῶσσαν
καὶ τὸν νόον τουτεῖ καταγράφω · Τιμαρέ-
  τας τὰν γλῶσσαν καὶ τὸν νόον τουτεῖ κα-
    ταγράφω . . . .
. . . . τω φαίν(ε)ται

. . . I register the mind and tongue of Silanos with this, and the tongue and mind of the witnesses of Silanos with this. I register with this the tongue and mind of Epainetos. I register the tongue and mind of Agēn. I bind the tongue and mind of Timaretē with this . . . it seems

DT 89 (Chapter 9)

Origin: Black Sea, Olbia
Date: Third century BCE (Audollent 1904)
Text: Audollent (1904); tablet folded and pierced with a nail

Side A:
Ἀγασικλῆς
Ἡρα(κλ)είδης
Ἀριστομένιος
[Ἀ]πολλᾶς
Ἀντικρ[α]τίδης

And, written sideways running along the right-hand side of the text, parallel to the last four lines: Ἡρόδωρος

Side B:
[τούτους καταδῶ]
καὶ μ[αρτυρίας καὶ δί-]
  κας καὶ ἀσεβ[ε]ιαν
πάντ[ω]ν

Side A:
Agasiclēs, Hēracleidēs, Aristomenios, Apollas, Antikratidēs;
(written sideways) Herodōros

Side B:
I bind these men and the witnesses and law cases and impiety of all of them

DT 90

Origin: Black Sea, Olbia
Date: Fourth century BCE (Audollent 1904)
Text: Audollent (1904)

Ἱεροκλεά Χαβρίαν
τοὺς συνδίκους

Hieroclēs, Chabrias, the co-advocates

DT 92 (Chapters 7, 10, 12)

Origin: Chersonesos, northern shores of the Black Sea; discovered in a grave
Date: Third century BCE (Audollent 1904)
Text: Audollent (1904)

Βίττα[λ]ος	τούτων τὴν ἐργασίην [ἐναν-
Βακίων	τ]ίαν γίνεσθαι καὶ ζόης
Ζωγέν[η]ς τιρακη	καὶ βίου μὴ ὄναιντο
. . . . .	Αἶσα ἀναιροῦσι κἀ[δι]κοῦσι
. . . . .	[. . . . . ἄ]φρονε[ς]
Βακίων	μὴ [τ]ις αὐτοῖς εἴη πη κτῆσις
	[ἀλλ'] ἀπολλύο[ι]ντο [κα]ὶ πα[ῖδες]
	αὐτοῖς

Column 1:
Bittalos, Bakiōn, Zōgenēs . . . Bakiōn

Column 2:
May the work of these men go against them, and do not let them profit from their living and life. O Fate, they destroy and they do wrong . . . mindless. Do not let there be any profit for these men, but may they and their children perish

DT 212 (Chapter 12)

Origin: Bronze tablet, South Italy, Bruttium
Date: Third century BCE (Versnel 1991a: 73)
Text: Audollent (1904)

[Ἀνιαρίζει Κολλύρα] ταῖς προπόλοις
[τᾶς θεῶ τὸ ἱμάτιον] τὸ πελλόν, τὸ
[ἔλαβε . . . . καὶ ο]ὐκ ἀποδίδωτι καὶ
[. . . . . κ]αὶ χρῆται καὶ ἴσατι
. . ἐσ[τι ἀ]νθε[ίη τᾶι] θεῶ δυωδεκαπλοῦν
σὺν ἠμεδίμν[ωι λιβάν]ω ὦι πόλις νομίζει
μὴ πρότερον δὲ [τ]ὰ[ν ψ]υχὰν ἀ<ι>νε[ίη . .] ἔχ[ω]ν
τὸ ἱμάτιον, ἔστε ἀνθε[ί]η τᾶι θεῶ .
Ἀνιαρίζει Κολλύρα ταῖς προπόλοις τᾶς θεῶ
τὼς τρῖς χρυσέως τὼς ἔλαβε Μ[ε]λίτα
καὶ οὐκ ἀποδίδωτι · ἀνθείη τᾶι θεῶι
δυωδεκαπλόα σὺν [μ]εδίμνωι λιβάνω<ι>
ὦι πόλις νομίζει · μὴ πρότερον δὲ τὰν
ψυχὰν ἀνείη ἔστε ἀνθείη τᾶι θεῶ.
Εἰ δὲ συνπίοι ἢ συμφάγοι μὴ <η> ἰσαώσα
ἀθῶιος εἴην, ἢ ὑπὸ τὸν αὐτὸν ἀετὸν ὑπέλ-
                                            θοι

Kollyra dedicates to the temple servants the dark-coloured cloak, which (Melita?) . . . took . . . and did not return and . . . and is using and she (Kollyra or the goddess?) knows . . it is. Let her dedicate to the goddess twelve-times the amount with a measure of incense as is the city custom. But do not let her release her breath/spirit, while she has the cloak, until she makes the dedication to the goddess. Kollyra dedicates to the temple servants the three gold coins that Melita took and did not return. Let her dedicate twelve-times the amount to the goddess, with a measure of incense that city custom dictates. But do not let her release her breath/spirit, until she makes the dedication to the goddess. And if they drink or eat together or if she comes under the same roof, let her not know and may she remain unharmed

SGD 3 (Chapters 7, 10)

Location: Greece, Athens, Kerameikos Museum
Origin: Kerameikos, near the grave plots of the Potamians and of Hegeso
Date: Second half of fifth century BCE (Peek 1941: 89); middle of fourth century BCE (Jeffery 1955)
Text: Peek (1941: 89–90, no. 1); written backwards

Λυσανίας ἐκ τô ἀργυ
ροκοπίο φυσētḗs
καὶ αὐτὸς καὶ ἑ γυνὲ καί
τὰ χρḗματα καὶ hότι ἐργά-
ζεται καὶ τὰ χρḗματα

καὶ χἐρες καὶ πόδε[ς] κα[ὶ νô]ς
κεφαλέ ῥὶν ἄνθεμ. . . ν .
γês hιερâς ·

Lysanias the blower from the silverworks, both him and his wife and (his) possessions, and whatever work he does, and (his) possessions and hands and feet and mind, head, nose . . . of holy earth.

SGD 4 (Chapters 7, 10)

Location: Greece, Athens, Kerameikos Museum
Origin: Kerameikos, near the grave plots of the Potamians and of Hegeso
Date: Second half of fifth century BCE (Peek 1941: 89); middle of fourth century BCE (Jeffery 1955)
Text: Peek (1941: 89–90, no. 2); written left to right, letters retrograde

[Λ]υσαν[ίας]
[ἐ]κ τὸ ἀργυροκοπ[ί]
[ο κ]αὶ γυνὲ αὐτō ῡ [κα]
[τα] δέω καὶ hότι ῡ
[ἐρ]γάζεται καὶ hότι
[πρ]άσεικαὶ hότι διαχ[ει]
[ρί]ζεται καὶ hό[τι - -]
. . . . ι καὶ . . . . ιν - -
- - -

Lysanias . . . from the silverworks, both him and his wife, I bind whatever he produces and whatever he makes and whatever he melts (?), makes fast (?) and whatever . . . and

SGD 6 (Chapters 7, 9)

Location: Greece, Athens, Kerameikos Museum
Origin: Kerameikos, near the grave plots of the Potamians and of Hegeso
Date: Later fifth century; early fourth century BCE (Jordan); early fourth century BCE (Peek 1941: 94)
Text: Peek (1941: 94); lead shaped as a box

Πυθέας
Πύθιππος
Ἡγέστρατος
Σμιδυρίδης
ὁπόσοί ἰσιν
ἀντίδικοι
Εὐόπηι
μετὰ Πυθέο

Pytheas, Pythippos, Hēgestratos, Smidyridēs, whoever are co-advocates with Pytheas opposing Euopēs

SGD 9 (Chapter 9)

Location: Greece, Athens, Kerameikos Museum
Origin: Greece, Athens, Kerameikos; grave 40 near the plot of Antidosis, daughter of Iatrokles
Date: Early fourth century BCE (Jordan)
Text: Trumpf (1958: 94–102); doll and coffin set
 Oval box with inscribed lid; doll was found outside the box; doll's arms bound behind its back; Μνησίμαχος scratched on its right leg:

Βαρβυριτίδης Ξώφυγος
Νικόμαχος Οἰνοκλῆς
Μνησίμαχος
Χαμαῖος Τεισωνίδης
Χαρίσανδρος
Δημοκλῆς
καὶ ἔ τις ἄλλος μετ' ἐκένων
ξύνδικός ἐστι ἔ μάρτυς

Barbyritidēs, Xōphygos, Nikomachos, Oinoklēs, Mnēsimachos, Chamaios, Teisōnidēs, Charisandros, Dēmoklēs, and any other co-advocate with those men, or witness

On the right leg of the doll: Mnēsimachos

SGD 10 (Chapter 9)

Location: Greece, Athens, Kerameikos Museum
Origin: Greece, Athens, Kerameikos; a grave near the 'Round Bath'
Date: Later fourth century BCE (Jordan 1985b)
Text: Peek (1957: 206)

Column 1:
Διοδώρα .
Χρυσίς .
Ἀμύντωρ

Column 2 (upside down in relation to the first):
Ξενότιμος
Πατρώ

Upwards along the left of the first column: Διόδ[ωρος?]

Column 1:
Diodōra, Chrysis, Amyntōr

Column 2:
Xenotimos, Patrō

Upwards along the left of the first column: Diodōros

SGD 11 (Chapters 7, 10)

Location: Greece, Athens, Kerameikos Museum
Origin: Greece, Athens, Kerameikos; a grave near the 'Round Bath'
Date: Later fourth century BCE (NGCT)
Text: Peek (1957: 207) with emendations by Jordan (NGCT)

Σώδ[ημος] Σωστράτου
Σώνιχ[ος καὶ :] Τεισέ[ας οἱ]
Σων[ίκου ? - - - - - - -]
Ζη[ν - - - -⁹⁻¹⁰ - - - - -] φάνους
Κυ[δ]α[ντίδης ?] : Τύχων
ὁ σκηνίτης : ὁ Καλλιτελους
οἰκέτης : ᵛ ᵛ ᵛ ᵛ ? Μυρτάλη
γραῦς καπηλίς : Θεογένης
εμ Μελ[ίτ]ει : οἰκῶν κάπηλος.
Φίλων Θεοφίλου Πλωθέως
οἰκέτης. Εὔπραξις
πορν[ο]βοσκ[ός]
τούτων καταδῶ τὴν γλῶτταν
καὶ τὸν νοῦν καὶ ψυχήν καὶ
σῶμα καὶ ἔργα τὰ τούτων καὶ
νοῦν καὶ φρένας καὶ διάνοιαν
καὶ βου[λ]ὴν το[υτων]

Sōdēmos, son of Sōstratos, Sōnichos and Teiseas, sons of Sōnikos ... Zēn- ... -phanous of Kydantidai, Tuchōn, the stallholder, the household slave of Kalliteles; the old woman Myrtales, who keeps an inn, Theotenes, the innkeeper, who lives in Melitē; Philōn, the son of Theophilos, the household slave of Plōtheōs; Eupraxis, the pimp. Of these men I bind the tongue and mind and spirit and body and the actions of these men, and the sense of their mind, and understanding and their plan

SGD 14 (Chapter 9)

Location: Greece, Athens, Kerameikos Museum, inv. I 460
Origin: Greece, Athens, Kerameikos; the bottom of Dipylon Well, B1
Date: 313/12–307 BCE (Jordan)
Text: Jordan (1980: 230); a column of five names; to the lower right of the column and upside down, the misspelled beginning of the first name

1:
Πλείσταρχον
Εὐπόλεμον
Κάσσα[ν]δρον
Δημήτ[ριον]
Φ[αλ]η[ρέα]
[-¹⁻²-] Κ Ν Η . [-¹⁻³-] Πειρ⟨α⟩ιέα

2:
Π Λ Ε Ι̣ [Σ] Τ Ε Α

1:
Pleistarchon, Eupolemon, Kassandron,
Demetrion, Phalerea, K N H Peiraiea

2:
PLEISTEA

Pleistarchos (younger brother of Kassander); Eupolemos (Kassander's general in Greece); Kassandros (succeeded Alexander, 319–297 BCE); Demetrios of Phalera (appointed governor of Athens by Kassander) ... and of Peiraeus

SGD 18 (Chapters 7, 9)

Location: Greece, Athens, National Museum, inv. 13083
Date: Fourth century BCE (Wilhelm 1904)
Text: Strÿd (1903: cols. 57 ff., no. 5)

θεοί· ἀγαθῇ τύχῃ   Ἀντίφανος   Πατροκλέος
                                καὶ
καταδῶ καὶ οὐκ ἀναλύσω Ἀντικλέα καὶ Ἀντιφάνην καὶ Φιλοκλέα καὶ
Κλεοχαρην
καὶ Φιλοκλέα   καὶ Σμικρωνίδης   καὶ Τιμάνθην   καὶ Τιμάνθην
καταδῶ τούτος ἅπαντας πρὸς τὸν Ἑρμῆν τὸν {τὸν} χθόνιον καὶ τὸν δόλιον καὶ τὸν
κάτοχον καὶ τὸν ἐριούνιον καὶ οὐκ ἀναλύσω.

Gods. Good luck Antiphanos, son of Patroklēs and I bind also and I do not release Antiklēs and Antiphanēs and Philoklēs and Kleocharēs and Philoklēs and Smikrōnidēs and Timanthē and Timanthē. I bind all of these in the presence of Hermēs of the underworld, the Trickster and the Binder, Erionios, and I do not release them.

SGD 19 (Chapters 7, 9)

Location: Greece, Athens, National Museum, inv. 13083
Date: Fourth century BCE (Jordan)
Text: Strÿd (1903: cols. 57 ff., no. 4); retrograde

Εὐρυκράτης
Μνησίεργος
Αἰσχίνης
Νικόστρατος
καὶ τὸς
ἄλλος
τὸς μετ' ἐκένο
[ἀ]ντ[ιδ]ίκος
[ἅπαν]τας

Eurykratēs (or Euthykratēs)*, Mnēsiergos (or Praxiergos or Euergos)*, Aischinēs, Nikostratos (or Philostratos or Peisistratos)* and the others, those on his side, all the opposing litigants

* Alternatives suggested by Strÿd 1903

SGD 20 (Chapters 7, 10)

Location: Greece, Athens; Stoa of Attalos, Agora inv. IL 997
Origin: Greece, Athens; 'House D' in industrial area of Agora
Date: Fourth century BCE (Young 1951: 222)
Text: Curbera and Jordan (1988*a*: 215–18); rolled up and pierced with a nail

Καταδῶ Ἀρίσταιχμον τὸ<ν> χλακέα
πρὸςς τὸς κάτω καὶ Πυρρίαν τὸν χαλκειά
καὶ τὴν ἐργασίαν αὐτῶ καὶ τὰς ψυχὰς
αὐτῶν καὶ Σωσία<ν> τὸν Λάμιον
καὶ τὴν ἐργασία<ν> καὶ τὴν ψυχὴν αὐτῶ
καὶ ἃ λήγοσι καὶ ἃ δρῶσ<ι> {καὶ ἃ δρῶσ<ι>}
καὶ Ἁγῆσ<ι> τὴν βοιωτία<ν>

I bind Aristaichmos the bronze worker,* in the presence of those below, and Pyrrias the bronzeworker and his work and their spirits, and Sōsias of Lamia, and his work and his spirit and what they say and what they do (and what they do) and Hagēsias of Boiotia

* Chlakea and (l. 2) Chalkeia could be ethnics, i.e. 'of Chalkis' rather than descriptions of profession (see Curbera and Jordan 1988*a*: 215–18).

SGD 42 (Chapters 7, 9)

Origin: Greece, Athens, Dekeleia
Date: First half of fourth century BCE (Jordan)
Text: Robert (1936: 12, no. 11); rolled up around a nail

Καταδ[έω] τὸς ἐνθαῦτα ἐνγεγραμμένος καὶ ἄνδρας καὶ γυναῖκας ὅσοι ἐνθαῦτα ἐνγεγραμένοι εἰσίν, πρὸς Ἑρμῆν Κάτοχον καὶ Γ-
ῆν καὶ Περσεφόνειαν καὶ ὅσπερ οἳ παρ[ὰ] ταύτην ἀφικνôνται οἴκαδε νοστôσι ὅτως οἱ ἐνθαῦτα ἀντίδικοι τέλος λαβόντον τῆς [δίκ]ης

I bind those inscribed here, both men and women who are here inscribed, in the presence of Hermēs the Binder and Earth and Persephonē. And just as those who arrive at her side (Persephone's) make a journey home, in the same way may those co-advocates in the end pay the penalty

Following this text: 'There is a long list of men's names (nom., nom. + gen., or nom. + demotic) and an unnamed woman identified as θυγατήρ + gen. After one of the men's names, his profession, κροκοπώλης ('saffron seller'), is given.' (Jordan)

SGD 43 (Chapter 10)

Origin: Greece, Attika
Date: Fourth century BCE (Robert 1936: 14)
Text: Robert (1936: 14, no. 12); folded into quarters and pierced with a nail; against the same persons as *DT* 70–2 and *DTA* 70–1

Τὸ Ὠφιλίωνος καπήλιον
καὶ τὴν ἐργασίαν τὴν
Ὠφιλίωνος, τὸ Μελανθί-
ου καπήλιον καὶ τὴν ἐρ-
γασιαν, το Συρίσκο καπή-
λιον καὶ τὴν ἐργασίαν
τὸ Πιστίου καπήληον
καὶ τὴν ἐργασίαν,
τὸ Ἑκαταιου καπήλιον
καὶ τὴν ἐργασίαν,
τὸ Ζωπυρίωνος κα-
πήληον καὶ τὴν ἐρ-
γασίαν. Ὄλυμπος,
Ὠφιλίων, Ζωπυρίων,
Πιστίας, Μ[ά]νης, Ἑκαταῖ-
ος, Ἡρακλείδης,
Συρίσκος · τούτων
τὴν ἐργασίαν κα-
ταδήω καὶ τὰ καπή-
λια.

(I bind) the inn of Ōpheliōn and the work of Ōpheliōn, the inn of Melanthios and the work, the inn of Syriskos and the work, the inn of Pistios and the work, the inn of Hekataios and the work, the inn of Zōpyriōn and the work. Olympos, Ōpheliōn, Zōpyriōn, Pistias, Manēs, Hekataios, Hērakleidēs, Syriskos. I bind the work of all these men and their inns.

SGD 44 (Chapters 7, 10, 11)

Location: Greece, privately owned, bought at Athens
Date: Middle of fourth century BCE (Peek 1941: 98)
Text: Peek (1941: 98)

Λιτίαν καταδ[ῶ] πρὸς τὸν Ἑρμῆν τὸν κάτο[χ]ον [καὶ τή]
ν Φε[ρ]σεφόνην, γλῶταν τὴ<ν> Λιτίου χεῖρας τὰς Λιτίου ψυχ[ὴν τήν]
Λιτίου πόδας τοὺς Λιτίου σῶμα τὸ Λιτ[ί]ου τὴν κεφα[λήν]
τὴν Λιτίου. Νικίαν καταδῶ, τὰς χεῖρας τοῦ Ἀρεοπαγίτ[ου]
[πρὸς] τὸν Ἑρμῆν{εν} τὸν κάτοχον, πόδας τὲν γλῶταν τὸ σῶμα
τὸ Νικίου. Δημέτρ[ι]ον καταδῶ πρὸς τὸν Ἑρμῆν τὸν κάτοχον, τὸ
           [σῶ]μα τὲ̄<ν> ἐργασία<ν> τὴ<ν> Δη[μέ̄]

τ<ρί>ου τοῦ [κε]ραμοδέτου τὰς χεῖρα<ς> τοὺ<ς> πόδας τὴ<ν> ψυχ[ήν].
Ἐπιχ[αρῖ]ν[ο]ν καταδῶ π[ρ]ὸς τὸν Ἑρμê<ν> τ<ὸν κ>άτοχον. Δη-
[μ]άδ[ην τὸ]ν κηραμοδήτēν <κα>ταδῶ πρὸς τὸ[ν Ἑ]ρμêν τόν
[κά]τοχον, [τὸ] σῶμα τēν ἐ[ργασ]ίαν τὴν ψ[υ]χήν. ///H ⋏ /// ///
/// /// ☉ Ι καταδῶ. Δάφνιν [κ]α[τα]δ[ῶ] πρὸς [τὸν] Ἑρμῆν [τὸν] κάτοχον.
[Φ]ιλωνίδην κ[α]ταδῶ πρὸς τὸν Ἑρμêν τὸ<ν> κάτοχον.
Σιμάλēν Πίστēν κα{κα}ταδῶ 7 καταδῶ πρὸς τὸν Ἑρμ[êν]
τὸν κάτο[χ]ον.
Λιτίαν καταδῶ, τοὺς πόδας τὰς χεῖρας τὲ<ν> ψυχέν {κ}
τὸ σῶμα τὸ Λιτίου τὴ<ν> γλῶταν τὲ<ν> Λιτίου τὴ<μ> βουλὲν τὴ<ν> Λιτίου ἃ
  ἐργάζεται
πρὸ[ς] τὸν Ἑρμêν τὸν κάτοχον καὶ τήν
Φερσεφόνēν καὶ τὸν Ἅιδην.

I bind Litias in the presence of Hermēs the Binder, and Persephonē, the tongue of Litias, the hands of Litias, the spirit of Litias, the feet of Litias, the body of Litias, the head of Litias. I bind Nikias, the hands of the Areopagite, in the presence of Hermēs the Binder, the hands, feet, the tongue, the body of Nikias. I bind Dēmetrios in the presence of Hermēs the Binder, the body, the work of Dēmetrios the potter, the hands, the feet, the spirit. I bind Epicharinon in the presence of Hermēs the Binder. I bind Dēmadēs, the potter in the presence of Hermēs the Binder. The body, the work, the spirit. I bind Daphnis I bind in the presence of Hermēs the binder. I bind Philōnidēs in the presence of Hermēs the Binder. I bind Simalē Pistē, I bind in the presence of Hermēs the Binder. I bind Litias, the feet, the hands, the spirit, and the body of Litias, the tongue of Litias, the plan of Litias, which he is working on, in the presence of Hermēs the Binder and Persephonē and Hades.

SGD 46 (Chapter 9)

Location: privately owned
Origin: Greece, Athens, Dekeleia
Date: Fourth century BCE (Jordan)
Text: Couilloud (1967: 513–15); nail hole at the bottom left

Side A:
Μυτίς,
τὴν γλῶ-
ταν αὐτῆς
καὶ τὴν
ψυχὴν
καὶ τὰ
ἔργα · ἐναν[τία]
[γ]ένοιτο
ἅπαντα ·

Side B:
Τελησίας
Μοσχίνη,
[Σ]ωσίας
Ἀρμένιος
Γ[λ]αυκέτης
Δημόστρατος
Ἀνφ[ί]νικος,
Γλαύ(κ)ιππος,
Παμφίλη ·

Side A:
Mytis, [I bind] her tongue and spirit and actions. May they all go against her

Side B:
Telēsias, Moschinē, Sōsias, Armenios, Glauketēs, Dēmostratos, Anphinikos, Glaukippos, Pamphilē

SGD 48 (Chapters 7, 9, 10; see overleaf)

Location: Greece, Athens, National Museum, inv. 14470
Date: c.323 BCE (Ziebarth 1934: 4, no. 1)
Text: Ziebarth (1934: 4, no. 1)

Catalogue of Binding Curses

Side A:

καταδῶ, κατορύττω, ἀφανίζω ἐξ ἀνθρώπων
Εὔνομον Π(ε)ρα   [Καλ]λίαν Πειραι.   Cτόμβιχος Εὐ(ων)
Ἀριστοτέλην   . . . .δην Πειραι   Cτρομβιχίδης Εὐ
Λυσικλέα Ἀχαρν   . . . . .δρος Πειρα   55
5 Δημοκρά[την] Αἰ(ξ)   . . . . .ος Πειρα   Cώστρατος Cφή
Κίρωνα Πρα(σιέα)   35 . . . .[C]υπ(αλ)(ήττιος)   Πολύευκτος Cφήτ
Φιλωνίδην Ἀρ(αφ) οἰκ(ῶν)   Εὐκράτης Εὐων.
Cαω . ν ἐ[ξ] . Ἀρ[αφ]   Καρ . . .δευς Ἐπικηφ
Μη . . . Μ[υ]ρριν
10 Τ{σ}[ιμ]ήν[ωρ?]   Φαινίππη
Τα   . . . . . . .να Ἀχ(α)ρ   60 θεμιστία
Δημ[έ]αν Π[α]ι[αν]   . . . . . . ηδης ἐκ Κερα   Νοήμων
Ναυσι . . . . .κλῆς Cουνι   Cτρομβιχίδης
Ἱερο . . . [θ]ορικι.   δον (?)
15 Ἀρχιάδην Ὀ(τ)ρ(υ)ν   Κοπυνης (?) Ῥα[μν]
Δημοχαρίδην Ὀ(τ)ρ(υ)ν   40 λης Πειρα   Κρατῖνος Ἀχα
Χαιρέαν Αἰθαλ   [Κ]αλλ[ίας] Ἀγ[κυ]λ.   65 Καλλιτέλης [Ἀχα]
Ὑγιαίν[ο]ν[τ]α   Κύλωνα (Ἱ)φιστι
Ξενοκλέα Με(λ)ιτ   . . ων Κυδα
20 Κόνωνα Τυ[ρ]μ   Καλλιφάνης Α[ἴξων]
Ξενοκλῆς ἐν . . . [οἰκ(ῶν)]   Ξενοκλέα   [Κυ]δαν Ξενοκλῆς
Κράτην Τον   70 Κυδαν Νικοκλῆ[ς]
Ξείνινος (?) . η   Π[υθό]δωρος Πειρα   Κυδαν Δε(ι)ν[ο]μ-
Ξενοκλ[έ]α Cφήτ.   [Ἀρί]σταρχος μέτοι(κος)   ένης Κυδαντι
25 Δημοχαρίδης Πόρι{στ}ος   45 Ἀριστάρχου   Δημομένης Κυδ
Παυσίαν Ἀναγ   Μνησίθεος Κυδαντ
(Λ)άκωνα [Πε]ρα   Φιλωτὶς Κικ   75 Φίλων Κυδαντιδ
Ἀρίσ[τω]να Ῥ[αμν]   ς Ἀχαρν   Πολυκλ(ε)ίδης Κυ(δαν)
Χα{ι}ρίδημ[ον Αἰγ]ιλ   Ἔρχιευ   Κυδαν Δημοκήδης
30 Δει(ν)ίαν Κυδαντίδην   ν Ἀχαρν   ηριονη
50 . . . .κλῆς Ἀχαρν
δης Κυδαν   Φειδ . . .
α γραμματέα

Side B:

Columns 3 and 4 are at right angles to the first two:

Δημόφιλος
[Δ]ημοσθέν[ης]   Πα[ια]ν
[Π]άμφιλος
Ἐπίχαρμος
5   .ημακτ   [Π]αμβ(ωτάδ)
[Κ]αλλι[άδης   ἐξ] Ἀνα<γ>α
νκ .   . πικαιερ
λη
α . . . α   υμν
10   τ
καὶ Ἀμφ . . .   κατα[δῶ]
(κ)αὶ ἔπη καὶ ἔ[ρ]γα καὶ Ἀρίσ-
[ταν]δρον Ἀ[ραφ]ήν(ιον)
λυ. . . .ην

Columns 3 and 4:
15 Μενέστρατος [Ἀ]γ[γελ]   [Δ]ιο[νύ]σιος [Τρι](κο)ρ
   Κλ(ει)νὶς Λαικάς {τερα}   ...ν.μ[ω]ν Παλλην
   Ἔκυλλα Λαικάς   [Ὀ]ν[ή]σανδρος Πειραι
   Cωφρονὶς Λαικάς   25 Δημοχαρίδης θορικ
   Ἀρχὶς Λαικάς   Χαρίδημος Πειραε
20 Εὐφρονίσκος Λα[κι]   Φίλωνος Ἀχερδούσ
   Ξενοφῶν Ἀναφ   28 Φιλοκήδης (Ἰφ)ιστιάδ

Side A:
I bind, I bury, I wipe out from the sight of man

Column 1
Eunomos from Peiraeus, Aristotelēs, Lusiklēs of Acharnai, Dēmokratēs of Aixone, Kirōn of Prasiai, Philōnidēs living in Araphen, Sao-..-n from . Araphen, Mē-... of Myrrhinous, Tsimēnōr... Dēmeas of Paiania, Nausi-....., Iero-... of Thorikos Archiadēs of Otryne, Dēmocharidēs of Otryne, Chaireas of Aithalidai, Hyiainon, Xenoklēs of Melite, Konōn of Tyrmeidai, Xenoklēs who lives in..., Kratēs... (sons) of Xeinis... Xenoklēs of Sphettos, Dēmocharidēs of Poros, Pausias of Anagyrous, Lakōn of Peiraeus, Aristōn of Rhamnous, Charidēmos of Aigilia, Deinias of Kydantidai

Column 2
Kallias of Peiraeus, ... -dēn of Peiraeus. .... -dros of Peiraeus .... -os of Peiraeus ... from Sypalettos, ... -na of Acharnai, ... -ēdēs from Kerameis, ... klēs of Sounion, ... -don, ... -lēs of Peiraeus, Kallias of Angele, Xenoklēs, Pythodōros of Peiraeus, Aristarchos the resident foreigner, of Aristarchos, Philōtis of Kikynna, ... -s of Acharnai, of Erchia, ... -n of Acharnai, ... -klēs of Acharnai, ... -dēs of Kydantidai, the office of scribe

Column 3
Strombichos of Euonymon, Strombichidēs of Euonymon, Sōstratos of Sphettos, Poleuktos of Sphettos, Eukratēs of Euonumon, Kar ... -deus of Epikephisia, Phainnippē, Themistia, Noēmōn, Strombichidēs, Kopynēs of Rhamnous, Kratinos of Acharnai, Kallitelēs of Acharnai, Kylon of Iphistiadai, .. -ōn of Kydantidai, Kalliphanēs of Aixone, Xenoklēs of Kydantidai, Nikoklēs of Kydantidai, Deinomenēs of Kydantidai, Mnēsitheus of Kydantidai, Philōn of Kydantidai, Polykleidēs of Kydantidai, Dēmokēdēs of Kydantidai ..., Pheid-...

Side B:
Column 1
Dēmophilos. Dēmosthenēs of Paiania, Pamphilos, Epicharmos . -ēmakt Kalliadēs, from Anagyrous, and ... I bind both the words and deeds and Aristandros, from Araphen, lu....ēn

Column 3
Menestratos of Angele, Kleinis, the tart,* Hekylla the tart, Sōphrones the tart, Archis the tart, Euphroniskos of Lakiadai, Xenophōn of Anaphlystos

Column 4
Dionysios of Trikorynthos, . . .n . -mōn of Pallene, Onēsandros of Peiraeus, Dēmocharidēs of Thorikos, Charidēmos of Peiraeus, Philōnos of Acherdous, Philokēdēs of Iphistiadai

* For this interpretation of *laikasteria* see Robert (1936: 14).

SGD 49 (Chapter 9)
Location: Germany, Munich Antiquarium, Alter Bestand, inv. III 1146
Origin: Greece, Athens, Dekeleia
Date: Late fourth century/early third century BCE (Abt 1911: 155)
Text: Abt (1911: 155)

Μἐνω . . . . ι̣ . . [ἔν]
δειξιν . . . νι̣ζω καὶ . . . . . . να . . . .
ην ἀγωνίζεσθαι μέλλει ἐν τῷ Μαιμα[κτ]
ηριῶνι μηνὶ καὶ αὐτὸν ἐπικατορύ[ττω]
. . καὶ τὸς συνδίκος αὐτοῦ|

Menōn (I bind) . . . *endeixis** . . . which he is about to contest in the month of Maimakterion and I will bury him utterly . . . and his co-advocate

* A writ of legal indictment against a disqualified public official.

SGD 51 (Chapter 9)
Location: Canada, Toronto, Royal Ontario Museum
Origin: Greece, Athens, Dekeleia
Date: Late fourth century BCE (Jordan)
Text: Fox (1913: 74–6); originally folded and pierced with a nail

The first column: 17 lines fill most of the tablet; the second column: seven lines just to the left of the first; the third column: five lines beneath and at right angles to the second.

Column 1:
καταδῶ καταδῶ
Ἀρισ[τ]οβούλο(υ)
. . . . το(υ)ς γλῶτ(τ)αν
κα̣[ὶ σῶμα] πόδας χεῖρας.
καταδῶ πόδας
καὶ [γλῶττ]αν
οἰκ[ία]ν <πόδας>

καταδῶ γλῶτταν
καὶ σῶμα
καὶ [πόδας δύναμ]ιν συν-
[δίκου]ς μετὰ Ἀρι-
στο[βούλου] πάντας τοὺς.

[κα]τ[αδῶ πόδας]
οἰκία[ν] γλῶτταν
[χεῖρας σῶμα] δύνα[μ]ιν
[Ἀριστοβούλου ἀ]ντ[ι]-
[δίκ]ο(υ)

Column 2:
[δ]ύνα-
μιν
καὶ σῶ-
μα Ἀ-
ριστοβού-
λο(υ) ἀν(τι)δί-
κο(υ).

Column 3:
καταδῶ Ἀρισ[τ]ό-
βουλον τὸν ἀ-
ντίδικον γλ-
ῶτταν
τοὺ[s]

Column 1:
I bind I bind, of Aristoboulos those men, tongue and body, feet, hands. I bind feet and tongue, household, feet (Go to Column 2) I bind tongue and body and feet, power, co-advocates with Aristoboulos, all of them. I bind feet, household, tongue, hands, body, power of Aristoboulos, opposing litigant. (Go to Column 3)

Column 2:
power and body of Aristoboulos, opposing litigant

Column 3:
I bind Aristoboulos, the opposing litigant, his tongue

SGD 52 (Chapter 10)

Location: Greece, Athens, National Museum, inv. 14470
Date: Third century BCE (Ziebarth 1934: 5)
Text: Ziebarth (1934: 5)

Κίττον τὸν στ[ι]γματίαν δικτυοπ(λόκον)
καὶ τὴν ἐργασίαν αὐτοῦ καὶ τὸ ἐργασ(τήριον)
Εὐφροσύνην τὴν δικτυοπλόκον
καὶ τὴν ἐργασίαν αὐτης καὶ τὸ ἐρ-
γαστή(ριον), Φιλόμηλον Φιλομήλο(υ)
[Με]λιτέα καὶ Φιλ-
. α Μελιτέα [Εὐ]γείτονα Εὐ-
γείτονος Ἀχαρνέα.

(I bind) Kittos, branded slave, netmaker, and his work and the workshop; Euphrosunē, the netmaker and her work and workshop, Philomēlos the son of Philomēlos, from Melitē, and Phil- . a, from Melitē, Eugeitōn, from Acharnai, son of Eugeitōn.

SGD 57 (Chapters 7, 11)

Location: Greece, Nemea Museum, inv. IL 327
Origin: Greece, Nemea; a pit on west side of interior of building at the southwest corner of the sanctuary
Date: Fourth century (Miller 1980: 196–7)
Text: Miller (1980: 196–7) from reading by Jordan; rolled up

ἀποστρέφω Εὔβουλαν
ἀπὸ Αἰνέα, ἀπὸ τοῦ ʷ
προσώπου, ἀπὸ τῶν ὀφ-
θαλμῶν, [ἀπὸ] τοῦ στόμα-
τος, ἀπὸ τῶν τιθθίαν, ᵛ
ἀπὸ τᾶς ψυχᾶς, ʷʷʷ
ἀπὸ τᾶς γάστρος, ἀπὸ
[τ]οῦ . . . . ., ἀπὸ τοῦ πρω-
κτου, ἀφ' ὅλου τοῦ σώμα
τος. Ἀποστρέφω Εὔβου-
λαν ἀπ' Αἰνέα.

l. 8 Miller says: 'Jordan believes, perhaps correctly, that the strokes visible in the middle of l. 8 yield the reading ψωλίου, or 'penis'.

I turn Euboula away from Aineas, from his face, from his eyes, from his mouth, from his breasts, from his spirit, from his stomach, from his . . . from his anus, from his whole body. I turn Euboula away from Aineas.

SGD 58 (Chapters 11, 12)

Location: Greece, Delos, Delos Museum, inv. B 7539
Origin: Greece, Delos; a shaft or well in a house at the foot of the rue du l'Inopos
Date: First century BCE to first century CE (Jordan)
Text: Bruneau (1970: 649–53)

Side A:
Κύριο[ι] θεοὶ Συκ(ο)ναῖοι Κ[- -
[Κ]υρί(α) θε(ὰ) Συρία ἡ Συκονα ϛ - -
ΕΑ ἐκδικήσετε καὶ ἀρετὴν
γεννήσετε κὲ διοργιάσετε
τὸν ἄραντα, τὸν κλέψαντα τὸ δρ-
άκι(ο)ν, τοῦ(ς) συνιδότες, τοὺς μέ-
ρ[ο]ς λαβόντες ἴδε γυνὴ ἴτε ἀ-
νήρ.

Side B:
[Κύριοι] θεοὶ οἱ Συκοναιο͂[ι ? -] ΤΟΙΚΟΥΡΙ-
- - Κυρ]ία θε(ὰ) Συρία ΗΙ - - ΤΟΙ - - Συκο̣[να
[ἐκδικ]ήσετε κὲ (ἀ)ρετὴν γεν(ν)ήσετε ·
[κατα]γράφο τὸν ἄραντα, τὸν κλέψαντα τὸ δραύκι(ο)ν · καταγρόφο τοὺς
συνιδότε(ς), τοὺς μέρο[ς] λα[βό]ντες ·
καταγράφο αὐτ[ὸ]ν, τὸν ἐνκέφαλον,
τὴν ψυχὴν [α]ὐ[τοῦ, τὰ] νεῦρα τοῦ
κλέψαντο[ς] τ[ὸ δράκ]ι(ο)ν, τὸν συν̣ι-
δότον, τὸ(ν) μ(έ)ρος λαβόντον · καταγράφο τοῦ ἄραντος ΤΑΟΙΔΕ\, τὰ ἀνανκê-
α αὐτοῦ, τὰς χῖρε αὐτôν τôν ἀράντον
κὲ κλεψάντον τὸ δράκι(ο)ν ΤΑΤΟΝΟ
ΤΑ τοὺς πόδος ἀπὸ κεφαλὴν - -
ΧΙΡΑΝ - - - | ὀνύχον ΑΕΛΤ - -
αὐτὸν τὸν ἀράντ[ον] τὸ δραύ[κι(ο)ν],
τô[ν σ]υνιδ[ό]τον - - -
- - - ἴ]δ[ε] γυνὴ ἴ[δε ἀνήρ.

Side A:
Lords, gods, Sykonaioi, Mistress, goddess, Syria, Sykona, punish and show your excellence and show your range to the one who took, who stole the necklace, and those who know about it, those who took a share, male or female.

Side B:
Lords, gods, Sykonaioi . . . mistress, goddess, Syria . . . Sykona. Punish and show your excellence. I register the one who took, who stole the necklace. I register the ones who know about it, those who are taking a share. I register him, his brain, his spirit, the sinews of the man who stole the necklace, of those who know, of those who took a share. I register the . . . of the man who took (the necklace), his private parts* . . ., the hands of those who took it, who stole the necklace . . . them from foot to head(?) . . . fingernail . . . him, the man who took the necklace. Of those who know about it . . . whether they are women or men.

 * Following Versnel (1991a: 66 ff.).

SGD 60 (Chapters 7, 10, 11, 12)
Origin: Sicily, near town of Amorgos
Date: No earlier than the second century BCE (Homolle 1901: 412); early second century BCE (Zingerle 1924)
Text: Bömer (1963: 992 ff.; line breaks from Homolle 1901: 412 ff.); once rolled up and pierced with a nail

Side A:
Κυρία Δημήτηρ, Βασίλισσα, ἱκέτης σου, προσπίπτω δὲ ὁ δοῦλός σου· τοῦ(ς) ἐμοὺς δούλος ὑπεδέξατο, τοῦ(ς) κακοδιδασκάλησε, ἐγνωμοδότησε, συνεβούλευσε,

ὑπενόθευσε, κατέχαρε, ἀνεπτέρωσε ἀγοράσαι, ἐγνωμοδότησε φυγῖν
τις Ἐφαφρόδ[ει]τ[ος], συνεπέθελγε τὸ παιδίσκην αὐτός, ἵνα, ἐμοῦ μὴ θέ-
λοντος, ἔχειν αὐτὸν γυναῖκα αὐτήν. δι' ἐκήνην τὴν αἰτίαν δὲ αὐτὴν πεφευ-
γέναι σὺν καὶ τοῖς ἄλλοις. - Κυρία Δημήτηρ, ἐγὼ ὦ ταῦτα παθὼν ἔρημος
ἔων ἐπί σε καταφεύγω σοῦ εὐγιλάτου τυχεῖν καὶ ποῖσαί με τοῦ δικαίου τυχεῖν·
ποιήσαις τὸν τοιαῦτά με διαθ[έ]μενον μὴ στάσιν μὴ βάσιν μηδ(αμ)οῦ ἐμπλησθῆναι
μὴ σώματος μήτε {ο}νοῦ, μὴ δούλων μὴ παιδισκῶν μὴ δουλεύθοιτο, μὴ ὑπὸ μυ[κρ]-
ῶν μὴ ὑπὸ μεγάλου μὴ ἐπιβαλομένος τι ἐκτελέ{σε}σαιτο, καταδε{ε}σμό(ς) αὐτοῦ
τὴν οἰκίαν λάβοιτο ἔχ[ο]ι, μὴ παιδὶν κλαύσετο, μὴ τράπεζαν ἱλαρὰν θῦτο. μὴ κύων
εἰλακτήσαιτο, μὴ ἀλέκτωρ κοκκύσαιτο, σπείρας μὴ θερίσαιτο, καταντίσας καρποὺς
μὴ ἐπι[στα]ιτο ετεραν(?), μὴ γῆ μὴ θάλασσα καρπὸν ἐνένκαιτο, μὴ χαρὰν μ[ακ]αρίαν
ἔχ[ο]ιτο, αὐτός τε κα[κ]ῶς ἀπόλοιτο καὶ τὰ παρ' αὐτοῦ πάντα.

Side B:
Κυρία Δημήτηρ, λιτανεύω σε παθὼν ἄδικα, ἐπάκουσον, θεά, καὶ κρῖναι
τὸ δίκαιον, ἵνα τοὺς τοιαῦτα ἐνθυμουμένους καὶ καταχαίροντε(ς) καὶ λύπας
ἐπιθε(ῖ)ναι κἀμοὶ καὶ τῇ ἐμῇ γυναικὶ Ἐπικτήσι, καὶ μισοῦσιν ἡμᾶς ποιῆσαι αὐτοῖς τὰ δινότατα καὶ χαλεπώτερα δινά. Βασίλισσα, ἐπάκουσον ἡμῖν
παθοῦσι, κολάσαι τοὺς ἡμᾶς τοιούτους ἡδέως βλέποντες.

Side A:
Mistress Dēmētēr, O queen, I, your suppliant, throw myself before you, your slave. A slave, a certain Ephaphroditus, has inveigled my slaves, he has taught them evil, he has counselled them, he has hatched conspiracies, he has corrupted them, he has celebrated with them, he has incited them to run about, he has counselled them to run away. He has bewitched a slave girl, without my permission, so that he can have her as his. For that reason she fled with the other runaways. Mistress Dēmētēr, I have suffered these things and, all alone, I run to you, may you be merciful and help me find justice. May you make this man who has perpetrated these acts against me, find no fulfilment, neither at rest, nor in motion, neither of the body, nor of the spirit, let him not be served either by slave boys or girls, let him not achieve anything, whether he takes on something small or great. May a binding spell seize his household, let no child cry for him and let him not prepare a gracious table. Let no dog howl, let no rooster crow. When he sows, let him not reap, if he produces a good harvest, let him produce (another?), let neither land nor sea bring forth fruit. Let him have no delight or bliss. But let him be horribly destroyed and everything with him.

Side B:
Mistress Dēmētēr, I, who have suffered injustice, pray to you, hear me, goddess and make a just judgement, so that on those who think such things and rejoice and bring grief on me and on my wife Epiktēsis, and hate us, on them you make the most terrible and painful horrors. O Queen, listen to us, who suffer, punish those who look happily on mortals like us.

SGD 61 (Chapter 9)

Location: Greece, Athens, National Museum
Origin: Eretria
Date: Fourth century BCE (Ziebarth 1934: 4)
Text: Ziebarth (1934: 4)

Side A:
Νίκωνα καταδῶ καὶ [Name καὶ γλῶτταν]
αὐτῶν καὶ ἐρ-
γασ[ίαν]
Ἀντιχάρ[ην]
καταδῶ [καὶ . . . . . . καὶ ἀ-]
κ[ρ]α{ν} ποδῶν

Side B:
Νικο . .
κ λ ο ν ε ισ
ἀντιδίκους.

Side A:
I bind Nikōn and . . . and their tongues and work. I bind Anticharēs and . . . and the end of their feet

Side B:
Niko . . . co-advocates

SGD 64 (Chapter 11)

Location: Froehner Collection, Cabinet des Médailles, Bibliothèque Nationale, Paris
Origin: Karystos, Euboia; exact location unknown
Date: Fourth century (Guarducci 1978: 248–9)
Text: Robert (1936: 17); flat figurine with both texts on one side: the first text is written on the right arm and top part of the body; the second text, at right angles to the first, on the left leg and lower part of the body

1:
καταγράφω Εἰσιάδα τὴν
Ἀτοκλέας πρὸς τὸν
Ἑρμῆ τὸν κά-
τοχον · κα-
τεχε αὐτ–
ἡ παρὰ σα-
(υ)τὸν

2:
Καταδεσμεύω
Εἰσιάδα
πρὸς τὸν Ἑρ

μὴ τὸν κά-
τοχον ·
[χ]έρες,
πόδες, Εἰσιάδα, σ-
ῶμα
ὅλον

1: I register Isias, the daughter of Autoklea, in the presence of Hermēs the binder. Bind her near him

2: I bind Isias, in the presence of Hermēs the binder, hands, feet, Isias, whole body

SGD 68 (Chapter 9)

Location: Greece, Athens, National Museum, inv. 14470
Date: Fourth century BCE (Bravo 1987: 185–218)
Text: Ziebarth (1934: 2)

Καταδῶ Καλλί-
στρατον καὶ τοὺς
συνηγόρου[s] αὐτοῦ
πάντας κατα-
    δῶ

I bind Kallistratos and his co-speakers; I bind them all

SGD 71 (Chapter 9)

Location: Greece, Athens, National Museum, inv. 14470, N.3
Text: Ziebarth (1934: 3)

Κράτων[α], Δη[μ](έ)αν
{λ}[κ]αταδῶ [σ]υνδίκους
    Δη[μ]ίαν

Kratōn, Dēmeas, I bind co-advocates, Dēmias

SGD 72 (Chapters 7, 10)

Location: Greece, Athens, National Museum
Date: No date given
Text: Ziebarth (1934: 7); two nail holes

[ὡς ὁ μόλυβδος] οὗτος ἀδύ[νατος κεῖται]
[οὕτω   καὶ ἄχρηστα ἔστω ἃ] ἂν Νικα[σ]ὼ [πράξηι]
                    νημο επ   πόδας γ[λῶσσαν]
        . . . . ταται πάντα δικα[στὴν?]
            [Διο]νυσ{ι}όδοτο[ν]
            [καὶ τὰς π](ρ)άξε[ις ἐκείνου]
                    [κατα]δῶ
                καὶ τὴν ἀκέστριαν κ[αὶ τὸν]
                 . . . . . κέντην

Just as this lead lies powerless, in the same way, let the business which Nikasos does be useless . . . feet, tongue . . . all things (the) judge. Dionysiodotos and the acts of that man. I bind also the seamstress, and the . . .

SGD 73 (Chapter 10)

Location: Greece, Athens, National Museum
Date: Classical/Hellenistic (Faraone 1991*a*: 27 n. 47)
Text: Ziebarth (1934: 8); one big nail hole

   Νίκων[α]
[Ἐφ]έσιον
   υσο νοῦ[ν] αὐτ[οῦ]
     [κ]αὶ τὴν ἐργασίαν α[ὐτοῦ]
       καὶ τὴν εικι

Nikōn, Ephesios . . . his mind and his work and the . . .

SGD 75 (Chapters 7, 9, 10, 11)

Location: Greece, Athens, National Museum
Date: Classical/Hellenistic (Faraone 1991*a*: 27 n. 47)
Text: Ziebarth (1934: 13)

Side A:
Ἑρμη κά[τ]οχε κα(ὶ) Γῆ κάτοχε κα(ὶ) Φρεσσ[ε]φόνη
Κάτεχε Ἀφροδίτην καὶ (?) - - -καὶ - - - [ἀ]κοήν
[κ]αὶ [ἐ]νκ[έ]{κν}<φ>αλον πο· Ἀφ<ροδ>ίτ{ο}ες - - - μ κα/// - -
     αις τοκα
    ηνε Νι<κ>οκλεῖ χ . . . ωλους . . . . . ε . . ελαικαι - -
                                 ιαν
κάτε(χ)ε (αὐ)τὴν καὶ οἰκίαν τὴν ἐκείνης καὶ ε . ει . . καὶ ἄδ[ικον]
καὶ σκεύη τὰ Ἀ(φ)ροδ[ίτης] καὶ αιχ - - - -ντια - - -
καὶ ειδαικ ^ιππαι

Side B:
[- -κ]α(ὶ) Φρεσεφόνη κάτεχε
   αννο . . . ατη ἄδικον αὐτῆ[ς]
      ενης καὶ γλῶταν καὶ δίκαιον καὶ ἄ[δικον?]
   [κα]ὶ πόδας κα(ὶ) ψυχὴ(ν) καὶ σκεύη τὰ κέρδ-
     η ἐκείνη[ς] αἵματι α . . ται ἐκείνης
ἄ[παν]τες ἐκείνης ἄπρακτ[α(?)] σοι
   καὶ . . θε εντος υυα αιν.
      τος και ηκε

Side A:
O Hermēs Binder and Earth Binder and Persephonē, bind Aphroditē and . . . and . . . hearing, and . . . ever. Of Aphroditē . . . to Nikoklēs . . . Bind her and her home and . . . both unjust and her tools an . . . and . . .

Side B:
And Persephonē bind ... unjust of her ... and her tongue, both just and unjust, and feet and spirit and tools, her profits. May all her activities be undone by you and ...

SGD 81 (Chapters 7, 10)

Location: Greece, Athens, National Museum
Text: Ziebarth (1934: 29); side B contains magical words

Side A:
[Κα]τέχετε Τιμαθεν Ὀλύμπω
--ρη καὶ φοβερὴ κατ' Ὄλυμπον
  υνα κατὰ Νικάνδρα<ς> ὁρκί[ζω]

Side B:
Ματμαράκου
  Ιατρακω
  ρ . ρμου

Side A:
Restrain Timathes, son of Olympos, ... and fear against Olympos, ... against Nikandras I swear an oath

Side B:
Of Matmarakos, of Iatrakos ...

SGD 82 (Chapter 9)

Location: Croatia, Zagreb, National Museum
Origin: Croatia, Siscia (Sisak); bed of River Kupa (ancient Kolapis)
Text: Hoffiller and Saria (1938: 526); folded six times and pierced with a nail

Γενηάλις.
Ἰανουαρία
Σηρᾶνος. Εὔπορ
ἐπιτεύξας
ἀπόσιμα. Φήστα
Οὐιτᾶλες Κόσμος.
Φίλητος Ὀπτ<τ>άτα
Κάρπη. Μάμμος
Πρείβατος Εὐτύχας
Ἡρακλᾶς Ἀπρήων.
Φῆλιξ, Ἀττικός. Εὔπλους
Κάλλιστ<τ>ος Ἑρμῆς Σόσις
Λαβερίς. Δωρυφόρος. Κρήσκης
Γρᾶτος. Κέρτ<τ>α Γραπ(...) Φλα(...)

Genēalis, Ianouaria. Sēranos, Eupor who has served a legal summons Phēsta, Itales, Kosmos. Philētos, Optata, Karpē, Mammos, Preibatos, Eutychas, Hēraklas, Apērōn. Phēlix, Attikos, Euplous, Kallistios, Hermēs, Sosis, Laberis, Dōryphoros, Krēskēs, Gratos, Kretta, Grap- ... Phla- ...

SGD 88 (Chapters 7, 10)

Location: Sicily, Syrakuse Museum, inv. 24086
Date: Mid–late fifth century BCE (Dubois)
Text: Dubois (1989: 127–9, no. 121); written boustrophedon

[Hοί]δε γεγράβαται
ἐπὶ δυσπραγ[ίαι]
Κέρδōν Ἐλαχ [- - -] -
ιξ ho Τοπερκō
Πύθōν, Διοκλ[ês]
Τίτᾱ,
Ἐξάκō[ν hυι] -
ὸς Ἐξάκōνος,
[- Μελάνθιο[ς - - -] -
[.]ατίμō,
Δίōν Π[αρ]-
[με]νōνος
Ονάσιμ[ος]
[Ἀθ]άνιος,
Δαρχōν,
[Τ]έλλōν,
Εὔθυμο[ς]
[Ε]υφραίō
Γελōιος[- - - -] -
δᾱς Γελōίō,
Γῆρυς, Παρ[- -] -
[- - - -]ρ, Ἄγνος,
Χαῖρις Διο[- - -] -
[- - -]ιβείō,
Ξήνιππος Μ[- - - -] -
-]ίō Ναραονίδα·
ἀναίμα[τοι ἔστōν]
[hοί]δε πάντες
δύσσοοι

These people are registered for misfortune: Kerdon,* Elach- ..., ... ix, the son of Toperkos, Python, Dioklēs, Tita, Hexakon, the son of Hexakōn, Melanthios, ...-atimo, Diōn, son of Parmenos. Onasimos, Athanios, Darchōn, Tellōn, Euthymos, son of Euphraios, Gelōios, ...-das, son of Gelōios. Gērys, Par- ..., ...r, Hagnos. Chairis, Dio-..., ...-ibeio, Xēnippos, M-..., ...-io, Naraonidas. Let them be, all of these evil men

* Jeffery (1955: 67–84, no. 18) reads *KEPΔON* as the accusative form of a name (Kerdos or Kerdon?). But Faraone (1991a: 11) reads δυσπραγί[αι [οἵ]δε γεγράβαται ἐπι τον] κέρδον, that is, 'These people are registered for bad luck/a downturn in their profit' citing *DTA* 86 for another example of *kerdos*, 'profit' as an object of binding.

SGD 89 (Chapters 7, 9)

Location: Sicily, Syrakuse Museum, inv. 24089
Origin: Sicily, exact provenance unknown
Date: Second century BCE (Ribezzo 1927: 147)
Text: Ribezzo (1927: 147 ff.)

Ὧτ[οι Θεοδω]ρίδ[ας (?) τοῦ Ἀρ]ιστ[ομάχου]
[Ἡρακλί]δας (?) Ἀ[ρι]στομάχου
Ἀπολλωνίδα[ς...]φύνου Ν-
άρων Α(ἰ)σχύλο[υ] Πασίων τοῦ Σ[ώσ]ου Ν-
εμέρατος Ἀριστομάχου Ἀπολλόδο[τ]ος
Ἀριστομάχου Ἀρίστων Ἐπιγόνου
καὶ [ἄ]λλος ὅστ[ις μ]αρτυρήσῃ Ἀριστομάχωι
ἐ[ν]γέγραντ[αι] καὶ τῆνοι καὶ τῆνος
Ἀ[ρι]στόμαχος Ἀρίστω [ὄλ]λυστα[ι

These men, Theodōridas, son of Aristomachos, Hēraklidas, son of Aristomachos, Apollōnidas, son of ...-phunos, Nearōn, son of Aischylos, Pasiōn, son of Sōsos, Nemeratos, son of Aristomachos, Apollodotos son of Aristomachos, Aristōn, son of Epigonos, and whoever else is a witness for Aristomachos, and is inscribed on this tablet, may both they and he, Aristomachos son of Aristōn, perish

SGD 91 (Chapters 7, 8, 11)

Εὐχὰ Ἀπέλλι<ο>ς ἐπὶ φιλότᾱτι τᾶι Εὐνίϙō· μēδέν' [Ε]ὐνίϙō σπευ-
δ[αι]ότερον ἔμεν μēδὲ Φίντōνα, ἀλλ' ἐπαινê ⟨ν κ⟩ αἰ ἐϙόντα κ' ἀεϙ-
οντα, καὶ Φιλέταν · ἐπὶ φιλότᾱτι τᾶι Εὐνίϙō ἀπογράφō τṑ-
ς χορᾱγṑς πάντας ἐπ' ἀτελείᾱ<ι> κ' ἐπέōν καὶ ἔργōν καὶ τ-
ōς παῖδ{ι}ας ἀπὸ τέϙōν καὶ τṑς πατέρας κ' ἀπρακτίαι κ' ἐν ἀγō-
νι κ' ἐχθὸς ἀγṑνōν, οἵτινές με παρ' ἐμ' ἀπολείποιεν · Καλεδιαν
[ἀπογ]αράφō ἀπ' Ἀπέλλιος καὶ τṑς {σ} τēνεῖ πάντας ἐπὶ μεσοτερ-
[....] εντάδα Σōσίαν ἀπογράφō ἀπὸ τō̂ καπēλείō · Ἀλκιάδαν ἐπὶ τᾱ̂-
[ι Μελ]ανθίō φιλότᾱτι · Πυρ(ρ)ία<μ>, Μύσσκελον, Δαμόφαντον καὶ τὸν
[....] ον ἀπογράφō ἀπὸ τōν παίδōν καὶ τōμ πατέρōν καὶ τṑς ἄλλ-
[ōς πά]ντας οἵτινες ἐντάδε ἀφικνοίατο. Μēδέν' Εὐνίκō σπευδαιό-
[τερο]ν γενέσθαι μέτ' ἄνδρεσι μέτε γυναίκεσσι. Τοσούτōς βολίμōς τṑς τē-
[νεῖ, β]ολίμō τιμᾶν ἐρύσαιντο Εὐνίκōι ἀὲ νίκαν παντε<ί> *PMOAY* ... ἐπ-
[ὶ φιλ]ότᾱτι τᾶι Εὐνίκō γάρφō.

See Chapter 8 for more details and translations.

SGD 95 (Chapters 7, 9)

Origin: Sicily, Selinous; Necropolis at Buffa
Date: End of sixth century BCE (Brugnone 1976: 75); c.500 BCE (Raubitschek, private communication reported in SGD)
Text: Brugnone (1976: 75); side A written boustrophedon

Side A:
→ τὰν Ε[ὐ]κλέος γλō(σ)σαν κ-
← αἰ τὰν Ἀριστοφάνιος
→ καὶ τὰν Ἀνγείλιος κα-
← ὶ τ[ὰν] Ἀλκ[ί]φρονο[ς] κ-
→ αἰ τὰν ἁγεστράτō· τὸ-
← ν συνδιϙōν τōν [·]υ[·]λι-
→ ος κα[ὶ τ]ōν Ἀριστοφάνε-
← ος [τὰς γ]λό[(σ)σ]ας· κα[ὶ τ]ὰν
→ [....]λ[·]ονος [γλō(σ)σαν]

Side B:
→ καὶ τὰν Ὀ[ι]νο[θ]έō καὶ τ-
→ ὰν α[...γ]λō[(σ)σ]αν.

Side A:
The tongue of Euklēs and the tongue of Aristophanēs and the tongue of Angeles and the tongue of Alkiphrōn and the tongue of Hegestratos. I bind the tongues of the co-advocates of ... and of Aristophanes. And the tongue of ...

Side B:
And the tongue of Oinotheos and the tongue of A ...

SGD 99 (Chapters 7, 9)

Origin: Sicily, Selinous; Sanctuary of Demeter Malophoros at Gaggara
Date: Fifth/sixth century BCE (Comparetti 1918); early fifth century BCE (Schwyzer 1924); earlier than 450 BCE? (Gàbrici 1927); c.500–475 BCE? (Jeffery 1955 and Miller 1973)
Text: Arangio-Ruiz and Olivieri (1925: 162); circular tablet

Side A (written in lines):
Σελινόνντιος
[κ]αὶ ha Σελινō-
ντίō γλόσα ἀπεσ-
στραμέν' ἐπ' ἀτλ-
είαι ἐνγραφō τᾶι <τε> νε̄[ν]
καὶ τōν ξένōν συν-
δίκōν τὰς γλόσας ἀπε
στραμένας ἐπ' ἀτε-
λείαι τᾶι τε νῦν
ἐνγράφō

Side B (written in a spiral):
Τιμασόι καὶ //a Τιμασō̂ς γλόσα ἀπεστραμέ-
ναν ἐπ' ἀτελείαι τᾶι τε νε̂ν ἐ<ν>γράφō.
Τυρρανὰ καὶ ha Τ[υ]ρ[ρ]ανᾶς γλόσα [ἀπε]-
στραμέναν ἐπ' ἀτελείαι τᾶ[ι] τε νε̂ν ἐ<ν>γ[ράφō]

The text curves around the tablet, in a semicircle, the first line of text is on the edge of the tablet, the last line towards the centre. In the space between the beginning and end of the first line of text, at the bottom of the tablet, but written upside down: πάντōν

Side A:
Selinōntios ('the one from Selinous') and the tongue of Selinōntios, which has been twisted to uselessness, I inscribe here and now, and the tongues of the foreign co-advocates, which have been twisted to uselessness, here and now, I inscribe

Side B:
Timasōs and the tongue of Timasōs, twisted to uselessness, I inscribe here and now. Tyranna and the tongue of Tyranna, twisted to uselessness, I inscribe here and now

And, on the bottom part of the tablet: 'of them all'.

SGD 100 (Chapters 7, 9)

Origin: Sicily, Selinous; Sanctuary of Demeter Malophoros at Gaggara
Date: Fifth/sixth century BCE (Comparetti 1918); early fifth century BCE (Schwyzer 1924); earlier than 450 BCE? (Gàbrici 1927: no. 13); c.500–475 BCE? (Jeffery 1955 and Miller 1973)
Text: Gàbrici (1927: no. 13); circular tablet

Side A:
Ἔνορμος καὶ hα [Ἐνόρμō γλόσα ἀ]πεστραμένα· Σ[ωσίας (?)
καὶ hα Σω]σίō γλόσᾱ ἀπεσ[τραμένα] · Δάμαρχος καὶ ξ[έ-
νοι σύνδικοι καὶ hα τούτōν] γλόσα ἀπεστ[ραμένα.

Side B:
Δάμαρχος καὶ hα Δαμάρ]χō γλό[σα ἀπεστραμένα· Π . . . . .]
καὶ hα Π . . . . . [γλόσα ἀπεστρα]μένα · [Δάμαρχος καὶ]
hα Δαμαχō [γλόσα ἀπεστραμένα].

Side A:
Enormos and the tongue of Enormos, which has been twisted, and the tongue of Sōsios which has been twisted. Damarchos and the foreign co-advocates and their tongues which have been twisted

Side B:
Damarchos and the tongue of Damarchos, which has been twisted, and the tongue (of) P-... which has been twisted. Damarchos, and the tongue of Damarchos, which has been twisted.

SGD 101 (Chapter 8)

Origin: Sicily, Selinous; Sanctuary of Demeter Malophoros at Gaggara
Location: Sicily, Palermo Museum
Date: Fifth/sixth century BCE (Comparetti 1918); early fifth century BCE (Schwyzer 1924 and Miller 1973); first half of fifth century BCE (Jeffery 1955 and Miller 1973)
Text: Gàbrici (1927: no. 16)

Πολυκλῆς Ἀρ͞ειάδας
Ὀνέρο͞ν Ἐξάκεστος
Ἀδείμαντος
Μύχα
Μείχυλος hιστίαρχος

To the left of the names, the sign >, interpreted by the editors as the initial of γ(ράφο), indicating the verb ἐνγραφω, I inscribe

Polyklēs Arēiadas, Onērōn, Exakestos, Adeimantos, Mycha, Meichylos, Histiarchos

SGD 107 (Chapters 7, 9)

Location: Sicily, Palermo Museum
Origin: Sicily, Selinous; Sanctuary of Demeter Malophoros at Gaggara
Date: 450 BCE/earlier (Ferri); c.475–450 BCE (Jeffery 1955 and Miller 1973)
Text: Ferri (1944–5: 168–73); tablet originally folded down the middle

First part:
ἄ]πελον τὸν λυκίνο <κα>καταγράφο πὰρ τὰν ηαγνὰν
θ]εὸν τὰν ψυχὰν αὐτō καὶ τὰν δύνασιν καὶ λυκῖνον
τὸν hάλο hυιὸν καὶ τὸν ἀδελφεὸν αὐτō· καὶ αὐτὸν
πὰρ τὰν ηαγνὰν θεὸν τὸν ναυέροτον hάλο hυιὸν
καὶ .ότυλον τὸν ταμίραντος καὶ τὸς hυιὸς καὶ σάριν
καὶ ἄπελον καὶ ρομιν · τὸν haίλιον πὰρ τὰν ηαγνὰν θεὸν καὶ τὸς hυιὸς καὶ σάριν τὸν πυρίνο καὶ πύρον·
τὸν πύρον πὰρ τὰν ηαγνὰν θεὸν καὶ τὸς· ροτύ-
λο hυιὸς· τô πύρο πὰρ τὰν ηαγνὰν θεὸν καὶ
δύνασιν καὶ γλόσας πλακίταν· τὸν ναννέλαιο[ν
καὶ hάλον τὸν πυκελεί(ο) ἐγὸ τὰν ψυχὰν καταγράφο πὰρ τὰν ηαγνὰν θεὸν καὶ δύνασιν αὐτôν·
κάδοσιν τὸν ματυλαίο καὶ ἐκοτιν τὸν μάγο[νος]
ἐ]νκαταγραόφο πὰρ τὰν ηαγνὰν θεὸν τὰ(ν) ψυχὰν
αὐτôν · τὸν φο(ί)νικος hυιὸν τô καιλίο καταγράφο
πὰρ τὰν ηαγνὰν θεὸν.

Second part, separated by a horizontal line:
    ἄπελος λυκίνο, λυκῖνος πύρο
νανέλαιος, εϙοτις μάγονος, hάλος πυκελείο<ν>, ρομις καιλ
ίο<ν>, ἄπελος ho φοίνιϙος, τίτελος φοίνιϙος, ἄτος ναυεριάδα,
τίτελος νανελαίο<ν>, σάρις ρόμιος.

First part:
I register Apelos, son of Lykinos, in the presence of the holy goddess, his spirit and his power; and Lykinos, the son of Halos, and his brother. And (I register) in the presence of the holy goddess, the man Nauerotos, the son of Halos, and . . .-otylos (the son) of Tamiras and their sons. And (I register) Saris, and Apelos and Romis, the son of Hailios.ˇ [I register] before the holy goddess, and his/their sons and Saris, the son

of Pyrinos, and Pyros. (I register) Pyros in the presence of the holy goddess and the sons of Rotylos, the son of Pyros in the presence of the holy goddess, both their power and tongues. (I register) Plakitas, the son of Nannelaios, and Halos, the son of Pykeleios, I register the spirit in the presence of the holy goddess and their power. (I register) Kadosis, the son of Matulaios and Ekotis, the son of Magon, I register, their spirit in the presence of the holy goddess. I register the son of Phoinix, the son of Kailios, in the presence of the holy goddess.

  * Gager (1992: 140, no. 50) reads Hailios, following Masson, *BCH* 96 (1972), 375–88.

Second part:
Apelos, son of Lykinos, Lykinos, son of Pyros, Nanelaios, Ekotis, son of Magon, Halos, son of Pykeleios, Romis, son of Kailios, Apelos, son of Phoinix, Titelos, son of Phoinix, Atos, son of Naueridas, Titelos, son of Nanelaios, Saris, son of Romis.

SGD 108 (Chapters 7, 9)

Location: Sicily, Palermo Museum
Origin: Sicily, Selinous; Sanctuary of Demeter Malophoros at Gaggara
Date: c.475–450 BCE (Jeffery 1955 and Miller 1973)
Text: Ferri (1944–5: 174)

vac.] τôι σοπάτροι
vac.] ος καὶ ha σοπάτρο γλō[σα vac.
vac.] φρῦνις νοαβαρίλο (?) καὶ ha[vac.
vac.] γ] λôσα γλôσα: αλτε[vac.
vac.] μεκολυισυνδικε[vac.
vac.] τας γ[. . .]λο λ

Seems to curse one Sopatros and his tongue. And there may be mention (l. 5) of a *sundikos*.

SGD 109 (Chapters 7, 11)

Origin: Sicily, Lilybaion
Date: Second century BCE (Jordan)
Text: Gàbrici (1942–3: 133); line breaks Gàbrici (1941: 296–9); letters written from right to left

Side A:
Δέομαί σου κά
τω Ἑρμῆ κάτωχε,
Ἑρμῆ, σοῦ καὶ οἱ πολλοὶ παραιτηταὶ
δὲ ἀνικόνοι Τελχῖνες.
Δῶρον τοῦτο πέμπω
παιδ[ίσκην] ἱκνουμένην [Πρ]ῖμα[ν]
ἐρωτῶ.
Παιδίσκην καλήν,
δορούμαι σοι [δῶρον] καλόν,

ὦτα νοετά, θώρακα καλή[ν],
Πρῖμα Ἄλλια, ἔχοντ-
α τρίχας καλάς, πρόσωπο-
ν καλόν, μέτωπον καλόν, ὄ-
φρυς καλαί, ὀφθα[λ]μοὶ καλοί,
δύο ὦπα λεῖα, δύο μυκτῆρ[ες], σῶμα, ὀδόντες ὦτα λεῖα,
τράχηλος, ὦμοι ἀκρωτήρια.
Κατορύσσω, σείω, εὐοῖ.
Μνῆμα εἶε τὸ ἐπαφρόδειτον
Ἄλλια Πρῖμα· τα-
ύτης τὴν ἐπιστολὴν γράφω.
Καὶ τὸ ψομ....

Side B:
... φθιτὸς
[Ἐρα]στοὶ δύο, κ-
[ήδουσιν] ἕνα καρδείαν
..... φει ὁ Κέρβερος.
Ἀλλίας Πρίμας
.... [λό]φος καλὸς σῶμ-
[α καλὸν] ἡμηροι καλοί..α
......[κ]νῆμαι καλαὶ ἀκρ-
[οτέρ]ια καλὰ ἅπαντα
..... [τ]ὰ ειλατη καλά. Ἀλ
λ[ια Πρ]ῖμα παραδείδο
[μι....ν] Ἑρμῆς ἵνα αὐτὴν
[παραδό]σει τῇ κυρείᾳ ἀδευ-
[κεῖ]....οιε. Ἐρωτῶ, Ἑρμῇ κάτωχε,
[καταχθ]όνειε, [ὑποχθόνειε] ἵνα ἀποξέῃς
[Πρ]ῖμαν Ἄλλιαν
.....α δωρέω τῇ κυρεί-
[ᾳ Περσε]φόνῃ. Κατορύσσω εἰς
[Ἅιδην].

Side A:
I beseech you, O Hermēs Binder, Hermes, you and the many intercessors, and the...
Telchines. I send this gift, I submit the maiden Prima as (a) fitting (gift), a beautiful maiden.

I present this fine gift to you. Ears that listen (?), beautiful chest. Prima Allia, who has beautiful hair, a beautiful face, a fine brow, beautiful eyebrows, gorgeous eyes, two smooth eyelids, two nostrils..., body,* teeth, smooth ears, neck and throat, shoulders, hands and feet. I bury, I shake, *euoi*.** Let her tomb be charming. Allia Prima. Of this woman, I send the letter. And the...

Side B:
... dead (?). Two lovers, taking care of one heart... Kerberos, of Allia Prima. A fine ..., a beautiful body, beautiful cultivated... beautiful legs, all her fine hands and feet,

beautiful ... I register Allia Prima ... Hermēs, so that you might give her up to the cruel mistress ... I ask, O Hermēs Binder, of the underworld, of the world below, that you cut off Prima Allia ... I give to the mistress Persephonē, I bury her below in Hades.

[*] Versnel (1998: 228) following Gordon reads στόμα, 'mouth'.
^{**} LSJ s.v. εὐοῖ an exclamation used in the cult of Dionysos.

SGD 118 (Chapter 11)

Location: Sicily, Aidone, Museo di Morgantina, inv. 62–17240
Origin: Sicily, Morgantina; 'The uppermost section of the well-altar or immediately outside it' (Nabers 1979: 463–4)
Date: Second century BCE to first part of first century BCE (Nabers 1979: 463–4)
Text: Nabers (1979: 463–4); ten tablets found in total, one was uninscribed, five restored on the basis of one complete text

Γᾶ, Ἑρμᾶ,
θεοὶ κατα
χθόνιοι, πο
τιδέξεσθε
τὰν Βενού
σταν τοῦ
Ῥούφου τὰ
ν θεράπαι
ναν.

Earth, Hermēs, Gods below the earth, receive Venousta the maidservant.

SGD 119 (Chapter 11)

Location: Sicily, Aidone, Museo di Morgantina, inv. 62–1730
Origin: Sicily, Morgantina; 'The uppermost section of the well-altar or immediately outside it' (Nabers 1979: 463–4)
Date: Second century BCE to first part of first century BCE (Nabers 1979: 463–4)
Text: Nabers (1979: 463–4); see SGD 118

Γᾶ καὶ Ἑρμᾶ,
καὶ [θ]εο[ὶ]
·κατα[χ]θό
νιοι, ποτι
δέκεσθ[ε]
τὰν Βεν[ο]ύ
σταν τ[οῦ]
Ῥούφου τὰ
ν θεράπαι
ναν.

Earth, Hermēs, Gods below the earth, receive Venousta the maidservant of Rufus.

Catalogue of Binding Curses 433

SGD 120 (Chapter 11)

Location: Sicily, Aidone, Museo di Morgantina, inv. 62–1728
Origin: Sicily, Morgantina; 'The uppermost section of the well-altar or immediately outside it' (Nabers 1979: 463–4)
Date: Second century BCE to first part of first century BCE (Nabers 1979: 463–4)
Text: Nabers (1979: 463–4); see SGD 118

Γᾶ, Ἑρμᾶ, θεοὶ
κα[τ]αχθόνιοι
ἀπ{αγ}άγετε τὰν Βενού[σταν]
τοῦ Ῥουφο[υ . . .ιου
(and then traces of other letters)

Earth, Hermēs, Gods below the earth, snatch away Venousta who belongs to Rufus . . .

SGD 121 (Chapter 11)

Location: Sicily, Aidone, Museo di Morgantina, inv. 62–1725
Origin: Sicily, Morgantina; 'The uppermost section of the well-altar or immediately outside it' (Nabers 1979: 463–4)
Date: Second century BCE to first part of first century BCE (Nabers 1979: 463–4)
Text: Nabers (1979: 463–4); see SGD 118

Γᾶ, [Ἑ]ρμᾶ, θ[ε]οὶ κατ[α]χθό
νιοι ποτιδ[έ]ξεσθε [Βε]
νούσ[τ]αν τὰ[ν] Σέξ[του τ]ὰν
θεραπαίν[αν]

Earth, Hermēs, Gods below the earth, receive Venousta the maidservant of Sextus

SGD 124 (Chapters 7, 10)

Location: Italy, Museo Nazionale di Taranto, inv. 109295
Origin: Italy, Metapontion; a cemetery
Date: Late fourth/early third century BCE (Jordan)
Text: LoPorto (1980: 282–8); originally folded

κα<τα>δίδημι τῶνδ<ε>
πρῶτον ἐργαστήρ[ι]
ον· καταδίδημι ὥ[στε]
μὴ ἐργάζεσθαι ἀλλὰ
ἀεργεῖν καὶ ἀτυχειν.
Τῶν τοῦδε κακῶν
[πά]λιν καταδίδημι τοὺ[ς]
[τ]ῶν ἰατρῶν ὥστε μὴ ἐρ-
[γάζε]σθαι ἀλλ' ἀργεῖν
[τ]οὺς ἐν τῶι βολίμωι γε-
[γρα]μένους πάντας· Φίλω[ν]

Νέαρχος Δικάϊς Θεύδ[ωρος]
Ε[- - -]ης Σιμυλίων Τρη[- - -
Λέων Ἀγίας Θευδωρίδ[ας]
[βά]καλλες Φιλοκλῆς
- -]οῦχος Τερπ[- - -
   - -]ων Ζωΐλο[ς
   Ξε[- -

I bind first of all the workshop of these men. I bind it so that it will not function but will be useless and without success. Second, of the wicked men of this (workshop?) I bind these men (slaves?) of the doctors, so that they will not work but will be useless, all those who are written on the lead tablet. Philōn, Nearchos, Dikais, Theudōros, E. . . ēs, Simyliōn, Trē. . ., Leōn, Agias, Theudōridas, Bakalles, Philoklēs, . . . ouchos, Terp. . ., . . .on, Zōilos, Xe . . .

SGD 133 (Chapter 9)

Location: Spain, Empúries Museum
Origin: Spain, Emporion; a Hellenistic level above the necropolis of the Campus Martius
Date: Third century BCE (Jordan)
Text: Almagro Basch (1952: 31)

Πάντα τοὺς ὑπέρ Ἀριστάρχ[ου . . .]
Ἀρίστραχος
Ἀριστοτέλης
Σωζίδημος
Ἐπίκορος
Παρμένων
Καύστριος
Δημήτριο[ς]
Πυ[. . .]νης

(I bind) all those who are on Aristarchos' side . . . Aristarchos, Aristotelēs, Sōzidēmos, Epikoros, Parmenōn, Kaustrios, Dēmētrios, Pu-. . .-nēs

SGD 136 (Chapter 11)

Location: Algeria, Algiers, Archaeological Museum
Origin: Africa, Theveste
Date: The beginning of the Empire at the latest (Roesch 1966–7)
Text: Roesch (1966–7: 231–7)

[Σατορνί]ναν [κ]αταδῶ, καθάψω νοεῖ πικρὸν
- - α, κατ[αδῶ] αὐτὴν ἐν τῇ εἰδίᾳ γονῇ,
[καὶ γένο?]ιτο τῇ Σατορνίνᾳ πικρὰ καὶ δι-
[νὰ ἕως Σατο]ρνίνα ἔσται πρὸς τὸν δάνατον,
- - - - - - - - - τῇ Σατορνίνᾳ. Ἀπολλύω

[τὴν Σατο]ρνίνα(ν) διὰ μανίας ἀπὸ τῆς ἄρτι ὥρας
   [ἤδ]η ἰς τὸν ἅπαντα χρόνον ἤδη ἤδη ἤδη
   ταχὺ ταχὺ ταχύ · ἀποκόπτω π̣ᾶσαν αὐ-
   [τὴν] ταχὺ διὰ τῶν αἰώνων
      ταχὺ ταχὺ τ̣αχύ.

I bind Satornina, I will attach bitterness to her mind . . . I bind her in her descendants (or her womb?) and may there be for Satornina bitterness and danger until she is close to death . . . for Satornina. I destroy Satornina on account of her madness, from the present time, for all time, already already already quickly quickly quickly. I cut up all of her quickly, for all time, quickly quickly quickly.

SGD 150 (Chapters 7, 11)

Origin: Kyrenaika
Date: Third century BCE (Gallavotti 1963)

The curse targets a woman, asking Praxidike to bind her tongue, hands, and feet, in the presence of Tyche, Zeus, the Charites. Jordan reports a 'hexametric base for the formulaic part'.

SGD 170 (Chapters 7, 10)

Location: Russia, Kerch State, Historico-archaeological museum?
Origin: Southern Russia, Pantikapaion; from the necropolis
Text: Pharmakowsky (1907: 126–8); Jordan reports that one of the three columns has been obliterated, and the other two have only partially survived; originally folded

Side A:
Column 1
κατορύσσω Νευμήνιον
καὶ Δήμαρχον καὶ Χαρίξενον
καὶ Μοιρικῶντα καὶ Νευμήνιον
τὸν κυβερνήτην κ[αὶ] Ἀρίσταρχον
παρ' Ἑρμᾶν (χ)θόνιον καὶ Ἑκάτα[ν] χθονία[ν]
καὶ παρὰ Πλούτωνα χθόνιον
καὶ παρὰ Λευκ(ο)θέαν χθονίαν
καὶ παρὰ Φερσεφόναν χθονίαν
καὶ παρὰ Ἀρτέμιδα στροφαίαν

Column 2
καὶ παρὰ Δήμη-
τρα χθονίαν καὶ
παρ' ἥρωας χθονίους.
τούτων μηδεὶ[ς] θεῶν
λύσιν ποιήσαιτο μη-
δὲ δαίμονας
τούτων μήτε Μαιήτας

παραιτήσαιτο
  μηδὲ μηρία τιθ(έ)ντες

Side B:
Column 1
κατορύσ(σ)ω Ξενομένην
καὶ τὰ ἔργα Ξενομένους
καὶ παίδων τῶν Ξενομένους
περὶ Ἑρμᾶν (χ)θόνιον καὶ παρ' Ἑρμᾶν (χ)θόνιον καὶ παρὰ Πλουτοδό-
ταν χθόνιον καὶ παρὰ Πραξιδί-
καν χθονίαν καὶ πα(ρὰ) Φερσεφόναν
χθονίαν· τούτων μὴ λύσιν γενέσθαι
Ξενομένῃ μὴ αὐτῷ μὴ τέκνοις μὴ γυναικί

Column 2
. . . .
παρὰ ἥρωας
χθονίους καὶ παρὰ Δήμητρα χθονίαν
. . . .

Side A:
Column 1
I utterly bury Neumēnios, and Dēmarchos, and Charixenos, and Moirikōn, and Neumēnios the navigator, and Aristarchos in the presence of Hermes of the underworld and Hekatē of the underworld, and in the presence of Pluto of the underworld and in the presence of the White Goddess of the underworld, and in the presence of Persephonē of the underworld, and in the presence of Artemis *Strophaia*

Column 2
And in the presence of Demeter of the underworld and the heroes of the underworld. May none of these gods release (this curse), nor their daimons, not even if Maiētas[*] begs this as a favour, not even if they offer thigh meat (as a sacrifice)

Side B:
Column 1
I utterly bury Xenomenēs, and the works of Xenomenēs, and of the children/slaves of Xenomenēs, in the vicinity of Hermēs of the underworld, and in the presence of Hermēs of the underworld, in the presence of Ploutodotos of the underworld, in the presence of Praxidika of the underworld, and in the presence of Persephonē of the underworld. From these gods let there be no release for Xenomenēs not for him, nor for his children nor for his wife

Column 2
. . . in the presence of heroes of the underworld and Dēmētēr of the underworld.

[*] Maietas does not appear in the *LGPN*; it is possible that it is related to the name of the local tribe, an ethnic as a personal name. See LSJ s.v. *Maiotis* (Ion. *Maietai*), a Skythian tribe to the north of the Black Sea (Hdt. 4.123, Xen. *Mem.* 2.1.10).

SGD 171 (Chapter 9)
Location: Russia, Odessa Archaeological Museum, inv. 44309
Origin: Black Sea, Olbia
Text: See Yailenko *VDI* 153 (1980: 86 ff.)

Jordan records a list of men's names in the nomitive and genitive and the phrase καὶ τὸς αὀτῶι συνιόντας πάντας, 'And all those who stand alongside him'.

SGD 173 (Chapters 7, 9)
Origin: Black Sea, Olbia
Date: Between third and first century BCE (Bravo 1987: 185–218)
Text: Bravo (1987: 188–9)

[ὥ]σπερ σε ἡμεῖς οὐ γεινώσκομε-
ν οὕτως Εὔπο[λ]ις καὶ Διονύσιος
Μακαρεύς, Ἀρι[σ]τοκράτης
κα Δημόπολις, [Κ]ωμαῖος
Ἡραγόρης ἐπὶ [δ]ινὸν πρᾶγμα παρα-
γείνονται κ[α]ὶ Λεπτίνας,
Ἐπικράτης, Ἑστιαῖος
ἐπ' ὅ τι πρᾶγμα [π]αρ<αγ>είνονται, ἐπ' ὅτι-
να μαρτυρίην ο[ὗ]τοι <ἐκοι>νώ<ν>ησαν,
ὥ[σπε]ρ ἡμεῖς σε. [ἤ]ν δὲ αὐτοὺς
κατάσχῃς καὶ κ[ατα]λάβῃς (or π[αρα]λάβῃς?) ἐ<γ>ὼ δέ σε
τειμήσω καὶ σο[ὶ] ἄριστον δ[ῶ]ρ-
ρον παρασκε[υῶ]

Just as we do not know you, in the same way (we know) Eupolis, and Dionysios, Makareus, Aristokratēs and Dēmopolis, Kōmaios, Hēragorēs are going to support a terrible case and Leptinas. Epikratēs, Hestiaios (we know) for whatever business they are going to support, for whatever act of witness they are coming together, in the same way that we (do not know) you. But if you restrain and hold down these men, I will honour you and I will give you the best present

SGD 176 (Chapter 9)
Location: Belgium, Brussels, Musée du Cinquantenaire, inv. A 1858
Origin: Black Sea, Olbia
Date: Late fourth century BCE/very early third century BCE (Jordan)
Text: Jordan (1987: 162–6); originally folded

Μενέστρατος, Κάλλιππος,
Ἡρακλείδης, Λεωδάμας,
Ἡρότοδος, καὶ ὅσοι συνηγοροῦσι^{ΑΥ}
καὶ παρατηροῦσι

Menestratos, Kallippos, Hērakleidēs, Leōdamas, Hērotodos, and those who are co-speakers and stand around

NGCT 1 (Chapter 10)

Location: Greece, Athens, Kerameikos Museum, inv. JB 15
Origin: Greece, Athens, Kerameikos Eckterrasse, sarcophagus
Date: 360–350 BCE (Willemsen 1990)
Text: Willemsen (1990: 142–3), except for l. 1 and l. 6 (from [κ] to 8 men's names (Jordan 2001)

Εὐκράτης ΦΕΡΣΙΘΕΦΙΩΝΙ
Διοκλῆς Πιθε(ύς) : Ἀριστοκράτη[ς
Πό(ριος?) : Δημόστρατος Κεφι(σιεύς) : Αὐτο
μένης Κηφι(σιεύς) : Καλλίας Εὐπυ(ρίδης)
Μνησίθεος Ἀγρυ(λῆθεν) : Κόνων
]υ : Αἰσχί[νης] Ὀῆθ[εν] : [κ
αὶ τὸς ἄ[λλ]ος τὸς
συνδί[κο]ς τὸς Εὐ
κράτος

Eukratēs (PHERSITHEPHIONI); Dioklēs of Pitthis, Aristokratēs, son of Porosi(?), Dēmostratos of Kephisia, Automenēs of Kephisia, Kallias of Eupyridai, Mnēsitheos of Agrylē, Konōn . . . Aeschinēs of Oē, and the other co-advocates of Eukratos

NGCT 5 (Chapter 9)

Location: Greece, Athens, Kerameikos Museum, inv. I 516
Origin: Greece, Athens, Kerameikos; Grave circle VIII
Date: Before Lykourgos' death in 325/4 BCE (Willemsen 1990)
Text: Willemsen (1990: 148–9)

Μειξίας
Λυσανίας
Εὐβουλίδης
Παρπακίδης
Λυκôργος
Ἀριστομήδης
Καλλισθένης
Ὑπερείδ|ης

Meixias, Lysanias, Euboulidēs, Parpakidēs, Lykourgos, Aristomēdēs, Kallisthenēs, Hypereidēs

NGCT 9 (Chapter 9)

Location: Greece, Athens, Kerameikos Museum inv. JB 24 + 42
Date: Earlier fourth century BCE (Jordan 2002)
Text: Columns 1 and 2, Jordan (2002); Column 3 (Costabile 2000); names of targets spelled backwards

Catalogue of Binding Curses

Column 1:
[Καταδέω] [Ἀ]θηνόδωρο[ν πρ-]
[ὸς τὸν Ἑρ]μῆν τὸν ἐρι[όνι-]
[ον καὶ] πρὸς τὴν Φερσ[εφό-]
[νην] καὶ [πρ]ὸς τὴν Λή[θην κα-]
[ὶ νô]ν αὐτ[ô κ]αὶ γλῶσαν κ[αὶ ψυ-]
[χὴν] καὶ ἔργα τὰ πρὸς ἡμâ[ς ἐπ-]
ιβ[ο]λεύει (?) καὶ τὴν δίκην [βλά-]
[βης] (?) τὴν [Ἀθηνόδωρο [τὴν πρὸ-]
[ς] ἡμᾶς δικάζεται

Column 2:
Καταδ[έ]ω Σμινδυρίδην : <
πρὸς τὸ[ν Ἑρ]μῆν τὸν ἐρίονιον
κα[ὶ] πρὸς τ[ὴ]ν Φερσεφόνην
καὶ πρὸς τὴν Λήθην καὶ νôν
αὐτô καὶ γλῶσαν καὶ ψυχὴν
αὐτô [καὶ ἔρ]γα τὰ πρὸς ἡ-
μâς ἐ[πιβο]λεύει (?) καὶ τὴν
δίκην βλάβης· τὴν ἡμîν ἐ-
π[ι]φέρ[ει] Σμινδυρίδ[ης].

Column 3:
Καταδ[έ]ω Ἰρήνη{η}ν πρὸς τ[ὸ[ν]
Ἑρ]μῆν τὸν Ἐρίονιον καὶ [π-]
ρὸς τ[ὴ]ν Φερσεφόνην καὶ [π]
ρὸς τὴν Λήθην καὶ νôν αὐ-
τῆς καὶ ψυχὴν καὶ γλῶσαν
καὶ ἔργα τὰ περὶ τῆς π[ρ]ὸς ἡ-
μâς δίκης λέγει. Καταδέ-
ω ἅπαντ' αὐτῆς. Κ<α>ταδέ-
ω {δέω} δὲ καὶ τὸς μάρτυ-
ρας αὐ[τ]ῶν ἅπαντα[ς] καὶ
τον [πολ]έμαρχον κ[α]ὶ τὸ
δικαστ[ήρι]ον τὸ τô πολεμάρχο
πρὸς τὸν [Ἐ]ριούνιον Ἑρ[μ]ῆν
καὶ πρὸ[ς τη]ν Φερσεφόνη[ν]
καὶ πρὸς τὴν Λήθην. Κα[τ]αδ[έω]
κα[ὶ] συ[νδίκ]ος ἅπαντας τὸς μετὰ Ἰρήνη]ς καὶ ἅπα[ν]τας
[τὸ]ς [μετ' αὐτων.]

Column 1:
I bind Athēnodōros in the presence of Hermēs Erionios, both in the presence of Persephonē and in the presence of Lēthē, and his mind and tongue and spirit and the deeds which he is planning against us and the case for damages, which Athēnodōros is bringing against us

Column 2:
I bind Smindyridēs, in the presence of Hermēs Erionios, both in the presence of Persephonē and in the presence of Lēthē, his mind and his tongue and his spirit and the acts he is planning against me, and the suit for damages that Smindyridēs is bringing against us.

Column 3:
I bind Eirēnē in the presence of Hermēs Erionios and Persephonē and Lēthē, and his mind and spirit and tongue and the deeds which, concerning this case against us, he is discussing. I bind down everything to do with this. I bind down, I bind, also all their witnesses and the Polemarch, and the court of the Polemarch in the presence of Hermēs Erionios and in the presence of Persephonē and in the presence of Lēthē. I bind also all the co-advocates with Eirēnē, and all those with them.

NGCT 10 (Chapter 9)

Location: Greece, Athens, Kerameikos Museum, inv. JB 6
Origin: Greece, Athens, Kerameikos; above graves of Eupheros and Lissos
Date: Early fourth century BCE (Jordan)
Text: Costabile (2000: 91)

Side A:
ἐπλυ(σίη) (at right angles to the rest of the text and in the middle)
γυναῖκα (at right angles and to the left of the text)
Σ Ε
Τελέ{σ}στης
Μενεκλῆς
Πυρ[ρία]ς
(upside down and to the left) Πύρρος ὁ <ὠ>|μησ|τής

Side B:
Εὔθυμ[ο]ς δ'
ἀν<έ>θεμεν (κ?)αὶ
Τιμοκράτης
σύνδικ(οι)
ἐ<ξ> Ξυπεθῆς
Εὔθυμ[ο]ς ὁ
Λεπτ[ίνου]

Side A:
Bewitchment, Woman, Telestēs, Menekles, Pyrrias, Pyrros, the savage

Side B:
Euthymos, we dedicate and Timokratēs, co-advocates from Xypetē. Euthymos from Leptinos

NGCT 11 (Chapters 7, 9)

Location: Greece, Athens, Kerameikos Museum, inv. JB 4
Origin: Greece, Athens, Kerameikos; above graves of Eupheros and Lissos
Date: Early fourth century BCE (Costabile 2000)
Text: Costabile (2000: 113); box and doll
Inner side of hinged lid of box:
Μικίνης
Καλλίας Ἀντιφάν[ης?
Πεδιεύς Ἄνδριππος

Mikinēs, Kallias, Antiphanēs, Pedieus, Andrippos

NGCT 12 (Chapters 7, 9)

Location: Greece, Athens, Kerameikos Museum, inv. JB 4
Origin: Greece, Athens, Kerameikos; above graves of Eupheros and Lissos
Date: Early fourth century BCE (Costabile 2000)
Text: Costabile (2000: 108); box and doll

Box—inner side of base inscribed:
Θεοχάρης ὁ κηδεστὴς ὁ Θ<ε>οχάρο(υ)ς
Σωσί·στρατος, Φιλοχάρης,
Διοκλῆς καὶ οἱ ἄλλοι ἀντίδικοι.
Doll:
On the right arm: ΘΥ
On the left arm (Jordan): Θοχάρης (Θ<ε>ο<χ>άρης· Costabile)

Theocharēs, the father/brother-in-law of Theocharēs, Sōsistratos, Philocharēs, Dioklēs and the other co-advocates

On the right arm of the doll: ThY
On the left arm of the doll: Thocharēs

NGCT 13 (Chapters 7, 9)

Location: Greece, Athens, Kerameikos Museum, inv. JB 5
Origin: Greece, Athens, Kerameikos; above graves of Eupheros and Lissos
Date: Early fourth century BCE (Costabile 2000)
Text: Costabile (2000: 101); box and doll

Box—inner side of base inscribed:
Θεοζοτίδης
Διοφάνης
Διόδ<ω>ρος
Κ<η>φισοφ<ῶ>ν
Down left arm and also outer side of right leg: Θεοζοτίδης
Down right arm: Διόδω<ρο>ς·
Down neck and shoulders from back of head: Διόδω<ρος>

Outer side of right leg: Διοφάνης
Down its back and left leg: Κ<η>φισοφ<ῶ>ν

Theozotidēs, Diophanēs, Diodōros, Kephisophōn

Down left arm and also outer side of right leg: Theozotidēs

Down right arm: Diodŏros

Down neck and shoulders from back of head: Diodŏros

Outer side of right leg: Diophanēs

Down its back and left leg: Kephisophōn

NGCT 14 (Chapters 7, 9, 12)

Location: Greece, Athens, First Ephoreia
Origin: Greece, Athens; Sanctuary of Pankrates
Date: Later fourth century BCE (Jordan)
Text: Jordan (forthcoming); retrograde.

Jordan provides the following Greek phrases from the curse (the translations are mine): καταδῶ πρὸς τ[ὸν Π]αλαίμονα, 'I bind in the presence of Palaimon'; καὶ δέομαί σου, ὦ Παλαῖμον, τιμωρὸς γένοιο, 'and I beg you, O Palaimon, that you may become an avenger'; Ἄδικα γὰρ καὶ ποιοῦσιν καὶ λέγουσι, 'for they are saying and doing unjust things'.

Jordan records that the curse asks that the victims should seem 'to judges' (δικασταῖ<ς>) to speak unjustly ...

NGCT 15 (Chapter 9)

Location: Greece, Athens, Stoa of Attalos, inv. IL 1695
Origin: Greece, Athens; dump fill in well in front of Royal Stoa
Date: Fourth century BCE (Jordan 1995)
Text: Jordan (1995); retrograde

Μενεκράτης Κ[ρά-]
τητος, Καλλίστρατος
Παυσιστράτου,
Νικόστρατος Γνί-
φωνος,
Θεοκλῆ<ς> συνήγορ-
ος, Αὐτόλυκος Ἐπιλύ-
κου, Τιμόστρατος, Ἱε-
ροκλείδου, καὶ πάν
τας τοὺς συνηγόρους τοὺς
Μενεκράτους

Menekratēs, son of Kratēs, Kallistratos, son of Pausistratos, Nikostratos, son of Gniphon, Theoklēs, co-speaker. Autolykos, son of Epilykos, Timostratos, son of Hierokleis and all the other co-speakers with Menekratēs

NGCT 22 (Chapter 9)

Location: Greece, Oropos, excavation storerooms, inv. ω 540
Origin: Greece, Oropos; grave
Date: Fourth century BCE?/ third century BCE? (Jordan)
Text: Petrakos (1997: 477, no. 745)

[Κ]α[τα]δέομεν Καλλιφάνην Ὀψιά-
δου καὶ πόδας καὶ γλῶταν καὶ χεῖρας καὶ ε[ἴ] τι ἐστὶν α-
ὑτοῦ ΕΚΤΙΜ[... c.6 ...] ΕΑΥ[.]ΗΝ Καλλι[φ]άνην [.]Η [... c.5 .] Ε [1-2]
ΠΑ[...... c.15 ....]ς καὶ γλῶταν καὶ πόδας καὶ χεῖρα-
ς καὶ ε[ἴ] τι [ἐστὶν - - -] vacat

vacat (;)   [- - -]ΕΔΗΜ[.]ΝΔΕΞ[- -] vacat

Εὔκτημ[. c.5 . .]Σ[. . c.3 . .]άτου καὶ [γλ]ῶταν καὶ πόδας
καὶ [χεῖρα]ς vacat

We bind Kalliphanēs, son of Opsias, his feet, tongue and hands and if there is anyone of his ... Kalliphanēs ... and tongue and feet and hands and if there is anyone ... and tongue and feet and hands

NGCT 23 (Chapter 12)

Location: Greece, Oropos, excavation storerooms, inv. ω 541
Origin: Greece, Oropos; Grave 4
Date: Second century BCE (Jordan)
Text: Petrakos (1997: 477, no. 745A); text is 50 lines long, 1–22 on side A and 23–50 on side B. Relevant extracts below.

Side A ll. 1–6:
Καταγράφω
Θεόξενον [ἀ]πήγυτον [Πλούτω]νι
κ[αὶ] Μουνογόνει καὶ Κλ[ει]τίαν
καὶ [. c.3 .[ΖΗΜ[1-2] καὶ Εὔπολι[ν] καὶ Δη-
μη[τ]ρίαν τὴν μητέρα ἔτι [τοῦ π]αιδὸς καὶ
Ἱεροκλείδην αὐτὸς καὶ τέκνα ἐξαίρετα ΤΟΔ

Side B ll. 25–9:
ἀξιῶι οὖν ἀδικού-
μενος καὶ οὐκ ἀδικῶν
πρότερος, ἐπιτελ[ῆ] γενέσ-
θα(ι) ἃ καταγράφω καὶ ἃ πα-
ρατίθεμαι ὑμῖν

Side A:
I bind Theoxenos the buttock-less* to Pluto and Persephone** and Kleitias and ... and Eupolis and Dēmētria the mother still of his child and Hierokleides himself and selected children

Side B:
So may he who is wronged without having done wrong first be judged worthy. Let them come to fruition, these things I write down and which I entrust to you

* Petrakos reads *apugos* for *apegutos*.
** Cf. Opp. *Hal.* 3.489, *IG* ix 2, 305.

NGCT 24 (Chapters 7, 9, 12)

Location: England, Oxford, Ashmolean Museum, inv. G. 514.3
Origin: Greece, Attika
Date: Very early fourth century BCE (Jordan 1999)
Text: Jordan (1999: 115–17)

Side A:
Εἴ τις ἐμὲ κατέδεσεν
ἒ γυνὴ ἢ <ἀ>νὴρ ἒ δ<ο>ῦλος ἒ ἐ-
λεύθερος ἒ ξένος ἒ ἀσ-
`σ´τος ἒ οἰκεῖος ἒ ἀλλώτ-
ρτος ἒ ἐπὶ φθόνον τὸν
ἐμεῖ ἐργασίαι ἒ ἔργοις,
εἴ τις ἐμὲ κατέδεσ-
εν πρὸς τὸν Ἑρμέν τὸ-
ν ἐρ̣ιονιον ἒ πρὸ`ς´ τὸν
κάτοχον ἒ πρὸς τὸν δό-
λιον ἒ ἄλλοθι πο, ἀντι-
καταδε`σ´μεύω τὸς ἐχ`ρ´θ-
ὸς ἄπαντας.

Side B:
Καταδεσμεύω ἀτίδικον Δί-
ωνα καὶ Γράνικον μὲ ΑΠ[.] Δ². Ε-
ΣΤΑΙ αὐτὸν τοῦ ἐλά[τον]ο (?) μέρος πλείονος ἒ ἐγὼ ἀνεδόμεν.

Side A:
If anyone has cursed me, whether woman or man or slave or free or stranger or citizen or household member or stranger, from envy for me, my work and deeds. If anyone has cursed me in the presence of Hermēs the Erionos or in the presence of (Hermēs) the Binder or in the presence of (Hermēs) the Trickster or elsewhere, I curse in turn all my enemies.

Side B:
I curse my court opponent Diōn, and Granikos, do not . . . him . . . a share of the greater part than I give up.

NGCT 37 (Chapter 9)

Location: Greece, Thessaloniki, Thessaloniki Museum, inv. Μακρυγίαλος, Αγροτεμάχιο 951, Tomb 187
Origin: Greece, Pydna
Date: Fourth century BCE (Jordan)
Text: Curbera and Jordan ('Curse Tablets from Pydna', forthcoming)

Jordan reports that the text comprises the names of men and women in the nominative, arranged in two columns.

NGCT 38 (Chapter 9)

Location: Greece, Thessaloniki, Thessaloniki Museum, inv. Μακρυγίαλος 95, Αγροτεμάχιο 480
Origin: Greece, Pydna
Date: Fourth century BCE (Jordan)
Text: Curbera and Jordan ('Curse Tablets from Pydna', forthcoming)

Jordan records a list of men's names in the nominative case, including Σιμμίας Κρατεύας, Παυσανίας, +καὶ ὅστις Σιμμίαι καὶ Τρόχαι {ΣΥΝ} καὶ Κρατεύαι καὶ Παυσανίαι σύνδικο[ς]. Καταγράφω τὰς γ[λ]ώσσας ἐκείνων πάντων ἀνδρῶ[ν].

Simmias, Krateuas, Pausanias, and whoever is a co-advocate with Simmias and Trochas and Krateuas and Pausanias. I curse the tongues of all these men.

NGCT 39 (Chapter 9)

Location: Greece, Thessaloniki, Thessaloniki Museum, inv. Μακρυγίαλος 94, Αγροτεμάχιο 480
Origin: Greece, Pydna
Date: Fourth century BCE (Jordan)
Text: Curbera and Jordan ('Curse Tablets from Pydna', forthcoming)

Jordan reports a list of men's names in the nominative case and the phrase καὶ ἄν τις ἄλλος ὑ'πὲρ ἐκείνου, 'And anyone else who takes his part'

NGCT 40 (Chapter 9)

Location: Greece, Thessaloniki, Thessalonikik Museum, inv. Μακρυγίαλος, Αγροτεμάχιο 480, north of Tomb 224
Origin: Greece, Pydna
Date: Fourth century BCE (Jordan)
Text: Curbera and Jordan ('Curse Tablets from Pydna', forthcoming); tablet has nail holes with impressions of flat round nailheads

Jordan reads a list of men's names in the genitive case, preceded by the phrase Καταδεσσμεύω τὰς γλώσσας, and followed by the phrase εἴ τις ἄλλος τι μαίνεται ἐχθρὸς μ[ὴ] δυνάσσθω ἀν[τ]ιλέγε[ι]ν μήδ[ε - - -]

I bind the tongues (of men's names) if there is anyone else, an enemy who is angry for any reason, let him not be able to say anything against me, and not . . .

NGCT 46 (Chapter 9)

Location: Greece, Thessaloniki, Thessaloniki Museum
Origin: Greece, Arethousa; disturbed fill in cemetery
Date: Fourth/third century BCE (*SEG* 47. 885)
Text: *SEG* 47. 885; folded eight times

Side A:
[----------] τον κ]αταγράφω ------------]
[----------] ους ξέ[νους καὶ ἐγχωρίους?]
[------------]ΣΑΔ[..] . N [------------------]
[----------] ραταν κατα[γράφω---------]
[----------] πάντα [----------------------]
[---καταγρ]άφω [...] . Ο Σ [---------------]

Side B:
[---καταγρ]άφω ὅσο[υς ...] . Ι [..] Α [..] Ν [...] Α Σ ουδ[---]
[---πά]ντας καὶ τὰ .Η[...] T A [--c.5---]
[-------] A B[...] Ω Λ . Ο Ι .. Ν Ο Ι [..] κ[αταγράφω ---]
[------] δικαστὰς ὅσα ἔγ<ρ>αφο[ν -- c.5 ---]
[----- πάντ]ων καὶ πασᾶν [βίο]ν κ[ατ]αγ[ράφω ---]
[-----] Ε.. Ξ Α Μ [---------------------------------]
[-----] δικ [-- c.7 ---π]αντὸ[s ..] Β [-----------]

Side C:
.. Ο Α [-------]
ἔγραψ[α ---]
καὶ τοὺς [---]
καὶ τὰ .. [---]
Α [----------]

Side D:
[---] Ο [-----------------]
[--- τῶ]ν συνδ[ίκων ---]
[---]ν ὅσοι ἐρ[γάζονται ---]
[---] Β . Ι καὶ δ[------------]
[---] τοὺς [----------------]
[---] κατὰ πά[ντων ------]

Side E:
[------------------]
[---] υἱὸ[ν --------]
[---] ἐρ[γασίαν?--]
Very fragmentary.

Side A includes the phrases: (l. 1) Him I bind; (l. 2) strangers and locals; (l. 4) I bind; (l. 5) all; (l. 6) I register

Side B: (l. 1) I register those who; (l. 2) and all those; (l. 3) I register; (l. 4) judges whatever they wrote; (l. 5) of all and all their life I bind

Side C: (l. 2) I have written; (l. 3) and them; (l. 4) and the

Side D: (l. 2) of the co-advocates; (l. 3) whoever are working; (l. 4) and; (l. 5) them; (l. 6) against them all

Side E: (l. 2) son; (l. 3) work

NGCT 48 (Chapter 9)

Location: Greece, Mytilene Museum, inv. 24254
Origin: Greece, Mytilene; Akropolis, Sanctuary of Demeter, foot of altar
Date: Fourth/third century BCE (Curbera and Jordan 1998*b*)
Text: Curbera and Jordan (1998*b*); retrograde; folded three times

Δίης Ἡρακλε[ί]δαος, Διογένη Ἡ[ρ-]
ακλίδαος, Θεόδωρο Ἡρακλ[ε-]
ίδαος, Χαιρ[.]ησκλε Ἕρμειος,
Νίκων Νημοφάνειος, Παν-
τάκλη Μελάνταος, Φ[¹⁻²] δα-
μος Ἱροίτ[α]ος, Ἱροίτας Ἡρ[ακ-]
[λίδ]αος, Πανтακλη s Ἱροίταος,
καὶ ὅσοι μελλ'ἐ'οι[σι] περὶ
αὔτων ἔρην ἢ πό[ην].

(I bind) Diēs son of Herakleis, Diogenēs son of Herakleidas, Theodōros son of Herakleidas. Chair . ēskles, son of Hermos, Nikon, son of Nēmophanēs, Pantaklēs, son of Melantas, Ph . . damos son of Hiroitas, Hiroitas son of Herakleidas, Pantaklēs son of Hiroitas, and whoever else is about to ask or act on their behalf.

NGCT 49 (Chapter 9)

Location: Greece, Mytilene Museum, inv. 24256
Origin: Greece, Mytilene; Akropolis, Sanctuary of Demeter, foot of altar
Date: Late fourth/early third century BCE (Curbera and Jordan 1998*b*)
Text: Curbera and Jordan (1998*b*); spelled backwards; folded three times

Δίης, Δαμόχαρις, Μέλων,
Δι[ο]νύ[σ]ιος, Πυθέδαμος
καὶ ἄλλος ἤ τις μετ'α[ὔ]των.

Diēs . , Damocharis, Melōn, Dionysios, Pythedamos, and anyone else who is with them.

NGCT 50 (Chapter 9)

Location: Greece, Mytilene Museum, inv. 24253
Origin: Greece, Mytilene; Akropolis, Sanctuary of Demeter, foot of altar
Date: Late fourth/early third century BCE (Curbera and Jordan 1998*b*)
Text: Curbera and Jordan (1998*b*); syllables in reversed order

Γε[.]α̣[.]ν [c. 2]
Ἀδωνικ[λ]ε̣ίδας
Ζίης
Μάτρων
Δάμαρχος
Ἀ̣σπασία
Μαλοίσιος
⟦κ⟧αλ⟦λος ? - - - - - c. 9 - - - - - ς̣ 1⟧
κἄλλος ἤ ἐστι μετ' αὔτων

l. 8 cancelled with fine horizontal strokes. Jordan supposes that the writer 'was correcting an unsuccessful attempt at a generalizing phrase'.

. . . Adōnikleidas, Ziēs, Matrōn, Damarchos, Aspasia, Maloisios, and anyone else . . . . and anyone else who is with them

NGCT 66 (Chapters 7, 9, 12)

Location: Germany, University of Würzburg, Martin-von-Wagner-Museum, inv. K2100
Origin: Sicily, Selinous
Date: Fifth century BCE (Weiss 1989)
Text: Weiss (1989: 201)

Side A:
Τὰν Εὐκλέος τō̂δειμάντō
τὰν γλ{λ}ο̂σαν καταγ<ρ>άφō, hō̄ς με̄-
δὲν . . . Μέστōρι ὀφελέσ<ε>ι·
τὰν Σιμία τō̂ Μιǫύθō γλο̂σα-
ν καταγράφō, hō̄ς με̄δὲν Μέστōρι ὀφελέ̣σει· τὰν Πιθάqō τ-
ō̂ Λ- - -όô τὰν γλο̂σαν καταγράφō, hō̄ς με̄δὲν Μέστō-
ρι ὀφελέσε[ι] · τὰν - - -φō τō̂ ΡΛΙΛ-
πō τὰν γλο̂σαν καταγράφō,
hō̄ς με̄δὲν Μέστōρι ὀφελέσει·
Φιλόνδαν τὸν Χοιρίνα κα{ιχ}τα-
{α}γράφō καὶ .ο..κλ[έ]α̣, hοὶ μ-
[ε̄]δὲν Μ̣έστōρι ὸ̣φ[ελέσ-]
ον[τι ·]

Side B:
Τὰν Μέστōρος τō̂ Ε̣-
ικέλō τὰν γλο̂σαν κ̣-
αταγράφō · τō̂ς ΟΠ..
Εἰκέλō πάντας γλο̂σ-
ας καταγράφō τὰ<ς> γλο̂σ-
α̣ξ, hō̄ς μ<ε̄δ>ὲν Μέστōρι ο̣̂-

φελέσοντι· κἀρχέστρα-
τον τὸν Αἰσχίνα καταγ-
ράφō, ἀντ' hō̄ν γλō̄σα-
ις Μέστο̄ρι ὀ[φ]ελέ̣ι-
λ[ε̄]σαν

Side A:
I register the terrible tongue of Euklēs, ... let him not be useful to Mēstōr. I register the tongue of Simias, the son of Mikythos, let him not be useful to Mēstōr. I register the tongue of ... Pitheus, (the son of?) ... let him not be useful to Mēstōr. I register the tongue of ..., the son of ..., let him not be useful to Mēstōr. I register Philondas, the son of Choirinas, and I register ..., let them not be useful to Mēstōr

Side B:
The tongue of Mēstōr, the son of Eikelos, I register. The ... of Eikelos, all their tongues I register, let them not be useful to Mēstōr. And Archestratos, the son of Aischinēs I register, because they have been useful to Mēstōr with their tongues

NGCT 78 (Chapters 7, 9)

Location: Sicily, Marsala, Museo Baglio Anselmi, inv. 1649
Origin: Sicily, Lilybaion; grave
Date: Late third century BCE (Jordan 1997*b*)
Text: Jordan (1997*b*: 387–96)

{τὰν πρᾶξιν τὰν Απιθαμβ . αλ ποτὶ Νυμήριον}
Καταδίδημι παρὰ καταχθονίοισι θεοῖσι <τὰν πρᾶξιν τὰν Απιθαμβ . αλ ποτὶ
         Νυμήριον>
καὶ Δαμ[έ]αν, ὅπως [μ]ὴ δύναται ἀντία / λεγειν,
ὅπως μ[ὴ] δύναται
ποτὶ πᾶ[σα] πρᾶξι ἀντία λέγειν
μ[η] {δ}δὲ μισῖν

The business of Apithamb ... against Numērios, I bind in the presence of the gods of the underworld, the business of Apithamb ... against Numērios and Dameas, so that he is unable to speak in opposition, so that he is not able to speak in opposition regarding this whole business, nor is he able to hate.

NGCT 79 (Chapters 7, 9)

Location: Sicily, Marsala, Museo Baglio Anselmi, inv. 1647
Origin: Sicily, Lilybaion; grave
Date: Late third century BCE (Jordan 1997*b*)
Text: Jordan (1997*b*: 387–96); retrograde

Καταδέω Ζωπυρίωνα τᾶς Μυμβυρ παρὰ Φερσε-
Φόναι καὶ παρὰ Τίτανεσσι καταχθονίοις καὶ παρ' ἀ-
π[ε]υχομένοισι νεκροῖς <Καταδέω δὲ νιν> {ἐς τοὺς ἀτελέστους} καὶ παρ-
α[ὶ]αρίαις Δάματρος <καὶ> παρ' ἀπευχομέ[ν]α[ισ]ιν-

Καταδέω δέ νιν ἐμ βολίμωι, α[ὐτὸν καὶ νοῦ]ν
αὐτοῦ καὶ ψυχὴν αὐτοῦ ὡς μὴ δύν[αται ἀντία]
λαλῖν.   Καταδέω δέ νιν ἐμ βολίμωι, Σ [-max. c.5-]
[.] . ΥΝ, [α]ὐτὰν καὶ νοῦν καὶ ψυ[χὴν αὐτᾶς]

I bind Zōpyrion, son of Mymbyr in the presence of Persephonē and in the presence of the Titans of the underworld, and in the presence of the despised dead (male) . . . I bind him among the unfulfilled, and in the presence of the priestesses of Dēmēter, and in the presence of the despised dead (female). I bind him on the lead, him and his mind and his spirit so that he is unable to speak (?) against me. I bind her on the lead . . . her and her mind and her spirit

NGCT 82 (Chapter 9)

Location: Italy, Calabria, Tirolo, Antiquarium of Comune
Origin: Italy, Calabria, Tiriolo; cemetery
Date: Fourth/third century BCE (Lazzarini 1994)
Text: Lazzarini (1994), with emendations by Dettori 1997

[--] Α Τ Ι Σ Α Ν ἐνδίδ[η] μι πὰρ Ἑρμᾶι
[ἐπ]ὶ παρκάτθεμα καὶ ψυχάν, γλώσας
[--σῶ]μα, ἰσχύν, δύναμι<ν> τὰν κριτᾶν Ω ΝΚΥΣ
[--]ΥΩΣ μυσαρὰ, ψυχρά, μ[ι]σετά

. . . I give up to Hermes for safekeeping spirit, tongues, body, strength, power, the judge . . . loathsome, cold, hated *

> * Dettori (1997) finds parallels for this abusive language in comedy, used of prostitutes.

NGCT 83 (Chapter 9)

Origin: Italy, Lokroi Epizephyroi; near *bothros* in Parapezza
Date: Later fourth century BCE (Jordan 2000)
Text: Jordan (2000: 95–103)

Θεστίας, Κα[λλ]ικράτης, Γνᾶθις,
οἱ ἄλλοι ἀντανταθ[έ]ντες,
καὶ εἴ τις ἀντα[ντ]ᾶ[ι] ἁμῖν ·

Thestias, Kallikratēs, Gnathis, and all the others opposed (by us), and anyone else who opposes us.

NGCT 88 (Chapter 9)

Origin: Gaul, Olbia; west sanctuary
Date: Second/first century BCE (Bats–Giffault)
Text: Bats–Giffault (1997: 459–62); retrograde; folded and pierced with a bronze nail (preserved).

Διονύσι[ος   ]
Διονύσιο[ς   ]δο[
Ποσιδων[   ]λεω[.] ε[

Καλλίστρ[ατος] Ἀριστίων[ος]
Ἥρυλος [   ]νακτος
πάντας [τοὺς ἀν]τιδίκους
[καταδῶ]

Dionysios, Dionysios ... Posidōn ... Kallistratos, Aristiōn, Hērylos ... All the opposing litigants I bind

NGCT 89 (Chapter 12)

Location: Spain, Cuenca, Museo Provincial
Origin: Spain, Cuenca, Barchín del Hoyo; near gateway of settlement abandoned around third/second century BCE
Date: First century BCE to first century CE (Curbera 1999)
Text: Curbera (1999: 279–83); small lead disk, text spirals inwards; bilingualism (as opposed to Latin texts written in Greek letters or vice versa) is very rare

Side A:
ὑπερ ἐμοῦ κα[ὶ] ὑπὲρ τῶν ἐμῶν τοῖς κατὰ Ἅδην δίδωμι, παραδίδωμι Νεικίαν καὶ Τειμὴν
καὶ τοὺς ἄ[λ]λους οἷς δικαίως κατηρασά-
μην

Side B:
pro me pro meis devotos defixos inferis,
devotos defixos inferis, Timen et Nici-
am et ceteros quos merito
devovi supr[a . pro] me,
pro mei[s],
Timen,
Nician,
Nicia[n]

Side A:
On behalf of me and mine to those below in Hades I give, I hand over Neikias and Teimēs and the others whom I have justly cursed

Side B:
For me, for mine those accursed, bound men to the powers below, accursed, bound men to the powers below, Times and Nikias and the others whom I have deservedly cursed above, for me, for mine, Timen, Nikias, Nician

NGCT 116 (Chapter 9)

Location: Russia, Kiev, Ukrainian Academy Institute of Archaeology, inv. 0/1982, Necr. -19
Origin: Black Sea, Olbia; the Olbian necropolis
Date: Early fourth century BCE (Vinogradov 1994)
Text: Vinogradov (1994: 103–8)

Side A:
In the middle of this side, three letters, negatively cast—A P I. Text written over these letters.

Ἀρτεμίδωρος Ἡροφίλο,
Θαλαιώ, δύο παῖδες,
Ἐπικράτης Ἡροσῶντος,
Διοσκορίδης Φιλογήθεος, Κίλλ(ος?),
Εὔκαρπος, Ἡρόφιλος,

Last three names at right and perpendicular to rest of text.

Θατόρακο/s,
Ἡραγόρη (s?),
Ἡγησαγό-
ρης

Side B:
In the middle of this side, three letters, positively cast—N I K. Text written over these letters.

καὶ οἱ ἄλλοι οἱ ἐναντίοι ἐ/μοί·
Καφακης, Δημοκῶν, Ἀτάης,

Side A:
Artemidōrus, son of Hērophilos, Thalaiō, two children, Epikratēs, son of Hērosōn, Dioskoridēs, son of Philgēthēs, Killos, Eukarpos, Herophilos, Thatorakos, Hēragorēs, Hēgēsagorēs

Side B:
And the others who oppose me Kaphakēs, Dēmokōn, Ataēs

Makedonia, Pella (Chapters 7, 11)

Origin: Makedonia, Pella; next to upper part of right thigh bone of skeleton in grave in cemetery east of agora of city
Date: 380 and 350 BCE (Voutiras 1998)
Text: Voutiras (1998: 8); tightly rolled up

[Θετί]μας καὶ Διονυσοφῶντος τὸ τέλος καὶ τὸν γάμον καταγράφω καὶ τᾶν ἀλλᾶν πασᾶν γυ-
[ναικ]ῶν καὶ χηρᾶν καὶ παρθένων, μάλιστα δὲ Θετίμας, καὶ παρκαττίθεμαι Μάκρωνι καὶ

[τοῖς] δαίμοσι. καὶ ὁπόκα ἐγὼ ταῦτα διελ<ί>ξαιμι καὶ ἀναγνοίην πάλ{L}ιν
   ἀνορ<ύ>ξασα,
[τόκα] γᾶμαι Διονυσοφῶντα, πρότερον δὲ μή · μὴ γὰρ λάβοι ἄλλαν γυναῖκα ἀλλ' ἢ ἐμέ,
[ἐμὲ δ]ὲ συνκαταγηρᾶσαι Διονυσοφῶντι καὶ μηδεμίαν ἄλλαν. ἱκέτις ὑμῶ<ν> γίνο-
[μαι · Φίλ ?]αν οἰκτίρετε δαίμονες φίλ[ο]ι, *ΔΑΓΙΝΑΓΑΡΙΜΕ* φίλων πάντων καὶ
   ἐρήμα· ἀλλὰ
[---]α φυλάσσετε ἐμὶν ὅ[π]ως μὴ γίνηται τα[ῦ]τα καὶ κακὰ κακῶς Θετίμα ἀπόληται.
[---] . *ΑΛ* [---] . *ΥΝΜ* . . *ΕΣΠΛΗΝ* ἐμός, ἐμὲ δὲ [ε]ὐ[δ]αίμονα καὶ μακαρίαν γενέσται.
[---] *ΤΟ* [.] . [---] . [. .] . . *Ε* . *Ε Ω* [ ] *A* . [.] *Ε* . . *ΜΕΓΕ* [---]

Of Thetima and Dionysophōn the ritual wedding and the marriage I bind by a written spell, as well as (the marriage) of all other women (to him), both widows and maidens, but above all of Thetima; and I entrust (this spell) to Makrōn and to the *daimones*. And were I ever to unfold and read these words again after digging (the tablet) up, only then should Dionysophōn marry, not before. Let him not marry any other woman but me, but let me alone grow old by the side of Dionysophōn and no one else. I implore you: have pity for [Phila?] dear *daimones*, [for I am indeed bereft?] of all my dear ones and abandoned. But please keep this (piece of writing) for my sake so that these events do not happen and wretched Thetima perishes miserably. [- - -] but let me become happy and blessed. [- - -]

Makedonia, Akanthos (Chapter 11)

Location: Greece, Thessaloniki, Thessaloniki Museum, inv. I. 160.79/1987
Origin: Makedonia, Akanthos, 'in the vicinity of graves' (Jordan 1999: 120)
Date: Late fourth century or early third century, except for the first line on side B which is possibly slightly earlier (Jordan 1999: 122)
Text: Jordan (1999: 122)

Side A:
1 Παυσανίας Σίμην τὴν Ἀν -
7 Ταῦτα δεὶ μηδεὶς ἀναλύσαι ἀλλ' ἢ Παυσανίας.
2 φιτρίτου καταδεῖ, μέχρι ἂν Παυ-
3 σανίαι ποήσῃ ὅσα Παυσανίας βούλεται.
4 Καὶ μήτι ἱερείου Ἀθηναίας ἅψασθαι
5 δύναιτο, μήτηι Ἀφροδίτη ἱλέως αὐτῇ
6 εἴη, πρὶν ἂν Παυσανίαν ἐνσχῇ Σίμη.

Side B:
(earlier text?)
Μελίσσης Ἀπολλωνίδος.
(curse)
Παυσανίας καταδεῖ Αἶνιν. Μήτι ἱερ -
είου ἄψασθαι δύναιτο μήτε ἄλλου ἀγα -
θοῦ ἐπήβολος δύναιτο γενέσθαι, πιρὶν
ἂν Παυσανίαν ἰλάσηται Αἶνις
Ταῦτα δε[ὶ] μηδεὶς ἀναλύσαι ἀλλ' ἢ Παυσανίας.

Side B, l. 1 Addition, inserted at the top of the tablet because of lack of room at the bottom; indicating the mother of Pausanias. Curbera has suggested that because there is no article after Μελίσσης, this is likely to be an ethnic rather than a metronym. Jordan suggests that whoever Melissa is, she is likely to have been from Apollonia in the Chalkidike, a city with which Akanthos had military alliances in the 380s.

Side A:

Pausanias binds Simē, daughter of Amphitritēs, until she does for Pausanias whatever Pausanias wants. And may she not be able to touch a sacrifice to Athena, nor may Aphrodite be gracious to her, before Simē clings to Pausanias. (l. 7) Let no one release these (words) except for Pausanias.

Side B:

Of Melissa of Apollōnia (?)

Pausanias binds Ainis. Let her/him not be able to touch a sacrifice nor be able to be recipient of any other good, until Ainis is gracious to Pausanias. Let no one release these (words) other than Pausanias.

Kovs. 3 (Chapter 10)

Origin: Greece, Athens, Kerameikos
Date: 317/307 BCE
Text: Kovacsovics (1990: 145)

Γλυκέραν τὴ Δίωνος
γυναῖκα κατωδῶμεν
πρὸς τοὺς χθονίους
ὅπως τιμωρηθεῖ
καὶ [ἀ]τε[λ]ὴς γάμου
Α . . .

to the right:]ηνως
to the right: Μαίτης for Μάρτης
on the left: Ἀρ[ι]στάδ(η)ς
ης : Κρατερει

We bind Glykera, the wife of Diōn, in the presence of the underworld (gods), so that she might be punished and unsuccessful in marriage . . .

to the right: . . . ēnōs

to the right: Maitēs, for Martēs

On the left: Aristadēs, ēs Kraterei

Glossary

chrēsmologos (*chresmologoi* pl.) literally, oracle-collector, sometimes translated 'oracle-monger'; usually found selling verse oracles from collections attributed to early prophets and poets; one of the itinerant band of men and women offering supernatural services

dike (*dikai* pl.) literally 'justice'; a 'private' legal suit, concerning a matter that affected a particular individual. *Dikai* (pl.) could only be brought by the injured party or his immediate relative or representative, and they would receive any compensation arising from the outcome of the case.

ethnikos found in inscriptions, added to the name of a person to indicate their origin, city or region, usually when they are abroad

ethnos (*ethnē* pl.) a tribal state organization

genos (*genē* pl.) family or association

goēs a spirit-raiser, but also offered other supernatural services

goēteia the art of spirit-raising, but might also cover other supernatural arts

graphē (*graphai* pl.) literally 'writing'; a 'public' legal suit, which could be brought by any citizen. Used in cases where offences had implications for the community, *graphai* carried more severe punishments than *dikai*. Resulting fines were usually paid to the state, but some forms of *graphai* rewarded the successful prosecutor. To discourage abuse of this system, plaintiffs who failed to win the support of 20 per cent of the *dikastai* also faced penalties.

hetaira an independent sex-worker, often hired to entertain at parties

kapēleion a tavern, sometimes a shop

kapēlis a tavern owner

katadesmos (*katadesmoi* pl.) an ancient Greek binding curse

koinon (*koina* pl.) a political federation

Magna Graecia the coastal region of Italy colonized by the Greeks

magos (*magoi* pl.) a specialist in supernatural engagements, spells, incantations, etc.

mantis (pl. *manteis*) a seer (may offer various supernatural services)

nekuomanteion (*nekuomanteia* pl.) an oracle of the dead

pharmakeia the practice of creating drugs, potions, or spells

pharmakon (*pharmaka* pl.) a drug or potion, but can also mean a spell

phthonos Envy; a disturbing pain resulting from the well-being of another

polis the Greek city state

thiasoi organizations created around the worship of particular gods

Bibliography

ABT, A. (1911), 'Bleitafeln aus Münchener Sammlungen', *ARW* 14: 155, no. 5.
ADAMS, J. (1995), *Risk* (London).
ALMAGRO BASCH, M. (1952), 'Las Inscripciones Ampuritanas Griegas, Ibéricas y Latinas', *Monografías ampuritanas*, 2 (Barcelona).
AMANDRY, P. (1950), *La Mantique Apollinienne à Delphes: Essai sur le Fonctionnement de l'Oracle* (Paris).
—— (1959), 'Oracles, Littérature et Politique', *REA* 61, 400–13.
—— (1997), 'Propos sur l'oracle de Delphes', *Journal des Savants*, 195–209.
APPADURAI, A. (1986) (ed.), *The Social Life of Things* (Cambridge).
ARANGIO-RUIZ, V., and OLIVIERI, A. (1925), 'Inscriptiones Graecae Siciliae et Infimae Italiae ad Ius', *Fondazione Guglielmo Castelli*, 3 (Milan).
ARENA, R. (1989), *Iscrizioni Greche Arcaiche di Sicilia e Magna Grecia: Iscrizioni di Megara Iblea e Selinunte* (Milan).
ASHFORTH, A. (2005), *Witchcraft, Violence and Democracy in South Africa* (Chicago).
AUPERT, P., and JORDAN, D. R. (1981), 'Magical Inscriptions on Talc Tablets from Amathous', *AJArch.* 85: 184.
BAKHUIZEN, S. C. (1987), 'The Continent and the Sea: Notes on Greek Activities in Ionic and Adriatic Waters', in P. Cabanes (ed.), *L'Illyrie Méridionale et l'Épire dans l'Antiquité, Actes du Colloque International de Clermont-Ferrand*, 22–25 Octobre 1984 (Paris), 185–94.
BASCOM, W. (1969), *Ifa Divination* (Indiana).
BATS, M., and GIFFAULT, M. (1997), 'Une Tablette d'Envoûtement en Plomb à Olbia de Provence', *REA* 99: 459–62.
BECK, U. (1992), *Risk Society: Towards a New Modernity* (London).
—— (1995), *Ecological Politics in the Age of Risk* (Cambridge).
—— GIDDENS, A. and LASH, S. (1994) (eds.), *Reflexive Modernization: Politics, Tradition and Aesthetics in the Modern Social Order* (Cambridge).
BELL, C. R. (1979) (ed.), *Uncertain Outcomes* (Lancaster).
BERNSTEIN, P. L. (1998), *Against the Gods: The Remarkable Story of Risk* (London).
BERS, V. (1985), 'Dikastic Thorubos', in P. A. Cartledge and F. D. Harvey (eds.), *Crux: Essays in Greek History Presented to G. E. M. de Ste. Croix* (London), 1–15.
BETEGH, G. (2004), *The Derveni Papyrus: Cosmology, Theology and Interpretation* (Cambridge).
BETHE, E. (1967), *Pollucis Onomasticon* (Stuttgart).
BLUNDELL, S. (1995), *Women in Ancient Greece* (London).
BOARDMAN, J. (1989), *Athenian Red Figure Vases: The Classical Period* (London).
—— GRIFFIN, J., and MURRAY, O. (1986) (eds.), *The Oxford History of the Classical World* (Oxford).

BOEGEHOLD, A. L. (1967), 'Philokleon's Court', *Hesperia*, 36: 111–20.
—— et al. (1995), 'The Lawcourts at Athens', *The Athenian Agora*, vol. 28 (Princeton).
BOHANNON, P. (1975), 'Tiv Divination', in J. Beattie and R. G. Lienhardt (eds.), *Essays in Social Anthropology in Memory of E. E. Evans-Pritchard* (Oxford), 149–66.
BOHOLM, Å. (1996), 'Risk Perception and Social Anthropology: Critique of Cultural Theory', *Ethnos*, 61 (1–2): 64–84.
BÖMER, F. (1963), *Untersuchungen über die Religion der Sklaven in Griechenland und Rom*, iv (Wiesbaden), 992–4.
BONNER, C. (1932), 'Witchcraft in the Lecture Room of Libanius', *TAPA* 63: 34–44.
BONNER, R. J. (1905), *Evidence in Athenian Courts* (Chicago).
BOUCHÉ-LECLERCQ, A. (1879–82), *Histoire de la Divination dans l'Antiquité* (New York; repub. 1975).
BOURDIEU, P. (1977), *Outline of a Theory of Practice* (Cambridge).
BOURGUET, E. (1929), 'Inscriptions de l'Entrée du Sanctuaire au Trésor', *Fouilles de Delphes*, III (1) (Paris).
BOUVIER, H. (1985), 'Hommes de Lettres dans les Inscriptions Delphiques', *ZPE* 58: 119–35.
BOWDEN, H. (2003), 'Oracles for Sale', in P. Derow and R. C. T. Parker (eds.), *Herodotus and his World* (Oxford), 256–74.
—— (2005), *Classical Athens and the Delphic Oracle: Divination and Democracy* (Cambridge).
BRAARVIG, J. (1999), 'Magic: Reconsidering the Grand Dichotomy', in D. Jordan, H. Montgomery, and E. Thomassen (eds.), *The World of Ancient Magic: Papers from the First International Samson Eitrem Seminar at the Norwegian Institute at Athens, 4–8 May 1997* (Bergen), 21–54.
BRASHEAR, W. M. (1995), 'The Greek Magical Papyri: An Introduction and Survey with an Annotated Bibliography', *ANRW* II. 18. 5: 3380–3684.
BRAUN, K. (1970), 'Der Dipylon—Brunnen B1—Die Funde', *MDAI(A)* 85: 129–290.
BRAUNER, S. (1995), *Fearless Wives and Frightened Shrews: The Construction of the Witch in Early Modern Germany* (Amherst).
BRAVO, B. (1987), 'Une Tablette Magique d'Olbia Pontique, les Morts, les Héros et les Démons', in J. Chase, *Poikilia: Études Offertes à Jean-Pierre Vernant* (Paris), 185–218.
BREMMER, J. (1993), 'Prophets, Seers and Politics in Greece, Israel, and Early Modern Europe', *Numen*, 40: 150–83.
—— (1994), 'Greek Religion' (Greece and Rome New Surveys in the Classics, 24; Oxford).
—— (1996), 'The Status and Symbolic Capital of the Seer', in R. Hägg (ed.), *The Role of Religion in the Early Greek Polis* (Stockholm), 97–109.
BRIGGS, R. (1996), *Witches and Neighbours: The Social and Cultural Context of European Witchcraft* (London).
BROWN, P. (1970), 'Sorcery, Demons, and the Rise of Christianity from Late Antiquity into the Middle Ages', in M. Douglas (ed.), *Witchcraft: Confessions and*

Accusations (London), 17–45; repr. in P. Brown, *Religion and Society in the Age of Augustine* (London, 1972), 119–46.

BROWN, P. G. McC. (1990), 'Plots and Prostitutes in New Comedy', *Papers of the Leeds International Latin Seminar*, 6: 241–66.

BROWNE, G. M. (1983) (ed.), *Sortes Astrampsychi* (Leipzig).

BRUGNONE, A. (1976), 'Defixiones Inedite da Selinunte', in *Studi di Storia Antica Offerti dagli Allievi a Eugenio Manni* (Rome), 67–90.

BRUNEAU, P. (1970), *Recherches sur les Cultes de Délos* (Paris).

BRUNER, J. S. (1986), *Actual Minds, Possible Worlds* (Harvard).

BURFORD, A. (1965), 'The Economics of Greek Temple-building', *PCPS* 191, NS 11: 21–34.

—— (1969), *The Greek Temple Builders at Epidauros: A Social and Economic Study of Building in the Asklepian Sanctuary during the Fourth and Early Third Centuries B.C.*, Liverpool Monographs in Archaeology and Oriental Studies (Liverpool).

—— (1972), *Craftsmen in Greek and Roman Society* (London).

BURKERT, W. (1962), 'GOES: Zum griechischen "Schamanismus"', *Rh. Mus.* NS 105: 36–55.

BURN, L. (1987), *The Meidias Painter* (Oxford).

BURROW, J. A., and WEI, I. (2000), *Medieval Futures: Attitudes to the Future in the Middle Ages* (Woodbridge).

BURY, R. G. (1926), *Plato's Laws, Books VII–XII, with an English Translation by R. G. Bury* (Harvard).

BUXTON, R. G. A. (1982), *Persuasion in Greek Tragedy: A Study in Peitho* (Cambridge).

—— (1999) (ed.), *From Myth to Reason? Studies in the Development of Greek Thought* (Oxford).

CABANES, P. (1976), *L'Épire de la Mort de Pyrrhos à la Conquête Romaine (272–167 BCE)* (Paris).

—— (1983), 'La Place de la Femme dans l'Épire Antique', *Iliria*, 2: 201–9.

—— (1987*a*), 'Réflexions sur Quelques Problèmes Historiques des Confins Illyro-Épirotes: IVe–Ier siècles avant J.-C.', in P. Cabanes (ed.), *L'Illyrie Méridionale et l'Épire dans l'Antiquité, Actes du Colloque International de Clermont-Ferrand, 22–25 Octobre 1984* (Paris), 17–27.

—— (1987*b*), *L'Illyrie Méridionale et l'Épire dans l'Antiquité, Actes du Colloque International de Clermont-Ferrand, 22–25 Octobre 1984* (Paris).

—— (1993) (ed.), *L'Illyrie Méridionale et l'Épire dans l'Antiquité, 2: Actes du IIe Colloque International de Clermont-Ferrand, 25–27 Octobre 1990* (Paris).

—— (1997) (ed.), Ἀφιέρωμα στον *N. G. L. Hammond:* Εταιρεία Μακεδονικῶν Σπουδῶν, Παράθημα Μακεδονικῶν, 7 (Thessaloniki).

—— (1999*a*), 'États Fédéraux et *KOINA* en Grèce du Nord et en Illyrie Méridionale', in P. Cabanes (ed.), *L'Illyrie Méridionale et l'Épire dans l'Antiquité, 3: Actes du IIIe Colloque International de Clermont-Ferrand, 16–19 Octobre 1996* (Paris), 373–82.

—— (1999*b*) (ed.), *L'Illyrie Méridionale et l'Épire dans l'Antiquité, 3: Actes du IIIe Colloque International de Clermont-Ferrand, 16–19 Octobre 1996* (Paris).

—— (2004) (ed.), *L'Illyrie Méridionale et l'Épire dans l'Antiquité*, 4: *Actes du IVe Colloque International de Clermont-Ferrand*, 10–12 Octobre 2002 (Paris).
CALDER, W. M. III (1963), 'The Great Defixion from Selinus', *Philologus*, 197: 163–72.
CAMERON, A., and KUHRT, A. (1983) (eds.), *Images of Women in Antiquity* (London).
CAPLAN, P. (2000) (ed.), *Risk Revisited* (London).
CAPPS, E. (1896), 'The Dramatic Synchoregia at Athens', *AJPhil*. 17: 319–28.
—— (1943), 'Greek Inscriptions: A New Fragment of the List of Victors at the City Dionysia', *Hesperia*, 12: 1–11.
CAREY, C. (1994), 'Legal Space in Classical Athens', *G&R* 41: 172–86.
CARTLEDGE, P. (1990), 'Fowl Play: A Curious Lawsuit in Classical Athens (Antiphon XVI, frr. 57–9 Thalheim)', in P. Cartledge, P. Millett, and S. Todd (eds.), *Nomos: Essays in Athenian Law, Politics and Society* (Cambridge) 41–61.
—— MILLETT, P., and TODD, S. (1990) (eds.), *Nomos: Essays in Athenian Law, Politics and Society* (Cambridge).
—— MILLETT, P., and von REDEN, S. (1998) (eds.), *Kosmos: Essays in Order, Conflict and Community in Classical Athens* (Cambridge).
CEKA, N. (1987), 'Le Koinon des Bylliones', in P. Cabanes (ed.), *L'Illyrie Méridionale et l'Épire dans l'Antiquité, Actes du Colloque International de Clermont-Ferrand*, 22–25 Octobre 1984 (Paris) 135–50.
CHAMPEAUX, J. (1997), 'De la Parole de l'Écriture: Essai sur la Langage des Oracles', in Jean-Georges Heintz (ed.), 'Oracles et Prophéties dans l'Antiquité', *Actes du Colloque de Strasbourg*, 15–17 Juin 1995 (Paris), 405–38.
CHANIOTIS, A. (1992), 'Watching a Lawsuit: A New Curse Tablet from South Russia', *GRBS* 33: 69–73.
—— (1995), 'Illness and Cures in the Greek Propitiatory Inscriptions and Dedications of Lydia and Phrygia', in P. J. van der Eijk, H. F. J. Horstmanshoff, and P. H. Schrijvers (eds.), *Ancient Medicine in its Socio-Cultural Context* (Atlanta), 322–43.
—— (2004), 'Justifying Territorial Claims in Classical and Hellenistic Greece: the Beginnings of International Law', in E. Harris and L. Rubinstein (eds.), *The Law and the Courts in Ancient Greece* (London), 185–213.
CHRIST, M. R. (1998), *The Litigious Athenian* (Baltimore and London).
CHRISTIDIS, A. Ph., and JORDAN, D. R. (1997) (eds.), Γλώσσα και Μαγεία. Κείμενα από την Αρχαιότητα (Athens).
CHRISTIDIS, A. Ph., DAKARIS, S., and VOKOTOPOULOU, J. (1999), 'Magic in the Oracular Tablets from Dodona', in D. R. Jordan, H. Montgomery, and E. Thomassen (eds.), *The World of Ancient Magic: Papers from the First International Samson Eitrem Seminar at the Norwegian Institute at Athens, 4–8 May 1997* (Bergen), 67–72.
CLARKE, JOHN R. (1998), *Looking at Lovemaking: Constructions of Sexuality in Roman Art* (Berkeley).
CLIFFORD, JAMES, and MARCUS, GEORGE (1986) (eds.), *Writing Culture: The Poetics and Politics of Ethnography* (Berkeley).

COHEN, D. (1992), 'Honour, Feud and Litigation in Classical Athens', *ZRG* 109: 100–15.
—— (1995), *Law, Violence and Community in Classical Athens* (Cambridge).
COLLITZ, H., and BECHTEL, F. (1899) (eds.), *Sammlung der Griechischen Dialekt-Inschriften* (Göttingen).
Compact Oxford English Dictionary, The (1991), ed. J. A. Simpson and E. S. C. Weiner, 2nd edn. (Oxford).
COMPARETTI, D. (1918), 'Defissioni di Selinunte e di Cuma', *Rend. Linc.* V. 27: 193–7.
CONNOR, W. R. (1971), *The New Politicians of Fifth-Century Athens* (Princeton).
CORMACK, J. M. R. (1951), 'A *Tabella Defixionis* in the Museum of the University of Reading, England', *Harv. Theol. Rev.* 44: 25–34.
CORVISIER, J. N. (1993), 'Quelques Remarques sur la Mise en Place de l'Urbanisation en Illyrie du Sud et en Épire', in P. Cabanes (ed.), *L'Illyrie Méridionale et l'Épire dans l'Antiquité*, 2: *Actes du IIe Colloque International de Clermont-Ferrand*, 25–27 Octobre 1990 (Paris).
COSTABILE, F. (2000), 'Defixiones dal *Kerameikos* di Atene, II, Maledizioni Processuali', *Minima Epigraphica et Papyrologica*, 4: 17–122.
COUILLOUD, M. T. (1967), 'Deux Tablettes d'Imprécation', *BCH* 91: 513–15.
COULOUBARITSIS, L. (1990), 'L'Art Divinatoire et la Question de la Vérité', *Kernos*, 3: 122–33.
COURBY, F. (1927), '*Le Sanctuaire d'Apollon*, fasc. 2: *La terrasse du Temple*' Fouilles de Delphes Vol. 2, pt. 2 (Paris).
CRAHAY, R. (1956), *La Littérature Oraculaire chez Hérodote* (Paris).
CSAPO, E. and SLATER, W. (1995), *The Context of Ancient Drama* (Michigan).
CURBERA, J., (1999) 'Defixiones', *Annali della Scuola Normale Superiore di Pisa*, Serie IV, Quaderni I (Pisa).
—— and JORDAN, D. (1998a), 'A Curse Tablet from the "Industrial District" near the Athenian Agora', *Hesperia*, 67: 215–18.
—— and JORDAN, D. (1998b), 'Curse Tablets from Mytilene', *Phoenix*, 52: 31–41.
——, SIERRA, M. DELAGE, and VELÁZQUEZ, I. (1999) 'A Bilingual Curse Tablet from Barchín del Hoyo (Cuenca)', *ZPE* 125: 279–83.
CURNOW, T. (2004), *The Oracles of the Ancient World* (London).
CURTIS, J., and TALLIS, N. (2005), *Forgotten Empire: The World of Ancient Persia* (London).
DAKARIS, S. (1968), 'Ἀνασκαφὴ τοῦ Ἱεροῦ τῆς Δωδώνης', *PAE* 42–59.
—— (1987), 'Organisation Politique et Urbanistique de la Ville dans l'Épire Antique', in P. Cabanes (ed.), *L'Illyrie Méridionale et l'Épire dans l'Antiquité, Actes du Colloque International de Clermont-Ferrand*, 22–25 Octobre 1984 (Paris), 71–80.
—— (1996), *Dodona*, 2nd edn. (Athens).
—— CHRISTIDIS, A. Ph., and VOKOTOPOULOU, J. (1993), 'Les Lamelles Oraculaires de Dodone et les Villes de l'Épire du Nord', in P. Cabanes (ed.), *L'Illyrie Méridionale et l'Épire dans l'Antiquité*, 2: *Actes du IIe Colloque International de Clermont-Ferrand*, 25–27 Octobre 1990 (Paris) 55–60.

—— Tzouvara-Souli, C., Vlachopoulou-Oikonomou, A., and Gravani-Katsiki, K. (1999), 'The Prytaneion of Dodona', in P. Cabanes (ed.), *L'Illyrie Méridionale et l'Épire dans l'Antiquité*, 3: *Actes du IIIe Colloque International de Clermont-Ferrand*, 16–19 Octobre 1996 (Paris), 149–60.

D'Andria, F. (1987), 'Problèmes du Commerce Archaïque entre la Mer Ionienne et l'Adriatique', in P. Cabanes (ed.), *L'Illyrie Méridionale et l'Épire dans l'Antiquité*, *Actes du Colloque International de Clermont-Ferrand*, 22–25 Octobre 1984 (Paris), 35–8.

Daux, G. (1957), 'Dodone', *BCH* 81: 583–5.

—— (1960), 'Dodone', *BCH* 84: 746–52.

Davidson, J. (1998), *Courtesans and Fishcakes* (London).

—— (2001), 'Dover, Foucault and Greek Homosexuality: Penetration and the Truth of Sex', *Past and Present*, 173: 3–51.

Davies, J. K. (1967), 'Demosthenes on Liturgies: A Note', *JHS* 87: 33–41.

—— (1981a), *Wealth and the Power of Wealth in Classical Athens* (New York).

—— (1981b), 'A Wholly Non-Aristotelian Universe: The Molossians as Ethnos, State, and Monarchy', in R. Brock and S. Hodkinson (eds.), *Alternatives to Athens: Varieties of Political Organization and Community in Ancient Greece* (Oxford).

—— (1994), 'The Tradition about the First Sacred War', in S. Hornblower (ed.), *Greek Historiography* (Oxford), 193–212.

Davis, N. (1987), *Society and Culture in Early Modern France: Eight Essays* (Cambridge).

Dean-Jones, L. (1992), 'The Politics of Pleasure: Female Sexual Appetite in the Hippocratic Corpus', *Helios*, 19: 72–91.

—— (1994), *Women's Bodies in Classical Greek Science* (Oxford).

De Gennaro, R., and Santoriello, A. (1994), 'Dodona', *Studi di Antichita*, 7: 383–408.

De Romilly, J. (1975), *Magic and Rhetoric in Ancient Greece* (Cambridge, Mass., and London).

Derrida, J. (1981), 'Plato's Pharmacy', *Disseminations* (Chicago) 51–4.

De Ste. Croix, G. (1974), 'Ancient Greek and Roman Maritime Loans', in H. Edey and B. S. Yamey (eds.), *Debits, Credits, Finance and Profits: Essays in Honour of W. T. Baxter* (London), 41–59.

Dettori, E. (1997), 'Annotazioni sulla Defixio di Tiriolo', *ZPE* 119: 132–4.

Devisch, R. (1985), 'Perspectives on Divination in Contemporary Sub-Saharan Africa', in Wim van Binsbergen and Matthew Schoffeleers (eds.), *Theoretical Explorations in African Religion* (London), 50–83.

Dick, H. (1955) (ed.), *Selected Writings of Francis Bacon* (New York).

Dickie, M. W. (2000), 'Who Practised Love-Magic in Classical Antiquity and in the Late Roman World?', *CQ* 50 (2): 563–83.

—— (2001), *Magic and Magicians in the Greco-Roman World* (London).

Dietrich, B. C. (1990), 'Oracles and Divine Inspiration', *Kernos*, 3: 157–74.

DIGGLE, J. (2004), *Theophrastus: Characters*, ed. with Introd., Trans., Comm. (Cambridge).
DILLERY, J. (2005), 'Chresmologues and *Manteis*: Independent Diviners and the Problem of Authority', in S. I. Johnston and P. Struck (eds.), *Mantike: Studies in Ancient Divination* (Leiden), 167–232.
DILLON, M. (1994), 'The Didactic Nature of the Epidaurian Iamata', *ZPE* 101: 239–60.
DODDS, E. R. (1951), *The Greeks and the Irrational* (Cambridge).
DÖRNER, F. K. (1940), 'Eine neue Fluchtafel', *JÖAI* 32: 63–72.
DOUGLAS, M. (1966; 2000), *Purity and Danger: An Analysis of Concepts of Pollution and Taboo* (London, 1966/69).
—— (1986), *Risk Acceptability according to the Social Sciences* (London).
—— (1992), *Risk and Blame: Essays in Cultural Theory* (London).
—— (1996), *Natural Symbols: Explorations in Cosmology*, new edn. (London).
—— (1999*a*), *Leviticus as Literature* (Oxford).
—— (1999*b*), *Implicit Meanings: Selected Essays in Anthropology* (2nd edn.) (London).
—— and WILDAVSKY, A. (1982), *Risk and Culture* (London).
DOVER, K. (1965), *Thucydides, Book VI: Introduction and Commentary* (Oxford).
—— (1974), *Greek Popular Morality in the Time of Plato and Aristotle* (Oxford).
—— (1978), *Greek Homosexuality* (London).
DUBOIS, L. (1989), *Inscriptions Grecques Dialectales de Sicile* (Rome).
DUNANT, C. (1978), 'Sus aux Voleurs!' *Museum Helveticum*, 35: 241–4.
DUNBABIN, T. (1948), *The Western Greeks: The History of Sicily and South Italy from the Foundation of the Greek Colonies to 480 BC* (Oxford).
DUNBAR, N. (1995), *Aristophanes' Birds* (Oxford).
EDELSTEIN, E. J., and EDELSTEIN, L. (1945), *Asclepius: A Collection and Interpretation of the Testimonies* (Baltimore).
EDMONDS, J. (1957–), *The Fragments of Attic Comedy*, vols. 1– (Leiden).
EDWARDS, C. (1985), *The Politics of Immorality in Ancient Rome* (Cambridge).
EIDINOW E. (2007) 'Why the Athenians Began to Curse', in R. Osborne (ed.), *The Anatomy of Cultural Revolution: Athenian Art, Literature, Language, and Politics, c. 430–380 BCE* (Cambridge).
EITREM, S. (1936), Review of E. Ziebarth, 'Neue Verfluchungstafeln aus Attika, Boiotien und Euboia' (*SBBerl. Phil.-hist. Kl.* 1934, 33), *Gnomon*, 12: 558–9.
ELSTER, J. (1983), *Sour Grapes: Studies in the Subversion of Rationality* (Cambridge).
ENGELMANN, H. (1975), 'The Delian Aretalogy of Serapis', *EPRO* 44 (Leiden) 53–4.
ERXLEBEN, E. (1974), 'Die Rolle der Bevölkerungsklassen in Aussenhandel Athens in 4 Jahrhundert v.u. 2', in E. C. Welskopf (ed.), *Hellenische Poleis*, i (460–520) (Berlin).
EVANGELIDIS, D. (1929), 'Ἀνασκαφὴ τοῦ Ἱεροῦ τῆς Δωδώνης', *PAE* 104–29.
—— (1931), 'Ἀνασκαφὴ τοῦ Ἱεροῦ τῆς Δωδώνης', *PAE* 192–260.
—— (1932), 'Ἀνασκαφὴ τοῦ Ἱεροῦ τῆς Δωδώνης', *PAE* 47–52.
—— (1935), 'Ἠπειρωτικαὶ Ἔρευνα', *Ἠπειρωτικὰ Χρονικά*, 10: 192–260.

—— (1952), 'Ἀνασκαφὴ τοῦ Ἱεροῦ τῆς Δωδώνης', PAE 279–306.
—— (1958), 'Ἀνασκαφὴ τοῦ Ἱεροῦ τῆς Δωδώνης', PAE 103–6.
—— (1965), 'Ἀνασκαφὴ τοῦ Ἱεροῦ τῆς Δωδώνης', PAE 53–65.
—— (1967), 'Ἀνασκαφὴ τοῦ Ἱεροῦ τῆς Δωδώνης', PAE 33–54.
—— (1968), 'Ἀνασκαφὴ ἐν Δωδώνῃ', PAE 42–59.
—— (1973), 'Ἀνασκαφὴ τοῦ Ἱεροῦ τῆς Δωδώνης', PAE 87–98.
EVANS-PRITCHARD, E. E. (1937), *Witchcraft, Oracles and Magic among the Azande* (Oxford).
FALCONER, W. A. (1996) (trans.), *Cicero: de Divinatione* (Cambridge, Mass.).
FARAONE, C. (1985), 'Aeschylus' ὕμνος δέσμιος (*Eum*. 306) and Attic Judicial Curse Tablets', *JHS* 105: 150–4.
—— (1989), 'An Accusation of Magic in Classical Athens (Aristophanes' *Wasps* 946–8)', *TAPA* 119: 149–60.
—— (1991*a*), 'The Agonistic Context of Early Greek Binding Spells', in C. A. Faraone and D. Obbink (eds.), *Magika Hiera: Ancient Greek Magic and Religion* (Oxford), 3–32.
—— (1991*b*), 'Binding and Burying the Forces of Evil: The Defensive Use of "Voodoo Dolls" in Ancient Greece', *CA* 10: 165–205.
—— (1993), 'Molten Wax, Spilt Wine, and Mutilated Animals: Sympathetic Magic in Near Eastern and Early Greek Oath Ceremonies', *JHS* 113: 60–80.
—— (1995), 'The "Performative Future" in Three Hellenistic Incantations and Theocritus' Second Idyll', *CPh*. 90: 1–15.
—— (1999), *Ancient Greek Love Magic* (Harvard).
—— (2005), 'Necromancy goes Underground: The Disguise of Skull- and Corpse-Divination in the Paris Magical Papyri (*PGM* IV 1928–2144)', in S. I. Johnston and P. Struck (eds.), *Mantike: Studies in Ancient Divination* (Leiden), 255–82.
FARDON, R. (1999), *Mary Douglas* (London).
FARNELL, L. R. (1909), *The Cults of the Greek States* (Oxford).
FAVRET-SAADA, J. (1980), *Deadly Words* (Cambridge).
FERGUSON, W. S. (1911), *Hellenistic Athens* (London).
FERNANDEZ, J. W. (1991), 'Afterword', in Philip M. Peek (ed.), *African Divination Systems: Ways of Knowing* (Bloomington).
FERRI, S. (1944–5), 'Nuova "Defixio" Greca dalla Gàggera', *Not. Scav.* VII. (5–6): 168–74.
FINLEY, M. I. (1983), *Politics in the Ancient World* (Cambridge).
—— (1973; 1999), *The Ancient Economy* (Berkeley; London).
FISCHER, M. (1977), 'Interpretive Anthropology', *Reviews in Anthropology*, 4 (4): 391–404.
FISHER, N. (1993), *Slavery in Classical Greece* (London).
—— (1998), 'Gymnasia and the Democratic Values of Leisure', in P. Cartledge, P. Millett, and S. von Reden (eds.), *Kosmos: Essays in Order, Conflict and Community in Classical Athens* (Cambridge).
—— (2001), '"Let Envy be Absent": Envy, Liturgies and Reciprocity in Athens', in

D. Konstan and N. K. Rutter (eds.), *Envy, Spite and Jealousy: The Rivalrous Emotions in Ancient Greece* (Edinburgh), 181–216.

FOLEY, H. (1981) (ed.), *Reflections of Women in Antiquity* (London).

FONTENROSE, J. (1978), *The Delphic Oracle: Its Responses and Operations with a Catalogue of Responses* (University of California).

—— (1988), *Didyma: Apollo's Oracle Cult and Companions* (Berkeley).

FORREST, G. (1957), 'Colonisation and the Rise of Delphi', *Historia*, 6: 160–75.

FORSTER, E. M. (1927), *Aspects of the Novel* (London).

FOUCAULT, M. (1985), *The Use of Pleasure: Volume 2 of the History of Sexuality*, trans. Robert Hurley (New York).

—— (1986), *The Care of the Self: Volume 3 of the History of Sexuality*, trans. Robert Hurley (New York).

—— (1997), *The Archaeology of Knowledge* (London).

FOWLER, B. H. (1989), *The Hellenistic Aesthetic* (Bristol).

FOWLER, R. L. and HUGHES, B. (1995), 'Greek Magic, Greek Religion', *ICS* 20: 1–22.

FOX, W. S. (1913), 'Two Tabellae Defixionum', *AJPhil.* 34: 74–80.

FOXHALL, L., and LEWIS, A. D. E. (1996) (eds.), *Greek Law in its Political Setting* (Oxford).

FRANKE, P. R. (1961), *Die Antiken Münzen von Epirus*, vols. i and ii (Wiesbaden).

FRAZER, J. G. (1911–15), *The Golden Bough* (London).

GÀBRICI, E. (1927), 'Il Santuario della Malophoros a Selinunte', *Mon. Ant.* 32: 379–400.

—— (1941), 'Sicilia', *Not. Scav.* VII. (2): 296–9.

—— (1942–3), *Epigraphica*, 5–6: 133, no. 1929.

GAGARIN, M. (2004), 'The Rule of Law in Gortyn', in E. Harris and L. Rubinstein (eds.), *The Law and the Courts in Ancient Greece* (London), 173–84.

GAGER, J. G. (1992), *Curse Tablets and Binding Spells from the Ancient World* (Oxford).

GALLAGHER, C. and GREENBLATT, S. (2000), *Practising New Historicism* (Chicago and London).

GALLANT, T. W. (1991), *Risk and Survival: Reconstructing the Rural Domestic Economy* (Cambridge).

GALLAVOTTI, C. (1963), 'Una *Defixio* Dorica e Altri Nuovi Epigrammi Cirenaici', *Maia*, 15: 450–4.

GARNER, R. (1987), *Law and Society in Classical Athens* (London).

GARNSEY, P. (1988), *Famine and Food Supply in the Graeco-Roman World: Responses to Risk and Crisis* (Cambridge).

—— and MORRIS, I. (1989), 'Risk and the *Polis*: The Evolution of Institutionalised Responses to Food Supply Problems in the Ancient Greek State', in P. Halstead and J. O'Shea (eds.), *Bad Year Economics: Cultural Responses to Risk and Uncertainty* (Cambridge), 98–105.

GAUTHIER, P. (1990), 'Quorum et Participation Civique dans les Démocraties Grecques', *Cahiers du Centre Glotz*, 1: 77–84.

GEERTZ, C. (1973), *The Interpretation of Cultures* (New York).

GIDDENS, A. (1990), *Runaway World* (London).

—— (1991), *Modernity and Self-Identity: Self and Society in the Late Modern Age* (Cambridge).
GILMOUR, G. (1997), 'The Nature and Function of Astragalus Bones from Archaeological Contexts in the Levant and Eastern Mediterranean', *Oxford Journal of Archaeology*, 16 (2): 167–76.
GOLDHILL, S. (1994), 'Representing Democracy: Women at the Great Dionysia', in R. Osborne and S. Hornblower (eds.), *Ritual, Finance and Politics* (Oxford), 351–68.
GONZALES, M. (2005), 'The Oracle and Cult of Ares in Asia Minor', *GRBS* 45: 3.
GOODY, E. (1970), 'Legitimate and Illegitimate Aggression in a West African State', in M. Douglas (ed.), *Witchcraft Confessions and Accusations* (London).
GORDON, R. (1995), 'The Healing Event in Graeco-Roman Folk Medicine', in P. J. van der Eijk, H. F. J. Horstmanshoff, and P. H. Schrijvers, *Ancient Medicine in its Socio-Cultural Context* (Atlanta), 363–76.
—— (1997), 'Reporting the Marvellous: Private Divination in the Greek Magical Papyri', in P. Schäfer and H. G. Kippenberg, *Envisioning Magic: A Princeton Seminar and Symposium* (Leiden), 65–92.
—— (1999a), 'What's in a List?', in D. R. Jordan, H. Montgomery, and E. Thomassen (eds.), *The World of Ancient Magic: Papers from the First International Samson Eitrem Seminar at the Norwegian Institute at Athens, 4–8 May 1997* (Bergen), 239–78.
—— (1999b), 'Imagining Greek and Roman Magic', in B. Ankarloo and S. Clark (eds.), *Witchcraft and Magic in Europe*, ii: *Ancient Greece and Rome* (London), 159–276.
GOULD, J. (2001), *Myth, Ritual Memory and Exchange: Essays in Greek Literature and Culture* (Oxford).
GOW, A. S. F. (1965) (ed.), *Machon: The Fragments* (Cambridge).
—— and PAGE, D. L. (1965) (eds.), *The Greek Anthology, Hellenistic Epigrams* (Cambridge).
GRAF, F. (1994), *Magie dans l'Antiquité Gréco-romaine: Idéologie et Pratique* (Paris).
—— (1996), *Gottesnähe und Schadenzauber: Die Magie in der griechisch-römischen antike* (Munich).
—— (1997a), *Magic in the Ancient World*, trans. F. Philip (London).
—— (1997b), 'How to Cope with a Difficult Life: A View of Ancient Magic', in P. Schäfer and H. G. Kippenberg, *Envisioning Magic: A Princeton Seminar and Symposium* (Leiden), 93–114.
—— (1999), 'Magic and Divination', in D. R. Jordan, H. Montgomery, and E. Thomassen (eds.), *The World of Ancient Magic: Papers from the First International Samson Eitrem Seminar at the Norwegian Institute at Athens, 4–8 May 1997* (Bergen), 283–98.
GRAHAM, A. J. (1964), *Colony and Mother City in Ancient Greece* (Manchester).
GRIFFITH, M. (1978), 'Aeschylus, Sicily, and Prometheus', in R. D. Dawe, J. Diggle, and P. E. Easterling (eds.), *Dionysiaca: Nine Studies in Greek Poetry by Former Pupils, Presented to Sir Denys Page* (Cambridge), 105–39.
GRIFFITHS FREDERICK, T. (1981), 'Home before Lunch: The Emancipated Woman in Theocritus', in H. Foley (ed.), *Reflections of Women in Antiquity* (London), 247–73.

GUARDUCCI, M. (1935–50) (ed.), *Inscriptiones Creticae*, vols. 1–4 (Rome).
—— (1978), *Epigrafia Greca*, iv: *Epigrafi Sacre Pagane e Cristiane* (Rome).
GÜNTHER, W. (1971), *Das Orakel von Didyma in Hellenistischer Zeit: Eine Interpretation von Stein-Urkunden*, Istanbuler Mitteilungen, 4 (Deutsches Archäologisches Institut, Abteilung Istanbul; Tübingen).
HABICHT, C. (1993), 'Attische Fluchtafeln aus der Zeit Alexanders des Großen', *ICS* 18: 113–18.
—— (1997), *Athens from Alexander to Antony* (Cambridge, Mass., and London).
HACKING, I. (1990), *The Taming of Chance* (Cambridge).
HALL, E. (1995), 'Lawcourt Drama: The Power of Performance in Greek Forensic Oratory', *BICS* 40: 39–58.
HALLIWELL, S. (1991), 'The Uses of Laughter in Greek Culture', *CQ* 41 (ii): 279–96.
HALPERIN, D. M. (1990a), *One Hundred Years of Homosexuality: And Other Essays on Greek Love* (London).
—— (1990b), 'Why is Diotima a Woman? Platonic Eros and the Figuration of Gender', in D. Halperin, J. Winkler, and F. Zeitlin (eds.), *Before Sexuality: The Construction of Erotic Experience in the Ancient Greek World* (Princeton), 257–308.
—— WINKLER, J., and ZEITLIN, F. (1990) (eds.), *Before Sexuality: The Construction of Erotic Experience in the Ancient Greek World* (Princeton).
HALSTEAD, P. (1987), 'Traditional and Ancient Rural Economy in Mediterranean Europe: Plus Ça Change?', *JHS* 107: 77–87.
——(1989), 'The Economy has a Normal Surplus: Economic Stability and Social Change among Early Farming Communities of Thessaly, Greece', in P. Halstead and J. O'Shea (eds.), *Bad Year Economics: Cultural Responses to Risk and Uncertainty* (Cambridge), 68–80.
—— and JONES, G. (1989), 'Agrarian Ecology in the Greek Islands: Time Stress, Scale and Risk', *JHS* 109: 41–55.
—— and O'SHEA, J. (1989a), 'Introduction: Cultural Responses to Risk and Uncertainty', in *Bad Year Economics: Cultural Responses to Risk and Uncertainty* (Cambridge), 1–7.
—— and O'SHEA, J. (1989b), 'Conclusion: Bad Year Economics', in *Bad Year Economics: Cultural Responses to Risk and Uncertainty* (Cambridge), 123–6.
HAMMOND, N. (1967), *Epirus: The Geography, the Ancient Remains, the History, and the Topography of Epirus and Adjacent Areas* (Oxford).
HANSEN, M. H. (1985), 'Two Notes on the Pnyx', *GRBS* 26: 129–35.
—— (1989), *The Athenian Ekklesia*, ii: *A Collection of Articles 1983–9* (Copenhagen).
—— (1991), *The Athenian Democracy in the Age of Demosthenes: Structure, Principles and Ideology* (Oxford).
HANSON, A. (1991), 'Continuity and Change: Three Case Studies in Hippocratic Gynaecological Therapy and Theory', in S. Pomeroy (ed.), *Women's History and Ancient History* (Chapel Hill), 48–110.
HARRIS, E. (1994), 'Law and Oratory', in Ian Worthington (ed.), *Persuasion: Greek Rhetoric in Action* (London), 130–50.

Harris, M. (1968), *The Rise of Anthropological Theory* (London), 568–604.
Harrison, A. R. W. (1968), *The Law of Athens: The Family and Property* (Oxford).
—— (1971), *The Law of Athens*, vols. i and ii (Oxford).
Harrison, T. (2000), *Divinity and History: The Religion of Herodotus* (Oxford).
Hart, H. L. A. (1994), *The Concept of Law* (Oxford).
Harvey, D. (1990), 'The Sykophant and Sykophancy: Vexatious Redefinition', in P. Cartledge, P. Millett, and S. Todd (eds.), *Nomos: Essays in Athenian Law, Politics and Society* (Cambridge), 103–22.
Hasebroek, J. (1928), *Staat und Handel im alten Griechenland* (Tübingen), trans. L. M. Fraser and D. C. McGregor (1933), as *Trade and Politics in Ancient Greece* (London).
Hatzopoulos, M. B., and Mari, M. (2004), 'Dion et Dodone', in P. Cabanes (ed.), *L'Illyrie Méridionale et l'Épire dans l'Antiquité*, 3: *Actes du IVe Colloque International de Clermont-Ferrand*, 10–12 Octobre 2002 (Paris), 505–13.
Haussoullier, B. (1905), 'Offrande à Apollon Didyméen', *Mém. de la Délég. en Perse*, 2nd ser. vol. 7, ed. J. de Morgan (Paris).
Hawley, R., and Levick, B. (1995), *Women in Antiquity: New Assessments* (London).
Hermary, A., Cassimatis, H., and Vollkommer, R. (1986), 'Eros', in *Lexicon Iconographicum Mythologiae Classicae*, 3: 850–942.
Hoffiller, V., and Saria, B. (1938), *Antike Inschriften aus Jugoslavien*, i (Zagreb), 526.
Hoffman, G. (1999), 'De La Politeia des Femmes en Épire et en Attique', in P. Cabanes (ed.), *L'Illyrie Méridionale et l'Épire dans l'Antiquité*, 3: *Actes du IIIe Colloque International de Clermont-Ferrand*, 16–19 Octobre 1996 (Paris).
Homolle, T. (1901), 'Inscriptions d'Amorgos', *BCH* 25: 412–30.
Hopkins, K. (1965), 'Contraception in the Roman Empire', *Comparative Studies in Society and History*, 8: 124–57.
Horden, P., and Purcell, N. (2000), *The Corrupting Sea: A Study of Mediterranean History* (Oxford).
Hornblower, S. (1982), *Mausolus* (Oxford).
—— (2005), *Thucydides and Pindar: Historical Narrative and the World of Epinikian Poetry* (Oxford).
—— and Spawforth, A. (1999) (eds.), *The Oxford Classical Dictionary*, 3rd edn. (Oxford).
Humphreys, S. C. (1978), *Anthropology and the Greeks* (London).
—— (1985), 'Social Relations on Stage: Witnesses in Classical Athens', *History and Anthropology*, 1: 313–69.
—— (1986), 'Kinship Patterns in the Athenian Courts', *GRBS* 27: 57–91.
—— (1993), *The Family, Women and Death* (Michigan).
Hunter, V. (1989), 'Women's Authority in Classical Athens', in *Echos du Monde Classique/Classical Views*, 8 (1): 39–48.
Hunter, V. (1994), *Policing Athens: Social Control in the Attic Lawsuits, 420–320B.C.* (Princeton).

HUPPERTS, Ch. A. M. (1988), 'Greek Love: Homosexuality or Paederasty? Greek Love in Black-Figure Vase-painting', in J. Christiansen and T. Melander (eds.), *Proceedings of the 3rd Symposion on Ancient Greek and Related Pottery* (Copenhagen).
ISAGER, S., and HANSEN, M. H. (1975), *Aspects of Athenian Society in the Fourth Century* (Odense).
JACKSON, M. (1978), 'An Approach to Kuranko Divination', *Human Relations*, 31 (2): 117–38.
JACQUEMIN, A. (1995), 'Ordre des Termes des Dédicaces Delphiques', *Annali di Archeologia e Storia Antica*, 2: 141–57.
—— (1999), *Offrandes Monumentales à Delphes* (Athens: École Française d'Athènes).
JAMES, A., HOCKEY, J. L., and DAWSON, A. H. (1997), *After Writing Culture: Epistemology and Praxis in Contemporary Anthropology* (London).
JAMESON, M. H. (1983), 'Famine in the Greek World', in P. Garnsey and C. R. Whittaker (eds.), *Trade and Famine in Classical Antiquity*, Cambridge Philological Society Supplementary Volume viii: 6–16.
—— (1991), 'Sacrifice before Battle', in Victor Davis Hanson (ed.), *Hoplites: The Classical Greek Battle Experience* (London), 197–227.
—— JORDAN D., and KOTANSKY, D. (1993), 'A *Lex Sacra* from Selinous', *Greek, Roman and Byzantine Monographs* (Durham, NC).
JANKO, R. (2002), 'The Derveni Papyrus: An Interim Text', *ZPE* 141: 1–62.
JEFFERY, L. H. (1955), 'Further Comments on Archaic Greek Inscriptions', *BSA* 50: 67–84.
—— (1990), *The Local Scripts of Archaic Greece*, rev. edn. with a supplement by A. W. Johnston (Oxford).
JOHNSTON, SARAH ILES (1999), *Restless Dead: Encounters between the Living and the Dead in Ancient Greece* (Berkeley).
—— (2004) (ed.), *Religions of the Ancient World: A Guide* (Harvard).
JONES, H. L. (2001) (trans.), *Strabo: Geography, Books 6–7* (Cambridge, Mass.).
JONES, N. F. (1999), *The Associations of Classical Athens: The Response to Democracy* (Oxford).
JORDAN, D. R. (1980), 'Two Inscribed Lead Tablets from a Well in the Athenian Kerameikos', *MDAI(A)* 95: 225–39.
—— (1985), 'Fourteen Defixiones from a Well in the SW Corner of the Athenian Agora', *Hesperia*, 54: 205–55.
—— (1987), 'A Greek Defixio at Brussels', *Mnemosyne* 162–7.
—— (1988), 'New Archaeological Evidence for the Practice of Magic in Classical Athens', in *Praktika of the 12th International Congress of Classical Archaeology, Athens, 4–10 September 1983*, vol. 4: 273–77.
—— (1995), 'A Curse Tablet Against Opponents at Law', in A. L. Boegehold (ed.), *The Lawcourts at Athens: Sites, Buildings, Equipment, Procedure and Testimonia* (Princeton), 55–7.
—— (1997a), Πρώιμη Γραφή ως Μαγεία in D. Jordan and A. Ph. Christidis (eds.) Γλώσσα καί Μαγεία. Κείμενα από την Αρχαιότητα (Athens).
—— (1997b), 'Two Curses from Lilybaeum', *GRBS* 40: 387–96.

—— (1999), 'Three Curse Tablets', in D. R. Jordan, H. Montgomery, and E. Thomassen (eds.), *The World of Ancient Magic: Papers from the First International Samson Eitrem Seminar at the Norwegian Institute at Athens, 4–8 May 1997* (Bergen), 115–24.

—— (2000), 'Three Texts from Lokroi Epizephyrioi', *ZPE* 130: 95–103.

—— (2002), 'Towards the Text of a Curse Tablet from the Kerameikos', in A. P. Matthaiou (ed.), Ἀττικαί Ἐπιγραφαί: Πρακτικά Συμποσίου εἰς Μνημην Adolf Wilhelm (1864–1950) (Athens), 291–312.

—— (forthcoming), 'A Curse Tablet Addressing Palaimon', in A. Kaloyeropoulou (ed.), Το Ἱεροόν του Παγκράτου (Athens).

—— and ROTROFF, S. I. (1999), 'A Curse in a Chytridion: A Contribution to the Study of Athenian Pyres', *Hesperia*, 68: 147–54.

JOUAN, F. (1990), 'L'Oracle, Thérapeutique de l'Angoisse', *Kernos*, 3: 11–28.

JUST, R. (1989), *Women in Athenian Law and Life* (London).

KAGAROW, E. G. (1929), 'Griechische Fluchtafeln', *Eos Supplementa*, 4 (Leopoli).

KAMBITSIS, S. (1976), 'Une Nouvelle Tablette Magique d'Égypte, Musée du Louvre, Inv. E 27145, 3e/4e siècle', *Bulletin de l'Institut Français d'Archéologie Orientale* (Cairo), 76: 213–23.

KAMPEN, N. (1996) (ed.), *Sexuality in Ancient Art* (New York).

KAPROW, M. (1985), 'Manufacturing Danger: Fear and Pollution in Industrial Society', *American Anthropologist*, 87 (2) June, 342–56.

KARAPANOS, C. (1878), *Dodone et ses Ruines* (Paris).

—— (1890), 'Dodone. Inscriptions de l'Oracle et Statuettes', *BCH* 14: 115–61.

KATZ, M. (1995), 'Ideology and "the Status of Women" in Ancient Greece', in R. Hawley and B. Levick (eds.), *Women in Antiquity: New Assessments* (London), 21–43.

KEKULE VON STRADONITZ, R., and WINNEFELD, H. (1909), *Bronzen aus Dodona in den Königlichen Museen zu Berlin* (Berlin).

KENNEDY, B. H. (1994), *A New History of Classical Rhetoric* (Princeton).

KEULS, E. C. (1985), *The Reign of the Phallus* (Berkeley).

KNIGHT, F. (1921), *Risk, Uncertainty, and Profit* (Cambridge, Mass.).

KOCK, K. T. (1880–8) (ed.), *Comicorum Atticorum Fragmenta*, 2 vols. [in 3] (Leipzig).

KONSTAN, D. (2001), 'Before Jealousy', in D. Konstan and N. K. Rutter (eds.), *Envy, Spite and Jealousy: The Rivalrous Emotions in Ancient Greece* (Edinburgh), 7–28.

KOTANSKY, R. (1991), 'Incantations and Prayers for Salvation on Inscribed Greek Amulets', in C. Faraone and D. Obbink, *Magika Hiera: Ancient Greek Magic and Religion* (Oxford), 107–37.

KÜHN, K. G. (1821–33) (ed.), *Claudii Galeni Opera Omnia. Medicorum Graecorum opera quae extant*, vol. 20 (Leipzig; repr. Hildesheim, 1964–9).

KUHN, T. S. (1977), *Essential Tensions* (Chicago).

KURKE, L. (1998), 'The Cultural Impact on (of) Democracy: Decentering Tragedy', in I. Morris and K. A. Raaflaub (eds.), *Democracy 2500? Questions and Challenges* (Dubuque, Ia.), 155–69.

LANE FOX, R. (1986), *Pagans and Christians* (San Francisco).

LANNI, A. M. (1997), 'Spectator Sport or Serious Politics? οἱ περιεστηκότες and the Athenian Lawcourts', *JHS* 117: 183–9.
LATTE, K. (1940), 'The Coming of the Pythia', *Harv. Theol. Rev.* 33: 9–18.
LAZZARINI, M. L. (1994), 'Una Nuova *Defixio* Greca da Tiriolo', in A. C. Cassio and P. Poccetti (eds.), *Forme di Religiosità e Tradizioni Sapienzali in Magna Grecia. Atti di Convegno, Napoli 14–15 Dicembre 1993* (Pisa and Rome), 163–9.
LECHAT, H. (1889), 'Inscription Imprécatoire Trouvée à Athènes', *BCH* 13: 77–80.
LEONARD, H. (1917–23, repr. 1988–9), *The Geography of Strabo* (Harvard).
LEVI, G. (1997), 'On Microhistory', in P. Burke (ed.), *New Perspectives on Historical Writing* (Cambridge), 93–113.
LEWIS, D. M. (1959), 'Attic Manumissions', *Hesperia*, 28: 208–38.
LIDONNICI, L. R. (1995), *The Epidaurian Miracle Inscriptions* (Atlanta).
LIENHARDT, G. (1956), 'Religion', in H. Shapiro (ed.), *Man, Culture and Society* (London; rev. edn. 1971), 382–401.
LLOYD, G. E. R. (1999*a*), *Science, Folklore and Ideology* (Bristol).
—— (1999*b*), *Magic, Religion and Experience* (Bristol).
—— (2003), *In the Grip of Disease: Studies in the Greek Imagination* (Oxford).
LLOYD-JONES, H. (1976), 'The Delphic Oracle', *G&R* 23: 60–73.
LOOMIS, W. T. (1995), 'Pay Differentials and Class Warfare in Lysias' *Against Theozotides*: Two Obols or Two Drachmas?', *ZPE* 107: 230–6.
LOPEZ-JIMENO, MARIA DEL AMOR (1991), *Las Tabellae Defixionis de la Sicilia Griega* (Amsterdam).
—— (1999), *Nuevas Tabellae Defixionis Aticas* (Amsterdam).
LOPORTO, F. G. (1980), 'Medici Pitagorici in una Defixio Greca da Metaponto', *La Parola del Passato*, 35: 282–8.
LOWE, N. (2000), *The Classical Plot and the Invention of Western Narrative* (Cambridge).
LUHMANN, N. (1993), *Risk: A Sociological Theory* (New York).
LUHRMANN, T. (1989), *Persuasions of the Witch's Craft: Ritual Magic and Witchcraft in Present-Day England* (Oxford).
LUPTON, D. (1999), *Risk* (London).
MACDOWELL, D. M. (1963), *Athenian Homicide Law* (Manchester).
—— (1978), *The Law in Classical Athens* (London).
MAEHLER, H. (1987), *Pindari Carmina cum Fragmentis* (Leipzig).
—— (1989), *Pindari Carmina cum Fragmentis, Pars II* (Leipzig).
MCKECHNIE, PAUL R. (1989), *Outsiders in the Greek Cities in the Fourth Century BC* (London).
MALINOWSKI, B. (1922), *Argonauts of the Western Pacific* (London).
—— (1967), *A Diary in the Strict Sense of the Term* (London).
MALKIN, I. (1987), *Religion and Colonisation in Ancient Greece* (London).
MARCUS, GEORGE E., and FISCHER, MICHAEL M. J. (1999), *Anthropology as Cultural Critique* (Chicago).
MARTINEZ, D. (1995), '"May she neither eat nor drink": Love Magic and Vows of Abstinence', in M. Meyer and P. Mirecki (eds.), *Ancient Magic and Ritual Power* (Leiden) 335–60.

MARWICK, M. (1982), *Witchcraft and Sorcery: Selected Readings* (London).
MAURIZIO, L. (1995), 'Anthropology and Spirit Possession: A Reconsideration of the Pythia's Role at Delphi', *JHS* 115: 69–86.
MEIGGS, R. (1972), *The Athenian Empire* (Oxford).
MEYER, M., and MIRECKI, P. (1995), 'Ancient Magic and Ritual Power', *Religions in the Graeco-Roman World*, vol. 129 (Leiden and New York).
—— (2002), 'Magic and Ritual in the Ancient World', *Religions in the Graeco-Roman World*, vol. 141 (Leiden).
MILLER, A. P. (1973), 'Studies in Early Sicilian Epigraphy: An Opisthographic Lead Tablet' (Ph.D. diss. University of North Carolina, Chapel Hill), no. 36.
MILLER, S. G. (1980), 'Excavations at Nemea: 1979', *Hesperia*, 49: 196–7.
—— (1981), 'Excavations at Nemea: 1980', *Hesperia*, 50: 60–4.
MILLETT, P. (1983), 'Maritime Loans and the Structure of Credit in Fourth Century Athens', in P. Garnsey, K. Hopkins, and C. R. Whittaker, *Trade in the Ancient Economy* (London), 36–52.
—— (1991), *Lending and Borrowing in Ancient Athens* (Cambridge).
MORAND, A.-F. (2001), *Etudes sur les Hymnes Orphiques* (Leiden).
MORAUX, P. (1960), 'Une Défixion Judiciaire au Musée d'Istanbul', *Acad. Roy. Belg. Mém.* 54 (2) (Brussels), 3–61.
MORETTI, L. (1967) (ed.), *Iscrizioni Storiche Ellenistiche*, i: *Attica, Peloponneso, Beozia: Testo, Traduzione e Commento* (Florence).
MORGAN, C. (1989), 'Divination and Society at Delphi and Didyma', *Hermathena*, 147: 17–42.
—— (1990), *Athletes and Oracles* (Cambridge).
MORSTEIN-MARX, R. (2004), *Mass Oratory and Political Power in the Late Roman Republic* (Cambridge).
MUCHEMBLED, R. (1985), *Popular Culture and Elite Culture in France, 1400–1750* (Baton Rouge).
NABERS, N. (1966), 'Lead Tabellae from Morgantina', *AJArch.* 70: 67–8.
—— (1979), 'Ten Lead Tabellae from Morgantina', *AJArch.* 83: 463–4.
NAFISSI, M. (1995), 'La Religione della *Pólis* al di Fuori del suo Territorio, n. 8 Zeus (Dodona)' in 'Parte Terza: La Documentazione Letteraria ed Epigrafica' of E. Lippolis, S. Garraffo, and M. Nafissi (eds.), *Culti Greci Occidente*, i: Taranto (Taranto), 155–335.
NAUCK, A. (1926), *Tragicorum Graecorum Fragmenta* (Leipzig).
NEEDHAM, R. (1972), 'Polythetic Classification: Convergence and Consequences', *Man*, 10: 349–69.
—— (1980), *Reconnaissances* (Toronto).
NEILS, J. (2000), 'Others within the Other: An Intimate Look at Hetairai and Maenads', in B. Cohen (ed.), *Not the Classical Ideal: Athens and the Construction of the Other in Greek Art* (Leiden), 203–26.
NEWTON, C. T. (1862–3), *A History of Discoveries at Halicarnassus, Cnidus and Branchidae* (London).

NIETO, F. (1989) (ed.), *Symposion 1982: Vorträge zur Griechischen und Hellenistischen Rechtsgeschichte* (Cologne and Vienna).

NIXON, L., and PRICE, S. (1990), 'The Size and Resources of Greek Cities', in O. Murray and S. Price (eds.), *The Greek City from Homer to Alexander* (Oxford), 137–70.

NOBLE, V. (1965), *Techniques of Painted Attic Pottery* (New York).

OAKLEY, J. H. (2004), *Picturing Death in Classical Athens: The Evidence of the White Lekythoi* (Cambridge).

OBER, J. (1989), *Mass and Elite in Democratic Athens* (Princeton).

—— (1994), 'Power and Oratory in Democratic Athens: Demosthenes 21, Against Meidias', in I. Worthington (ed.), *Persuasion: Greek Rhetoric in Action* (London), 85–108.

OGDEN, D. (1996), *Greek Bastardy in the Classical and Hellenistic Periods* (Oxford).

—— (1999), 'Binding Spells: Curse Tablets and Voodoo Dolls', in B. Ankarloo and S. Clark (eds.), *Witchcraft and Magic in Europe,* ii: *Ancient Greece and Rome* (London), 1–90.

—— (2001), *Greek and Roman Necromancy* (Princeton).

OMITOWOJU, R. (2002), *Rape and the Politics of Consent in Classical Athens* (Cambridge).

ONIANS, J. (1979), *Art and Thought in the Hellenistic Age* (London).

OSBORNE, M. J. (1981, 1982), *Naturalisation in Athens* (Brussels), i. 43–51 and ii. 45–8.

—— and BYRNE, S. G. (1996), *The Foreign Residents of Athens, An Annex to the Lexicon of Greek Personal Names: Attica*, Studia Hellenistica, 33 (Louvain).

OSBORNE, R. (1985), 'Law in Action in Classical Athens', *JHS* 105: 40–58.

—— (1987), *Classical Landscape with Figures* (London).

—— (1990), 'Vexatious Litigation in Classical Athens: Sykophancy and the Sykophant', in P. Cartledge, P. Millett, and S. Todd (eds.), *Nomos: Essays in Athenian Law, Politics and Society* (Cambridge), 83–102.

—— (1991), 'Pride and Prejudice, Sense and Subsistence: Exchange and Society in the Greek City', in J. Rich and A. Wallace-Hadrill (eds.), *City and Country in the Ancient World* (London), 119–45.

—— (1994), 'Looking on Greek Style: Does the Sculpted Girl Speak to Women Too?', in I. Morris (ed.), *Classical Greece: Ancient Histories and Modern Archaeologies* (Cambridge), 81–96.

—— (1996), *Greece in the Making: 1200–479 BC, the Greek City under Construction* (London).

—— (1998), *Archaic and Classical Greek Art* (Oxford).

—— (2000), 'Religion, Imperial Politics and the Offering of Freedom to Slaves', in V. Hunter and J. Edmondson (eds.), *Law and Social Status in Classical Athens* (Oxford), 75–92.

—— and HORNBLOWER, S. (1994), *Ritual, Finance, and Politics: Athenian Democratic Accounts Presented to David Lewis* (Oxford).

PARKE, H. W. (1939), *A History of the Delphic Oracle* (Oxford).
—— (1967a), *The Oracles of Zeus* (Oxford).
—— (1967b), *Greek Oracles* (Oxford).
—— (1967c), 'Three New Enquiries from Dodona', *JHS* 87: 132–3.
—— (1976), 'The Problem of an Oracle in Heraclides Ponticus', *Hermathena*, 120.
—— (1985), *The Oracles of Apollo in Asia Minor* (London).
——, and WORMELL, D. E. (1956a), *The Delphic Oracle vol. 1: The History* (Oxford).
—— —— (1956b), *The Delphic Oracle vol. 2: The Oracular Responses* (Oxford).
PARKER, H. N. (1992), 'Love's Body Anatomized: The Ancient Erotic Handbooks and the Rhetoric of Sexuality', in A. Richlin (ed.), *Pornography and Representation in Greece and Rome* (Oxford) 90–111.
PARKER, R. (1983), *Miasma* (Oxford).
—— (1985), 'Greek States and Greek Oracles', in P. Cartledge and D. Harvey (eds.), *Crux: Essays in Greek History Presented to G. E. M. de Ste. Croix* (London), 298–326.
—— (1995), 'Early Orphism', in A. Powell (ed.), *The Greek World* (London), 483–510.
—— (1996), *Athenian Religion: A History* (Oxford).
—— (2005a), 'ὡς ἥρωι ἐναγίζειν', in R. Hägg and B. Alroth (eds.), *Greek Sacrificial Ritual, Olympian and Chthonian. Proceedings of the Sixth International Seminar on Ancient Greek Cult, organized by the Department of Classical Archaeology and Ancient History, Göteborg University, 25–27 April 1997* (Stockholm) 37–45.
—— (2005b), *Polytheism and Society at Athens* (Oxford).
PATON, W. R. (1916–18), *The Greek Anthology*, 5 vols. (London).
PEEK, PHILIP M. (1991), *African Divination Systems: Ways of Knowing* (Bloomington).
PEEK, W. (1941), 'Inschriften, Ostraka, Fluchtafeln', *Kerameikos: Ergebnisse der Ausgrabungen*, 3 (Berlin), 87–100.
—— (1942), 'Attische Inschriften', *Ath. Mitt.* 67: 166 ff.
—— (1957), 'Attische Grabschriften, II: Unedierte Grabinschriften aus Athen und Attika', *Abhandlungen der Deutschen Akademie der Wissenschaften zu Berlin, Klasse für Sprachen, Literatur und Kunst* 1956, no. 3.
—— (1978), 'Orakel aus Dodona für den Piratenkönig Zeniketes', *ZPE* 30: 247–8.
PETRAKOS, V. (1997), 'Οι επιγραφές του Ωρωπού' (Athens).
PETROPOULOS, J. (1988), 'The Erotic Magical Papyri', *Proceedings of the XVIII International Congress of Papyrology*, vol. 2 (Athens) 215–22.
PFEIFFER, R. (1949, 1953), *Callimachus Edidit Rudolfus Pfeiffer*, vols. 1–2 (Oxford).
PHARMAKOWSKY, B. (1907), 'Archäologische Funde im Jahre 1906', *Arch. Anz.* 22: 126–8.
PICKARD-CAMBRIDGE, A. W. (1988), *The Dramatic Festivals of Athens*, 2nd edn. rev. J. Gould and D. M. Lewis (Oxford).
PLEKET, H. W. (1969), *Epigraphica*, ii: *Texts on the Social History of the Greek World* (Leiden).

POLLITT, J. J. (1972), *Art and Experience in Classical Greece* (Cambridge).
—— (1986), *Art in the Hellenistic Age* (Cambridge).
POMEROY, S. (1975), *Goddesses, Whores, Wives and Slaves: Women in Classical Antiquity* (New York).
POUILLOUX, J. (1976), 'Les inscriptions de la Terrasse du Temple et de la Région Nord du Sanctuaire', *Fouilles de Delphes*, vol. 3, pt. 4 (Paris).
POWELL, J. U. (1925), *Collectanea Alexandrina* (Oxford), 68–71.
PREISENDANZ, K. (1972), 'Fluchtafel (Defixion)', *RAC* 8: 1–29.
PRICE, S. (1985), 'Delphi and Divination', in P. E. Easterling and J. V. Muir (eds.), *Greek Religion and Society* (Cambridge), 128–54.
—— (1999), *Religions of the Ancient Greeks* (Cambridge).
RADERMACHER, L. (1951), 'Artium Scriptores (Reste der Voraristotelischen Rhetorik)', *Österreichische Akademie der Wissenschaften*, 227: 3.
REDDY, S. (1996), 'Claims to Expert Knowledge and the Subversion of Democracy: The Triumph of Risk over Uncertainty', *Economy and Society*, 25 (2): 222–54.
REED, C. M. (2003), *Maritime Traders in the Ancient World* (Cambridge).
REYNOLDS WHYTE, S. (1997), 'Questioning Misfortune: The Pragmatics of Uncertainty in Eastern Uganda', *Cambridge Studies in Medieval Anthropology*.
RHODES, P. J. (1980), 'Athenian Democracy after 403 BC', *CJ* 75: 305–23.
—— (1981), *A Commentary on the* Athenaion Politeia (Oxford).
—— (1986), 'Political Activity in Classical Athens', *JHS* 106: 132–44.
—— and LEWIS, D. M. (1996), 'Vetting Procedures and the Law Courts', in *The Decrees of the Greek States* (Oxford), 34.
—— and OSBORNE R. (2003), *Greek Historical Inscriptions 404–323 BCE* (Oxford).
RIBEZZO, F. (1927) (ed.), 'Defissioni greche di Sicilia', *Rivista Indo-Greco-Italica di Filologia, Lingua, Antichità*, 11, fasc. I–II, 147.
RICHLIN, A. (1991), 'Zeus and Metis: Foucault, Feminism, Classics', *Helios*, 18: 160–80.
—— (1992a) (ed.), *Pornography and Representation in Greece and Rome* (Oxford).
—— (1992b), 'Introduction' and 'Foucault's *History* of Sexuality: A Useful Theory for Women', in A. Richlin (ed.), *Pornography and Representation in Greece and Rome* (Oxford), 1–13 and 112–70.
ROBERT, L. (1936), *Collection Froehner*, i: *Inscr. Gr.* (Paris).
—— (1954), *Les Fouilles de Claros: Conférence Donnée l'Université d'Ankara le 26 Octobre 1953 sous les Auspices de la Société Turque d'Histoire* (Paris).
—— (1959), Review of T. Wiegand, *Didyma 2 Teil: Die Inschriften*, Bearb. von Albert Rehm, *Gnomon*, 31: 657–74.
—— (1967), 'Sur des Inscriptions d'Ephèse: fêtes, athlètes, empereurs, épigrammes' *Rev. Phil.* 7–84.
—— (1968), 'Trois Oracles de la Théosophie et un Prophète d'Apollon', *CR Acad. Inscr.* 568–99.
—— (1973), 'Xenion' *OMS* 5: 137–54.
—— (1979–80), 'Athenian Democracy after 403 BC', *CJ* 75: 305–23.

—— (1981), 'Amulettes Grecques', *Journ. Sav.* 3–44.
—— and ROBERT, J. (1989), *Claros*, i: *Décrets Hellénistiques* (Paris).
ROESCH, P. (1966–7), 'Une Tablette de Malédiction de Tébessa', *Bulletin d'Archéologie Algérienne*, 2: 231–7.
ROSE, V. (1886) (ed.), *Aristotelis qui Ferebantur Librorum Fragmenta* (Lipsiae).
RUBINSTEIN, L. (2000), *Litigation and Cooperation: Supporting Speakers in the Courts of Classical Athens* (Stuttgart).
RUSCHENBUSCH, E. (1989), 'Drei Beiträge zur Öffentlichen Diaita in Athen', in F. Nieto (ed.), *Symposion 1982: Vorträge zur Griechischen und Hellenistischen Rechtsgeschichte* (Cologne and Vienna), 31–40.
RZACH, A. (1913) (ed.), *Hesiodi Carmina* (Leipzig).
SALVIAT, F. (1993), 'Timodamos et son Gaulos, Oracles et Marchands à Dodone', in P. Cabanes (ed.), *L'Illyrie Méridionale et l'Épire dans l'Antiquité*, 2: *Actes du IIe Colloque International de Clermont-Ferrand, 25–27 Octobre 1990* (Paris), 61–4.
SCHACHTER, A. (1976), 'Homeric Hymn to Apollo, ll. 231–238 (The Onchestos Episode): Another Interpretation', *BICS* 23: 102–14.
—— (1981), *Cults of Boeotia*, vols. 1–3 (London).
—— (1994), 'The Politics of Dedication: Two Athenian Dedications at the Sanctuary of Apollo Ptoieus in Boeotia', in R. Osborne and S. Hornblower (eds.), *Ritual, Finance, and Politics: Athenian Democratic Accounts Presented to David Lewis* (Oxford), 291–306.
SCHAPS, D. (1977), 'The Woman Least Mentioned: Etiquette and Women's Names', *CQ* 27: 323–30.
—— (1979), *Economic Rights of Women in Ancient Greece* (Edinburgh).
SCHELER, M. (1998), *Ressentiment*, trans. Lewis B. Coser and William W. Holdheim (Wisconsin).
SCHLÖRB-VIERNEISEL, B. (1964), 'Zwei Klassische Kindergräber im Kerameikos', *MDAI(A)* 79: 85–113.
SCHWYZER, E. (1924), 'Zu Griechischen Inschriften', *Rh. Mus.* 73: 426–9.
SCOTT-KILVERT, I. (1979) (trans.), *Polybius: The Rise of the Roman Empire* (London).
SCULLION, S. (1994), 'Olympian and Chthonian', *CA* 13 (1): 75–199.
SEAFORD, R. (1994), *Reciprocity and Ritual* (Oxford).
SEALEY, R. (1984), 'On Lawful Concubinage in Athens', *CA* 3: 111–33.
—— (1990), *Women and Law in Classical Greece* (Chapel Hill).
SEGRÈ, F. (1980), *From X-rays to Quarks* (San Francisco).
SHAPIRO, H. (1956) (ed.), *Man, Culture and Society* (London; rev. edn. 1971).
—— (1981), 'Courtship Scenes in Attic Vase-Painting', *AJArch.* 85: 133–43.
—— (1990), 'Oracle-Mongers in Peisistratid Athens', *Kernos*, 3: 335–45.
—— (1992), 'Eros in Love: Pederasty and Pornography in Greece', in A. Richlin (ed.), *Pornography and Representation in Greece and Rome* (Oxford), 53–72.
SIMON, E. (1986), 'Dione', in *Lexicon Iconographicum Mythologiae Classicae*, 3: 411–13.

SIMON, E. (1989) (ed.), *Die Sammlung Kiseleff im Martin-von-Wagner-Museum der Universität Würzburg*, 2: *Minoische und griechische Antiken* (Mainz).
SINCLAIR, R. K. (1988), *Democracy and Participation in Athens* (Cambridge).
SLOVIC, P. (2000), *The Perception of Risk* (London).
SMITH, JONATHAN Z. (1978), 'Map is not Territory: Studies in the History of Religions', *Studies in Judaism in Late Antiquity*, vol. 23 (Leiden).
SMITH, N. D. (1989), 'Diviners and Divination in Aristophanic Comedy', *CA* 8 (1): 140.
SNOEK, J. A. M. (1987), *Initiations: A Methodological Approach to the Application of Classification and Definition Theory in the Study of Rituals* (diss. Leiden).
SNYDER, J. M. (1989), *The Woman and the Lyre* (Bristol).
SOKOLOWSKI, F. (1949), 'Sur un Passage de la Convention Delphes-Skiathos. Mélanges Charles Picard', *Revue Archéologique*, 31/32: 981–4.
SOMMERSTEIN, A. H. (1980), *Acharnians*, edited with Translation and Notes (Warminster).
—— (1987), *Birds* (Warminster).
—— (1989) (ed.), *Eumenides by Aeschylus* (Cambridge).
—— (1996), 'Aeschylus', in S. Hornblower and A. Spawforth (eds.), *Oxford Classical Dictionary*, 3rd edn. (Oxford).
SOURVINOU-INWOOD, C. (1991), *Reading Greek Culture* (Oxford).
—— (1995), *Reading Greek Death* (Oxford).
STADTMÜLLER, H. (1894–1906), *Anthologia Graeca*, vol. i (Leipzig).
STEWART, C. (1991), *Demons and the Devil* (Princeton).
STILLWELL, R. (1976) (ed.), *The Princeton Encyclopedia of Classical Sites* (Princeton).
STONE, L. (1987), *The Past and the Present Revisited* (London and Boston).
STRAUSS, B. S. (1985), 'Ritual, Social Drama and Politics in Classical Athens', *AJAH* 10: 73.
STROUD, R. (1971), 'Greek Inscriptions: Theozotides and the Athenian Orphans', *Hesperia*, 40: 280–301.
STRUBBE, J. H. M. (1991), 'Cursed be he that Moves my Bones', in C. Faraone and D. Obbink (eds.), *Magika Hiera: Ancient Greek Magic and Religion* (Oxford), 33–60.
STRȲD, J. H. W. (1903), '*Ἀττικὰ μετ' Ἀρῶν Μολύβδινα Ἐλάσματα*', *Ἀρχ. Ἐφ*. 55–60.
SUTTON ROBERT, F. Jr. (1992), 'Pornography and Persuasion on Attic Pottery', in A. Richlin (ed.), *Pornography and Representation in Greece and Rome* (Oxford), 3–35.
TAMBIAH, S. J. (1968), 'The Magical Power of Words', *Man*, 3: 175–208.
—— (1973), 'Form and Meaning of Magical Acts', in R. Horton and R. Finnegan (eds.), *Modes of Thought: Essays on Thinking in Western and Non-Western Societies* (London), 199–229.
TARTARON, T. F. (2004), 'Bronze Age Landscape and Society in Southern Epirus, Greece', *BAR Internationl Series* 1290 (Oxford).
THOMAS, R. (1992), *Literacy and Orality in Ancient Greece* (Cambridge).
—— (2000), *Herodotus in Context* (Cambridge).

THOMPSON, H. A., and WYCHERLEY, R. E. (1972), 'The Agora of Athens', in *The Athenian Agora*, vol. 14 (Princeton).

THÜR, G. (1977), *Beweisführung vor den Schwurgerichtshöfen Athens: Die* Proklesis zur Basanos (Vienna).

TODD, S. (1990), 'The Purpose of Evidence in Athenian Courts', in P. Cartledge, P. Millett, and S. Todd (eds.), *Nomos: Essays in Athenian Law, Politics and Society* (Cambridge), 19–39.

—— (1993), *The Shape of Athenian Law* (Oxford).

—— and MILLETT, P. (1990), 'Law, Society and Athens', in P. Cartledge, P. Millett, and S. Todd (eds.), *Nomos: Essays in Athenian Law, Politics and Society* (Cambridge), 1–18.

TODISCO, L. (2002), *Teatro e Spettacolo in Magna Graecia e Sicilia: Testi, Immagini, Architettura* (Milan).

TOMLIN, R. S. O. (1988), 'Tabellae Sulis: Roman Inscribed Tablets of Tin and Lead from the Sacred Spring at Bath', *Monograph (University of Oxford. Committee for Archaeology)*, no. 16, fasc. 1 (Oxford).

TOWNSEND, R. F. (1995), 'The East Side of the Agora: The Remains beneath the Stoa of Attalos', in *The Athenian Agora*, vol. 27 (Princeton).

TRAVLOS, J. (1974), 'The Law Court ΕΠΙ ΠΑΛΛΑΔΙΩΙ', *Hesperia*, 43: 500–11.

TREDENNICK, H., and WATERFIELD, R. (1990) (trans.), *Xenophon: Conversations of Socrates* (London).

TRENDALL, A. D. (1991), 'Farce and Tragedy in South Italian Vase Painting', in T. Rasmussen and N. Spivey, *Looking at Greek Vases* (Cambridge), 151–82.

TRUMPF, J. (1958), 'Fluchtafel und Rachpuppe', *MDAI(A)* 73: 94–102.

TYLOR, E. B. (1871), *Primitive Culture*, 2 vols. (Gloucester, Mass.).

TZOUVARA-SOULI, C. (1993), 'Common Cults in Epirus and Albania', in P. Cabanes (ed.), *L'Illyrie Méridionale et l'Épire dans l'Antiquité*, 2: *Actes du IIe Colloque International de Clermont-Ferrand*, 25–27 Octobre 1990 (Paris), 65–82.

—— (2004), 'The Cult of Zeus in Ancient Epirus', in P. Cabanes (ed.), *L'Illyrie Méridionale et l'Épire dans l'Antiquité*, 4: *Actes du IVe Colloque International de Clermont-Ferrand*, 10–12 Octobre 2002 (Paris), 515–42.

VAN BREMEN, R. (1983), 'Women and Wealth', in A. Cameron and A. Kuhrt (eds.), *Images of Women in Antiquity* (London), 223–42.

VAN DER EIJK, P. J., HORSTMANSHOFF, H. F. J., and SCHRIJVERS, P. H. (1995), *Ancient Medicine in its Socio-Cultural Context* (Atlanta).

VAN DER VALK, M. (1979) (ed.), *Eustathii Archiepiscopi Thessalonicensis Commentarii ad Homeri Iliadem Pertinentes*, vol. iii (Brill).

VAN STRATEN, F. T. (1976), 'Daikrates' Dream', *BABesch*. 51: 1–38.

VERNANT, J.-P. (1974), 'Paroles et Signes Muets', in J.-P. Vernant *et al.* (eds.), *Divination et Rationalité* (Paris), 9–25.

—— (1991), *Mortals and Immortals: Collected Essays* (Princeton), 303–17.

VERSNEL, H. (1985), '"May he not be Able to Sacrifice": Concerning a Curious Formula in Greek and Latin Curses', *ZPE* 58: 247–69.

VERSNEL, H. (1991*a*), 'Beyond Cursing: The Appeal to Justice in Judicial Prayers', in C. Faraone and D. Obbink, *Magika Hiera: Ancient Greek Magic and Religion* (Oxford), 60–106.
—— (1991*b*), 'Some Reflections on the Relationship between Magic–Religion', *Numen*, 38: 177–97.
—— (1998), 'An Essay on Anatomical Curses', in F. Graf (ed.), *Ansichten Griechischer Rituale: Geburtstag-Symposium für Walter Burkert* (Stuttgart), 219–67.
—— (1999), 'κόλασαι το τοὺς ἡμᾶς τοιούτους ἡδέως βλέποντες: 'Punish Those who Rejoice in our Misery': On Curse Tablets and Schadenfreude', in D. R. Jordan, H. Montgomery, and E. Thomassen (eds.), *The World of Ancient Magic: Papers from the First International Samson Eitrem Seminar at the Norwegian Institute at Athens, 4–8 May 1997* (Bergen), 125–62.
—— (2002), 'The Poetics of the Magical Charm: An Essay on the Power of Words', in P. Mirecki and M. Meyer (eds.), *Magic and Ritual in the Ancient World* (Leiden), 105–58.
VEYNE, P. (1988), *Did the Greeks Believe in their Myths? An Essay on the Constitutive Imagination* (Chicago).
—— (1990), *Bread and Circuses* (London).
VINOGRADOV, J. G. (1994), 'New Inscriptions on Lead from Olbia', *Ancient Civilisations from Scythia to Siberia*, 1: 103–11.
VLACHOPOULOU-OIKONOMOU, A. (2003), *Επισκόπηση της Τοπογραφίας της Αρχαίας Ηπείρου Νομοί Ιωαννίνων-Θεσπρωτίας και Νότια Αλβανία* (Ioannina).
VOKOTOPOULOU, J. (1987), 'Vitsa, Organisation et Cimetières d'un Village Molosse', in P. Cabanes (ed.), *L'Illyrie Méridionale et l'Épire dans l'Antiquité, Actes du Colloque International de Clermont-Ferrand*, 22–25 Octobre 1984 (Paris), 53–64.
—— (1992), 'Dodone et les Villes de la Grande Grèce et de la Sicile', in *La Magna Grecia e i Grandi Santuari della Madrepatria*. Atti del Trentunesimo Convegno di Studi sulla Magna Grecia 4–8 Ottobre 1991 (Taranto), 64–90.
VOUTIRAS, E. (1998), *ΔΙΟΝΥΣΟΦΩΝΤΟΣ ΓΑΜΟΙ: Marital Life and Magic in Fourth Century Pella* (Amsterdam).
—— (1999), 'Euphemistic Names for the Powers of the Nether World', in D. R. Jordan, H. Montgomery, and E. Thomassen (eds.), *The World of Ancient Magic: Papers from the First International Samson Eitrem Seminar at the Norwegian Institute at Athens, 4–8 May 1997* (Bergen), 73–82.
WALCOT, P. (1978), *Envy and the Greeks* (Warminster).
WARNER, R. (1972) (trans.), *Xenophon*: The Persian Expedition (London).
—— (1972) (trans.), *Thucydides*: History of the Peloponnesian War (London).
WATERFIELD, R. (1988) (trans.), *Herodotus*: The Histories (Oxford).
WEHRLI, F. (1944), *Die Schule des Aristoteles: Texte und Kommentar*, vols. i–x (Basle).
WEISS, P. (1989), 'Fluchtafel', in E. Simon (ed.), *Die Sammlung Kiseleff im Martin-von-Wagner-Museum der Universität Würzburg*, 2: *Minoische und Griechische Antiken* (Mainz), 200–6.

WEST, M. (1978), *Hesiod's Works and Days, Edited with Prolegomena and Commentary* (Oxford).
—— (2003), *Homeric Hymns, Homeric Apocrypha, Lives of Homer, Edited and Translated* (London).
WEST, W. C. III (1999), 'New Light on an Opisthographic Lead Tablet in Chapel Hill', *International Congress of Greek and Latin Epigraphy* XI 1997 (Rome), 205–14.
WHITEHEAD, D. (1977), 'The Ideology of the Athenian Metic', *PCPS* Suppl. vol. 4.
—— (1986), *The Demes of Attica 508/7–ca. 250 BCE: A Political and Social Study* (Princeton).
—— (2000), *Hypereides: The Forensic Speeches, Introduction, Translation, and Commentary* (Oxford).
WHITTAKER, C. R. (1965), 'The Delphic Oracle', *Harv. Theol. Rev.* 58: 21–47.
WILHELM, A. (1904), 'Über die Zeit einiger Attische Fluchtafeln', *JÖAI* 7: 105–26.
WILLEMSEN, F. (1990), 'Die Fluchtafeln', in W. K. Kovacsovics (ed.), 'Die Eckterrasse an der Gräberstrasse des Kerameikos', *Kerameikos*, 14: 142–51.
WILKINSON, A., ELAHI, S., and EIDINOW, E. (2003), 'Special Issue: Riskworld', *Journal of Risk Research*, 6(4–6): 289–579.
WILSON, P. J. (1991), 'Demosthenes 21 (Against Meidias): Democratic Abuse', *PCPS* 37: 164–95.
—— (2000), *The Athenian Institution of the Khoregia: The Chorus, the City, and the Stage* (New York).
WINKLER, J. (1990a), 'The Ephebes' Song: *Tragoidia* and *Polis*', in J. Winkler and F. Zeitlin (eds.), *Nothing to do with Dionysos? Athenian Drama in its Social Context* (Princeton), 20–62.
—— (1990b), *The Constraints of Desire* (London).
—— and ZEITLIN, F. (1990) (eds.), *Nothing to do with Dionysos? Athenian Drama in its Social Context* (Princeton).
WITTGENSTEIN, L. (1969), *On Certainty*, trans. D. Paul and G. E. M. Anscombe, (eds.) G. E. M. Anscombe and G. H. von Wright (New York).
WOODHEAD, A. G. (1956–83), 'Dodona', in *Supplementum Epigraphicum Graecum*.
WORDSWORTH, CHRISTOPHER (1840), *Greece, Pictorial, Descriptive, and Historical, with Upwards of Three Hundred and Fifty Engravings by Copley Fielding, etc.* (London, William S. Orr & Co.).
WORTHINGTON, I. (1994) (ed.), *Persuasion: Greek Rhetoric in Action* (London).
WÜNSCH, R. (1900), 'Neue Fluchtafeln', *Rh. Mus.* 55: 62–85, 232–71.
YOUNG, R. S. (1951), 'An Industrial District of Ancient Athens', *Hesperia*, 20: 222–3.
YOUTIE, H. C., and BONNER, C. (1937), 'Two Curse Tablets from Beisan', *TAPA* 68: 43–78.
ZIEBARTH, E. (1899), 'Neue Attische Fluchtafeln', *Gött. Nachr.*, 1028–32.
—— (1934), 'Neue Verfluchungstafeln aus Attika, Boiotien und Euboia', *Sitzungsberichte der Preussischen Akademie der Wissenschaften, Phil.-hist. Klasse*, 33: 1022–50.

ZINGERLE, J. (1924), *Strena Buliciana* (Zagreb).
ZWEIG, B. (1992), 'The Mute Nude Female Characters in Aristophanes' Plays', in A. Richlin (ed.), *Pornography and Representation in Greece and Rome* (Oxford), 73–89.

Index Locorum

Acts 19.19 329 n.13
AENEAS THE TACTICIAN
  10.4 253 n.20
AESCHINES
  1.47–8 312 n.71
  1.74 338 n.67
  1.77 317 n.105
  1.86 311 n.63
  1.114 284 n.2
  1.117 318 n.108
  1.124 326 n.34
  1.158 338 n.67
  1.159 310 n.56
  1.173 317 n.105
  1.177 317 n.105
  1.9 297 n.26
  2.4 310 n.56
  2.5 317 n.105
  2.142 314 n.84
  2.152 316 n.94
  2.153 310 n.56
  2.179 316 n.93, 94
  2.184 316 n.93
  2.5 318 n.107
  2.87 284 n.2
  2.155 309 n.46
  3.1 311 n.63
  3.8 317 n.105
  3.56 317 n.105
  3.110 334 n.45
  3.125 317 n.105
  3.205–6 310 n.56
  3.207 317 n.105
  3.244 310 n.56; 317 n.105
  3.247 318 n.108
AESCHYLUS
  TGF 20 276 n.69
  Agamemnon (Ag.)
  1269–74 253 n.21
  Eumenides (Eu.)
  303–6 285 n.8; 321 n.129
  835 335 n.49
  Seven Against Thebes (Sept.)
  43–54 284 n.2
  Prometheus Bound (PV)
  829 268 n.35, 270 n.4

AESOP
  Hausrauth=Perry 56 254 n.24
ALEXIS (K–A)
  fr. 33 311 n.59
  206 332 332 n.28
ALKMAION
  fr. 283.5–9 337 n.63
ANAXIMENES
  *Rhet. ad Alex.*1437a 312 n.70
ANDROTION
  FGrH 324 F 30 263 n.73
ANAKREON
  fr. 13 333 n.31
ANDOKIDES
  1 319 n.120
  1.6 316 n.92
  1.11–68 310 n.49
  1.69 311 n.69
  1.105 317 n.105
  1.112–16 311 n.65
  1.20 310 n.49
  1.61–4 315 n.89
  1.140 318 n.108
  1.146 325 n.25
  1.150 315 n.89, 316 n.93
  4 333 n.33
  4.16 313 n.80
  4.20–1 297 n.22
ANTIGONOS OF KARYSTOS
  117 338 n.67
ANTIPHANES
  25 K–A 327 n.51
ANTIPHON
  1 255 n.24; 318 n.118; 332 n.28
  2.b.12 (the first tetralogy) 297 n.18
  1.2 313 n.80
  5.64 313 n.80, 316 n.92
  5.94 313 n.80
  6 297 n.22
  6.11 297 n.25
  6.14 317 n.105; 318 n.107
  6.24 317 n.105
Anthologia Palatina (AP)
  5.129 238 n.5
  5.131 238 n.5
  5.187 339 n.75
  6.276 335 n.49

7.649   292 n.53
11.161   283 n.37
11.163   283 n.37
12.46   339 n.75
12.47   339 n.75
APF
  222–3   306 n.28
  11234   309 n.44
  3188   309 n.44
APOLLODOROS
  Bibliotheca (Bibl.)
  1.7.2   272 n.25
  3.4.3   290 n.45
APOSTOLIUS
  6.82   261 n.58
APOLLONIOS
  Mirab. 40   299 n.32
APPIAN
  Syr.
  56   268 n.34
  63   268 n.34
APOLLONIOS RHODIOS
  1.525   276 n.69
  4.580   276 n.69
Archaiologike Ephemeris
  1952:40   268 n.42
ARISTOPHANES (K–A)
  Fr. 101   311 n.59
  Fr. 285   327 n.51
  Fr. 607   323 n.13
  Acharnians (Ach.)
  703–18   302 n.3
  1128–9   252 n.9
  Birds (Av.)
  32–41   303 n.9
  109–11   303 n.9
  436   323 n.13
  521   251 n.5, 255 n.26, 255 n.26, 258 n.37
  618   256 n.29
  716   256 n.29
  959–91   258 n.39
  962   250 n.2, 255 n.26
  967–8   255 n.25
  982   250 n.2
  988   253 n.18, 258 n.37
  Ecclesiazousai (Eccl.)
  253   325 n.25
  Knights (Eq.)
  44   325 n.25
  116–49   258 n.39
  123   250 n.2, 251 n.5
  129   325 n.25
  641   317 n.105

837   310 n.54
997–1089   258 n.39
1084–5   253 n.18, 258 n.37
1229–53   258 n.39
1389   340 n.81
Lysistrata (Lys.)
189   284 n.2
770–6   258 n.39
Clouds (Nub.)
206–8   303 n.9
332   255 n.26, 258 n.37
Peace (Pax)
11   332 n.28
164   332 n.28
692   325 n.25
1026   251 n.4
1026–32   256 n.28
1043–1126   255 n.25, n.26
1045   258 n.39
1046–7   251 n.5
1047   253 n.18, 258 n.37
1052–1126   258 n.39
1069   258 n.39
1071   250 n.2
1084   255 n.26
1095   250 n.2
1120   258 n.37, 258 n.39
1121   258 n.37, 258 n.39
1125   253 n.18
Wealth (Plut.)
1–55   258 n.40
435   327 n.51
820   279 n.23
Frogs (Ran.)
148   336 n.55
405   301 n.45
1028   299 n.31
1031–5   250 n.2
Triphales
fr. 564.2 (K–A)   300 n.36
Wasps (Vesp.)
106–9   303 n.9
158–60   258 n.40, 303 n.9
380   253 n.18, 258 n.37
562–75   311 n.68; 316 n.93
568–75   316 n.94
579–86   311 n.68
946–8   302 n.3
978–1008   303 n.9
1113   303 n.9
[ARIST.]
Athenian Constitution
  (Ath. Pol.)
3.5   335 n.49

21.6   263 n.73
27.3   297 n.18
27.5   311 n.63
42.1   313 n.80
57.3   293 n.69
58.2–3   309 n.45
63–5   311 n.63
ARISTOTLE
Magna Moralia
1188b31–7   254 n.24
On the Heavens (Cael.)
279b9   304 n.15
Nikomachean Ethics
1108a33–b7   264 n.1
1122a34   297 n.18
1122b35   297 n.18
1122b23   297 n.18
1123a20   297 n.18
Poetics (Poet.)
1448a28–40   298 n.30
Politics (Pol.)
1310a7   315 n.89
1314b39–1315a4   264 n.2
1316a37   297 n.28
Pr.
876a39   337 n.65
Rhetoric (Rhet.)
1386b18–19 . 2.9   296 n.17
1387b 23–24 . 2.10   296 n.17
1398a   312 n.70
1400b   299 n.32
1403b31–5   295 n.8
1411a24   327 n.51
ARRIAN
Anab.
2.3.3–4   252 n.13
ARTEMIDOROS
4.2.5   283 n.40
ARV[2]
86a   339 n.72
372.31   339 n.72
444.241   339 n.72
ASKLEPIADES
7 (Gow–Page)   333 n.31
15   339 n.75
ATHENODOROS
6.246b   332 n.28
12.523f–524b   264 n.84
12.534c   300 n.38
13.584b   332 n.28
13.590d   332 n.28
13.591de   332 n.28
14.632[a]   299 n.32

CASSIUS DIO
9 fr.39.5   299 n.32
CICERO
Letters to Brutus (Brut.)
46–8   287 n.14
217   288 n.28, 302 n.4
About the Divine (Div.)
1.18.34   250 n.2
1.19.37   258 n.41
1.34.76   272 n.37, 277 n.81
1.41.91   252 n.13
1.42.94   252 n.13
1.43.95   250 n.2
1.54.122   267 n.31
2.32.69   272 n.37, 277 n.81
About the Invention of Rhetoric (de Inv.)
2.1.1   339 n.72
Letters to Atticus (Att.)
7.2.1   275 n.59
Carmina Epigraphica Graeca (CEG)
454   284 n.2
CGFP
220.98–103   258 n.37
CLEMENT OF ALEXANDRIA
Stromateis
1.132, 398 P   250 n.2
1.132, 399 P   250 n.2
Protrepticus
2, p.4   274 n.50
2.11.1   276 n.75, 277 n.80
COM. ADESP.
192 K–A   332 n.28

DEMOSTHENES (including [DEM.])
2.22   265 n.8
7.32   270 n.8
15.19   301 n.43
18.52   310 n.56
18.129   337 n.65
18.134   313 n.80
18.138   311 n.62
18.196   317 n.105
18.253   273 n.37
18.257   297 n.20
18.265   310 n.58
19.1   311 n.63
19.17   317 n.105
19.29   273 n.37
19.70   284 n.2
19.75   310 n.56
19.128   280 n.26
19.146   309 n.46
19.216   312 n.72
19.281   254 n.23

19.309　317 n.105
20　296 n.17; 315 n.92
20.10　296 n.17
20.131　310 n.56
20.146　313 n.80
20.165　317 n.105; 318 n.108
21.47　310 n.46
21.51–3　259 n.49
21.51　273 n.37
21.53　276 n.68
21.64　316 n.92
21.112　312 n.72
21.139　312 n.72; 315 n.89
21.151–9　297 n.20
21.159　297 n.18
21.226　311 n.58
22　315 n.92
22.25–7　308 n.41
23.53　334 n.41
23.67–8　284 n.2
23.71　284 n.2
23.95–9　310 n.56
23.199　278 n.6
23.206　313 n.80; 315 n.89
24　315 n.92
24.36　313 n.80
25　252 n.17
25.76–8　297 n.20
25.78　316 n.94
25.79　253 n.23, 293 n.69
25.98　317 n.105; 318 n.108
25.162　309 n.46
27.8–9　311 n.65
27.9　326 n.34
27–30　318 n.118
27.11　245 n.35
27.12　316 n.98
27.40　319 n.119
27.51　312 n.72
29.28　312 n.72
30.32　317 n.105; 318 n.107
32　245 n.35, 38
32.29　309 n.45
33.4　245 n.35
33.30–1　311 n.65
33.35–6　310 n.56
34　245 n.35; 316 n.96, 99
34.5–10　279 n.19
34.6–7　245 n.37
34.18–20　312 n.72
34.24　297 n.20
34.51　245, n.38
35　245 n.35, 38

35.14　309 n.46
35.20　309 n.46
35.23　309 n.46
35.33　309 n.46
35.18　245 n.35
36.13–14　279 n.19
37.52–4　245 n.38
39.2　254 n.23
40.9　254 n.23
40.10　319 n.119
41　318 n.118
43.57　316 n.96
43.66　259 n.49
45.7　316 n.98
45.41　317 n.105
45.71–86　319 n.120
45.78　297 n.18
45–6　312 n.73
47　316 n.98
48　318 n.118
48.53–5　332 n.28
49.18–21　313 n.74
49.10　314 n.84
49.22　314 n.84
52.20　245 n.35
55.23–5　318 n.118
55.27　318 n.118
55.24　319 n.119
56　245 n.35; 316 n.96
56.37　316 n.99
56.48　317 n.105
57.8　318 n.118
57.31–45　340 n.83
57.67–8　316 n.94
58.31　311 n.60
59　315 n.92; 332 n.28; 333 n.30
59.24　336 n.61
59.33　336 n.61
59.48　336 n.61
59.29　332 n.28
59.59–60　316 n.97
59.66　309 n.46
59.110–11　319 n.121
59.109　318 n.108, 118
59.117　316 n.93
59.122　333 n.29
Derveni Papyrus　252 n.10
　Col. 20, 4　344 n.4
　Col. 20, 1–12　257 n.34
Didyma II
　7　269 n.47
　11　269 n.45
　479　263 n.76

Index Locorum

505.6–10 268 n.44
DIKAIARCHOS
  FHG II.239, fr. 14 261 n.64
DINARCHOS
  1.22 318 n.108
  1.27 318 n.108
  1.30 317 n.105; 318 n.107
  1.46 317 n.105
  1.51 316 n.92
  1.58 316 n.92
  1.66 317 n.105
  1.78 273 n.37
  1.98 273 n.37
  1.114 316 n.92
  2.6 316 n.92
  2.15 317 n.105
  2.16 284 n.2
  2.19 317 n.105; 318 n.108
  3.1 317 n.105
  3.22 318 n.108
DIO CHRYSOSTOM
  17.17 273 n.37
  30–5, fr. 101.2 274 n.47
DIODOROS OF SICILY
  4.66.5–6 250 n.2
  12.10.3–4 254 n.26
  14.13.4 268 n.36
  15.14.2 276 n.66
  15.17.3 272 n.37
  26.17 269 n.4
DIOGENES LAERTIUS
  2.50 267 n.31
DIONYSIOS OF HALIKARNASSOS
  1.19.3 277 n.75
  Din 11 254 n.23
DT
  1 236
  4 236
  5 213; 224
  10 350
  1–13 289 n.35; 333 n.34; 341 n.4; 349
  4 236
  5 212; 213; 215; 221; 224; 287 n.16; 333 n.35; 336 n.50; 336 n.63
  15 294 n.4; 343 n.15
  18–21 287 n.17
  27 343 n.15
  38 329 n.11
  39 304 n.17; 313 n.77; 314 n.81
  43 148; 167; 304 n.17
  44 167; 287 n.16, 304 n.17
  45 286 n.12
  47 201; 287 n.20; 322 n.4; 323 n.18; 326 n.33; 328 n.54
  49 145; 168; 171; 177; 185; 187; 288 n.24; 289 n.31, 32, 304 n.17; 307 n.32; 305 n.17; 307 n.31; 311 n.64 318 n.110
  50 147; 151; 184; 318 n.110; 326 n.33
  52 149; 151; 199; 200; 287 n.23, 293 n.63; 307 n.32; 322 n.4; 323 n.18; 325 n.25; 326 n.36; 328 n.53; 325 n.23; 349
  60 167; 292 n.60, 304 n.17; 305 n.20
  61 185; 318 n.110
  62 304 n.17; 305 n.17; 313 n.77; 314 n.81
  63 178; 304 n.12, 17; 305 n.17; 311 n.64; 313 n.76; 314 n.83
  66 326 n.33
  67 168; 183; 305 n.18; 317 n.100
  68 149; 201; 207; 212; 218; 219; 221; 286 n.41; 333 n.35; 349
  69 146; 207; 212
  70 199; 322 n.4; 326 n.36; 328 n.53
  71 200; 322 n.4; 323 n.18; 326 n. 32; 326 n.36; 328 n.53
  72 144; 148; 322 n.4; 323 n.18; 326 n.36, 37; 334 n.45
  73 287 n.19; 326 n.36. 37
  74 349
  75 349
  77 304 n.17; 305 n.17
  85 207; 212; 216; 219; 220; 221; 284 n.1, 287 n.18; 333 n.35; 334 n.44
  86 143; 146; 207; 212; 217; 220; 221; 223; 238 n.5; 329 n.12; 333 n.35
  87 146; 177; 185; 307 n.31; 311 n.64; 318 n.110; 325 n.25
  87–90 304 n.17
  89 177; 311 n.64
  90 313 n.77; 314 n.81, 82
  92 151; 199; 293 n.63; 322 n.4; 323 n.18; 326 n.36
  93 285 n.3
  129 285 n.3
  135 322 n.4
  155 324 n.24
  156 352
  159 352
  160 352
  161 352
  166 352
  174 352
  178 352
  187 352
  188 324 n.24
  196 285 n.5

198 210; 329 n.11
212 341 n.4
227 329 n.11
230–1 329 n.11
238 352
239 352
240 352
248 352
264–71 329 n.11
265 334 n.44
266 334 n.44
270 334 n.44
304 329 n.11

DTA
11 287 n.20; 305 n.20
12 196; 322 n.4; 324 n.22; 328 n.55
24 184; 249 n.61, 287 n.20; 305 n.17; 305 n.20; 318 n.110
25 177; 187; 287 n.20, 304 n.17; 311 n.64; 319 n.122
26 304 n.17; 305 n.20
30 184; 305 n.20; 318 n.110; 322 n.4; 324 n.22; 327 n.55
33 156; 163; 287 n.20, 294 n.2
34 156; 163; 287 n.20, 294 n.2, 302 n.44
38 179; 304 n.17; 313 n.77
39 179; 185; 287 n.20, 304 n.17; 313 n.77; 314 n.81; 318 n.110
42 146; 287 n.20, 289 n.33; 305 n.20
45 156; 157; 287 n.20, 294 n.2
47–50 287 n.20; 305 n.17, 20
51 305 n.20
53 326 n.37
55 146; 196; 197; 284 n.1, 285 n. 5, 287 n.17, n.20, 289 n.33, 302 n.63; 323 n.21
57 287 n.20; 305 n.20; 322 n.4
63 179; 304 n.17; 313 n.77; 326 n.37
64 326 n.37
65–8 304 n.17
65 151; 175; 177; 187; 287 n.20, 305 n.17, 20; 307 n.31; 310 n.54; 311 n.64; 313 n.77; 319 n.122; 320 n.128;
66 167; 287 n.20, 305 n.17; 307 n.31; 313 n.77; 314 n.81
67 150; 175; 185; 310 n.48, 54; 318 n.110
68 177; 185; 187; 196; 197; 198; 200; 287 n.20, n.23, 294 n.75; 303 n.6; 307 n.31, 32; 311 n.64; 318 n.110; 322 n.4; 327 n.50; 328 n.3; 349; 352
69 196; 197; 199; 201; 287 n.20; 319 n.4; 326 n.36; 327 n.50
70 199; 322 n.4; 326 n.36; 327 n.42

71 200; 322 n.4; 323 n.18; 326 n.32; 326 n.34, 36
72 322 n.4; 328 n.53
73 199; 200; 288 n.23; 322 n.4; 328 n.53
74 199; 200; 201; 289 n.33; 307 n. 32; 322 n.4; 323 n.18; 328 n. 54
75 151; 198; 199; 200; 287 n.20; 288 n.23, 288 n.25; 307 n.32; 322 n.4; 326 n.32; 328 n.53; 329 n.11; 349
77 293 n.63; 325 n.33; 327 n.46; 352
78 207; 212; 215; 219; 221; 224; 333 n.35
79 168; 183; 307 n.31; 317 n.100
81 179; 304 n.17; 313 n.77; 314 n.81
84 184; 287 n.20, 289 n.33; 305 n.20; 307 n.32; 318 n.110; 322 n.4; 326 n.35, 38; 352
85 290 n.41; 322 n.4; 323 n.18; 351, 352
86 199; 200; 307 n.32; 322 n.4; 325 n.29; 326 n.36; 327 n.50, 52; 328 n.54
87 184; 187; 196; 198; 199; 203; 287 n.20, 303 n.6; 305 n.20; 307 n.32; 318n.110; 319 n.122; 326 n.36; 327 n.50; 329 n.11, 122; 322 n.4; 323 n.21; 349
88 147; 287 n.16, 303 n.6, 304 n.11, 12, 17; 307 n.31; 313 n.77; 314 n.83
89 184; 207; 290 n.42; 305 n.20; 318 n.110, 352
93 207, 352
94 168; 177; 178; 179; 287 n.20, 304 n.12, 17; 307 n.31; 310 n.47; 311 n.64; 313 n.77; 320 n.128
95 179; 185; 304 n.17; 305 n.17; 307 n31; 313 n.77; 318 n.110; 326 n.35
97 307 n.32; 322 n.4; 327 n.45
98 229; 292 n.54; 326 n.35; 341 n.4
100 148; 168; 229; 230, 232; 287 n.16, 290 n.44, 304 n.12; 341 n.4; 349
102 146; 148; 229; 293 n.63; 341 n.4; 342 n.5; 351
103 146; 167; 179; 229; 230; 302 n.51, 304 n.12, 17; 305 n.17, 22; 310 n.47; 313 n.77; 314 n. 81; 321 n.134; 341 n.4
104 326 n.33
105–7 150; 304 n.17; 307 n.31
105 147; 168; 290 n.42, 290 n.43; 326 n.35
106 147; 185; 313 n.77; 314 n.81; 318 n.110; 326 n.35
107 304 n.17; 307 n.31; 313 n.77; 202; 314 n.83
108 148; 202; 285 n.7, n.9; 322 n.4
109 148; 286 n.9, 288 n.25; 322 n.4; 326 n.37; 341 n.4

Index Locorum

120 322 n.33; 338 n.4; 339 n.5
129 304 n.17; 313 n.77
137 326 n.35
158 168; 229; 230; 283 n.1; 341 n. 4; 342 n. 5
160 234; 325 n.33; 327 n.46; 344 n.1

EMPEDOKLES
  31 B 111 D–K 279 n.21
EPHOROS
  FGrH 70 F 206 268 n.36
EPICHARMOS (K–A)
  103 300 n.35
  187 279 n.23
EUBOULOS (K–A)
  67 332 n.28; 336 n.54
  74 317 n.105
  80 327 n.51
  82 332 n.28; 336 n.54
EUPOLIS
  231 (K–A) 251 n.5
EURIPIDES
  Alkmeon
  TGF 67 321 n.132
  Alkestis (Alk.)
  112 255 n.29
  1127–8 279 n.21
  The Bacchai (Bacch.)
  233–8 279 n.21
  255–7 258 n.35
  Elektra (El.)
  734 256 n.29
  900 f. 294 n.72
  Erechtheus
  TrGF 367–88 268 n.35
  Children of Herakles (Her.)
  639 278 n.6
  Hippolytos (Hipp.)
  1038–40 279 n.21
  Medea (Med.)
  290–7 294 n.72
  Rhesos (Rhes.)
  941–7 250 n.2
  The Suppliants (Supp.)
  240–2 294 n.72
EUSEBIUS
  Praeparatio Evangelica (PE)
  2.3.1 (61d) 276 n.75
EUSTATHIOS
  Od.
  14.327 p.1760 269 n.2
  Il.
  16: 233–5, p.1057.61 ff. 269 n.2; 277 n.83

EPIMENIDES
  FGrH 457 279 n.21

Fontenrose
  H2 262 n.70
  H3 262 n.69, 268 n.39
  H4 262 n.69
  H5 262 n.69, 70
  H10 262 n.69
  H11 262 n.69
  H12 262 n.69, 267 n.33
  H21 262 n.69
  H25 262 n.70, 268 n.38
  H27 262 n.69, n.70
  H 36 268 n.40
  H45 262 n.70
  H47 262 n.70
  H54 262 n.70, 268 n.41
  H 61 262 n.70
  H66 262 n.70
  H74 262 n.70, 268 n.42
  Q21 267 n.24
  Q28–31 266 n.20
  Q78 267 n.26
  Q92 266 n.19
  Q103 266 n.19
  Q135 267 n.22
  Q140 266 n.20
  Q162 267 n.23
  Q201 266 n.19
  Q213 267 n.27
  Q216 267 n.27
  Q224 267 n.21
  Q225 266 n.20
  L4 266 n.20
  L5 266 n.20
  L6 267 n.25
  L8 267 n.22
  L10 266 n.20
  L11 266 n.23
  L14 267 n.26
  L17 266 n.20
  L18 266 n.20
  L23 266 n.20
  L28 266 n.20
  L31 267 n.26
  L34 266 n.20
  L40 267 n.22
  L79 267 n.26
  L80 266 n.20
  L82 266 n.20
  L85 267 n.26
  L87 267 n.26

488 *Index Locorum*

L90   267 n.24
L99   266 n.20, 267 n.24
L107   267 n.26
L109   267 n.22, 267 n.26
L114   267 n.22
F10   266 n.20
F13   267 n.23
Fouilles de Delphes (FD)
3.1.560   268 n.39

Gager
97, 27   288 n.30
97, 28   288 n.30
GAIUS
Dig.
47.22.4   325 n.28
GALEN
Anat. Adm. 2.1 (II p.280 Kühn)   252 n.11
Comp. Med. 9.4 (XIII p.276 Kühn)   252 n.11
De Usu Partium 3.1 (III p.169 Kühn)   257 n.31
Introductio seu Medicus 1.1 (XIV p.675 Kühn)   257 n.31
De Simplicium Medicamentorum Temperamentis ac Facultatibus 10.1 (XII p.251 Kühn)   288 n.26

HARPOKRATION
Θεωρίς   254 n.23
Ἰσοδαίτης   254 n.23
κλώζετε   311 n.59
HEKATAIOS
FGrH 1 F 168   270 n.4
HERAKLEIDES PONT.
Fr. 50   264 n.84
HERAKLEITOS
B92 D–K   253 n.20
HERODOTOS
1.5.4   242 n.14
1.19.1   267 n.22
1.29–34   281 n.2
1.32.4   241 n.3
1.32.6   241 n.4
1.32.9   241 n.5
1.46   268 n.36
1.46.3   281 n.11
1.46–7   264 n.85
1.53.3   260 n.49
1.62   255 n.25
1.62.4   250 n.2
1.66.1   260 n.49

1.78   252 n.13
1.91   241 n.6, 266, n.19
1.92.2   264 n.85
1.157–60   260 n.52
1.157.3   264 n.84
1.158   283 n.46
1.159   264 n.85, 266 n.19
1.174   261 n.55
1.209.4   241 n.8
2.18.1   312 n.71
2.52   270 n.4
2.55   276 n.70
2.56   276 n.73
2.56.1   271 n.19
2.57   276 n.74
2.135   337 n.65
2.159.3   264 n.85
3.50.3   262 n.60
3.64.3–5   266 n.19
3.124–5   241 n.8
3.132.2   253 n.18
4.123   293 n.65
4.150–64   283 n.35
4.155   259 n.49
4.159   277 n.3
5.42–3   267 n.26
5.42.2   259 n.49
5.43.1   250 n.2
5.44.2   253 n.18
5.63   261 n.55
5.67   259 n.49
5.71   273 n.37
5.72   273 n.37
5.83   300 n.37
5.90   261 n.55
5.90.2   250 n.2
5.92   261 n.60, 266 n.20, 281 n.11
6.34.6   266 n.21
6.57   278 n.11
6.57.2   250 n.2
6.57.4   250 n.2
6.66   260 n.55
6.76.1   260 n.49
6.86c2   266 n.19
6.123   261 n.55
7.6   255 n.25
7.6.3   250 n.2
7.6.4   255 n.26
7.10   241 n.8
7.76   261 n.57
7.139.5–143   283 n.46
7.143.3   250 n.3
7.155   297 n.28

7.228 253 n.18
8.20.1–2 250 n.2
8.27.3 253 n.18
8.77.2 250 n.2
8.96.2 250 n.2
8.132.2 281 n.2
9.33.1 253 n.18
9.33.2 252 n.12, 266 n.20
9.37.1 253 n.18
9.43.1 250 n.2
9.43.2 250 n.2
9.93.4 243 n.23, 261 n.56, 275 n.57
9.95 252 n.16
[HERODOTOS]
Life of Homer 32 321 n.2
HELENOS
FGrH 274 F 1 270 n.8
HESIOD (MW)
Great Eoiai
fr. 261 252 n.15
Melampodia
frr. 270–9 252 n.15
'Catalogue of Women'
fr. 240.1 272 n.30
fr. 302 321 n.2
Works and Days (Op.)
20–6 322 n.7
HESYCHIOS
Γεφυρίς 332 n.28
Θριαί 261 n.67
Πέλειαι 276 n.72
Hippokratics
Epidemics (Epid.)
5.63 253 n.20
7.28 253 n.20
27 278 n.12
On the Sacred Disease (Morb. Sacr.)
II–III in particular 243 n.22
III.2 244 n.24
On Women (Mul.) 278 n.16
HOMER
Epigram 14 321 n.2
Hymn to Apollo
3.229–8 258 n.43
Iliad (Il.)
1.147 333 n.39
1.386 333 n.39
1.472 333 n.39
2.635 270 n.10
5.370 238 n.3
16.220 272 n.29
16.233 (Schol. B) 269 n.2, 276 n.68, 76

16.234 (Schol. A) 272 n.24, 272 n.29
16.235 (Schol. T) 272 n.29
Odyssey (Od.)
1.57 350
3.419 333 n.39
5.47 350
5.334 291 n.46
11.72–6 291 n.53
12.40 350
14.1760 269 n.2
14.327 271 n.19; 272 n.24, n.29
15.225 253 n.15
16.195 350
17.521 350
19.296 271 n.19; 272 n.29
20.74 335
n.49
24.378 270 n.10
HYPERIDES
1 fr. Vi cols. 25–26 321 n.130
Against Demosthenes fr. 4, col. 17 245 n.35
1.20 311 n.60
2.10 316 n.93
3.1–12 246, n.39
3.5–6 308 n.41
3.12 313 n.80
4 315 n.92
4.8 315 n.89
4.12 315 n.89
5.22 317 n.105
5.33 309 n.46
Eux. 24 273 n.37

IAMATA FROM EPIDAUROS
Stele B, 22; T 3.11 243 n.23
Stele B, 36 243 n.23
IC
III.4, 9.27 317 n.103
ICos
60 269 n.50
IDOMENEUS
FGrH
338 F 14 332 n.28
Inscriptiones Graecae (IG)
i³.40.64–9 255 n.26
i³.61.4–5 253 n.18
i³.71 310 n.57
i³.78 255 n.26
i³.969 297 n.20
i³.104.20–3 316 n.96
ii².17 253 n.20
ii².204 263 n.71
ii².226 280 n.27

490 *Index Locorum*

ii².649 302 n.48
ii².657 302 n.48
ii².749 302 n.48
ii².850 310 n.57
ii².1138 297 n.21
ii².1139 279 n.21
ii².1147 297 n.21
ii².1157 297 n.21
ii².1158 297 n.21
ii².1196 313 n.80
ii².1197 313 n.80
ii².1258 316 n.96, 97, 99
ii².1629 310 n.57
ii².1554–9 325 n.27
ii².9536 333 n.38
ii².10850 280 n.27
ii².13209–10 289 n.35
ii².16420 256 n.29
ii².2318 295 n.8, 300 n.40
ii².3073 301 n.48
ii².3092 306 n.26
ii².3095 301 n.45
ii².3098 301 n.45
iv 1299 288 n.27
iv².95 280 n.27
iv².128 268 n.38
ix.2.106 334 n.45
xii.3.248 268 n.41
IL
  367 338 n.68
  369 338 n.68
  370 338 n.68
  372 338 n.68
  373 338 n.68
Isaios
  3 318 n.118
  3.13–14 336 n.61
  4.27 297 n.20
  5 306 n.24; 316 n.96, 99
  5.2 289 n.38
  5.20 317 n.105
  6 332 n.28
  6.21 332 n.28
  9 312 n.71
  11 306 n.24
  12.5 316 n.94; 319 n.121
  12.11 316 n.97
  12.9 319 n.119
Isokrates
  Antidosis 296 n.17
  6.25 304 n.15
  15.246 265 n.8
  16.35 297 n.20

  17.20 289 n.38
  17.42 245 n.35
  18.11 311 n.63
  18.42 318 n.108
  18.52–7 312 n.72
  18.58 297 n.203
  19.5–9 253 n.18
  20.2 316 n.96

Josephus
  Against Apion (Ap.)
  2.267 254 n.23
Justin
  12.2.3 268 n.36
  14 268 n.36
  17.3.1–22 271 n.17

Kallias
  fr. 20 K–A 258 n.37
Kallisthenes
  FGrH 124 F 14 264 n.86
  FGrH 124 F 22 277 n.81
  FGrH 124 F 22a, b 272 n.37
Kallimachos
  Hymn to Apollo 45 262 n.67
  Hymn to Apollo 286 277 n.78
  Aitia fr. 229 252 n.11
Karapanos 1878
  Pl. 36, 2 238 n.1
  Pl 26, 8 274 n.48
  Pl. 34, 3 275 n.62
  Pl. 34, 4 274 n.53
  Pl. 39, 2 275 n.63
  p. 39.7 274 n.53
Konon
  Narr.
  33 252 n.11
  44 252 n.11
Kovacsovics 1990 (Kovs.)
  3 322 n.4; 350
Kratinos (K–A)
  Fr. 62 258 n.37
  Fr. 66 258 n.37

Lois Sacrées des Cités Grecques: Supplement
  (LSS)
  115 279 n.21
Lactantius Placidus
  On Statius' Thebais (Theb.)
  8.198 252 n.11
Leges Graecorum Sacrae (LGS)
  II.1.42 273 n.37

Index Locorum

LIBANIUS
  Speeches (Or.)
    1.43 303 n.7; 344 n.5
    1.62 303 n.7; 344 n.5
    1.71 303 n.7; 344 n.5
    1.243–50 288 n.30
    1.245–9 288 n.28, 293 n.66, 302 n.5
  Life of Aeschylus (Vit.)
    9–11 299 n.31
    10, 11 299 n.34
    18 299 n.31
LIVY
  8.24.1 268 n.36
  45.34 274 n.46
  45.43.10 276 n.66
LYNKEUS OF SAMOS
  ap. Ath. 6.246b 332 n.28
  ap. 13.584b 332 n.28
LYKOURGOS
  1.14 318 n.108
  1.135 316 n.93
  1.138 316 n.93
  1.139 297 n.20
LYKOPHRON
  Alex.
    856–8 299 n.32
    1131 299 n.32
    fr. 233 (van der Valk) 277 n.83
LYSIAS
  fr. 82 333 n.30
  fr.182 306 n.26
  1 318 n.118; 334 n.41; 334 n.42
  1.24 327 n.51
  3.47 297 n.19
  6 315 n.92
  6.48, 49 297 n.19
  7 310 n.51
  7.11 313 n.80
  7.13 313 n.80
  7.16 310 n.49
  10.24–5 312 n.73
  12.35 317 n.105
  12.43–4 315 n.89
  12.87 312 n.72
  12.91 318 n.108
  13 310 n.49, 51; 315 n.92
  14 310 n.51, 315 n.92
  14.19–22 316 n.93
  15 315 n.92
  16.6–7 313 n.80
  16.18 297 n.18
  17.2 311 n.69
  19 296 n.16
  19.2 313 n.80; 316 n.92
  19.7 312 n.72
  19.61 313 n.80
  20.7 316 n.92
  20.26 311 n.65
  20.35 316 n.94
  21 296 n.16, 297 n.18
  21.1–2 300 n.40
  21.20 313 n.80
  21.20–1 316 n.92
  22.19–21 318 n.108
  23.2 309 n.45
  25.5 316 n.92
  26.3 297 n.18 and 19
  27 315 n.92
  27.7 317 n.105
  27.12 314 n.89; 316 n.94
  27.14 316 n.92
  29 310 n.51
  29.6 310 n.49
  30.31 316 n.93
  30.34 316 n.92
  32 318 n.118; 319 n.119
  32.6 245 n.35
LYSIPPOS
  fr. 6 K-A 258 n.37

MACHON
  fr. 6 332 n.28
  fr. 7 332 n.28
MACROBIUS
  Saturnalia (Sat.)
    1.7.2874 277 n.75
MAMA VIII
  544 334 n.45
  547 334 n.45
  550 334 n.45
  553 334 n.45
  555 334 n.45
  557 334 n.45
  559 334 n.45
  565 334 n.45
  568 334 n.45
  578 334 n.45
Marmor Parium (Marm. Par.) 299 n.31
MAXIMUS OF TYRE
  8.2 260 n.58
MELEAGER
  15 339 n.75
  58 339 n.75
MENANDER
  fr. 65 (K–A) 277 n.78
  Arbitration (Epit.)

794 332 n.28
Hated Man (Mis.) 332 n.28
Man from Sikyon (Sikyon.) 332 n.28
Girl with Her Hair Cut Short (Pk.) 332 n.28
Girl from Samos (Sam.)
390 332 n.28
Milet.
  1.3.141 249 n.59, 263 n.76
  1.3.155 249 n.59, 264 n.84
  1.3.178 268 n.44
  1.7.205a and b 268 n.43
ML
  1 284 n.2
  5 284 n.2
  30 284 n.2
  33 253 n.20
  52 255 n.26
  69 310 n.57
  73 255 n.26

NEPOS
  1.3 267 n.21
NIKOSTRATOS
  22 K–A 327 n.51
NGCT
  1 304 n.12, 305 n.19, 313 n.77; 314 n.81, 82; 324 n.22
  5 305 n.22; 306 n.25; 321 n.134
  9 167; 173; 304 n.12; 305 n.19
  10 185; 305 n.19; 318 n.110
  11–13 293 n.61
  11 169; 306 n.25
  12 187; 304 n.12; 305 n.19; 306 n.25; 314 n.85
  13 169; 306 n.25
  14 148; 175; 229; 230; 304 n.12; 305 n.19
  15 179; 304 n.12; 305 n.19; 313 n.77
  22 307 n.33
  23 229; 230; 342 n.4; 342 n.6
  24 179; 225; 229; 230;235; 288 n.25, 304 n.12; 305 n.19; 342 n.4
  28 328 n.8
  29 328 n.8
  37 318 n.110
  38 304 n.12; 305 n.19; 313 n.77; 314 n.81, 83
  39 172; 313 n.75
  40 171
  46 304 n.12; 307 n.54; 313 n.77; 314 n.81
  48 172
  49 172; 313 n.75
  50 172; 184; 313 n.75, 318 n.110
  66 171; 225; 229; 303 n.8

  78 303 n.8
  79 149; 171; 303 n.8
  82 304 n.12
  83 171
  88 304 n.12; 314 n.85
  89 341 n.4; 342 n.4
  116 171; 303 n.8

OVID
  Metamorphoses (Met.)
  1.163–413 272 n.25
  1.379 272 n.26
  7.614 276 n.69

PA
  4309 258 n.37
Parke
  Private oracle consultations at Dodona
  2 283 n.42
  11 238 n.1
  28 280 n.30
  State oracle consultations at Dodona
  1 274 n.55
  2 274 n.52
  3 274 n.53
  4 275 n.62
  5 275 n.60
  6 274 n.54
  7 243 n.23; 275 n.57
  8 275 n.63
  9 273 n.39, 275 n.61
Parke and Wormell
  35–6 266 n.19
  43–5 266 n.20
  56 266 n.19
  85 267 n.22
  110 266 n.20
  141 266 n.20
  145 267 n.26
  148 266 n.20
  149 266 n.20
  156 266 n.20
  174 267 n.33
  180 266 n.19
  190 266 n.20
  194 267 n.26
  198 266 n.20
  202 267 n.22
  229 266 n.20
  266 267 n.27
  275 266 n.20
  279 268 n.38
  313 267 n.26

Index Locorum

317–19 266 n.20
322 266 n.20
325 267 n.26
334 268 n.39
335 268 n.40
372 266 n.20
375 267 n.26
383 267 n.24
406 266 n.20; 267 n.25
411 267 n.26
421 267 n.21
427 268 n.41
442 267 n.26
444 267 n.26
445 267 n.22
450 267 n.22
484 266 n.20
494 267 n.26
602 267 n.22

PARTHENIUS
1.2 268 n.34

PAUSANIAS
1.34.4 251 n.5
1.44.7 290 n.45
2.1.3 290 n.45
3.17 262 n.60
3.11.5 253 n.20
3.18.3 257 n.29
3.21.8 257 n.29
5.25.2–5 299 n.34
7.21.5 261 n.61
7.22.2–4 262 n.62
7.25.1 272 n.37; 277 n.75
7.25.6 261 n.57
8.11.12 273 n.37
9.38.5 279 n.21
9.39 261 n.58
10.7.3 266 n.20
10.9.1 263 n.81
10.10.1 263 n.73
10.12.1 251 n.5
10.12.2 250 n.2
10.12.10 276 n.72; 277 n.75

PGM (Greek Magical Papyri)
I.262 352
III.35 352
III.85 352
III.123 352
IV.296–303 328 n.9
IV.296–466 286 n.8
IV.325–35 286 n.9
IV.327 337 n.63
IV.335–84 288 n.30
IV.351–2 330 n.19
IV.396 330 n.19
IV.449–56 344 n.19
IV.973 352
IV.1502 330 n.19
IV.1533–5 330 n.19
IV.1593 352
IV.2037 352
IV.2145 285 n.5
IV.2176–7 286 n.10
IV.2740–58 331 n.18
IV.2755–66 331 n.18
IV.2756 337 n.63
IV.2910 330 n.19
IV.2931–3 330 n.19
V.314 286 n.9
VII.411–16 280 n.32
VII.429 286 n.9
X.24–35 285 n.5
XV.4 337 n.63
XVI.3–8 330 n.19
XIXa 56 337 n.63
XIXb.53–4 330 n.19
XXXIIa 330 n.18; 337 n.67
XXXVI.81 329 n.18; 330 n.19
XXXVI.147 330 n.19
XXXVI.151–2 330 n.19
XXXVI.161 286 n.9
LXI.29–30 330 n.18; 337 n.63
LXVIII 329 n.18

PHibeh (Hibeh Papyri)
14 306 n.28

PHILIPPIDES
fr. 38 (K–A) 252 n.9

PHILOCHOROS
FGrH 328 F 60 254 n.23
FGrH 328 F 78 253 n.20
FGrH 328 F 155 262 n.73
FGrH 328 F 195 262 n.67

PHILOSTRATOS
Life of Apollonius 8.19 261 n.58
*Im.*2.33 272 n.24

PHOTIOS
Lex
διδάσκαλον 300 n.41
νέμεσις ὑποκριτῶν 295 n.8

PINDAR
frr. 57–60 (Maehler) 269 n.4, 275 n.71
fr. 59.3 (Maehler) 272 n.30
fr. 60 (Maehler) 271 n.20
Olympian Odes (Ol.)

1.75–8 285 n.7, 294 n.5
6.7 (schol.) 261 n.64
8.2 282 n.37
Nemean Odes (Nem.)
4.51 270 n.8
7 270 n.8
Pythian Odes (Pyth.)
4.71 288 n.24
11.2 291 n.46
11.28 294 n.72
PHILO JUDAEUS
2.468 276 n.69
PHRYNICHOS
fr. 34 K–A 332 n.28
PLATO
Alkibiades (Alk.)
148b 283 n.41
148d 256 n.29
Apologia (Ap.)
24e–25b 317 n.105
35b 317 n.105
Charmides (Charm.)
163b 331 n.25; 338 n.67
Epinomis (Ep.)
325c5–d5 315 n.89
Euthydemos (Euthyd.)
303a 321 n.133
Gorgias (Grg)
483e6 279 n.21
Ion
536a 300 n.41
Laches (Lach.)
195e 251 n.4
Laws (Leg.)
637b 299 n.32
700c1–4 311 n.61
731a 294 n.72
738c 256 n.29
853e5–6 257 n.33
866a5–6 257 n.33
873a5–6 257 n.33
876b1–6 311 n.62
909a–d 344 n.3
932e6–933a5 293 n.70
932e–933e 344 n.9
933a 286 n.10
933a–c 285 n.5
933a5 279 n.21
933b 257 n.32
933b2–3 292 n.57
933c–d 251 n.4, 252 n.9
933d7–e5 257 n.33
933e 252 n.8

937 312 n.73
Meno (Men.)
80a2 279 n.21
80a2–3 252 n.8
80a-b 321 n.133
80b6 279 n.21
90a 325 n.25
92c 251 n.4
234a–b 317 n.105
Phaido (Phd.)
1c 333 n.39
64b 301 n.43
69c 291 n.53
Phaidros (Phdr.)
244b 276 n.75
270c 252 n.11
Protagoras (Prt.)
309b 338 n.67
311b 252 n.11
316d 250 n.2
Republic (Resp.)
364b–365a 250 n.2
364b–c 308 n.43
364c–e 286 n.10, 287 n.17
364c 251 n.5
381d4–7 253 n.21
427b–c 259 n.49
492b5–c1 311 n.62
Sophist (Soph.)
234c5–6 279 n.21
Theagenes (Theag.)
124d 250 n.20
Theaitetos (Theaet.)
173d4 315 n.89
PLAUTUS
The Comedy of Asses (Asin.)
746 332 n.28
The Bacchis Sisters (Bacch.)
fr. 10 332 n.28
896 332 n.28
Threepence (Trin.)
858 300 n.36
The Businessman (Merc.) 332 n.28
The Persian (Persa)
159–60 300 n.36
The Man From Karthage (Poen.)
34.1 332 n.28
488 334 n.45
PLINY
Natural History (HN)
3.152 276 n.66
7.151 267 n.28

28.4.19 322 n.10
29.81 280 n.32
32.49 280 n.32
35.61 339 n.72
PLUTARCH
  Moral Matters (Mor.)
  Consolatio ad Apollonium
  109 261 n.58
  Bellone an pace clariores fuerint Athenienses
  349b 297 n.21
  De E apud Delphos
  386c 266 n.12, 283 n.37
  De Pythiae Oraculis
  398c 250 n.2
  399a 250 n.2
  406b 260 n.54
  407c 260 n.52, n.53
  408c 259 n.49, 266 n.11
  De Fraterno Amore
  492a 263 n.72
  De sera numinis vindicta
  555c 262 n.60, 279 n.21
  De genio Socratis
  580d-e 317 n.105
  590–2 261 n.58
  Amatorius
  770c 338 n.67
  Praecepta gerendae reipublicae
  812d 255 n.26
  De Musica
  1146b 279 n.21
  Phok.
  28 273 n.37
  Proverbs
  1.51 261 n.58
  Life of Aemilius (Aem.)
  29 274 n.46
  Life of Aristides (Ar.)
  27.4 252 n.9
  Life of Agesilaos (Ag.)
  11 265 n.3
  Life of Alkibiades (Alk.)
  8 333 n.33
  16 297 n.22
  Lives of the 10 Orators (Vit. X orat.)
  833e-f 316 n.95
  Life of Cato the Younger (Cat. Min.)
  61 333 n.39
  Life of Demosthenes (Dem.)
  14.4 254 n.23; 293 n.69
  21.3 315 n.89
  Life of Kimon (Kim.)
  6 262 n.60
  18 256 n.28
  18.7 257 n.29
  Life of Lysander (Lys.)
  22.5–6 253 n.18
  25 268 n.36
  Life of Nikias (Nik.)
  13 256 n.28, 29; 273 n.37
  23.5 256 n.28
  29 299 n.30
  Life of Perikles (Per.)
  24.1–6 333 n.30
  32.1–2 253 n.18; 333 n.30
  32.2–5 258 n.37
  38.2 253 n.22
  Life of Pyrrhos (Pyrrh.)
  1.3 280 n.27
  Life of Themistokles (Them.)
  28.5 268 n.36
POLYBIOS
  2.8.4 276 n.66
  4.6.2 276 n.66
  4.6.8 276 n.66
  4.16.6 276 n.66
  4.67.3 270 n.4
  5.9.2 274 n.45
  8.28.2 299 n.32
  30.16 274 n.46
  36.17 259 n.49
  36.17.2–4 265 n.9
  36.17.2 265 n.10
  36.17.6 265 n.10
POxy. (Oxyrynchos Papyri)
  1176 fr. 39, col. 19 (Satyrus *Life of Euripides*) 298 n.30
POLLUX
  Onomastics (Onom.)
  3.38 335 n.49
  4.122 311 n.61
  7.108 322 n.10; 323 n.13
  8.110 263 n.73
  9.41–2 299 n.35
Pomtow (1887)
  1 274 n.52
  2 274 n.53
  3 274 n.55
PORPHYRY
  On Abstinence (Abst.)
  2.16 267 n.28, 281 n.2
PROXENOS
  FGrH 703 271 n.17
  FGrH 703 272 n.24

Roman Inscriptions of Britain (RIB)
  6–7   323 n.11

SAPPHO
  fr. 16   37 n.63
SEG
  4.31   293 n.62
  9.45.28   333 n.38
  9.72   279 n.21
  26.1717   288 n.30
  28.1245   253 n.18
  29.361   253 n.18, 253 n.20
  35.626   253 n.20
  40.919   291 n.51
  42.846   298 n.28
  47.823   271 n.21
SEMONIDES
  7   340 n.82
SERVIUS
  Commentary on Virgil's Aeneid (Aen.)
  3.466   276 n.68
  Commentary on Virgil's Eclogues (Ecl.)
  9.11   276 n.72
SGD
  1   285 n.6
  2   285 n.6
  3   196; 201; 287 n.20; 322 n.4; 327 n.50
  4   201; 287 n.20
  6   180; 304 n.11, 12, 17; 313 n.77
  9   142; 169; 293 n.61, 304 n.17
  10   184; 318 n.110
  11   196; 197; 288 n.20, 328 n.55
  14   169; 249 n.59; 305 n.17, 20
  18   151; 289 n.37; 305 n.20
  19   180; 284 n.1, 304 n.12, 17; 305 n.17; 313 n.77
  20   149; 195; 322 n.4
  21   232; 343 n.19
  30–2   207; 328 n.8
  31   334 n.44
  42   168; 187; 290 n.44, 304 n.12, 17; 305 n.17, 22; 313 n.77; 314 n.86
  43   199; 326 n.34, 36
  44   195; 287 n.20; 322 n.4
  46   184; 318 n.110
  48   145; 173; 184; 196; 198; 287 n.18, n.20; 304 n.17; 305 n.20; 314 n.86; 318 n.110; 321 n.134; 323 n.18; 324 n.23; 328 n.55
  49   168; 304 n.12, 17; 313 n.77; 314 n.81
  51   179; 304 n.12, 17; 305 n.17; 313 n.77; 314 n.81, 83
  52   196; 197; 200; 322 n.4; 327 n.50; 328 n.53
  54   289 n.36
  57   207; 212; 218; 220; 224; 287 n.20; 328 n.8; 333 n.35; 338 n.68
  58   229; 230; 342 n.4, 8; 352
  60   290 n.44; 322 n.4; 328 n.4; 334 n.45; 341 n.4; 342 n.8;
  61   304 n.12, 17; 313 n.77; 350
  68   179; 304 n.12, 17; 313 n.77
  71   304 n.12, 17; 313 n.77; 314 n.81
  72   196; 287 n.20; 324 n.22; 328 n.55
  73   322 n.4; 326 n.38
  75   199; 202; 290 n.44; 307 n.32; 322 n.4; 328 n.54
  81   289 n.34; 322 n.4
  82   304 n.12
  86   292 n.60
  87   292 n.60
  88   146; 200; 322 n.4; 323 n.18; 328 n.53
  89   151; 285 n.3, 305 n.8, 307, n.17; 314 n.64
  91   146; 155; 156; 157; 161; 284 n.1, 294 n.2; 328 n.2; 331 n.2
  95   295 n.60, 303 n.8, 304 n.12, 17; 307 n.31; 313 n.77; 314 n.81
  99   150; 292 nn.54, 60, 303 n.8, 304 n.12, 17; 307 n.31; 313 n.77; 314 n.81
  100   292 n.57, n.59, 60; 303 n.8, 304 n.17; 307 n.31; 313 n.77; 314 n.81
  101   299 n.34
  103   299 n.34
  107   146; 169; 305 nn.17, 20; 314 n.86
  108   292 n.60; 304 n.17; 307 n.31
  109   287 n.20, 289 n.36; 328 n.4; 349; 350
  116   285 n.4
  118–21   328 n.4, 349
  124   196; 200; 287 n.20, n.23; 322 n.4; 326 n.34; 327 n.50, 53
  133   172; 303 n.8; 304 n.17; 313 n.77
  136   352
  150   285 n.7
  151–3   329 n.11
  152   292 n.57
  154   207; 328 n.8
  155–6   329 n.11
  158–61   329 n.11
  167   294–5 n.4
  170   148; 151; 196; 287 n.20, 290 n.43; 324 n.23; 328 n.55
  171   172; 303 n.8; 317 n.100, 104
  173   287 n.18; 304 n.17; 311 n.64
  176   179; 304 n.12; 304 n.17; 313 n.77; 317 n.100, 101
  179–80   283 n.3

186–7 329 n.11
191 329 n.11
192 329 n.11
SGDI
117 280 n.31
1336 271 n.21
1565a 238 n.1
1590 260 n.49
Skylax
28 276 n.66
28–32 270 n.14
30 276 n.66
Skymnos
Travels (Perieg.)
50–64 268 n.43
442–3 270 n.8
Sophokles
Antigone (Ant.)
998–1032 291 n.53
1033–47 258 n.35
1055 258 n.35
1061 258 n.35
1241 335 n.49
Oidipous the King (OT)
298–9 258 n.36
387–9 258 n.36
380–403 258 n.35
The Women of Trachis (Trach.)
46 268 n.35, 277 n.76
170 276 n.71
1159 268 n.35, 277 n.76
Sophronius
PG 87.3, col. 3625
Narratio Miraculorum Sanctorum Cyri et Joann 288 n.30, 293 n.67
Soranus
Gynaecology (Gyn.) 278 n.16
Sortes Astrampsychi
No.89 279 n.20
Stephanos of Byzantion
Βύλλις 270 n.8
Γαλεῶται 252 n.14
Δωδώνη 269 n.2
Θρῖα 262 n.67
Πανδοσία 277 n.75
Strabo
Geography (Geog.)
6.1.5 268 n.36
7.5.5 277 n.4
7.5.6–12 270 n.12
7.7.3 274 n.46
7.7.5 270 n.8, 275 n.59
7.7.9 274 n.49
7.7.10 271 n.19
7, fr. 1a 276 n.72, 277 n.77
7, fr. 3 277 n.79
8.7 267 n.33
9.3.9 252 n.11
17.2.43 264 n.86
Suda
Αἰσχύλος 299 n.31
Βάκις 250 n.2
Δωδώνη 276 n.69, 75, 277 nn.75, 79
Δωδωναῖον χαλκεῖον 269 n.2
Ὀρφεύς 250 n.2
Πυθώ 262 n.67
Τροφονίου 261 n.58
Suetonius
On Augustus (Aug.)
31.1 329 n.13
Supplementum Magicum (Suppl. Mag.)
37.47 343 n.16
39.1 343 n.16
42.12 343 n.15
42.14 343 n.17
44 285 n.5
44.13 343 n.15
45 291 n.56
45.4 343 n.15, 16
45.6–7 343 n.18
46 291 n.56
47 288 n.30
47.18 343 n.16
49.12 343 n.15
49.19–23 343 n.18
50.17–19 343 n.17
53.12–22 343 n.18
54.22 343 n.15
57.1 343 n.15
*Syll.*³
73 273 n.37
977 268 n.41
1044.20 278 n.12
1157 277 n.82
1219 334 n.45
1237 334 n.45
TAM
318 344 n.8
Terence
Phormio (Phorm.) 277 n.7
Theokritos
2.44 337 n.63
3.31–3 280 n.32
4 339 n.75
16.35 278 n.6

THEODORETUS
  Graecarum Affectionum Curatio
  10.3.5 276 n.75, 277 n.80
  10.3.11 261 n.58
THEOPHRASTOS
  Characters
  6.9 246 n.39
  16 293 n.68
  16.2–5 265 n.1
  16.3 253 n.21
  26.5–6 296 n.17
THEOPOMPOS (FGrH)
  FGrH 115 F 77 250 n.2
  115 F 314 281 n.2
  115 F 213 332 n.28
  115 F 225 332 n.28
  115 F 344 267 n.28
THUCYDIDES
  1.134 279 n.21
  1.5.2–3 270 n.10
  1.5.3 276 n.66
  1.8.1 312 n.71
  1.25.1 260 n.49
  1.41 304 n.15
  1.47.3 270 n.10
  1.77 303 n.9
  1.118.3 260 n.49
  2.8.2 251 n.3
  2.15.2 273 n.40
  2.21.3 251 n.3, n.6
  2.43 340 n.85
  2.54.2 251 n.6
  2.68 272 n.36
  2.68.3 281 n.13
  2.68.9 282 n.13
  2.80.5 282 n.13
  2.80.6 280 n.27
  2.81 282 n.13
  2.82 282 n.13
  3.38 310 n.54
  3.92.5 292 n.49
  3.94.3 270 n.10
  3.94.4 270 n.14
  3.102.6 270 n.10
  3.114.4 270 n.10
  5.16.2 261 n.55
  5.19.2 255 n.26
  5.24.1 255 n.26
  5.26.4 251 n.6
  5.47 280 n.26
  6.9.1 256 n.29
  6.16 296 n.17
  6.27.2 313 n.46
  7.50.4 251 n.4
  8.1.1 250 n.2, 251, n.6
  8.54 343 n.13
  8.54.4 315 n.89
  8.63 343 n.13
  8.66 343 n.13
  8.92.10 256 n.29
TIMOKLES
  24.1–2 (K–A) 332 n.28
Tod
  200 310 n.57
TZETZES
  Scholia on Lycophron (Lyc.)
  1385 268 n.34.
  Chiliades (Chil.)
  13.111–12 268 n.34
VALERIUS FLACCUS
  1.302 276 n.69
  5.65 276 n.69
VALERIUS MAXIMUS
  7.1.2 267 n.28
VARRO
  fr. 252 252 n.11
XENARCHOS
  4 (K–A) 331 n.28; 336 n.54
XENOPHON
  Agesilaos (Ages.)
  2.1–2 265 n.2
  8 265 n.2
  The Expedition (An.)
  1.7.4 302 n.41
  1.8.15 242 n.10
  2.2.3 242 n.10
  2.4 284 n.2
  2.5.7 243 n.15
  2.5.21 243 n.15
  3.1.5–8 242 n.13, 267 n.31, 283 n.46
  3.1.6 262 n.69
  3.1.8 262 n.69
  3.1.11 242 n.11, 257 n.30
  3.1.13 242 n.12
  3.1.41 241 n.7
  3.2.8 257 n.30
  4.3.8 242 n.11
  5.2.24 242 n.11
  5.3.7 267 n.33
  5.6.28 242 n.10
  5.6.29 253 n.20, 256 n.27
  6.1.21 12
  6.1.22–4 256 n.27

6.1.22 267 n.31
6.1.23 252 n.9
6.1.24 242 n.13, 267 n.32
6.2.15 242 n.12, 267 n.32
6.4.14 256 n.27
6.4.15 242 n.10
6.5.2 257 n.30
7.6.44 242 n.13, 267 n.32
Life of Kyros (Kyr.)
1.6.2 242 n.10, 256 n.27
1.6.4 243 n.15
1.6.46 242 n.9
3.5.58 265 n.2
On Horsemanship (Eq. mag.)
6.6 242 n.10
A History of Greek Affairs (Hell.)
2.3.36 278 n.6
3.2.22 265 n.3
4.7.2 265 n.3
3.3.3 253 n.18
4.7.2 261 n.56
6.1.11 278 n.6
Socratic Memoirs (Mem.)
1.1.6 265 n.5
1.4.15 265 n.4
2.1.10 293 n.65
2.2.4 332 n.28
2.7.4 301 n.43
3.11.7 252 n.8
4.4.11 312 n.72
Oikonomikos (Oik.)
5.19–20 241 n.10
11.8 265 n.8
12.2–3 279 n.19
Symposion (Symp.)
4.12–35 338 n.67
Ways and Means (Vect.)
6.2 273 n.37
[Xen.] (Old Oligarch)
Athenian Constitution (Ath. Pol.)
 303 n.9
22.5 chapter 8

ZENOBIOS
Proverbs
3.62 298 n.30
5.75 262 n.67
Ziebarth (1899)
 no. 16 291 n.53
 (1934)
 nos. 21–22 284 n.1
 no. 22 238 n.4
 no. 23 284 n.1
Makedonia, Akanthos
 Jordan 1999, no.3 213; 287 n.16; 333 n.37
Makedonia, Pella 213; 215; 286 n.16
Museum (Ceramics) Catalogue Numbers
 Athens
 1975 291 n.53
 Berlin
 2294 323 n.14
 Boston, Museum of Fine Arts
 03.800 291 n.53
 03.802 339 n.74
 Frankfurt, Liebig-Haus
 538 339 n.76
 London
 BM 1185.6–13 284 n.2
 Munich
 Antikensammlungen 1717 323 n.14
 Naples, Museo Archeologico
 Stg.316 339 n.76
 2296 339 n.76
 New York, Flechmann coll. F93 300 n.36
 Oxford, Ashmolean museum
 1966.714 339 n.76
Oracle Tablet Catalogue Numbers (Ioannina Museum)
 M-22 275 n.60
 M-33 274 n.54
 M-177 275 n.59
 M-186 344 n.2
 M-827 274 n.56
 M-957 275 n.64
 M-1099 275 n.64

General Index

NOTES: An asterisk * signifies a name from a *katadesmos*.
Where relevant, names are followed by the name of the oracular sanctuary at which they have consulted, e.g. Agelochos (Dodona)

abecedaria 129
Abrasax 291n51
Achaia 389
Acheron river 49
Acheron, Thesprotia 261n59
Achilles 60
    see also Selloi (or Helloi)
actors: curses against 156–7
Adriatic Sea 73
Aeneas the Tactician 253n20
Aeschines 179
Aeschylus
    Aitnaiai in Sicily 299n31
    honoured by Hieron of Gela 162
    Kassandra in *Agamemnon* 29
    lost play 276n69
    oral binding curse in *Eumenides* 141, 301n3, 321n129, 341n2
    Persians in Sicily 299n31
    psychagogoi and spirit-raising 280n21
    in Sicily 299n31
Africa: curse from 434
Agariste (of Alkmaionid family) 310n49
Agelochos (Dodona) 128
*Agenos 186
Agesipolis, Spartan king 261n56
Agios, Tisamenos' grandson 253n20
*Agnotheos 184
agonistic context 4, 154, 156, 239n12, 294n73, 294n3
agonothetai 164
agriculture
    and risk 16–17
    see also farmwork; Theophrastos
agyrtriai 29
AIDS, see HIV/AIDS
Aigeus of Athens 266n20
Aigina (Dorian) 162, 300n37
Aigospotami 253n20
*Aineas 219, 224
*Ainis 213–14

Aipytos, king 266n20
Aitolians 24, 62, 66
Akanthos, Makedonia 212–14, 221, 329n11, 452
Akrisios, king of Argos 266n20
Aletes 49
Aleuas the Red, Thessalian king 37
Alexander the Great 40, 47, 49, 169, 267n27, 268n36
Alexander, king of the Molossians 83
*Alkiadas 157–9
Alkibiades 30, 160, 256n29, 296n17, 300n38, 316n93, 333n33
Alkinoos (Dodona) 108–9
Alkmaion 266n22
*Allia Prima 350
Alyattes, Lydian king 46
Amandry, P. 34
Amantia 274n44
Amathous, see Hagios Tychonas
Ambrakia 270nn8, 15, 272n36, 274n44
Ambrakiots 128
Ammon (Egypt): oracle 32, 67–8, 256n29
Amorgos, Sicily 419
Amphiaraos, Oropos: oracle 261n59
Amphilochos: oracle 36
Amphilytos 250n3
Amphyktionic oath 334n45
amulets 139
Amyntas (Dodona) 136
Anaktorion 270n8
Anaxippos (Dodona) 134
Andromachos 310n49
Annyla (Dodona) 1–2, 88, 120
*Antheira 216–17, 220
Anthemion 139
antidikoi (adversaries) 180–2
Antigonos of Karystos 338n67
Antiochos (Seleucid king) 113, 263n76
Antipater 273n37

General Index

Antiphon 152, 316n95
Anyte 291n53
Anytos 251n4, 316n93, 324n25
*Apelles 157–9, 162, 328n2
Aphrodite 213–14, 222
Apollo
  Euenios claims inheritance from 28
  Glaukos consults 46
  Homeric Hymn to 39
  as oracle 26, 35, 50–2, 70, 110–11, 260n56, 275n57
  see also Loxias
Apollodoros, 245n38, 313n73, 316n98, 332nn28, 29
Apollonia, Apollonians 64, 128, 264n84, 270n8, 274n44, 275n57
apophasis 180
apotropaic practice 194–5
Appheion (or Heronas) of Alexandria (Didyma) 268n43
Arcadians 272n37
Archephon (Dodona) 110–11
Archeptolemos 316n95
*Archestratos 226
Archias 128
Archidamos 251n6, 272n37
Archilochos 53
Archippe of Kyme 340n84
Ares: oracle dedicated to 35, 261n57
Arethousa, Greece 445
Argonauts 67
Argos 272n36
Argos Amphilochikon 270n8, 281n13
Aristandros 253n18
Aristarchos 172
Aristoboulos 179, 314n83
Aristodikos 40
Aristokydes 216
Aristolaos (Dodona) 119–20, 136
Aristolochos (Didyma consultant) 54
*Aristomachos 151, 321n130
Ariston (Dodona) 74, 129
Aristophanes
  on agriculture 244n30
  on allocation of *dikastai* 311n63
  on behaviour of witnesses 176
  on Hierokles and Lampon 255n25, 258n37
  mocks oracle-peddlers 27, 29, 32
  names occupations 198
  on Thucydides son of Melesias 165, 341n2
Aristophantes (Dodona) 108

Aristotle
  on character 265n1
  on *choregia* 301n45
  on marriage 335n49
  on megaloprepeia 297n18
  on Megarians 298n30
Aristoxenes of Taras 299n32
*Aristylla 185
Arkes, Illyrian bandit chief 63
Artabanus 241n8
Artemidorus 135
Artemis 48
  Phakelitis 299n32
  Strophaia 148
Arybbas 115
Ashforth, Adam 191, 230
Asia Minor: catalogue of curses from 388–9
*Asklapiadas 236
Asklepios 35, 243n23, 252n11
*Aspasia 172
Aspasia, wife of Perikles 211
*Asteas, son of Euandros 157
astragaloi (knuckle-bones) 54, 55, 69–70
atelestoi 148–9
Athena: Chaonian temple of 65
Athena Polias 347
Athenaios 244n30
Athens
  Agora 149, 195
  Areopagos 29, 317n105
  books of oracles 250n2
  border with Megara 36–7
  choral competitions in 162–3
  citizenship 82, 324n22
  city archives 146
  consultants at Dodona 128
  consults Delphic oracle before Persian invasion 137
  consults oracle at Ammon 256n29
  court witnesses 176–7
  curses from 147, 151, 156–7, 197, 201, 240n20; (catalogued, 364, 367, 378, 390–2, 405–11, 415–16, 437–42, 453)
  effects of literacy 24
  judicial curses from 166, 168, 172–3, 176, 180–1
  Kerameikos cemetery 145, 169, 184–5, 197, 333n35, 350, 405–8, 437–41, 453
  legal procedures 182–4, 228, 284n2, 293n69, 303n9, 304n16, 319n124
  manumission in 282n24
  oracle interpreters in 30
  Pankrates sanctuary 148

General Index

Peloponnesian war 26, 29–30, 231, 305n20
political structure 181
position of women in 130
revolts against Makedonian rule 305n22, 321n134
seeks control of Epirus 61
and sibling marriage 83
Sicilian expedition 26, 30, 272n37
Stoa of Attalos 410, 442
Theatre of Dionysos 301n46
athletes: as targets of curses 156–9
Attika, curses from 141, 145–7, 149, 157, 166, 180, 183–4, 198, 200–1, 212, 215, 218, 225, 234, 342n4, 350; (catalogued, 352–63, 365–6, 368–86, 391, 393–9, 411, 443)
attraction curses 154–5, 207
Audoleon 268n37
Audollent, A. 144, 154, 185, 212, 291n53, 305n17, 349
Avernos, Campania 260n59
Azande people, Sudan 33, 241n1
  poison oracle 239n9, 258n46

Bacchiadai family 46
Bakis 26
Barbaroi 281n13
Barchin del Hoyo, Cuenca, Spain 450
Battos 134
Bdelykleon 165
behaviour (human): and regularities 19
Bendis (goddess) 273n37
Berkeley, Busby: 'Gold Diggers of 1933' (etc.) 330n22
binding, *see* curse tablets
black magic: as explanation of curse tablets 3–4, 154, 307n35
Black Sea 151, 403–4, 436–7, 451
*Blastos 349
bodies and body parts 3, 104, 216–17
  binding, *see* curse tablets
  see also tongues
Bohr, Niels 257n31
Boiotia 147, 212, 216–17, 265n3
  curses from 399–400, 402
Boiotians
  consultations at Dodona 70
  as *sunegoroi* 179
bottomry 17, 245n38, 403
Bouthrotos 270n8, 282n14
Bowden, H. 29
Branchidai 28, 46, 264n84
Branchos 252n11

bronze work 96
brothels 216, 328n3, 331n25
Bruttium, south Italy 404
Buffa, Selinous, Sicily 426
Burnett, Anne 162
business ventures 109–10
  see also commercial curses
Buto: oracle 46
Bylliones, League of 274n43, 274n44, 275n65, 346
Byllis (or Bylliake) 64, 270n8, 274n56

Calabria 449
Carnuntum 334n45
centaurs 257n31
Chalke, near Larissa 195
Chalkidia: colony of Rhegion 65
Chalkis (Euboea) 195
chance, games of 54
Chaniotis, A. 183
Chaonia and Chaonians 58, 63, 65, 347
*Charias 202, 218–19
Charikles 266n20
charioteers: targeted 172
charis 297n20
chastity 83
Chersikrates 270n8
Chersonese, Thrakian 267n21
Chersonesos Taurica 404
childlessness: consultations on 45–6, 48–9, 131–2
children
  catalogue of questions 89–93
  cursed 293n63
  in oracular questions 83, 87–9, 120, 126–7, 133–5
  questions on paternity 138
Chionides 298n30
Chiron 194, 257n31
choregoi (*choregia*) 156–64, 228
chresmologoi (oracle-collectors) 26–7, 29–30
Christianity: and abolition of oracles 33
Christidis, A.-Ph. 6, 71, 82, 87–8, 94, 96, 100–1, 104, 110, 113–16, 126, 131, 269n51
chthonian, *see* gods
Cicero
  Brutus 165
  Verrine Orations 309n44
circus curses 156, 172
city affairs and politics 63–6, 115–16, 126
Clement of Alexandria 63
colonists: and oracles 34

comedies 31–2
commercial curses 154, 191–205, 228–9
competition
　between *choregoi* 160–1
　as an explanation of cursing 172, 192–3, 227, 236
　in oracular questions 126, 128
　see also agonistic context; Faraone, C.; rivalries
corpses, *see* dead, the
courtesans, *see* hetairai
courts of law
　cursing in 187–90
　see also judicial curses
craftsmen: and curses 191–6
crime 116, 126, 132, 138
Croatia: curse from 424
Curio the Consul 165–6
Curnow, Trevor 32
curse tablets (*katadesmoi*)
　adversarial function 4, 154, 156, 239n12, 294n73, 294n3
　in ancient literature 141
　binding 140, 142–52, 195, 201
　categories 154–5
　composers/authors 142–3
　and cultural context 8–9
　and the dead 148–50, 232
　efficacy 152, 165
　formulae 144, 147
　interpretation 7–9, 24
　language 142–4, 167, 199–202
　motivation for 4, 8, 154, 229–30
　and nailing 145
　origin and development of 140–2, 232
　possibilities of lifting 151–2
　and risk 4, 189–90, 203–5, 221–4
　role in ancient society 154–5, 173, 230
　targets 144, 173–87, 189, 195–9, 213–19
　techniques of creation 141
　writing and selling 6, 139, 141, 143, 234
curses, conditional 140

daimones 148, 191, 193–4, 232
Dakaris, S. 60, 61
Damagetos, king of Ialysos 47, 267n24
Darios, Perian king 241n8, 279n21
Daux, G. 50
Davies, J.K. 59
dead, the 148–50, 152, 232

death
　in curse tablets 151
　in oracular questions 121, 126
defigens 239n12, 295n6
defigere 283n1, 323n11
defixio 140, 169, 284n1, 291n52, 334n45, 349
Deinokles (Dodona) 128
Deinomenes of Syrakuse 266n20
Deiphonos 28, 275n57
deisidaimon 29, 42, 265n2, 293n68
Delian League 310n57
Delos
　curse from 18, 342n4
　Serapis cult 145
Delphi
　Athenians consult on eve of Persian invasion 137
　on Athens' wooden walls 29
　cult activity 39
　and development of local settlement system 39
　epigraphic evidence 50–3
　founding myth 39, 60
　individual consultations of oracle 45–7, 137
　instructs Athenians to establish choric dances 69
　Kroisos consults 10
　oracle 3, 6, 32–8, 42
　Plutarch's priesthood 45
　Sophocles refers to 32
　waning role 40
　Xenophon consults 12
Delphic Amphiktiony 39
Demades (Athenian statesman) 305n20
*Demades (potter) 195
Demeter
　chthonic god 148, 290n43
　Knidos sanctuary 213, 236, 333n34
　Malophoros 299n33, 427–9
　Mytilene sanctuary 172, 446–7
　oracle dedicated to 35
　Thermasia 106
Demetrios of Phaleron 164, 169, 340n83
*Demetrios (potter) 195
Demoklos the Delphian 267n26
*Demokrates 167
Demophilos 311n63
Demosthenes
　Aeschines' defence speech 179
　and *choregia* 160, 301n45, 302n50

compared by Dinarchos 321n130
    on Ninon 254n23
    on popular responses to court verdicts 186
    recovery of patrimony 318n118
Derveni Papyrus 28, 31, 234, 252n10
desire, see relationship magic and curses
despised dead, the 150
De Ste. Croix, G. 17
Deukalion 59–60
Dickie, Matthew W. 202, 208–9, 216
Didaskaliai 295n8
didaskalos (chorus trainer) 162–3
Diodoros (Dem.22) 315n92
Didyma
    Branchidai 28
    epigraphic evidence 50, 53–5, 69
    founding myth 40
    oracle 6, 32, 37–8, 42, 48
    sacked by Persians 40
dikai 181–2, 188
Dikaiogenes family 306n24
dikastai, see judges
dike pseudomarturion 312n73
Dinarchos 141
Diogenes of Sinope 266n19
Diognetos (Dodona consultant) 128, 283n41
Diokleidis 310n49
*Diokles 168, 177–9, 324n21
*Dion 179, 350
Dione (goddess) 2, 62–6, 87, 120, 129, 135, 273n37
Dionysiac festival 272n37, 300n40
Dionysios (slave-owner; Dodona consultant) 100–1, 103, 312n73
*Dionysophon 143, 214–15, 221
Dionysos 69
Diopeithes 139, 253n18, 258n37
disease
    and supernatural intervention 15
    see also health
divination
    methods 67, 252n9
    and nature of oracular questions 133
    in ordinary lives 4
    Sokrates and 43
    use of *astragaloi* in 70
    varying attitudes to 30–1
divine punishment 243n23
Dodds, E.R.: *The Greeks and the Irrational* 239n6
Dodona
    accounts of foundation 59–61, 67–8, 128
    bronze tripods 69

buildings 61–2
consulted on behalf of others 136–7
decline and extinction 63
divination 261n68
formulae of inquiry 121
Hiera Oikia (Holy House) 56, 61
individual consultants 137–8
international clientele 61
language of tablets 128–9
magic workers 28
manner and style of questioning 131–7
method of divination 67–71, 262n68
oracular dove 61, 66–8, 71
oracular oak 61, 63–4, 66–7, 71
oracular sanctuary 2, 6, 24, 32, 40–2, 61–3
personal names 129
political role 62
priestesses 68–9
question tablets 5–6, 23, 38, 57, 62, 233
questions about
    children 87–93, 120
    city affairs and politics 115–16
    crime 116–19
    death 121
    health and disease 104–7, 120
    judicial activity 114–15
    military campaigns 113–14
    property 107–10
    prosperity 110–12
    requests for truth 119
    ritual activity 112–13
    slavery 100–4
    travel 72–81
    treasure 120
    women 82–7
    work 93–100
    wrongdoing in an oracle consultation 119
questions presented by communities 345–8
rediscovery of site 56–9
responses 123, 138
sacked by Aetolians, Romans and Thrakians 62
spring 67, 71
state consultations 63–6, 345–8
subject matter and timing of questions 125–8
Dodona (Oceanid daughter of Zeus) 60
dolls: used in cursing 142–3, 145, 151, 170, 233
Dolonkoi tribe (Thrake) 46, 47
Dorieus 47

Dorios (the spirit-raiser; Dodona oracle question) 112–13, 234
*Dorothea 350
Dorystomphoi 298n28
Douglas, Mary 20–2, 259nn46, 47
dreams: interpretation of 35, 70, 135
Dropion, king of the Paeonians 268n37
Dubois, L. 157–9
dumbness *see* speaking; tongues

Eëtion of Petra 46
Egypt
   curses and spells from 329n11, 337n67
   and love-magic 340n87
   oracles 32–3
Eikades 316n96
Ekbatana 46
Elea 270n8
Eleusis 36–7
Elpenor 270n8
emic: defined 14
Emmenids 298n28
Empedokles 287n14
Emporion, Spain 433
engastrimuthoi 29
envy (*phthonos*)
   and *choregia* 160, 296n17
   and others' good fortune as threat 204–5, 229
   and witchcraft 230–1, 235
*Epainetos 186
Epainetos (Dem.59) 309n46
*Epaphroditos 350
Ephesos 48
Ephyra: oracle, 261n59, 262n60
Epicharmos 298n30, 300n35
Epidamnos 270n8
Epidauros, 300n37, 327nn48, 49
epilepsy 15
Epimenides 279n21
Epiros
   coastal harbours 65
   curses from 403
   and Dodona cult 62
   ethnê (tribes) 58
   kômas 58
   place and people 56–9
   Romans ravage (167 BCE) 24
   serfs in 75
   and sibling marriage 83
   women in 130
epodoi 27
eranos, *see* loans

Eretria 420
Ergetion, Sicily 128
Erginos, king of Orchomenos 266n20
Eridanos river 171
Erinyes (Eumenides; Furies), 141, 148, 285nn7, 8, 302n3, 321n129, 341n2
Eros: and risk 221–3
etic: defined 14, 246n42
Etruria 323n14
Etymologicum Magicum 276n68
Euadne 266n20
*Euandros 110–11, 130, 157
Euathlos, son of Kephisodenos 165
Euboia 255n26, 420
*Euboula 219, 224
Euboulos (Aesch.2) 316n93
Euenios 28
Euergos (Dem.47) 316n98
*Eukairos 185
*Eukles 226
*Eukrates 324n22
Eukrates (Dem.59) 332n28
Euktemon (Dem.24) 315n92
Euktemon (Isai.6.21) 332n28
Eumenides, *see* Erinyes
Eumolpos 295n4
*Eunikos 157–9, 162, 328n2
*Eupolemos 169
Euripides
   on Egyptian priestesses at Dodona 276n71
   on Ino in *Medea* 290n46
   Phaedra's nurse in *Hippolytos* 29
   on *psychagogos* in *Alkestis* 279n21
   saves lives after Sicilian expedition 298n30
Europa 47, 267n23
Eustathios 70
euthynai 313n80
Euxitheos (Dem.57) 340n83
Evans-Pritchard, E.E. 33
eyes: in oracular questions 104, 107

'Faithless' (music group) 238n5
Faraone, C. 4, 154, 170, 208–9, 216
farmwork
   in oracular questions 95–6
   see also agriculture
festivals: competitors cursed 156–64, 228
Finley, Moses I. 17
First Sacred War 263n82
fishing: in oracular questions 96
Fontenrose, J. 40, 266n17
Forster, E.M. 8

General Index

fortune (good) 98–100, 102, 114, 120, 204–5, 242n14
  see also misfortune
Foucault, Michel 21
funeral songs 299n32
Furies, the, *see* Erinyes
future: oracular questions about 72–116, 126

Gager, J.G. 168
Gaggara, Selinous, Sicily 427–9
Gaia 148, 264n83
Galen 244n30, 257n31
Galeotai (clan) 28, 49
Gambreion 334n45
Gaul: curse tablet from 450
Ge, *see* Gaia
Gela, Sicily 157, 161–3
Geta 278n7
Gilula, Dwora 162
Gitana (Goumani), Thesprotia 271n15
Glaukos the Spartan 46–7
Glaukothea (Dem.19.281) 254n23
*Glykanthe (or Malthake) 185
*Glykera 349, 350
Gnathaena 332n28
gods
  called as witnesses in *katadesmoi* 147–8
  chthonic 147–8
  omniscience 11–12
  see also names of individual gods
goeteis (male) and *goetides* (female) 27
Gordios, King 252n13
Gordon, R. 24, 144
Gorgias 302n4
Gorgos, son of Kypselos 270n8
Gould, John 14
Graf, Fritz 145
graphai 181–2, 188
graves: and curse burial 140–1, 291n53
Greek language: on Dodona tablets 128–9
Greek Magical Papyri 141, 208, 286n9, 288n30
Gytheion 256n29

Hadrumetum 329n11, 351
Hagios Tychonas (ancient Amathous) 287n17
Hagnon family 306n24
Halai, Attika 353
Hammond, N. 59, 128
Harpokration
  on binding 79
  on noise made by audience 311n59
  on Theoris 29, 153

Hatshepsut 32
healing 31
health
  catalogue of questions 105–7
  in oracular questions 104, 120–1, 126, 128, 130–1, 133, 136, 235
  see also prosperity/safety
*Hedyle, wife of Timokrates 185
Hegestratos (Dem.32) 245n38
Hekataios: on Epirote tribes 270n12
Hekate: invoked 147–8, 185, 290n43
Hekatomnids 278n9
Helenos 270n8
Hera 291n46
Herakleia 74, 128, 270n8
Herakleia Pontike, Black Sea 35, 261n59
Herakleitos: criticises traditional religiosity 257n34
Herakles 69, 261n59, 267nn22, 26
  oracle dedicated to 35
herding 95
Hermes
  Binder 184
  Chthonios 148, 151, 290n43
  invoked in *katadesmoi* 146–9, 151, 185, 225
  Katochos 148, 349
  Pharai oracle 35
Hermion 134, 138
Hermon (Dodona) 89–90
Hermon of Thasos 243n23
Herms: mutilation 310n49
Herodotos
  on Apollonians 64
  on Battos 134
  on *choregoi* in Aigina 162
  on Deiphonos 28
  on Dodona foundation 67–8
  on Glaukos 47
  on Kroisos 10–13, 46
  on Kymaeans consulting oracle 40
  on oracle-mongers 27, 29
  on oracles 135
  on Themistokles 256n27
  on witnesses 312n71
Hesiod
  describes Dodona in *Eoiai* 60, 67
  on diviner Melampos and descendants in *Melampodia* 252n15
  'Potter's Hymn' in *Life of Homer* 321n2
  on strife and competition in *Works and Days* 192–3, 204
hetairai 208–11, 216–18, 332n28
hetaireiai 315n89

Hiera Oikia (holy house) 56, 61–2
Hierapolis 334n45
Hierapytna 317n103
Hierokles, 251n5, 253n18, 255nn25, 26, 258n37
Hieron, tyrant of Gela 161–2
Hipparchos 250n2
Hipparete 333n33
Hippeis 306n29
Hippokrates 297n28
   On the Sacred Disease 15, 31
Hippotoxotai 170
HIV/AIDS: in Africa 9
Homer 26, 60, 87, 191, 266n20
   Iliad 61, 253n20
   Odyssey 60–1, 67, 252n15
Homeric Hymn to Pythian Apollo 39
homosexuality 218, 221, 338n67, 339n77
honour, love of, *see philotimia*
houses: in oracular questions 107–9
Hyperbolos 324n25
Hyperides
   gives examples of misfortunes 321n130
   mistresses 332n28
   opposition to Makedon 321n134

Iamata 245n23
Iamidai (of Olympia) 28
Ikarion 301n45
*Ilara 184
Illyria, Illyrians 66, 75
Inachos 267n26
incubation, *see* dreams
informers 174, 186
inheritance: in oracular questions 128
innkeepers: cursed 196–7
Ino (sea-goddess), 290nn45 46
Io 267n26
Iphitos 267n22
Isodemos (Dodona) 82, 127
Isomachos 265n8
Isyllos 50
Italy: curse tablets from 449–50
Itanos 317n103

Jason 67, 276n69
jealousy 230–1
   see also envy
Jordan, David 157–9, 168–9
Josephus 254n23
journeys, *see* travel
judges (*dikastai*) 172, 313n78
   as curse targets 175–6

judicial activities
   in *katadesmoi* 154, 227, 230
   in oracular questions 114–15, 126
   participants 178–84
judicial curses 154, 166–83, 227–9
justice and revenge: in *katadesmoi* 154, 229
Justin 49

*Kabeira 2, 217–18
Kadmos 47, 267n23
*Kaledias 146, 157–9
*Kallias
   DTA 65, 175, 179
   DTA 87, 184, 323n21
   DTA 88, 314n83
Kallisthenes
   on revival of Didyma 40
   on Spartan consultation of Dodona 70
*Kallistrate 293n63
*Kallistratos 179
Kamarina 298n28
Kambyses, king of Persia 46, 243n15, 256n27
kapeloi 196, 198, 203
Karapanos, Konstantine 57
Karia: curses from 388–9
Karkinos 47
Karpos (Didyma) 268n43
Karthage 322n4, 329n11
   amphitheatres 172
Karystos, Euboia 420
*Kassander of Makedonia 169, 305n20
Kassandra 28–9, 36
Kassopaians 270n14
Kassope 271n15
Kastritsa 271n15
katadesmoi, *see* curse tablets
katapugon 338n67
kategoroi (accusers) 178, 181
Kephalos 266n20, 324n25
Kephisias 243n23
Kerberos 261n59
*Kerkis 349
Kerkyra (Corfu)
   curse text from 185, 403
   founded 270n8
   oracular questions at Dodona 63–4, 345–6
   trade with Epiros 58
kidnapping 116–17
Kimon 256n29
kinaidos 338n67
*Kineas 185
Kirke 194
*Kittos 100–1, 103, 187, 323n21

General Index

Kleandros 297n28
Klearchos 243n15
Kleisthenes 37, 260n55
Kleoboule 318n118
Kleomenes of Sparta 260n55, 272n37
Kleon 175, 324n25
Kleonike 35
Kleophon 324n25
kleromancy 3
Klytiadai (of Olympia) 28
Knidos 212–13, 222, 236, 289n35, 349
 curses from 388–9
Knight, F. 19
knuckle-bones, *see astragaloi*
Kolias 251n3
Konon of Paiania 321n130
Korax 287n14
Korinth 39, 46
 trade with Epiros 58
Korope, Thessaly 70
Kourion, Kypros 287n17
*Krates 185
Kretaia (Dodona) 89–90
Krison, Molossian general 273n43
Kroisos, Lydian king 10–13, 40, 46, 267n36, 281n2
Kroton 74, 107
Kydippe 267n24
Kyesti (Molossian tribe) 274n43
Kylon 272n37, 279n21
Kyme and Kymaeans 40, 94, 95, 100, 128, 260n52
Kypselos, tyrant of Korinth 46
Kyrenaika 434
Kyrene 46, 284n2
Kyrikos of Ancona 274n51
Kyros, Persian king 10, 12, 243n15, 256n27, 260n52
Kyrus the Great, Persian king 11
Kyzikos 278n5

Labda, wife of Eëtion 46
Laios, king of Thebes 266n20
Lais, younger and elder 332n28
Lakonia 256n29
Lampon, 139, 255nn25, 26, 258n37
lamprotes (brilliance) 160
law courts, *see* courts of law
Lele (people), Zaire 22
Leon, son of Leontios (Dodona) 136
Leontios (Dodona) 136
Leton (Dodona) 123
Leuka (Dodona) 101–2, 131

Leuktra, battle of (371 BCE) 272n37
Leviticus: oracles in 259n46
Libanius 152, 166, 236
Libya 67–9
Lilybaion, Sicily 150, 289n36, 430, 449
*Litias 195
litigation, *see* judicial curses
Livy 49
loans 17–18, 20
 see also bottomry
logistai 313n80
Lokroi Epizephyroi, Italy: curse tablet from 450
lots and lottery 36–7, 70–1
love curses 154
 see also relationship magic and curses
love poetry 238n5
Loxias 10–11
Lucian: *Conversations of the Hetairai* 222, 333n31
Lucilius 283n36
Lucius of Tarrha 277n79
Luhrmann, T. 31
Lydos 310n49
Lykourgos 301n48, 305n22
Lynkeus of Samos 332n28
Lyrkos, son of Phoroneus 48–9
Lysander 268n36
Lysanias (Dodona) 1–2, 56, 88, 120
Lysias 169–70, 174, 211
Lysikles 211
Lysippos 267n23
Lysitheos 312n73

Machon 332n28
MacIntyre, Alasdair 13, 241n1
McKechnie, Paul R. 203
Mages 298n30
magic
 analogical 151
 as concept 14–16, 244n26
 for love and attraction 207–9
 in oracle consultation 13
 see also black magic
Magnesia 317n103
magoi 27
*Maietas 152
Makedonia
 Athens revolts against 305n22, 321n134
 curses from 28, 143, 212, 333n35, 452
 and Hellenization 340n83
 trade with Epiros 75
*Makron 148

*Manes 147–8, 326n37
*Mania the inn-keeper 185
Maniea 332n28
manteia (sorcery) 234
manteis (seers)
  practitioners and activities 1, 6, 26–31, 139, 141, 143, 234–5
  see also Aristophanes; Diopeithes; Hierokles; Lampon
Mantia 163
Mardonios, Persian general 47, 267n23
maritime loans, *see* bottomry
marriage
  among siblings 83, 85
  catalogue of questions 83–7
  in oracular questions 82–3, 126–7, 228, 235
  role 221
  see also women
Marvell, Andrew: 'To his Coy Mistress' 238n5
Medea 291n46
Megalopolis 317n103
Megara
  border with Athens 36
  cited in travel question 73
  and invention of comedy 298n30
Megiddo, battle of (608 BCE) 40
Megistias 253n18
Meidias 69, 160, 302n50
Melampodids 28, 253n18
*Melanthios 157, 159
Melanthos the Messenian 267n26
Meleos 47, 267n26
Melos 389
men
  and attraction magic 208
  at Dodona 130
Menander 222
  Samia 332n28
*Menedemos 325n27
Menedhi 393
*Menekrates 179
Menelaos 47, 266n20, 267n24
*Menon, son of Aristokles 185
Messene 74, 162
*Mestor 171, 226–7
Metapontion, Italy 128, 200, 433
metics 82, 173, 189, 324n22
*Mikines 169
Miletos 40, 48, 249n59, 264n84, 278n5
military campaigns: in oracular questions 12–13, 47–8, 113–14, 126
Millett, P. 17
Milon, cavalry general 274n43

Miltiades the Elder 46–7
misfortune 166, 235–7
  see also fortune (good)
mistresses 332n28
Mithridates VI, king of Pontos 62
Mnesarchos of Samos 267n26
Mnesiboulos (Dem.47) 316n98
Mnesiepes of Paros (Delphi) 52–3
*Mnesimachos 142, 169
Molossia and Molossians
  dominance 58–9, 61, 65
  erect *Hieria Oikia* 61
  and founding of Dodona 68
  language 128
  settlements 270nn14 15
  and sister-marriage 83
  see also Arybbas
Mondaeans 348
Mopsos, Mallos (Kilikia): oracle 36
Mopsuestia 334n45
Morgan, Catherine 38, 40
Morgantina, Sicily 285n4, 431–2
Mousaios 26–7, 250n2
murder: in oracular questions 116, 118–19
Mykale expedition (479 BCE) 28
*Myrrine 147, 184
*Myrtale 197
Myskellos of Ripai 47
Mytilene
  curse tablet from 184, 446–7
  Demeter sanctuary 172, 446–7
  punishment 310n54
*Mytis 184

Naia 274n51
nailing: in *katadesmoi* 145
Nais 332n28
names
  on Dodona oracle tablets 129
  and identification in *katadesmoi* 142, 197–9
  on Sicilian *katadesmoi* 309n44
Neaira (Dem.59), 186, 211, 332n28, 333n29
Necho, Egyptian pharaoh 40
Neileos, founder of Miletos 48–9
nekuodaimon, 232, 343nn15 16
nekuomanteia 35
Nemea 212, 218, 328n8, 338n68, 417
Neodike 185
Neoptolemus 270n8
Nepos 266, 21
Nestor's cup 140

New Historicism 249n57
Nietzsche, Friedrich 232
Nikandra (priestess) 68
*Nikandros 349
Nikeas (Dodona) 108
Nikias 251n4, 256n29, 296n17
Nikokrateia (Dodona) 130
Nikomachos (Dodona) 74, 128
Nikomedes III, king of Bithynia 268n43
*Nikos of Ephesos 326n38
*Nikostratos 179–80
Nikostratos (Aesch.1.86) 311n63
Ninon 29, 153
Nomentum 322n4
Nostoi 270n8
nude female figures 339n72
Nuer people 241n1

Odysseus 49, 60
Oidipous 31, 266n20
oikists (founders of colonies) 38
Olbia, Black Sea
   curses from 171–2, 240n19, 403–4, 436–7, 451
   law in 183, 317n104
   shared citizenship with Miletos 278n5
Olbia, Gaul 450
Olympia
   Iamidai and Clytiadai at 28
   oracle 35, 48, 265n3, 283n36
Olympias 83
Olympos, Lykia: oracle 35, 261n56, 283n36
omens: interpretation of 30
Onchesimoi 64, 346
Onchesmos, Chaonia 275n59
Onchestos, Boiotia 258n43
*Onesime 287n16
Onomakritos 250n2, 255n25
oracles (messages)
   and ambiguity of responses 34–5, 235
   formulae of inquiry 121, 132
   about future 72–5, 126–7
   illegitimate questions 46, 137
   interpretation of 34, 251n3
   in literature 45–9
   method of transmission 67–71
   about past/present 126–7
   responses 123–4, 134, 138
   and risk 131–2, 137, 235
   series of questions 136–7
   see also chresmologoi
oracles (sanctuaries)
   consultation of 4, 42–8, 67, 233

   as disseminators of international information 3, 33
   foundation and development 38–41
   identity of consultants 127–31
   individual consultations, 43–53 (Delphi); 53–5 (Dodona)
   methods of divination 3–38
   priestesses 68–9
   sites across ancient world 32–6
   state consultation of 63–6, 137, 164
   see also names of individual oracles
oratory: and seizure 165
Orestes 141, 267n22, 302n3, 321n129
Orikos (Pascha Liman) 63–4, 270n8, 346
Oropos, Greece 342n4, 442–3
Orpheus 27
Osborne, R. 174, 187, 222

Pactyes the Lydian 40, 46, 260n52
*Palaimon 148
Palatine Anthology 238n5
Pankleon (Lys.23.2) 309n45
Pankrates, Sanctuary of 441
Pantikapaion, southern Russia 435
Paris 267n24
Parke, H.W. 53, 60, 70116
Parker, R. 37
Paros 74
*Pasianax 148–9
Pasikles (Didyma) 54
Passaron 273n41
past/present: oracle questions about 116–21, 126
Patissia, Attika 352–3, 357, 363, 373–4, 377, 384
Patrae 317n103
Patrai, Achaia: oracle of Demeter 35
Pausanias 69, 162
Pausanias, king of Sparta 35, 279n21
Pausanias (of Akanthos) 213–14, 223, 237, 287n16
Peiraieus 201, 355, 362, 376, 380, 391, 395
Pelasgia 68
Pella, Makedonia 148, 151, 212–14, 221, 224, 452
penestai (Thessalian serfs) 75
Perachora, Korinthian Gulf 263n78
Periallas, Pythian prophetess 260n55
Periander 262n60, 262n22
Perikles 29, 165, 211, 340n85
Persephone 146–8, 184, 290n43
Perses 193
Persia: Kroisos invades 10–11

Pharai: oracle of Hermes 35
pharmaka 152, 251n8, 254n23
pharmakeis (male) and *pharmakides* (female) 27, 236–7
Pharos 74
*Pherekles 177
*Pherenikos 314n83
phialai 37–8, 324n22
*Phila 143, 148, 151, 214–15, 219–21, 224, 237
*Philetas 157–8
Philip II, king of Makedonia 47, 267n27
Philip V, king of Makedonia 62
Philippides (poet) 302n48
Philippides, son of Philomelos 302n48
Philistas (Dodona) 130, 139
Philochoros
  on divination 253n20
  on Eleusis 263n73
  on lot oracle 262n67
  on Theoris 254n23
Philokrates (Lys.29) 310n51
*Philon 327n45
*Philondas 226
Philoneas (Antiph.1) 152
Philotas (Dodona) 282n14
philotimia (love of honour) 160
*Phinton 157–8
Phoenikians 67–8
  as *sunegoroi* 179
Phokion 316n93
Phormio 278n7
Phormion (Dem.45–6) 313n73
Phryne 29, 153, 332n28
phthonos, *see* envy
phyletai 313n80
Pindar: and founding of Dodona 68
Pisistratidae 29
Pisistratos 251n3, 255n25
Pistos (Dodona) 118
*Pitheus 226
*Pithios 185
Plataea, battle of (479 BCE) 253n18
*Plathane 185
Plato
  on belief 31
  on curses 141, 143, 173, 229, 287n17
  Diotima (in *Symposion*) 29, 253n20
  on Dodona priestesses 69
  on fatal and non-fatal injuries caused by natural and supernatural means 153, 237

on prayer 135
on 'signs of the future' 26
on speaker as magician 302n4
on spirit-raisers 234, 279n21
on suffering of uninitiated 291n53
on travelling spell-sellers 141, 143, 229
*Pleistarchos 169
Pleistoanax, king of Sparta 261n55
Pliny: on maleficent magic 192, 194
plot 8
Plutarch
  on Ammon 256n29
  on defeated *choregoi* 160
  on Dodona 273n37
  on individual consultations 45, 114, 283n37
  on oracular responses, 34, 38, 260nn52 53
  on Pausanias's ghost 279n21
  on Pausanias's visit to oracle of the dead 35
  on poetic diction 260nn53, 54
  on political advice of seers 30
  priesthood at Delphi 45
  on Themistokles 49
Pluto 149, 290n43
poets: and chorus training 163
polis: development 20, 23
politicians: as curse targets 173
Pollux: *Onomasticon* 192, 194
Polybios: on individual oracle consultation 44–5
Polykrates of Samos 241n8, 253n18
Polykrates of Thebes 47, 267n23
Polymnestos of Thera ('Battos') 46
Polyxenos 316n96
Pompeii: frescoes 261n68
Porinos of Kymae (Dodona) 94, 100, 128, 130
Poseidon: sanctuary at Onchestos 258n43
Poseidonios of Halikarnassos (Delphi) 50–3
possessions in oracular questions, *see* property
pots: and iconography 221–2
Potter's Hymn, The 191–5
Prasaiboi 282n14
Praxidikai (goddesses) 148
Praxiteles 332n28, 339n72
prayers: in oracular questions 122–3
Priam 36
priestesses: and prophecy 68–9, 276n75
priesthood 126
professions
  in *katadesmoi* 196–9, 203
  see also work: in oracular questions
Promeneia (priestess) 68

property
  catalogue of questions 108–10
  in oracular questions 107–8, 126, 133
prophecy 70–1
*Prosodion 215, 219, 221, 224, 287n16
prosperity/safety
  catalogue of questions 110–12
  in oracular questions 72, 110, 126, 133, 135, 137
  see also health
prostitutes
  in brothels, 216, 331nn25, 28
  in court cases 184
  as curse targets 173, 189, 196, 198, 330n21
  male 331n25, 333n31, 338n67
  see also hetairai
psychagogoi (spirit-raisers) 112, 234, 279n21
public performers: as objects of curses 156–60
Pydna, Greece 171–2, 444–5
Pyrrhos, king of Epiros 56–7, 61–2
Pyrrhos (Neoptolemus), son of Achilles 59
Pythagoras 267n26
*Pytheas 180
Pythia (priestess) 11, 33–4, 36–7, 47, 68
  see also Delphi
Pytho (she-dragon) 39

rape 329n16, 334n42
Razia (Dodona) 131
relationship magic and curses 207–8, 228
  excluded texts 349–51
religion
  and cult activity 38–9
  Greek 14–15
  and magic 15–16
religious matters: as oracular questions 126, 128
Rhegion 65
rhetoric 286n14
riddles 34, 260n50
risk
  and agriculture 16
  commercial 204
  concept and meanings 4–5, 18–19, 22, 237
  and control of desire 219–20
  cultural-symbolic 21
  and Dodona oracle tablets 6
  and eros 221–3
  governmentality 21
  and Greeks 22–5
  human causes 248n54

  and *katadesmoi* 225–6, 235–6
  management 9, 16, 18, 25, 232, 236
  maritime 247n43
  and Mary Douglas 20–1
  origins 19
  and sexual experience 210–12
  socially determined 5, 20–2, 233–5, 237–15
  society 21
  and uncertainty and probability 13, 16–17, 19–20
ritual activities: in oracular questions 112–13, 126
rivalries
  in assembly 171
  in business and professions 191–4, 201–5
  in court 168, 172, 180–1
  in love 207
  in relationships 159, 207
  in sport 156–7
  in theatre 160–3
  see also competition
rizotomoi 27
Roman Empire: oracles closed down 33
Rome
  amphitheatres 172
  curses from 351
Rubinstein, L. 181
Russia
  curse tablets from 183, 196, 435
  see also Black Sea

Sacred *Orgas* ('Land') decree 36
sacred places: and cutting of trees in oracular questions 126
sacrifice
  and decision-making 242n10
  in *katadesmoi* 213–14
sacrificial cakes 37
safety, see prosperity/ safety
Sardis: fall of 10
Sartre, Jean-Paul 231
Saturnina 351
Satyra of Larissa 29, 185, 253n20
Scheler, Max 232
sea: in oracular travel questions 73
Seleukos I 48–9
Selinous, Sicily
  curses from 150, 169, 171, 179, 226, 284n1, 426–9, 447
  earliest tablets found 141, 240n19, 288n22
Selloi (or Helloi) 60, 70, 252n15
separation curses 154, 207

Serapis: cult of 145
Servius Marius Honoratus: commentaries on Virgil 67
sexual experience: and risk 210–12
sexual intercourse
  abstention and prospect of children 88, 93
  penetration 330n23
Shakespeare, William: Sonnets 238n5
ship-related work: in oracular questions 97–8
Sicily
  Athenian expedition and defeat 26, 30, 273n37
  curses from 28, 150–1, 154, 155, 309n44, 419, 425–32, 447–9
  in oracular question 74
  and origins of rhetoric 287n14
sickness, *see* health
*Silanos 185–6
Sime 213–14, 223
*Simias, son of Mikythos 226
similia similibus, *see* magic, analogical
Sinope 332n28
Siscia (Sisak), Croatia: curse from 424
Skiathos 37
Skillos, Selinous river 48
slaves and slavery
  catalogue of oracular questions 101–4, 126
  as curse targets 198
  cursed in court cases 189
  in law cases 174, 186
  as oracle consultants 100–1, 131, 135–6
  torture 174
Sokrates
  on Anytos as *mantis* 251n4
  and divination 43–4
  and Xenophon's question to Delphic oracle 12, 48, 137
Sokrates of Anagyrous 297n20
Sokrates (Dodona) 119–20, 128, 136
Solon 10–11, 13, 281n2, 325n28
Sophocles
  Dodona oracle tablets 49, 68–9
  on Tiresias 32
Sophronios 152
sorcerers
  practitioners and activities 27–9
  see also manteia
Sortes Astrampsychi 279n20
Sosias (Dodona) 120, 136, 146, 157–9
*Sosio 334n45, 335n46
Sotirios Dakaris 56
Sounion 334n45

Soweto, South Africa 7, 9, 230, 237, 321n1, 341n1
Spain: curses from 433, 450
Sparta
  books of oracles 250n2
  consults Dodona oracle 272n37
  dedications at Delphi 39
  Leuktra defeat (371 BCE) 70
  seeks control of Epiros 61
  and sibling marriage 278n9
  war with Athens ends 305n20
speaking
  prevention of 152, 165–6, 170–1, 177, 189
  see also tongues
spells 139
spirit-raisers, *see psychagogoi*
Stephanos (Dem.59) 309n46, 313n73, 332n28
Stesichoros 162
Sthorys of Thasos 253n20
stolen property: in oracular questions 117–18
story 8
Strabo 58, 63, 68–70
Straton 267n23
'subjectivising' 240n21
sundikoi (advocates) 178–82, 184, 185
sunegoroi: in court cases 179, 181–2
supernatural
  and envy 235
  human engagements with 5–6, 11–13
  legality 152
  relations with mortals 10–13, 235
  use in commercial and craft competition 191, 193–5
  and women 236
  see also manteis
superstition 42
Sybil, the 26, 253n20
Symmachos 253n18
Syrakuse 74

Tainaron, Mani 261n59
talismans: apotropaic, 323nn13 14
Taras (Tarento) 63–4, 74, 128, 347
Tatias 237
Taureas 160
technitikon 197, 324n22
technology: and risk 248n54
Teisamenos of Elis 46
Telenikos 253n20
Telephos 266n20
Telesilla 267n22
Telmessoi 28, 49

Telmessos, Karia 50–1
Telmessos, Lykia 28
Teos 284n2
Termessos, Pisidia (southern Turkey) 35
*Tethys 290n41, 291n53
Tetraskopoi 27
Teukros 267n26, 310n49
Thais 332n28
Thaletas 279n21
Thasos 278n5
thaumatopoioi 27
*Theagenes 163–4
theatre: and curses 154, 156, 172, 227–8
Thebes
  curses from 399
  as threat to Athens 305n20
  Zeus temple 67–8
Themis 65, 264n83, 348
Themistokles 49, 256n27, 268n36
*Theodora 149–50, 185, 202, 218–20, 349
Theodoros 343n18
Theodosios the Great 33
*Theokles 179
Theokritos
  on Simaetha's use of magic 331n26
  women in the *Idylls* 222
Theomnestos (Lys.10.24–5) 312n73
*Theon 200
*Theonnastos 216
*Theophemos 293n63
Theophilos 152
Theophrastos
  on agriculture 244n30
  on the superstitious man 29, 42, 293n68
Theopompos 270n12
Theoris 29, 153
Theozotides 170
Theramenes 316n95
Thermon 62
Thersis 292n53
Theseus 267n26
Thesprotia 261n59
Thesprotians (tribe) 58–9, 68, 270n14
Thessaly 39, 75
*Thetima 143, 214–15
Theveste, Africa 434
Thourioi (colony) 123
*Thraitta 184, 325n27
Thrason (Didyma) 54
Thrasyllos 28
Thucydides
  on citizens' love of city 340n85
  description of Athens 26, 29, 231

  language 128
  on oracle-peddlers 27, 256n29
  on witnesses 312n71
Thucydides, son of Melesias 165
Thuria 317n103
Timanoridas (Dem.59) 332n28
*Timareta 186
Timarete (priestess) 68
Timodamos (Dodona) 94, 97–8, 134, 137
*Timokles 216
*Timostratos 200
Timotheos of Anaphe (Delphi) 48, 51
Tiphys 276n69
Tiresias 32
Tirolo, Calabria, Italy 449
Tisias 287n14
Tissaphernes 243n15
Tlepolemos 267n26
tongues: binding 152, 165–6, 170–1, 177, 184–6, 189, 195, 199, 201
tools: identified in work curses 200
torture: of slaves 174
trade
  lending and borrowing in 17–18, 20
  see also bottomry; commercial curses; travel
tragedies 31–2
translation 8
travel
  catalogue of questions 75–81
  in oracular questions 72–5, 93, 126–7, 138, 235
treasure 120, 126
trees: cutting of in oracular questions 126
tripods (bronze) 61, 69
Trophonios: oracle at Lebadeia 35, 263n75
Troy: fate foretold 36
truth: requests for 119, 126
Tyre 329n11

ubuntu 341n1
uncertainty 121–2, 233–4, 237, 247n48
  see also risk
unfulfilled dead, the 149
uninitiated dead, the 149
unmarried dead, the 149
untimely dead, the 148

Veliani 271n15
*Venusta 285n4
Versnel, H. 154
Victor Lists 295n8, 300n40
Virgil 67

Voutiras, E. 149

Wilamowitz-Moellendorff, Ulrich von 240n14
Winch, Peter 13, 241n1
Winkler, J. 208
wishes: in curses 150–1
witchcraft
    accusations of, 293n71, 294n72
    belief in 31
    fear of 194
    and gossip 344n7
    and misfortune 191
    in South Africa 7, 9, 230, 237, 321n1
    and women 294n72
    see also black magic
witnesses (legal): as curse targets 176–8, 198, 320n128
wives
    attitudes to sex-workers 212
    cursed 293n63
    see also marriage
women
    and attraction magic 108–9
    catalogue of oracular questions 83–7
    in court cases 167, 184–7
    as curse targets 184–7, 349–50
    as curse writers 214–16, 228
    and eroticism 221–3
    iconography 221–3
    as oracle consultants 130–1
    in oracular questions 74, 82–3, 126–8, 228
    and prospects of children 87–9
    and relationship curses 206
    and risk 228
    as seers 28–9
    sex-workers 210–13, 217–18, 349
    and speaking 171
    status 130, 222–3
    in supernatural activities 236
    and witchcraft 294n72
Wordsworth, Christopher, Bishop of Lincoln 56–7, 67

work
    catalogue of oracle questions 95–100
    in oracular questions 72–3, 93–5, 126–7
    vocabulary of 199–202
wrongdoing: in an oracular consultation, in oracular questions 119, 126, 137
Wünsch, R. 149

*Xanthios 158–9
xenia (guest-friendship) 20
Xenokles 301n48, 309n44
Xenophon
    on consulting oracles 43–4
    goes to war 12–13
    and oracle-peddlers 27
    personal consultation of oracle 47–8, 137
    reads sacrifices 256n27
    on seers 253n20
    on Sokrates 43, 47–8, 338n67
Xerxes 241n8
xunomosia 315n89
Xuthos of Athens 266n20

Yoruba people, West Africa 33

Zankle 162
Zeniketes, Lykian chief (Dodona) 62, 348
Zeno of Kition 267n21
Zenobius 298n30
Zenothemis (Dem.32) 245n38
Zeus
    abducts Europa 47
    Ammon 67–9
    Theban 67
Zeus Naios
    bronze tripods dedicated to at Dodona 61
    Dodonean cult 60, 62–6
    epithet 67
    as oracle 35, 67, 87, 120, 134–5, 275n57
    questions posed to 2, 6, 129
*Zoilos 216–17, 220
*Zois the Eretrian, wife of Kabeira 2–3, 217–18
*Zois (*hetaira*) 143, 147, 220, 223, 237